Ismaili Literature

Ismaili Literature

A Bibliography of Sources and Studies

Farhad Daftary

I.B.Tauris *Publishers*
LONDON • NEW YORK
in association with
The Institute of Ismaili Studies
LONDON

Published in 2004 by I.B.Tauris & Co Ltd
6 Salem Rd, London W2 4BU
175 Fifth Avenue, New York NY 10010
www.ibtauris.com

In association with The Institute of Ismaili Studies
42–44 Grosvenor Gardens, London SW1W 0EB
www.iis.ac.uk

In the United States of America and in Canada distributed by
St Martin's Press, 175 Fifth Avenue, New York NY 10010

ISBN 1 85043 439 5
EAN 978 1 85043 439 9

A full CIP record for this book is available from the British Library
A full CIP record for this book is available from the Library of Congress

Library of Congress catalog card: available

Typeset in Minion Tra for The Institute of Ismaili Studies

Printed and bound in Great Britain by MPG Books Ltd, Bodmin

The Institute of Ismaili Studies

The Institute of Ismaili Studies was established in 1977 with the object of promoting scholarship and learning on Islam, in the historical as well as contemporary contexts, and a better understanding of its relationship with other societies and faiths.

The Institute's programmes encourage a perspective which is not confined to the theological and religious heritage of Islam, but seeks to explore the relationship of religious ideas to broader dimensions of society and culture. The programmes thus encourage an interdisciplinary approach to the materials of Islamic history and thought. Particular attention is also given to issues of modernity that arise as Muslims seek to relate their heritage to the contemporary situation.

Within the Islamic tradition, the Institute's programmes seek to promote research on those areas which have, to date, received relatively little attention from scholars. These include the intellectual and literary expressions of Shiʿism in general, and Ismailism in particular.

In the context of Islamic societies, the Institute's programmes are informed by the full range and diversity of cultures in which Islam is practised today, from the Middle East, South and Central Asia, and Africa to the industrialized societies of the West, thus taking into consideration the variety of contexts which shape the ideals, beliefs and practices of the faith.

These objectives are realized through concrete programmes and activities organized and implemented by various departments of the Institute. The Institute also collaborates periodically, on a programme-specific basis, with other institutions of learning in the United Kingdom and abroad.

The Institute's academic publications fall into several distinct and interrelated categories:

1. Occasional papers or essays addressing broad themes of the relationship between religion and society in the historical as well as modern contexts, with special reference to Islam.
2. Monographs exploring specific aspects of Islamic faith and culture, or the contributions of individual Muslim figures or writers.
3. Editions or translations of significant primary or secondary texts.
4. Translations of poetic or literary texts which illustrate the rich heritage of spiritual, devotional and symbolic expressions in Muslim history.
5. Works on Ismaili history and thought, and the relationship of the Ismailis to other traditions, communities and schools of thought in Islam.
6. Proceedings of conferences and seminars sponsored by the Institute.
7. Bibliographical works and catalogues which document manuscripts, printed texts and other source materials.

This book falls into category seven listed above.

In facilitating these and other publications, the Institute's sole aim is to encourage original research and analysis of relevant issues. While every effort is made to ensure that the publications are of a high academic standard, there is naturally bound to be a diversity of views, ideas and interpretations. As such, the opinions expressed in these publications must be understood as belonging to their authors alone.

To my colleagues and students at
The Institute of Ismaili Studies

Contents

Preface

I started to compile a bibliography of Ismaili sources and studies more than three decades ago when I began my research on the history of the Ismailis. By then, publications in this field of Islamic studies had already grown significantly since the 1920s and 1930s when Louis Massignon (1883–1962) and Asaf A.A. Fyzee (1899–1981) made the earliest attempts to take stock of modern scholarship on the Ismailis. The rapid increase in the number of Ismaili-related publications since the middle of the twentieth century is, indeed, a reflection of the impressive progress of modern Ismaili studies during that period. Aspects of the progress made in the field have been recorded, partially but on a regular basis, in the *Index Islamicus*, conceived by James D. Pearson (1911–1997), and its continuation in the *Quarterly Index Islamicus*, while Nagib Tajdin attempted a sketchy and uncritical compilation in his *A Bibliography of Ismailism* (1985).

As is now well-known, modern scholarship in Ismaili studies has been almost exclusively due to the recovery and study of an increasing number of Ismaili manuscript sources preserved privately in India, Central Asia, Syria and Yaman, amongst other regions. The improvement in our knowledge of Ismaili texts and in their recovery may be readily traced by a comparative analysis of *A Guide to Ismaili Literature* (1933), compiled by W. Ivanow (1886–1970) partially on the basis of the medieval *Fihrist al-Majdūʿ*, and its second revised edition,

Ismaili Literature: A Bibliographical Survey (1963) with I.K. Poonawala's monumental *Biobibliography of Ismāʿīlī Literature* (1977), which identifies some 1,300 titles attributed to more than 200 authors. It may be noted here that the present bibliography relates only to 'published' primary sources, by or about the Ismailis (Chapter 3), as well as secondary studies (Chapter 4) and as such, it complements the works of Ivanow and Poonawala which refer mostly to unpublished Ismaili texts. A most valuable undertaking accomplished by Professor Poonawala is the identification of the locations of the various manuscripts of each text.

The coverage of secondary studies in the present bibliography is not limited to Ismaili history and thought, although these areas do represent its focus. Ismailism is defined rather broadly here to cover what some scholars designate more specifically as Fatimid studies, including Fatimid political history, institutions, art and archaeology. In addition, certain peripheral yet highly relevant subjects and areas of study have been covered to various extents, notably the Ikhwān al-Ṣafāʾ and their *Rasāʾil* as well as the Cairo Geniza documents and the Druzes who originally split away from the Ismailis in the time of the Fatimid Ismaili caliph-imam al-Ḥākim (d. 411/1021). In the case of the Druzes, particular emphasis has been placed on major monographs and publications related to the earlier history of this community in Fatimid times (but without covering the Druze writings which are not always readily accessible) together with the earliest studies of the orientalists who sometimes also covered the Ismailis in their investigations of the Druzes. Druze studies are currently experiencing a breakthrough as attested by two recent bibliographies compiled by Samy S. Swayd (1998) and Talal Fandi and Ziyad Abi-Shakra (2001). A selection of recent publications on Imāmī Shiʿism, covering the early history and teachings of the Shiʿi imams recognized by the Ismailis, as well as some major genealogical works and biographical dictionaries, are also included.

An attempt at comprehensive coverage of Arabic, Persian and Tajik (Cyrillic) publications has been made. Similarly, all major publications in the main European languages, especially English, French, German, Italian, Spanish and Russian, have been included, in addition to a selection in other languages such as Dutch and Polish. The coverage of publications in Urdu and Turkish is less certain. With few exceptions, publications in Gujarātī and other Indian languages have been excluded, although a selection of the religious literature of the Khojas, the *ginān*s, in English translation has been included. Ismaili publications in South Asian languages would indeed require a separate annotated bibliography. Also excluded is most of the literature of a popular or polemical kind produced by different Ismaili groups as well as numerous 'open letters' and legal proceedings of court cases. Chapter 4: Studies, with few exceptions deals exclusively, or at least primarily, with books, contributions to collective volumes, articles, encyclopedia articles, etc., on the Ismailis. Consequently, chapters or sections on Ismailis appearing in single-authored books devoted to other Islamic subjects have not been covered. A selection of Ismaili-related theses is covered in Chapter 5. The system of transliteration used in this book for the Arabic, Persian, Turkish and Urdu scripts, as well as the Cyrillic characters, is essentially the same as that adopted in the second edition of *The Encyclopaedia of Islam*, with the usual modifications.

It remains for me to express my gratitude to a number of colleagues and friends who assisted me in various ways in this endeavour. Sophia Vasalou, my research assistant in 2002, meticulously and tirelessly checked the bibliographical details of the entries which I had not undertaken myself, at the British Library, the SOAS Library, and other libraries in Oxford and Cambridge; without her, this bibliography would have contained many (perhaps even more) errors. Samer F. Traboulsi checked a selection of my Arabic entries using the collections of the American University in Beirut and Princeton University, while Dr Leila R. Dodikhudoeva did the same in Moscow, St. Petersburg and Dushanbe for the entries in Russian and Tajik, transcribed in Cyrillic; I would like to thank them both very sincerely. I am also grateful to Dr Sergei Andreyev who called my attention to a number of Russian publications, and to Alnoor Merchant, Senior Librarian and Keeper of the Ismaili Collection at our Institute, for his help throughout the years.

I received valuable comments and suggestions from Professor W. Madelung; as always, I remain very grateful to him. I would also like to thank Kutub Kassam and Patricia Salazar of the editorial team at the Institute's Department of Academic Research and Publications who helped in various ways to improve this work. Finally, I am indebted to Julia Kolb who produced the earlier drafts of the bibliography and to Nadia Holmes who meticulously prepared its final typescript for publication. Needless to reiterate that the inclusion of any item in this bibliography does not necessarily imply its endorsement by the author or The Institute of Ismaili Studies.

F.D.

July 2004

Abbreviations

AIEO	*Annales de l'Institut d'Études Orientales*
AI	*Annales Islamologiques*
AI(U)ON	*Annali dell'Istituto (Universitario) Orientale di Napoli*
APP	S.H. Nasr and M. Aminrazavi (ed.), *An Anthology of Philosophy in Persia.* Volume II. Oxford: Oxford University Press, 2001.
BEO	*Bulletin d'Études Orientales*
BIE	*Bulletin de l'Institut d'Égypte*
BIFAO	*Bulletin de l'Institut Français d'Archéologie Orientale du Caire*
BSO(A)S	*Bulletin of the School of Oriental (and African) Studies*
CT	*Les Cahiers de Tunisie*
DDI	*Dānishnāma-yi Djahān-i Islām* [*Encyclopaedia of the World of Islam*], ed., S.M. Mīrsalīm et al. Tehran: Encyclopaedia Islamica Foundation, 1375 Sh.-/1996-
DIFM	*Darülfünun Ilâhiyat Fakültesi Mecmuası* (Istanbul)
DKGI	Muḥammad Karīmī Zanjānī Aṣl, ed., *Darāmadī bar kashākish-i Ghazālī va Ismāʿīliyān.* Tehran: Kavīr, 1381 Sh./2002.
DMBI	*Dāʾirat al-Maʿārif-i Buzurg-i Islāmī* [*The Great Islamic Encyclopaedia*], ed., K. Musavi Bojnurdi. Tehran: The Centre of Great Islamic Encyclopaedia, 1367 Sh.–/1989–.

DT *Dā'irat al-Maʿārif-i Tashayyuʿ* [*Encyclopaedia of Shiʿa*], ed., A. Ṣadr Ḥāj-Sayyid-Jawādī et al. Tehran: Nashr-i Shahīd Muḥibbī, 1375 Sh.–/1996–.

EF M. Barrucand (ed.), *L'Égypte Fatimide, son art et son histoire.* Paris: Presses de l'Université de Paris-Sorbonne, 1999.

EAL *Encyclopedia of Arabic Literature,* ed., J.S. Meisami and P. Starkey. London and New York: Routledge, 1998.

EI *The Encyclopaedia of Islam*, ed., M. Th. Houtsma et al. 1st edition, Leiden: E.J. Brill; London: Luzac, 1913–38; reprinted, Leiden: E.J. Brill, 1987; also published in French and German.

EI2 *The Encyclopaedia of Islam*, ed., H.A.R. Gibb et al. New edition, Leiden: E.J. Brill, 1960–2004; also published in French.

EII *Encyclopaedia of Iran and Islam* [*Dānish-nāma-yi Īrān va Islām*], ed., E. Yarshater. Tehran: The Institute of Translation and Publication, 1354–70 Sh./1975–91.

EIR *Encyclopaedia Iranica,* ed., E. Yarshater. London: Routledge and K. Paul; New York: Encyclopaedia Iranica Foundation, 1982–.

EJ *Eranos Jahrbuch*

ER *Encyclopedia of Religion*, ed., M. Eliade. New York: Macmillan; London: Collier Macmillan, 1987.

ERE *Encyclopaedia of Religion and Ethics*, ed., J. Hastings. Edinburgh: T. and T. Clark, 1908–26.

ESFAM U. Vermeulen and D. de Smet (ed.), *Egypt and Syria in the Fatimid, Ayyubid and Mamluk Eras.* Orientalia Lovaniensia Analecta, 73. Louvain: Peeters, 1995.

ESFAM 2 U. Vermeulen and D. de Smet (ed.), *Egypt and Syria in the Fatimid, Ayyubid and Mamluk Eras II.* Orientalia Lovaniensia Analecta, 83. Louvain: Peeters, 1998.

ESFAM 3 U. Vermeulen and J. Van Steenbergen (ed.), *Egypt and Syria in the Fatimid, Ayyubid and Mamluk Eras III*. Orientalia Lovaniensia Analecta, 102. Louvain: Peeters, 2001.

EUDI *Encyclopaedia Universalis: Dictionnaire de l'Islam, religion et civilisation.* Paris: Encyclopaedia Universalis and A. Michel, 1997.

GIH	*The Great Ismaili Heroes.* Karachi: Prince Aly S. Khan Colony Religious Night School, 1973.
HI	*Handwörterbuch des Islam,* ed., A.J. Wensinck and J.H. Kramers. Leiden: E.J. Brill, 1941.
IA	*Islâm Ansiklopedisi.* Istanbul, 1940–86.
IA2	*Türkiye Diyanet Vakfi Islām Ansiklopedisi.* Istanbul: Türkiye Diyanet Vakfi, 1988–.
IAW	F. Daftary (ed.), *al-Ismāʿīliyyūn fi'l-ʿaṣr al-wasīṭ,* tr., Sayf al-Dīn al-Qaṣīr. Damascus and Beirut: Dār al-Madā, 1998.
IC	*Islamic Culture*
ICIC	S.H. Nasr (ed.), *Ismāʿīlī Contributions to Islamic Culture.* Tehran: Imperial Iranian Academy of Philosophy, 1977.
IJMES	*International Journal of Middle East Studies*
IMM	The Department of Islamic Denominations, The Center for Religious Studies, *Ismāʿīliyya: majmūʿa-yi maqālāt.* Qom, Iran: Center for Religious Studies, 1381 Sh./2002.
JA	*Journal Asiatique*
JASB	*Journal and Proceedings of the Asiatic Society of Bengal*
JAOS	*Journal of the American Oriental Society*
JBBRAS	*Journal of the Bombay Branch of the Royal Asiatic Society*
JESHO	*Journal of the Economic and Social History of the Orient*
JIMMA	*Journal, Institute of Muslim Minority Affairs*
JIS	*Journal of Islamic Studies*
JRCA	*Journal of the (Royal) Central Asian Society*
JRAS	*Journal of the Royal Asiatic Society*
JSS	*Journal of Semitic Studies*
MIHT	F. Daftary (ed.), *Mediaeval Ismaʿili History and Thought.* Cambridge: Cambridge University Press, 1996.
NP	*Nāme-ye Pārsī: Quarterly of the Center for Expansion of Persian Language and Literature*
MW	*The Muslim World*
NS	New Series
OE	*The Oxford Encyclopedia of the Modern Islamic World,* ed., John L. Esposito. Oxford: Oxford University Press, 1995.
REI	*Revue des Études Islamiques*
RIS	F. Sezgin, et al. (ed.), *Rasāʾil Ikhwān aṣ-Ṣafāʾ wa-Khillān*

	al-Wafā' (2nd half 4th/10th cent.): Texts and Studies Collected and Reprinted. Frankfurt am Main: Institute for the History of Arabic-Islamic Science at the Johann Wolfgang Goethe University, 1999.
RSO	*Rivista degli Studi Orientali*
SEI	*Shorter Encyclopaedia of Islam*, ed., H.A.R. Gibb and J.H. Kramers. Leiden: E.J. Brill, 1953.
SI	*Studia Islamica*
TAI	F. Daftary (ed.), *Ta'rīkh va andīshahā-yi Ismāʿīlī dar sadahā-yi miyāna*, tr., Farīdūn Badra'ī. Tehran: Farzān, 1382 Sh./2003.
WI	*Die Welt des Islams*
WO	*Die Welt des Orients*
YNK	*Yādnāma-yi Nāṣir-i Khusraw.* Mashhad: Dānishkada-yi Adabiyyāt va ʿUlūm-i Insānī, Dānishgāh-i Firdawsī, 2535 [1355 Sh.]/1976.
ZDMG	*Zeitschrift der Deutschen Morgenländischen Gesellschaft*

1

Ismaili History and its Literary Sources

The Ismailis, a major Shiʿi Muslim community who have subdivided into a number of branches and minor groups, have had a long and complex history dating back to the middle of the 2nd/8th century. Currently, the Ismailis, who belong to the Nizārī and Ṭayyibī Mustaʿlī branches, are scattered as religious minorities in numerous countries of Asia, the Middle East, Africa, Europe and North America. Numbering several millions, they also represent a diversity of ethnic groups and speak a variety of languages, including Persian, Arabic and Indic languages, as well as a number of European languages.*

Early Shiʿism

At least during the first three centuries of their history, Muslims lived in an intellectually dynamic and fluid milieu. The formative period of Islam was, indeed, characterized by a multiplicity of communities of interpretation and schools of thought, representing a diversity of views on the major religio-political issues faced by the early Muslims after the death of the Prophet Muḥammad in 11/632. At the time, the Muslims were confronted by many gaps in their religious knowledge and understanding of Islam, revolving around issues such as the unity and attributes of God, nature of religious authority and definitions of true believers. Different religious communities and schools of thought, which were later enumerated in heresiographical writings, elaborated their doctrines in stages and eventually acquired their distinctive identities and names. In terms of political loyalties, which remained closely linked to theological perspectives, pluralism in early Islam ranged from the stances of those later designated as Sunnis, who endorsed the historical caliphate and the authority-power structure that had actually evolved in the nascent Muslim community (*umma*), to various religio-political opposition communities, notably the Khawārij and the Shīʿa, who aspired towards new orders.

The Shīʿa themselves eventually subdivided into a number of major communities, notably the Ithnāʿasharīs or Twelvers, the Ismailis and the Zaydīs, and several minor groupings. It is the fundamental belief of the Shīʿa of all branches, however, that the Prophet himself had designated his cousin and son-in-law ʿAlī b. Abī Ṭālib (d. 40/661), married to his daughter Fāṭima, as his successor – a designation or *naṣṣ* instituted through divine command and revealed by the Prophet at Ghadīr Khumm shortly before his death. A minority group originally holding to this view gradually expanded and became generally designated as the *Shīʿat ʿAlī*, party of ʿAlī, or simply as the Shīʿa. The Shīʿa also came to hold a particular conception of religious authority that set them apart from other Muslims. They held that the message of Islam as revealed by the Prophet Muḥammad contained inner truths that could not be grasped directly through common reason. Thus, they recognized the need for a religiously authoritative guide, or imam, as the Shīʿa have traditionally preferred to call their spiritual leader. A person qualified for such an important task of spiritual guidance, according to the Shīʿa, could belong only to the Prophet's family, the *ahl al-bayt*, whose members provided the sole, authoritative channel for elucidating and interpreting the teachings of Islam.[1] Before long, however, the Shīʿa disagreed among themselves regarding the precise definition and composition of the *ahl al-bayt*, causing internal divisions within Shiʿism.

Initially, for some fifty years, Shiʿism represented a unified community with limited membership comprised mainly of Arab Muslims. The Shīʿa had then recognized successively ʿAlī and his sons al-Ḥasan (d. 49/669) and al-Ḥusayn (d. 61/680) as their imams. This situation changed with the movement of al-Mukhtār who, in 66/685, briefly launched an open revolt in Kūfa, the cradle of Shiʿism, against the

Umayyads. Aiming to avenge al-Ḥusayn's murder, al-Mukhtār organized his own Shiʿi movement in the name of ʿAlī's third son and al-Ḥusayn's half-brother Muḥammad, known as Ibn al-Ḥanafiyya (d. 81/700), as the Mahdi, 'the divinely-guided one', the messianic saviour imam and restorer of true Islam who would establish justice on earth and deliver the oppressed from tyranny. The new eschatological concept of imam-Mahdi proved particularly appealing to the *mawālī*, the non-Arab converts to Islam who under the Umayyads (41–132/661–750) were treated as second-class Muslims. As a large and underprivileged social class aspiring to the establishment of a social order based on the egalitarian precepts of Islam, the *mawālī* provided a significant recruiting ground for any movement opposed to the exclusively Arab hegemony of the Umayyads and their social structure. Starting with the movement of al-Mukhtār that survived his demise in 67/687, however, the *mawālī* became particularly drawn to Shiʿism and played a key role in transforming it from an Arab party of limited membership and doctrinal basis to a dynamic movement. Henceforth, different Shiʿi communities and lesser groups, consisting of both Arabs and *mawālī*, came to coexist, each with its own line of imams and elaborating its own ideas. The Prophet's family, whose sanctity was supreme for the Shīʿa, was still defined broadly in its tribal sense to include not only all major branches of the extended ʿAlid family – descendants of his sons al-Ḥasan, al-Ḥusayn and Ibn al-Ḥanafiyya – but also members of other branches of the Prophet's clan of Banū Hāshim. It was not until after the Abbasid revolution that the *ahl al-bayt* came to be defined more narrowly to include only certain ʿAlids.

It was under such circumstances that the Shiʿism of the later Umayyad period developed mainly in terms of two branches or trends, the Kaysāniyya and the Imāmiyya, each with its own internal groupings. In time, another ʿAlid movement led to the foundation of a third major Shiʿi community, the Zaydiyya. There were also those Shiʿi *ghulāt*, individual theorists with often small followings, who existed within or on the margins of the major Shiʿi communities. A radical branch, in terms of both doctrine and policy, evolved out of al-Mukhtār's movement accounting for the bulk of the early Shīʿa until shortly after the Abbasid revolution. This branch, comprised of a number of interrelated groups recognizing various ʿAlids and other Hāshimids as their imams, was generally designated as the

Kaysāniyya by heresiographers who were responsible for coining the names of many of the early Muslim communities. The Kaysānī groups drew mainly on the support of the *mawālī* in southern Iraq, Persia and elsewhere. Many of the Kaysānī doctrines were propounded by the *ghulāt* amongst them, who were accused by the more moderate Shiʿis of later times of 'exaggeration' (*ghuluww*) in religious matters. In addition to their condemnation of the early caliphs before ʿAlī, the commonest feature of the ideas propagated by the early Shiʿi *ghulāt* was the attribution of superhuman qualities, or even divinity, to imams. The Kaysāniyya also pursued an activist anti-establishment policy against the Umayyads, aiming to transfer the leadership of the Muslim *umma* to ʿAlids. By the end of the Umayyad period, the main body of the Kaysāniyya, known as the Hāshimiyya, had transferred their allegiance to the Abbasids, descendants of the Prophet's uncle al-ʿAbbās, who had been cleverly conducting an anti-Umayyad campaign on behalf of an anonymous member of the *ahl al-bayt* with much Shiʿi appeal.

In the meantime, there had developed another major branch of Shiʿism, later designated as the Imāmiyya. This branch, the early common heritage of the Ismailis and the Twelvers, had acknowledged a particular line of Ḥusaynid ʿAlids, descendants of al-Ḥusayn b. ʿAlī b. Abī Ṭālib, as imams and remained completely removed from any political activity. Indeed, the Imāmiyya adopted a quiescent policy in the political field while doctrinally they subscribed to some of the radical views of the Kaysāniyya, such as the condemnation of ʿAlī's predecessors as caliphs. The Imāmiyya, who like other Shiʿis of the Umayyad times were centred in Kūfa, traced the imamate through al-Ḥusayn b. ʿAlī's sole surviving son ʿAlī b. al-Ḥusayn (d. 95/714), with the honorific title of Zayn al-ʿĀbidīn (the Ornament of the Pious). But it was with Zayn al-ʿĀbidīn's son and successor Muḥammad al-Bāqir (d. ca. 114/732) that the Ḥusaynid line of ʿAlid imams and the Imāmī branch began to acquire prominence among the early Shīʿa. The Imam al-Bāqir, too, refrained from political activity and concerned himself with the religious aspects of his imamate. In particular, he elaborated the rudiments of some of the ideas which later became the legitimate principles of Imāmī Shiʿism. He is also credited with introducing the important principle of *taqiyya*, or precautionary dissimulation of one's true religious belief under adverse circumstances, which was later adopted widely by both the Ismailis and the Twelvers. In spite of many difficulties, al-Bāqir succeeded during his imamate of some twenty years in increasing his following. It was, however, during the long and eventful imamate of al-Bāqir's son and successor, Jaʿfar al-Ṣādiq, that the Imāmiyya expanded significantly and became a major religious community with a distinct identity. The foremost scholar and teacher of the Ḥusaynid line of imams, al-Ṣādiq acquired prominence rather gradually during this turbulent period in early Islam when the Umayyads were finally uprooted by the Abbasids.

The Abbasid revolution marked a turning point in early Islamic history, ushering in many socio-political and economic changes, including the disappearance of distinctions between the Arab Muslims and the *mawālī*. But the Abbasid victory proved a source of deep disillusionment for all Shīʿa who had expected an ʿAlid to succeed to the caliphate after the demise of the Umayyads. The Shīʿa were further disappointed when the Abbasids, soon after seizing the caliphate in 132/750, began to persecute their former Shiʿi supporters as well as many of the ʿAlids. In fact, the Abbasid caliph became in due course the spiritual spokesman of Sunni Islam. It was under such circumstances that many Shiʿis, including those Kaysānīs who had not joined the Abbasid party, rallied to the side of Jaʿfar al-Ṣādiq, who had gradually acquired a widespread reputation as a religious scholar. He was a reporter of *ḥadīth* and was later cited as such even in the chain of authorities accepted by Sunnis. He also taught *fiqh* or jurisprudence and has been credited, after the work of his father, with founding the Imāmī Shiʿi school of religious law or *madhhab*, named Jaʿfarī after him. By the final decade of his imamate, al-Ṣādiq had gathered a noteworthy group of religious scholars and associates around him which included some of the most eminent jurists, traditionists and theologians of the time, such as Hishām b. al-Ḥakam (d. 179/795), the foremost representative of Imāmī *kalām* or scholastic theology. As a result of the intense intellectual activities of Jaʿfar al-Ṣādiq and his circle, the Imāmī Shiʿis came to possess a distinctive body of ritual as well as theological and legal doctrines. Above all, they now elaborated the basic conception of the doctrine of the imamate (*imāma*), which was essentially retained by later Ismaili and Twelver Shiʿis.[2] This doctrine enabled al-Ṣādiq to consolidate Shiʿism, after its numerous earlier defeats, on a quiescent basis, as it no longer required the imam to rebel against actual rulers to assert his claims. The last imam recognized by both the Twelvers and the Ismailis, Jaʿfar al-Ṣādiq died in 148/765. The dispute over his succession led to historic divisions in Imāmī Shiʿism, also marking the emergence of independent Ismaili groups.[3]

Origins and early development of the Ismaili *Daʿwa*

A persistent research problem in Ismaili studies relates to the dearth of reliable information. The Ismailis were often persecuted and were, thus, obliged to observe *taqiyya* in their daily life. Furthermore, the authors who produced the Ismaili literature of different periods were generally trained as theologians who normally also served secretly as their community's *dāʿīs*, missionaries or religio-political agents, in hostile milieus. As a result of these realities, the Ismaili *dāʿī*-authors were not particularly interested in compiling historical records of their activities. This general lack of interest in historiography is attested to by the fact that only a handful of historical works have come to light in the modern recovery of Ismaili texts. It is also noteworthy that in medieval times only one general history of Ismailism was compiled by an Ismaili author, namely, the *ʿUyūn al-akhbār* of Idrīs ʿImād al-Dīn (d. 872/1468), the nineteenth *dāʿī* of the Ṭayyibī Mustaʿlī Ismailis.

The pre-Fatimid period of Ismaili history in general and the opening phase of Ismailism in particular remain rather obscure in Ismaili historiography. It is highly probable that the early Ismailis, conducting a revolutionary movement in an extremely hostile environment, did not produce any substantial volume of literature, preferring instead to propagate their doctrines mainly by word of mouth. The modern recovery of Ismaili literature has confirmed this suspicion. In addition, much of the meagre literature of the early Ismailis was evidently discarded or subjected to revisions in the Fatimid period. Nevertheless, a small collection of early Ismaili doctrinal works has survived to the present day. These include fragments of the *Kitāb al-rushd wa'l-hidāya*, attributed to the *dāʿī* Ibn Ḥawshab, better known as Manṣūr al-Yaman (d. 302/914); the *Kitāb al-ʿālim wa'l-ghulām* of Manṣūr al-Yaman's son Jaʿfar (d. ca. 346/957), who is also credited with compiling the *Kitāb al-kashf*, a collection of six short treatises. The religious texts of the Ismailis produced in later times are themselves invaluable for tracing their early doctrinal history. There are also those brief but highly significant historical accounts of specific early Ismaili events, notably the *Istitār al-imām* of the *dāʿī* Aḥmad b. Ibrāhīm al-Nīsābūrī (d. after 386/996), dealing with the settlement of the early Ismaili Imam ʿAbd Allāh in Salamiyya and the flight of ʿAbd Allāh al-Mahdī, the founder of the Fatimid caliphate, from Salamiyya to North Africa. However, for the initial phase of Ismaili history, the brief accounts of the earliest Imāmī Shiʿi heresiographers al-Ḥasan b. Mūsā al-Nawbakhtī (d. after 300/912) and Saʿd b. ʿAbd Allāh al-Qummī (d. 301/913–14), who were much better informed than Sunni heresiographers about the internal divisions of Shiʿism, remain our main sources of information. The anti-Ismaili polemical writings, too, despite their malicious intentions, serve as important sources on aspects of early Ismailism. In this context, particular mention should be made of the highly influential works of Ibn Rizām and the Sharīf Abu'l-Ḥusayn Muḥammad b. ʿAlī, better known as Akhū Muḥsin, who flourished in the 4th/10th century. Their refutations of the Ismailis have not been recovered, but they were widely available to several generations of Muslim scholars and historians who have preserved them fragmentarily. In modern times, after the pioneering efforts of W. Ivanow (1886–1970), S.M. Stern (1920–1969) and W. Madelung produced ground-breaking studies on early Ismailism. However, scholars still disagree on certain aspects of the early Ismaili *daʿwa*, and some of the outstanding issues may never be resolved due to a lack of reliable sources.

According to most sources, both Ismaili and non-Ismaili, the Imam al-Ṣādiq had originally designated his second son Ismāʿīl, the eponym of the Ismāʿīliyya, as his successor to the imamate by the rule of the *naṣṣ*. There cannot be any doubt regarding the historicity of this designation, which provides the basis of the Ismaili claims. However, matters are rather confused as Ismāʿīl apparently predeceased his father, and three of al-Ṣādiq's sons simultaneously laid claim to his heritage. According to the Ismaili religious tradition and as reported in some of its sources, Ismāʿīl survived his father and succeeded him in due course. But most non-Ismaili sources relate that he died before his father, the latest date mentioned being 145/762–63. These sources also add that during Ismāʿīl's funeral procession in Medina, Jaʿfar al-Ṣādiq made several attempts to show the face of his dead son to witnesses, though some of the same sources also state that Ismāʿīl was later seen in Baṣra.[4] At any rate, Ismāʿīl was not present in Medina or Kūfa on Jaʿfar al-Ṣādiq's death in 148/765 when three other sons, ʿAbd Allāh al-Afṭaḥ (d. 149/766), Muḥammad al-Dībāj (d. 200/815) and Mūsā al-Kāẓim (d. 183/799) laid open claims to the imamate. As a result, al-Ṣādiq's Imāmī Shiʿi following split into six groups, two of which may be identified as proto-Ismailis or earliest Ismailis. These splinter groups, based in Kūfa and supporting the claims of Ismāʿīl b. Jaʿfar and his son Muḥammad, had evidently appeared in the lifetime of the Imam al-Ṣādiq, but they separated from other Imāmīs only in 148/765.

One of these groups denied the death of Ismāʿīl and awaited his return as the Mahdi, as did another Imāmī group now believing in the Mahdiship of al-Ṣādiq himself. The members of this group, designated as 'al-Ismāʿīliyya al-khāliṣa' or the 'Pure Ismāʿīliyya' by al-Nawbakhtī and Saʿd b. ʿAbd Allāh al-Qummī,[5] held that the Imam al-Ṣādiq had announced Ismāʿīl's death merely as a ruse to protect him against Abbasid persecution as he had been politically active against them. Indeed on the basis of sketchy biographical details available on Ismāʿīl, there is sufficient evidence to indicate that he had close ties with the more activist circles of the Imāmiyya.[6] Evidently, there were also contacts between Ismāʿīl and Abu'l-Khaṭṭāb al-Asadī, the most prominent of all early Shiʿi *ghulāt* who was for a while in the entourage of Jaʿfar al-Ṣādiq before being repudiated by him for his extremist views. Soon afterwards in 138/755, Abu'l-Khaṭṭāb and a number of his followers were attacked and killed in the mosque of Kūfa where they had gathered for rebellious purposes. Ismāʿīl's association with Abu'l-Khaṭṭāb is also alluded to in an obscure Persian treatise called *Umm al-kitāb*, which states that the Ismaili religion (*madhhab*) was founded by the disciples of Abu'l-Khaṭṭāb.[7] However, Abu'l-Khaṭṭāb is generally condemned as a 'heretic' in the Ismaili literature of the Fatimid times.[8] The second proto-Ismaili splinter group, known as the Mubārakiyya, affirmed Ismāʿīl's death in the lifetime of his father and now recognized his eldest son Muḥammad b. Ismāʿīl as their imam. It seems likely that the Mubārakiyya, derived from Ismāʿīl's epithet al-Mubārak, 'the blessed one', were originally supporters of Ismāʿīl before acknowledging his son Muḥammad as their imam. Be that as it may, Mubārakiyya – a term coined later by heresiographers – was, thus, one of the original names of the nascent Ismāʿīliyya.

As in the case of Ismāʿīl b. Jaʿfar, little is known about the life and career of Muḥammad b. Ismāʿīl, the seventh imam of the Ismailis. The relevant biographical information contained in early Ismaili sources has been reproduced by the *dāʿī* Idrīs ʿImād al-Dīn in his *ʿUyūn al-akhbar*.[9] After the recognition of the imamate of his uncle Mūsā al-Kāẓim, soon after al-Ṣādiq's death, Muḥammad b. Ismāʿīl left Medina, seat of the ʿAlids, and went into hiding, marking the initiation of the *dawr al-satr*, or the period of concealment, in early Ismailism which lasted until the foundation of the Fatimid state and the emergence of the Ismaili imams from their concealment. Henceforth, Muḥammad acquired the epithet of al-Maktūm, 'the hidden one', in addition to al-Maymūn, 'the fortunate one'. Nevertheless, Muḥammad maintained his contacts with the Kufan-based Mubarakiyya from different localities in Iraq and Persia. He died not long after 179/795, during the caliphate of the Abbasid Hārūn al-Rashīd (170–193/786–809).

No details are available on the relations between the 'Pure Ismāʿīliyya' and the Mubārakiyya or any particular connections between these two groups and the Khaṭṭābīs, the followers of Abu'l-Khaṭṭāb, some of whom may have joined the supporters of Muḥammad b. Ismāʿīl, as claimed by al-Nawbakhtī and Saʿd b. ʿAbd Allāh.[10] It is certain, however, that all these groups were politically active against the Abbasids and they originated within the radical fringes of Imāmī Shiʿism in Kūfa. At any rate, on the death of Muḥammad b. Ismāʿīl, the Mubārakiyya split into two groups. The majority, identified by Imāmī heresiographers as the immediate predecessors of the dissident Qarmaṭīs, refused to accept his death; they recognized him as their seventh and last imam, and awaited his return as the Mahdi or *qāʾim* (riser) – terms which were synonymous in their early usage by the Ismailis and other Shiʿis. A second small and obscure group acknowledged Muḥammad b. Ismāʿīl's death and now began to trace the imamate in his progeny. Almost nothing is known with certainty regarding the subsequent history of these earliest Ismaili groups until shortly after the middle of the 3rd/9th century, when a unified Ismaili movement appeared on the historical stage.

Drawing on different categories of sources, including the Ismaili literature of the early Fatimid period, the heresiographical works of Imāmī scholars and even the anti-Ismaili treatises of polemicists, especially the works of Ibn Rizām and Akhū Muḥsin, modern scholarship has to a large extent succeeded in clarifying the circumstances leading to the emergence of the Ismaili movement in the 3rd/9th century. It is certain that for almost a century after Muḥammad b. Ismāʿīl, a group of leaders, well placed within the earliest Ismailis, worked secretly for the creation of a unified, revolutionary Shiʿi movement against the Abbasids. Initially attached to one of the earliest Ismaili groups, and in all probability the imams of that obscure group issued from the Mubārakiyya who maintained continuity in the imamate in the progeny of Muḥammad b. Ismāʿīl, these leaders did not openly claim the Ismaili imamate for three generations. They had, in fact, hidden their true identity in order to escape Abbasid persecution. ʿAbd Allāh, the first of these hidden leaders, had organized his campaign around the central doctrine of the majority of the earliest Ismailis, namely the Mahdiship of Muḥammad b. Ismāʿīl.

The existence of such a group of early Ismaili leaders is confirmed by both the official version of Ismailis of the Fatimid period regarding the pre-Fatimid phase of their history, as reflected in the *ʿUyūn al-akhbār* of the *dāʿī* Idrīs ʿImād al-Dīn, as well as the hostile accounts of the anti-Ismaili polemicists, Ibn Rizām and Akhū Muḥsin, as preserved by later Sunni historians such as Ibn al-Dawādārī, al-Nuwayrī and al-Maqrīzī, among others. Indeed, with minor variations, the names of these leaders (ʿAbd Allāh, Aḥmad, Ḥusayn or Muḥammad, and ʿAbd Allāh al-Mahdī), who were members of the same family and succeeded one another on a hereditary basis, are almost identical in the accounts of the later Fatimid Ismailis,[11] and in the lists traceable to Akhū Muḥsin and his source Ibn Rizām.[12] However, in the Ismaili sources these central leaders are presented as ʿAlids descending from Jaʿfar al-Ṣādiq while in the anti-Ismaili accounts their ancestry is traced to a certain Maymūn al-Qaddāḥ. Modern scholarship has shown that the Qaddāḥid ancestry attributed to the early Ismaili leaders was a construct of the polemicists who aimed to refute the ʿAlid genealogy of the Fatimid caliph-imams. Maymūn al-Qaddāḥ and his son ʿAbd Allāh were, in fact, associates of the Imams al-Bāqir and al-Ṣādiq and had nothing to do with early Ismailism.

ʿAbd Allāh, designated in later Ismaili sources as al-Akbar (the elder), the first of the early Ismaili leaders after Muḥammad b. Ismāʿīl, settled in ʿAskar Mukram, in Khūzistān, south-western Persia, where he disguised himself as a merchant. It should be noted that

Muḥammad b. Ismāʿīl himself had spent the latter part of his life in Khūzistān; and several early *dāʿīs* including al-Ḥusayn al-Ahwāzī and ʿAbdān also hailed from that part of Persia adjacent to southern Iraq. The Ismaili *dāʿī* Aḥmad b. Ibrāhīm al-Nīsābūrī relates important details on ʿAbd Allāh al-Akbar and his successors down to ʿAbd Allāh al-Mahdī in his *Istitār al-imām*. It was from that locality that he began to organize a reinvigorated Ismaili *daʿwa* sending *dāʿīs* to different districts around Khūzistān. At an unknown date in the first half of the 3rd/9th century, ʿAbd Allāh found refuge in Syria, where he re-established contact with some of his *dāʿīs*, and settled in Salamiyya, continuing to pose as a Hāshimid merchant. Henceforth, Salamiyya served as the secret headquarters of the Ismaili *daʿwa*.

The efforts of ʿAbd Allāh and his successors began to bear fruit in the 260s/870s, when numerous *dāʿīs* appeared in southern Iraq and adjacent regions. In 261/874 Ḥamdān Qarmaṭ was converted to Ismailism by the *dāʿī* al-Ḥusayn al-Ahwāzī. Ḥamdān, in turn, organized the *daʿwa* in the Sawād of Kūfa, his native locality, and in other districts of southern Iraq. His chief assistant was his brother-in-law ʿAbdān. A learned theologian, ʿAbdān was responsible for training and appointing numerous *dāʿīs*, including Abū Saʿīd al-Jannābī, who later founded the Qarmaṭī state of Baḥrayn. The Ismailis of southern Iraq became generally known as the Qarāmiṭa, after their first local leader. This term was soon applied to other Ismaili communities not organized by Ḥamdān and ʿAbdān. At the time, there was a single Ismaili movement directed from Salamiyya in the name of Muḥammad b. Ismāʿīl as the Mahdi. In fact, in order to prepare the ground for the emergence of the Mahdi, in 277/890 Ḥamdān established a *dār al-hijra*, or abode of migration, near Kūfa, where his followers gathered weapons and other provisions. The abode was to serve as the nucleus of a new society for the Ismailis. Later, similar *dār al-hijra*s were established for the Ismaili communities of Yaman, Baḥrayn and North Africa. The Ismailis (Qarmaṭīs) now referred to their movement simply as *al-daʿwa* (the mission) or *al-daʿwa al-hādiya* (the rightly guiding mission), in addition to using expressions such *daʿwat al-ḥaqq* (summons to the truth) or *ahl al-ḥaqq* (people of the truth). Aside from the narratives traceable to Ibn Rizām and Akhū Muḥsin, valuable details on the history of the early Ismaili (Qarmaṭī) movement in Iraq are related by al-Ṭabarī who had access to Qarmaṭī informants.[13]

In the meantime, the Ismaili *daʿwa* had appeared in many other regions in the 260s/870s. Centred on the expectation of the imminent return of Muḥammad b. Ismāʿīl as the Mahdi who would establish justice in the world, the revolutionary and messianic Ismaili movement appealed to underprivileged groups of different social strata; and it achieved particular success among those Imāmī Shiʿis who had been disillusioned with the quietist policies of their imams and were, furthermore, left without a manifest imam after al-Ḥasan al-ʿAskarī (d. 260/874). The *daʿwa* in Yaman was initiated by Ibn Ḥawshab, later known as Manṣūr al-Yaman, where he arrived in 268/881 accompanied by his collaborator ʿAlī b. al-Faḍl. By 293/905, when ʿAlī occupied Ṣanʿāʾ, the Ismaili *dāʿīs* were in control of almost all of Yaman. South Arabia also served as a base for the extension of the *daʿwa* to other regions such as Yamāma, Baḥrayn and Egypt as well as Sind. By 280/893, on Ibn Ḥawshab's instructions, the *dāʿī* Abū ʿAbd Allāh al-Shīʿī was already active among the Kutāma Berbers of the Lesser Kabylia mountains in the Maghrib. And in 273/886, or a few years later, Abū Saʿīd al-Jannābī was sent to Baḥrayn by Ḥamdān and ʿAbdān; he rapidly won converts there from among the bedouins and the Persian emigrants.[14]

In a chapter on the Ismailis, added to his *Siyāsat-nāma* shortly before his assassination in 485/1092, the Saljūq vizier Niẓām al-Mulk provides important details on the early *daʿwa* in Persia and Khurāsān. It was in the same decade of 260s/870s that the *daʿwa* was taken to the region of the Jibāl in Persia by Khalaf al-Ḥallāj, who established his base of operations in Rayy where an important Imāmī community already existed. Under Khalaf's successors as chief *dāʿīs* of the Jibāl, the *daʿwa* spread to Qumm, another major Imāmī centre of learning, Iṣfahān, Hamadān and other towns of that region. Ghiyāth, the third *dāʿī* of the Jibāl, extended the *daʿwa* to Khurāsān and Transoxania on his own initiative. Ghiyāth's chief deputy was the learned theologian Abū Ḥātim al-Rāzī, who in time became the chief *dāʿī* of Rayy, his native land. Abū Ḥātim further extended the *daʿwa* to Ādharbāyjān, in north-western Persia, and to various parts of Daylam in the Caspian region of northern Persia. He succeeded in converting several Daylamī amirs. But the Ismaili *daʿwa* was officially established in Khurāsān only during the last decade of the 3rd century/903–12 by Abū ʿAbd Allāh al-Khādim, who set up his secret headquarters at

Nīshāpūr. A later chief *dāʿī* of Khurāsān, al-Ḥusayn b. ʿAlī al-Marwazī, was an eminent amir in the service of the Sāmānids, and he succeeded in extending the *daʿwa* to Harāt, Ghūr, Maymana and other localities in eastern Iranian lands under his control. Al-Ḥusayn al-Marwazī's successor as chief *dāʿī* of Khurāsān was the Central Asian Muḥammad b. Aḥmad al-Nasafī, who introduced a form of Neoplatonism into Ismaili thought. He moved his base of operations to his native town of Nakhshab (Arabic, Nasaf) and then to Bukhārā, the Sāmānid capital. Al-Nasafī's success in Transoxania was crowned by his conversion of the Sāmānid amir Naṣr II b. Aḥmad (301–331/914–943), as well as other dignitaries at the Sāmānid court. But in 332/943, in the aftermath of the revolt of the Turkish soldiers who deposed Naṣr, al-Nasafī and his close associates were executed in Bukhārā. Their co-religionists too were persecuted under Naṣr's son and successor Nūḥ I (331–343/943–954), who called for a *jihād* or religious war against the Qarmaṭī 'heretics'. Despite these setbacks, the *daʿwa* survived in Khurāsān and Transoxania under the leadership of other *dāʿīs*, including especially Abū Yaʿqūb al-Sijistānī.[15]

Meanwhile, by the early 280s/890s, a unified Ismaili movement had replaced the earlier Ismaili splinter groups. But in 286/899, soon after ʿAbd Allāh, the future Fatimid caliph al-Mahdī, had succeeded to leadership in Salamiyya, Ismailism was rent by a major schism.[16] Ḥamdān Qarmaṭ now noticed significant changes in the doctrinal instructions he received from Salamiyya, and dispatched ʿAbdān there to investigate the matter. In due course, Ḥamdān found out that instead of advocating the Mahdiship of Muḥammad b. Ismāʿīl, the new leader claimed the imamate for himself and his predecessors, the very central leaders of the Ismaili *daʿwa* in the *dawr al-satr*. Refusing to accept this doctrinal change, Ḥamdān and ʿAbdān renounced their allegiance to the central leadership of Ismailism and suspended their *daʿwa* activities. Soon after, ʿAbdān was murdered at the instigation of the *dāʿī* Zikrawayh b. Mihrawayh, and Ḥamdān disappeared. Evidently, as reported by Ibn Ḥawqal, Ḥamdān later changed his mind, joined the faction loyal to ʿAbd Allāh al-Mahdī and surfaced as a *dāʿī* in Egypt with a new identity, calling himself Abū ʿAlī.[17]

ʿAbd Allāh al-Mahdī's reform is explained in the above-mentioned letter he later sent to the Ismailis of Yaman, in which an attempt is made to reconcile his reform with the actual course of events in pre-Fatimid Ismaili history. He explains that as a form of *taqiyya* the central leaders of the early *daʿwa* had assumed different pseudonyms, such as al-Mubārak and al-Maymūn, also assuming the rank of the *ḥujja*, proof or full representative, of the absent Imam Muḥammad b. Ismāʿīl. It is further explained that the earlier propagation of the Mahdiship of Muḥammad b. Ismāʿīl was itself another dissimulating veil, and that this was in reality a collective code-name for every true imam in the progeny of Jaʿfar al-Ṣādiq.

The doctrinal reform of ʿAbd Allāh al-Mahdī split the Ismaili movement into two rival factions. One faction remained loyal to the central leadership and acknowledged continuity in the imamate, recognizing ʿAbd Allāh al-Mahdī (d. 322/934) and his ʿAlid ancestors as their imams, which in due course became the official Fatimid Ismaili doctrine of the imamate. These Ismailis allowed for three hidden imams (*al-aʾimma al-mastūrīn*) between Muḥammad b. Ismāʿīl and ʿAbd Allāh al-Mahdī. This loyalist faction included the bulk of the Ismailis of Yaman and those communities in Egypt, North Africa and Sind founded by *dāʿī*s dispatched by Ibn Ḥawshab. On the other hand, a dissident faction, originally led by Ḥamdān Qarmaṭ, rejected ʿAbd Allāh's reform and maintained their belief in the Mahdiship of Muḥammad b. Ismāʿīl. Henceforth, the term Qarmaṭī came to be applied more specifically to the dissidents who did not acknowledge ʿAbd Allāh al-Mahdī, as well as his predecessors and successors in the Fatimid dynasty, as their imams. The dissident Qarmaṭīs, who lacked central leadership, soon acquired their most important stronghold in Baḥrayn in eastern Arabia, where a Qarmaṭī state had been founded in the same eventful year 286/899 by Abū Saʿīd al-Jannābī who had sided with Ḥamdān and ʿAbdān. The Qarmaṭī state of Baḥrayn survived until 470/1077–78. There were also Qarmaṭī communities in Iraq, Yaman, Persia and Central Asia.

Abū Saʿīd was murdered in 300/913 and, subsequently, several of his sons rose to leadership of the Qarmaṭī state in Baḥrayn. Under his youngest son Abū Ṭāhir Sulaymān (311–332/923–944), the Qarmaṭīs of Baḥrayn became infamous for their regular raids into Iraq and their pillaging of the Meccan pilgrim caravans. Abū Ṭāhir's ravaging activities culminated in his attack on Mecca during the pilgrimage season in 317/930, when the Qarmaṭīs committed numerous desecrating acts and dislodged the Black Stone (*al-ḥajar al-aswad*) from the corner of the Kaʿba and carried it to al-Aḥsāʾ, their new capital in eastern Arabia. Sunni polemicists who condemned the entire Ismaili movement as a conspiracy to destroy Islam, capitalized on these events and alleged that Abū Ṭāhir had secretly received his instructions from ʿAbd Allāh al-Mahdī who was then reigning as the first Fatimid caliph-imam in Ifrīqiya. Modern scholarship has shown, however, that the Qarmaṭīs of Baḥrayn were at the time, like other Qarmaṭī communities, still predicting the imminent appearance of the Mahdi and did not acknowledge the first Fatimid caliph, or any of his successors, as their imams. This also explains why after sacking Mecca, Abū Ṭāhir recognized the expected Mahdi in a young Persian, to whom he handed over the rule in 319/931. The Persian Mahdi embarked on strange behaviour, he abolished the *sharīʿa* and Islamic worship, and as he started to execute the notables of Baḥrayn, too, Abū Ṭāhir admitted that the Mahdi had been an impostor and had him killed. The obscure episode of the 'Persian Mahdi' seriously demoralized the Qarmaṭīs. Subsequently, the Qarmaṭīs of Baḥrayn reverted to their former beliefs and their leaders, once again, claimed to be acting on the orders of the hidden Mahdi. They eventually returned the Black Stone to Mecca in 339/950, for a large ransom paid by the Abbasids and not, as alleged by anti-Ismaili sources, in response to the Fatimid caliph's request.

In Yaman, by 291/904, or perhaps earlier, Ibn Ḥawshab's collaborator, the *dāʿī* ʿAlī b. al-Faḍl displayed signs of disloyalty. In 299/911, after occupying Ṣanʿāʾ, Ibn al-Faḍl openly renounced his allegiance to ʿAbd Allāh al-Mahdī and declared war on Ibn al-Ḥawshab, who remained loyal to the Fatimids until his death in 302/914. On Ibn al-Faḍl's demise in 303/915, the Qarmaṭī movement in Yaman disintegrated rather rapidly. In Persia, Qarmaṭism spread widely after 286/899. The *dāʿī*s of the Jibāl did not generally recognize ʿAbd Allāh al-Mahdī's imamate, and awaited the return of Muḥammad b. Ismāʿīl as the expected Mahdi. Abū Ḥātim al-Rāzī, too, like Qarmaṭīs elsewhere, prophesied the Mahdi's advent for the year 316/928 on the basis of certain astrological calculations. As Abū Ḥatim's predictions did not materialize, he encountered hostilities from his co-religionists and was obliged to seek refuge with an amir in Ādharbāyjān, where he died in 322/934. Later, as attested by coins dating from 343/954–55, some rulers of Ādharbāyjān and Daylam, belonging to the Musāfirid (or Sallārid) dynasty, adhered to Qarmaṭism and recognized Muḥammad b. Ismāʿīl as the Mahdi. In Khurāsān and Transoxania, as well, dissident Qarmaṭism persisted after the establishment of the Fatimid state. The *dāʿī* al-Nasafī affirmed the Mahdiship of Muḥammad b. Ismāʿīl in his major treatise, *Kitāb al-maḥṣūl*, which acquired a prominent status within the Qarmaṭī circles of different regions.[18]

Meanwhile, the *dāʿī* Zikrawayh b. Mihrawayh had gone into hiding following the events of the year 286/899, possibly fearing reprisals by ʿAbdān's supporters in Iraq. From 288/901, however, he sent several of his sons as *dāʿī*s to the Syrian desert where large numbers of bedouins were converted. Zikrawayh now aimed to establish a Fatimid state in Syria for ʿAbd Allāh al-Mahdī without his authorization. Soon Zikrawayh's sons summoned their bedouin followers to proceed to Salamiyya and declare their allegiance to the imam who was still guarding his identity. In the event, ʿAbd Allāh, whose position had now been dangerously compromised, secretly left Salamiyya in 289/902 to escape capture by the Abbasid agents sent after him. He first went to Ramla, in Palestine, and then in 291/904, following the defeat of Zikrawayh's movement in Syria by an Abbasid army, he embarked on a historic journey which ended several years later in North Africa where he founded the Fatimid caliphate. Important details on ʿAbd Allāh al-Mahdī's fateful journey to North Africa are contained in the autobiography, *Sīra*, of his chamberlain Jaʿfar b. ʿAlī who accompanied the imam. After their defeat in Syria in 291/904, Zikrawayh and his sons turned against ʿAbd Allāh al-Mahdī and in fact established a separate wing of the dissident camp. Zikrawayh was finally defeated and killed in 294/907 by the Abbasids while his Qarmaṭī movement lingered on for a while longer.[19]

The early Ismailis elaborated the basic framework of a system of religious thought which was further developed or modified in the Fatimid period. As only a handful of Ismaili texts have survived from this period, and as the literature of the Qarmaṭīs has disappeared almost completely, it is not possible to trace the development of early Ismaili thought in any great detail. It is nevertheless possible to convey in broad terms the distinctive intellectual traditions and the central teachings of the early Ismailis, as expounded by the unified Ismaili movement during 261–286/874–899. Subsequently, the early doctrines were further developed, modified, or even discarded, by the Ismailis of the Fatimid times while the Qarmaṭīs followed a separate course. Central to the early Ismaili system of thought was a fundamental distinction between the exoteric (*ẓāhir*) and the esoteric (*bāṭin*) aspects of the sacred scriptures and religious commandments and prohibitions. Accordingly, the Ismailis held that the Qur'an and other revealed scriptures, and their laws (*sharīʿa*s), had their apparent or literal meaning, the *ẓāhir*, which had to be distinguished from their inner meaning hidden in the *bāṭin*. They further held that the *ẓāhir*, or the religious laws enunciated by prophets, underwent periodical changes while the *bāṭin*, containing the spiritual truths (*ḥaqāʾiq*), remained immutable and eternal. These truths, indeed, represented the message common to the religions of the Abrahamic tradition, namely, Judaism, Christianity and Islam. However, the truths hidden in the *bāṭin* of these monotheistic religions had been veiled by different exoteric laws or *sharīʿa*s as required by different temporal circumstances. The hidden truths were explained through the methodology of *taʾwīl* or esoteric interpretation, which often relied on the mystical significance of letters and numbers. In every age, however, the esoteric truths would be accessible only to the elite (*khawāṣṣ*) of humankind as distinct from the ordinary people (*ʿawāmm*), who were only capable of perceiving the apparent meaning of the revelations. Consequently, in the era of Islam, the eternal truths of religion could be explained only to those who had been properly initiated into the Ismaili *daʿwa* and as such recognized the teaching authority of the Prophet Muḥammad and, after him, that of his *waṣī*, ʿAlī b. Abī Ṭālib, and the rightful imams who succeeded him; these authorities were the sole possessors of *taʾwīl* in the era of Islam. The centrality of *taʾwīl* for the Ismailis is attested by the fact that a good portion of the literature produced by them during the early and Fatimid times, notably the writings of Jaʿfar b. Manṣūr al-Yaman, is comprised of the *taʾwīl* genre which seeks justification for Ismaili doctrines in Qur'anic verses.

Initiation into Ismailism, known as *balāgh*, was gradual and took place after the novice had taken an oath of allegiance known as *ʿahd* or *mīthāq*. There were, however, no fixed seven or more stages of initiation as claimed by the polemicists. The initiates were obliged to keep secret the *bāṭin* imparted to them by a hierarchy (*ḥudūd*) of teachers. Such ideas provide the subject matter of the *Kitāb al-ʿālim wa'l-ghulām*, one of the few surviving early Ismaili texts attributed to

Jaʿfar b. Manṣūr al-Yaman. By exalting the *bāṭin* aspects of religion, the Ismailis came to be regarded by the rest of the Muslim community as the most representative of the Shiʿis propounding esotericism in Islam and, hence, their common designation as the Bāṭiniyya. This designation was, however, used in a derogatory sense accusing the Ismailis of generally ignoring the *ẓāhir*, or the *sharīʿa*. The available evidence, including the fragmentary texts of the Ismaili oath of allegiance,[20] clearly show that the early Ismailis were not exempted in any sense from the commandments and prohibitions of Islam. Indeed, early Ismaili teachings accorded equal significance to the *ẓāhir* and the *bāṭin* and their inseparability, ideas that were further elaborated in the Ismaili teachings of the Fatimid period. Such generalized accusations of *ibāḥa* or antinomianism against the Ismailis seem to have been rooted in the polemics of their enemies, who also blamed the entire Ismaili movement for the anti-Islamic views and practices of the Qarmaṭīs.

The esoteric truths or *ḥaqāʾiq* formed a gnostic system of thought for the early Ismailis, representing a distinct world-view. The two main components of this system, developed by the 280s/890s, were a cyclical history of revelations or prophetic eras and a gnostic cosmological doctrine. The Ismailis applied their cyclical interpretation of time and the religious history of humankind to Judaeo-Christian revelations as well as a number of other pre-Islamic religions such as Zoroastrianism with much appeal to non-Muslims. This conception of religious history, reflecting a variety of influences such as Hellenic, Judaeo-Christian, Gnostic as well as eschatological ideas of the earlier Shiʿis, was developed in terms of the eras of different prophets recognized in the Qurʾan. This cyclical conception was also combined with the Ismaili doctrine of the imamate inherited from the Imāmīs.

According to their cyclical view, the Ismailis held that the religious history of humankind proceeded through seven prophetic eras (*dawr*s) of various durations, each one inaugurated by a speaker or enunciator (*nāṭiq*) of a divinely revealed message which in its exoteric (*ẓāhir*) aspect contained a religious law (*sharīʿa*). The *nāṭiq*s of the first six eras of human history were Adam (Ādam), Noah (Nūḥ), Abraham (Ibrāhīm), Moses (Mūsā), Jesus (ʿĪsā) and Muḥammad. These *nāṭiq*s had announced only the outer (*ẓāhir*) aspects of each revelation with its rituals, commandments and prohibitions, without explaining details of its inner (*bāṭin*) meaning. Each *nāṭiq* was, therefore, succeeded by a spiritual legatee (*waṣī*), also called the 'silent one' (*ṣāmit*) and later the 'foundation' (*asās*), who explained to the elite the esoteric truths (*ḥaqā'iq*) contained in the *bāṭin* dimension of that era's message. Each *waṣī* was, in turn, succeeded by seven imams, also called *atimmā'* (singular, *mutimm*), who guarded the true meaning of the sacred scriptures and laws in their *ẓāhir* and *bāṭin* aspects. The seventh imam of every era would rise in rank to become the *nāṭiq* of the following era, abrogating the *sharī'a* of the previous era and enunciating a new one in its place. This pattern would change only in the seventh, final era of history. As the seventh imam of the sixth era, the era of the Prophet Muḥammad and Islam, Muḥammad b. Ismā'īl was initially expected to return as the Mahdi (or *qā'im*) as well as the *nāṭiq* of the seventh eschatological era when, instead of promulgating a new law, he would fully divulge to all humankind the esoteric truths of all the preceding revelations. He would, thus, unite in himself the ranks of *nāṭiq* and *waṣī*, being also the last of the imams as the eschatological Imam-Mahdī. In the final, millenarian age, the *ḥaqā'iq* would be completely freed from all their veils and symbolisms; there would no longer be any distinction between the *ẓāhir* and the *bāṭin* in that age of pure spirituality. On his advent, Muḥammad b. Ismā'īl would rule in justice before the physical world is consummated. This original cyclical view of religious history was modified after 'Abd Allāh al-Mahdī's doctrinal reform, which allowed for more than one heptad of imams in the era of Islam. Recognizing continuity in the imamate, the advent of the seventh era now lost its earlier messianic appeal for the Fatimid Ismailis, for whom the final eschatological age, whatever its nature, was postponed indefinitely into the future; while the functions of the Mahdi who would initiate the Day of Resurrection (*qiyāma*) at the end of time, were to be similar to those envisaged by other Muslim communities. On the other hand, the Qarmaṭīs of Baḥrayn and elsewhere continued to consider Muḥammad b. Ismā'īl as their Mahdi who on his reappearance as the seventh *nāṭiq* was expected to initiate the final age.[21]

The cosmological doctrine of the early Ismailis, which was evidently propagated orally, has been reconstructed from the fragmentary evidence preserved in later Ismaili texts by S.M. Stern and H. Halm.[22] This doctrine, representing a gnostic cosmological myth, was evidently espoused by the entire Ismaili (Qarmaṭī) movement until it was superseded by a new cosmology of Neoplatonic provenance. According to this doctrine, through His intention (*irāda*) and will (*mashī'a*), God first created a light (*nūr*) and addressed it with the Qur'anic creative imperative *kun* (Be!). Through duplication of its two letters, *kāf* and *nūn*, the name acquired its feminine form Kūnī. On God's command, Kūnī created from its light Qadar, its male assistant. Kūnī and Qadar were, thus, the first two principles (*aṣlān*) of creation. It was out of the original heptad of consonantal letters of Kūnī-Qadar, also called the higher letters (*al-ḥurūf al-ʿulwiyya*), interpreted as the archetypes of the seven *nāṭiq*s and their messages, that all other letters and names emerged; and with the names there simultaneously appeared the very things they symbolized. The doctrine explained how God's creative activity, through the intermediary of Kūnī and Qadar, brought forth the beings of the spiritual world, also accounting for the creation of the lower physical world which culminated in the genesis of Man. The early cosmology also had a key soteriological purpose. Man, who appears at the end of the process of creation, is far from his origins and his Creator. This cosmology, thus, aimed at showing the path for removing this distance and bringing about Man's salvation. This could be achieved only if Man acquired knowledge (*gnosis*) of his origin and the causes for his distance from God, a knowledge that had to be imparted from the above by God's messengers (*nāṭiq*s), as recognized in the Qur'an, and their legitimate successors in each era of human history.

The Fatimid period in Ismaili history

The Fatimid period represents the 'golden age' of Ismailism, when the Ismailis possessed an important state of their own and Ismaili scholarship and literature attained their summit. The foundation of the Fatimid caliphate in 297/909 in North Africa indeed marked the crowning success of the early Ismailis. The religio-political *daʿwa* of the Ismāʿīliyya had finally led to the establishment of a state or *dawla* headed by the Ismaili imam. In line with their universal claims, the Fatimid caliph-imams did not abandon their *daʿwa* activities on assuming power. They particularly concerned themselves with the affairs of the Ismaili *daʿwa* after transferring the seat of their state to

Egypt. The *daʿwa* achieved particular success outside the domains of the Fatimid state, and, as a result, Ismailism outlived the downfall of the Fatimid dynasty and caliphate in 567/1171, also surviving the challenges posed by the Sunni revival of the 5th-6th/11th-12th centuries. Be that as it may, Cairo, founded by the Fatimids upon their conquest of Egypt in 358/969, became the headquarters of the complex hierarchical Ismaili *daʿwa* organization in addition to serving as the capital of the Fatimid state. In Egypt, the Fatimids patronized intellectual activities. They founded major institutions of learning and libraries in Cairo, and the Fatimid capital soon became a flourishing centre of Islamic scholarship, sciences, art and culture, in addition to playing a prominent role in the Indian Ocean as well as the Mediterranean trade and commerce. All in all, the Fatimid period marked not only a glorious age in Ismaili history, but also one of the greatest eras in Egyptian and Islamic histories – a milestone in the development of Islamic civilizations.

It was during this period that the Ismaili *dāʿī*s, who were at the same time the scholars and writers of their community, produced what were to become the classical texts of Ismaili literature dealing with a multitude of exoteric and esoteric subjects, as well as *taʾwīl* which became the hallmark of Ismaili thought. The *dāʿī*s of the Fatimid period elaborated distinctive intellectual traditions. In particular, certain *dāʿī*s of the Iranian lands, notably Abū Yaʿqūb al-Sijistānī and Ḥamīd al-Dīn al-Kirmānī, amalgamated Ismaili theology with Neoplatonism and other philosophical traditions into elegant and complex metaphysical systems of thought as expressed in numerous treatises written in Arabic. Only Nāṣir-i Khusraw, the last major proponent of that Iranian Ismaili school of philosophical theology, produced all of his works in Persian. With the establishment of the Fatimid state the need had also arisen for promulgating a legal code, even though Ismailism was never to be imposed on all Fatimid subjects as their official religion. Ismaili law, which had not existed during the pre-Fatimid, secret phase of Ismailism, was codified during the early Fatimid period as a result of the efforts of al-Qāḍī al-Nuʿmān, the foremost jurist of the Ismailis. The Fatimid Ismailis now came to possess their own school of religious law or *madhhab*, similarly to the principal Sunni systems of jurisprudence (*fiqh*) and the Jaʿfarī system of the Imāmī (Twelver) Shiʿis. It was indeed during the Fatimid period that Ismailis made their contributions to Islamic theology and philosophy in general and to Shiʿi thought in particular. Modern recovery of their literature clearly attests to the richness and diversity of the literary and intellectual heritage of the Ismailis of Fatimid times.

The Fatimid period is one of the best documented in Islamic history. Many medieval Muslim historians have written about the Fatimid dynasty and state, and there are also memoirs and a multitude of non-literary sources of information on the Fatimids. In the latter category, Fatimid monuments and works of art have been thoroughly studied, and much progress has been made on the scholarly investigations of numismatic, epigraphic and other types of evidence related to the Fatimids. There are also valuable letters, documents and other types of archival materials from Fatimid Egypt – materials which are rarely available for other Muslim dynasties of medieval times. These sources have been categorized and explained in Paul E. Walker's *Exploring an Islamic Empire: Fatimid History and its Sources* (2002). Furthermore, the extensive Ismaili literature of the period, recovered in modern times, contains some historical details in addition to shedding light on various aspects of Ismaili doctrines propagated during this period. As a result of this relative abundance of the primary sources, Fatimid history and Ismailism of the Fatimid period represent the best studied and understood areas of research within the entire spectrum of modern Ismaili studies.

As a rare instance of its kind in Ismaili literature, for the Fatimid period we also have a few historical works written by Ismaili authors. These include al-Qāḍī al-Nuʿmān's *Iftitāḥ al-daʿwa* (*Commencement of the Mission*), completed in 346/957, the oldest known historical work in Ismaili literature covering the background to the establishment of the Fatimid state; and Ibn al-Haytham's *Kitāb al-munāẓarāt* on the first year of Fatimid rule in North Africa which was recently brought to light. There are also a number of short treatises on specific Ismaili events, such as the *dāʿī* al-Nīsābūrī's *Istitār al-imām*. The Fatimid caliph-imams are, of course, treated by the *dāʿī* Idrīs in volumes 5–7 of his *ʿUyūn al-akhbār*. Aside from strictly historical sources, Ismailis of the Fatimid period produced a few biographical works of the *sīra* genre with great historical value. Amongst the extant examples in this category, mention may be made of the *Sīra*s of the chamberlain Jaʿfar b. ʿAlī; the courtier Jawdhar, and the chief *dāʿī* al-Muʾayyad fi'l-Dīn al-Shīrāzī. A wide variety of archival documents, such as treatises, letters, decrees and epistles (*sijillāt*) of historical value issued through the Fatimid chancery of state, or *dīwān al-inshā'*, such as *al-Sijillāt al-Mustanṣiriyya,* and the documents included in Jamāl al-Dīn al-Shayyāl's *Majmūʿat al-wathāʾiq al-Fāṭimiyya* (1958) and in S.M. Stern's *Fāṭimid Decrees* (1964), have survived directly or been preserved in later literary sources, notably in al-Qalqashandī's encyclopedic *Ṣubḥ al-aʿshā*. The Geniza documents, consisting of thousands of letters, contracts, petitions, etc., written in Judaeo-Arabic and recovered in an old synagogue in Cairo in 1890, should also be mentioned in this context. Studied extensively by S.D. Goitein (1900–1985), Cl. Cahen (1909–1991) and others, they provide an invaluable source of information on the socio-economic and cultural life of Fatimid Egypt.

The Fatimid caliph-imams did concern themselves with historiography, and they commissioned or encouraged works which may have been regarded as official chronicles. Indeed, the events and achievements of the Fatimid state needed to be recorded by reliable chroniclers, and this became an important concern of the Fatimids, especially after the transference of the seat of their state from Ifrīqiya to Egypt in 362/973. Henceforth, numerous histories of the Fatimid state and dynasty were compiled by contemporary chroniclers, both Ismaili and non-Ismaili. But with the exception of a few fragments, these chronicles did not survive the downfall of the dynasty.

Ibn Zūlāq (d. 386/996) is one of the earliest Fatimid chroniclers whose works have been lost completely. The tradition of Fatimid historiography was maintained by al-Musabbiḥī (d. 420/1030), an official in the service of the Fatimids who may have been an Ismaili himself. He produced a vast history of Fatimid Egypt and its ruling dynasty, but only a small fraction of the fortieth volume of his *Akhbār Miṣr* has survived in a unique manuscript. Amongst other Fatimid chroniclers whose works have not survived directly, mention may be made of Muḥammad b. Salāma al-Quḍāʿī (d. 454/1062), al-Murtaḍā al-Muḥannak (d. 549/1154) and Ibn al-Maʾmūn al-Baṭāʾiḥī (d. 588/1192). Portions of these Fatimid chronicles have been preserved by later Egyptian historians, notably al-Maqrīzī. Indeed, the only extant contemporary account of the Fatimids is the history of Yaḥyā b. Saʿīd al-Anṭākī (d. 458/1066). Amongst later Egyptian historians, who were mostly functionaries in Fatimid administration, mention should be made of Ibn al-Ṣayrafī (d. 542/1147), a prolific writer who headed the Fatimid chancery of state for more than four decades. A history written by Ibn al-Ṣayrafī has not survived, but two of his other works on Fatimid viziers and institutions have been preserved. During the 7th/13th century, after the demise of the Fatimids, several other histories of the dynasty were written, such as the *Akhbār mulūk Banī ʿUbayd* of Ibn Ḥammād (d. 628/1231), a Berber *qāḍī* of North Africa, and the history of the Fatimid and Ayyūbid dynasties by Ibn al-Ṭuwayr (d. 617/1220), a high-ranking official of the later Fatimids. Ibn Ẓāfir (d. 613/1216), a secretary in the chancery of the early Ayyūbids, produced a universal history in terms of dynasties, with a section on the Fatimids. However, the most extensive history of Fatimid Egypt produced in the 7th/13th century under the early Mamlūks is the *Akhbār Miṣr* of Ibn Muyassar (d. 677/1278), which has survived in an incomplete form.

The Fatimids were treated in a number of regional chronicles and in several universal histories written by Egyptian authors of the later Mamlūk period. Ibn ʿIdhārī, a Maghribī historian who died after 712/1312, included an important account of the early Fatimids in his chronicle of Ifrīqiya entitled *al-Bayān al-mughrib*. Ibn al-Dawādārī, an Egyptian historian and a Mamlūk officer, produced an extensive universal history in 736/1335, *Kanz al-durar*, of which the sixth part is devoted to the Fatimids. Ibn al-Dawādārī has preserved extracts from the anti-Ismaili polemical work of the Sharīf Akhū Muḥsin, as well as the history of Ibn Zūlāq and other earlier sources. More extensive paraphrases from Akhū Muḥsin, as well as a detailed history of the Fatimids, are contained in the encyclopedic *Nihāyat al-arab* of al-Nuwayrī (d. 733/1333). Later, Ibn Taghrībirdī (d. 874/1470) wrote a voluminous history of Islamic Egypt, *al-Nujūm al-zāhira fī mulūk Miṣr wa'l-Qāhira*, which includes an elaborate account of Fatimid Egypt. There were other Egyptian historians, such as Ibn al-Furāt (d. 807/1405), writing on the Fatimids. However, the only Sunni author to have produced a separate and substantial history of the Fatimids was Taqī al-Dīn Aḥmad b. ʿAlī al-Maqrīzī (d. 845/1442), the dean of the medieval Egyptian historians. He produced an extensive account of the Fatimid dynasty in his *Ittiʿāẓ al-ḥunafāʾ*. In his topographic work, *al-Mawāʿiẓ wa'l-iʿtibār bi-dhikr al-khiṭaṭ wa'l-āthār*, generally known as the *Khiṭaṭ*, too, al-Maqrīzī provides many details on the

Fatimids and their achievements. In both these works, al-Maqrīzī has preserved substantial quotations from Ibn Zūlāq, al-Muḥannak, al-Musabbiḥī, Ibn al-Ṭuwayr and many other earlier authorities whose writings have been lost. Finally, al-Maqrīzī compiled a biographical dictionary, *Kitāb al-muqaffā al-kabīr*, with many entries on persons connected to Fatimid Egypt.

Much valuable information on the Fatimids and the Ismailis of that period are contained in the universal histories of Muslim authors, starting with the *Ta'rīkh* of al-Ṭabarī (d. 310/923) and its continuation by ʿArīb b. Saʿd (d. 370/980), the Andalusian historian and poet. More significantly, al-Ṭabarī's continuation became the collective work of Thābit b. Sinān (d. 365/975) and some of his relatives belonging to the learned family of Sabean scholars who hailed from Ḥarrān but settled in Baghdad. These histories, too, are almost completely lost, but they are quoted in later universal histories, such as *al-Muntaẓam* of Ibn al-Jawzī (d. 597/1200). The most important early universal history containing information on the Ismailis is, however, the *Tajārib al-umam* of Miskawayh (d. 421/1030), who made extensive use of the histories of Thābit and his nephew Hilāl b. al-Muḥassin al-Ṣābiʾ (d. 448/1056). The tradition of compiling universal histories found its culmination in *al-Kāmil fi'l-ta'rīkh* of Ibn al-Athīr (d. 630/1233), representing the peak of Muslim annalistic historiography. Ibn al-Athīr's history is rich in information on both the Fatimids and the Nizārī Ismailis of Persia and Syria.

In modern times, Ferdinand Wüstenfeld (1808–1899) was the first European orientalist to have produced an independent history of the Fatimids, *Geschichte der Faṭimiden Chalifen* (1880–81), based on Arabic chronicles, but without using any Ismaili sources. Several subsequent works on the Fatimids, such as S. Lane-Poole's *History of Egypt in the Middle Ages* (1901), De Lacy O'Leary's *A Short History of the Fatimid Khalifate* (1923), and G. Wiet's early publications, were all written before the modern advances in Ismaili studies and as such were based exclusively on hostile Sunni sources. Meanwhile, with the initiation of modern scholarship in Ismaili studies, a number of specialists began to investigate the religious dimensions of the Fatimids and the religio-political milieu in which they rose to power. In this context, particular mention should be made of B. Lewis's *The Origins of Ismāʿīlism: A Study of the Historical Background of the Fāṭimid*

Caliphate (1940) and W. Ivanow's *Ismaili Tradition Concerning the Rise of the Fatimids* (1942). It was under such circumstances that Zāhid ʿAlī (1888–1958), a learned Ismaili Bohra, produced the first history of the Fatimids in Urdu, *Taʾrīkh-i Fāṭimiyyīn-i Miṣr* (1948), using his ancestral collection of Ismaili manuscripts. In the meantime, Egyptian authors themselves had started to compose histories of the Fatimids, starting with Ḥasan Ibrāhīm Ḥasan (1892–1968), who in 1932 published his doctoral thesis on the Fatimids, *al-Fāṭimiyyūn fī Miṣr*, and in the subsequent editions of this book also drew on Ismaili sources. The progress made since then is amply reflected in the much more comprehensive *al-Dawla al-Fāṭimiyya fī Miṣr* (1992; rev. ed., 2000), written by Ayman Fuʾād Sayyid, the dean of contemporary Egyptian historians who has edited numerous Arabic texts on the Fatimids. A number of Egyptian scholars have also written biographies of individual Fatimid caliph-imams. Meanwhile, Western scholarship in Fatimid studies has continued unabated, after the earlier studies of P. Casanova (1861–1926) and M. Canard (1888–1982) who contributed the entry 'Fāṭimids' to the revised edition of *The Encyclopaedia of Islam*, as reflected in a growing number of articles and monographs devoted to different aspects of Fatimid history or Ismaili teachings and activities under the Fatimids. In the latter category, special mention should be made of the contributions of H. Halm, who fully uses Ismaili and non-Ismaili sources in his historical studies, and P.E. Walker, who has produced major work on aspects of Ismaili thought in the Fatimid age. Amongst other contemporary scholars who are specifically contributing to Fatimid studies, mention may be made of the Tunisian scholars F. Dachraoui and M. Yalaoui, as well as M. Brett, Y. Lev and Th. Bianquis, while I.K. Poonawala has concerned himself, after the pioneering work of Asaf A.A. Fyzee (1899–1981), with Ismaili jurisprudence under the Fatimids. At the same time, Jonathan M. Bloom and other art historians have been investigating aspects of Fatimid art and architecture, after the initial studies of K.A.C. Creswell (1879–1974), P. Balog (1900–1982), E.J. Grube and others. Much new research in Fatimid-Ismaili studies found expression in the papers presented at an international colloquium, *L'Égypte Fatimide, son art et son histoire*, held in Paris in 1998.

The ground for the establishment of the Fatimid state was meticulously prepared by the *dāʿī* Abū ʿAbd Allāh al-Shīʿī (d. 298/911), who had been active among the Kutāma Berbers of the Maghrib since 280/893.[23] Meanwhile, after leaving Salamiyya, the Ismaili Imam ʿAbd Allāh al-Mahdī had arrived in Egypt in 291/904, where he spent a year. Subsequently, he was prevented from going to the Maghrib because the Aghlabid rulers of the region had discovered the Ismaili imam's plans and were waiting to arrest him. ʿAbd Allāh instead headed for the remote town of Sijilmāsa, in southern Morocco, where he lived quietly for four years (292–296/905–909), maintaining his contacts with Abū ʿAbd Allāh who had already commenced his conquest of Ifrīqiya with the help of his Kutāma soldier-tribesmen. By 296/908, this Kutāma army had achieved much success signalling the fall of the Aghlabids. On 1 Rajab 296/25 March 909, Abū ʿAbd Allāh entered Raqqāda, the royal city outside of the Aghlabid capital of Qayrawān, from where he governed Ifrīqiya as al-Mahdī's deputy, for almost a whole year. In Ramaḍān 296/June 909, he set off at the head of his army for Sijalmāsa to hand over the reins of power to the Ismaili imam himself. ʿAbd Allāh al-Mahdī was acclaimed as caliph in a special ceremony in Sijilmāsa on 7 Dhu'l-Ḥijja 296/27 August 909. With these events the *dawr al-satr* in early Ismailism had also ended. ʿAbd Allāh al-Mahdī entered Raqqāda on 20 Rabīʿ II 297/4 January 910 and was immediately acclaimed as caliph there. An eyewitness account of the establishment of Fatimid rule is contained in Ibn al-Haytham's *Kitāb al-munāẓarāt*. The Ismaili Shiʿi caliphate of the Fatimids had now officially commenced in Ifrīqiya. The new dynasty was named Fatimid (Fāṭimiyya) after the Prophet's daughter Fāṭima to whom al-Mahdī and his successors traced their ʿAlid ancestry.

The Fatimids did not abandon their Ismaili *daʿwa* on assuming power, as they entertained universal aspirations aiming to extend their rule over the entire Muslim community. However, the first four Fatimid caliph-imams, ruling from Ifrīqiya, encountered numerous difficulties while consolidating their power with the help of the Kutāma Berbers who were converted to Ismailism and provided the backbone of the Fatimid armies. In particular, they confronted the hostility of the Khārijī Berbers and the Sunni Arab inhabitants of Qayrawān and other cities of Ifrīqiya led by their Mālikī jurists, in addition to their rivalries and conflicts with the Umayyads of Spain, the Abbasids and the Byzantines. Under these circumstances, the Ismaili *daʿwa* remained rather inactive in North Africa for some time.[24] Fatimid rule was established firmly in the Maghrib only under al-Muʿizz li-Dīn Allāh (341–365/953–975), who succeeded in transforming the Fatimid caliphate from a regional state into a great empire. He was also the first Fatimid caliph-imam to concern himself significantly with the propagation of the Ismaili *daʿwa* outside the Fatimid dominions, especially after the transference of the seat of the Fatimid state in 362/973 to Egypt, where he founded Cairo as his new capital city. The *daʿwa* policy of al-Muʿizz was based on a number of religio-political considerations. In particular, he was apprehensive of the success of the Qarmaṭī propaganda in the eastern regions, which not only undermined the efforts of the Fatimid Ismaili *dāʿī*s operating in the same lands, notably Iraq, Persia and Transoxania, but also aroused the general anti-Ismaili sentiments of the Sunni Muslims who did not distinguish the Ismailis from the Qarmaṭīs who had acquired a reputation for extremism and lawlessness. Al-Muʿizz's policies soon bore fruit as the Ismaili *daʿwa* and Fatimid cause were reinvigorated outside the Fatimid state. However, he was only partially successful in undermining the Qarmaṭīs and their *daʿwa* activities. Most notably, Abū Yaʿqūb al-Sijistānī (d. after 361/971), the *dāʿī* of Sīstān, Makrān and Khurāsān, who had earlier belonged to the dissident faction, transferred his allegiance to the Fatimids; and, consequently, many of his followers in Persia and Central Asia acknowledged the Fatimid caliph-imam. Ismailism also acquired a permanent stronghold in Multān, Sind, where an Ismaili principality was established for a few decades.

The caliph-imam al-Muʿizz permitted the assimilation of the Neoplatonic cosmology elaborated by the *dāʿī*s of the Iranian lands into the teachings of the Fatimid *daʿwa*. Henceforth, this Neoplatonized cosmology was advocated by the Fatimid *dāʿī*s in preference to the earlier doctrine of creation. In the course of the 4th/10th century, Muḥammad b. Aḥmad al-Nasafī, Abū Ḥātim al-Rāzī and Abū Yaʿqūb al-Sijistānī set about harmonizing their Ismaili Shiʿi theology with Neoplatonic philosophy which led to the development of a unique intellectual tradition of philosophical theology in Ismailism. These *dāʿī*s wrote for the educated classes of society and aimed to attract them intellectually. This is why they expressed their theology, always revolving around the central Shiʿi doctrine of the imamate, in terms of the then most intellectually fashionable terminologies and themes. After the initial efforts of al-Nasafī and al-Rāzī, the Iranian *dāʿī*s elaborated complex metaphysical systems of thought with a distinct Neoplatonized emanational cosmology. In this cosmology, fully elaborated in al-Sijistānī's *Kitāb al-yanābīʿ* and other works, God is described as absolutely transcendent, beyond being and non-being, and thus unknowable. Here, the Neoplatonic dyad of universal intellect (*ʿaql*) and universal soul (*nafs*) in the spiritual world replace Kūnī and Qadar of the earlier cosmology; and the emanational chain of creation is traced finally to Man, while recognizing that God created everything in the spiritual and physical worlds all at once.[25] These *dāʿī*s also expounded a doctrine of salvation as part of their cosmology. In their soteriology, the ultimate goal of salvation is the human soul's progression towards its Creator in quest of a spiritual reward in an eternal afterlife. This, of course, would depend on guidance provided by the authorized sources of wisdom in every era of history.[26]

Sharing a common interest in philosophy, a number of major Iranian *dāʿī*s became involved in a long-drawn theological debate with important juridical implications. Al-Nasafī's main work, *Kitāb al-maḥṣūl* (*Book of the Yield*), written around 300/912 and representing the earliest work of a *dāʿī* to contain Greek philosophical materials, has not survived. This book circulated widely in Qarmaṭī circles, and was soon afterwards criticized by al-Nasafī's contemporary *dāʿī* of Rayy, Abū Ḥātim al-Rāzī, who wrote his own *Kitāb al-iṣlāḥ* (*Book of the Correction*) to correct certain antinomian aspects of al-Nasafī's teachings including the view that the final seventh era of history had already commenced on the first appearance of Muḥammad b. Ismāʿīl. Al-Rāzī's *al-Iṣlāḥ* was, in turn, attacked by al-Nasafī's successor in Khurāsān, al-Sijistānī, who wrote a book entitled *Kitāb al-nuṣra* (*Book of the Support*) to defend al-Nasafī's views against the criticisms of al-Rāzī. It is mainly on the basis of al-Sijistānī's numerous extant writings, however, that scholars have recently studied the early development of what Paul Walker has termed philosophical Ismailism, with its Neoplatonized emanational cosmology, elaborated during the 4th/10th century. Later, Ḥamīd al-Dīn al-Kirmānī acted as an arbiter in the prolonged debate that had taken place earlier among the Iranian *dāʿī*s. He reviewed this debate from the perspective of the Fatimid *daʿwa* in his *Kitāb al-riyāḍ* (*Book of the Meadows*), and in particular upheld certain views of Abū Ḥātim al-Rāzī against those of al-Nasafī in affirming the indispensability of both the *ẓāhir* and the *bāṭin*, the letter of the law as well as its inner meaning. This explains perhaps why Abū Ḥātim al-Rāzī's *al-Iṣlāḥ* was the only text related to this disputation that was preserved by the Fatimid *daʿwa*.

Neoplatonic philosophy also influenced the cosmology elaborated by the Ismaili-connected Ikhwān al-Ṣafā', a group of anonymous authors in Baṣra who produced an encyclopedic work of fifty-two epistles, *Rasā'il Ikhwān al-Ṣafā'*, on a variety of sciences during the 4th/10th century, or just before the foundation of the Fatimid state as argued in numerous studies by Abbas Hamdani. At any rate, the Ikhwān al-Ṣafā', usually translated as the 'Sincere Brethren' or 'Brothers of Purity', drew on a wide variety of Greek and other pre-Islamic sources and traditions which they combined with Islamic teachings, especially as upheld by the Shiʿis. Like the contemporary Iranian *dāʿīs*, they aimed to harmonize religion and philosophy, but they do not seem to have had any discernible influence on Ismaili thought of the Fatimid period. It was only in the 6th/12th century that the *Rasā'il* were introduced into the literature of the Ṭayyibī Mustaʿlī *daʿwa* in Yaman. Henceforth, these epistles were widely studied by the Ṭayyibī *dāʿīs* of Yaman and, later, by their successors in the Dā'ūdī Bohra community of the Indian subcontinent.

It was also in al-Muʿizz's time that Ismaili law was finally codified. The process had started already in ʿAbd Allāh al-Mahdī's reign as caliph (297–322/909–934), when the precepts of Shiʿi law were put into practice. The promulgation of an Ismaili *madhhab* resulted mainly from the efforts of al-Qāḍī Abū Ḥanīfa al-Nuʿmān b. Muḥammad (d. 363/974), who was officially commissioned by al-Muʿizz to prepare legal compendia. Al-Nuʿmān had started serving the Fatimids in different capacities from the time of al-Mahdī. In 337/948, he was appointed by the Fatimid caliph-imam al-Manṣūr (334–341/946–953) as chief judge (*qāḍī al-quḍāt*) of the Fatimid state. It is to be noted that from the time of Aflaḥ b. Hārūn al-Malūsī, the Fatimid chief judge was also placed in charge of the affairs of the Ismaili *daʿwa*. Thus, responsibilities for explaining and enforcing the *ẓāhir*, or the commandments and prohibitions of the law, and interpreting its *bāṭin* or inner meaning, were united in the same person under the overall guidance of the Ismaili imam of the time.

Al-Nuʿmān codified Ismaili law by systematically collecting the firmly established *ḥadīth*s transmitted from the *ahl al-bayt*, drawing on existing collections of earlier Imāmī as well as Zaydī authorities.[27] His initial efforts resulted in a massive compendium entitled *Kitāb al-īḍāḥ*, which has not survived except for one fragment. Subsequently, he produced several abridgements of the *Īḍāḥ*, which was treated as semi-official by the Fatimids. Al-Nuʿmān's efforts culminated in the *Daʿāʾim al-Islām* (*The Pillars of Islam*), which was scrutinized closely by al-Muʿizz and endorsed as the official code of the Fatimid state. Similarly to the Sunnis and other Shiʿi communities, the Ismailis, too, now possessed a system of law and jurisprudence, also defining an Ismaili paradigm of governance. Ismaili law accorded special importance to the Shiʿi doctrine of the imamate. The authority of the infallible ʿAlid imam and his teachings became the third principal source of Ismaili law, after the Qurʾan and the *sunna* of the Prophet which are accepted as the first two sources by all Muslims. In the *Daʿāʾim*, al-Nuʿmān also provided Islamic legitimation for an ʿAlid state ruled by the *ahl al-bayt*, elaborating the *ẓāhirī* doctrinal basis of the Fatimids' legitimacy as ruling imams and lending support to their universal claims. The *Daʿāʾim al-Islām* has continued through the centuries to be used by Ṭayyibī Ismailis as their principal authority in legal matters.

The Ismailis had high esteem for learning and elaborated distinctive traditions and institutions of learning under the Fatimids. The Fatimid *daʿwa* was particularly concerned with educating the Ismaili converts in esoteric doctrine, known as the *ḥikma* or 'wisdom'. As a result, a variety of lectures or 'teaching sessions', generally designated as *majālis* (singular, *majlis*), were organized. The private lectures on Ismaili esoteric doctrine, known as the *majālis al-ḥikma* or 'sessions of wisdom', were reserved exclusively for the Ismaili initiates who had already taken the oath of allegiance and secrecy. The lectures, delivered by the *dāʿī al-duʿāt* at the Fatimid palace, were approved beforehand by the imam. Only the imam was the source of the *ḥikma*; and the *dāʿī al-duʿāt* or chief *dāʿī*, commonly called *bāb* (the gate) in Ismaili sources, was the imam's mouthpiece through whom the Ismailis received their knowledge of esoteric doctrines. Many of these *majālis* were in due course collected and committed to writing, such as al-Nuʿmān's *Taʾwīl al-daʿāʾim* and the *Majālis al-Mustanṣiriyya* delivered by al-Malījī. This Fatimid tradition of learning culminated in the

Majālis al-Mu'ayyadiyya of the *dā'ī* al-Mu'ayyad fi'l-Dīn al-Shīrāzī (d. 470/1078). Another of the main institutions of learning founded by the Fatimids was the Dār al-'Ilm, the House of Knowledge, sometimes also called the Dār al-Ḥikma. Established in 395/1005 by the caliph-imam al-Ḥākim (386–411/996–1021), a variety of religious and non-religious subjects were taught at this academy which was also equipped with a major library. Many Fatimid *dā'īs* received at least part of their training at the Dār al-'Ilm.[28]

Information on the structure and functioning of the Ismaili *da'wa* organization were among the most guarded secrets of the Ismailis. The religio-political messages of the *da'wa* were disseminated by networks of *dā'īs* within the Fatimid dominions as well as in other regions referred to as the *jazā'ir* (singular, *jazīra*, 'island'). Each *jazīra* was placed under the charge of a high-ranking *dā'ī* referred to as *ḥujja*; and every *ḥujja* had a number of *dā'īs* of different ranks working under him. Organized in a strictly hierarchical manner, the Fatimid *da'wa* was under the overall supervision of the imam and the *dā'ī al-du'āt*, or *bāb*, who acted as its administrative head. The *da'wa* organization developed over time and reached its full elaboration under the caliph-imam al-Mustanṣir. It was, however, in non-Fatimid regions, the *jazā'ir*, especially Yaman, Persia and Central Asia, that the Fatimid *da'wa* achieved lasting success.[29] The *da'wa* was intensified in Iraq and Persia under al-Ḥākim. Foremost among the *dā'īs* of this period was Ḥamīd al-Dīn al-Kirmānī (d. after 411/1020). A learned philosopher, he harmonized Ismaili theology with a variety of philosophical traditions in developing his own metaphysical system, presented in his *Rāḥat al-'aql*, completed in 411/1020. In fact, al-Kirmānī's thought represents a unique tradition within the Iranian school of philosophical Ismailism. In particular, he expounded a modified cosmology, replacing the Neoplatonic dyad of intellect and soul in the spiritual world by a system of ten separate intellects in partial adaptation of al-Fārābī's Aristotelian cosmic system.[30] Al-Kirmānī's cosmology, however, was not adopted by the Fatimid *da'wa*; it later provided the basis for the fourth and final stage in the evolution of Ismaili cosmology at the hands of Ṭayyibī *dā'īs* of Yaman. The Fatimid caliph-imam al-Ḥākim's reign also coincided with the opening phase of what was to become known as the Druze religion, founded by a number of *dā'īs* who had come to Cairo from Persia and Central Asia, notably al-Akhram, and al-Darazī. These *dāʿīs* proclaimed the end of the historical era of Islam and advocated the divinity of al-Ḥākim. Al-Kirmānī was officially invited to Cairo around 405/1014 to refute the new extremist doctrines from a theological perspective. He wrote several treatises in defence of the doctrine of imamate in general and al-Ḥākim's imamate in particular, including *al-Maṣābīḥ fī ithbāt al-imāma,* the *Risālat mabāsim al-bishārāt* and *al-Risāla al-wāʿiẓa.* In fact, the doctrine of the imamate provided an essential subject matter for a number of doctrinal treatises written by the Ismaili authors of different periods.

The Ismaili *daʿwa* activities outside the Fatimid dominions reached their peak in the long reign of al-Mustanṣir (427–487/1036–1094), even after the Sunnī Saljūqs replaced the Shīʿī Būyids as overlords of the Abbasids in 447/1055. The Fatimid *dāʿīs* won many converts in Iraq and different parts of Persia and Central Asia. One of the most prominent *dāʿīs* of this period was al-Muʾayyad fiʾl-Dīn al-Shīrāzī who after his initial career in Fārs, in southern Persia, settled in Cairo and played an active role in the affairs of the Fatimid *dawla* and Ismaili *daʿwa*. In 450/1058, al-Mustanṣir appointed him as *dāʿī al-duʿāt,* a post he held for twenty years, with the exception of a brief period, until his death in 470/1078. He has left an invaluable account of his life and early career in his *Sīra,*[31] which reveals this *dāʿī*'s central role as an intermediary between the Fatimids and the Turkish military commander al-Basāsīrī who briefly led the Fatimid cause in Iraq against the Saljūqs. Al-Basāsīrī seized Baghdad in 450/1058 and had the *khuṭba* read there for one whole year for al-Mustanṣir before he was eventually defeated by the Saljūqs. Al-Muʾayyad established closer relations between Cairo and several *jazīras,* especially Yaman where Ismailism had persisted in a dormant form throughout the 4th/10th century. By the time of al-Mustanṣir, the leadership of the *daʿwa* in Yaman had fallen into the hands of the *dāʿī* ʿAlī b. Muḥammad al-Ṣulayḥī, an important chieftain of the Banū Hamdān in the mountainous region of Ḥarāz. The *dāʿī* ʿAlī al-Ṣulayḥī rose in Ḥarāz in 439/1047, marking the effective foundation of the Ṣulayḥid dynasty ruling over different parts of Yaman as vassals of the Fatimids until 532/1138. On ʿAlī's death in 459/1067, Lamak b. Mālik al-Ḥammādī was appointed as chief *dāʿī* of Yaman while ʿAlī's son Aḥmad al-Mukarram (d. 477/1084) succeeded his father merely as head of the Ṣulayḥid state. The *dāʿī* Lamak had earlier spent five years in Cairo, staying and studying with the chief *dāʿī* al-Muʾayyad at his residence at the Dār al-ʿIlm. From the latter part of Aḥmad al-Mukarram's reign, during which time the Ṣulayḥids lost much of Yaman to Zaydīs there, effective authority in the Ṣulayḥid state was transferred to al-Mukarram's consort, al-Malika al-Sayyida Ḥurra (d. 532/1138). She played an increasingly important role in the affairs of the Yamanī *daʿwa* culminating in her appointment as the *ḥujja* of Yaman by al-Mustanṣir. This represented the first assignment of a high rank in the *daʿwa* hierarchy to a woman. These events, and the Ṣulayḥids in general, are treated in ʿUmāra al-Yamanī's *Taʾrīkh al-Yaman*, and in the seventh volume of the *dāʿī* Idrīs's *ʿUyūn al-akhbār*.[32] The Ṣulayḥids also played an active part in the renewed efforts of the Fatimids to spread the *daʿwa* on the Indian subcontinent. The Ismaili community founded in Gujarāt by *dāʿīs* sent from Yaman in the second half of the 5th/11th century evolved into the modern day Ṭayyibī Bohra community.

Meanwhile, the Ismaili *daʿwa* had continued to spread in many parts of the Iranian world, now incorporated into the Saljūq sultanate. By the early 460s/1070s, the Persian Ismailis in the Saljūq dominions were under the leadership of ʿAbd al-Malik b. ʿAṭṭāsh who had his secret headquarters in Iṣfahān, the main Saljūq capital. He was also responsible for launching the career of Ḥasan-i Ṣabbāḥ who in due course led the Ismaili *daʿwa* in Persia. In Badakhshān and other eastern parts of the Iranian world, too, the *daʿwa* had continued to spread after the downfall of the Sāmānids in 395/1005.[33] One of the most eminent *dāʿīs* of al-Mustanṣir's time, Nāṣir-i Khusraw (d. after 462/1070) played an important part in propagating Ismailism in Central Asia as the *ḥujja* of Khurāsān; he also spread the *daʿwa* to Ṭabaristān and other Caspian provinces.[34] It was mainly during his period of exile in Yumgān that Nāṣir extended the *daʿwa* throughout Badakhshān while maintaining his contacts with the *dāʿī* al-Muʾayyad and the *daʿwa* headquarters in Cairo. It was during those years in the midst of the Pamir mountains that Nāṣir produced the bulk of his poetry as well as his theological-philosophical writings, including the *Jāmiʿ al-ḥikmatayn*, his last known work completed in 462/1070 at the request of his Ismaili protector and amir of Badakhshān, Abu'l-Maʿālī ʿAlī b. al-Asad. The Ismailis of Badakhshān, now divided between Tajikistan and Afghanistan, and their offshoot groups in the Hindu Kush region, situated in Hunza and other northern areas of Pakistan, regard Shāh Nāṣir-i Khusraw as the founder of their communities. By the time the Qarmaṭī state of Baḥrayn was finally uprooted in 470/1077–78 by the local tribal chieftains, other Qarmaṭī groups in Persia, Iraq and elsewhere too had either disintegrated or switched their allegiance to the Ismaili *da'wa* of the Fatimids. There was now, once again, only one unified Ismaili *da'wa* under the supreme leadership of the Fatimid caliph-imam.

During the long reign of al-Mustanṣir the Fatimid caliphate had already embarked on its decline resulting from factional fighting in the Fatimid armies and other political and economic difficulties. The ravaging activities of the Turkish regiments which led to a complete breakdown of law and order finally obliged al-Mustanṣir to appeal for help to Badr al-Jamālī, an Armenian general in the service of the Fatimids. Badr arrived in Cairo in 466/1074 and soon assumed leadership of civil, judicial and religious administrations in addition to being 'commander of the armies' (*amīr al-juyūsh*), his main title and source of power. He managed to restore peace and relative prosperity to Egypt in the course of his long vizierate of some twenty years when he was the effective ruler of the Fatimid state. Badr died in 487/1094 after having arranged for his son al-Afḍal to succeed him in the vizierate. Henceforth, real power in the Fatimid state remained in the hands of viziers who were normally commanders of the armies, whence their title of 'vizier of the sword' (*wazīr al-sayf*), and normally also in charge of the *da'wa* organization and activities.

Al-Mustanṣir, the eighth Fatimid caliph and eighteenth Ismaili imam, died in Dhu'l-Ḥijja 487/December 1094, a few months after Badr al-Jamālī. Thereupon, the unified Ismaili *da'wa* split into two rival factions, as al-Mustanṣir's son and original heir-designate Nizār was deprived of his succession rights by al-Afḍal who quickly installed Nizār's younger half-brother to the Fatimid throne with the title of al-Musta'lī bi'llāh (487–495/1094–1101). The two factions were later designated as the Nizāriyya and Musta'liyya after al-Mustanṣir's sons who claimed his heritage. Al-Afḍal immediately obtained for al-Musta'lī the allegiance of the notables of the Fatimid court and most leaders of the Ismaili *da'wa* in Cairo who also recognized al-Musta'lī's imamate. Nizār refused to pay homage to al-Musta'lī and fled to Alexandria where he rose in revolt, but was defeated and killed in 488/1095. The imamate of al-Mustaʿlī was recognized by the Ismaili communities of Egypt, Yaman and western India. These Ismailis who depended on the Fatimid regime later traced the imamate in the progeny of al-Mustaʿlī. The bulk of the Ismailis of Syria, too, joined the Mustaʿlī camp. On the other hand, the Ismailis of Persia who were then already under the leadership of Ḥasan-i Ṣabbāḥ supported the succession rights of Nizār. The Central Asian Ismailis seem to have remained uninvolved in the Nizārī-Mustaʿlī schism for quite some time.

The Fatimid state survived for another 77 years after the Nizārī-Mustaʿlī schism of 487/1094. These decades witnessed the rapid decline of the Fatimid caliphate which was beset by continuing crises. Al-Mustaʿlī and his successors on the Fatimid throne, who were mostly minors and remained powerless in the hands of their viziers, continued to be recognized as imams by the Mustaʿlī Ismailis who themselves soon split into Ḥāfiẓī and Ṭayyibī branches. On al-Mustaʿlī's premature death in 495/1101, the all-powerful vizier al-Afḍal placed his five-year-old son on the throne with the caliphal title of al-Āmir bi-Aḥkām Allāh. Al-Afḍal was murdered in 515/1121; and when al-Āmir himself was assassinated in 524/1130, the Mustaʿlī Ismailis were confronted with a major crisis of succession. A son, named al-Ṭayyib, had been born to al-Āmir a few months before his death; and he had been designated as the heir apparent. But on al-Āmir's death, power was assumed by his cousin, ʿAbd al-Majīd, a grandson of al-Mustanṣir and the eldest member of the Fatimid family, and nothing more was heard of al-Ṭayyib. After a brief confusing period in Fatimid history, when Twelver Shiʿism instead of Ismailism was adopted as the official religion of the Fatimid state by al-Afḍal's son Kutayfāt who had succeeded to the vizierate, ʿAbd al-Majīd re-emerged on the scene in 526/1132 proclaiming himself as caliph and imam with the title of al-Ḥāfiẓ li-Dīn Allāh; and Ismailism was reinstated as the Fatimid state's religion.[35]

The irregular proclamation as imam of al-Ḥāfiẓ, whose father (Abu'l-Qāsim Muḥammad b. al-Mustanṣir) had not been imam previously, caused a major split in the Mustaʿlī Ismaili community. As in the case of the Nizārī-Mustaʿlī schism, the Mustaʿlī *daʿwa* headquarters in Cairo endorsed the imamate of al-Ḥāfiẓ, who claimed al-Āmir had personally designated him.[36] Therefore, it was also acknowledged by the Mustaʿlī Ismailis of Egypt and Syria as well as a portion of the

Mustaʿlīs of Yaman. These Ismailis, who recognized al-Ḥāfiẓ and the later Fatimid caliphs as their imams, became known as the Ḥāfiẓiyya. On the other hand, the Ṣulayḥid queen of Yaman, al-Sayyida Ḥurra, who had already drifted away from Cairo, upheld al-Ṭayyib's cause and recognized him as al-Āmir's successor to the imamate. As a result, the Mustaʿlī community of the Ṣulayḥid state, too, recognized al-Ṭayyib's imamate. These Mustaʿlī Ismailis of Yaman, with some minority groups in Egypt and Syria, initially known as the Āmiriyya, became later designated as the Ṭayyibiyya. The Ismaili traditions of the earlier times were maintained during the final decades of the Fatimid dynasty. These included the appointment of chief *dāʿī*s as administrative heads of the Ḥāfiẓī *daʿwa*, the regular holdings of the *majālis al-ḥikma*, and the activities of the Dār al-ʿIlm, which was moved to a new location in Cairo in 526/1132. The Ḥāfiẓī theologians of this period must have, therefore, concerned themselves with literary activities. However, after the demise of the Fatimid dynasty and caliphate, there were no longer any Ḥāfiẓī communities left in Egypt or elsewhere to preserve their literature. The extant anonymous *al-Qaṣīda al-Shāfiya,* originally composed by a Ḥāfiẓī poet, may be a sole exception.

The Ayyūbid Ṣalāḥ al-Dīn, who had acted as the last Fatimid vizier, ended Fatimid rule on 7 Muḥarram 567/10 September 1171, when he had the *khuṭba* read in Cairo in the name of the reigning Abbasid caliph al-Mustaḍīʾ. A few days later, al-ʿĀḍid (555–567/1160–1171), the fourteenth and final Fatimid caliph, died after a brief illness. The Fatimid *dawla* had, thus, ended after 262 years.[37] On the collapse of the Fatimid caliphate, Egypt's new Sunni Ayyūbid masters began to persecute the Ismailis, also suppressing the Ḥāfiẓī *daʿwa* organization and all the Fatimid institutions. The immense treasures of the Fatimids and their vast libraries were pillaged or sold. For a while longer, however, certain direct descendants of al-Ḥāfiẓ and a few false pretenders claimed the imamate of the Ḥāfiẓīs. Some of them led revolts which received limited support in Egypt. Al-ʿĀḍid had appointed his eldest son, Dāʾūd, as his heir apparent; and, after al-ʿĀḍid, the Ḥāfiẓīs recognized him as their next imam. But Dāʾūd, like other members of the Fatimid family, had been placed in permanent captivity in Cairo. In 569/1174, a major conspiracy to overthrow Ṣalāḥ al-Dīn and restore Fatimid rule was discovered in Cairo. The chief conspirators included ʿUmāra, the famous Yamanī poet and historian, a former chief *dāʿī* as well as several Ismaili jurists and Fatimid commanders. ʿUmāra and several others were executed on Ṣalāḥ al-Dīn's order. A few more minor revolts, led by Fatimid pretenders or Ismailis, occurred during the final decades of the 6th/12th century. After Dāʾūd b. al-ʿĀḍid (d. 604/1207), his son Sulaymān (d. 645/1248), conceived secretly in prison, was evidently acknowledged as the imam of the Ḥāfiẓī Ismailis.

The Ḥāfiẓiyya had disintegrated almost completely in Egypt by the end of the 7th/13th century, when the Fatimid prisoners were finally released by the Mamlūks who had succeeded the Ayyūbids. In Yaman, the Zurayʿids of ʿAdan and some of the Hamdānids of Ṣanʿāʾ had adhered to Ḥāfiẓī Ismailism until the Ayyūbid conquest of southern Arabia in 569/1173. The main source for the history of the Zurayʿids, who also acted as the chief *dāʿī*s of the Ḥāfiẓī *daʿwa*, is the *Taʾrīkh al-Yaman* of ʿUmāra al-Yamanī, who personally knew some members of the dynasty.[38] The Ḥāfiẓīs may still have enjoyed some prominence in Yaman by the beginning of the 7th/13th century when the fifth *dāʿī* of the Ṭayyibīs, ʿAlī b. Muḥammad b. al-Walīd (d. 612/1215), found it necessary to write a polemical work, *Tuḥfat al-murtād*, refuting the claims of al-Ḥāfiẓ and his successors to the imamate and defending the legitimacy of the Ṭayyibī *daʿwa*. For all practical purposes, on the collapse of the Fatimid caliphate, Mustaʿlī Ismailism survived only in its Ṭayyibī form.

The Yamanī and Indian phases of Ṭayyibī Ismailism

The Ṭayyibī Ismailis recognized al-Āmir's infant son, al-Ṭayyib, as their imam after al-Āmir, rejecting the claims of al-Ḥāfiẓ and the later Fatimids to the imamate. Ṭayyibī Ismailism found its permanent stronghold in Yaman, where it received the initial support of the Ṣulayḥids. The Ṭayyibīs divide their history into succeeding eras of concealment (*satr*) and manifestation (*kashf* or *ẓuhūr*), during which the imams are concealed or manifest. The first era of *satr*, coinciding with the pre-Fatimid period in Ismaili history, ended with the appearance of ʿAbd Allāh al-Mahdī. This was followed by an era of *ẓuhūr* which continued in the Fatimid period until the concealment of the twenty-first Ṭayyibī Imam al-Ṭayyib, soon after al-Āmir's death in 524/1130. Al-Ṭayyib's concealment, it is held by the Ṭayyibīs, initiated another era of *satr*, during which the Ṭayyibī imams have all remained hidden (*mastūr*) from the eyes of their followers; and the current *satr* will continue until the appearance of an imam from al-Ṭayyib's progeny. The current period of *satr* in Ṭayyibī Ismailism has, in turn, been further divided into a Yamanī phase, extending from 526/1132 to around 997/1589, when the Ṭayyibīs were split into Dā'ūdī and Sulaymānī factions, and an Indian phase, covering essentially the history of the Dā'ūdī Ṭayyibī *da'wa* during the last four centuries. There were essentially no doctrinal differences between the two Ṭayyibī communities, which were to follow separate lines of *dā'ī*s.

The history of the Yamanī phase of Ṭayyibī Ismailism is essentially a history of the activities of the various *dā'ī*s and their relations with the Zaydīs and other local dynasties of medieval Yaman. The literary sources for this phase have been fully discussed in the relevant sections of A. Fu'ād Sayyid's bio-bibliographical survey of the sources on Yaman's Islamic history.[39] For the earliest period in Ṭayyibī history, the chief authority is once again 'Umāra al-Yamanī's *Ta'rīkh al-Yaman*. Ismaili historiography on the subject, as expected, is rather meagre with the major exception of the works of the *dā'ī* Idrīs 'Imād al-Dīn (d. 872/1468). The still unpublished *Tuḥfat al-qulūb* of the *dā'ī* Ḥātim b. Ibrāhīm al-Ḥāmidī (d. 596/1199) is another important source on the history of the early Ṭayyibī *da'wa* in Yaman. Professor Abbas Hamdani has prepared a critical edition of the *Tuḥfa*, which will be published in the near future.

Idrīs 'Imād al-Dīn b. al-Ḥasan remains our major source on the history of Ṭayyibī Ismailism in medieval Yaman. He hailed from the prominent Banū al-Walīd clan of Quraysh, who led the Ṭayyibī *da'wa* in Yaman for more than three centuries. In 832/1428, Idrīs succeeded his uncle, 'Alī b. 'Abd Allāh b. 'Alī al-Walīd, as the nineteenth *dā'ī muṭlaq* of the Ṭayyibīs. Idrīs, who took special interest in the affairs of the *da'wa* in Gujarāt, was also a warrior and participated in several battles against the Zaydīs. Idrīs produced three extensive historical works. As the head of the Ṭayyibī *da'wa*, Idrīs was very well-informed about the affairs of the Ismaili community in Yaman. He also has extensive quotations from numerous Ismaili sources and archival documents which have not survived. In the seventh and final volume of his *'Uyūn al-akhbār*, he provides valuable information on the Ṣulayḥids and the *da'wa* in Ṣulayḥid Yaman, as well as on the later Fatimids and the opening phase of Ṭayyibī Ismailism. His second historical work, *Nuzhat al-afkār*, deals especially with the history of the Ismaili *daʿwa* in Yaman from the collapse of the Ṣulayḥid dynasty in 532/1138 until 853/1449. In the *Nuzhat al-afkār*, which is still in manuscript form, particular attention is paid to the Ṭayyibī *daʿwa* in India and the relations between the Ṭayyibī communities of Yaman and India. Thirdly, in the *Rawḍat al-akhbār*, which is a continuation of the previous history, Idrīs relates the events of his own time, from the year 854/1450 to 870/1465. This is also an important source on the history of the Ṭāhirids (858–923/1454–1517) who ruled over Yaman after the Rasūlids (626–858/1229–1454) and were allied with the *dāʿī* Idrīs. The recently published *Rawḍat al-akhbār* is also an important autobiographical source on Idrīs's career. Ḥusayn F. al-Hamdānī was the first modern scholar to indicate the importance of Idrīs's historical works for studying Ismailism in Yaman while also pointing out their occasional biases.[40]

The history of the Indian phase of Ṭayyibī Ismailism, too, revolves around the activities of different *dāʿīs*, in addition to the polemical accounts of various disputes and minor schisms in the Dāʾūdī Bohra community arising mainly from competing claims to the leadership of the *daʿwa*. A number of Dāʾūdī *dāʿīs* and authors have produced historical works on the Ṭayyibī *daʿwa* in India, some of which have been written in a form of Arabicized Gujarātī, i.e., Gujarātī transcribed in Arabic script, adopted as the language of the Dāʾūdī *daʿwa* and Bohras. The majority of the Ismaili sources produced in South Asia, however, mix legend and reality rather indiscriminately. As a result, the history of Ṭayyibī Ismailism in India, especially for the earlier centuries, remains shrouded in mystery. Among the few accurate Ismaili histories produced in India, is the *Muntazaʿ al-akhbār*, in two volumes, written in Arabic by Quṭb al-Dīn Sulaymānjī Burhānpūrī (d. 1241/1826), a Dāʾūdī Ṭayyibī Bohra with a high rank in the *daʿwa* organization. The first volume of this work deals with the history of the twenty-one imams recognized by the Ṭayyibī Mustaʿlīs, and the second volume covers the history of the Ṭayyibīs and their (Dāʾūdī) *dāʿīs* until 1240/1824. Another noteworthy history of Ismailism in South Asia is the *Mawsim-i bahār* of Muḥammad ʿAlī b. Mullā Jīwābhāʾī Rāmpūrī, a functionary of the Dāʾūdī *daʿwa* who died in 1315/1897 or a year later. This three-volume work, in Arabicized Gujarātī and drawing on the *Muntazaʿ al-akhbār* and a number of earlier sources which have not survived, is considered by the Dā'ūdī Bohras as an authentic source of their history. The first volume on the stories of the prophets and the second volume on the imams were completed during 1302–11/1885–93, after the third volume on the history of the *dā'īs* in Yaman as well as the *da'wa* in India from its origins until the time of the author. The third volume was compiled in 1299/1882 and lithographed shortly afterwards.

The Ṭayyibīs of Yaman and South Asia have preserved a good portion of the literary heritage of the Ismailis, including the classical works of the Fatimid period and the texts written by Yamanī Ṭayyibī authors. These manuscript sources, collectively designated as *al-khizāna al-maknūna* 'the guarded treasure', were mostly transferred after the 10th/16th century from Yaman to India, where they continued to be copied by better-educated Bohras of Gujarāt and elsewhere. This literature was classified and described for the first time in the *Fahrasat al-kutub wa'l-rasā'il* of al-Majdū', a Dā'ūdī Bohra scholar who died in 1183/1769 or a year later. All this, as well as the devotional sectarian and polemical writings of the Dā'ūdī Bohras themselves, are also listed in the relevant sections of I.K. Poonawala's *Biobibliography of Ismā'īlī Literature* (1977). At present, there are major libraries of Ismaili manuscripts in Sūrat, Bombay and Baroda, seats of the Dā'ūdī, Sulaymānī and 'Alawī Bohras in India, and in some private collections in Yaman within the Sulaymānī community there. The largest collections of such manuscripts in the West is located at The Institute of Ismaili Studies Library in London.

In modern times, a number of Dā'ūdī Bohras, who account for the overwhelming majority of the Ṭayyibī Ismailis, have written on various aspects of their community. But historical works of any value have remained rather few in number. The *Gulzare Daudi* (1920), written by Mullā Abdul Husain, a Dā'ūdī functionary who became a dissident, served as one of the most popular and influential books in English on Ṭayyibī Ismailism in India. Several other Dā'ūdī authors, such as Hasan Ali Badripresswala Ismailji and Najm al-Ghani Khan, wrote historical works in Gujarātī or Urdu. The late Zāhid 'Alī produced in Urdu the fullest contemporary account of the Ṭayyibī doctrines in his *Hamāre Ismā'īlī madhhab* (1954). Several members of the distinguished al-Hamdānī family, descendants of Muḥammad 'Alī b. Fayḍ Allāh al-Ya'būrī al-Hamdānī (d. 1315/1898), a prominent

Dā'ūdī scholar from Sūrat, have written on Ṭayyibī Ismailism and on the *da'wa* in India. Muḥammad 'Alī's grandson Ḥusayn b. Fayḍ Allāh al-Hamdānī (1901–1961) and the latter's son Abbas Hamdani have also made their family collections of Ismaili manuscripts available to libraries and scholars at large. Asaf A.A. Fyzee (1899–1981), a learned Sulaymānī Bohra, produced pioneering work on Ismaili jurisprudence – a field of enquiry later adopted by I.K. Poonawala, himself from another learned Bohra family. With a few exceptions, notably John N. Hollister's *The Shi'a of India* (1953), Western scholars and Ismaili specialists have not produced major works on Ṭayyibī Ismailism. On the other hand, a number of dissident Dā'ūdīs, led by Asghar Ali Engineer, who have been involved in various reformist groups organized against the *dā'ī* and his policies have written on Bohra institutions and practices.[41]

The Ṭayyibī *da'wa*, as noted, survived the downfall of the Fatimids, because from early on it had developed independently of the Fatimid state. It received its initial support from the Ṣulayḥid queen, al-Sayyida Ḥurra, who had been looking after the affairs of the Musta'lī *da'wa* in Yaman with the help of the *dā'ī* Lamak b. Mālik al-Ḥammādī (d. ca. 491/1098) and then his son Yaḥyā (d. 520/1126). It was soon after 526/1132 that the Ṣulayḥid queen broke her relations with Cairo and declared Yaḥyā's successor al-Dhu'ayb b. Mūsā al-Wādi'ī as the *dā'ī muṭlaq*, or *dā'ī* with absolute authority, to lead the affairs of the Ṭayyibī Musta'lī *da'wa* on behalf of their concealed Imam al-Ṭayyib. This marked the foundation of the Ṭayyibī *da'wa* independently of the Ṣulayḥid state as well. On al-Dhu'ayb's death in 546/1151, Ibrāhīm b. al-Ḥusayn al-Ḥāmidī succeeded to the leadership of the Ṭayyibī *da'wa* as the second *dā'ī muṭlaq*. The Ṭayyibī *da'wa* spread successfully in the Ḥarāz region of Yaman even though it did not receive the support of any Yamanī rulers after the death of the Ṣulayḥid queen in 532/1138.[42] After Ibrāhīm al-Ḥāmidī (d. 557/1162), the position of *dā'ī muṭlaq* remained hereditary among his descendants until 605/1209 when it passed to 'Alī b. Muḥammad b. al-Walīd of the Banū al-Walīd al-Anf family of the Quraysh and remained in this family, with minor interruptions, until 946/1539. During the Yamanī period, the Ṭayyibīs maintained their unity in Yaman and won an increasing number of converts in western India.

In the doctrinal field, the Ṭayyibīs maintained the Fatimid

traditions, and, in like manner, they emphasized the equal importance of the *ẓāhir* and *bāṭin* aspects of religion, also retaining the earlier interest of the Ismailis in cyclical history and cosmology which served as the basis of their gnostic, esoteric *ḥaqāʾiq* system of religious thought with its distinctive eschatological themes. This system was, in fact, founded largely by Ibrāhīm al-Ḥāmidī who drew extensively on al-Kirmānī's *Rāḥat al-ʿaql* and synthesized its cosmological doctrine of the ten separate intellects with gnostic mythical elements. The Ṭayyibī modification of al-Kirmānī's system, first elaborated in Ibrāhīm al-Ḥāmidī's *Kanz al-walad*, in effect, represents the fourth and final stage in the development of the Neoplatonized cosmology in Ismaili thought. By astronomical and astrological speculations, the Yamanī Ṭayyibīs also introduced certain innovations into the earlier cyclical conception of religious history, expressed in terms of the seven prophetic eras. They conceived of countless cycles leading the sacred history of humankind from its origins to the Great Resurrection (*qiyāmat al-qiyāmāt*). The Ṭayyibī *ḥaqāʾiq*, explained in many sources such as the *Tāj al-ʿaqāʾid* of ʿAlī b. Muḥammad b. al-Walīd (d. 612/1215), find their fullest description in Idrīs ʿImād al-Dīn's *Zahr al-maʿānī*, an extensive compendium of esoteric doctrines completed in 838/1435. Subsequently, the Ṭayyibīs made few further doctrinal contributions while copying the earlier texts. From early on, the Ṭayyibīs also used al-Qāḍī al-Nuʿmān's *Daʿāʾim al-Islām* as their most authoritative legal compendium. In modern times, Henry Corbin has studied extensively the various aspects of Ṭayyibī thought, especially its cosmology and eschatology with what he called its 'drama in heaven', also discussing important parallels between these doctrines and those found in Manichaeism and other Iranian religions.[43]

The Ṭayyibī *daʿwa* organization has drawn on Fatimid antecedents with certain modifications. As in the case of imams, every *dāʿī muṭlaq* has appointed his successor by the rule of the *naṣṣ*. The Ṭayyibī *dāʿīs* in Yaman were among the most educated members of their community; many became outstanding religious scholars and produced the bulk of the classical Ṭayyibī literature related to the *ḥaqāʾiq*. The *dāʿī muṭlaq* was normally assisted in the affairs of the *daʿwa* by several subordinate *dāʿīs* designated as *maʾdhūn* and *mukāsir*. Meanwhile, the Yamanī *dāʿī muṭlaqs* had maintained close relations with the Ṭayyibī community of western India. There, the Ismaili converts, mostly of Hindu descent, were known as Bohras, a name believed to have been derived from the Gujarātī term *vohorvū* meaning 'to trade', since the *da'wa* originally spread among the trading community of Gujarāt. The Ismaili Bohras of Gujarāt were persecuted under the Sunni sultans of the region from 793/1391, obliging them to observe *taqiyya* in the guise of Sunnism. With the establishment of Mughal rule in 980/1572, however they began to enjoy a certain degree of religious freedom in India and conversions to Sunni Islam ceased.

On the death of the twenty-sixth *dā'ī muṭlaq*, Dā'ūd b. 'Ajabshāh, in 997/1589 or 999/1591, his succession was disputed leading to the Dā'ūdī-Sulaymānī schism in the Ṭayyibī *da'wa* and community. By then, the Ṭayyibī Bohras in India, who greatly outnumbered their Yamanī co-religionists, desired to attain their independence from Yaman. As a result, they acknowledged Dā'ūd Burhān al-Dīn (d. 1021/1612) as their next *dā'ī* and became known as Dā'ūdīs. A small number of Yamanī Ṭayyibīs, too, supported the Dā'ūdī cause. On the other hand, a minority of Ṭayyibīs, who accounted for the bulk of the community in Yaman, recognized Sulaymān b. Ḥasan (d. 1005/1597) as their new, twenty-seventh *dā'ī*; they became known as Sulaymānīs. Henceforth, the Dā'ūdī and Sulaymānī Ṭayyibīs followed separate lines of *dā'īs*. The Dā'ūdī *dā'īs* continued to reside in India, while the headquarters of the Sulaymānī *da'wa* were established in Yaman. Subsequently, the Dā'ūdī Bohras were further subdivided in India due to periodical challenges to the authority of their *dā'ī muṭlaq*. As one such instance, in 1034/1624, 'Alī b. Ibrāhīm (d. 1046/1637) founded the 'Alawī splinter group who established their own line of *dā'īs*. At present, the 'Alawī Bohras are a very small community centred in Baroda (Vadodara), Gujarāt. The present 'Alawī *dā'ī*, the forty-fourth in the series, is Sayyidnā Abū Ḥātim Ṭayyib Ḍiyā' al-Dīn Ṣāḥib who succeeded his father in 1394/1974.

In 1200/1785, the headquarters of the Dā'ūdī *da'wa* was transferred to Sūrat, where the forty-third *dā'ī*, 'Abd 'Alī Sayf al-Dīn (1213–1232/1798–1817), founded a seminary known as Sayfī Dars, also Jāmi'at Sayfiyya, for the education of Dā'ūdī scholars and functionaries. This seminary, with a major library, has continued to serve as an institution of traditional Islamic learning for the Dā'ūdī Bohras. Since 1232/1817, the office of the *dā'ī muṭlaq* of the Dā'ūdī Ṭayyibīs has remained among the descendants of Shaykh Jīwanjī Awrangābādī, while the community has experienced intermittent strife and crisis rooted in opposition to the *dāʿī*'s authority. The present *dāʿī muṭlaq* of the Dāʾūdī *daʿwa*, Sayyidnā Muḥammad Burhān al-Dīn, succeeded his father Sayyidnā Ṭāhir Sayf al-Dīn (1333–1385/1915–1965) as the fifty-second in the series. The total Dāʾūdī population of the world is currently (2004) estimated at around 900,000 persons, located mainly in India. Since the 1920s, Bombay (Mumbai), with its largest single concentration of Bohras, has served as the permanent administrative seat of the Dāʾūdī *dāʿī muṭlaq*. The Ṭayyibī Bohras, together with the Nizārī Khojas, were also among the earliest Asian communities to settle, during the nineteenth century and subsequently, in East Africa. Their settlement received particular encouragement from Sultan Saʿīd (1220–1273/1806–1856), of the Āl Bū Saʿīd dynasty of ʿUmān and Zanzibar, who aimed to expand his trade relations with India. In time, the Indian Ismaili traders, who had originally emigrated to Zanzibar, the sultan's capital since 1256/1840, moved to the growing urban centres of East Africa. But from the early 1970s, due to the anti-Asian policies of Ugandan and other African governments, many Ismailis left Africa for the West.

In Yaman, the leadership of the Sulaymānī Ṭayyibīs has remained hereditary, since 1088/1677 with few exceptions, in the same Makramī family. Unlike the Dāʾūdīs, the Sulaymānīs have not experienced succession disputes and schisms. The Sulaymānī *dāʿī*s established their headquarters in Najrān, in north-eastern Yaman, and ruled over that region with the military support of the local Banū Yām. In the twentieth century, the political prominence of the Sulaymānī *dāʿī*s, checked earlier by Zaydīs and the Ottomans, was further curtailed by the Saʿūdī family; Najrān was, in fact, annexed to Saudi Arabia in 1353/1934. The present *dāʿī muṭlaq* of the Sulaymānīs, the fiftieth in the series, Sayyidnā al-Ḥusayn b. Ismāʿīl al-Makramī, succeeded to office in 1413/1992 and lives in Saudi Arabia. At present, the Sulaymānī Ṭayyibī Ismailis of Yaman number around 70,000 persons. The Sulaymānī Bohras represent a very small community of a few thousands in India. Similarly to the Dāʾūdīs, the Sulaymānīs withhold their religious literature from outsiders.

Nizārī Ismailism of the Alamūt period

By the time of the Nizārī-Mustaʿlī succession dispute of 487/1094, Ḥasan-i Ṣabbāḥ, who preached the Ismaili *daʿwa* within the Saljūq dominions in Persia, had emerged as the leader of the Persian Ismailis. He was then clearly following an independent policy, and his seizure of the fortress of Alamūt in 483/1090 had, in fact, signalled the initiation of the Persian Ismailis' open revolt against the Saljūqs as well as the foundation of what would become the Nizārī Ismaili state. The Nizārī state, centred at Alamūt, with its territories scattered in different parts of Persia and Syria, lasted some 166 years until it was destroyed by the Mongols in 654/1256.

The circumstances of the Nizārīs of the Alamūt period were radically different from those faced by the Ismailis of the Fatimid state and the Ṭayyibīs of Yaman. From early on, the Nizārīs were preoccupied with a revolutionary campaign and their survival in an extremely hostile environment. As a result, they produced military commanders rather than learned theologians. Futhermore, Ḥasan-i Ṣabbāḥ and his seven successors at Alamūt used Persian as the religious language of their community. This made it very difficult for the Nizārīs of Persia and adjacent Persian-speaking, eastern lands to have ready access to the Ismaili literature produced in Arabic during the Fatimid period, although the Syrian Nizārīs using Arabic did preserve some of the earlier texts. At any rate, the Persian Nizārīs did not produce a substantial literature;[44] the bulk of their literature, including the collections of the famous library at Alamūt, was either destroyed in the Mongol invasions or lost soon afterwards during the Mongol Īlkhānid rule over Persia (654–754/1256–1353). The Syrian Nizārīs were spared the Mongol catastrophe and were permitted by the Mamlūks to remain in their traditional strongholds. Subsequently, many of the literary sources, produced or preserved by the Syrian Nizārīs, perished in the course of prolonged hostilities with their Nuṣayrī (ʿAlawī) neighbours.

The Nizārī Ismailis of the Alamūt period did, nevertheless, maintain a sophisticated intellectual outlook and a literary tradition, elaborating their teachings in response to changing circumstances. Ḥasan-i Ṣabbāḥ himself was a learned theologian and was credited with founding an impressive library at Alamūt. Later, other major Nizārī fortresses in Persia and Syria were equipped with significant collections of books, documents and scientific instruments. In the doctrinal field, only a handful of Nizārī works have survived directly from that period. These include the *Haft bāb-i Bābā Sayyidnā*, or the *Seven Chapters* of Bābā Sayyidnā, two honorific titles reserved for Ḥasan-i Ṣabbāḥ. This is an anonymous work written around 596/1200, several decades after Ḥasan-i Ṣabbāḥ's death in 518/1124. There are also those Ismaili works written during the final decades of the Alamūt period and attributed to Naṣīr al-Dīn al-Ṭūsī (d. 672/1274), who spent some three decades in the Nizārī fortress communities of Persia. Among the Ismaili corpus of al-Ṭūsī's works, mention should be made of the *Rawḍat al-taslīm*, which is the single most important source on the Nizārī teachings of the Alamūt period. A few Nizārī texts, which are not extant otherwise, have been fragmentarily preserved in the *Kitāb al-milal wa'l-niḥal* of Ḥasan-i Ṣabbāḥ's contemporary, Muḥammad b. ʿAbd al-Karīm al-Shahrastānī (d. 548/1153), the famous heresiographer and theologian who was influenced by Ismaili ideas if not an Ismaili himself, as well as in some post-Alamūt Nizārī writings. Al-Shahrastānī himself wrote several works, including a partial Qur'an commentary called *Mafātīḥ al-asrār wa-maṣābīḥ al-abrār*, and a philosophical treatise in refutation of Ibn Sīnā's metaphysics, *Kitāb al-muṣāraʿa*, using Ismaili ideas and the methodology of *ta'wīl* or esoteric interpretation.

The Nizārī Ismailis of the Alamūt period, too, maintained a historiographical tradition in Persia. They compiled chronicles in the Persian language recording the events of their state according to the reigns of the successive lords of Alamūt.[45] This historiographical tradition commenced with the *Sargudhasht-i Sayyidnā*, covering the biography of Ḥasan-i Ṣabbāḥ, designated as Bābā and Sayyidnā ('our master') by the contemporary Nizārīs, and the events of his rule as the first lord of Alamūt. The reign of Ḥasan's successor, Kiyā Buzurg-Umīd (518–532/1124–1138), was covered in another chronicle known as the *Kitāb-i Buzurg-Umīd*. The chronicle of Buzurg-Umīd's son and successor, Muḥammad (532–557/1138–1162), was compiled by a certain Dihkhudā ʿAbd al-Malik Fashandī, who was also the commander of the Nizārī fortress of Maymūndiz, near Alamūt. The events of the Nizārī state during the later Alamūt period, when the imams themselves were leading the affairs of their community, were recorded by other official chroniclers, such as Ra'īs Ḥasan Munshī Bīrjandī who was also a poet and secretary (*munshī*) to Shihāb al-Dīn Manṣūr, the Nizārī chief in Quhistān during the first half of the 7th/13th century.

All the Nizārī chronicles, kept at Alamūt and other strongholds in Persia, perished in the period of Mongol rule. However, some of these chronicles and other Nizārī documents, such as the *fuṣūl* or epistles of the lords of Alamūt, were seen and used extensively by three Persian historians of the Īlkhānid period, namely, ʿAṭā-Malik Juwaynī (d. 681/1283), Rashīd al-Dīn Faḍl Allāh (d. 718/1318), and Abu'l-Qāsim ʿAbd Allāh Kāshānī (d. ca. 738/1337). The Ismaili histories of these authorities remain our main sources on the Nizārī *daʿwa* and state in Persia during the Alamūt period. Having joined the entourage of Hülegü, Juwaynī accompanied the Mongol conqueror on his military campaigns against the Nizārīs in 654/1256; he also participated in the peace negotiations between Hülegü and the Nizārī Imam Rukn al-Dīn Khurshāh. Juwaynī received permission to visit the Alamūt library before the destruction of that fortress by the Mongols. As a result, he succeeded in saving a number of what he called 'choice books', including the *Sargudhasht-i Sayyidnā*, and used these Ismaili sources in writing his history of Ḥasan-i Ṣabbāḥ and his successors at Alamūt, who he labelled the *daʿwa* of the 'heretics' (*malāḥida*) and the 'new preaching' (*daʿwat-i jadīd*). He composed this account soon after the fall of Alamūt and added it to the end of his *Taʾrīkh-i jahān-gushā* on Mongol victories, completed in its present form in 658/1260. Juwaynī's history of the Persian Nizārīs, permeated with invective and curses against them, is preceded by sections relating to the earlier history of the Ismailis, a pattern adopted by later Persian historians. Rashīd al-Dīn's history of the Ismailis is contained in the second volume of his vast *Jāmiʿ al-tawārīkh* (*Collection of Histories*) completed in 710/1310. More detailed than Juwaynī's account, Rashīd al-Dīn doubtless had direct access to the same Ismaili sources in addition to his predecessor's work. Rashīd al-Dīn quotes more extensively from the Nizārī chronicles and also displays a sense of relative objectivity rarely found in other Sunni historians writing on the Ismailis. Few details are known about the life of Kāshānī, a Persian (Twelver) Shiʿi historian belonging to the Abū Ṭāhir family of leading potters from Kāshān. It is known, however, that he was associated with Rashīd al-Dīn and was probably involved in producing parts of the *Jāmiʿ al-tawārīkh,* although his claim to the entire authorship of that work is very doubtful.[46] At any rate, he included a section on the Ismailis in his *Zubdat al-tawārīkh*, a general history of the Muslim world until the demise of the Abbasids. Kāshānī's account, which came to light in 1964, is the fullest of the three sources.

Later Persian historians who produced summary accounts of Ḥasan-i Ṣabbāḥ and his successors, based themselves mainly on Juwaynī and Rashīd al-Dīn, occasionally drawing also on sources of legendary nature. Amongst such authors writing general histories with sections devoted to the Ismailis, the earliest and perhaps the most famous is Ḥamd Allāh Mustawfī Qazwīnī (d. after 740/1339), who benefited from the patronage of Rashīd al-Dīn himself. In 730/1330, he completed his *Ta'rīkh-i guzīda*, a general history of Islam and the dynasties ruling over Persia, with a section on the Fatimids and the Ismailis (*malāḥida*),[47] and dedicated it to Rashīd al-Dīn's son and successor as Īlkhānid vizier, Ghiyāth al-Dīn Muḥammad. Ḥamd Allāh Mustawfī included a section on the lords of Alamūt also in his versified history, *Ẓafar-nāma*, recently published for the first time.[48] Among later Persian chroniclers writing on the Ismailis, Ḥāfiẓ-i Abrū (d. 833/1430), court historian of the Tīmūrid ruler Shāhrukh (807–850/1405–1447), is one of the most important. In 826/1423, he began to compile a vast universal history, *Majmaʿ al-tawārīkh*, at the request of Shāhrukh's son Bāysunghur (d. 837/1433), a patron of poets and of the arts. In the third volume of his history, Ḥāfiẓ-i Abrū devoted an extensive section to the Fatimids and the Nizārī state of Persia, following closely the account of Rashīd al-Dīn. Muḥammad b. Khwāndshāh, known as Mīrkhwānd (d. 903/1498), is a later historian of note who wrote a detailed account of the Persian Nizārīs of the Alamūt period, which was first published in Paris in 1813.[49] This represented one of the earliest accounts of the Persian Ismailis made accessible to European orientalists. Mīrkhwānd's grandson, Ghiyāth al-Dīn b. Humām al-Dīn Muḥammad, known as Khwānd Amīr (d. 942/1535–36) also wrote on the Ismailis in his own general history which was completed in 930/1524.[50] The Nizārī rulers of Alamūt continued to be treated, in later medieval times, and to various extents, by Persian historians such as Qāḍī Aḥmad b. Muḥammad al-Ghaffārī (d. 975/1567).

Another category of literary sources on the Persian Nizārīs of the Alamūt period are the contemporary chronicles of the Saljūqs. ʿImād al-Dīn Muḥammad al-Kātib al-Iṣfahānī (d. 597/1201) was evidently the author of the earliest Saljūq history with references to the Nizārīs, *Nuṣrat al-fatra,* which has survived only in an abridgement compiled in 623/1226.[51] Mention should also be made of Ẓahīr al-Dīn Nīshāpūrī's (d. 582/1187) *Saljūq-nāma,* composed around 580/1184 and used by many later chroniclers; the *Akhbār al-dawla al-Saljūqiyya,* written around 622/1225 and ascribed to Ṣadr al-Dīn ʿAlī al-Ḥusaynī, and al-Rāwandī's *Rāḥat al-ṣudūr,* a history of the Great Saljūqs completed around 601/1204 with many references to the Persian Nizārīs.[52] The medieval regional histories of Daylam and other Caspian provinces in northern Persia, starting with Ibn Isfandiyār's *Ta'rīkh-i Ṭabaristān* written in 613/1216–17,[53] provide another category of historical sources on the Persian Nizārīs. Finally, both Syrian and Persian Nizārīs are treated in many general histories of the Muslim world by Arab authors, most notably in *al-Kāmil fi'l-ta'rīkh* of Ibn al-Athīr (d. 630/1233) whose biography of Ḥasan-i Ṣabbāḥ is independent of the official *Sargudhasht-i Sayyidnā,* compiled at Alamūt perhaps on the basis of an autobiographical account.

The Nizārīs of Syria produced their own religious literature, including numerous poetical works in Arabic, during the Alamūt period.[54] This literature has not been sufficiently studied in modern times, as the relevant manuscript sources are not readily accessible. The Syrian Nizārīs have also preserved many of the Ismaili texts of the Fatimid period, works of al-Qāḍī al-Nuʿmān, Jaʿfar b. Manṣūr al-Yaman and others. The Persian Nizārī works of the Alamūt period were evidently not translated into Arabic in Syria, and, similarly the religious literature of the Syrian Nizārīs was not rendered into Persian. Nor did the Syrian Nizārīs compile official chronicles like those produced by their Persian co-religionists. Amongst the few surviving Syrian Nizārī works, a special place is occupied by the *Faṣl min al-lafẓ al-sharīf,* which includes a biographical account of Rāshid al-Dīn Sinān (d. 589/1193), the most famous *dāʿī* of the community, in addition to sayings attributed to him. This hagiographic work containing various anecdotes based on the oral tradition of the Syrian Nizārīs, may have been compiled much later by the *dāʿī* Abū Firās Shihāb al-Dīn al-Maynaqī (d. 937/1530 or 947/1540), or possibly by another Syrian Abū Firās who lived two centuries earlier. The main literary sources on the history of the Syrian Nizārīs, from the arrival of the first *dāʿīs* dispatched from Alamūt in the earliest years of the 6th/12th century until the complete subjugation of the Nizārī castles by Mamlūks in 671/1273, are the local histories of Syria as well as general Arab chronicles.[55] Amongst the relevant authorities, the most important are Ibn al-Qalānisī (d. 555/1160), the Damascene chronicler, Ibn al-ʿAdīm (d. 660/1262), the historian of Aleppo, and Ibn al-Jawzī's grandson known as Ṣibt (d. 654/1256).[56] Of particular interest here are also works of several lesser known historians, notably al-ʿAẓīmī (d. after 556/1161). For the later decades, the histories of Abū Shāma (d. 665/1267) and Ibn Wāṣil (d. 697/1298), amongst others, are of significance.

The non-literary sources on the Persian Nizārīs of the Alamūt period are rather insignificant. The Mongols demolished the major Nizārī fortresses of Persia, which may have provided valuable archaeological evidence. At any rate, these fortresses have not been scientifically studied; and, the few excavations undertaken in modern times probably caused more damage to the sites than they yielded results. All in all, no epigraphic evidence has been recovered from the Nizārī castles of Persia, which were equipped with impressive defence and water supply systems, while relatively limited hoards of Nizārī coins minted at Alamūt have also been recovered.[57] On the other hand, the Nizārī castles of Syria, which have been much better preserved, have yielded valuable archaeological, including epigraphic, information.[58]

The development of Nizārī studies in broad terms is covered in the next chapter. Here it is sufficient to recall that the distorted image of the Nizārīs, made famous in medieval Europe as the Assassins, was retained by the orientalists until at least the 1930s, when W. Ivanow, the founder of modern Nizārī studies, began to produce his numerous publications based on genuine Nizārī source materials. Subsequently, Marshall G.S. Hodgson (1922–1968) produced the first scholarly monograph on the Nizārīs of Alamūt period in his *The Order of Assassins* (1955), a misleading title which he himself later recanted.[59] After these pioneering efforts, few Islamicists have concerned themselves with the medieval history of the Nizārīs. On the other hand, there have periodically appeared 'sensational' and popular types of monographs on the so-called 'Assassins' – a misnomer for the Nizārī Ismailis which has continued to be used by many Western authors, as in W.B. Bartlett's *The Assassins: The Story of Medieval Islam's Secret Sect* (2001), to name a recent example.

By 487/1094, Ḥasan-i Ṣabbāḥ, as noted, had emerged as the leader of the Persian Ismailis. As an Ismaili Shiʿi, he could not tolerate the anti-Shiʿi policies of the Saljūqs, who as the new champions of Sunni Islam aimed to uproot the Fatimids. Ḥasan's revolt was also an expression of Persian 'national' sentiments, as the alien rule of Saljūq Turks was greatly detested by the Persians of different social classes. This may explain why he substituted Persian for Arabic as the religious language of the Persian Ismailis, accounting also for the popular success of his movement.[60] It was under such circumstances that in al-Mustanṣir's succession dispute, Ḥasan supported Nizār's cause and severed his relations with the Fatimid regime and the *daʿwa* headquarters in Cairo which had lent their support to al-Mustaʿlī. By this decision, Ḥasan founded the independent Nizārī Ismaili *daʿwa* on behalf of the Nizārī imam who then remained inaccessible; and, as a result, the Nizārī *daʿwa* survived the downfall of the Fatimid dynasty, similarly to the subsequent fate of the Ṭayyibī *daʿwa* in Yaman.

The revolt of the Persian Ismailis soon acquired a distinctive pattern and method of struggle, suited to the decentralized power structure of the Saljūq sultanate and their much superior military power. Ḥasan devised a strategy to overwhelm the Saljūqs locality by locality, amir by amir, and from a multitude of impregnable mountain strongholds. Ḥasan-i Ṣabbāḥ did not divulge the name of Nizār's successor to the imamate. In fact, numismatic evidence shows that Nizār's own name appeared on coins minted at Alamūt for about seventy years after his death in 488/1095, while his progeny were blessed anonymously. The early Nizārī Ismailis were, thus, left without an accessible imam in another *dawr al-satr*; and, as in the pre-Fatimid period of concealment, the absent imam was represented in the community by a *ḥujja*, his chief representative. Ḥasan and his next two successors as heads of the Nizārī *daʿwa* and state, were indeed recognized as such *ḥujjas*. It seems that already in Ḥasan-i Ṣabbāḥ's time many Nizārīs believed that a son or grandson of Nizār had been secretly brought from Egypt to Persia, and he became the progenitor of the line of the Nizārī imams who later emerged at Alamūt.

From early on in the Alamūt period, outsiders had the impression that the Persian Ismailis had initiated a 'new preaching' (*al-daʿwa al-jadīda*) in contrast to the 'old preaching' (*al-daʿwa al-qadīma*) of the Fatimid times. The 'new preaching' did not, however, represent any new doctrines; it was merely a reformulation of the old Shiʿi doctrine of *taʿlīm*, or authoritative teaching by the imam. It was mainly Ḥasan-i Ṣabbāḥ himself who restated this doctrine in a more rigorous form in a theological treatise entitled *al-Fuṣūl al-arbaʿa*, or *Four Chapters*. This treatise, originally written in Persian, has been preserved only fragmentarily by al-Shahrastānī and our Persian historians.[61] The doctrine of *taʿlīm*, emphasizing the autonomous teaching authority of each imam in his own time, became the central doctrine of the Nizārīs who, henceforth, were designated as the Taʿlīmiyya. The intellectual challenge posed to the Sunni establishment by the doctrine of *taʿlīm*, which also refuted the legitimacy of the Abbasid caliph as the spiritual spokesman of all Muslims, called forth the reaction of the Sunni establishment. Many Sunni scholars, led by Abū Ḥāmid al-Ghazālī (d. 505/1111), attacked the Ismaili doctrine of *taʿlīm*. It is to be noted that the Nizārīs, as a matter of general policy, do not seem to have responded to these polemics.

By 489/1096, when the fortress of Lamasar was seized, Ḥasan had acquired or built numerous mountain strongholds in Rūdbār, Daylamān, the centre of Nizārī power in northern Persia. Meanwhile, the Ismailis had come to possess a network of fortresses and several towns in Quhistān, in south-eastern Khūrāsān, which remained the second most important territory of the Nizārī state in Persia. Later, the Nizārīs acquired Girdkūh and other fortresses in the regions of Qūmis, Arrajān and Zagros. In the opening years of the 6th/12th century, Ḥasan began to extend his activities also to Syria by sending Persian *dāʿīs* from Alamūt, led by al-Ḥakīm al-Munajjim (d. 496/1103). In Syria, the *dāʿīs* confronted many difficulties in the initial phases of their operations in Aleppo and Damascus; and it took them several decades before they succeeded in various ways to acquire a network of castles, collectively referred to in the sources as the *qilāʿ al-daʿwa*, in the Jabal Bahrāʾ (present-day Jabal Anṣāriyya), a mountainous region between Ḥamā and the Mediterranean coastline in central Syria. These castles included Qadmūs, Kahf and Maṣyāf, which often served as the headquarters of the chief *dāʿī* of the Syrian Nizārīs. There, the Nizārīs confronted the enmity of various local Sunni rulers as well as the Crusaders who were active in adjacent territories belonging to the Latin states of Antioch and Tripoli. By the final years of Ḥasan's life, however, the anti-Saljūq revolt of the Nizārīs had lost its momentum, much in the same way that the Saljūqs under Barkiyāruq (d. 498/1105) and Muḥammad Tapar (d. 511/1118) had failed in their prolonged military campaigns to uproot the Persian Ismailis from their mountain strongholds.[62] Ismaili-Saljūq relations had now entered a new phase of 'stalemate'.

On Ḥasan-i Ṣabbāḥ's death in 518/1124, Kiyā Buzurg-Umīd succeeded him as the head of the Nizārī *da'wa* and state. A capable administrator like his predecessor, Buzurg-Umīd (518–532/1124–1138) maintained the policies of Ḥasan and further strengthened and extended the Nizārī state. The Ismaili-Saljūq stalemate essentially continued during the long reign of Buzurg-Umīd's son Muḥammad (532–557/1138–1162) as the third lord of Alamūt. By then, the Nizārī state had acquired its distinctive administrative structure. Each Nizārī territory was placed under the overall leadership of a chief *dā'ī* appointed from Alamūt; the leader of the Quhistānī Nizārīs was known as *muḥtasham*. These *dā'īs* as well as the commanders of major fortresses enjoyed a large degree of independence and local initiative, contributing to the dynamism and resilience of the Nizārī movement. Highly united with a remarkable sense of mission, the Nizārīs acknowledged the supreme leadership of Alamūt and obeyed without any dissent the religious policies initiated at that fortress by the imam's *ḥujjas* and, subsequently, by the Nizārī imams themselves. Meanwhile, the Nizārīs had been eagerly expecting the appearance of their imam, who had remained inaccessible since Nizār's murder in 488/1095.

The fourth lord of Alamūt, Ḥasan II to whom the Nizārīs refer with the expression *'alā dhikrihi'l-salām* (on his mention be peace), succeeded to leadership in 557/1162 and, soon after, declared the *qiyāma* or resurrection initiating a new phase in the religious history of the Nizārī community. On 17 Ramaḍān 559/8 August 1164, in the presence of the representatives of different Nizārī territories who had gathered at Alamūt, he delivered a sermon in which he proclaimed the *qiyāma*, the long awaited Last Day. About two months later, a similar ceremony was held at the fortress of Mu'minābād, near Bīrjand, and the earlier *khuṭba* and message were read out by Ra'īs Muẓaffar, the *muḥtasham* in Quhistān. There, Ḥasan II's position was more clearly equated with that of al-Mustanṣir as God's caliph (*khalīfa*) on earth, implicitly claiming the status of imam for the lord of Alamūt.[63]

Ḥasan II relied heavily on Ismaili *ta'wīl* and earlier traditions, interpreting *qiyāma* symbolically and spiritually for the Nizārīs. Accordingly, *qiyāma* meant nothing more than the manifestation of unveiled truth (*ḥaqīqa*) in the person of the Nizārī imam; it was a spiritual resurrection only for those who acknowledged the rightful imam of the time and were now capable of understanding the truth, the esoteric and immutable essence of Islam. It was in this sense that Paradise was actualized for the Nizārīs in this world. They were now to rise to a spiritual level of existence, transcending from *ẓāhir* to *bāṭin*, from *sharīʿa* to *ḥaqīqa*, or from the literal interpretation of the law to an understanding of its spirituality and the eternal truths of religion. On the other hand, the 'outsiders', the non-Nizārīs who were incapable of recognizing the truth, were rendered spiritually non-existent. The imam proclaiming the *qiyāma* would be the *qāʾim al-qiyāma*, 'lord of resurrection', a rank which in Ismaili religious hierarchy was always higher than that of an ordinary imam.

Ḥasan II's son and successor Nūr al-Dīn Muḥammad devoted his long reign (561–607/1166–1210) to a systematic elaboration of the *qiyāma* in terms of a doctrine. The exaltation of the autonomous teaching authority of the present imam now became the central feature of Nizārī thought; and *qiyāma* came to imply a complete personal transformation of the Nizārīs who were expected to perceive the imam in his true spiritual reality. Nūr al-Dīn Muḥammad also made every Nizārī imam potentially a *qāʾim*, capable of inaugurating an era of *qiyāma*. In the spiritual world of resurrection, there would remain only three categories of persons, ranked in terms of their relationship to the Nizārī imam. These include the 'people of opposition' (*ahl-i taḍādd*), the non-Nizārīs who exist only in the realm of appearances (*ẓāhir*) and are spiritually non-existent. Secondly, there are the ordinary followers of the Nizārī imam, the 'people of gradation' (*ahl-i tarattub*), who have penetrated the *sharīʿa* to its inner meaning. However, they have access only to partial truth, as they still do not fully understand the *bāṭin*. Finally, there are the 'people of union' (*ahl-i waḥdat*), the Nizārī super-elite, or the *akhaṣṣ-i khāṣṣ*, who perceive the imam in his true spiritual reality as the epiphany (*maẓhar*) of the word (*kalima*) of God; only they arrive at the realm of *ḥaqīqa*, in a sense the *bāṭin* behind the *bāṭin*, where they find full truth and as such, enjoy salvation in the paradisal state actualized for them in this world.[64] Nūr al-Dīn Muḥammad also explicitly affirmed the Nizārid

Fatimid descent of his father and, therefore, of himself. He explained that Ḥasan II was in fact an imam and the son of a descendant of Nizār b. al-Mustanṣir who had earlier found refuge in Alamūt. Henceforth, the Nizārīs recognized the lords of Alamūt, beginning with Ḥasan II, as their imams.[65]

Meanwhile, the Syrian Nizārīs had entered into an important phase of their own history under the leadership of Rāshid al-Dīn Sinān, their most famous leader who had been appointed as chief *dāʿī* in Syria by Ḥasan II soon after his own accession in 557/1162. Sinān reorganized and strengthened the Syrian Nizārī *daʿwa*, also consolidating their network of fortresses in the Jabal Bahrāʾ. Furthermore, he organized an independent corps of *fidāʾī*s, designated more commonly in Syria and in the Arabic sources as *fidāwī*s (*fidāwiyya*), self-sacrificing devotees of the community who were sent on dangerous missions to remove selected enemies who had posed serious threats to the survival of the Nizārīs in particular localities. Aiming to safeguard his community, Sinān entered into intricate and shifting alliances with the major neighbouring powers and rulers, notably the Crusaders, the Zangids and Ṣalāḥ al-Dīn. The Syrian Nizārīs had intermittent conflicts with the Templars and the Hospitallers, Frankish military orders which often acted independently in the Latin East. The only one of the Syrian *dāʿī*s to act somewhat independently of Alamūt, Sinān evidently taught his own version of the doctrine of *qiyāma*. He led the Syrian Nizārīs for almost three decades to the peak of their power and fame until his death in 589/1193.[66]

Nūr al-Dīn Muḥammad's son and successor, Jalāl al-Dīn Ḥasan (607–618/1210–1221), was concerned largely with redressing the isolation of the Nizārīs from the larger world of Sunni Islam. Consequently, he publicly repudiated the doctrine of *qiyāma* and ordered his followers to observe the *sharīʿa* in its Sunni form, inviting Sunni jurists to instruct his people. Indeed, Jalāl al-Dīn Ḥasan did his utmost to convince the outside world of his new policy. In 608/1211, the Abbasid caliph al-Nāṣir acknowledged the imam's rapprochement with Sunni Islam and issued a decree to that effect. Henceforth, the rights of Jalāl al-Dīn Ḥasan to Nizārī territories were officially recognized by the Abbasid caliph, as well as the Khwārazm Shāhs, who were then establishing their own empire in Persia as successors to the Saljūqs, and by other Sunni rulers. The Nizārīs evidently viewed Jalāl al-Dīn

Ḥasan's declarations as a restoration of *taqiyya*, which had been lifted in the *qiyāma* times; the observance of *taqiyya* could imply any type of accommodation to the outside world as deemed necessary by the infallible imam. Be that as it may, the Nizārī imam had now successfully achieved peace and security for his community and state.

Under ʿAlāʾ al-Dīn Muḥammad (618–653/1221–1255), Jalāl al-Dīn Ḥasan's son and successor as the penultimate lord of Alamūt, gradually the Sunni *sharīʿa* was relaxed within the community and the Nizārī traditions associated with *qiyāma* were once again revived, although the Nizārīs continued to appear to outsiders in Sunni guise. The Nizārī leadership now also made a sustained effort to explain the different doctrinal declarations and religious policies of the lords of Alamūt. As a result, all these teachings were interpreted comprehensively within a coherent theological framework, aiming to provide satisfactory explanations for the seemingly contradictory policies adopted at Alamūt. Intellectual life indeed flourished in the long reign of ʿAlāʾ al-Dīn Muḥammad, receiving a special impetus from the influx of outside scholars who fled the first waves of the Mongol invasions and took refuge in the Nizārī fortress communities. Foremost among such scholars, who availed themselves of the Nizārī libraries and patronage of learning, was Naṣīr al-Dīn al-Ṭūsī (d. 672/1274), who made major contributions to the Nizārī Ismaili thought of the late Alamūt period during his prolonged stay amongst them.

It is mainly through al-Ṭūsī's extant Ismaili writings, notably the *Rawḍat al-taslīm*, that we have an exposition of the Nizārī thought of the Alamūt period, especially as it developed after the declaration of the *qiyāma*. Al-Ṭūsī explained that *qiyāma* was not necessarily a final, eschatological event, but a transitory condition of life when the veil of *taqiyya* would be lifted so as to make the unveiled truth accessible. In the current cycle of history, however, the full *qiyāma*, or Great Resurrection (*qiyāmat-i qiyāmāt*) would still occur at the end of the era initiated by the Prophet Muḥammad. The identification between *sharīʿa* and *taqiyya*, implied by the teachings of Ḥasan II, was now made explicit by al-Ṭūsī who also identified *qiyāma* with *ḥaqīqa*. Thus, the imposition of the Sunni *sharīʿa* by Jalāl al-Dīn Ḥasan was presented as a return to *taqiyya*, and to a new period of *satr* or concealment, when the truth (*ḥaqīqa*) would be once again concealed in the *bāṭin* of religion. The condition of *qiyāma* could, in principle, be granted by the current Nizārī imam at any time, because every imam was potentially also an *imām-qā'im*. In his integrated theological presentation, human life could alternate between periods of *qiyāma*, when reality is manifest, and *satr*, when it would be concealed requiring the observance of *taqiyya*. In this sense, the term *satr* was redefined to imply the concealment of the religious truths and the true spiritual reality of the imam, and not just the physical inaccessibility of the imam, as had been the case in the pre-Fatimid and early Alamūt times.[67] The teachings of the late Alamūt period brought the Nizārīs even closer to the esoteric traditions more commonly associated with Sufism.

Nizārī fortunes in Persia were rapidly reversed after the collapse of the Khwārazmian empire which brought them into direct confrontation with the invading Mongols. When the Great Khan Möngke decided to complete the Mongol conquests of western Asia, he assigned first priority to the destruction of the Nizārī Ismaili state, a task completed with some difficulty in 654/1256 by his brother Hülegü who led the main Mongol expedition into Persia. Shortly before, in 653/1255, 'Alā' al-Dīn Muḥammad had been succeeded by his eldest son Rukn al-Dīn Khurshāh, who would rule for exactly one year as the last lord of Alamūt. The youthful imam engaged in a complex, and ultimately futile, series of negotiations with Hülegü. Finally, on 29 Shawwāl 654/19 November 1256, Khurshāh descended from the fortress of Maymūndiz in Rūdbār in the company of Naṣīr al-Dīn al-Ṭūsī and Nizārī dignitaries, and surrendered to the Mongols. With the fall of Alamūt a month later, the fate of the Nizārī state was sealed. Alamūt and many other fortresses were demolished, though Girdkūh resisted its Mongol besiegers for another fourteen years. In the spring of 655/1257, Khurshāh himself was killed by his Mongol guards in Mongolia, where he had gone in order to meet the Great Khan. By then, the Mongols had massacred large numbers of Nizārīs who had been placed in their protective custody.

In the meantime, the Syrian Nizārīs had been led by other *dā'īs* after Rāshid al-Dīn Sinān. From the time of the Imam Jalāl al-Dīn Ḥasan's rapprochement with Sunni Islam, relations between the Syrian Nizārīs and their Muslim neighbours had improved significantly, while periodic encounters of different kinds continued with the Franks. The last important encounter between the Nizārīs and the Crusaders, who still held the Syrian coastline, occurred in the early 650s/1250s in connection with embassies exchanged with Louis IX, the French king better known as St. Louis (d. 1270), who led the Seventh Crusade (1248–1255) to the Holy Land. John of Joinville (d. 1317), the king's biographer and secretary, has left a valuable account of these dealings, including a curious disputation between an Arabic-speaking friar and the chief *dāʿī* of the Syrian Nizārīs.[68] Subsequently, the Nizārīs collaborated with the Mamlūks and other Muslim rulers in defeating the Mongols in Syria. Baybars, the victorious Mamlūk sultan, now resorted to various measures for bringing about the submission of the Nizārī strongholds in Syria. Kahf was the last Nizārī outpost there to fall in 671/1273. However, the Syrian Nizārīs were permitted to remain in their traditional abodes as loyal subjects of the Mamlūks and their Ottoman successors. Having lost their political prominence, the Nizārīs henceforth lived secretly as religious minorities in numerous communities scattered in Syria, Persia, Afghanistan, Central Asia and the Indian subcontinent.

Nizārī Ismailism of the post-Alamūt period

The post-Alamūt period in Nizārī Ismailism covers more than seven centuries, from the fall of Alamūt in 654/1256 to the present time. The Nizārī communities, scattered from Syria to Persia, Central Asia and South Asia, now elaborated a diversity of religious and literary traditions in different languages. The first five centuries after the fall of Alamūt represent the longest obscure phase of Ismaili history. Many aspects of Ismaili activity in this period are not still sufficiently studied due to a scarcity of primary sources. A variety of factors, related to the very nature of Nizārī Ismailism of this period, have caused special research difficulties here. In the aftermath of the destruction of their state and fortress communities in Persia, the Nizārīs were deprived of the centralized leadership they had enjoyed during the Alamūt period. After Rukn al-Dīn Khurshāh's son and successor, Shams al-Dīn Muḥammad, there was a split in the line of the Nizārī imams and their followers, dividing the community into rival Muḥammad-Shāhī and Qāsim-Shāhī branches. The Nizārī imamate was, thus, handed down through two parallel lines while the imams remained in hiding and were inaccessible to most of their followers for about two centuries.

More complex research difficulties arise from the widespread practice of *taqiyya* by the Nizārīs of different regions. During much of the post-Alamūt period of their history, the Nizārīs were obliged to dissimulate rather strictly to safeguard themselves against rampant persecution. They concealed their true beliefs and literature in addition to resorting to Sunni, Sufi, Twelver Shiʿi and Hindu disguises in different parts of the Iranian world and the Indian subcontinent. It is important to note that in many regions, the Nizārīs observed *taqiyya* for very long periods with lasting consequences. Although this phenomenon has only recently been studied by a few scholars, notably cultural anthropologists, it is certain that long-term dissimulation under any guise would eventually result in irrevocable changes in the traditions and the very religious identity of the dissimulating community. Such influences might have manifested themselves in a variety of manners, ranging from total acculturation or full assimilation of the Nizārīs of a particular locality into the community chosen originally as a protective cover, to various degrees of interfacing and admixture between Ismaili and 'other' traditions without necessarily the loss of their Ismaili identity. Probabilities for complete assimilation or disintegration were particularly high during the early post-Alamūt times when the Nizārīs were effectively deprived of any form of central leadership, including especially the guidance of their imams. In the event, for several centuries, the Nizārī communities developed independently of one another under the local leadership of their *dāʿī*s, *pīr*s, *shaykh*s, *khalīfa*s, etc., who often established their own hereditary dynasties.

Under the circumstances, it is not surprising that the dissimulating Nizārī Ismailis did not generally attract the attention of outsiders and historians during much of this period. The difficulties of studying post-Alamūt Nizārī Ismailism are further aggravated by the fact that the Nizārīs produced relatively few religious texts, while, following the demise of their state in 654/1256, they had lost their earlier interest in historiography as well. The difficult conditions under which the Nizārīs have often lived and the generally limited standards of education attained by the community until recent times made it impossible for the Nizārīs to produce outstanding theologians and authors comparable to their contemporary Ṭayyibī *dāʿī*s in Yaman. Furthermore, already from the Alamūt period the Persian-speaking Nizārīs did not have much access to the Arabic Ismaili literature of the Fatimid times, which was preserved and used extensively by the Ṭayyibī Ismailis. Of all the Nizārī communities, only the Syrians were able to preserve a certain number of the Arabic texts of the classical Ismaili literature.

In the light of these problems, further progress here would require the acquisition of better understanding of the historical developments as well as the religious and literary traditions of major Nizārī communities of this period, especially those in South Asia and different parts of the Iranian world. The Nizārī Ismaili literature of the post-Alamūt period can be classified into four main categories, namely, the Persian, the Badakhshānī or Central Asian, the Syrian, and the South Asian or the *ginān* literature. The Nizārī sources produced in Persia, Afghanistan and the upper Oxus region are written entirely in the Persian language, while the Syrian texts are in Arabic. The Nizārīs of South Asia, designated as Khojas, who elaborated a distinctive Ismaili tradition known as Satpanth or 'true path', have used various Indian languages in committing their doctrines to writing in the form of devotional hymns known as *ginān*s and using the Khojkī script developed by themselves.

The Nizārīs of Persia and adjacent regions did not produce any doctrinal works during the earliest post-Alamūt centuries. Only the versified works of Ḥakīm Saʿd al-Dīn Nizārī Quhistānī (d. 720/1320), a poet and government functionary from Bīrjand in south-eastern Khurāsān, remain extant from that period. He was perhaps also the first post-Alamūt Nizārī author to have chosen verse and Sufi forms of expression to conceal his Ismaili ideas, a model adopted by later Nizārī authors in Persia. The revival of the *daʿwa* activities during the Anjudān period also encouraged the literary activities of the community, and a number of better educated Persian Nizārīs began to produce the first doctrinal works of the period. The earliest amongst these authors were Abū Isḥāq Quhistānī (d. after 904/1498), and Khayrkhwāh-i Harātī (d. after 960/1553), a *dāʿī* and poet who visited the contemporary Nizārī imam in Anjudān. The writings of these authors contain important historical references as well. Amongst later authors, mention may be made of the poet Imām Qulī Khākī Khurāsānī (d. after 1056/1646) and his son ʿAlī Qulī, better known as Raqqāmī Khurāsānī; they, too, resorted to poetry and Sufi expressions. More doctrinal works by Persian Nizārī authors appeared during the 13th/19th century and later times, marking a modern revival in Nizārī literary activities. This revival was encouraged by the Nizārī imams following the transference of their residence to India. Amongst such works written in Persian mention may be made of the *Risāla dar ḥaqīqat-i dīn* and the *Khiṭābāt-i ʿāliya* of Shihāb al-Dīn Shāh al-Ḥusaynī (d. 1302/1884), the eldest son of Āqā ʿAlī Shāh, Āghā Khān II, and the works of Muḥammad b. Zayn al-ʿĀbidīn, known as Fidāʾī Khurāsānī (d. 1342/1923), who was also the only Persian Nizārī author of modern times to have written a history of Ismailism, *Hidāyat al-muʾminīn al-ṭālibīn*, a work permeated with anachronisms and inaccuracies.[69] The Nizārīs of Persia did not attract the attention of Persian historians of the post-Alamūt period until modern times. Only a few chroniclers writing during the first three post-Alamūt centuries, including Sayyid Ẓahīr al-Dīn Marʿashī (d. after 893/1488) and other historians of the Caspian region, occasionally have important references to the Persian Nizārīs. It was after the middle of the 12th/18th century, when the Nizārī imams had acquired political prominence in Persia, that the chroniclers of the Zand and Qājār dynasties there, such as Aḥmad ʿAlī Khān Vazīrī Kirmānī (d. 1295/1878), Riḍā Qulī Khān Hidāyat (d. 1288/1871) and Muḥammad Taqī Lisān al-Mulk Sipihr (d. 1297/1880), made frequent references to those imams and their activities.

The Nizārī Ismailis of Badakhshān and the adjacent areas in the upper Oxus have retained their distinctive literary tradition, drawing on the Persian Ismaili literature of different periods with particular reference to the writings of Nāṣir-i Khusraw (d. after 462/1070) as well as the Sufi traditions of Central Asia. Consequently, the Badakhshānī Nizārīs have preserved and transmitted the anonymous *Umm al-kitāb*, which does not contain any specific Ismaili ideas, the genuine and spurious writings of Nāṣir-i Khusraw, all written in Persian, as well as the Nizārī literature of later times representing the coalescence of Nizārī Ismailism and Sufism; they have also preserved many anonymous works as well as the writings of the great mystic poets of Persia, who are regarded as their co-religionists. The Nizārīs of these remote regions in the Pamirs do not seem to have produced many noteworthy authors in the post-Alamūt period, with some exceptions such as Sayyid Suhrāb Valī Badakhshānī (d. after 856/1452); but they have preserved the bulk of the Ismaili literature of different periods written in Persian elsewhere. These manuscript sources have been held in numerous private collections, especially by the local religious leaders known as *khalīfa*s, in Shughnān, Rūshān, Ishkāshīm and other districts of the Gorno-Badakhshān province of Tajikistan. The Nizārīs of Afghan Badakhshān, too, have extensive collections of manuscripts, about which information is not readily available. The Nizārīs of Hunza, Chitral, and the districts of Gilgit, now all situated in northern areas of Pakistan, have preserved a selection of Persian Nizārī works, although they themselves speak a host of local languages and dialects such as Burushaski and Wakhi rather than Persian. This literature was originally made available to them by their Badakhshānī neighbours, who themselves speak a number of local dialects, like Shughni, in addition to a Tajik version of Persian. The Ismailis of Badakhshān do not seem to have compiled histories of their community, but there are references to Ismailis in a few local histories of the region.

The Syrian Nizārīs, who adhered almost entirely to the Muḥammad-Shāhī branch of Nizārī Ismailism until the 13th/19th century, developed their own limited literature in Arabic. As they also preserved some of the Ismaili works of the Fatimid period, certain earlier Ismaili traditions continued to be represented in the Nizārī texts of the Syrian provenance.[70] The most famous Syrian *dāʿī*-author of this period was Abū Firās Shihāb al-Dīn al-Maynaqī, who died in 937/1530 or ten years later. However, the attribution by ʿĀrif Tāmir of a number of Ismaili works, such as the *Kitāb al-īḍāḥ*, to this author, has proven incorrect. The Nizārīs of Syria were evidently not persecuted by the Ottomans, who mention them and their castles in their land registers of the region. In fact, the Syrian Nizārīs did not attract much outside attention until the early decades of the nineteenth century, when they became entangled in recurrent conflicts with their Nuṣayrī neighbours. It was around the same time that European travellers and orientalists began to make references to them. In the 1840s, the Syrian Nizārīs successfully petitioned the Ottoman authorities for permission to restore Salamiyya, then in ruins, for the settlement of their community. Meanwhile, the Syrian Nizārīs belonging to the Muḥammad-Shāhī line had not heard, since 1210/1796, from their last known imam, Muḥammad al-Bāqir, who lived in India. As they failed to locate him, the majority of the Muḥammad-Shāhī Nizārīs of Syria transferred their allegiance in 1304/1887 to the Qāsim-Shāhī line, then represented by Aga Khan III. An Ismaili minority, centred in Maṣyāf and Qadmūs, remained loyal to the Muḥammad-Shāhī line, and are still awaiting the reappearance of their imam. In modern times, ʿĀrif Tāmir (1921–1998), a Muḥammad-Shāhī Nizārī, and Muṣṭafā Ghālib (1923–1981), a Qāsim-Shāhī Nizārī, have written extensively on the history of the Syrian Nizārī Ismailis in addition to producing editions (alas often defective) of many Arabic Ismaili texts.

The Nizārī Khojas of the Indian subcontinent, as noted, elaborated their own literary tradition in the form of the *ginān*s, containing a diversity of mystical, mythological, didactic, cosmological and eschatological themes.[71] Many *ginān*s contain ethical and moral instructions for the conduct of religious life and guiding the spiritual quest of the believer. As an oral tradition, some *ginān*s also relate anachronistic, hagiographic and legendary accounts of the activities of *pīr*s, as the chief *dāʿī*s in India were called, and their converts; and, as such, they are not generally reliable as historical sources. The *ginān*s are composed in verse form and are meant to be sung and recited melodically. The earlier Ismaili literature, produced in Arabic and Persian, was not until recently available to the Khojas. The authorships of the *ginān*s are attributed to Pīr Shams al-Dīn, Pīr Ṣadr al-Dīn and a few other early *pīr*s. Originally transmitted orally, the *ginān*s began to be collected and recorded from the 10th/16th century. The *ginān*s exist in a mixture of Indian languages, including Sindhī, Gujarātī, Hindī, Panjābī and Multānī. The bulk of the recorded corpus of the *ginān* literature, comprised of about one thousand separate compositions, has survived in the specific Khojkī script developed and used extensively by the Nizārī Khojas. Since the middle of the nineteenth century, an increasing number of *ginān*s have been published in India.

Drawing mainly on the *ginān*s and their oral traditions, the Nizārī Khojas and related communities like the Imām-Shāhīs compiled a few historical works in Gujarātī during the nineteenth century. There also appeared the *Noorum Mobin* (1935) of Alimahomed J. Chunara (1881–1966), which was treated for several decades as the quasi-official history of the Nizārī Khojas. In more recent times, a number of Khojas have studied various aspects of their Satpanth tradition and its literature. Foremost among such scholars, mention should be made of Azim Nanji, Ali S. Asani, Aziz Esmail, Zawahir Moir (Noorally) and Tazim Kassam. At the same time, several European scholars, notably Françoise Mallison and Dominique-Sila Khan, have contributed to this field of South Asian religious studies from social and anthropological perspectives. All in all, numerous aspects of Nizārī Ismailism of the post-Alamūt period remain obscure; and modern scholars, after the initial efforts of W. Ivanow, have not produced major studies dealing with this phase of Ismailism. As noted, further progress here would require studying the individual Nizārī communities and their separate literary and intellectual traditions.

As a result of modern progress in Nizārī studies, three main periods may be distinguished in the history of post-Alamūt Nizārī Ismailism: (a) an obscure early period covering the first two centuries after the fall of Alamūt in 654/1256; (b) the Anjudān revival in Nizārī *daʿwa* and literary activities, from around the middle of the 9th/15th century until the 12th/18th century; and (c) the modern period dating to the middle of the 13th/19th century when the residence of the Nizārī imams was transferred from Persia to India and subsequently to Europe. This chronological categorization provides the frame for our brief discussion of post-Alamūt Nizārī Ismailism.

In the aftermath of the Mongol debacle, contrary to Juwaynī's claim, the Nizārī Ismailis of Persia survived the downfall of their state. Many migrated to Badakhshān and Sind, where Ismaili communities already existed. Other isolated Nizārī groups soon disintegrated or were assimilated into the religiously dominant communities of their locality. The centralized *daʿwa* organization also disappeared, to be replaced by a loose network of autonomous *dāʿī*s and *pīr*s in the regions. Under these circumstances, scattered Nizārī communities developed independently while resorting to *taqiyya* and different external guises. Many Nizārī groups in the Iranian world, where Sunnism prevailed until the rise of the Safawids, disguised themselves as Sunni Muslims. Meanwhile, a group of Nizārī dignitaries had managed to hide Rukn al-Dīn Khurshāh's minor son, Shams al-Dīn Muḥammad, who succeeded to the imamate in 655/1257. Shams al-Dīn was taken to Ādharbāyjān, in north-western Persia, where he and his next few successors to the imamate lived clandestinely. Certain allusions in the unpublished versified *Safar-nāma* (*Travelogue*) of the contemporary poet Nizārī Quhistānī indicate that he may have seen the Nizārī imam in Tabrīz in 679/1280. Shams al-Dīn, who in certain legendary accounts has been confused with Mawlānā Jalāl al-Dīn Rūmī's spiritual guide Shams-i Tabrīz, died around 710/1310. An obscure dispute over his succession split the line of the Nizārī imams and their following into the Qāsim-Shāhī and Muḥammad-Shāhī (or Mu'min-Shāhī) branches.[72] The Muḥammad-Shāhī imams, who initially had more followers in Persia and Central Asia, transferred their seat to India in the 10th/16th century and by the end of the 12th/18th century this line had become discontinued. The sole surviving Muḥammad-Shāhī Nizārīs, currently numbering about 15,000, are to be found in Syria where they are locally known as the Jaʿfariyya. The Qāsim-Shāhī community has persisted to the present time, and their last four imams have enjoyed prominence under their hereditary title of Āghā Khān (also Āqā Khān and Aga Khan). It was in the early post-Alamūt times that Persian Nizārīs, as part of their *taqiyya* practices, disguised themselves under the cover of Sufism, without establishing formal affiliations with any of the Sufi *ṭarīqa*s then spreading in Persia and Central Asia. The practice soon gained wide currency among the Nizārīs of Central Asia and Sind as well.

In early post-Alamūt times, the Nizārīs had some success in regrouping in Daylam, where they remained active throughout the Īlkhānid and Tīmūrid periods. A certain Khudāvand Muḥammad (d. 807/1404), a Muḥammad-Shāhī imam, even occupied Alamūt for a while, before he was dislodged by Sayyid ʿAlī, the powerful Zaydī ruler of Daylamān. The Nizārīs did not survive in the Caspian region after the 10th/16th century.[73] Sulṭān Muḥammad b. Jahāngīr (d. 998/1589) and his son Sulṭān Jahāngīr (d. 1006/1597), belonging to the Banū Iskandar rulers of Kujūr, adhered to Nizārī Ismailism and spread it in their dominions; they represent the last known references in the sources to Ismailis in northern Persia. Only a few isolated Nizārī groups survived a while longer in Daylam during the Safawid period when Alamūt was used as a prison. In Badakhshān and other parts of Central Asia, the Ismailis evidently acknowledged the Nizārī imamate only during the late Alamūt period as a result of the activities of *dāʿī*s dispatched from Quhistān.[74] These *dāʿī*s founded dynasties of *pīr*s and *mīr*s who ruled over Shughnān and other districts of Badakhshān. In 913/1507, Shāh Raḍī al-Dīn b. Ṭāhir, a Muḥammad-Shāhī imam, established his rule briefly over a part of Badakhshān with the help of his followers there. Subsequently, the Badakhshānī Nizārīs were severely persecuted by the local Tīmūrid, and then, Özbeg rulers.

By the middle of the 9th/15th century, Ismaili-Sufi relations had become well established in the Iranian world. Indeed, a type of coalescence had emerged between Persian Sufism and Nizārī Ismailism, two independent esoteric traditions in Islam which shared close affinities and common doctrinal grounds. As an early instance of this coalescence, mention may be made of the celebrated Sufi *mathnawī* poem, *Gulshan-i rāz* (*The Rose-Garden of Mystery*), composed by the Sufi master Maḥmūd-i Shabistarī (d. after 740/1339), and its later commentary, *Baʿḍī az taʾwīlāt-i Gulshan-i rāz*, by an anonymous Persian Nizārī author. Among other examples, Central Asian Nizārīs consider ʿAzīz al-Dīn Nasafī (d. ca. 661/1262), a local Sufi master, as a co-religionist, and they have preserved his treatise *Zubdat al-ḥaqāʾiq* as an Ismaili work. Owing to their close relations with Sufism, the Persian-speaking Nizārīs have also regarded several of the great mystic poets of Persia, such as Sanāʾī, ʿAṭṭār and Jalāl al-Dīn Rūmī, as their co-religionists. The Nizārī Ismailis of Persia, Afghanistan and Central Asia have preserved their works and continue to use their poetry in their religious ceremonies. Soon, the dissimulating Persian Ismailis adopted the more visible aspects of the Sufi way of life. Thus, the imams appeared to outsiders as Sufi masters or *pīr*s, while their followers adopted the typically Sufi appellation of disciples or *murīds*.[75] By then, the Nizārī imams of the Qāsim-Shāhī line had emerged in the village of Anjudān, in central Persia, and initiated the Anjudān revival in Nizārī Ismailism. With Mustanṣir bi'llāh (II) (d. 885/1480), who carried the Sufi name of Shāh Qalandar, the Qāsim-Shāhī imams became definitely established in the locality where a number of their tombs are still preserved.[76] Taking advantage of the changing religio-political climate of Persia, including the spread of ʿAlid loyalism and Shiʿi tendencies through Sunni Sufi orders, the imams successfully began to reorganize and reinvigorate their *daʿwa* activities to win new converts and reassert their authority over various Nizārī communities, especially in Central Asia and India where the Ismailis had been led for long periods by independent dynasties of *pīr*s. The imams gradually replaced these powerful autonomous figures with their own loyal appointees who would also regularly deliver the much needed religious dues to the imam's central treasury.

The Anjudān period witnessed a revival in the literary activities of the Nizārīs, especially in Persia, where the earliest doctrinal works of the post-Alamūt period were now produced. In the context of

Nizārī-Sufi relations during the Anjudān period, valuable details are preserved in a book entitled *Pandiyāt-i jawānmardī*, containing the religious admonitions of Imam Mustanṣir bi'llāh (II). In this book, later translated into Gujarātī for the benefit of the Khojas, the Nizārīs are referred to with common Sufi expressions such as *ahl-i ḥaqīqat*, or the 'people of the truth', while the imam is designated as *pīr* or *murshid*. The imam's admonitions start with the *sharīʿat-ṭarīqat-ḥaqīqat* categorization of the Sufis, describing *ḥaqīqat* as the *bāṭin* of *sharīʿat* which could be attained only by the believers (*muʾmins*). The *Pandiyāt* further explains, in line with the earlier Nizārī teachings of the *qiyāma* times, that *ḥaqīqat* consists of recognizing the spiritual reality of the imam of the time.[77] The Nizārīs now essentially retained the teachings of the Alamūt period, especially as elaborated after the declaration of the *qiyāma*. The current imam retained his central importance in Nizarı doctrine, and the recognition of his true spiritual reality remained the prime concern of his followers.[78]

The advent of the Safawids and the proclamation of Twelver Shiʿism as the state religion of their realm in 907/1501, promised more favourable opportunities for the activities of the Nizārīs and other Shiʿi communities in Persia. The Nizārīs were, in fact, now able to reduce the intensity of their *taqiyya* practices. However, this new optimism was short-lived as the Safawids and their *sharīʿat*-minded *ʿulamāʾ* soon suppressed all popular forms of Sufism and those Shiʿi movements which fell outside the confines of Twelver Shiʿism. The Nizārīs, too, received their share of persecutions. Shāh Ṭāhir al-Ḥusaynī (d. ca. 956/1549), the most famous imam of the Muḥammad-Shāhī line whose popularity had proved unacceptable to the founder of the Safawid dynasty, was persecuted in Shāh Ismāʿīl's reign (907–930/1501–1524). However, Shāh Ṭāhir fled to India in 926/1520 and permanently settled in the Deccan where he rendered valuable services to the Niẓām-Shāhs of Aḥmadnagar. It is interesting to note that from early on in India, Shāh Ṭāhir advocated Twelver Shiʿism, which he had obviously adopted as a form of disguise. He achieved his greatest success in the Deccan when Burhān Niẓām-Shāh, after his own conversion, proclaimed Twelver Shiʿism as the official religion of his state in 944/1537. Shāh Ṭāhir's successors as Muḥammad-Shāhī imams continued to observe *taqiyya* in India under the cover of Twelver Shiʿism.[79] In this connection, it is to be noted that in the *Lamaʿāt al-ṭāhirīn*, one of the few extant Muḥammad-Shāhī texts composed in India around 1110/1698, the author (a certain Ghulām ʿAlī b. Muḥammad) conceals his Ismaili ideas under the double cover of Twelver Shiʿi and Sufi expressions; he eulogizes the Ithnāʿasharī imams whilst also alluding to the Nizārī imams of the Muḥammad-Shāhī line.

Meanwhile, the second Safawid monarch Shāh Ṭahmāsp persecuted the Qāsim-Shāhī Nizārīs of Anjudān and had their thirty-sixth imam, Murād Mīrzā, executed in 981/1574. By the time of Shāh ʿAbbās I (995–1038/1587–1629), the Persian Nizārīs, too, had successfully adopted Twelver Shiʿism as a second form of disguise, which was now widely adopted by the Qāsim-Shāhī Nizārī imams and their followers in Persia and adjacent lands.[80] By the end of the 11th/17th century, the Qāsim-Shāhī *daʿwa* had gained the allegiance of the bulk of the Nizārīs at the expense of the Muḥammad-Shāhīs. The *daʿwa* had been particularly successful in Afghanistan, Central Asia and several regions of the Indian subcontinent.

In South Asia, the Hindu converts originally belonging to the Lohana caste, became known as Khoja, derived from the Persian word *khwāja*, an honorary title meaning lord or master corresponding to the Hindi term *thākur* by which the Lohanas were addressed. As noted, the Nizārī Khojas developed a religious tradition, known as Satpanth or the 'true path' (to salvation), as well as a devotional literature, the *ginān*s. The earliest Nizārī *pīr*s, missionaries or preacher-saints, operating in India concentrated their efforts in Sind. Pīr Shams al-Dīn is the earliest figure specifically associated in the *ginān* literature with the commencement of the Nizārī *daʿwa* there. By the time of Pīr Ṣadr al-Dīn, a great-grandson of Pīr Shams, the *pīr*s in India had established a hereditary dynasty. Pīr Ṣadr al-Dīn, who died around the turn of the 9th/15th century, consolidated and organized the *daʿwa* in India; he is also credited with building the first *jamāʿat-khāna* (literally, community house), in Kotri, Sind, for the religious and communal activities of the Khojas. In India, too, the Nizārīs developed close relations with Sufism. Multān and Ucch in Sind, in addition to serving as centres of Satpanth *daʿwa* activities, were the headquarters of the Suhrawardī and Qādirī Sufi orders. Ṣadr al-Dīn was succeeded as *pīr* by his son Ḥasan Kabīr al-Dīn, who reportedly visited the Nizārī Imam Mustanṣir bi'llāh (II) in Anjudān. Ḥasan Kabīr al-Dīn's brother Tāj al-Dīn was evidently the last person appointed as *pīr* by the Nizārī imams who were then making systematic efforts to end the hereditary authority of the *pīr*s in India.

Periodically the Khojas experienced internal dissensions, while many reverted back to Hinduism or converted to Sunnism, the dominant religions of the contemporary Indo-Muslim society. It was under such circumstances that a group of Nizārī Khojas of Gujarāt seceded and recognized the imamate of Nar Muḥammad (d. 940/1533); they became known as Imām-Shāhīs, named after Nar Muḥammad's father Imām Shāh (d. 919/1513), one of Ḥasan Kabīr al-Dīn's sons who had attempted in vain to become a *pīr* in Sind. The Imām-Shāhīs, who produced their own *ginān* literature and split into several groups following different *pīr*s, soon denied any connections with Ismailism. Meanwhile, in the absence of *pīr*s, the Nizārī imams maintained their contacts with the Khoja community through lesser functionaries known as *wakīl*s or *bābā*s. The origins and early development of the indigenous form of Ismailism known as Satpanth on the Indian subcontinent remain obscure. In particular, it is not clear whether Satpanth Ismailism resulted from the conversion policies developed locally by the early *pīr*s who operated in India at least from the 7th/13th century, or whether it represented a tradition that had evolved gradually over several centuries dating further back, possibly even to Fatimid times. Be that as it may, Satpanth Ismailism may be taken to represent an indigenous tradition reflecting certain historical, social, cultural and political circumstances prevailing in the medieval Indian subcontinent, especially in Sind. On the evidence of the *ginān*s, it seems plausible that the *pīr*s did attempt ingeniously to maximize the appeal of their message to a Hindu audience of mainly rural and uneducated lower castes. Hence, they turned to Indian vernaculars, rather than Arabic and Persian used by the educated classes. And for the same reasons, they used Hindu idioms and mythology, interfacing their Islamic and Ismaili tenets with myths, images and symbols already familiar to the Hindus. The teachings of Satpanth Ismailism are clearly reflected in the *ginān* literature.[81]

In the meantime, with the fortieth Qāsim-Shāhī imam, Shāh Nizār (d. 1134/1722), the seat of this branch of the Nizārī *daʿwa*, then representing the only branch in Persia, was transferred from Anjudān to the nearby village of Kahak, in the vicinity of Qumm and Maḥallāt, effectively ending the Anjudān period in post-Alamūt Nizārī Ismailism.

By the middle of the 12th/18th century, in the unsettled conditions of Persia after the demise of the Safawids and the Afghan invasion, the Nizārī imams moved to Shahr-i Bābak in Kirmān, a location closer to the pilgrimage route of Khojas who then regularly travelled from India to see their imam and deliver the religious dues, the *dassondh* or tithes, to him. The Khojas were by then acquiring increasing influence in the Nizārī community, both in terms of their numbers and financial resources. Soon, the imams acquired political prominence in the affairs of Kirmān. The forty-fourth imam, Abu'l-Ḥasan ʿAlī, also known as Sayyid Abu'l-Ḥasan Kahakī, was appointed around 1170/1756 to the governorship of the Kirmān province by Karīm Khān Zand (1164–1193/1751–1779), founder of the Zand dynasty in Persia; earlier the imam had been the *beglerbegi* or governor of the city of Kirmān.[82] It was in his time that the Niʿmat Allāhī Sufi order was revived in Persia. Imam Abu'l-Ḥasan had close relations with Nūr ʿAlī and Mushtāq ʿAlī Shāh among other Niʿmat Allāhī Sufis then active in Kirmān. On Abu'l-Ḥasan's death in 1206/1792, his son Shāh Khalīl Allāh succeeded to the Nizārī imamate and eventually settled in Yazd. Shāh Khalīl Allāh was murdered in 1232/1817, and was succeeded by his eldest son Ḥasan ʿAlī Shāh, who was later appointed to the governorship of Qumm by Fatḥ ʿAlī Shāh (1212–1250/1797–1834) and also given properties in Maḥallāt. In addition, the Qājār monarch of Persia gave one of his daughters in marriage to the youthful imam and bestowed upon him the honorific title of Āghā Khān (Āqā Khān), meaning 'lord' or 'master' – this title has remained hereditary among Ḥasan ʿAlī Shāh's successors. This Nizārī imam, who maintained his own close relations with the Niʿmat Allāhī Sufi order, has left a valuable autobiographical account of his early life and career in Persia in a work entitled *ʿIbrat-afzā*.[83]

Ḥasan ʿAlī Shāh was appointed to the governorship of Kirmān in 1251/1835 by the third Qājār monarch, Muḥammad Shāh. Subsequently, after some prolonged confrontations between the imam and the Qājār establishment, Āghā Khān I, also known as Āghā Khān Maḥallātī, left Persia permanently in 1257/1841. After spending some years in Afghanistan, Sind, Gujarāt and Calcutta, the imam finally settled in Bombay in 1265/1848, marking the commencement of the modern period of Nizārī Ismailism. As the spiritual head of a Muslim community, Āghā Khān I received the full protection of the British establishment in India. The Nizārī imam now launched a widespread campaign for defining and delineating the distinct religious identity of his Khoja following. The Nizārī Khojas were not always certain about their religious identity as they had dissimulated for long periods as Sunnis and Twelver Shiʿis, while their Satpanth tradition had been influenced by Hindu elements. With the help of the British courts in India, however, the Āghā Khān's followers were, in due course, legally defined as Shiʿi Imāmī Ismailis. In the event, the bulk of Khojas reaffirmed their allegiance to Āghā Khān I and acknowledged their Ismaili identity while minority groups seceded and joined Twelver Khoja and other communities.

Āghā Khān I died in 1298/1881, and was succeeded by his son Āqā ʿAlī Shāh who led the Nizārīs for only four years (1298–1302/1881–1885). The latter's sole surviving son and successor, Sulṭān Muḥammad Shāh, Aga Khan III, led the Nizārīs for seventy-two years, and also became internationally known as a Muslim reformer and statesman. Aga Khan III, too, made systematic efforts to set his followers' identity apart from those of other religious communities, particularly the Twelvers who for long periods had provided dissimulating covers for Nizārīs of Persia and elsewhere. The Nizārī identity was spelled out in numerous constitutions that the imam promulgated for his followers in different regions, especially in India, Pakistan and East Africa. Furthermore, the Nizārī imam became increasingly engaged with reform policies that would benefit not only his followers but other Muslims as well. He worked vigorously to consolidate and reorganize the Nizārīs into a modern Muslim community with high standards of education, health and social well-being, for both men and women, also developing a new network of councils for administering the affairs of his community. The participation of women in communal affairs was a high priority in the imam's reforms. Aga Khan III, who established his residence in Europe in the early part of the twentieth century, has left an interesting account of his life and public career in his *Memoirs*.[84]

Aga Khan III died in 1376/1957 and was succeeded by his grandson, known to his followers as Mawlana Hazar Imam Shah Karim al-Husayni. The present, Harvard-educated imam of the Nizārī Ismailis, the forty-ninth in the series, has continued and substantially expanded the modernization policies of his predecessor, also developing numerous new programmes and institutions of his own which are of wider interest to Muslims and Third World countries at large. He has created a complex institutional network generally referred to as the Aga Khan Development Network (AKDN), which implements projects in a variety of social, economic and cultural areas. In the field of higher education and educational institutions, his major initiatives include The Institute of Ismaili Studies, founded in London in 1977 for the promotion of general Islamic as well as Ismaili studies, and the Aga Khan University, set up in Karachi in 1985. More recently, he established in Tajikistan the University of Central Asia to address the specific educational needs of the region's mountain-based societies.

Prince Karim Aga Khan IV, as he is known internationally, has his secretariat near Paris. By 2004, when the Nizārīs celebrated the forty-seventh anniversary of his imamate, Aga Khan IV had established an impressive record of achievement not only as an Ismaili imam but also as a Muslim leader deeply aware of the demands of modernity and dedicated to promoting a better understanding of Islamic civilizations with their diversity of traditions and expressions.[85] Numbering several millions, the Nizārī Ismailis have emerged as progressive and prosperous Muslim minorities in more than twenty-five countries of Asia, the Middle East, Africa, Europe and North America.

Notes

* This chapter is partially based on the author's *The Ismāʿīlīs: Their History and Doctrines* (Cambridge, 1990) and *A Short History of the Ismailis* (Edinburgh, 1998).

1. The issues surrounding the succession to the Prophet and ʿAlī's legitimate claims to leadership are thoroughly investigated in W. Madelung, *The Succession to Muḥammad: A Study of the Early Caliphate* (Cambridge, 1997). For a modern exposition of the traditional Shiʿi view on the origins of Shiʿism, see Sayyid Muḥammad Ḥusayn Ṭabāṭabāʾī, *Shiʿite Islam*, ed. and tr., S.H. Nasr (London, 1975), especially pp. 39–73, 173–190.

2. See Abū Jaʿfar Muḥammad b. Yaʿqūb al-Kulaynī, *al-Uṣūl min al-kāfī*, ed., ʿA.A. al-Ghaffārī (Tehran, 1388/1968), vol. 1, pp. 168–548, containing the earliest Shiʿi *ḥadīth*s on the imamate reported mainly from Jaʿfar al-Ṣādiq. Many of the same *ḥadīth*s are reiterated in al-Qāḍī al-Nuʿmān's *Daʿāʾim al-Islām*, ed. A.A.A. Fyzee (Cairo, 1951–61), vol. 1, pp. 3–98; English trans., A.A.A. Fyzee, completely revised by I.K. Poonawala, as *The Pillars of Islam*:

Volume I, *Acts of Devotion and Religious Observances* (New Delhi, 2002), pp. 5–122. See also S. Husain M. Jafri, *Origins and Early Development of Shīʿa Islam* (London, 1979), pp. 235–300, and Ayatollah Jaʿfar Sobhani, *Doctrines of Shiʿi Islam: A Compendium of Imami Beliefs and Practices*, ed. and tr., R. Shah-Kazemi (London, 2001), pp. 96–120.

3. Many interesting ideas on the origins and early development of Shiʿism are contained in M.A. Amir-Moezzi, *The Divine Guide in Early Shiʿism: The Sources of Esotericism in Islam*, tr., D. Streight (Albany, NY, 1994). See also A.R. Lalani, *Early Shīʿī Thought: The Teachings of Imam Muḥammad al-Bāqir* (London, 2000), and W. Madelung "Shīʿa", *EI2*, vol. 9, pp. 420–424. A number of classical studies on the Imāmiyya may be found in E. Kohlberg, ed., *Shiʿism* (Aldershot, 2003), pp. 1–167.

4. Al-Qāḍī al-Nuʿmān, *Sharḥ al-akhbār*, ed., S.M. al-Ḥusaynī al-Jalālī (Qumm, 1409–12/1988–92), vol. 3, p. 309; Jaʿfar b. Manṣūr al-Yaman, *Sarāʾir wa-asrār al-nuṭaqāʾ*, ed., M. Ghālib (Beirut, 1984), pp. 262–263; Idrīs ʿImād al-Dīn, *Zahr al-maʿānī*, ed., M. Ghālib (Beirut, 1991), pp. 200–201; his *ʿUyūn al-akhbār*, ed., M. Ghālib (Beirut, 1973), vol. 4, p. 334, and Muḥammad b. Muḥammad al-Mufīd, *Kitāb al-Irshād: The Book of Guidance*, tr., I.K.A. Howard (London, 1981), p. 431.

5. Al-Ḥasan b. Mūsā al-Nawbakhtī, *Kitāb firaq al-Shīʿa*, ed., H. Ritter (Istanbul, 1931), pp. 57–61, and Saʿd b. ʿAbd Allāh al-Qummī, *Kitāb al-maqālāt wa'l-firaq*, ed., M.J. Mashkūr (Tehran, 1963), pp. 80–81, 83. On the relationships between these two closely connected heresiographies, see W. Madelung, "Bemerkungen zur imamitischen Firaq-Literatur", *Der Islam*, 53 (1967), pp. 37–52; reprinted in his *Religious Schools and Sects in Medieval Islam* (London, 1985), article XV; English trans., "Some Remarks on the Imāmī Firaq Literature", in Kohlberg, ed., *Shiʿism*, pp. 153–167. See also F. Daftary, "The Earliest Ismāʿīlīs", *Arabica*, 38 (1991), pp. 220 ff.; reprinted in Kohlberg, ed., *Shiʿism*, pp. 235 ff.

6. Al-Qāḍī al-Nuʿmān, *Sharḥ al-akhbār*, vol. 3, pp. 302, 309–310; Jaʿfar b. Manṣūr al-Yaman, *Sarāʾir wa-asrār al-nuṭaqāʾ*, pp. 256–257, 258; Idrīs ʿImād al-Dīn, *ʿUyūn*, vol. 4, pp. 332–350; Abū ʿAmr Muḥammad b. ʿUmar al-Kashshī, *Ikhtiyār maʿrifat al-rijāl*, as abridged by Muḥammad b. al-Ḥasan al-Ṭūsī, ed., Ḥ. al-Muṣṭafawī (Mashhad, 1348 Sh./1969), pp. 217–218, 244–245, 321, 325–326, 354–356, 376–382, 390, and F. Daftary, "Esmāʿīl b. Jaʿfar al-Ṣādeq", *EIR*, vol. 8, pp. 625–626.

7. *Umm al-kitāb*, ed., W. Ivanow, in *Der Islam*, 23 (1936), text p. 11; see also H. Halm, *Die islamische Gnosis* (Zurich and Munich, 1990), pp. 113–198.

8. See, for example, al-Qāḍī al-Nuʿmān, *Daʿāʾim al-Islām*, vol. 1, pp. 49–50; tr., Fyzee and Poonawala, vol. 1, p. 65.

9. Idrīs ʿImād al-Dīn, *ʿUyūn,* vol. 4, pp. 351–356; see also his *Zahr al-*

maʿānī, pp. 204–208.

10. Al-Nawbakhtī, *Firaq al-Shīʿa*, pp. 60–61, and Saʿd b. ʿAbd Allāh al-Qummī, *Kitāb al-maqālāt*, p. 83.

11. See ʿAbd Allāh al-Mahdī's letter to the Ismailis of Yaman, as preserved by Jaʿfar b. Manṣūr al-Yaman, edited by Ḥusayn F. al-Hamdānī under the title of *On the Genealogy of Fatimid Caliphs* (Cairo, 1958), text pp. 10–12.

12. Ibn al-Nadīm, *Kitāb al-fihrist*, ed., M.R. Tajaddud (2nd ed., Tehran, 1973), p. 238; Ibn al-Dawādārī, *Kanz al-durar*, vol. 6, ed., Ṣ. al-Munajjid (Cairo, 1961), pp. 17–20; Aḥmad b. ʿAlī al-Maqrīzī, *Ittiʿāẓ al-ḥunafāʾ*, ed., J. al-Shayyāl and M.Ḥ.M. Aḥmad (Cairo, 1967–73), vol. 1, pp. 22–26; Aḥmad b. ʿAbd al-Wahhāb al-Nuwayrī, *Nihāyat al-arab*, vol. 25, ed., M.J. ʿA. al-Ḥīnī et al. (Cairo, 1984), p. 189, and Muḥammad b. Mālik al-Ḥammādī al-Yamānī, *Kashf asrār al-Bāṭiniyya*, ed., S. Muḥammad Zāhid al-Kawtharī (Cairo, 1357/1939), pp. 16 ff. See also A. Hamdani and F. de Blois, "A Re-examination of al-Mahdī's Letter to the Yemenites on the Genealogy of the Fatimid Caliphs", *JRAS* (1983), pp. 173–207.

13. See Muḥammad b. Jarīr al-Ṭabarī, *Taʾrīkh al-rusul waʾl-mulūk*, ed., M.J. de Goeje et al. (Leiden, 1879–1901), III, pp. 2124, 2126–2127; English trans., *The History of al-Ṭabarī:* Volume XXXVII, *The ʿAbbāsid Recovery*, tr., Philip M. Fields (Albany, NY, 1987), pp. 169, 171–173.

14. Al-Ṭabarī, *Taʾrīkh*, III, pp. 2188 ff., 2196–2197, 2205, 2232; tr., Fields, pp. 77 ff., 86–89, 98, 128–129; ʿAlī b. al-Ḥusayn al-Masʿūdī, *Murūj al-dhahab*, ed. and tr., C. Barbier de Meynard and A. Pavet de Courteille (Paris, 1861–76), vol. 8, pp. 191 ff.; Ibn al-Dawādārī, *Kanz*, vol. 6, pp. 55–62, 91 ff.; al-Maqrīzī, *Ittiʿāẓ*, vol. 1, pp. 159 ff., and al-Nuwayrī, *Nihāyat al-arab*, vol. 25, pp. 233 ff.

15. The best modern treatment of the early *daʿwa* in Khurāsān and Central Asia, with a survey of the sources, is to be found in S.M. Stern, "The Early Ismāʿīlī Missionaries in North-West Persia and in Khurāsān and Transoxania", *BSOAS*, 23 (1960), pp. 59–60; reprinted in his *Studies in Early Ismāʿīlism* (Jerusalem and Leiden, 1983), pp. 189–233.

16. For the issues and the sources, see W. Madelung, "Das Imamat in der frühen ismailitischen Lehre", *Der Islam*, 37 (1961), pp. 59–65, 69 ff., and F. Daftary, "A Major Schism in the Early Ismāʿīlī Movement", *SI*, 77 (1993), pp. 123–139.

17. Ibn Ḥawqal, *Kitāb ṣūrat al-arḍ*, ed., J.H. Kramers (2nd ed., Leiden, 1938–39), pp. 96, 295; French trans., *Configuration de la terre*, tr., J.H. Kramers and G. Wiet (Paris and Beirut, 1964), pp. 94, 289, and W. Madelung, "Ḥamdān Qarmaṭ", *EIR*, vol. 11, pp. 634–635.

18. For surveys of the Qarmaṭīs and the relevant sources, see W. Madelung, "Fatimiden und Baḥrainqarmaṭen", *Der Islam*, 34 (1959), pp. 34–88; English trans., "The Fatimids and the Qarmaṭīs of Baḥrayn", in *MIHT*, pp. 21–73; W.

Madelung, "Ḳarmaṭī", *EI2*, vol. 4, pp. 660–665, and F. Daftary, "Carmatians", *EIR*, vol. 4, pp. 823–832.

19. A detailed account of the activities of Zikrawayh and his sons is contained in al-Ṭabarī, *Ta'rīkh*, III, pp. 2218–2246, 2255–2275; English trans., *The History of al-Ṭabarī*: Volume XXXVIII, *The Return of the Caliphate to Baghdad*, tr., F. Rosenthal (Albany, NY, 1985), pp. 113–144, 157–179. See also ʿArīb b. Saʿd al-Qurṭubī, *Ṣilat ta'rīkh al-Ṭabarī*, ed., M.J. de Goeje (Leiden, 1897), pp. 9–18, 36, 137; ʿAlī b. al-Ḥusayn al-Masʿūdī, *Kitāb al-tanbīh wa'l-ishrāf*, ed., M.J. de Goeje (Leiden, 1894), pp. 370–376; Ibn al-Dawādārī, *Kanz*, vol. 6, pp. 69–90; al-Maqrīzī, *Ittiʿāẓ*, vol. 1, pp. 168–179, and al-Nuwayrī, *Nihāyat al-arab*, vol. 25, pp. 246–276. For the best modern study of the subject, see H. Halm, "Die Söhne Zikrawaihs und das erste fatimidische Kalifat (290/930)", *WO*, 10 (1979), pp. 30–53, and his *The Empire of the Mahdi: The Rise of the Fatimids*, tr., M. Bonner (Leiden, 1996), pp. 66–88, 183–190.

20. See H. Halm, "The Ismaʿili Oath of Allegiance (*ʿahd*) and the 'Sessions of Wisdom' (*majālis al-ḥikma*) in Fatimid Times", in *MIHT*, pp. 91–98.

21. See H. Corbin, *Cyclical Time and Ismaili Gnosis*, tr., R. Manheim and J.W. Morris (London, 1983), pp. 1–58; H. Halm, *Kosmologie und Heilslehre der frühen Ismāʿīlīya* (Wiesbaden, 1978), pp. 18–37, and F. Daftary, "Dawr", *EIR*, vol. 7, pp. 151–153.

22. S.M. Stern, "The Earliest Cosmological Doctrine of Ismāʿīlism", in his *Studies in Early Ismāʿīlism*, pp. 3–29; Halm, *Kosmologie*, pp. 38–127, 206–227, and his "The Cosmology of the Pre-Fatimid Ismāʿīliyya", in *MIHT*, pp. 75–83.

23. See al-Qāḍī al-Nuʿmān, *Iftitāḥ al-daʿwa*, ed., W. al-Qāḍī (Beirut, 1970), pp. 71–222; ed., F. al-Dashrāwī (Tunis, 1975), pp. 47–257; M. Talbi, *L'Émirat Aghlabide 184–296/800–909: Histoire politique* (Paris, 1966), pp. 579–672, and Halm, *Empire of the Mahdi*, pp. 9–128.

24. W. Madelung, "The Religious Policy of the Fatimids toward their Sunnī Subjects in the Maghrib", in M. Barrucand, ed., *L'Égypte Fatimide, son art et son histoire* (Paris, 1999), pp. 97–104.

25. See al-Sijistānī, *Kashf al-maḥjūb*, ed., H. Corbin (Tehran and Paris, 1949), pp. 4–15; his *Ithbāt al-nubū'āt*, ed., ʿĀ. Tāmir (Beirut, 1966), pp. 2–3, 28, and Nāṣir-i Khusraw, *Jāmiʿ al-ḥikmatayn*, ed., H. Corbin and M. Muʿīn (Tehran and Paris, 1953), pp. 210–232.

26. See P.E. Walker, *Early Philosophical Shiism: The Ismaili Neoplatonism of Abū Yaʿqūb al-Sijistānī* (Cambridge, 1993), pp. 67–142, and his *Abū Yaʿqūb al-Sijistānī: Intellectual Missionary* (London, 1996), pp. 26–103.

27. W. Madelung, "The Sources of Ismāʿīlī Law", *Journal of Near Eastern Studies*, 35 (1976), pp. 29–40; reprinted in his *Religious Schools and Sects*, article XVIII, and I.K. Poonawala, "Al-Qāḍī al-Nuʿmān and Ismaʿili

Jurisprudence", in *MIHT*, pp. 117–143.

28. Taqī al-Dīn Aḥmad b. ʿAlī al-Maqrīzī, *Kitāb al-mawāʿiẓ waʾl-iʿtibār bi-dhikr al-khiṭaṭ waʾl-āthār* (Būlāq, 1270/1853–54), vol. 1, pp. 390–391, 458–460; Halm, "The Ismaʿili Oath of Allegiance", in *MIHT*, pp. 98–112; his *The Fatimids and their Traditions of Learning* (London, 1997), pp. 23–29, 41–45, 71–77, and P.E. Walker, "Fatimid Institutions of Learning", *Journal of the American Research Center in Egypt*, 34 (1997), pp. 182–186, 189–193.

29. S.M. Stern, "Cairo as the Centre of the Ismāʿīlī Movement", in *Colloque international sur l'histoire du Caire* (Cairo, 1972), 437–450; reprinted in his *Studies in Early Ismāʿīlism*, pp. 234–256; A. Hamdani, "Evolution of the Organisational Structure of the Fāṭimī Daʿwah", *Arabian Studies*, 3 (1976), pp. 85–11; F. Daftary, "The Ismaili *Daʿwa* outside the Fatimid *Dawla*", in Barrucand, ed., *L'Égypte Fatimide*, pp. 29–43, and his "*Dāʿī*", *EIR*, vol. 6, pp. 590 592.

30. For studies of al-Kirmānī's system, see D. de Smet, *La Quiétude de l'intellect: Néoplatonisme et gnose Ismaélienne dans l'oeuvre de Ḥamîd ad-Dîn al-Kirmânî (Xe/XIes.)* (Louvain, 1995), pp. 35–377, and P.E. Walker, *Ḥamīd al-Dīn al-Kirmānī: Ismaili Thought in the Age of al-Ḥākim* (London, 1999), especially pp. 80–124. See also F. Daftary, "Ḥamid-al-Din Kermāni", *EIR*, vol. 11, pp. 639–641.

31. See also V. Klemm, *Die Mission des fāṭimidischen Agenten al-Muʾayyad fī d-dīn in Šīrāz* (Frankfurt, etc., 1989), pp. 2–63, 136–92, and her *Memoirs of a Mission: The Ismaili Scholar, Statesman and Poet al-Muʾayyad fiʾl-Dīn al-Shīrāzī* (London, 2003), especially pp. 19–86.

32. ʿUmāra al-Yamanī, *Taʾrīkh al-Yaman*, ed. and tr., H.C. Kay in his *Yaman, its Early Mediaeval History* (London, 1892), text pp. 1–102, translation pp. 1–137; Idrīs ʿImād al-Dīn, *ʿUyūn al-akhbār*, ed. and summary English trans., A.F. Sayyid, in collaboration with P.E. Walker and M.A. Pomerantz, as *The Fatimids and their Successors in Yaman: The History of an Islamic Community* (London, 2002), text pp. 5–174, translation pp. 33–73. For the best modern coverage of the Ṣulayḥids, see Ḥusayn F. al-Hamdānī, *al-Ṣulayḥiyyūn waʾl-ḥaraka al-Fāṭimiyya fiʾl-Yaman* (Cairo, 1955), especially pp. 62–231.

33. Ibn al-Athīr, *al-Kāmil fiʾl-taʾrīkh*, ed., C.J. Tornberg (Leiden, 1851–76), vol. 9, pp. 211, 358; vol. 10, pp. 122 ff., 165–166; V.V. Barthold, *Turkestan down to the Mongol Invasion*, ed., C.E. Bosworth (3rd ed., London, 1968), pp. 304–305, 316–318, and Daftary, *The Ismāʿīlīs*, pp. 167–169, 212–218.

34. W. Ivanow, *Nasir-i Khusraw and Ismailism* (Bombay, 1948); A.E. Bertel's, *Nasir-i Khosrov i ismailizm* (Moscow, 1959); H. Corbin, "Nāṣir-i Khusrau and Iranian Ismāʿīlism", in *The Cambridge History of Iran:* Volume 4, *The Period from the Arab Invasion to the Saljuqs*, ed., R.N. Frye (Cambridge, 1975), pp. 520–542, and A.C. Hunsberger, *Nasir Khusraw, The Ruby*

of Badakhshan: A Portrait of the Persian Poet, Traveller and Philosopher (London, 2000).

35. Ibn al-Qalānisī, *Dhayl ta'rīkh Dimashq*, ed., H.F. Amedroz (Leiden, 1908), pp. 203, 229, 242 ff., 262, 270, 272–273, 295–296; Ibn Ẓāfir, *Akhbār al-duwal al-munqaṭi'a*, ed. A. Ferré (Cairo, 1972), pp. 94–101; Ibn Muyassar, *Akhbār Miṣr*, ed., A. Fu'ād Sayyid (Cairo, 1981), pp. 113–141; Ibn al-Dawādārī, *Kanz al-durar*, vol. 6, pp. 505–556; al-Maqrīzī, *Itti'āẓ al-ḥunafā'*, vol. 3, pp. 135–192, and Ibn Taghrībirdī, *al-Nujūm al-zāhira* (Cairo, 1348–92/1929–72), vol. 5, pp. 237–287.

36. Shihāb al-Dīn Aḥmad b. 'Alī al-Qalqashandī, *Ṣubḥ al-a'shā fī ṣinā'at al-inshā'* (Cairo, 1332–38/1914–20), vol. 9, pp. 291–297; reprinted in *Majmū'at al-wathā'iq al-Fāṭimiyya*, ed., Jamāl al-Dīn al-Shayyāl (Cairo, 1958), text pp. 249–260, commentaries pp. 71–102.

37. The best modern study of the Fatimid dynasty after al-Āmir, and the Ḥāfiẓī -Ṭayyibī schism, is S.M. Stern's "The Succession to the Fatimid Imam al-Āmir, the Claims of the Later Fatimids to the Imamate, and the Rise of Ṭayyibī Ismailism", *Oriens*, 4 (1951), pp. 193–255; reprinted in his *History and Culture in the Medieval Muslim World* (London, 1984), article XI. See also P. Casanova, "Les derniers Fāṭimides", *Mémoires de la Mission Archéologique Française du Caire*, 6 (1897), pp. 415–445, and Daftary, *The Ismā'īlīs*, pp. 256–297, where full references to the sources are cited.

38. 'Umāra al-Yamanī, *Ta'rīkh al-Yaman*, in Kay, *Yaman, its Early Mediaeval History*, text pp. 48–59, translation pp. 64–80. 'Umāra's section on the Zuray'ids is cited more correctly by Ibn al-Mujāwir (d. 690/1291) in his *Ta'rīkh al-Mustabṣir*, ed., O. Löfgren (Leiden, 1951–54), vol. 1, pp. 121–127, also in O. Löfgren, ed., *Arabische Texte zur Kenntnis der Stadt Aden in Mittelalter* (Uppsala, 1936–50), vol. 1, pp. 40–47.

39. See A.F. Sayyid, *Maṣādir ta'rīkh al-Yaman fi'l-'aṣr al-Islāmī* (Cairo, 1974), especially pp. 99–219.

40. Al-Hamdānī, *al-Ṣulayḥiyyūn*, p. 5.

41. For further details, see J. Blank, *Mullahs on the Mainframe: Islam and Modernity among the Daudi Bohras* (Chicago, 2001), pp. 229–257, 301–307.

42. See A. Hamdani, "The Dā'ī Ḥātim Ibn Ibrāhīm al-Ḥāmidī (d. 596 H./ 1199 A.D.) and his Book *Tuḥfat al-Qulūb*", *Oriens*, 23–24 (1970–71), especially pp. 279 ff., and F. Daftary, "Sayyida Ḥurra: The Ismā'īlī Ṣulayḥid Queen of Yemen", in Gavin R.G. Hambly, ed., *Women in the Medieval Islamic World: Power, Patronage and Piety* (New York, 1998), pp. 117–130.

43. See, for instance, H. Corbin, *Histoire de la philosophie Islamique* (Paris, 1964), pp. 124–136; English trans., *History of Islamic Philosophy*, tr., L. Sherrard (London, 1993), pp. 84–93; his *Cyclical Time and Ismaili Gnosis*, pp. 37–58, 65 ff., 76 ff., 103 ff., 173–181, and his *L'imam caché* (Paris, 2003), pp.

57–67.

44. W. Ivanow, *Ismaili Literature: A Bibliographical Survey* (Tehran, 1963), pp. 127–136, and I.K. Poonawala, *Biobibliography of Ismāʿīlī Literature* (Malibu, CA, 1977), pp. 251–263.

45. F. Daftary, "Persian Historiography of the Early Nizārī Ismāʿīlīs", *Iran, Journal of the British Institute of Persian Studies*, 30 (1992), pp. 91–97.

46. See Abu'l-Qāsim Kāshānī, *Ta'rīkh-i Uljāytū*, ed., M. Hambly (Tehran, 1348 Sh./1969), pp. 4–5, 54–55, 240–241, and his *Zubdat al-tawārīkh: bakhsh-i Fāṭimiyān va Nizāriyān*, ed., M.T. Dānishpazhūh (2nd ed., Tehran, 1366 Sh./ 1987), pp. 3–4.

47. Ḥamd Allāh Mustawfī Qazwīnī, *Ta'rīkh-i guzīda*, ed., ʿAbd al-Ḥusayn Navā'ī (Tehran, 1339 Sh./1960), pp. 508–528. Ḥamd Allāh's section on the Persian Ismailis was first published in French translation in Charles F. Defrémery's "Histoire des Seldjoukides", *JA*, 4 série, 13 (1849), pp. 26–49. Subsequently, a partial edition with French translation was produced by Jules Gantin under the title of *Târîkhè Gozîdè. Les dynasties Persanes pendent la période Musulmane* (Paris, 1903), pp. 452–515 (covering the Ismailis). It was, however, Edward G. Browne (1862–1926) who for the first time produced a complete facsimile edition of this history for the E.J.W. Gibb Memorial Series, *The Ta'rīkh-i Guzīda; or, 'Select History'* (Leiden and London, 1910), pp. 509–527, with a later abridged English translation for the same series (Leiden and London, 1913), pp. 122–131.

48. Ḥamd Allāh Mustawfī Qazwīnī, *Ẓafar-nāma*, facsimile ed., N. Pūrjavādī and N. Rastigār (Tehran and Vienna, 1377 Sh./1999), vol. 1, pp. 655–656; vol. 2, pp. 859–872.

49. Different parts of Mīrkhwānd's *Rawḍat al-ṣafā'* were published in Europe during the nineteenth century. For the first edition of its Ismaili section, together with French translation, see *Histoire de la dynastie des Ismaéliens de Perse,* in *Le Jardin de la Pureté*, ed. and tr., Am. Jourdain, published in *Notices et Extraits des Manuscrits de la Bibliothèque Impériale et autres bibliothèques*, 9 (1813), especially pp. 143–248.

50. Khwānd Amīr, *Ḥabīb al-siyar*, ed., J. Humā'ī (Tehran, 1333 Sh./1954), vol. 2, pp. 450–479.

51. See al-Fatḥ b. ʿAlī al-Bundārī, *Zubdat al-nuṣra*, ed., M. Th. Houtsma (Leiden, 1889).

52. Ẓahīr al-Dīn Nīshāpūrī, *Saljūq-nāma*, ed., Ismāʿīl Afshār (1332 Sh./ 1953); Ṣadr al-Dīn ʿAlī b. Nāṣir al-Ḥusaynī, *Akhbār al-dawla al-Saljūqiyya*, ed., M. Iqbāl (Lahore, 1933), and Muḥammd b. ʿAlī al-Rāwandī, *Rāḥat al-ṣudūr*, ed., M. Iqbāl (London, 1921). For more details on Saljūq chronicles, see Cl. Cahen, "The Historiography of the Seljuqid Period", in B. Lewis and P.M. Holt, ed., *Historians of the Middle East* (London, 1964), pp. 68–76, and

Julie Scott Meisami, *Persian Historiography to the End of the Twelfth Century* (Edinburgh, 1999), pp. 141–280.

53. Ibn Isfandiyār, *Ta'rīkh-i Ṭabaristān*, ed., ʿAbbās Iqbāl (Tehran, 1320 Sh./1941); abridged English trans., E.G. Browne as *An Abridged Translation of the History of Ṭabaristān* (Leiden and London, 1905).

54. See Ivanow, *Ismaili Literature*, pp. 169–173, and Poonawala, *Biobibliography*, pp. 287 ff.

55. See Claude Cahen, *Syrie du nord à l'époque des Croisades* (Paris, 1940), pp. 33–93; J. Sauvaget, *Introduction to the History of the Muslim East: A Bibliographical Guide*, based on the second edition as recast by Cl. Cahen (Berkeley, 1965), pp. 162 ff., and F. Gabrieli, "The Arabic Historiography of the Crusades", in Lewis and Holt, ed., *Historians of the Middle East*, pp. 98–107. For a survey of different categories of sources on the Syrian Nizārīs, see B. Lewis, "The Sources for the History of the Syrian Assassins", *Speculum*, 27 (1952), pp. 475–489; reprinted in his *Studies in Classical and Ottoman Islam (7th–16th Centuries)* (London, 1976), article VIII.

56. Ibn al-Qalānisī, *Dhayl ta'rīkh Dimashq*, ed., Amedroz; also ed., S. Zakkār (Damascus, 1403/1983); Kamāl al-Dīn Ibn al-ʿAdīm, *Zubdat al-ḥalab min ta'rīkh Ḥalab*, ed., S. al-Dahhān (Damascus, 1951–68), 3 vols., and Sibṭ Ibn al-Jawzī, *Mir'āt al-zamān*, ed., J.R. Jewett (Chicago, 1907); ed. A. Sevim (Ankara, 1968).

57. P. Casanova, "Monnaie des Assassins de Perse", *Revue Numismatique*, 3 série, 11 (1893), pp. 343–352, and G.C. Miles, "Coins of the Assassins of Alamūt", *Orientalia Lovaniensia Periodica*, 3 (1972), pp. 155–162.

58. Most of the inscriptions at Maṣyāf and several other major Nizārī castles in Syria were studied by Max van Berchem (1863–1921); see his "Épigraphie des Assassins de Syrie", *JA*, 9 série, 9 (1897), pp. 453–501; reprinted in his *Opera Minora* (Geneva, 1978), vol. 1, pp. 453–501; also reprinted in Bryan S. Turner, ed., *Orientalism: Early Sources*, Volume I, *Readings in Orientalism* (London, 2000), pp. 279–309. See also P. Thorau, "Die Burgen der Assassinen in Syrien und ihre Einnahme durch Sultan Baibars", *WO*, 18 (1987), pp. 132–158.

59. M.G.S. Hodgson, "The Ismāʿīlī State", in *The Cambridge History of Iran:* Volume 5, *The Saljuq and Mongol Periods*, ed., J.A. Boyle (Cambridge, 1968), p. 424, n.1.

60. F. Daftary, "Ḥasan-i Ṣabbāḥ and the Origins of the Nizārī Ismaʿili Movement", in *MIHT*, pp. 181–204, and his "Ḥasan Ṣabbāḥ", *EIR*, vol. 12, pp. 34–37.

61. Muḥammad b. ʿAbd al-Karīm al-Shahrastānī, *Kitāb al-milal wa'l-niḥal*, ed., W. Cureton (London, 1842–46), pp. 150–152; French trans., *Livre des religions et des sectes*, tr., D. Gimaret et al. (Paris and Louvain, 1986–93),

vol. 1, pp. 560–565; partial English trans., *Muslim Sects and Divisions*, tr., A.K. Kazi and J.G. Flynn (London, 1984), pp. 167–170; ʿAṭā-Malik Juwaynī, *Taʾrīkh-i jahān-gushā*, ed., M. Qazwīnī (Leiden and London, 1912–37), vol. 3, pp. 195–199; English trans., *The History of the World-Conqueror*, tr., J.A. Boyle (Manchester, 1958), vol. 2, pp. 671–673; Rashīd al-Dīn, *Jāmiʿ al-tawārīkh: qismat-i Ismāʿīliyān*, ed., M.T. Dānishpazhūh and M. Mudarrisī Zanjānī (Tehran, 1338 Sh./1959), pp. 105–107, and Abu'l-Qāsim Kāshānī, *Zubdat al-tawārīkh: bakhsh-i Fāṭimiyān va Nizāriyān*, pp. 142–143.

62. Carole Hillenbrand, "The Power Struggle Between the Saljuqs and the Ismaʿilis of Alamūt, 487–518/1094–1124: The Saljuq Perspective", in *MIHT*, pp. 205–220.

63. Juwaynī, vol. 3, pp. 222–239; tr., Boyle, vol. 2, pp. 686–697; Rashīd al-Dīn, pp. 162–170; Kāshānī, pp. 199–208; Hodgson, *The Order of Assassins* (The Hague, 1955), pp. 146–159, and Daftary, *The Ismāʿīlīs*, pp. 385–391.

64. Naṣīr al-Dīn al-Ṭūsī, *Rawḍat al-taslīm*, ed. and tr., W. Ivanow (Leiden, 1950), text pp. 104–105, 112, translation pp. 119, 128–129, and his *Sayr va sulūk*, ed. and tr., S.J. Badakhchani as *Contemplation and Action: The Spiritual Autobiography of a Muslim Scholar* (London, 1998), text pp. 17–18, translation pp. 47–48.

65. See *Haft bāb-i Bābā Sayyidnā*, ed., W. Ivanow, in his *Two Early Ismaili Treatises* (Bombay, 1933), pp. 4–42; English trans., Hodgson, in his *Order of Assassins*, pp. 279–324; al-Ṭūsī, *Rawḍa*, text pp. 42, 44–45, 47–56, 98–99, 101–102, translation pp. 46–47, 49–50, 52–63, 111–112, 115–116; Juwaynī, vol. 3, pp. 240–242; tr., Boyle, vol. 2, pp. 697–699; Rashīd al-Dīn, pp. 170–173, and Kāshānī, pp. 208–214.

66. See *Faṣl min al-lafẓ al-sharīf* (attributed to Rāshid al-Dīn Sinān), ed. and tr., S. Guyard, in his "Un grand maître des Assassins au temps de Saladin", *JA*, 7 série, 9 (1877), pp. 387–489; B. Lewis, "Kamāl al-Dīn's Biography of Rāšid al-Dīn Sinān", *Arabica*, 13 (1966), pp. 225–267; reprinted in his *Studies*, article X, and his *The Assassins* (London, 1967), pp. 110–118; Hodgson, *Order of the Assassins*, pp. 185–209; F. Daftary, *The Assassin Legends: Myths of the Ismaʿilis* (London, 1994), pp. 67–74, 94 ff., and his "Rāshid al-Dīn Sinān", *EI2*, vol. 8, pp. 442–443.

67. Al-Ṭūsī, *Rawḍa*, text pp. 61–63, 101–102, 110, 117–119, 132–133, 143, 145, 147, translation pp. 67–69, 115–116, 126, 136–138, 154–155, 173 and elsewhere.

68. John of Joinville, *Memoirs of John Lord de Joinville*, tr., T. Johnes (Hafod, 1807), vol. 1, pp. 194–197, also in John of Joinville and Geoffroy of Villehardouin, *Chronicles of the Crusades*, tr., M.R.B. Shaw (New York, 1963), pp. 277–280, and Daftary, *Assassin Legends*, pp. 79–82.

69. For the Persian literarature of the Alamūt period, see Ivanow, *Ismaili Literature*, pp. 137–154, and Poonawala, *Biobibliography*, pp. 263–286.

70. Ivanow, *Ismaili Literature*, pp. 168–173, and Poonawala, *Biobibliography*, pp. 293–297.

71. See Azim Nanji, *The Nizārī Ismāʿīlī Tradition in the Indo-Pakistan Subcontinent* (Delmar, NY, 1978), pp. 50–96, and Ali S. Asani, *Ecstasy and Enlightenment: The Ismaili Devotional Literature of South Asia* (London, 2002), pp. 1–53 and 124–152 (on the Khojkī script).

72. This schism was first brought to the attention of modern scholars in W. Ivanow's "A Forgotten Branch of the Ismailis", *JRAS* (1938), pp. 57–79. See also ʿĀrif Tāmir, "Furūʿ al-shajara al-Ismāʿīliyya al-Imāmiyya", *al-Mashriq*, 51 (1957), pp. 581–612.

73. See Ẓahīr al-Dīn Marʿashī, *Taʾrīkh-i Gīlān va Daylamistān*, ed., M. Sutūda (Tehran, 1347 Sh./1968), pp. 52–68, 69–70, 76 ff., 81 ff., 89, 121, 123–30

74. Mīrzā Sang Muḥammad Badakhshī and Mīrzā Faḍl ʿAlī Beg Surkh Afsar, *Taʾrīkh-i Badakhshān*, ed., A.N. Boldyrev (Leningrad, 1959), pp. 227–253, and Ghurbān Muḥammad-Zāda and Muḥabbat Shāh-Zāda, *Taʾrīkh-i Badakhshān*, ed., A.A. Yigāna (Moscow, 1973), pp. 87–91.

75. F. Daftary, "Ismāʿīlī-Sufi Relations in Early Post-Alamūt and Safavid Persia", in L. Lewisohn and D. Morgan, ed., *The Heritage of Sufism:* Volume III, *Late Classical Persianate Sufism (1501–1750)* (Oxford, 1999), pp. 275–289.

76. On Anjudān and its Nizārī antiquities, which are rapidly disappearing, see W. Ivanow, "Tombs of Some Persian Ismaili Imams", *JBBRAS*, NS, 14 (1938), pp. 49–62, and F. Daftary, "Anjedān", *EIR*, vol. 2, p. 77.

77. Mustanṣir bi'llāh (II), *Pandiyāt-i jawānmardī*, ed. and tr., W. Ivanow (Leiden, 1953), text pp. 2–3, 11, 13, 14, 34–36, 54–58, 65–68 and elsewhere.

78. Abū Isḥāq Quhistānī, *Haft bāb*, ed. and tr., W. Ivanow (Bombay, 1959), text pp. 19–20, 37–38, 53–54, 58, 67–68, translation pp. 19–20, 37–38, 53–54, 58, 67–68; Khayrkhwāh-i Harātī, *Kalām-i pīr*, ed. and tr., W. Ivanow (Bombay, 1935), text pp. 46, 72–73, 86, 95–96, 100, 114–116, and his *Taṣnīfāt*, ed., W. Ivanow (Tehran, 1961), pp. 18 ff.

79. Muḥammad Qāsim Hindū Shāh Astarābābī, better known as Firishta, *Taʾrīkh-i Firishta*, ed., J. Briggs (Bombay, 1832), vol. 2, pp. 213–231; ʿAlī b. ʿAzīz Ṭabāṭabā, *Burhān-i maʾāthir* (Hyderabad, 1936), pp. 251–270, 274 ff., 281 ff., 291, 308, 314, 324–326, 338–339, 361, 381, 433, 448–450, 502–503 and elsewhere; Qāḍī Nūr Allāh al-Shūshtarī, *Majālis al-muʾminīn* (Tehran, 1375–76/1955–56), vol. 2, pp. 234–240; Poonawala, *Biobibliography*, pp. 271–275, and F. Daftary, "Shāh Ṭāhir and the Nizārī Ismaili Disguises", in T. Lawson, ed., *Reason and Inspiration in Islam: Essays in Honour of Hermann Landolt* (London, forthcoming).

80. Daftary, *The Ismāʿīlīs*, pp. 471–474, 487–491.

81. For some listings of the *ginān*s, see Ivanow, *Ismaili Literature*, pp. 174–181; Poonawala, *Biobibliography*, pp. 298–311, and Ali S. Asani, *The Har-*

vard Collection of Ismaili Literature in Indic Languages (Boston, 1992). The *ginān* collection of The Institute of Ismaili Studies Library, numbering some 150 items, has not yet been catalogued; see Asani, *Ecstasy and Enlightenment*, pp. 130–131.

82. ʿAlī Riḍā b. ʿAbd al-Karīm Shīrāzī, *Taʾrīkh-i Zandiyya*, ed., E. Beer (Leiden, 1888), pp. 52–56; ed., Ghulām Riḍā Varahrām (Tehran, 1365 Sh./1986), pp. 74–77; Aḥmad ʿAlī Khān Vazīrī, *Taʾrīkh-i Kirmān*, ed., M.I. Bāstānī Pārīzī (2nd ed., Tehran, 1352 Sh./1973), pp. 543–565; Riḍā Qulī Khān Hidāyat, *Rawḍat al-ṣafā-yi Nāṣirī* (Tehran, 1339 Sh./1960), vol. 9, pp. 250, 252, 255; Muḥammad Ḥasan Khān Iʿtimād al-Salṭana, *Taʾrīkh-i muntaẓam-i Nāṣirī* (Tehran, 1298–1300/1881–83), vol. 3, pp. 53–54, and Daftary, *The Ismāʿīlīs*, pp. 499–503.

83. On Āghā Khān I, in addition to his *ʿIbrat-afzā* (Bombay, 1278/1862), pp. 8–49; ed., Ḥ. Kūhī Kirmānī (Tehran, 1325 Sh./1946), pp. 1–86, see Vazīrī, *Taʾrīkh*, pp. 602–604, 608–13; Fidāʾī Khurāsānī, *Kitāb-i hidāyat al-muʾminīn al-ṭālibīn*, ed., A.A. Semenov (Moscow, 1959), pp. 146–176; Hidāyat, *Rawḍat al-ṣafāʾ*, vol. 10, pp. 169, 249–253, 259–261; Muḥammad Taqī Lisān al-Mulk Sipihr, *Nāsikh al-tawārīkh: taʾrīkh-i Qājāriyya*, ed., M.B. Bihbūdī (Tehran, 1344 Sh./1965), vol. 2, pp. 248, 334–335, 350–356, 358–360, 364; Iʿtimād al-Salṭana, *Muntaẓam-i Nāṣirī*, vol. 3, pp. 165, 167, 173–174, 175–176, 177; N.M. Dumasia, *A Brief History of Aga Khan* (Bombay, 1903), pp. 62–95; H. Algar, "Maḥallātī, Āghā Khān", *EI2*, vol. 5, pp. 1221–1222, and Daftary, *The Ismāʿīlīs*, pp. 504–516, 717–720, where full references to the sources and studies are cited.

84. See *The Memoirs of Aga Khan: World Enough and Time* (London and New York, 1954). Several biographies of this imam have also been published.

85. See Daftary, *The Ismāʿīlīs*, pp. 518–532, 537–548, and his *A Short History of the Ismailis*, pp. 206 ff.

2

Ismaili Studies: Medieval Antecedents and Modern Developments

Ismaili historiography and the perceptions of the Ismailis by others, in both Muslim and Christian milieus, as well as stages in modern Ismaili studies have had their own fascinating evolution, of which we shall present a brief survey here. In the course of their history the Ismailis have often been accused of various heretical teachings and practices and, at the same time, a multitude of myths and misconceptions circulated about them. This state of affairs reflected mainly the unfortunate fact that the Ismailis were, until the middle of the twentieth century, perceived, studied and judged almost exclusively on the basis of evidence collected or often fabricated by their enemies. As the most revolutionary wing of Shiʿism with a religio-political agenda that aimed to uproot the Abbasids and restore the caliphate to a line of ʿAlid imams, the Ismailis from early on aroused the hostility of the Sunni establishment of the Muslim majority. With the foundation of the Fatimid state in 297/909, the Ismaili challenge to the established order had become actualized, and thereupon the Abbasid caliphs and the Sunni *ʿulamāʾ* launched what amounted to nothing less than a widespread and official anti-Ismaili propaganda campaign. The overall objective of this systematic and prolonged campaign was to discredit the entire Ismaili movement from its origins so that the Ismailis could be readily condemned as *malāḥida*, heretics or deviators from the true religious path.

Sunni polemicists, starting with Abū ʿAbd Allāh Muḥammad b. ʿAlī b. Rizām al-Ṭāʾī al-Kūfī, better known as Ibn Rizām, who lived in Baghdad during the first half of the 4th/10th century, now began to fabricate evidence that would lend support to the condemnation of the Ismailis on specific doctrinal grounds. Ibn Rizām's anti-Ismaili tract, *Kitāb radd ʿalāʾl-Ismāʿīliyya* (or *al-Naqḍ ʿalāʾl-bāṭiniyya*), does not seem to have survived, but it is quoted by Ibn al-Nadīm in his catalogue of Arabic books, *al-Fihrist*. More importantly, it was used extensively a few decades later by another polemicist, the Sharīf Abuʾl-Ḥusayn Muḥammad b. ʿAlī, an ʿAlid from Damascus better known as Akhū Muḥsin, whose own anti-Ismaili work, consisting of historical and doctrinal parts written around 372/982, has also not survived. However, the Ibn Rizām and Akhū Muḥsin accounts have been preserved fragmentarily by several later historians, notably al-Nuwayrī (d. 733/1333), Ibn al-Dawādārī (d. after 736/1335), and al-Maqrīzī (d. 845/1442) who was the first authority to have identified Ibn Rizām as the principal source of Akhū Muḥsin while condemning both writers as unereliable.[1] The polemicists concocted detailed accounts of the sinister teachings and practices of the Ismailis, while refuting the ʿAlid genealogy of their imams, descendants of the Imam Jaʿfar al-Ṣādiq (d. 148/765) and the last of the early Shiʿi imams recognized jointly by the Ismaili and the Twelver (Ithnāʿasharī) Shiʿis. Anti-Ismaili polemical writings provided a major source of information for Sunni heresiographers, such as al-Baghdādī (d. 429/1037), who produced another important category of writing against the Ismailis.[2] On the other hand, the Imāmī Shiʿi heresiographers al-Ḥasan b. Mūsā al-Nawbakhtī (d. after 300/912) and Saʿd b. ʿAbd Allāh al-Qummī (d. 301/913–14), who were better informed than their Sunni counterparts on the internal divisions of Shiʿism, were notably less hostile towards the Ismaili Shiʿis.[3] In fact, these earliest Imāmī heresiographers provide our main source of information on the opening phase of Ismailism.

A number of polemicists fabricated travesties in which they attributed a variety of shocking beliefs and practices to the Ismailis; these forgeries circulated widely as genuine Ismaili treatises and were used as source materials by subsequent generations of polemicists and heresiographers. One of these forgeries, the anonymous *Kitāb al-siyāsa* (*Book of Methodology*), acquired wide popularity as it contained all the ideas needed to condemn the Ismailis as heretics on account of their libertinism and atheism. Akhū Muḥsin claims to have read this book and quoted passages from it; the same book, or another forgery entitled *Kitāb al-balāgh* was seen shortly afterwards by Ibn al-Nadīm who mentions it in his *al-Fihrist* completed in 377/987.[4] The heresiographer al-Baghdādī even claims that the *Kitāb al-siyāsa* was sent by ʿAbd Allāh (ʿUbayd Allāh) al-Mahdī (d. 322/934), the founder of the Fatimid dynasty, to Abū Ṭāhir al-Jannābī (d. 332/944), the leader of the Qarmaṭī state in Baḥrayn.[5] By this claim al-Baghdādī not only attempted to accord authenticity to this forgery, but also made the Qarmaṭīs subservient to the Fatimids in order to defame all Ismailis. This book, which has survived only fragmentarily in later Sunni sources, and was partially reconstructed by S.M. Stern,[6] is reported to have candidly expounded the procedures that were supposedly followed by Ismaili *dāʿīs* for winning new converts and instructing them through some seven stages of initiation or *balāgh* leading ultimately to unbelief and atheism. Needless to add that the Ismaili tradition knows of these fictitious accounts only from the polemics of its enemies. The anti-Ismaili polemical and heresiographical traditions, in turn, influenced the Muslim historians, theologians and jurists who had something to say about the Ismailis.

The Sunni authors, who were generally not interested in collecting accurate information on the internal divisions of Shiʿism and treated all Shiʿi interpretations of Islam as 'heterodoxies' or even 'heresies', also readily availed themselves of the opportunity of blaming the Fatimids and indeed the entire Ismaili community for the atrocities perpetrated by the Qarmaṭīs of Baḥrayn who, in 317/930, attacked Mecca, massacred the pilgrims there and then carried away the Black Stone (*al-ḥajar al-aswad*). The Qarmaṭīs, it may be recalled, seceded from the rest of the Ismāʿīliyya, in 286/899, and never recognized continuity in the imamate which was the central doctrine of the Fatimid Ismailis. They continued to await the return of their seventh and last imam, Muḥammad b. Ismāʿīl, as the initiator of the final era of history. At any rate, the dissemination of hostile accounts and misrepresentations contributed significantly to turning the Sunni Muslims at large against the Ismailis.[7]

By spreading defamations and forged accounts, the anti-Ismaili authors, in fact, produced a 'black legend' in the course of the 4th/10th century. Ismailism was now depicted as the arch-heresy, *ilḥād*, of Islam, carefully designed by a certain ʿAbd Allāh b. Maymūn al-Qaddāḥ or some other non-ʿAlid impostors, or possibly even a Jewish magician disguised as a Muslim, aiming at destroying Islam from within.[8] By the 5th/11th century, this fiction, with its elaborate details and stages of initiation, had been accepted as an accurate and reliable description of Ismaili motives, beliefs and practices, leading to further anti-Ismaili polemics and heresiographical accusations as well as intensifying the animosity of other Muslim communities towards the Ismailis. It is interesting to note that the same 'black legend' served as the basis of the famous Baghdad manifesto issued in 402/1011 against the Fatimids. This declaration, sponsored by the reigning Abbasid caliph al-Qādir (381–422/991–1031), was essentially a public refutation of the ʿAlid ancestry of the Fatimid caliphs. The same was reiterated in a second anti-Fatimid document sponsored in 444/1052 by the Abbasid caliph al-Qāʾim (422–467/1031–1075).

By the end of the 5th/11th century, the widespread anti-Ismaili campaign of the Sunni authors had been astonishingly successful throughout the central Islamic lands. The revolt of the Persian Ismailis led by Ḥasan-i Ṣabbāḥ (d. 518/1124) against the Saljūq Turks, the new overlords of the Abbasids, called forth another vigorous Sunni reaction against the Ismailis in general and the Nizārī Ismailis in particular. The new literary campaign, accompanied by military attacks on Alamūt and other Nizārī strongholds in Persia, was initiated by Niẓām al-Mulk (d. 485/1092), the Saljūq vizier and virtual master of their dominions for more than two decades. Niẓām al-Mulk himself devoted a long chapter in his *Siyāsat-nāma* (*The Book of Government*) to the condemnation of the Ismailis who, according to him, aimed 'to abolish Islam, to mislead mankind and cast them into perdition'.[9] However, the earliest polemical treatise against the Persian Ismailis and their doctrine of *taʿlīm*, propounding the necessity of authoritative teaching by the Ismaili imam, was written by no lesser a figure than Abū Ḥāmid Muḥammad al-Ghazālī (d. 505/1111), the most renowned contemporary Sunni theologian and jurist. He was, in fact, commissioned by the Abbasid caliph al-Mustaẓhir (487–512/1094–1118) to write a treatise in refutation of the Bāṭinīs – another designation, meaning 'esotericists', coined for the Ismailis by their enemies who accused them of dispensing with the *ẓāhir,* or the commandments and prohibitions of the *sharīʿa,* because they claimed to have found access to the *bāṭin,* or the inner meaning of the Islamic message as interpreted by the Ismaili imam. In this widely circulating book, completed around 488/1095 and generally known as *al-Mustaẓhirī,* al-Ghazālī fabricated his own elaborate 'Ismaili' system of graded initiation leading to the ultimate stage (*al-balāgh al-akbar*) of atheism.[10] Subsequently, al-Ghazālī wrote several shorter works in refutation of the Ismailis, and his defamations were adopted by other Sunni writers who, like Niẓām al-Mulk, were familiar with the earlier 'black legend' as well. It is interesting to note that the Nizārīs never responded to al-Ghazālī's polemics, but a detailed refutation of the *Mustaẓhirī* was much later written in Yaman by the fifth Ṭayyibī Mustaʿlī *dāʿī* who died in 612/1215.[11] In any case, Sunni authors, including especially Saljūq chroniclers, participated actively in the renewed propaganda against the Ismailis, while Saljūq armies failed to dislodge the Nizārīs from their mountain fortresses.

By the opening decades of the 6th/12th century, the Ismaili community became divided and embarked on its own internal, Nizārī versus Mustaʿlī, feuds. It is reported that Ḥasan-i Ṣabbāḥ sent secret agents to Egypt to undermine the Mustaʿlī *daʿwa* there, while the Mustaʿlī Ismailis, now supported by the Fatimid state, initiated their own campaign to refute the claims of Nizār b. al-Mustanṣir (d. 488/1095) to the Ismaili imamate. In one anti-Nizārī polemical epistle, *al-Hidāya al-Āmiriyya,* issued in 516/1122 by the Fatimid caliph al-Āmir (495–524/1101–1130), the Nizārī Ismailis of Syria were for the first time referred to with the abusive designation of *ḥashīshiyya,* without any explanation.[12] This term was later applied to Syrian Nizārīs by a few Sunni historians, notably Abū Shāma (d. 665/1267) and Ibn Muyassar (d. 677/1278), without accusing them of actually using *ḥashīsh,* a product of hemp.[13] The Persian Nizārīs, too, were designated as *ḥashīshīs* in some Zaydī Arabic sources written in northern Persia during the Alamūt period.[14] It is important to note that in all the Muslim sources in which the Nizārīs are referred to as *ḥashīshīs,* this term is used only in its abusive, figurative sense of 'low-class rabble' and 'irreligious social outcast'. The literal interpretation of the term for the Nizārīs as users of *ḥashīsh* is rooted in the fantasies of medieval Europeans and their 'imaginative ignorance' of Islam and the Ismailis. At any event, the Fatimids and the Syrian Nizārīs soon found a common enemy in the Christian Crusaders, who arrived in the Holy Land to liberate their co-religionists. The Crusaders seized Jerusalem, their primary target, in 492/1099, and subsequently, they founded four principalities in the Near East and engaged in extensive military and diplomatic encounters against the Fatimids in Egypt and the Nizārī Ismailis in Syria, with lasting consequences in terms of the distorted image of the Nizārīs in Europe.

The Syrian Nizārīs attained the peak of their power and fame under the leadership of Rāshid al-Dīn Sinān, who was their chief *dāʿī* for some three decades until his death in 589/1193. It was in the time of Sinān, the original 'Old Man of the Mountain' or 'Le Vieux de la Montagne' of the Crusader sources, that occidental chroniclers of the Crusades and a number of European travellers and diplomatic emissaries began to write about the Nizārī Ismailis, designated by them as the 'Assassins'. The very term Assassin, evidently based on the variants of the Arabic word *ḥashīshī* (plural, *ḥashīshiyya*) that was applied to the Nizārī Ismailis in a derogatory sense by other Muslims, was picked up locally in the Levant by the Crusaders and their European observers. At the same time, the Frankish circles and their occidental chroniclers, who were not interested in collecting accurate information about Islam as a religion and its internal divisions despite their proximity to Muslims, remained completely ignorant of Muslims in general and the Ismailis in particular. It was under such circumstances that the Frankish circles themselves began to fabricate and put into circulation both in the Latin Orient and in Europe a number of tales about the secret practices of the Ismailis. It is important to note that none of the variants of these tales are to be found in contemporary Muslim sources, including the most hostile ones, produced during the 6th/12th and 7th/13th centuries.

The Crusaders were particularly impressed by the highly exaggerated reports and rumours of the Nizārī assassinations and the daring behaviour of their *fidāʾī*s, the self-sacrificing devotees who carried out targeted missions in public places and normally lost their own lives in the process. It should be recalled that in the 6th/12th century, almost any assassination of any significance committed in the central Islamic lands was readily attributed to the daggers of the Nizārī *fidāʾī*s. This explains why these imaginative tales came to revolve around the recruitment and training of the *fidāʾīs*; for they were meant to provide satisfactory explanations for behaviour that would otherwise seem irrational or strange to the medieval European mind. These so-called Assassin legends consisted of a number of separate but interconnected tales, including the 'paradise legend', the '*ḥashīsh* legend', and the 'death-leap legend'.[15] The legends developed in stages, receiving new embellishments at each successive stage, and finally culminated in a synthesis popularized by Marco Polo (d. 1324). The famous Venetian traveller added his own original contribution in the form of a 'secret garden of paradise', where bodily pleasures were supposedly procured for the *fidāʾīs* with the aid of *ḥashīsh* by their mischievous and beguiling leader, the Old Man, as part of their indoctrination and training.[16]

Marco Polo's version of the Assassin legends, offered as a report obtained from reliable contemporary sources in Persia, was reiterated to various degrees by subsequent European writers, such as Odoric of Pordenone (d. 1331), as the standard description of the 'Old Man of the Mountain and his Assassins'. Strangely enough, it did not occur to any European that Marco Polo may have actually heard the tales in Italy after returning to Venice in 1295 from his journeys to the East – tales that were by then widespread in Europe and could already be at least partially traced to European antecedents on the subject – not to mention the possibility that the Assassin legends found in Marco Polo's travelogue may have been entirely inserted, as a digressionary note, by Rustichello of Pisa, the Italian romance writer who was actually responsible for committing the account of Marco Polo's travels to writing. No more can be said on this subject given the present state of our knowledge, especially as the original version of Marco Polo's travelogue written by Rustichello in a peculiar old French mixed with Italian has not been recovered. In this connection, it may also be noted that Marco Polo himself evidently revised his travelogue during the last twenty years of his life, at which time he could readily have appropriated the Assassin legends regarding the Syrian Nizārīs then current in Europe. In fact, it was Marco Polo who transferred the scene of the legends from Syria to Persia. The contemporary historian ʿAṭā-Malik Juwaynī (d. 681/1283), an avowed enemy of the Nizārīs who accompanied the Mongol conqueror Hülegü to Alamūt in 654/

1256 and personally inspected that fortress and its library before their destruction by the Mongols, does not report that he discovered any 'secret garden of paradise' there, as claimed in Marco Polo's famous account.

Different Assassin legends or components of particular tales were 'imagined' independently and at times concurrently by different authors, such as Arnold of Lübeck (d. 1212) and James of Vitry (d. 1240), and embellished over time. Starting with Burchard of Strassburg who visited Syria in 570/1175 as an envoy of the Hohenstaufen emperor of Germany, European travellers, chroniclers and envoys to the Latin East who had something to say about the 'Assassins' participated, as if in tacit collusion, in the process of fabricating, transmitting and legitimizing the legends. By the 8th/14th century, the legends had acquired wide currency and were accepted as reliable descriptions of secret Nizārī Ismaili practices, in much the same way as the earlier 'black legend' of Sunni polemicists had been accepted as accurate explanation of Ismaili motives, teachings and practices. Henceforth, the Nizārī Ismailis were portrayed in medieval European sources as a sinister order of drugged assassins bent on indiscriminate murder and terrorism.

In the meantime, the word 'assassin', instead of signifying the name of the Nizārī community in Syria, had acquired a new meaning in French, Italian and other European languages. It had become a common noun designating a professional murderer. With the advent of this usage, the origin of the term was soon forgotten in Europe, while the 'oriental sect' designated by that name in the Crusader sources continued to arouse interest among Europeans, mainly because of the enduring popularity of the Assassin legends which had indeed acquired an independent mythical life of their own. In this connection, mention should be made of Denis Lebey de Batilly's book, the first Western monograph devoted entirely to the subject.[17] Having become apprehensive of the existence of would-be assassins in the religious orders of Christendom, after the 1589 stabbing of Henry III of France by a Jacobian friar, the author had set out to compose this short treatise on the true origin of the word *assasin* and the history of the sect to which it originally belonged. Needless to add that this work represented a confused medley of a number of European accounts with Marco Polo's narrative. Henceforth, a number of European philologists and lexicographers began to collect the variants of the term 'assassin', such as *assassini, assissini* and *heyssessini*, occurring in medieval occidental sources, also proposing many strange etymologies. By the 12th/18th century, numerous etymologies of this term had become available, while the Ismailis in question had received a few more notices from the pens of travellers and missionaries to the East. In sum, by the beginning of the 13th/19th century, Europeans still perceived the Ismailis in an utterly confused and fanciful manner. [18]

The orientalists of the nineteenth century, led by Silvestre de Sacy (1758–1838), began their more scholarly study of Islam on the basis of the Arabic manuscripts which were written mainly by Sunni authors. As a result, they studied Islam according to the Sunni viewpoint and, borrowing classifications from Christian contexts, treated Shiʿism as the 'heterodox' interpretation of Islam by contrast to Sunnism which was taken to represent 'orthodoxy'. It was mainly on this basis, as well as the continued attraction of the seminal Assassin legends, that the orientalists launched their own study of the Ismailis. Nevertheless, Étienne M. Quatremère (1782–1857), one of the most learned orientalists of the period, did manage to produce a number of historical studies on the Fatimids. It was left for de Sacy, however, to finally solve the mystery of the name 'Assassin' in his famous *Memoir*;[19] he also produced important studies on early Ismailis as background materials for his major work on the Druze religion, *Exposé de la religion des Druzes* (1838). Although the orientalists correctly identified the Ismailis as a Shiʿi Muslim community, they were still obliged to study them exclusively on the basis of the hostile Sunni sources and the fictitious occidental accounts of the Crusader circles. Consequently, the orientalists, too, tacitly lent their own seal of approval to the myths of the Ismailis, namely, the anti-Ismaili 'black legend' of the medieval Sunni polemicists and the Assassin legends of the Crusaders.

Indeed, de Sacy's distorted evaluation of the Ismailis, though unintentional, set the frame within which other orientalists of the nineteenth century studied the medieval history of the Ismailis. The orientalists' interest in the Ismailis had now received a fresh impetus from the anti-Ismaili accounts of the then newly-discovered Sunni chronicles which seemed to complement the Assassin legends contained in the occidental sources familiar to them. It was under such circumstances that misrepresentation and plain fiction came to permeate the first Western book devoted exclusively to the Persian Nizārīs of the Alamūt period written by Joseph von Hammer-Purgstall (1774–1856). This Austrian orientalist-diplomat endorsed Marco Polo's narrative in its entirety as well as all the medieval defamations levelled against the Ismailis by their Sunni enemies. Originally published in German in 1818, this book achieved great success in Europe and continued to be treated as the standard history of the Nizārī Ismailis until the 1930s.[20] With rare exceptions, notably the French orientalist Charles F. Defrémery (1822–1883) who produced valuable historical studies on the Nizārīs of Syria and Persia,[21] the Ismailis continued to be misrepresented to various degrees by later orientalists such as Michael J. de Goeje (1836–1909), who made valuable contributions to the study of the Qarmaṭīs of Baḥrayn but whose incorrect interpretation of Fatimid-Qarmaṭī relations was generally adopted.[22] Orientalism, thus, gave a new lease of life to the myths surrounding the Ismailis; and this deplorable state of Ismaili studies remained essentially unchanged until the 1930s. Even an eminent scholar like Edward G. Browne (1862–1926), who covered the Ismailis rather tangentially in his magnificent survey of Persian literature, could not resist reiterating the orientalistic tales of his predecessors on the Ismailis.[23] As a result, Westerners continued unwittingly to refer to the Nizārī Ismailis as the Assassins, a misnomer rooted in a medieval pejorative neologism.[24]

The breakthrough in Ismaili studies had to await the recovery and study of genuine Ismaili texts on a large scale – manuscript sources which had been preserved secretly in numerous private collections. A few Ismaili manuscripts of Syrian provenance had already surfaced in Paris during the nineteenth century, and some fragments of these works were studied and published there by Stanislas Guyard (1824–1884) and other orientalists.[25] At the same time, Paul Casanova (1861–1926), who produced important studies on the Fatimids and the Nizārī coins, was the first European orientalist to have recognized the Ismaili affiliation of the *Rasāʾil Ikhwān al-Ṣafāʾ*, a portion of which had found its way to the Bibliothèque Nationale in Paris.[26] Earlier, the German orientalist Friedrich Dieterici (1821–1903) had published many portions of the *Rasāʾil*, with German translation, without recognizing their Ismaili connection. More Ismaili manuscripts preserved in Yaman and Central Asia were recovered in the opening decades of the twentieth century by Giuseppe Caprotti (1869–1919), Ivan I. Zarubin (1887–1964) and others.[27] In particular, a number of Nizārī texts were collected from Shughnān, Rūshān and other districts of Badakhshān (now divided by the Oxus River between Tajikistan and Afghanistan)and studied by Aleksandr A. Semenov (1873–1958), the Russian pioneer in Ismaili studies from Tashkent.[28] The Ismaili manuscripts of Central Asian provenance found their way to the Asiatic Museum in St. Petersburg, now part of the collections of the Institute of Oriental Studies there. However, by 1922, when the first Western bibliography of Ismaili writings was prepared by the foremost French pioneer in Shiʿi and Ismaili studies, Louis Massignon (1883–1962), knowledge of European libraries and scholarly circles about Ismaili literature was still very limited.[29]

Modern scholarship in Ismaili studies was actually initiated in the 1930s in India, where significant collections of Ismaili manuscripts have been preserved by the Ismaili Bohra community. This breakthrough resulted mainly from the pioneering efforts of Wladimir Ivanow (1886–1970), and a few Ismaili Bohra scholars, notably Asaf A.A. Fyzee (1899–1981), Ḥusayn F. al-Hamdānī (1901–1962) and Zāhid ʿAlī (1888–1958), all of whom based their original studies on their family collections of manuscripts.[30] Asaf Fyzee, who studied law at Cambridge University and belonged to the most learned Sulaymānī Ṭayyibī family of Ismaili Bohras in India, in fact, made modern scholars aware of the existence of an independent Ismaili school of jurisprudence. Among his numerous publications on the subject,[31] Fyzee produced a critical edition of al-Qāḍī al-Nuʿmān's major work, *Daʿāʾim al-Islām*, which served as the legal code of the Fatimid state and is still used by the Ṭayyibī Ismailis of India, Pakistan, Yaman and elsewhere. Ḥusayn al-Hamdānī, belonging to an eminent Dāʾūdī Ṭayyibī family of scholars with Yamanī origins and who received his doctorate from London University, was a pioneer in producing a number of studies based on Ismaili sources, calling the attention of modern scholars to the existence of this unique literary heritage. Zāhid ʿAlī hailed from another learned Dāʾūdī Bohra family and was for many years the principal of the Niẓām College at Hyderabad after receiving his doctorate from Oxford University, where he produced a critical edition of the *Dīwān* of the Ismaili poet Ibn Hāniʾ as his doctoral thesis. He was also the first author in modern times to have produced in Urdu, on the basis of a variety of Ismaili sources, a scholarly study of Fatimid history and a work on Ismaili doctrines.[32]

Wladimir Ivanow, who eventually settled in Bombay after leaving his native Russia in 1917, collaborated closely with the above-mentioned Bohra scholars and succeeded, through his own connections within the Khoja community, to gain access to Nizārī literature as well. Consequently, he compiled the first detailed catalogue of Ismaili works, citing some 700 separate titles which attested to the hitherto unknown richness and diversity of Ismaili literature and intellectual traditions. The initiation of modern scholarship in Ismaili studies may indeed be traced to the publication of this very catalogue in 1933, which provided a scientific frame for further research in the field.[33] In the same year, Ivanow founded in Bombay the Islamic Research Association with the help of Fyzee and other Ismaili friends. Several Ismaili works appeared in the series of publications sponsored by the Islamic Research Association which was subsequently transformed into the Ismaili Society of Bombay. Ismaili scholarship received a major impetus through the establishment in 1946 of the Ismaili Society under the patronage of Sulṭān Muḥammad Shāh, Aga Khan III (1877–1957), the forty-eighth imam of the Nizārī Ismailis. Ivanow played a crucial role in the creation of the Ismaili Society whose various series of publications were mainly devoted to his own monographs as well as editions and translations of Persian Nizārī Ismaili texts.[34] He also acquired a large number of Persian and Arabic manuscripts for the Ismaili Society's Library, which were transferred to The Institute of Ismaili Studies Library in London during the early 1980s.

By 1963, when Ivanow published a revised edition of his Ismaili catalogue, many more sources had become known and progress in Ismaili studies had accelerated considerably.[35] In addition to many studies by Ivanow and the Bohra pioneers in the field, numerous Ismaili texts now began to be critically edited by other scholars, preparing the ground for further progress in this relatively new area of Islamic studies. In this connection, particular mention should be made of the Ismaili texts of Fatimid and later times edited together with French translations and analytical introductions by Henry Corbin (1903–1978), published simultaneously in Tehran and Paris in his 'Bibliothèque Iranienne' series;[36] and the Fatimid texts edited by the Egyptian scholar Muḥammad Kāmil Ḥusayn (1901–1961) and published in his 'Silsilat Makhṭūṭāt al-Fāṭimiyyīn' series in Cairo.[37] It is interesting to note that it was in Cairo, the capital city founded by the Fatimids, that Paul Kraus (1904–1944), another pioneer in the field, kindled Corbin's interest in Ismailism, as M. Kāmil Ḥusayn was to do for Wilferd Madelung who, later, studied also under Rudolf Strothmann (1877–1960), an important German authority on Shiʿi and Ismaili studies.

Meanwhile, a number of Russian scholars, notably Andrey E. Bertel's and Lyudmila V. Stroeva (1910–1993), had maintained the earlier interests of their compatriots in Ismaili studies. In Syria, ʿĀrif Tāmir (1921–1998), who belonged to the small Muḥammad-Shāhī Nizārī community there, made the Ismaili texts of Syrian provenance available to scholars, as did his Qāsim-Shāhī Nizārī compatriot Muṣṭafā Ghālib (1923–1981). A number of European scholars, such as Marius Canard (1888–1982) and several Egyptians including Ḥasan Ibrāhīm Ḥasan (1892–1968), Jamāl al-Dīn al-Shayyāl (1911–1967), Muḥammad Jamāl al-Dīn Surūr (1911–1992) and ʿAbd al-Munʿim Mājid (1920–1999) made further contributions to Fatimid studies.[38] Ivanow himself as well as Bernard Lewis had earlier produced important studies on the Ismaili background to the establishment of Fatimid rule.[39] At the same time, Yves Marquet embarked on a lifelong study of the Ikhwān al-Ṣafā' and their *Rasā'il*. Subsequently, Alessandro Bausani (1921–1988) and his student Carmela Baffioni, among others, contributed to the Ikhwān al-Ṣafā' studies, while Abbas Hamdani expounded his own distinct views in a body of articles. Concentrating his research on the authorship and dating of the *Rasā'il*, Professor Hamdani has essentially maintained that these epistles were composed by a group of Ismaili *dāʿī*s just prior to the foundation of the Fatimid caliphate in 297/909.[40] There are other scholars, however, like I.R. Netton, who dispute the Ismaili origin of the *Rasā'il*.[41]

By the mid-1950s, progress in the field had already enabled Marshall G.S. Hodgson (1922–1968) to produce the first scholarly and comprehensive study of the Nizārī Ismailis of the Alamūt period, albeit mistitled as *The Order of Assassins* (1955). Soon, others representing a new generation of scholars, notably Samuel M. Stern (1920–1969) and Wilferd Madelung, produced pathbreaking studies, especially on the early Ismailis and their relations with the dissident Qarmaṭīs.[42] A number of Stern's major Ismaili articles, together with some of his unpublished work, were collected in his *Studies in Early Ismāʿīlism* (1983). Professor Madelung clarified many obscure aspects of early Ismailism in two seminal articles;[43] and, among his many later contributions to the field, he summed up the current state of research on Ismaili history in his article 'Ismāʿīliyya', written for the new edition of *The Encyclopaedia of Islam*. Progress in Ismaili studies has proceeded at a rapid pace during the last few decades through the efforts of yet another generation of scholars such as Pio Filippani-Ronconi, Ismail K. Poonawala, Heinz Halm, Paul E. Walker, Azim Nanji, Thierry Bianquis, Michael Brett, Yaacov Lev, Ayman Fu'ād Sayyid, Farhat Dachraoui and Mohammed Yalaoui, some of whom have devoted their attention mainly to Fatimid studies. The progress in the recovery and study of Ismaili literature is well reflected in Professor Poonawala's monumental *Biobibliography of Ismāʿīlī Literature* (1977), which identifies some 1300 titles written by more than 200 authors. This progress has received further impetus from the recovery, or accessibility, of yet more Ismaili manuscripts. For instance, hundreds of Ismaili manuscripts preserved by the Nizārīs of Tajik Badakhshān were recovered during 1959–63,[44] and in the 1990s many more manuscripts were identified in Shughnān and other districts of the same region through the efforts of The Institute of Ismaili Studies. Many Ismaili texts have now been published in critical editions, while numerous secondary studies of Ismaili history and thought have been produced by at least three successive generations of scholars. Meanwhile, the Satpanth Ismaili tradition of the Nizārī Khojas, as reflected in the *ginān* literature, has provided yet another highly specialized area within Ismaili studies. In particular, A. Nanji and Ali Asani have made valuable contributions here. There are also those newcomers to the field, such as Pieter Smoor, Daniel de Smet, Christian Jambet, Michel Boivin and Paula Sanders, who are already making contributions to different aspects of Ismailism.

Scholarship in Ismaili studies is set to continue at an ever greater pace as the Ismailis themselves are becoming increasingly interested in studying their literary heritage and history – a phenomenon attested by the growing number of Ismaili-related doctoral dissertations written in recent decades by Ismailis. In this context, a major contribution is made by The Institute of Ismaili Studies, established in London in 1977 by H.H. Prince Karim Aga Khan IV, the present imam of the

Nizārī Ismailis. This institution is already serving as the central point of reference for Ismaili studies while making its own contributions through various programmes of research and publications. Amongst these, particular mention should be made of the monographs appearing in the Institute's 'Ismaili Heritage Series' which aims to make available to wide audiences the results of modern scholarship on the Ismailis and their intellectual and cultural traditions; and the 'Ismaili Texts and Translations Series' in which critical editions of Arabic and Persian texts are published together with English translations and contextualizing introductions.[45] Numerous scholars worldwide participate in these academic programmes, as well as in the recently initiated series devoted to the *Rasā'il Ikhwān al-Ṣafā'* (critical edition and English translation), and many more benefit from the accessibility of the Ismaili manuscripts held at the Institute's library, representing the largest collection of its kind in the West.[46] With these modern developments, the scholarly study of the Ismailis, which by the closing decades of the twentieth century had already greatly deconstructed and explained the seminal anti-Ismaili legends of medieval times, promises to dissipate the remaining misrepresentations of the Ismailis rooted either in hostility or the imaginative ignorance of earlier generations.

Notes

1. Shihāb al-Dīn Aḥmad b. 'Abd al-Wahhāb al-Nuwayrī, *Nihāyat al-arab fī funūn al-adab*, vol. 25, ed., M.J.'A. al-Ḥīnī et al. (Cairo, 1984), pp. 187–317; Abū Bakr 'Abd Allāh b. al-Dawādārī, *Kanz al-durar wa-jāmi' al-ghurar*, vol. 6, ed., Ṣ. al-Munajjid (Cairo, 1961), pp. 6–21, 44–156, and Taqī al-Dīn Aḥmad b. 'Alī al-Maqrīzī, *Itti'āẓ al-ḥunafā' bi-akhbār al-a'imma al-Fāṭimiyyīn al-khulafā'*, vol. 1, ed., J. al-Shayyāl (Cairo, 1967), pp. 22–29, 151–202.

2. Abū Manṣūr 'Abd al-Qāhir b. Ṭāhir al-Baghdādī, *al-Farq bayn al-firaq*, ed., M. Badr (Cairo, 1328/1910), pp. 265–299; English trans., *Moslem Schisms and Sects*, part II, tr., A.S. Halkin (Tel Aviv, 1935), pp. 107–157.

3. See al-Ḥasan b. Mūsā al-Nawbakhtī, *Kitāb firaq al-Shī'a*, ed., H. Ritter (Istanbul, 1931), pp. 37–41, 57–60, and Sa'd b. 'Abd Allāh al-Qummī, *Kitāb al-maqālāt wa'l-firaq*, ed., M.J. Mashkūr (Tehran, 1963), pp. 50–55, 63–64, 80–83.

4. Ibn al-Nadīm, *Kitāb al-fihrist*, ed., M.R. Tajaddud (2nd ed., Tehran, 1973), pp. 238, 240.

5. Al-Baghdādī, *al-Farq*, pp. 277–279; tr., Halkin, pp. 130–132.

6. See Stern, "The 'Book of the Highest Initiation' and Other Anti-Ismāʿīlī Travesties", in his *Studies in Early Ismāʿīlism*, (Jerusalem and Leiden, 1983), pp. 56–83.

7. See W. Madelung, "Ḳarmaṭī", *EI2*, vol. 4, pp. 660–665, and F. Daftary, "Carmatians", *EIR*, vol. 4, pp. 823–832.

8. W. Ivanow produced a number of pioneering studies on this "black legend", see especially his *The Alleged Founder of Ismailism* (Bombay, 1946).

9. Niẓām al-Mulk, *Siyar al-mulūk* (*Siyāsat-nāma*), ed., H. Darke (2nd ed., Tehran, 1347 Sh./1968), p. 311; English trans., *The Book of Government; or, Rules for Kings*, tr., H. Darke (2nd ed., London, 1978), p. 231.

10. Abū Ḥāmid Muḥammad al-Ghazālī, *Faḍāʾiḥ al-Bāṭiniyya*, ed., ʿAbd al-Raḥmān Badawī (Cairo, 1964), pp. 21–36.

11. ʿAlī b. Muḥammad b. al-Walīd, *Dāmigh al-bāṭil wa-ḥatf al-munāḍıl*, ed., M. Ghālib (Beirut, 1403/1982), 2 vols.; see also H. Corbin, "The Ismāʿīlī Response to the Polemic of Ghazālī", in S.H. Nasr, ed., *Ismāʿīlī Contributions to Islamic Culture* (Tehran, 1977), pp. 69–98 and F. Mitha, *Al-Ghazālī and the Ismailis* (London, 2001).

12. Abū ʿAlī al-Manṣūr al-Āmir bi-Aḥkām Allāh, *Risālat īqāʿ ṣawāʿiq al-irghām*, in al-Āmir's *al-Hidāya al-Āmiriyya*, ed., A.A.A. Fyzee (London, etc., 1938), pp. 27, 32; reprinted in *Majmūʿat al-wathāʾiq al-Fāṭimiyya*, ed., J. al-Shayyāl (Cairo, 1958), pp. 233, 239.

13. Abū Shāma Shihāb al-Dīn b. Ismāʿīl, *Kitāb al-rawḍatayn fī akhbār al-dawlatayn* (Cairo, 1287–88/1870–71), vol. 1, pp. 240, 258, and Tāj al-Dīn Muḥammad b. ʿAlī Ibn Muyassar, *Akhbār Miṣr*, ed., A. Fuʾād Sayyid (Cairo, 1981), p. 102.

14. See W. Madelung (ed.), *Arabic Texts Concerning the History of the Zaydī Imāms of Ṭabaristān, Daylamān and Gīlān* (Beirut, 1987), pp. 146, 239.

15. For a survey of these legends, see F. Daftary, *The Assassin Legends: Myths of the Ismaʿilis* (London, 1994), especially pp. 88–127.

16. Marco Polo, *The Book of Ser Marco Polo, the Venetian, Concerning the Kingdoms and Marvels of the East*, ed. and tr., H. Yule, 3rd revised ed. by H. Cordier (London, 1929), vol. 1, pp. 139–146.

17. D. Lebey de Batilly, *Traité de l'origine des anciens Assasins porte-couteaux* (Lyon, 1603); reprinted in *Collection des meilleurs dissertations, notices et traités particuliers relatifs à l'histoire de France*, ed., C. Leber (Paris, 1838), vol. 20, pp. 453–501.

18. See, for instance, Camille Falconet, "Dissertation sur les Assassins, peuple d'Asie", in *Mémoires de Littérature, tirés des registres de l'Académie Royale des Inscriptions et Belles Lettres*, 17 (1751), pp. 127–170; English trans.,

"A Dissertation on the Assassins, a People of Asia", in John of Joinville, *Memoirs of John Lord de Joinville*, tr., T. Johnes (Hafod, 1807), vol. 2, pp. 287–328, and Simone Assemani, *Ragguaglio storico-critico sopra la setta Assissana, detta volgarmente degli Assassini* (Padua, 1806).

19. A.I. Silvestre de Sacy, "Mémoire sur la dynastie des Assassins, et sur l'étymologie de leur nom", in *Mémoires de l'Institut Royal de France*, 4 (1818), pp. 1–84; reprinted in Bryan S. Turner, ed., *Orientalism: Early Sources*, Volume I, *Readings in Orientalism* (London, 2000), pp. 118–169; English trans., "Memoir on the Dynasty of the Assassins, and on the Etymology of their Name", in Daftary, *Assassin Legends*, pp. 136–188.

20. J. von Hammer-Purgstall, *Die Geschichte der Assassinen aus Morgenländischen Quellen* (Stuttgart and Tübingen, 1818); French trans., *Histoire de l'ordre des Assassins*, tr., J. Hellert and P.A. de la Nourais (Paris, 1833; reprinted, Paris, 1961); English trans., *The History of the Assassins, derived from Oriental Sources*, tr., O.C. Wood (London, 1835; reprinted, New York, 1968).

21. C.F. Defrémery, "Nouvelles recherches sur les Ismaéliens ou Bathiniens de Syrie, plus connus sur le nom d'Assassins", *JA*, 5 série, 3 (1854), pp. 373–421; 5 (1855), pp. 5–76, and his "Essai sur l'histoire des Ismaéliens ou Batiniens de la Perse, plus connus sur le nom d'Assassins", *JA*, 5 série, 8 (1856), pp. 353–387; 15 (1860), pp. 130–210.

22. Michael Jan de Goeje, *Mémoire sur les Carmathes du Bahraïn et les Fatimides* (Leiden, 1862; 2nd ed., Leiden, 1886).

23. E.G. Browne, *A Literary History of Persia* (Cambridge, 1902–24), vol. 1, pp. 391–415; vol. 2, pp. 190–211, 453–460. See also the anonymous article "Assassins", in *EI*, vol. 1, pp. 491–492.

24. Freya Stark (1893–1993), the celebrated traveller to the Alamūt valley entitled her travelogue *The Valleys of the Assassins* (London, 1934), where she also cited von Hammer as a main authority on the Nizārī Ismailis (p. 228). Also, Professor Bernard Lewis, who has made valuable contributions to Ismaili studies, persistently designated the Nizārīs as the Assassins; see his "The Sources for the History of the Syrian Assassins", *Speculum*, 27 (1952), pp. 475–489; reprinted in his *Studies in Classical and Ottoman Islam* (London, 1976), article VIII, and *The Assassins: A Radical Sect in Islam* (London, 1967), which has been translated into a number of European languages, always retaining variants of the name Assassins, such as *Les Assassins* (Paris, 1982), *Die Assassinen* (Frankfurt, 1989) and *Gli assassini* (Milan, 1992).

25. S. Guyard (ed.), *Fragments relatifs à la doctrine des Ismaélîs* (Paris, 1874), and his "Un grand maître des Assassins au temps de Saladin", *JA*, 7 série, 9 (1877), pp. 324–489.

26. P. Casanova, "Notice sur un manuscript de la secte des Assassins", *JA*, 9 série, 11 (1898), pp. 151–159.

27. E. Griffini, "Die jüngste ambrosianische Sammlung arabischer Handschriften", *ZDMG*, 69 (1915), especially pp. 80–88, and V.A. Ivanov (W. Ivanow), "Ismailitskie rukopisi Aziatskago Muzeya. Sobranie I. Zarubina, 1916g.", *Bulletin de l'Académie Impériale des Sciences de Russie*, 6 série, 11 (1917), pp. 359–386; English summary in E. Denison Ross, "W. Ivanow, Ismaili MSS in the Asiatic Museum", *JRAS* (1919), pp. 429–435.

28. A.A. Semenov, "Opisanie ismailitskikh rukopisey, sobrannïkh A.A. Semyonovïm", *Bulletin de l'Académie des Sciences de Russie*, 6 série, 12 (1918), pp. 2171–2202.

29. L. Massignon, "Esquisse d'une bibliographie Qarmaṭe", in T.W. Arnold and R.A. Nicholson, ed., *A Volume of Oriental Studies Presented to Edward G. Browne on his 60th Birthday* (Cambridge, 1922), pp. 329–338; reprinted in L. Massignon, *Opera Minora*, ed., Y. Moubarac (Paris, 1969), vol. 1, pp. 627–639.

30. Subsequently, these collections were made available to scholars at large. Asaf Fyzee donated some 200 manuscripts to the Bombay University Library; see M. Goriawala, *A Descriptive Catalogue of the Fyzee Collection of Ismaili Manuscripts* (Bombay, 1965), and A.A.A. Fyzee, "A Collection of Fatimid Manuscripts", in N.N. Gidwani, ed., *Comparative Librarianship: Essays in Honour of Professor D.N. Marshall* (Delhi, 1973), pp. 209–220. Ḥusayn al-Hamdānī also donated part of his family's manuscript collection to the Bombay University, which remains uncatalogued, while a portion remains in the possession of his son, Professor Abbas Hamdani, who has generously made these texts accessible to scholars. The Zāhid ʿAlī collection of some 226 Arabic Ismaili manuscripts was donated in 1997 to The Institute of Ismaili Studies; see D. Cortese, *Arabic Ismaili Manuscripts: The Zāhid ʿAlī Collection in the Library of The Institute of Ismaili Studies* (London, 2003).

31. See F. Daftary, "The Bibliography of Asaf A.A. Fyzee", *Indo-Iranica*, 37 (1984), pp. 49–63.

32. Zāhid ʿAlī, *Taʾrīkh-i Fāṭimiyyīn-i Miṣr* (Hyderabad, 1367/1948), 2 vols., and his *Hamāre Ismāʿīlī madhhab kī ḥaqīqat awr uskā niẓām* (Hyderabad, 1373/1954).

33. W. Ivanow, *A Guide to Ismaili Literature* (London, 1933).

34. See the following articles by F. Daftary: "Bibliography of the Publications of the late W. Ivanow", *IC*, 45 (1971), pp. 56–67; 56 (1982), pp. 239–240; "W. Ivanow: A Biographical Notice", *Middle Eastern Studies*, 8 (1972), pp. 241–244; "Anjoman-e Esmāʿīlī", *EIR*, vol. 2, p. 84, and "Ivanow, Wladimir", *EIR* (forthcoming).

35. W. Ivanow, *Ismaili Literature: A Bibliographical Survey* (Tehran, 1963), covering some 929 titles.

36. This series was launched with Abū Yaʿqūb al-Sijistānī's *Kashf al-*

maḥjūb, ed., H. Corbin (Tehran and Paris, 1949).

37. The first text to be published here was *al-Majālis al-Mustanṣiriyya*, ed., M.K. Ḥusayn (Cairo, [1947]); as shown by S.M. Stern, this represents the collected lectures that Abu'l-Qāsim ʿAbd al-Ḥākim b. Wahb al-Malījī delivered as the *majālis al-ḥikma* in the Fatimid caliph-imam al-Mustanṣir's time.

38. See F. Daftary, "Marius Canard (1888–1982): A Bio-bibliographical Notice", *Arabica*, 33 (1986), pp. 251–262; A. Fu'ād Sayyid, *al-Dawla al-Fāṭimiyya fī Miṣr: tafsīr jadīd* (2nd ed., Cairo, 2000), pp. 76–92, and P.E. Walker, *Exploring an Islamic Empire: Fatimid History and its Sources* (London, 2002), pp. 186–202.

39. See, for instance, W. Ivanow, *Ismaili Tradition Concerning the Rise of the Fatimids* (London, etc., 1942), and B. Lewis, *The Origins of Ismāʿīlism* (Cambridge, 1940).

40. For summaries of A. Hamdani's views on this subject, see his "Abū Ḥayyān al-Tawḥīdī and the Brethren of Purity", *IJMES*, 9 (1978), pp. 345–353, and his "Brethren of Purity, a Secret Society for the Establishment of Fāṭimid Caliphate: New Evidence for the Early Dating of their Encyclopaedia", in M. Barrucand, ed., *L'Égypte Fatimide, son art et son histoire* (Paris, 1999), pp. 73–82.

41. Ian R. Netton, *Muslim Neoplatonists: An Introduction to the Thought of the Brethren of Purity (Ikhwān al-Ṣafā')* (London, 1982), especially pp. 95–108.

42. See J.D. Latham and H.W. Mitchell, "The Bibliography of S.M. Stern", *JSS*, 15 (1970), pp. 226–238; reprinted with additions in S.M. Stern, *Hispano-Arabic Strophic Poetry: Studies by Samuel Miklos Stern*, ed., L.P. Harvey (Oxford, 1974), pp. 231–245, and F. Daftary, "Bibliography of the Works of Wilferd Madelung", in F. Daftary and J.W. Meri, ed., *Culture and Memory in Medieval Islam: Essays in Honour of Wilferd Madelung* (London, 2003), pp. 5–40.

43. W. Madelung, "Fatimiden und Baḥrainqarmaṭen", *Der Islam*, 34 (1959), pp. 34–88; slightly revised English trans., "The Fatimids and the Qarmaṭīs of Baḥrayn", in *MIHT*, pp. 21–73, and his "Das Imamat in der frühen ismailitischen Lehre", *Der Islam*, 37 (1961), pp. 43–135.

44. See, for instance, A.E. Bertel's and M. Bakoev, *Alphabetic Catalogue of Manuscripts found by 1959–1963 Expedition in Gorno-Badakhshan Autonomous Region*, ed., B.G. Gafurov and A.M. Mirzoev (Moscow, 1967). The Persian Ismaili manuscripts of The Institute of Ismaili Studies Library are now in the process of being catalogued.

45. These series were launched, respectively, with P.E. Walker's *Abū Yaʿqūb al-Sijistānī: Intellectual Missionary* (London, 1996), and Ibn al-Haytham's *Kitāb al-munāẓarāt*, ed. and tr., W. Madelung and P.E. Walker as *The Advent of the Fatimids: A Contemporary Shiʿi Witness* (London, 2000).

For a complete listing, see The Institute of Ismaili Studies, Department of Academic Research and Publications, *Catalogue of Publications, 2003–2004* (London, 2003). See also P.E. Walker, "The Institute of Ismaili Studies", *EIR* (forthcoming).

46. See A. Gacek, *Catalogue of Arabic Manuscripts in the Library of The Institute of Ismaili Studies* (London, 1984), vol. 1; D. Cortese, *Ismaili and Other Arabic Manuscripts: A Descriptive Catalogue of Manuscripts in the Library of The Institute of Ismaili Studies* (London, 2000), and her already-cited *Arabic Ismaili Manuscripts: The Zāhid ʿAlī Collection in the Library of The Institute of Ismaili Studies.*

3

Primary Sources

The Ismailis have produced a relatively substantial and diversified literature on a variety of subjects and religious themes in different periods of their history. These texts range from a few historical and biographical works of the *sīra* genre, legal compendia, poetry, and treatises on the central Shiʿi doctrine of the imamate, to complex esoteric and metaphysical works culminating in the gnostic system of the Ismaili *ḥaqāʾiq*, with its cyclical history, cosmology, eschatology, soteriology, etc. From early on, a good portion of the Ismaili literature related to *taʾwīl*, esoteric or allegorical interpretation of the Qurʾanic passages and prescriptions of the *sharīʿa*. Some of the *dāʿī*s of the Iranian lands, such as Abū Yaʿqūb al-Sijistānī, Ḥamīd al-Dīn al-Kirmānī and Nāṣir-i Khusraw elaborated a distinct Shiʿi intellectual tradition amalgamating their Ismaili theology (*kalām*) with a variety of philosophical traditions.

After the classical texts of the Fatimid period, produced mainly by the Ismaili *dāʿī*s, works on the *ḥaqāʾiq* occupied a central place in the literary activities of the Ṭayyibī Ismailis of Yaman, who maintained many of the Fatimid traditions, while the Nizārī Ismailis concerned themselves more particularly with the doctrine of *taʿlīm*, or authoritative guidance of their imam, and ideas related to the declaration of *qiyāma*, or spiritual resurrection, in their community. In later medieval times, the Nizārīs of the post-Alamūt period often adopted

Sufi idioms and poetic forms for expressing their Ismaili ideas. At the same time, the Nizārīs of the Indian subcontinent elaborated a distinct literary tradition, in a variety of Indian languages, in the form of devotional hymns known as *ginān*s.

Many of the Ismaili manuscript resources, written mainly in Arabic and Persian languages, have been recovered, edited, translated and published since the middle of the twentieth century. These publications provide the subject matter of Section A of this chapter. It is to be noted that only published works are included here; for other Ismaili titles which remain unpublished, the reader should consult I.K. Poonawala's *Biobibliography of Ismāʿīlī Literature* (1977). Full details of the collective volumes in which some of the Ismaili texts have been published are cited in "Collective Ismaili Works" in Section B of this chapter. For other full references, see Chapter 4: Studies. With the major exception of the Syrian Nizārīs, the Nizārī authors of the post-8th/14th-century period named in Section A belong to the Qāsim-Shāhī, as distinct from the Muḥammad-Shāhī (Mu'minī), branch of Nizārī Ismailism.

In addition to covering a number of anonymous and pseudo-Ismaili works (Section C), and the publications related to the *Rasā'il Ikhwān al-Ṣafā'* (Section D), the final part (Section E) of this chapter is devoted to a selection of published works on Ismailis written by non-Ismaili Muslim authors. The Ismailis are treated rather pejoratively in numerous medieval works of Muslim heresiographers, polemicists, theologians, jurists and historians who were mostly of Sunni persuasion. Only a selection of the most important publications in this category are covered in this chapter. Medieval Europeans, especially chroniclers of the Crusades and travellers, too, have made brief and passing, often fanciful, references to the Ismailis, notably to the Syrian Nizārīs. These works provide another suitable field of bibliographical study but are excluded from our coverage.

A. Works by Ismaili Authors

Abu'l-Fawāris Aḥmad b. Yaʿqūb (d. ca. 411/1020), Ismaili *dāʿī* in Syria

- *al-Risāla fi'l-imāma*, ed. and English trans., Sami Nasib Makarem as *The Political Doctrine of the Ismāʿīlīs (The Imamate)*. Delmar, NY: Caravan Books, 1977. pp. x + 104 (English) + 41 (Arabic). Excerpt, ed. and French trans., André Ferré, in his "Le traité sur l'imâmat", *Études Arabes: Dossiers*, 84–85 (1993), pp. 80–89.

  A theological work containing replies to sixteen questions dealing with various aspects of the imamate.

Abū Firās Shihāb al-Dīn b. al-Qāḍī Naṣr al-Maynaqī (d. 937/1530 or 947/1540), Nizārī *dāʿī* in Syria

- *Faṣl min al-lafẓ al-sharīf*, *see* Rāshid al-Dīn Sinān
- *Kitāb al-īḍāḥ*, *see* Abū Tammām, *Kitāb al-shajara*
- *Risālat maṭāliʿ al-shumūs fī maʿrifat al-nufūs*, ed., ʿĀrif Tāmir, in his *Arbaʿ rasāʾil Ismāʿīliyya*, pp. 27–57.

  A short theological treatise on *tawḥīd*, the creation, the soul, eschatology (*maʿād*) and the Ismaili oath (*ʿahd*) of allegiance.

Abū Ḥātim al-Rāzī, *see* al-Rāzī, Abū Ḥātim

Abu'l-Haytham Aḥmad b. Ḥasan Jurjānī, Khwāja (fl. 4th/10th century), Persian Ismaili author

- *Qaṣīda*, ed., Mujtabā Mīnuvī, in *Yādigār*, 2, no. 8 (1325 Sh./1946), pp. 9–21; also in Nāṣir-i Khusraw, *Kitāb-i jāmiʿ al-ḥikmatayn*, ed., H. Corbin and M. Muʿīn, pp. 19–30; French trans., Isabelle de Gastines as *Le livre réunissant les deux sagesses*, pp. 50–57; also in Muḥammad b. Surkh Nīshāpūrī, *Sharḥ-i qaṣīda-yi Fārsī*, ed., H. Corbin and M. Muʿīn, scattered throughout the text, pp. 2–106.

  This *Qaṣīda*, in eighty-two verses in response to questions, deals with a variety of theological and philosophical subjects.

Abū Isḥāq (Ibrāhīm) Quhistānī (d. after 904/1498), Nizārī *dāʿī* in Persia

- *Haft bāb-i Abū Isḥāq*, ed. and English trans., Wladimir Ivanow. Ismaili Society Series A, no. 10. Bombay: Ismaili Society, 1959. pp. 27 (English) + 85 (English) + 68 (Persian).

One of the earliest doctrinal texts produced during the Anjudān revival in Persian Nizārī Ismailism. After an autobiographical *bāb*, this work in seven chapters (*haft bāb*) deals with the seventy-two erring sects, the Ismailis as the only salvaged community, prophethood, the revelation of the Qur'an and its esoteric interpretation (*ta'wīl*), imamate, era of concealment (*satr*), resurrection (*qiyāmat*), eschatology (*maʿād*), spiritual and physical worlds, hierarchy of ranks from *mustajīb* to imam, etc.

Abū Yaʿqūb al-Sijistānī (al-Sijzī), *see* al-Sijistānī, Abū Yaʿqūb

Abū Tammām [Yūsuf b. Muḥammad al-Nīsābūrī] (fl. 4th/10th century), Ismaili (Qarmaṭī) *dāʿī* in Khurāsān

- *Kitāb al-shajara*, partial ed. and English trans., Wilferd Madelung and Paul Ernest Walker as *An Ismaili Heresiography: The "Bāb al-shayṭān" from Abū Tammām's Kitāb al-shajara*. Islamic History and Civilization, Studies and Texts, 23. Leiden: E.J. Brill, 1998. pp. xi + 134 (English) + 143 (Arabic); partial edition, wrongly attributed to the Syrian Nizārī *dāʿī* Abū Firās Shihāb al-Dīn al-Maynaqī (d. 937/1530 or 947/1540), as *Kitāb al-īḍāḥ*, ed., ʿĀrif Tāmir. Beirut: al-Maṭbaʿa al-Kāthūlīkiyya, 1965. pp. 12 + 164; a second partial edition of the same second part of the *Kitāb al-shajara*, this time wrongly attributed to the early Ismaili *dāʿī* ʿAbdān (d. ca. 286/899), as *Shajarat al-yaqīn*, ed., ʿĀrif Tāmir. Beirut: Dār al-Āfāq al-Jadīda, 1402/1982. pp. 165.

The first part of the *Kitāb al-shajara* is comprised of a heresiography of the seventy-two erring sects in Islam in its third chapter on Satan. Other chapters of the first part relate to the following classes of beings: angels, jinn, devils and humans. The text of the second part, as edited by Tāmir, starts in the middle of the section on devils and continues to a discussion of humans in potentiality and actuality. Abū Tammām's heresiography, as edited by Madelung and Walker on the basis of its single known manuscript, contains information on the following communities: Muʿtazila (six sects), the Khawārij (fourteen sects), Ḥadīthiyya or *aṣḥāb al-ḥadīth* (four sects), Qadariyya or Mujbira (five sects), Mushabbiha (thirteen sects), Murjiʾa (six sects), Zaydiyya (five sects), Kaysāniyya (four sects), ʿAbbāsiyya (two sects), Ghāliya (eight sects), and Imāmiyya (five sects). Abū Tammām's descriptions of eight sects are unique, and for several others add much to known details about them; *see* Walker, "An Ismaʿili Version of the Heresiography of the Seventy-two Erring Sects", in *MIHT,* pp. 161–177.

Abu'l-Maʿālī Ḥātim b. ʿImrān (or Maḥmūd) b. Zahrā (d. 497 or 498/1103–5), Syrian Ismaili author

- *Risālat al-uṣūl wa'l-aḥkām,* ed., ʿĀrif Tāmir, in his *Khams rasāʾil Ismāʿīliyya*, pp. 99–143.

A theological treatise on prophetic eras and religious duties with their esoteric interpretations (*taʾwīl*).

Āghā Khān Maḥallātī, Ḥasan ʿAlī Shāh (d. 1302/1885), Nizārī imam

- *ʿIbrat-afzā,* lithographed, Bombay, 1278/1862. pp. 79; ed., Ḥusayn Kūhī Kirmānī. Intishārāt-i Rūznāma-yi Nasīm-i Ṣabā, 32. Tehran: n.p., 1325 Sh./1946. pp. xxxii + 100; also in M. Sāʿī, *Āqā Khān Maḥallātī*, pp. 25–68.

This biography of the first Āghā Khān, the forty-sixth (Qāsim-Shāhī) Nizārī imam, written in the manner of an autobiography, was evidently compiled in India by Mīrzā Aḥmad Viqār b. Viṣāl Shīrāzī (d. 1298/1881) who stayed briefly with the imam in Bombay in 1266/1850. This work is particularly valuable for details relating to the Āghā Khān's early life and the events leading to his conflict with the Qājār ruling establishment in Persia which culminated in his permanent settlement in British India in the 1840s.

ʿAlī b. Ḥanẓala b. Abī Sālim al-Maḥfūẓī al-Wādiʿī al-Hamdānī (d. 626/1229), Ṭayyibī *dāʿī muṭlaq* in Yaman

- *Ḍiyāʾ al-ḥulūm wa-miṣbāḥ al-ʿulūm,* ed., Muṣṭafā Ghālib, in his *Arbaʿ kutub ḥaqqāniyya*, pp. 77–111.

Divided into four chapters, this work on the *ḥaqāʾiq* deals with *tawḥīd*, the creation, eschatology (*maʿād*) and other theological issues.

- *Simṭ al-ḥaqāʾiq (fī ʿaqāʾid al-Ismāʿīliyya)*, ed., ʿAbbās al-ʿAzzāwī. Damascus: Institut Français de Damas, 1953. pp. 67.

This short versified work deals with *tawḥīd*, the creation, the seven spheres, eras of religious history and eschatology (*maʿād*), amongst other themes found normally in such Yamanī Ṭayyibī writings on the *ḥaqāʾiq*.

ʿAlī b. Muḥammad b. al-Walīd, *see* Ibn al-Walīd, ʿAlī b. Muḥammad

ʿĀmir b. ʿĀmir al-Baṣrī (d. after 700/1300), Syrian Ismaili poet

- *Tāʾiyyat ʿĀmir b. ʿĀmir al-Baṣrī*, ed., ʿAbd al-Qādir al-Maghribī. Damascus: Institut Français de Damas, 1367/1948. pp. 103; ed., ʿĀrif Tāmir as *al-Qaṣīda al-tāʾiyya*, in his *Arbaʿ rasāʾil Ismāʿīliyya*, pp. 103–133; ed. and French trans., Yves Marquet as *Poésie ésoterique Ismaïlienne. La Tāʾiyya de ʿĀmir b. ʿĀmir al-Baṣrī.* Islam d'hier et d'aujourd'hui, 26. Paris: Maisonneuve et Larose, 1985. pp. 242.

A long didactic poem in 506 verses on Ismaili subjects related to the *ḥaqāʾiq*, including *tawḥīd*, the creation, cycles of prophethood, imamate and eschatology.

al-Āmir bi-Aḥkām Allāh, Abū ʿAlī Manṣūr (d. 524/1130), Fatimid caliph and Mustaʿlī imam

- *al-Hidāya al-Āmiriyya fī ibṭāl daʿwat al-Nizāriyya*, ed., Asaf A.A. Fyzee. Islamic Research Association Series, no.7. London, etc.: Published for the Islamic Research Association by H. Milford, Oxford University Press, 1938. pp. 18 (English) + 26 (Arabic); reprinted in *Majmūʿat al-wathāʾiq al-Fāṭimiyya*, ed., J. al-Shayyāl, text pp. 203–230, analysis pp. 47–67.

The *Hidāya al-Āmiriyya*, based on the proceedings of a meeting held in Cairo at the Fatimid palace in 516/1122 and written down by Ibn al-Ṣayrafī (d. 542/1147), is a polemical epistle against the claims of Nizār b. al-Mustanṣir (d. 488/1095) to the Ismaili imamate. This epistle is the earliest official document upholding the rights of al-Āmir's father, al-Mustaʿlī, and refuting the claims of Nizār and his descendants to the imamate; *see* S.M. Stern, "The Epistle of the Fatimid Caliph al-Āmir", pp. 20–31.

- *Risālat īqāʿ ṣawāʿiq al-irghām*, ed., Asaf A.A. Fyzee, together with al-Āmir bi-Aḥkām Allāh's *al-Hidāya al-Āmiriyya*, pp. 27–39; reprinted in *Majmūʿat al-wathāʾiq al-Fāṭimiyya*, ed., J. al-Shayyāl, text pp. 231–247, analysis pp. 68–70.

This additional epistle against the Nizārī claims to the imamate was written in refutation of a Nizārī reply produced in Syria to the earlier *al-Hidāya al-Āmiriyya*.

Badakhshānī, Sayyid Suhrāb Valī (d. after 856/1452), Central Asian Nizārī author

- *Sī va shish ṣaḥīfa*, ed., Hūshang Ujāqī, with an English Foreword by W. Ivanow. Ismaili Society Series A, no.12. Tehran: Ismaili Society, 1961. pp. 15 (English) + 84 (Persian).

Preserved by the Nizārīs of Central Asia and in some of its manuscripts referred to also as the *Ṣaḥīfat al-nāẓirīn*, this work is a typical representation of the Badakhshānī Nizārī tradition. It deals with the creation, prophethood, revelation (*tanzīl*) and its esoteric interpretation (*taʾwīl*), resurrection (*qiyāmat*) and eschatology (*maʿād*), salvation, Paradise and Hell, with scattered references to Nāṣir-i Khusraw and his teachings.

al-Bharūchī (or al-Bharūjī), Ḥasan b. Nūḥ al-Hindī (d. 939/1533), Ṭayyibī Bohra author in India

- *Kitāb al-azhār wa-majmaʿ al-anwār*, vol. 1, ed., ʿĀdil al-ʿAwwā, in his *Muntakhabāt Ismāʿīliyya*, pp. 181–250; for part of vol. 6, see Ibn al-Haytham, *Kitāb al-munāẓarāt*.

Part of a seven-volume anthology of Ismaili literature compiled between 931/1524 and 933/1527. The first volume of the *Kitāb al-azhār* deals with prophethood, imamate and aspects of the Ismaili *daʿwa*; *see* I.K. Poonawala, *Biobibliography*, pp. 179–183.

Bīrjandī, Ra'īs Ḥasan b. Ṣalāḥ Munshī (fl. 7th/13th century), Persian Nizārī historian and poet

- *Ashʿār*, selection, ed. and English trans., Wladimir Ivanow, in his "An Ismaili Poem in Praise of Fidawis", *JBBRAS*, NS, 14 (1938), pp. 63–72.

  A poem in praise of *fidā'īs* who killed Atabeg Qizil Arslān, governor of Ādharbāyjān, in 587/1191. Other poems of Ra'īs Ḥasan, who served also as secretary (*munshī*) to the *muḥtasham* Shihāb al-Dīn Manṣūr and other Nizārī governors in Quhistān, are scattered in Khayrkhwāh-i Harātī's *Faṣl dar bayān-i shinākht-i imām*.

Burhānpūrī, Quṭb al-Dīn Sulaymānjī (d. 1241/1826), Dā'ūdī Bohra author in India

- *Muntazaʿ al-akhbār fī akhbār al-duʿāt al-akhyār*, partial ed., Samer F. Traboulsi. Beirut: Dār al-Gharb al-Islāmī, 1999. pp. 318.

  A partial edition covering the first part of the second volume of the *Muntazaʿ*, from the time of the first Ṭayyibī *dāʿī muṭlaq* al-Dhu'ayb (d. 546/1151)to the Dā'ūdī-Sulaymānī schism in the Ṭayyibī *daʿwa* and the period of the twenty-seventh Dā'ūdī *dāʿī muṭlaq* Dā'ūd b. Quṭbshāh (d. 1021/1612). Part of a two-volume history of the Ismaili *daʿwa* from earliest times until 1240/1824.

al-Dādīkhī, Qays b. Manṣūr (d. 655/1257), Syrian Nizārī author

- *Risālat al-asābīʿ*, ed., ʿĀrif Tāmir, in his *Khams rasā'il Ismāʿīliyya*, pp.157–179.

  A short treatise on esoteric interpretations (*ta'wīl*) of certain Qur'anic verses and Ismaili teachings related to the number seven.

Ḍiyā' al-Dīn Ismāʿīl b. Hibat Allāh b. Ibrāhīm (d. 1184/1770), Sulaymānī Ṭayyibī *dāʿī muṭlaq* in Yaman

- *Mizāj al tasnīm*, partial ed., Rudolf Strothmann as *Ismailitischer Koran-Kommentar*. Abhandlungen der Akademie der Wissenschaften in Göttingen, Philologisch-historische Klasse, Dritte Folge, 31. Göttingen: Vandenhoeck & Ruprecht, 1944–55. Fascicules, 1–4.

  Part of a commentary of the Qur'an composed by the thirty-third

Sulaymānī *dāʿī*, who was a learned religious scholar and made some original contributions to Ṭayyibī Ismaili thought.

Fidāʾī Khurāsānī, Muḥammad b. Zayn al-ʿĀbidīn Dīzābādī (d. 1342/1923), Persian Nizārī historian and poet

- *Kitāb-i hidāyat al-muʾminīn al-ṭālibīn,* ed., Aleksandr A. Semenov. Akademiya Nauk SSSR, pamyatniki literaturï narodov Vostoka, Tekstï, Malaya seriya, 1. Moscow: Izdatel'stvo Vostochnoy Literaturï, 1959. pp. 24 (Russian) + 222 (Persian); reprinted, Tehran: Asāṭīr, 1362 Sh./1983. pp. 222 (Persian text, without the Russian introduction).

  A history of Ismailism from its origins to modern times; the final sections on the Āghā Khāns were evidently added in Bombay around 1328/1910 by a certain Mūsā Khān Khurāsānī (d. 1937) who was in the service of the imams. Copies of this work, permeated with errors, have been preserved by the Nizārīs of Badakhshān in present-day Tajikistan and Afghanistan; *see* F. Daftary, "Fedāʾī Korāsānī", in *EIR*, vol. 9, p. 470.

- *Qaṣīda-yi Nigāristān*, ed. and Russian trans., Aleksandr A. Semenov, in his "Ismailitskiy panegirik obozhestvlyonnomu ʿAliyu Fedai Khorasanskogo" [An Ismaili Panegeric of ʿAli by Fidaʾi Khorasani], *Iran* (Leningrad), 3 (1929), pp. 51–70.

  Fidāʾī was also a poet and composed a large number of poems in different forms such as *mathnawī*, *qaṣīda* and *ghazal.* This *mathnawī* of 169 verses is in praise of ʿAlī b. Abī Ṭālib.

al-Ḥāmidī, Ḥātim b. Ibrāhīm (d. 596/1199), Ṭayyibī *dāʿī muṭlaq* in Yaman

- *Jāmiʿ al-ḥaqāʾiq,* an abridged version of al-Muʾayyad fiʾl-Dīn al-Shīrāzī's *al-Majālis al-Muʾayyadiyya,* partial ed., Muḥammad ʿAbd al-Qādir ʿAbd al-Nāṣir. Silsilat nafāʾis al-fikr al-Islāmī, 2. Cairo: Dār al-Thaqāfa, 1975. pp. 459.

  Contains selections in 18 chapters from the *dāʿī* al-Muʾayyad fiʾl-Dīn al-Shīrāzī's (d. 470/1078) *al-Majālis al-Muʾayyadiyya* on theological and other themes as well as esoteric interpretation (*taʾwīl*) of the Qurʾan.

- *Majālis Sayyidnā Ḥātim b. Ibrāhīm al-Ḥāmidī*, excerpt, ed. and

English trans., W. Ivanow, in his *Ismaili Tradition*, text pp. 107–113, translation pp. 305–313.

Excerpt from the 117th *majlis* on Ismaili imams.

- *Risālat zahr badhr al-ḥaqāʾiq*, ed., ʿĀdil al-ʿAwwā, in his *Muntakhabāt Ismāʿīliyya*, pp. 155–180.

  Divided into 18 sections, this is another Yamanī Ṭayyibī work on the *ḥaqāʾiq* dealing with the creation, the spheres, eschatology and other standard themes.

- *Tuḥfat al-qulūb*, *see* al-Nīsābūrī, *al-Risāla al-mūjaza al-kāfiya*

al-Ḥāmidī, Ibrāhīm b. al-Ḥusayn (d. 557/1162), Ṭayyibī *dāʿī muṭlaq* in Yaman

- *Kitāb kanz al-walad*, ed., Muṣṭafā Ghālib. Bibliotheca Islamica, 24. Wiesbaden: F. Steiner, 1391/1971. pp. 342; reprinted, Beirut: Dār al-Andalus, 1979. pp. 342.

  Drawing extensively on Ḥamīd al-Dīn al-Kirmānī's metaphysical system as contained in his *Rāḥat al-ʿaql*, this theological work provided the basis of the specific Ṭayyibī *ḥaqāʾiq* system, including its cosmology and eschatology with what H. Corbin called its mythical 'drama in heaven', and as such, it was used as a model for later Ṭayyibī writings on the subject. Divided into 14 chapters (*bābs*), this is also one of the earliest works in Yamanī Ṭayyibī tradition to refer to the *Rasāʾil Ikhwān al-Ṣafāʾ*.

Ḥasan b. Aḥmad al-Muʿaddil (d. ca. 658/1260), Syrian Nizārī author

- *Risālat maʿrifat al-nafs al-nāṭiqa,* ed., Muṣṭafā Ghālib, in his *Arbaʿ kutub ḥaqqāniyya,* pp. 113–121.

  A brief philosophical work on the rational soul.

- *Risālat mubtadaʾ al-ʿawālim wa-mabdaʾ dawr al-satr waʾl-taqiyya,* ed., Muṣṭafā Ghālib, in his *Arbaʿ kutub ḥaqqāniyya*, pp. 122–142.

  A brief *urjūza* on cosmogony and eras of prophets, from Ādam to Ibrāhīm.

Ḥasan Kabīr al-Dīn, Pīr (d. ca. 875/1470), Satpanth Nizārī preacher-saint in India

- *Ginān*s, selections, English trans., Vali Mahomed N. Hooda, in his "Some Specimens of Satpanth Literature", in W. Ivanow, ed., *Collectanea*, pp. 109–111; also in C. Shackle and Z. Moir, *Ismaili Hymns from South Asia*, pp. 97, 99, 127, 129, 137, 139; in A. Esmail, *A Scent of Sandalwood*, pp. 106–107, 121, 126, 133, 181–185, and in A.S. Asani, *Ecstasy and Enlightenment*, pp. 153–159, 165–166.

Ḥasan-i Ṣabbāḥ, Ḥasan b. ʿAlī b. Muḥammad al-Ṣabbāḥ (d. 518/1124), Ismaili *dāʿī* and founder of the Nizārī *daʿwa* and state in Persia

- *al-Fuṣūl al-arbaʿa* (*Fuṣūl-i arbaʿa*), fragmentarily quoted by Muḥammad b. ʿAbd al-Karīm al-Shahrastānī in his *Kitāb al-milal wa'l-niḥal*, ed., William Cureton. London: Printed for the Society for the Publication of Oriental Texts, 1842, part 1, pp. 150–152; on the margin of Ibn Ḥazm's *Kitāb al-fiṣal fi'l-milal wa'l-ahwāʾ wa'l-niḥal*. Cairo: al-Maṭbaʿa al-Adabiyya, 1317–21/1899–1903, part 2, pp. 32–36; reprinted (with the same pagination), Rawāʾiʿ al-turāth al-ʿArabī. Beirut: Maktabat Khayyāṭ, n.d.; ed. Aḥmad Fahmī Muḥammad. Cairo: n.p., 1368/1948, vol. 1, pp. 339–345; ed. Muḥammad b. Fatḥ Allāh Badrān. Silsila fi'l-dirāsāt al-falsafiyya wa'l-akhlāqiyya. 2nd ed., Cairo: Maktabat al-Anjlū al-Miṣriyya, 1375/1956, vol. 1, pp. 175–178; ed. ʿAbd al-ʿAzīz Muḥammad al-Wakīl. Cairo: Muʾassasat al-Ḥalabī, 1387/1968, vol. 1, pp. 195–198. Partial English trans., in Edward S. Salisbury, "Translation of Two Unpublished Arabic Documents", pp. 267–272; also in Marshall G.S. Hodgson, *The Order of Assassins*, pp. 325–328; partial English trans., A.K. Kazi and J.G. Flynn as *Muslim Sects and Divisions: The Section on Muslim Sects in Kitāb al-Milal wa'l-Niḥal*. London: K. Paul International, 1984, pp. 167–170. French trans., Daniel Gimaret, Guy Monnot and Jean Jolivet as *Livre des religions et des sectes*. Collection UNESCO d'oeuvres représentatives, série Arabe. Paris: UNESCO; Louvain: Peeters, 1986–93, vol. 1, pp. 560–565. Partial French trans., Jean-Claude Vadet as *Kitāb al-Milal, les dissidences de l'Islam*. Bibliothèque d'études Islamiques, 14. Paris: P. Geuthner, 1984, pp. 315–319. German trans., Theodor Haarbrücker as *Religionspartheien und Philosophen-Schulen*. Halle: C.A. Schwetschke, 1850–51, vol. 1, pp. 225–230. Persian trans., Afḍal al-Dīn Ṣadr Turka-yi Iṣfahānī (d.

850/1446), ed., Muḥammad Riḍā Jalālī Nā'īnī. Tehran: Iqbāl, 1350 Sh./1971, pp. 155–157. Persian trans., Muṣṭafā Khāliqdād Hāshimī as *Tawḍīḥ al-milal*. 2nd ed., Tehran: n.p., 1358 Sh./1979, vol. 1, pp. 259–269. Ottoman Turkish trans., *Tercüme-yi Milel ve nihal*. Istanbul: Tab'hane-yi Āmire, 1279/1862–63, pp. 43–47.

Ḥasan-i Ṣabbāḥ's *Fuṣūl* was seen and paraphrased also by three Persian historians of the Īlkhānid period, namely, ʿAṭā-Malik Juwaynī, *Ta'rīkh-i jahān-gushā*, ed., Muḥammad Qazwīnī. Leiden: E.J. Brill; London: Luzac, 1937, vol. 3, pp. 195–199; English trans., John A. Boyle as *The History of the World-Conqueror*. Manchester: Manchester University Press, 1958, vol. 2, pp. 671–673; Rashīd al-Dīn Faḍl Allāh, *Jāmiʿ al-tawārīkh: qismat-i Ismāʿīliyān*, ed., Muḥammad Taqī Dānishpazhūh and Muḥammad Mudarrisī Zanjānī. Tehran: Bungāh-i Tarjama va Nashr-i Kitāb, 1338 Sh./1959, pp. 105–107, reproduced with English trans. in R. Levy, "The Account of the Ismaʿili Doctrines", pp. 532–536, and Abu'l-Qāsim Kāshānī, *Zubdat al-tawārīkh: bakhsh-i Fāṭimiyān va Nizāriyān*, ed., Muḥammad Taqī Dānishpazhūh. 2nd ed., Tehran: Mu'assasa-yi Muṭālaʿāt va Taḥqīqāt-i Farhangī, 1366 Sh./1987, pp. 142–143.

Ḥasan-i Ṣabbāḥ's major theological treatise, *al-Fuṣūl al-arbaʿa*, written originally in Persian, has not survived directly, but it has been preserved fragmentarily by Ḥasan's contemporary al-Shahrastānī (d. 548/1153), in his heresiographical work written around 521/1127. This treatise was also seen and paraphrased by a number of Persian historians who had access to Nizārī Ismaili sources of the Alamūt period which have not survived. In the *Fuṣūl*, Ḥasan restated the Shiʿi doctrine of *taʿlīm*, establishing a logical basis in four propositions for the necessity of an authoritative and trustworthy teacher (*muʿallim-i ṣādiq*) as the spiritual guide of mankind, who would be none other than the Ismaili imam of the time.

- *Javāb-i Ḥasan-i Ṣabbāḥ bi ruqʿa-yi Jalāl al-Dīn Malik Shāh Saljūqī*, ed., Naṣr Allāh Falsafī (1901–1981), in his *Hasht maqāla-yi ta'rīkhī va adabī*. Intishārāt-i Dānishgāh-i Tehran, 104. Tehran: Dānishgāh-i Tehran, 1330 Sh./1951, pp. 208–216; reprinted in Naṣr Allāh Falsafī, *Chand maqāla-yi ta'rīkhī va adabī*. Intishārāt-i Dānishgāh-i Tehran, 903. Tehran: Dānishgāh-i Tehran, 1342 Sh./1963, pp. 416–425. This text is also published by Mehmet Şerefeddin (Yaltkaya), in *Darülfünun Ilâhiyat Fakültesi Mecmuası* (Istanbul), 1, no. 4 (1926), pp. 38–44.

The authorship of this reply (*javāb*), allegedly written by Ḥasan-i Ṣabbāḥ to the brief letter (*ruqʿa*) of the Saljūq sultan Malik Shāh (465–485/1073–1092), is very doubtful. In this letter, the author after relating some biographical details including his travel to Egypt where he encountered the animosity of the Fatimid vizier, Badr al-Jamālī (d. 487/1094) but was protected by the Fatimid caliph-imam al-Mustanṣir (d. 487/1094), defends his religious beliefs. Above all, the author rejects the idea that he is propagating a new religion.

- *Sargudhasht-i Sayyidnā*. This anonymous work was the official Nizārī account of Ḥasan-i Ṣabbāḥ's biography (*sargudhasht*) and reign, and its first part may have been autobiographical. The *Sargudhasht* has not survived, but it was seen by Juwaynī, Rashīd al-Dīn and Kāshānī, who used and paraphrased it in writing their accounts of the life and career of Ḥasan-i Ṣabbāḥ as part of their Ismaili histories. Rashīd al-Dīn and Kāshānī have fuller quotations from this work; see Juwaynī, *Taʾrīkh-i jahān-gushā*, vol. 3, pp. 186–216; tr., Boyle, vol. 2, pp. 666–683; Rashīd al-Dīn, *Jāmiʿ al-tawārīkh: qismat-i Ismāʿīliyān*, pp. 97–134, and Kāshānī, *Zubdat al-tawārīkh: bakhsh-i Fāṭimiyān va Nizāriyān*, 2nd ed., pp. 133–168.

Ibn Hāniʾ al-Andalusī, Abu'l-Qāsim Muḥammad (d. 362/973), Ismaili poet in the Maghrib

- *Dīwān*, lithographed, Būlāq, 1274/1858. pp. 160; Beirut: al-Maṭbaʿa al-Lubnāniyya, 1886; Beirut: Maṭbaʿat al-Maʿārif, 1326/1908; ed., Zāhid ʿAlī as *Tabyīn al-maʿānī fī sharḥ Dīwān Ibn Hāniʾ al-Andalusī al-Maghribī*. Cairo: Maṭbaʿat al-Maʿārif, 1352/1933. pp. 61 + 818; ed., with an introduction by K. Bustānī, Beirut: Dār Ṣādir, 1964. pp. 391; ed., Muḥammad al-Yaʿlāwī. Beirut: Dār al-Gharb al-Islāmī, 1995. pp. 503; ed., Anṭwān Nuʿaym. Beirut: Dār al-Jīl, 1416/1996. pp. 502; partial ed., Karam al-Bustānī. Beirut: Maktabat Ṣādir, 1952. pp. 435; partial ed. and English trans., Arthur Wormhoudt as *The Diwan of Abu Qasim Muhammad ibn Hani al Azdi al Andalusi*. Arab Translation Series, 79. [Oskaloosa, IA]: William Penn College, 1985. pp. 92 (Arabic and English on opposite pages). Selections, in R.P. Dewhurst, "Abu Tammam and Ibn Hani", pp. 629–642, and in H. Massé, "Le poème d'Ibn Hani", pp. 121–127.

The first great poet of the Maghrib, and a devout Ismaili, Ibn Hāniʾ eventually became the chief court poet to the Fatimid caliph-imam al-Muʿizz. Most of his collected poems are in praise of the Fatimids, notably al-Muʿizz himself, also defending the rights of the Fatimids against the claims of the Abbasids and the Umayyads of Spain. Ibn Hāniʾ was murdered on his way to Egypt in 362/973.

Ibn Ḥawshab (Manṣūr al-Yaman), Abu'l-Qāsim al-Ḥasan b. Faraḥ (Faraj) (d. 302/914), early Ismaili *dāʿī* in Yaman

- *Kitāb al-rushd wa'l-hidāya,* fragment, ed., Muḥammad Kāmil Ḥusayn. [Silsilat makhṭūṭāt al-Fāṭimiyyīn, 2], in W. Ivanow, ed., *Collectanea,* pp. 185–213. English trans., W. Ivanow as "The Book of Righteousness and True Guidance", in his *Studies in Early Persian Ismailism,* 1st ed., pp. 51 83; 2nd ed., pp. 29–59.

One of the earliest Ismaili texts, this exegesis of the Qur'an has survived only fragmentarily. This work also makes references to the reappearance of Muḥammad b. Ismāʿīl as the Mahdi and the seventh *nāṭiq,* which was the central doctrine of the bulk of the Ismāʿīliyya in pre-Fatimid times.

Ibn al-Haytham, Abū ʿAbd Allāh Jaʿfar b. Aḥmad al-Aswad (fl. 4th/10th), Ismaili *dāʿī* in North Africa

- *Kitāb al-munāẓarāt,* ed. and English trans., Wilferd Madelung and Paul Ernest Walker as *The Advent of the Fatimids: A Contemporary Shiʿi Witness.* Ismaili Texts and Translations Series, 1. London: I.B. Tauris in association with The Institute of Ismaili Studies, 2000. pp. xiv + 192 (English) + 134 (Arabic).

This work, on the first year of Fatimid rule in Ifrīqiya, has been preserved in the sixth volume of al-Bharūchī's *Kitāb al-azhār,* still in manuscript form. Composed around 334/945, it is a personal memoir of Ibn al-Haytham, a scholar from Qayrawān, who reconstructs his encounters and conversations with the Ismaili *dāʿī*s Abū ʿAbd Allāh al-Shīʿī and his brother Abu'l-ʿAbbās which took place between Rajab 296/March 909 and Rabīʿ II 297/January 910. This work also contains many biographical details on Ibn al-Haytham, who hailed from a Zaydī family and then converted to Imāmī (Twelver) Shiʿism before eventually becoming an Ismaili and a prominent *dāʿī.*

Ibn al-Walīd, ʿAbd Allāh b. ʿAlī b. al-Ḥasan (d. 886/1481), Yamanī Ṭayyibī author

- *Dīwān*, ed., Ghulam Ali Godharwī as *Sharḥ dīwān Sayyidnā ʿAbd Allāh b. ʿAlī al-mawsūm bi tanfīs al-mughram fī sharḥ Wasīlat al-muʾlam*. Bombay: Akbarī Press, 1336/1917.

  A collection of 28 poems, each consisting of 29 verses, in praise of the Prophet Muḥammad and dealing additionally with various religious matters.

Ibn al-Walīd, ʿAlī b. Muḥammad (d. 612/1215), Ṭayyibī *dāʿī muṭlaq* in Yaman

- *Dāmigh al-bāṭil wa-ḥatf al-munāḍil*, ed., Muṣṭafā Ghālib. Beirut: Muʾassasat ʿIzz al-Dīn, 1403/1982. 2 vols.

  A detailed refutation, in two volumes, of Abū Ḥāmid Muḥammad al-Ghazālī's polemical work, *Faḍāʾiḥ al-Bāṭiniyya,* better known as *al-Mustaẓhirī*, written around 488/1095 against the Ismailis.

- *Dīwān Sayyidnā ʿAlī b. Muḥammad al-Walīd*, excerpts, in R. Strothmann, "Kleinere ismailitische Schriften", pp. 145–146 and 153–163; excerpts with English trans., in Rabab Hamiduddin's doctoral thesis "The Qaṣīdah of the Ṭayyibī Daʿwah and the Dīwān of Syedna ʿAlī b. Muḥammad al-Walīd". A *qaṣīda* is edited by Yūsuf Najm al-Dīn, in *Nasīm rawḍat al-adab al-Fāṭimī*. Surat: al-Jāmiʿa al-Sayfiyya, 1380/1960, pp. 59–98.

  A collection of over 100 poems in praise of dignitaries and *dāʿī*s of the Ṭayyibī *daʿwa*, also covering a variety of themes such as a refutation of the Ḥāfiẓī claims to the Ismaili imamate and descriptions of the *ḥajj*.

- *Jalāʾ al-ʿuqūl wa-zubdat al-maḥṣūl*, ed., ʿĀdil al-Awwā, in his *Muntakhabāt Ismāʿīliyya,* pp. 87–153.

  Divided into three main parts, this theological work deals with *tawḥīd* and the creation, the spiritual world, and esoteric interpretations of certain Qurʾanic verses related mainly to eschatology.

- *Kitāb al-dhakhīra fiʾl-ḥaqīqa*, ed., Muḥammad Ḥasan al-Aʿẓamī. Beirut: Dār al-Thaqāfa, 1391/1971. pp. 156.

  This work on the *ḥaqāʾiq* in 33 chapters deals with numerous standard themes such as *tawḥīd*, cosmology, hierarchy of the Ismaili *daʿwa*, eschatology, speaker-prophets (*nuṭaqāʾ*) and imams, Muḥammad b.

Ismāʿīl, reward and punishment of the believers and their opponents.

- *Risāla [fī maʿnā] al-ism al-aʿẓam*, ed., R. Strothmann, in his *Gnosis-Texte*, pp. 171–177.

  Strothmann does not mention the author's name, treating this treatise as anonymous, but Poonawala, *Biobibliography*, p. 159 (no. 12) attributes it to ʿAlī b. Muḥammad al-Walīd.

- *Risālat al-īḍāḥ wa'l-tabyīn*, ed., R. Strothmann, in his *Gnosis-Texte*, pp. 137–158.

  A short treatise on the creation, ranks in the Ismaili hierarchy, eschatology and the imamate of al-Ṭayyib, the twenty-first and last manifest imam of Ṭayyibī Mustaʿlīs.

- *al-Risala al-mufīda fī sharḥ mulghuz al-quṣīdu li-Abī ʿAlī Sīnā*, ed., al-Ḥabīb al-Faqī, in *Ḥawliyyāt al-Jāmiʿa al-Tūnusiyya*, 17 (1979), pp. 117–182.

  A brief commentary on the *Qaṣīdat al-nafs* of Ibn Sīnā (d. 429/1037), a poem on the relationship between soul and body.

- *Risālat tuḥfat al-murtād wa-ghuṣṣat al-aḍdād*, ed., R. Strothmann, in his *Gnosis-Texte*, pp. 159–170.

  A polemical work defending the claims of al-Ṭayyib to the Ismaili imamate against those of the Ḥāfiẓī faction of the Mustaʿlī *daʿwa*.

- *Tāj al-ʿaqā'id wa-maʿdin al-fawā'id*, ed., ʿĀrif Tāmir. Recherches publiées sous la direction de l'Institut de Lettres Orientales de Beyrouth, Série 1: Pensée Arabe et Musulmane, XXXVII. Beirut: Dār al-Mashriq, 1967, pp. 11 + 193; 2nd ed., Beirut: Mu'assasat ʿIzz al-Dīn, 1403/1982. pp. 11 + 193. Summary English trans., Wladimir Ivanow as *A Creed of the Fatimids*. Bombay: Qayyimah Press, 1936. pp. viii + 82.

  A compendium of Ismaili doctrines in 100 sections (*iʿtiqāds*) intended for ordinary believers. The themes covered include cosmogony, prophethood, imamate, eschatology, religious practices, esoteric interpretations of the *sharīʿa*, and the necessity of observing *taqiyya*.

Ibn al-Walīd, al-Ḥusayn b. ʿAlī b. Muḥammad (d. 667/1268), Ṭayyibī *dāʿī muṭlaq* in Yaman

- *Risālat al-īḍāḥ wa'l-bayān ʿan masā'il al-imtiḥān*, excerpt, ed., B. Lewis, in his "An Ismaili Interpretation of the Fall of Adam", pp. 698–704.

  A compendium of responses to 25 theological questions from an

Ismaili perspective. This excerpt relates to the ninth question on Adam and his fall.

- *Risālat al-mabdaʾ waʾl-maʿād*, ed. and French trans., H. Corbin, in his *Trilogie Ismaélienne*, Arabic text pp. 99–130, trans. as *Cosmogonie et eschatologie*, pp. 129–200; ed., Khālid al-Mīr Maḥmūd. Damascus: Dār al-Takwīn, 2001. pp. 84.

  Divided into five chapters (*faṣl*s) and preceded by an introduction on *tawḥīd*, this short treatise summarizes Ismaili doctrines of the early Yamanī Ṭayyibī tradition; it deals with cosmogony, origination of the spiritual universe and its corresponding ranks in the physical world, creation of man, eschatology (*maʿād*) and the advent of the *qāʾim*, the imamate and the opponents of the imam, etc.

Idrīs b. al-Ḥasan b. ʿAbd Allāh b. al-Walīd, ʿImād al-Dīn (d. 872/1468), Ṭayyibī *dāʿī muṭlaq* and historian in Yaman

- *Kitab zahr al-maʿānī*, ed., Muṣṭafā Ghālib. Beirut: al-Muʾassasa al-Jāmiʿiyya liʾl-Dirāsa waʾl-Nashr waʾl-Tawzīʿ, 1411/1991. pp. 344. Selection covering chapter 17, ed. and English trans., W. Ivanow, in his *Ismaili Tradition*, text pp. 47–80, translation pp. 232–274.

  This work divided into 21 chapters (*bāb*s) and completed in 838/1435 represents the zenith of the Yamanī Ṭayyibī tradition of compiling compendia of esoteric Ismaili doctrines, drawing on the writings of the major authors of the Fatimid period, such as Abū Yaʿqūb al-Sijistānī, al-Qāḍī al-Nuʿmān and Ḥamīd al-Dīn al-Kirmānī.

- *Rawḍat al-akhbār wa-nuzhat al-asmār*, ed., Muḥammad b. ʿAlī al-Akwaʿ al-Ḥiwālī al-Ḥimyarī. Sanaa: Dār al-Maʿrifa liʾl-Ṭibāʿa waʾl-Nashr, 1995. pp. 258.

  A history of the Ṭayyibī *daʿwa* in Yaman from 853/1449 to 870/1465.

- *ʿUyūn al-akhbār wa-funūn al-āthār*, ed., Muṣṭafā Ghālib, vols. 4–6. Silsilat al-turāth al-Fāṭimī. Beirut: Dār al-Andalus, 1973–78; vol. 5 and part of vol. 6, ed., Muḥammad al-Yaʿlāwī as *Taʾrīkh al-khulafāʾ al-Fāṭimiyyīn biʾl-Maghrib: al-qism al-khāṣṣ min Kitāb ʿuyūn al-akhbār*. Beirut: Dār al-Gharb al-Islāmī, 1985. pp. 817; vol. 7, ed. and summary English trans., Ayman Fuʾād Sayyid in collaboration with Paul E. Walker and Maurice A. Pomerantz as *The Fatimids and their Successors in Yaman: The History of an Islamic Community*. Ismaili Texts and Translations Series, 4. London: I.B. Tauris in association with The

Institute of Ismaili Studies, 2002. pp. x + 109 (English) + 44 (Arabic) + 397 (Arabic).

Parts of a comprehensive, seven-volume history of the Ismaili *daʿwa* from its beginnings until the opening phase of the Ṭayyibī *daʿwa* in Yaman and the subsequent demise of the Fatimid dynasty in 567/1171; *see* Poonawala, *Biobibliography*, pp. 170–172. This is also an important history of the Prophet Muḥammad, the early Shiʿi imams, and the Fatimids and their state.

Imām Shāh, Imām al-Dīn ʿAbd al-Raḥīm (d. 919/1513), founder of the Imām-Shāhī Satpanth community in India

- *Dasa Avatāra*, complete English trans., G. Khakee, in her doctoral thesis "The Dasa Avatāra of the Satpanthi Ismailis and the Imam Shahis of Indo-Pakistan", pp. 62–478.

  This important *ginān* has been preserved and recorded in three separate versions attributed to Pīr Shams al-Dīn, Pīr Ṣadr al-Dīn and Imām Shāh. This *ginān* presents the imam as the long-awaited saviour of a Vaishnavite tradition concerning the ten descents (*dasa avatāra*) of the Hindu deity Vishnu through the ages.
- *Mōman Chetāmāni*, selection, English trans., Vali Mahomed N. Hooda, in his "Some Specimens of Satpanth Literature", in W. Ivanow, ed., *Collectanea*, pp. 97–101.
- *Gināns*, selections, English trans., in C. Shackle and Z. Moir, *Ismaili Hymns from South Asia*, pp. 91, 139, 141, and in A. Esmail, *A Scent of Sandalwood*, pp. 84, 87–88, 97–98, 99–100, 122, 123, 124–125, 127, 128, 134–135.

Jaʿfar b. Manṣūr al-Yaman, Abu'l-Qāsim (d. ca. 346/957), Ismaili *dāʿī* and author in North Africa

- *Kitāb al-ʿālim wa'l-ghulām*, ed. and English trans., James Winston Morris as *The Master and the Disciple: An Early Islamic Spiritual Dialogue*. Ismaili Texts and Translations Series, 3. London: I.B. Tauris in association with The Institute of Ismaili Studies, 2001. pp. xiii + 225 (English) + 180 (Arabic); ed., M. Ghālib, in his *Arbaʿ kutub ḥaqqāniyya*, pp. 13–75. Summary English trans., W. Ivanow as "The

Book of the Teacher and the Pupil", in his *Studies in Early Persian Ismailism.* 1st ed., pp. 61–86; 2nd ed., pp. 85–113. Summary French trans., H. Corbin, in his "L'initiation Ismaélienne ...", pp. 41–142. Summary English trans., H. Corbin, in his *Ismaili Initiation or Esotericism and the Word.*

One of the earliest Ismaili texts and an important source on pre-Fatimid Ismaili teachings and practices. This work is essentially the presentation of a series of personal encounters between various seekers of the spiritual truth and other individuals who act as their guides.

- *Kitāb al-farā'iḍ wa-ḥudūd al-dīn*, extract, *see* al-Mahdī bi'llāh, *Kitāb arsalahu ...*
- *Kitāb al-kashf*, ed., Rudolf Strothmann. Islamic Research Association Series, no.13. London, etc.: Published for the Islamic Research Association by G. Cumberlege, Oxford University Press, 1952. pp. 180 + 15 + 19; ed., Muṣṭafā Ghālib. Beirut: Dār al-Andalus, 1404/1984. pp. 153.

A collection of six short treatises, written separately in pre-Fatimid times but attributed to Ja'far, who apparently acted only as the compiler of the collection. Compiled probably during the reign of the second Fatimid caliph-imam al-Qā'im (322–334/934–946), this work contains allegorical exegesis of the Qur'an, in some passages in cipher, as well as allusions to early Ismaili doctrines, such as the expectation of the return of the Mahdi or *qā'im* as the the seventh *nāṭiq*.

- *Sarā'ir wa-asrār al-nuṭaqā'*, ed., Muṣṭafā Ghālib. Beirut: Dār al-Andalus, 1404/1984. pp. 264; selection, ed. and English trans., W. Ivanow, in his *Ismaili Tradition*, text pp. 81–106, translation pp. 275–304 (from *Asrār al-nuṭaqā'*).

The *Sarā'ir al-nuṭaqā'* and *Asrār al-nuṭaqā'* are two separate but closely related works edited together here by M. Ghālib. The *Sarā'ir* and its later expanded version, the *Asrār*, contain esoteric interpretations of mythological figures, and stories of the prophets (*nuṭaqā'*) recognized in the Qur'an and their eras. The *Asrār* also upholds the legitimacy of Ismā'īl b. Ja'far al-Ṣādiq's claim to the imamate.

al-Jawdharī, Abū 'Alī Manṣūr al-'Azīzī (d. ca. 386/996), Fatimid functionary and author in North Africa

- *Sīrat al-ustādh Jawdhar*, ed., Muḥammad Kāmil Ḥusayn and Muḥammad 'Abd al-Hādī Sha'īra. Silsilat makhṭūṭāt al-Fāṭimiyyīn,

11. Cairo: Dār al-Fikr al-ʿArabī, [1954]. pp. 198. French trans., Marius Canard as *Vie de l'ustadh Jaudhar (contenant sermons, lettres et rescrits des premiers califes Fâtimides)*. Publications de l'Institut d'Études Orientales de la Faculté des Lettres d'Alger, IIe série, XX. Algiers: La Typo-Litho et J. Carbonel, 1958. pp. 232.

This is the biography of Jawdhar, the eunuch (*ustādh*) and courtier who served the first four Fatimid caliph-imams and died in 363/973; it was compiled by Jawdhar's private secretary Abū ʿAlī Manṣūr al-ʿAzīzī al-Jawdharī, who was named after his master, in the time of the Fatimid caliph-imam al-ʿAzīz (365–386/975–996). This is an important source for early Fatimid history and the inner workings of the Fatimid court.

Khākī Khurāsānī, Imām Qulī (d. after 1056/1646), Persian Nizārī poet

- *Dīwān*, partial ed., Wladimir Ivanow as *An Abbreviated Version of the Diwan of Khaki Khorasani*. Islamic Research Association [Series], no.1. Bombay: A.A.A. Fyzee, 1933. pp. ii + 20 (English) + 128 (Persian).

  Part of Khākī's collection of popular *ghazal*s which occasionally also contain rural forms of the Khurāsānī dialect spoken in north-eastern Persia.

- *Nigāristān*, ed., W. Ivanow, in his edition of Khākī's *Dīwān*, pp. 109–124.

  A lengthy *qaṣīda* of 980 verses on the recognition of the imam, salvation and other religious themes.

- *Bahāristān*, ed., W. Ivanow, in his edition of Khākī's *Dīwān*, pp. 124–128.

  A *qaṣīda* of 79 verses on Adam and Satan, eras in religious history, piety, etc.

Khayrkhwāh-i Harātī, Muḥammad Riḍā b. Khwāja Sulṭān Ḥusayn Ghūriyānī (d. after 960/1553), Persian Nizārī *dāʿī* and poet

- *Faṣl dar bayān-i shinākht-i imām*, ed. and English trans., Wladimir Ivanow, in his *Ismailitica*, in *Memoirs of the Asiatic Society of Bengal*,

8 (1922), pp. 3–49; 2nd ed., Ismaili Society Series B, no.3. Leiden: Published for the Ismaili Society by E.J. Brill, 1949. pp. xvi (English) + 28 (Persian); 3rd ed., Ismaili Society Series B, no. 11. Tehran: Ismaili Society, 1960. pp. 11 (English) + 44 (Persian). English trans., Wladimir Ivanow as *On the Recognition of the Imam.* Ismaili Society Series B, no.4. 2nd ed., Bombay: Published for the Ismaili Society by Thacker & Co., 1947. pp. xii + 59.

Composed around 952/1545, this work contains a summary of the author's views on the imamate and other Nizārī teachings of the Anjudān period.

- *Kalām-i pīr*, ed. and English trans., Wladimir Ivanow as *Kalami Pir: A Treatise on Ismaili Doctrine, also (wrongly) called Haft-Babi Shah Sayyid Nasir.* Islamic Research Association [Series], no. 4. Bombay: A.A.A. Fyzee, 1935. pp. lxviii (English) + 146 (English) + 117 (Persian).

This is apparently a plagiarized version of Abū Isḥāq Quhistānī's *Haft bāb*, wrongly attributed to Nāṣir-i Khusraw; *see* W. Ivanow, *Ismaili Literature*, pp. 142–143.

- *Taṣnīfāt-i Khayrkhwāh-i Harātī,* ed., Wladimir Ivanow. Ismaili Society Series A, no.13. Tehran: Ismaili Society, 1961. pp. 14 (English) + 150(Persian). Includes *Risāla-yi Khayrkhwāh-i Harātī*, pp. 1–75 (originally lithographed by Sayyid Munīr Badakhshānī as *Kitāb-i Khayrkhwāh-i Muwaḥḥid Waḥdat*, Bombay, 1333/1915), *Qiṭaʿāt*, pp. 77–111, and *Ashʿār-i Gharībī*, pp. 113–132.

In his poetry, Khayrkhwāh adopted the pen-name (*takhalluṣ*) of Gharībī, after Mustanṣir bi'llāh (III) also known as Gharīb Mīrzā (d. 904/1498), a contemporary Nizārī imam. In the *Risāla*, Khayrkhwāh expounds his ideas on the status and attributes of the ranks of *pīr* and *ḥujjat*, also providing autobiographical details and relating how he travelled to Anjudān to see the Nizārī imam.

al-Kirmānī, Ḥamīd al-Dīn Aḥmad b. ʿAbd Allāh (d. after 411/1020), Ismaili *dāʿī* in Persia and Iraq

- *al-Aqwāl al-dhahabiyya,* ed., Ṣalāḥ al-Ṣāwī, with an English introduction by S. Hossein Nasr. Imperial Iranian Academy of Philosophy, Publication no. 32. Tehran: Imperial Iranian Academy of Philosophy, 1397/1977. pp. 5 (English) + xxiii (Persian) + 142 (Arabic); ed., Muṣṭafā

Ghālib. Beirut: Dār Miḥyū, 1977. pp. 200; ed., ʿAbd al-Laṭīf al-ʿAbd, in his *al-Ṭibb al-rūḥānī li-Abī Bakr al-Rāzī: al-Aqwāl al-dhahabiyya li'l-Kirmānī wa-maʿahā al-munāẓarāt li-Abī Ḥātim al-Rāzī*. Cairo: Maktabat al-Nahḍa al-Miṣriyya, 1978, pp. 148–283. Selections, in *Rasā'il falsafiyya li-Abī Bakr Muḥammad ibn Zakariyyā' al-Rāzī*, ed., Paul Kraus. Universitatis Fouadi I Litterarum Facultatis Publicationum, Fasc. XXII. Cairo: n.p., 1939, pp. 7–13 and 313–316.

A work on the nature of the soul and prophethood refuting the Persian physician and philosopher Abū Bakr Muḥammad b. Zakariyyā' al-Rāzī's (d. 313/925) *al-Ṭibb al-rūḥānī*, which had been earlier refuted by Abū Ḥātim al-Rāzī (d. 322/934) in his *Aʿlām al-nubuwwa*.

- *Kitāb al-riyāḍ fi'l-ḥukm bayna'l-ṣādayn ṣāḥibay al-Iṣlāḥ wa'l-Nuṣra*, ed., ʿĀrif Tāmir. Silsilat al-makhṭūṭāt al-ʿArabiyya, 1. Beirut: Dār al-Thaqāfa, [1960]. pp. 253.

In this work, divided into ten *bāb*s, al-Kirmānī acts as an arbiter, from the point of view of the Fatimid Ismaili *daʿwa*, in a controversial theological debate among Muḥammad b. Aḥmad al-Nasafī (d. 332/943), Abū Ḥātim al-Rāzī (d. 322/934) and Abū Yaʿqūb al-Sijistānī (d. after 361/971), and preserves fragments of al-Nasafī's *Kitāb al-maḥṣūl* and al-Sijistānī's *Kitāb al-nuṣra*, which have not survived. In many instances, al-Kirmānī upholds the views of al-Rāzī, as expressed in his *Kitāb al-iṣlāḥ* which is extant, against those of al-Nasafī and al-Sijistānī.

- *Majmūʿat rasā'il al-Kirmānī*, ed., Muṣṭafā Ghālib. Beirut: al-Mu'assasa al-Jāmiʿiyya li'l-Dirāsāt wa'l-Nashr wa'l-Tawzīʿ, 1403/1983. pp. 209.

A collection of eleven short *Risāla*s, starting with *al-Durriyya* and ending with *al-Kāfiya*. The attribution of two other *Risāla*s usually included in this collection (*Khazā'in al-adilla* and *Risāla fi'l-radd ʿalā man yunkir al-ʿālam al-rūḥānī*) to al-Kirmānī are doubtful. For English summaries of these epistles, see H. Haji, *A Distinguished Dāʿī*, pp. 22–67.

- (i) *al-Risāla al-durriyya fī maʿnā al-tawḥīd wa'l-muwaḥḥid wa'l-muwaḥḥad* (pp. 13–34), together with *Risālat al-nuẓum fī muqābalat al-ʿawālim* (pp. 35–59), ed., Muḥammad Kāmil Ḥusayn. Silsilat makhṭūṭāt al-Fāṭimiyyīn, 7, 8. Cairo: Maṭbaʿat al-Jāmiʿa, [1952]. pp. 59; ed., M. Ghālib, in al-Kirmānī, *Majmūʿat rasā'il*, pp. 19–26. Excerpt, English trans., Faquir M. Hunzai as *al-Risāla al-durriyyah* (*The Brilliant Epistle*), in *APP*, pp. 192–200.

On the literal and esoteric meanings of *tawḥīd*.

- (ii) *Risālat al-nuẓum* (or *al-naẓm*) *fī muqābalat al-ʿawālim*, ed., M. Kāmil Ḥusayn, together with *al-Risāla al-durriyya* (pp. 35–59); ed., M. Ghālib, in al-Kirmānī, *Majmūʿat rasāʾil*, pp. 27–34.

  A brief treatment of correspondences among coexisting realms so as to reconcile multiplicity of the creation with *tawḥīd*.

- (iii) *al-Risāla al-raḍiyya fī jawāb man yaqūlu bi-qidam al-jawhar wa-ḥudūth al-ṣūra*, ed., M. Ghālib, in al-Kirmānī, *Majmūʿat rasāʾil*, pp. 35–42.

  A short epistle in refutation of those who hold that substance is eternal and form is temporal.

- (iv) *al-Risāla al-muḍīʾa fiʾl-amr waʾl-āmir waʾl-maʾmūr*, ed., M. Ghālib, in al-Kirmānī, *Majmūʿat rasāʾil*, pp. 43–60.

  A short treatise on the divine command, the commander and the commanded. Here, al-Kirmānī also refutes the doctrine of *amr* discussed by al-Sijistānī in the 28th chapter of his *Kitāb al-maqālīd*, which still remains in manuscript form.

- (v) *al-Risāla al-lāzima fī ṣawm shahr Ramaḍān wa-ḥīnihi*, ed., Muḥammad ʿAbd al-Qādir ʿAbd al-Nāṣir, in *Majallat Kulliyyat al-Ādāb, Jāmiʿat al-Qāhira/Bulletin of the Faculty of Arts, Cairo University*, 31 (1969), pp. 1–52; ed., M. Ghālib, in al-Kirmānī, *Majmūʿat rasāʾil*, pp. 61–80; ed. and Urdu trans., Muḥammad Ḥasan al-Aʿẓamī, in his *Niẓām al-ṣawm ʿinda al-Fāṭimiyyīn*, pp. 18–54.

  An epistle on the suitable time for starting the fast of Ramaḍān, defending the Fatimid practice of relying on astronomical calculations in preference to sighting of the new moon.

- (vi) *Risālat al-rawḍa fiʾl-azal waʾl-azalī waʾl-azaliyya*, ed., M. Ghālib, in al-Kirmānī, *Majmūʿat rasāʾil*, pp. 81–91.

  On the literal and esoteric meanings of terms related to eternity. In this epistle, al-Kirmānī also refutes al-Sijistānī's ideas as elaborated in the 21st chapter of his *Kitāb al-maqālīd*.

- (vii) *al-Risāla al-zāhira fī jawāb masāʾil waʾl-naẓar fī abwāb al-rasāʾil*, ed., M. Ghālib, in al-Kirmānī, *Majmūʿat rasāʾil*, pp. 92–101.

  A series of questions and answers in refutation of a work wrongly attributed to al-Sijistānī.

- (viii) *al-Risāla al-ḥāwiya fiʾl-layl waʾl-nahār*, ed., M. Ghālib, in al-Kirmānī, *Majmūʿat rasāʾil*, pp. 102–112.

A short work on esoteric interpretation (*ta'wīl*) of night and day, written in 399/1009, in reply to a question raised by al-Kirmānī's deputy in Jīruft, Kirmān.

- (ix) *Risālat mabāsim al-bishārāt bi'l-imām al-Ḥākim bi-Amr Allāh*, ed., Muḥammad Kāmil Ḥusayn, in his *Ṭā'ifat al-Durūz*, pp. 55–74; ed., M. Ghālib, in al-Kirmānī, *Majmū'at rasā'il*, pp. 113–133; ed., M. Ghālib, in his *al-Ḥarakāt al-bāṭiniyya fi'l-Islām*, pp. 205–233.

  Composed in 405–406/1014–1016 in Egypt, this work deals with the imamate in general and al-Ḥākim's imamate (386–411/996–1021) in particular.

- (x) *al-Risāla al-wā'iẓa 'an masā'il al-māriq min al-dīn Ḥasan al-Farghānī al-Ajda'* (also as *al-Risāla al-wā'iẓa fi'l-radd 'alā'l-Akhram al-Farghānī*), ed., Muḥammad Kāmil Ḥusayn. Silsilat makhṭūṭāt al-Fāṭimiyyīn, 6, in *Majallat Kulliyyat al-Ādāb, Jāmi'at Fu'ād al-Awwal/ Bulletin of the Faculty of Arts, Fouad I University*, 14, part 1 (1952), pp. 1–29; ed., M. Ghālib, in al-Kirmānī, *Majmū'at rasā'il*, pp. 134–147.

  This epistle, written in 408/1017 in Egypt, aims to refute the views of al-Ḥasan al-Akhram (d. 408/1018), one of the founders of the Druze movement, on al-Ḥākim's divinity.

- (xi) *al-Risāla al-kāfiya fi'l-radd 'alā'l-Hārūnī al-Ḥusaynī*, ed., M. Ghālib, in al-Kirmānī, *Majmū'at rasā'il*, pp. 148–182.

  A polemical treatise written against the Zaydī Imam Abu'l-Ḥusayn al-Mu'ayyad bi'llāh Aḥmad al-Buṭḥānī al-Hārūnī (d. 411/1020). It was sent to al-Kirmānī's deputy, 'Abd al-Malik al-Māzīnī, in Kirmān, Persia.

- *al-Maṣābīḥ fī ithbāt al-imāma*, ed., Muṣṭafā Ghālib. Beirut: Manshūrāt Ḥamad, 1969. pp. 155. Extract, in P. Kraus, "Hebräische und syrische Zitate", pp. 243–263; reprinted in Kraus, *Alchemie, Ketzerei*, pp. 3–23.

  A treatise on the imamate in two parts (*maqāla*s), each subdivided into seven *maṣābīḥ*s. The ultimate aim of this treatise, composed around 404/1013, is to defend the legitimacy of al-Ḥākim's imamate. This work also contains quotations from Hebrew and Syriac writings in Arabic script.

- *Rāḥat al-'aql*, ed., Muḥammad Kāmil Ḥusayn and Muḥammad Muṣṭafā Ḥilmī. Ismaili Society Series C, no.1; Silsilat makhṭūṭāt al-Fāṭimiyyīn, 9. Leiden: Published for the Ismaili Society by E.J. Brill, 1953. pp. 45 + 438 + 48 (English index prepared by W. Ivanow); ed.,

Muṣṭafā Ghālib. Beirut: Dār al-Andalus, 1967. pp. 591; 2nd ed., Beirut: Dār al-Andalus, 1983. pp. 591. Russian trans., A.V. Smirnov as *Uspokoenie razuma*. Moscow: Ladomir, 1995. pp. 510. Excerpt, English trans., Daniel C. Peterson as *Rāḥat al-ʿaql, Repose of the Intellect*, in *APP*, pp. 175–192.

Completed in 411/1020 for advanced adepts, this work contains al-Kirmānī's metaphysical system, representing a unique syncretic tradition within the Iranian school of philosophical Ismailism. Al-Kirmānī was fully acquainted with Aristotelian and Neoplatonic philosophies as well as the metaphysical systems of Muslim philosophers, notably al-Fārābī (d. 339/950), known as the 'second teacher' (*al-muʿallim al-thānī*) of philosophy in the Islamic world after Aristotle, and Ibn Sīnā (d. 428/1037), or Avicenna of the medieval Europeans. He harmonized Ismaili theology with a diversity of philosophical traditions in elaborating his own system expounded in the *Rāḥat al-ʿaql*, which is comprised of seven ramparts (*suwar*s). In his cosmology, al-Kirmānī replaced the Neoplatonic dyad of intellect (*ʿaql*) and soul (*nafs*) in the spiritual world, adopted by al-Sijistānī and other Ismaili predecessors, by a system of ten separate intellects, in partial adaptation of al-Fārābī's school of philosophy. Al-Kirmānī's cosmology was later adopted by the Ṭayyibī *daʿwa* in Yaman.The *Rāḥat al-ʿaql* and its sources are thoroughly studied in D. de Smet, *La Quiétude de l'intellect*.

- *Risālat usbūʿ dawr al-satr*, ed., ʿĀrif Tāmir, in his *Arbaʿ rasāʾil Ismāʿīliyya*, pp. 59–66.

The attribution of this short work, on the seven cycles of prophethood, to al-Kirmānī is probably incorrect.

- *al-Risāla al-waḍīʾa fī maʿālim al-dīn wa-uṣūlihi*, ed., Muḥammad ʿĪsā al-Ḥarīrī. Kuwait: Dār al-Qalam, 1407/1987. pp. 231.

A short treatise on the necessity of maintaining balance between the exoteric (*ẓāhir*) and esoteric (*bāṭin*) dimensions of religion. The first part deals with prophethood, imamate, the creation, religious hierarchy, esoteric interpretation of the *sharīʿa*, while the second part relates to the pillars of Islam.

al-Mahdī bi'llāh, Abū Muḥammad ʿAbd Allāh (ʿUbayd Allāh) (d. 322/934), Fatimid caliph and Ismaili imam

- *Kitāb arsalahu al-Mahdī ilā nāḥiyat al-Yaman,* as preserved in Jaʿfar b. Manṣūr al-Yaman's *Kitāb al-farā'iḍ wa-ḥudūd al-dīn,* ed. and English trans., Ḥusayn F. al-Hamdānī as *On the Genealogy of Fatimid Caliphs* (*Statement on Mahdī's Communication to the Yemen on the Real and Esoteric Names of his Hidden Predecessors*). Publications of the American University at Cairo, School of Oriental Studies, Occasional Paper no.1. Cairo: American University at Cairo, 1958. pp. 14 (Arabic) + 22 (English). A more complete and literal English trans., in A. Hamdani and F. de Blois, "A Re-examination of al-Mahdī's Letter", pp. 175–178.

In this letter, sent to the Ismaili community in Yaman, al-Mahdī explains his genealogy and claim to the imamate as well as the *taqiyya* practices used by the central leaders of the early Ismaili *daʿwa*. The text of this letter, in paraphrased form, is preserved in Jaʿfar b. Manṣūr al-Yaman's *Kitāb al-farā'iḍ wa-ḥudūd al-dīn*, still in manuscript form.

al-Majdūʿ, Ismāʿīl b. ʿAbd al-Rasūl (d. 1183 or 1184/1769–71), Dā'ūdī Bohra author in India

- *Fahrasat al-kutub wa'l-rasā'il,* ed., ʿAlī Naqī Munzavī. Manshūrāt Maktabat al-Asadī bi-Ṭihrān, 9. Tehran: Tehran University Printing House, 1344 Sh./1966. pp. 419.

Divided into 12 chapters, this is the earliest known catalogue of Ismaili literature. Commonly known as the *Fihrist al-Majdūʿ*, it summarizes some 250 Ismaili works, and it served as the basis for W. Ivanow's *A Guide to Ismaili Literature.*

al-Malījī, Abu'l-Qāsim ʿAbd al-Ḥākim b. Wahb (fl. 5th/11th century), Fatimid chief *qāḍī* in Egypt

- *al-Majālis al-Mustanṣiriyya*, ed., Muḥammad Kāmil Ḥusayn. Silsilat makhṭūṭāt al-Fāṭimiyyīn, 1. Cairo: Dār al-Fikr al-ʿArabī, [1947]. pp. 229; ed., Muḥammad Zīnhum and Muḥammad ʿAzab. Cairo: Maktabat Madbūlī 1413/1992. pp. 223.

These 35 weekly lectures, containing sermons of al-Mustanṣir on different topics, were delivered by al-Malījī during 451/1059. Before Stern correctly identified the author of this work, in his "Cairo as the Centre of the Ismāʿīlī Movement", pp. 439–440, different individuals such as the Fatimid vizier Badr al-Jamālī (d. 487/1094) had been named as its author by various scholars.

Mazyad b. Ṣafwān b. al-Ḥasan al-Ḥillī al-Asadī, al-Amīr (d. 584/1188 or 592/1196), Syrian Nizārī poet

- *Dīwān*, ed., ʿĀrif Tāmir. Beirut: Dār al-Aḍwāʾ, 1418/1998. pp. 140.

  Originally belonging to the Banū Asad of Iraq before settling in Maṣyāf, the amir Mazyad's collected poems here are in the form of 33 *qaṣīda*s on a variety of ethical and religious subjects.

Manṣūr al-Yaman, *see* Ibn Ḥawshab

al-Muʾayyad fi'l-Dīn al-Shīrāzī, Abū Naṣr Hibat Allāh b. Abū ʿImrān Mūsā (d. 470/1078), Ismaili chief *dāʿī* and poet

- *al-Dawḥa,* ed., ʿĀrif Tāmir, in his *Thalāth rasāʾil Ismāʿīliyya*, pp. 35–52.

  A brief *qaṣīda* in defence of Ismailis, also containing esoteric interpretation (*taʾwīl*) of certain Ismaili teachings.

- *Dīwān al-Muʾayyad fi'l-Dīn dāʿī al-duʿāt,* ed., Muḥammad Kāmil Ḥusayn. Silsilat makhṭūṭāt al-Fāṭimiyyīn, 4. Cairo: Dār al-Kātib al-Miṣrī, 1949. pp. 372.

  Collected poems in praise of the Fatimid caliph-imams, also dealing with *tawḥīd*, esoteric interpretation of the Qur'an and other religious themes.

- *Khuṭba*, English trans., Jawad Muscati and Khan Bahadur A.M. Moulvi, in their *Life and Lectures of the Grand Missionary al-Muayyad-fid-Din al-Shirazi,* pp. 78–183; excerpt (pp. 174–178) reprinted in *APP*, pp. 281–290.

  Sermons on Paradise, the *walāya* of ʿAlī, *tawḥīd*, guidance of the imams and on certain *ḥadīth*s.

- *al-Majālis al-Muʾayyadiyya,* vols. 1 (*al-miʾa al-ūlā*) and 3 (*al-miʾa al-thālitha*), ed., Muṣṭafā Ghālib. Silsilat al-turāth al-Fāṭimī. Beirut: Dār al-Andalus, [1974] and 1984; vols. 1 and 2 (*al-miʾa al-thāniya*), ed.,

Ḥātim Ḥamīd al-Dīn. Bombay, 1395/1975 and Oxford, 1407/1986; vol. 1, ed., Muḥammad ʿAbd al-Ghaffār. Cairo: Maktabat Madbūlī, 1994. pp. 338. Selections: *Aḍwāʾ ʿalāʾl-rasāʾil al-mutabādala bayna dāʿī al-duʿāt al-Fāṭimī Hibat Allāh al-Shīrāzī, wa-Abiʾl-ʿAlāʾ al-Maʿarrī,* ed., ʿAlī Muḥammad Khalūf. Damascus: Dār Ḥūrān, 1996. pp. 95. For an abridged version of volume 1, *see* al-Ḥāmidī, Ḥātim b. Ibrāhīm. Selections, English trans., in Muscati and Moulvi, *Life and Lectures of the Grand Missionary al-Muayyad-fid-Din*, pp. 53–131.

Parts of a collection of eight volumes, with one hundred *majlis* in each volume. These lectures were delivered by al-Muʾayyad as the Ismaili *dāʿī al-duʿāt* as the *majālis al-ḥikma* at the Dār al-ʿIlm in Cairo. The lectures deal with a wide range of theological, philosophical and ethical issues as well as esoteric interpretation (*taʾwīl*) of the Qurʾan.

- *Sīrat al-Muʾayyad fiʾl-Dīn dāʿī al-duʿāt,* ed., Muḥammad Kāmil Ḥusayn. Silsilat makhṭūṭāt al-Fāṭimiyyīn, 5. Cairo: Dār al-Kātib al-Miṣrī, 1949. pp. 28 + 209; ed., ʿĀrif Tāmir as *Mudhakkirāt dāʿī duʿāt al-dawla al-Fāṭimiyya al-Muʾayyad fiʾl-Dīn Hibat Allāh ibn Abī ʿImrān Mūsā al-Shīrāzī.* Beirut: Muʾassasat ʿIzz al-Dīn, 1403/1983. pp. 228.

This is al-Muʾayyad's memoirs or autobiography covering the events of his life and times until around 450/1058; it also sheds particular light on al-Muʾayyad's role in the pro-Fatimid campaign of al-Basāsīrī in Iraq which culminated in the pronouncement of the *khuṭba* in Abbasid Baghdad in the name of the Fatimid al-Mustanṣir during 450–51/1058–59. Al-Muʾayyad's *Sīra* is paraphrased, summarized and studied in V. Klemm, *Memoirs of a Mission.*

Muḥammad ʿAlī b. Mullā Jīwābhāʾī Rāmpūrī (d. 1315 or 1316/1897–1899), Dāʾūdī Bohra functionary and historian in India

- *Mawsim-i bahār fī akhbār al-ṭāhirīn al-akhyār,* lithographed, Bombay: Maṭbaʿat Ḥaydarī Ṣafdarī, 1301–11/1884–93. 3 vols. (in Gujarati written in Arabic script). The first two volumes were reprinted in Bombay in 1335/1916–17 and thereafter; the third volume was reprinted only in the final decades of the twentieth century in Bombay.

A three-volume history of Ismailism, with volume two on the Ismaili imams until al-Ṭayyib, and volume three (completed in 1299/1882 and lithographed first soon afterwards) on the *daʿwa* in Yaman and

Gujarāt from its origins until the author's time. This history draws on the *Muntazaʿ al-akhbār* of Burhānpūrī and a number of earlier sources, some of which have not survived.

Muḥammad b. Saʿd (or Aḥmad) b. Dāʾūd al-Rafna (d. ca. 854/1450), Muḥammad-Shāhī Nizārī *dāʿī* in Syria

- *al-Risāla al-kāfiya,* ed., ʿĀrif Tāmir, in his *Khams rasāʾil Ismāʿīliyya,* pp. 89–97; reprinted in *Thalāth rasāʾil Ismāʿīliyya,* ed., ʿĀrif Tāmir, pp. 21–33.

  A brief treatise on Ismaili doctrine.

al-Muʿizz li-Dīn Allāh, Abū Tamīm Maʿadd (d. 365/975), Fatimid caliph and Ismaili imam

- *al-Munājāt aw adʿiyat al-ayyām al-sabʿa,* selections, ed. and French trans., S. Guyard, in his *Fragments relatifs à la doctrine des Ismaélîs,* in *Notices et Extraits des Manuscrits,* 22 (1874), text pp. 224–229, translation pp. 344–358; in Louis Massignon, *Recueil de textes inédits concernant l'histoire de la mystique en pays d'Islam.* Paris: P. Geuthner, 1929, p. 217. Selections with Urdu trans., in Zāhid ʿAlī, *Hamāre Ismāʿīlī madhhab,* pp. 90–96; also in Zāhid ʿAlī, *Taʾrīkh-i Fāṭimiyyīn,* vol. 2, pp. 254–264.

  A compilation of prayers, one for each day of the week. These prayers are traditionally attributed to al-Muʿizz.

- *al-Risāla al-Masīḥiyya,* excerpt, in Louis Massignon, *Recueil de textes inédits concernant l'histoire de la mystique en pays d'Islam.* Paris: P. Geuthner, 1929, pp. 215–217.

  This epistle is addressed to Bishop Paul of Damietta. The attribution of this work to al-Muʿizz may be doubtful.

- *Risālat al-Muʿizz ilā al-Ḥasan ibn Aḥmad al-Qarmaṭī,* as preserved by the Sharīf Abu'l-Ḥusayn Muḥammad b. ʿAlī, known as Akhū Muḥsin, quoted in al-Maqrīzī, *Ittiʿāẓ al-ḥunafāʾ,* ed., H. Bunz, pp. 133–143; ed., J. al-Shayyāl, 1948, pp. 251–265 (end of letter, pp. 200–201 in al-Shayyāl, 1967 ed., is missing in this edition); ed., J. al-Shayyāl, 1967, vol. 1, pp. 189–201; reprinted in *Akhbār al-Qarāmiṭa,* pp. 367–383; also in al-Walī, *al-Qarāmiṭa,* pp. 289–300; briefer versions are preserved in Ibn al-Dawādārī, *Kanz al-durar,* vol. 6, pp. 149–156; in al-Nuwayrī,

Nihāyat al-arab, vol. 25, pp. 308–311. French trans., in Silvestre de Sacy, *Exposé de la religion des Druzes*, vol. 1, introduction pp. 227–238.

The attribution of this letter to al-Muʿizz is doubtful. The author of this letter, sent to al-Ḥasan al-Aʿṣam around 363/973, reproaches the Qarmaṭī leader for having deviated from the creed of his forefathers. Al-Aʿṣam made this letter public and denounced the Fatimids before attacking Egypt in 363/974.

- *Sijill al-Muʿizz ilā Ḥalam (Jalam) ibn Shaybān*, as preserved in Idrīs ʿImād al-Dīn, *ʿUyūn al-akhbār*, ed., M. Ghālib, vol. 5, pp. 160–162; ed. and English trans., W. Ivanow, in his "Ismailis and Qarmatians", pp. 74–76, and in S.M. Stern, "Heterodox Ismāʿīlism", pp. 11–13, 26–27.

This *Sijill*, sent in 354/965 to the *dāʿī* of Sind, Ḥalam, who established an Ismaili state in Multān, explains the *taqiyya* practices of the early Ismaili imams before the foundation of the Fatimid state. This document, reasserting the ʿAlid genealogy of the Fatimid caliphs, represents the earliest Ismaili refutation of the myth of Ibn al-Qaddāḥ that portrayed a certain non-ʿAlid (ʿAbd Allāh b. Maymūn al-Qaddāḥ) as the progenitor of the Fatimid caliphs.

al-Mustanṣir bi'llāh, Abū Tamīm Maʿadd (d. 487/1094), Fatimid caliph and Ismaili imam

- *al-Sijillāt al-Mustanṣiriyya*, ed., ʿAbd al-Munʿim Mājid. Cairo: Dār al-Fikr al-ʿArabī, 1954. pp. 231. English summary, Ḥ.F. al-Hamdānī, in his "The Letters of al-Mustanṣir bi'llāh", pp. 307–324.

A collection of 66 *Sijill*s addressed, from 445/1053 to 489/1096, mainly by al-Mustanṣir to the Ṣulayḥids who propagated the Ismaili *daʿwa* in Yaman on behalf of the Fatimids. Ḥusayn F. al-Hamdānī has edited five additional *Sijillāt* in his *al-Ṣulayḥiyyūn*, pp. 302–307 and 319–320.

Mustanṣir bi'llāh [II] b. Muḥammad b. Islām Shāh (d. 885/1480), Nizārī imam

- *Pandiyāt-i jawānmardī*, ed. and English trans., Wladimir Ivanow as *Pandiyat-i Jawanmardi or "Advices of Manliness"*. Ismaili Society Series A, no.6. Leiden: Published for the Ismaili Society by E.J. Brill, 1953. pp. 19 (English) + 97 (English) + 102 (Persian).

Containing the sermons or religious admonitions of the thirty-second

(Qāsim-Shāhī) Nizārī imam, this is one of the earliest doctrinal works produced during the Anjudān revival in Persian Nizārī Ismailism. These sermons or advices (*pandiyāt*) to the true believers seeking exemplary standards of chivalry (*jawānmardī*) were evidently compiled by an anonymous Nizārī author during the imamate of Mustanṣir bi'llāh's son and successor ʿAbd al-Salām Shāh. The Nizārī Khojas, who have preserved Sindhī (Khojkī) and Gujarātī versions of the *Pandiyāt,* maintain that this book was sent to the Indian subcontinent for their religious guidance. This work preserves important evidence on Nizārī-Sufi relations during the early Anjudān period in Nizārī history.

Nāṣir-i Khusraw, Ḥakīm Abū Muʿīn Nāṣir b. Khusraw b. Ḥārith Qubādiyānī Marwazī (d. after 462/1070), Persian poet, traveller and Ismaili *dāʿī* in Khurāsān

- *Dīwān*, lithographed by Ibn al-Ḥusayn ʿAskar Urdūbādī. Tabrīz, 1280/1864. pp. 277; lithographed in Tehran, 1307/1889; lithographed by Zayn al-ʿĀbidīn al-Sharīf al-Ṣafawī. Tehran, 1314/1896. pp. 321 (together with *Safar-nāma*); lithographed in Tehran, 1318/1900; lithographed by Muḥammad Malik al-Kātib. Bombay, n.d. [1860?]. pp. 160 (together with *Savāniḥ-i ʿumrī*, pp. 2–14, and *Risāla dar taskhīr-i kavākib,* pp. 15–25); ed., Sayyid Naṣr Allāh Taqavī (1871–1947) et al., with an introduction by Ḥasan Taqīzāda (1878–1970). Tehran: Kitābkhāna-yi Tehran, 1304–7 Sh./1925–28. pp. 694 (together with *Rawshanāʾī-nāma, Saʿādat-nāma* and *Risāla dar javāb-i ...*); reprinted by Mahdī Suhaylī. Iṣfahān: Intishārāt-i Kitāb-furūshī-yi Ta'yīd, 1335 Sh./1956. pp. 8 + 96 + 694; reprinted by M. Darvīsh. Tehran: ʿIlmī, 1339 Sh./1960 (with subsequent reprints); ed., Mujtabā Mīnuvī and Mahdī Muḥaqqiq. Tehran: Dānishgāh-i Tehran, 1353 Sh./1974. pp. xxiii + 771; reprinted, Wisdom of Persia, 21. Tehran: McGill University, Institute of Islamic Studies, Tehran Branch; Tehran University, 1357 Sh./1978. pp. xxiii + 771; ed., Jaʿfar Shuʿār and Kāmil Aḥmad-Nizhād. Silsila intishārāt-i Nashr-i Qaṭra, 200. Tehran: Nashr-i Qaṭra, 1378 Sh./1999. pp. 769.

Partial editions and translations of the *Dīwān*

- *Diwan-i Nasir-i Khusraw, containing only the Portions Prescribed for the M.A. Examination of the Calcutta University,* ed., Āqā Muḥammad

Kāẓim Shīrāzī. Calcutta: University of Calcutta, 1926. pp. 100.

- *Pānzdah qaṣīda az Ḥakīm Nāṣir-i Khusraw Qubādiyānī*, ed., Mahdī Muḥaqqiq. Zabān va farhang-i Īrān, 63. Tehran: Ṭahūrī, 1340 Sh./1961. pp. 90; reprinted, 1341 Sh./1962 and later.
- *Barguzīda-yi ashʿār-i Nāṣir-i Khusraw*, with an introduction by Nāṣir ʿĀmilī. Tehran: Sāzimān-i Kitābhā-yi Jībī, 1344 Sh./1965. pp. 250.
- *Guzīda-yi qaṣāʾid-i Nāṣir-i Khusraw*, ed., Jaʿfar Shuʿār. Tehran: Nashr-i Nāshir, 1363 Sh./1964. pp. 262.
- *Gulchine az devoni ashʿor*, ed., Kamol Ainī. Stalinobod: Nashriyoti davlatii Tojikiston, 1957. pp. 179 (Persian text in Cyrillic script).
- Partial English trans., Edward G. Browne, in his "Nasir-i-Khusraw, Poet, Traveller, and Propagandist", pp. 313–352.
- Partial English trans., Peter L. Wilson and Gholam Reza Aavani as *Forty Poems from the Divan*. Imperial Iranian Academy of Philosophy, Publication no. 31. Tehran: Imperial Iranian Academy of Philosophy, 1977. pp. 144; excerpt (pp. 31–43) reprinted in *APP*, pp. 329–340.
- Partial English trans., Annemarie Schimmel as *Make a Shield from Wisdom: Selected Verses from Nāṣir-i Khusraw's Dīvān*. London: Kegan Paul International for The Institute of Ismaili Studies, 1993, pp. 44–96; reprinted, London: I.B. Tauris in association with The Institute of Ismaili Studies, 2001, pp. 44–96.
- Partial Urdu trans., Fidā ʿAlī Īthār Hunzaʾī Fāḍil as *Javāhir-i ḥikmat: muntakhab az dīvān-i ashʿār-i Sayyidnā Pīr Nāṣir-i Khusraw-i ʿAlavī*. Karachi: H.R.H. The Aga Khan Ismailia Association [for] Pakistan, 1976. pp. 103.

Comprising more than 10,000 verses (*bayts*), the poems collected in Nāṣir-i Khusraw's *Dīwān* are primarily odes composed in the *qaṣīda* form. They relate to a wide range of ethical, theological and philosophical themes; several *qaṣīda*s are autobiographical.

Other works by Nāṣir-i Khusraw

- *Gushāyish va rahāyish*, ed., Saʿīd Nafīsī (1895–1966). Ismaili Society Series A, no.5. Leiden: Published for the Ismaili Society by E.J. Brill, 1950. pp. xix (English) + 125 (Persian); 2nd ed., Ismaili Society Series A, no.11. Tehran: Ismaili Society, 1961. pp. 108; ed. and English trans., Faquir M. Hunzai, with an introduction and commentary by Parviz

Morewedge as *Knowledge and Liberation: A Treatise on Philosophical Theology*. London: I.B. Tauris in association with The Institute of Ismaili Studies, 1998. pp. xii (English) + 132 (English) + 92 (Persian); excerpt (pp. 24–53) reprinted in *APP*, pp. 311–329. Italian trans., Pio Filippani-Ronconi as *Il libro dello scioglimento e della liberazione*. Naples: Istituto Universitario Orientale di Napoli, 1959. pp. xxix + 102.

This concise work represents Nāṣir-i Khusraw's responses to a series of thirty questions on theological and philosophical topics, with special reference to the human soul, its relation to the world of nature and its quest for salvation.

- *Khwān al-ikhwān*, ed., Yaḥyā al-Khashshāb. Cairo: Institut Français d'Archéologie Orientale, 1359/1940. pp. xxvi + 265; ed., ʿAlī Qavīm. Tehran: Intishārāt-i Kitābkhāna-yi Bārānī, 1338 Sh./1959. pp. 14 + 294.

Divided into 100 chapters, this is another work on philosophical theology. Here, Nāṣir-i Khusraw paraphrases many of the ideas found in Abū Yaʿqūb al-Sijistānī's *Kitāb al-yanābīʿ*.

- *Kitāb jāmiʿ al-ḥikmatayn*, ed., Henry Corbin (1903–1978) and Muḥammad Muʿīn (1918–1971) as *Kitab-e Jamiʿ al-Hikmatain. Le livre réunissant les deux sagesses, ou harmonie de la philosophie Grecque et de la théosophie Ismaélienne*. Bibliothèque Iranienne, 3. Tehran: Département d'Iranologie de l'Institut Franco-Iranien; Paris: A. Maisonneuve, 1953. pp. 144 (French) + 348 (Persian) + 18 (Persian). Arabic trans., Ibrāhīm al-Dasūqī Shatā, *Jāmiʿ al-ḥikmatayn*. Silsilat al-nuṣūṣ al-falsafiyya, 5. Cairo: Dār al-Thaqāfa, 1974. pp. 432. French trans., Isabelle de Gastines as *Le livre réunissant les deux sagesses* (*Kitāb-e Jāmiʿ al-Ḥikmatayn*). Paris: Fayard, 1990. pp. 339. Selection, English trans., Latimah Parvin Peerwani as *Kitāb jāmiʿ al-ḥikmatayn*, *The Sum of the Two Wisdoms*, in *APP*, pp. 293–311.

This is a commentary, on Khwāja Abu'l-Haytham Jurjānī's *Qaṣīda*, composed by Nāṣir-i Khusraw in 462/1070 at the request of his patron and amir of Badakhshān, Abu'l-Maʿālī ʿAlī b. al-Asad. In this, the latest known work of Nāṣir-i Khusraw, the author attempts to harmonize the "two wisdoms" (*ḥikmatayn*), philosophy and religion, or more specifically Ismaili gnosis.

- *Rawshanāʾī-nāma*, ed. and German trans., Hermann Ethé, in his "Nâsir Chusrau's Rûśanâinâma oder Buch der Erleuchtung", in *ZDMG*,

33 (1879), pp. 645–665; 34(1880), pp. 428–464, 617–642; 36 (1882), pp. 96–106; ed., Sayyid Munīr Badakhshānī, together with Khayrkhwāh-i Harātī's *Risāla*, under the title of *Kitāb-i Khayrkhwāh-i Muwaḥḥid Waḥdat*, lithographed, Bombay, 1333/1915. pp. 52; ed., M. Ghanīzāda, together with *Safar-nāma*. Berlin: Kaviani, 1341/1922, pp. 36; ed., N. Taqavī et al., in Nāṣir-i Khusraw's *Dīwān*, pp. 508–542; ed., Aleksandr A. Semenov, "Shugnansko-ismailitskaya redaktsiya 'Knigi sveta' Nasïr-i Khosrova" in *Zapiski kollegii vostokovedov*, 5 (1930), pp. 589–610; ed. and Urdu trans., Naṣīr al-Dīn Naṣīr Hunzā'ī as *Nūr-i ʿirfān, yaʿnī tarjama-yi Rawshanā'ī-nāma*. Karachi: The Aga Khan Ismailia Association [for] Pakistan, 1976. pp. 99.

Composed around 440/1048, this *mathnawī* poem deals with *tawḥīd*, soul (*nafs*), and a number of other theological as well as ethical themes.

- *Risāla dar javāb-i navad va yak faqara as'ala-yi falsafī va manṭiqī va ṭabīʿī va naḥvī va dīnī va ta'wīlī*, ed., N. Taqavī et al., in Nāṣir-i Khusraw's *Dīwān*, pp. 561–583, with subsequent reprints.

  An abridged version of Nāṣir Khusraw's *Jāmiʿ al-ḥikmatayn*.

- *Risāla dar taskhīr-i kavākib*, lithographed, together with the spurious *Savāniḥ-i ʿumrī*, pp. 2–14, and the *Dīwān*. Bombay, n.d. [1860?], pp. 15–25.

  The attribution of this brief astronomical treatise in seven chapters (*faṣls*) to Nāṣir-i Khusraw is very doubtful.

- *Saʿādat-nāma*, ed. and French trans., Edmond Fagnan, in his "Le livre de la félicité par Nâçir ed-Dîn Khosroû", in *ZDMG*, 34 (1880), pp. 643–674; 36 (1882), pp. 96–114; ed., Sayyid Munīr Badakhshānī, together with *Rawshanā'ī-nāma* and Khayrkhwāh-i Harātī's *Risāla*, under the title of *Kitāb-i Khayrkhwāh-i Muwaḥḥid Waḥdat*, lithographed, Bombay, 1333/1915, pp. 53–78; ed., M. Ghanīzāda, together with *Safar-nāma* and *Rawshanā'ī-nāma*. Berlin: Kaviani, 1341/1922, pp. 18; ed., N. Taqavī et al., in *Dīwān*, pp. 543–561, and subsequent reprints. English trans., George M. Wickens, in his "The Saʿādatnāmah attributed to Nāṣir-i Khusrau", *Islamic Quarterly*, 2 (1955), pp. 117–132, 206–221.

  This *Saʿādat-nāma* is wrongly attributed to Nāṣir-i Khusraw. It was apparently composed by another Nāṣir, better known as Sharīf-i Iṣfahānī, who died in 735/1334.

- *Safar-nāma*, ed. and French trans., Charles Schefer (1820–1898) as

Sefer Nameh. Relation du voyage de Nassiri Khosrau en Syrie, en Palestine, en Égypte, en Arabie et en Perse, pendent les années de l'hégire 437–444 (1035–1042). Publications de l'École des Langues Orientales Vivantes, 2e série, I. Paris: E. Leroux, 1881. pp. lviii (French) + 348 (French) + 97 (Persian); reprinted, Amsterdam: Philo Press, 1970; lithographed by Khwāja Alṭāf Ḥusayn Ḥālī. Delhi, 1299/1882. pp. 136; lithographed by Muḥammad Malik al-Kātib. Bombay, 1309/1891–92. pp. 76; lithographed by Zayn al-ʿĀbidīn al-Sharīf al-Ṣafawī. Tehran, 1312/1894–95. pp. 261; lithographed by Zayn al-ʿĀbidīn al-Sharīf al-Ṣafawī. Tehran, 1314/1896. pp. 82 (together with *Dīwān*); ed., Maḥmūd Ghanīzāda. Berlin: Kaviani, 1341/1922. pp. 151 (together with *Rawshanāʾī-nāma* and *Saʿādat-nāma*); ed., ʿAlī Qavīm. Tehran: n. p., 1335 Sh./1956. pp. 112; ed., Muḥammad Dabīr Siyāqī. Tehran: Zavvār, 1335 Sh./1956. pp. xxxii + 156; reprinted, Zabān va farhang-i Īrān, 40. Tehran: Ṭahūrī, 1344 Sh./1965. pp. 169; 4th ed., by Muḥammad Dabīr Siyāqī. Tehran: Anjuman-i Āthār-i Millī, 1354 Sh./1975. pp. xlvi + 400; 5th ed., by M. Dabīr Siyāqī. Tehran: Zavvār, 2536 [1356 Sh.]/1977. pp. xxxxvi + 400; ed., Vaḥīd Dāmghānī. Tehran: Farāhānī, 1344 Sh./1965. pp. 153; ed., Nādir Vazīnpūr. Majmūʿa-yi sukhan-i Pārsī, 3. Tehran: Kitābhā-yi Jībī, 1350 Sh./1971. pp. xiv + 190; ed., Aḥmad Ibrāhīmī. Tehran: Vizārat Farhang va Hunar, 1355 Sh./1976. pp. 145; special edition produced by Shams al-Dīn Mīr Fakhrāʾī, in the handwriting of the calligrapher Kaykhusraw Khurūsh. Tehran: n.p., 1361 Sh./ 1982. pp. 122; ed., Jaʿfar Shuʿār as *Taḥlīl-i Safar-nāma-yi Nāṣir-i Khusraw*. Tehran: Nashr-i Qaṭra, 1371 Sh./1992. pp. 242. Persian text, based on Ghanīzāda's edition, transcribed in Cyrillic, as *Safarnoma*. Dushanbe, 1970.

- Translations of the *Safar-nāma*: Arabic trans., Yaḥyā al-Khashshāb, *Safarnāma*. Maṭbūʿāt Maʿhad al-Lughāt al-Sharqiyya, Kulliyyat al-Ādāb, Jāmiʿat Fuʾād al-Awwal. Cairo: Lajnat al-Taʾlīf waʾl-Tarjama waʾl-Nashr, 1364/1945. pp. 135; 2nd ed., Beirut: Dār al-Kitāb al-Jadīd, 1970. pp. 182; excerpt, in *Akhbār al-Qarāmiṭa*, ed., Suhayl Zakkar, pp. 193–199. English trans., Wheeler M. Thackston, Jr., as *Nāṣer-e Khosraw's Book of Travels (Safarnāma)*. Persian Heritage Series, 36. Albany, NY: State University of New York Press, 1986. pp. xii + 135; reprinted, with the Persian text, Bibliotheca Iranica, Intellectual Traditions Series, no. 6. Costa Mesa, CA: Mazda Publishers, 2001. pp. xv + 172. Partial English trans., Guy Le Strange (1854–1933) as *Diary of a*

Journey Through Syria and Palestine. Palestine Pilgrims' Text Society, Library, vol. IV, no. 1. London: [Palestine Pilgrims' Text Society], 1893. pp. xiv + 72. German trans., Manfred Mayrhofer as *Safarnāme: Das Reisetagebuch des persischen Dichters Nāṣir-i Husrau*. Vergleichende Sprachwissenschaft, 5. Graz: Leykam, 1993. pp. x + 132. German trans., Seyfeddin Najmabadi and Siegfried Weber as *Safarname. Ein Reisebericht aus dem Orient des 11. Jahrhunderts*. Munich: Diederichs, 1993. pp.187. Russian trans., Evgeniy Bertel's as *Nasir-i Khosrov: Kniga puteshestviya*. Leningrad, 1933. pp. 206. Selections, in Tajik trans., A. Adalis as *Khisrou Nosir: Izbrannoe*. Stalinabad, 1949. Turkish trans., Abd al-Wahab Tarzi, *Sefername*. Istanbul: Milli egitim basimevi, 1950. pp. 28 + 268. Urdu trans., Muḥammad Tharvat Allāh, *Safarnāma*. Lucknow, 1937. Urdu trans., ʿAbd al-Razzāq Kānīpūr, *Safarnāma*. Delhi: Anjuman-i Taraqī Urdu, 1941. pp. 15 + 223.

The *Safar-nāma* is the account of Nāṣir-i Khusraw's seven-year journey (437–444/1045–1052) to many parts of Central Asia, Persia, Near East, and Fatimid Egypt, where he furthered his education as an Ismaili *dāʿī*. He presents a vivid account of the splendour of Fatimid Cairo, in the reign of al-Mustanṣir, with its royal palaces, gates, gardens and shops.

- *Shish faṣl, yā Rawshanāʾī-nāma-yi nathr*, ed. and English trans., Wladimir Ivanow. Ismaili Society Series B, no. 6. Leiden: Published for the Ismaili Society by E.J. Brill, 1949. pp. 111 (English) + 47 (Persian).

  A short Ismaili treatise on *tawḥīd*, God's word (*kalima*), the soul (*nafs*), the intellect (*ʿaql*), *nāṭiq*, *asās*, *imām*, and reward and punishment in the hereafter.

- *Wajh-i dīn*, ed., Maḥmūd Ghanīzāda and Muḥammad Qazwīnī. Berlin: Kaviani, 1343/1924. pp. 304; reprinted, Zabān va farhang-i Īrān, 54, Tehran: Ṭahūrī, 1348 Sh./1969. pp. 304; ed., Gholam Reza Aavani with an English introduction by S. Hossein Nasr. Imperial Iranian Academy of Philosophy, Publication no. 34. Tehran: Imperial Iranian Academy of Philosophy, 1398/1977. pp. xvi + 362. Urdu trans., Naṣīr al-Dīn Naṣīr Hunzāʾī, *Vajh-i dīn*. Gilgit, Hunza: Dār al-Ḥikma al-Ismāʿīliyya, n.d. 2 vols. Urdu selections, Naṣīr al-Dīn Naṣīr Hunzāʾī, *Intikhāb az Vajh-i dīn*. Karachi: The Aga Khan Ismaili Association [for] Pakistan, 1976. pp. 132. Partial Russian trans. (covering the eleventh chapter), in Aleksandr Semenov, *K dogmatike pamirskogo ismailizma, XI glava "Litsa veri" Nasïr-i Khosrova*. Tashkent, 1926. pp. xiv + 52.

Divided into 51 sections (*guftārs*), this work contains esoteric interpretations of a range of religious commandments such as prayer, fasting, *ḥajj*, etc. This is Nāṣir-i Khusraw's major work on *ta'wīl*, preserved and read widely by the Nizārī Ismailis of Central Asia.

- *Zād al-musāfirīn*, ed., Muḥammad Badhl al-Raḥmān. Berlin: Kaviani, 1341/1923. pp. 520; ed., 'Alī Qavīm. Tehran: n.p., 1338 Sh./1960. pp. 322. Arabic trans., Yaḥyā al-Khashshāb, *Zād al-musāfirīn*. Cairo, 1364/1945.

  Composed in 453/1061, this is one of Nāṣir-i Khusraw's most important philosophical works dealing with a variety of metaphysical topics, with special reference to the voyage of the soul from the physical world in quest of salvation to the spiritual world. Here, Nāṣir also refutes the transmigration of souls (*tanāsukh*).

al-Nīsābūrī, Aḥmad b. Ibrāhīm (or Muḥammad) (d. after 386/996), Persian Ismaili *dā'ī* and author

- *Istitār al-imām wa-tafarruq al-du'āt fi'l-jazā'ir li-ṭalabihi*, ed., Wladimir Ivanow, in *Majallat Kulliyyat al-Ādāb,al-Jāmi'a al-Miṣriyya/ Bulletin of the Faculty of Arts, University of Egypt*, 4, part 2 (1936), pp. 93–107; ed., Suhayl Zakkār, in his *Akhbār al-Qarāmiṭa*, pp. 111–132. English trans., W. Ivanow, in his *Ismaili Tradition*, pp. 157–183.

  An important historical source, authorized by the Fatimids themselves, this work deals with the settlement of the early Ismaili Imam 'Abd Allāh in Salamiyya in the 3rd/9th century, and the eventful journey of 'Abd Allāh al-Mahdī, another early imam and the future founder of the Fatimid state, from Syria to North Africa.

- *Ithbāt al-imāma*, ed., Muṣṭafā Ghālib. Beirut: Dār al-Andalus, 1404/1984. pp. 94; ed. and English trans., Arzina R. Lalani as *Degrees of Excellence: A Fatimid Treatise on Leadership in Islam*. Ismaili Texts and Translations Series. London: I.B. Tauris in association with The Institute of Ismaili Studies, forthcoming.

  Composed in the reign of the Fatimid caliph-imam al-Ḥākim (386–411/996–1021), this short treatise argues for the legitimacy of the imamate and its necessity. Defining the imamate as the foundation of religion, the author resorts to a variety of arguments for establishing his thesis, ranging from the ten categories of the philosophers to several metaphors from minerals, plants and animals.

- *al-Risāla al-mūjaza al-kāfiya fī adab al-duʿāt*, facsimile ed., V. Klemm, in her *Die Mission des fāṭimidischen Agenten*, pp. 205–277. Summary English trans., V. Klemm, in her *Memoirs of a Mission*, Appendix 2, pp. 117–127.

  This work, on the attributes and functions of an ideal *dāʿī* which has not survived directly, is preserved at the end of Ḥātim b. Ibrāhīm al-Ḥāmidī's *Tuḥfat al-qulūb*, still in manuscript form, and also in the second volume of al-Bharūchī's *Kitāb al-azhār*.

Nīshāpūrī, Muḥammad b. Surkh (fl. 4th/10th century), Persian Ismaili author

- *Sharḥ i qaṣīda-yi Fārsī-yi Khwāja Abu'l-Haytham Aḥmad b. Ḥasan Jurjānī* (*Commentaire de la qasida Ismaélienne d'Abu'l-Haitham Jorjani*), ed., Henry Corbin and Muḥammad Muʿīn. Bibliothèque Iranienne, 6. Tehran: Département d'Iranologie de l'Institut Franco-Iranien; Paris: A. Maisonneuve, 1955. pp. 113 (French) + 125 (Persian) + 12 (Persian).

  This is another commentary using Ismaili *ta'wīl*, other than Nāṣir-i Khusraw's much more detailed *Jāmiʿ al-ḥikmatayn*, on Khwāja Abu'l-Haytham Jurjānī's *Qaṣīda* by one of his disciples.

Nizārī Quhistānī, Ḥakīm Saʿd al-Dīn b. Shams al-Dīn (d. 720/1320), Nizārī poet and *dāʿī* in Persia

- *Dastūr-nāma*, ed. and Russian trans., Evgeniy Bertel's, in *Vostochnïy Sbornik* (Leningrad), 1 (1926), pp. 37–104; also in Nizārī's *Dīwān*, ed., Maẓāhir Muṣaffā, vol. 1, pp. 257–299.

  Composed in 710/1310, this *mathnawī* poem of 576 verses (*bayts*) contains many Ismaili ideas.

- *Dīwān*, ed., Maẓāhir Muṣaffā and presented by Maḥmūd Rafīʿī, based on ten manuscripts as well as the doctoral thesis of Sayyid ʿAlī Riḍā Mujtahidzāda. Tehran: Intishārāt-i ʿIlmī, 1371–73 Sh./1992–94. 2 vols.

  Containing more than 10,000 verses (*bayts*) in *ghazal* form, Nizārī's collected poems contain numerous Ismaili ideas expressed in Sufi terminologies.

- *Safar-nāma*, excerpts, in Chingiz G.A. Bayburdi, *Zhizn' i tvorchestvo Nizārī*. Selections, English trans., in N. Eboo Jamal, *Surviving the*

Mongols (with the original verses in the Persian translation of N. Eboo Jamal's *Surviving the Mongols*, tr., F. Badra'ī, as *Baqā-yi baʿd az Mughūl*).

A *mathnawī* poem of 1200 verses (*bayts*) describing Nizārī's two-year (678–681/1280–1282) journey through Persia and Transcaucasia. This versified travelogue was evidently completed before Nizārī's appointment in 694/1294 as court poet to ʿAlī Shāh, the Mihrabānid governor of Quhistān in eastern Persia.

al-Nuʿmān b. Muḥammad b. Manṣūr al-Tamīmī al-Qayrawānī al-Maghribī, al-Qāḍī Abū Ḥanīfa (d. 363/974), Ismaili chief *dāʿī* and Fatimid chief *qāḍī*

- *Daʿā'im al-Islām fī dhikr al-ḥalāl wa'l-ḥarām wa'l-qaḍāyā wa'l-aḥkām*, ed., Āṣaf b. ʿAlī Aṣghar Fayḍī (Asaf A.A. Fyzee). Cairo: Dār al-Maʿārif, 1951–61. 2 vols; reprinted, Cairo, 1963–67. 2 vols; ed., ʿĀrif Tāmir. Beirut: Dār al-Aḍwā', 1416/1995. 2 vols. English trans., Asaf A. A. Fyzee, completely revised and annotated by Ismail K. Poonawala, as *The Pillars of Islam:* Volume I, *Acts of Devotion and Religious Observances*. New Delhi: Oxford University Press, 2002. pp. xxxiii + 558. Persian trans., ʿAbd Allāh Umīdvār as *Tarjama-yi Kitāb-i Daʿā'im al-Islām*. Tehran: al-Ḥājj Sayyid Manṣūr Nādirī and Mu'assasa-yi Maṭbūʿātī-yi Ismāʿīliyān, 1372 Sh./1993. 2 vols. Urdu trans., Yūnus Shakīb Mubārakpūrī as *Daʿā'im al-Islām*. Surat: Idāra-yi Adabiyyāt-i Fāṭimī, 1964–67. 2 vols.

- Selections from the *Daʿā'im al-Islām*: *Kitāb al-jihād*, ed., Āṣaf b. ʿAlī Aṣghar Fayḍī. Cairo: Dār al-Maʿārif, 1370/1951. pp. 23 (English) + 70 (Arabic). English trans., Gerald G. Salinger, in his "The *Kitāb al-Jihād* from Qāḍī Nuʿmān's *Daʿā'im al-Islām*" (Ph.D. thesis, Columbia University, 1953), pp. 1–107; also in Gerard G. Salinger, "A Muslim Mirror for Princes", *MW*, 46 (1956), pp. 24–39. *Kitāb al-waṣāyā*, ed. and English trans., A.A.A. Fyzee as *The Ismaili Law of Wills*. London, etc.: Published for the University of Bombay, H. Milford, Oxford University Press, 1933. pp. vii + 94. *Kitāb al-walāya*, English trans., A.A.A. Fyzee as *The Book of Faith*. Bombay: Nichiketa Publications, 1974. pp. xix + 116.

Commissioned by the Fatimid caliph-imam al-Muʿizz and supervised closely by him, the *Da'ā'im al-Islām* was composed around 349/960 in two volumes, with volume one on *'ibādāt* (acts of worship) and volume two on *mu'āmalāt* (worldly affairs and transactions). It served as the official, legal code of the Fatimid state. This work has continued to be used by the Ṭayyibī Ismailis of India and elsewhere as their principal authority in legal matters; *see* I.K. Poonawala, "al-Qāḍī al-Nu'mān and Isma'ili Jurisprudence", in *MIHT*, pp. 117–143.

- *Iftitāḥ al-da'wa,* ed., Wadād al-Qāḍī. Beirut: Dār al-Thaqāfa, 1970. pp. 310; ed., Farḥāt al-Dashrāwī (Farhat Dachraoui). Tunis: al-Sharika al-Tūnusiyya li'l-Tawzī', 1975. pp. 143 (French) + 396 (Arabic). Excerpt, ed. and English trans., W. Ivanow, in his *Ismaili Tradition*, text pp. 40–46, translation pp. 224–231.

  Completed in 346/957, this is the earliest known historical work in Ismaili literature covering the background to the establishment of the Fatimid caliphate. The *Iftitāḥ* was apparently partially based on the *Sīra* of the *dā'ī* Ibn Ḥawshab Manṣūr al-Yaman (d. 302/914), which has not survived. The *Iftitāḥ al-da'wa* is studied in T. Nagel, *Frühe Ismailiya und Fatimiden*.

- *Ikhtilāf uṣūl al-madhāhib*, ed., Sham'un T. Lokhandwalla. Simla: Indian Institute of Advanced Study, 1972. pp. xiv + 140 (English) + 262 (Arabic); ed., Muṣṭafā Ghālib. Beirut: Dār al-Andalus, 1393/1973. pp. 228.

  Composed after 343/954, this legal work in refutation of Sunni schools of law is one of al-Qāḍī al-Nu'mān's extant polemical treatises.

- *Kitāb asās al-ta'wīl*, ed., 'Ārif Tāmir. Silsilat al-makhṭūṭāt al-'Arabiyya, 2. Beirut: Dār al-Thaqāfa, [1960]. pp. 416.

  This work, on Ismaili *ta'wīl* of Qur'anic stories of prophets from Ādam to Muḥammad, was translated into Persian by al-Mu'ayyad fi'l-Dīn al-Shīrāzī under the title of *Bunyād-i ta'wīl*, which is still in manuscript form. Only two copies of this Persian translation, belonging to the Hamdānī and Zāhid 'Alī collections of Ismaili manuscripts, have come to light. The Hamdānī collection is now partly in the keeping of Professor Abbas Hamdani while the Zāhid 'Alī collection is housed at The Institute of Ismaili Studies Library in London.

- *Kitāb al-iqtiṣār*, ed., Muḥammad Waḥīd Mīrzā. Damascus: Institut Français de Damas, 1376/1957. pp. xxxviii (French) + 174 (Arabic); ed., 'Ārif Tāmir. Beirut: Dār al-Aḍwā', 1416/1996. pp. 128.

An abridgement of al-Qāḍī al-Nuʿmān's *Kitāb al-īḍāḥ* on *fiqh*, which was composed before the *Daʿāʾim al-Islām* but has not survived directly. The *Iqtiṣār* was used later by al-Nuʿmān's descendants as Fatimid chief judges (*qāḍī al-quḍāt*) in public sessions on law held in the mosques of Cairo.

- *Kitāb al-himma fī ādāb atbāʿ al-aʾimma*, ed., Muḥammad Kāmil Ḥusayn. Silsilat makhṭūṭāt al-Fāṭimiyyīn, 3. Cairo: Dār al-Fikr al-ʿArabī, [1948]. pp. 142; ed., Muṣṭafā Ghālib. Beirut: Dār wa-Maktabat al-Hilāl, 1979. pp. 216; ed., Muḥammad Sharīf ʿAlī Yamanī al-Ḥarāzī. Beirut: Dār al-Aḍwāʾ, 1416/1996. pp. 143. Abridged English trans., Jawad Muscati and Khan Bahadur A.M. Moulvi as *Selections from Qazi Noaman's Kitab-ul-Himma fi Adabi Ataba-el-aʾemma or Code of Conduct for the Followers of Imam*. Ismailia Association [W.] Pakistan Series, no. 1. Karachi: The Ismailia Association [W.] Pakistan, 1950. pp. ii + 135; reprinted, Mombasa: The Ismailia Association for Africa, n.d.

  Belonging to the *adab* genre in Arabic literature, on the code of conduct in different social contexts, this work explains proper behaviour towards the imam and in his presence. As a rare instance of its kind, in the final, fifteenth chapter, al-Nuʿmān explains the virtues and qualifications of an ideal *dāʿī*.

- *Kitāb al-majālis wa'l-musāyarāt*, ed., al-Ḥabīb al-Faqī (Habib Feki), Ibrāhīm Shabbūḥ and Muḥammad al-Yaʿlāwī (Mohammed Yalaoui). Tunis: al-Maṭbaʿa al-Rasmiyya li'l-Jumhūriyya al-Tūnusiyya, 1978. pp. 648; 2nd ed., revised by Muḥammad al-Yaʿlāwī. Beirut: Dār al-Gharb al-Islāmī, 1997. pp. 568.

  A collection of lectures and anecdotes on the activities of the first four Fatimid caliph-imams, this voluminous work also reports numerous conversations between al-Nuʿmān and the Fatimid caliph-imam al-Muʿizz on religious matters and affairs of the Fatimid state.

- *Mafātīḥ al-niʿma*, ed., Muhtadī Muṣṭafā Ghālib. Salamiyya: Dār al-Ghadīr, 1992. pp. 66.

  A short work written in reply to a certain Abu'l-Ḥasan al-Baghdādī, explaining the necessity of obeying the imam.

- *al-Manāqib wa'l-mathālib* (also known as *Kitāb al-manāqib li-ahl bayt rasūl Allāh wa'l-mathālib li-Banī Umayya*), ed., Mājid b. Aḥmad al-ʿAṭiyya. Beirut: Muʾassasat al-Aʿlamī li'l-Maṭbūʿāt, 1423/2002. pp. 445.

This work provides in typical Shiʿi fashion details on the virtues of the Prophet Muḥammad's clan of Banū Hāshim, his family (*ahl al-bayt*), the first Shiʿi Imam ʿAlī b. Abī Ṭālib, the ʿAlids and other Ṭālibids; and the impiety of the Banū Umayya and the Umayyad caliphs.

- *al-Risāla al-mudhhiba*, ed., ʿĀrif Tāmir, in his *Khams rasāʾil Ismāʿīliyya*, pp. 27–87.

This is a philosophical work, in three chapters, in the form of answers to a number of questions on cosmology, eschatology, ranks of the Ismaili hierarchy, etc. The attribution of this work to al-Qāḍī al-Nuʿmān may be doubtful.

- *Sharḥ al-akhbār fī faḍāʾil al-aʾimma al-aṭhār*, ed., al-Sayyid Muḥammad al-Ḥusaynī al-Jalālī. Qumm: Muʾassasat al-Nashr al-Islāmī, 1409–12/1988–92. 3 vols; reprinted, Beirut: Dār al-Thaqalayn, 1994. 3 vols. Excerpts, ed. and English trans., W. Ivanow, in his *Ismaili Tradition*, text pp. 1–34, translation pp. 97–122; partial ed., *al-Juzʾ al-awwal min kitāb sharḥ al-akhbār*. Surat: Al Jameatus-Saifiyah, n.d. [1960s]. pp. 49.

A collection of non-legal traditions (*ḥadīth*s) compiled during the reign of al-Muʿizz li-Dīn Allāh (341–365/953–975); it was revised and approved by the Fatimid caliph-imam himself. Divided into 16 parts, it contains about 1460 traditions, all of which, according to al-Nuʿmān, were well-known and authentic. Two-thirds of this work is related to the Imam ʿAlī b. Abī Ṭālib, with the remaining portion dealing with the *faḍāʾil* or virtues of the *ahl al-bayt* and the early imams up to Jaʿfar al-Ṣādiq (d. 148/765). The final parts (15–16) relate to the beginning of the Ismaili *daʿwa* in North Africa and the appearance of ʿAbd Allāh al-Mahdī there. Many of the sources used by al-Nuʿmān in producing this compendium are no longer extant.

- *Taʾwīl al-daʿāʾim*, (also known as *Tarbiyat al-muʾminīn*), ed., Muḥammad Ḥasan al-Aʿẓamī. Cairo: Dār al-Maʿārif, 1967–72. 3 vols.; ed., ʿĀrif Tāmir. Beirut: Dār al-Aḍwāʾ, 1415/1995. 3 vols. Selection, entitled *Tarbiyat al-muʾminīn*, ed., ʿĀdil al-ʿAwwā, in his *Muntakhabāt Ismāʿīliyya*, pp. 3–85.

This is the esoteric counterpart to the *Daʿāʾim al-Islām*, based on al-Nuʿmān's weekly lectures delivered as the *majālis al-ḥikma*. Divided into 12 parts (*juz*'s), each subdivided into 10 lectures (*majālis*), al-Nuʿmān here provides esoteric interpretation (*taʾwīl*) of *walāya*, *ṭahāra*, *ṣalāt* and other acts of worship (*ʿibādāt*).

- *al-Urjūza al-mukhtāra*, ed., Ismāʿīl Qurbān Ḥusayn Pūnāwālā (Ismail K. Poonawala). Montreal: McGill University, Institute of Islamic Studies, 1970. pp. 10 (English) + 357 (Arabic); ed., Yūsuf al-Biqāʿī, with an introduction by ʿĀrif Tāmir. Beirut: Dār al-Aḍwāʾ, 1419/1999. pp. 181.

  Written in the time of the Fatimid caliph-imam al-Qāʾim (322–334/934–946) and dealing with the issue of the imamate, this versified treatise defends the rights of the Fatimids against the arguments forwarded by their Muslim opponents, including the Sunnis, the Muʿtazila, the Khārijīs, the Zaydīs and several other Shiʿi groups. With 2375 verses, this work is one of the longest *arājiz* in the history of Arabic literature.

Raqqāmī Khurāsānī, ʿAlī Qulī b. Imām Qulī Khākī Khurāsānī (fl. 11th/17th century), Persian Nizārī poet

- *Qaṣīda-yi dhurriyya*, ed. and Russian trans., Aleksandr S. Semenov, in his "Ismailitskaya oda, posvyashchennaya voploshcheniyam ʿAliyaboga" [An Ismaili Ode dedicated to ʿAli], *Iran* (Leningrad), 2 (1928), pp. 1–24; partial ed. and English trans., W. Ivanow, in his *Ismailitica*, pp. 73–76.

  In some manuscripts, this *Qaṣīda*, comprised of a versified list of Nizārī imams, is attributed to Raqqāmī's father Khākī Khurāsānī. It seems that a later poet has continued the list of the Nizārī imams beyond those living in the 11th/17th century, as the enumeration ends with Sulṭān Muḥammad Shāh (1877–1957), who succeeded to the imamate in 1302/1885.

Rāshid al-Dīn Sinān b. Salmān (or Sulaymān) (d. 589/1193), Nizārī chief *dāʿī* in Syria

- *Faṣl min al-lafẓ al-sharīf, hādhihi manāqib al-mawlā Rāshid al-Dīn*, ed. and French trans., Stanislas Guyard, in his "Un grand maître des Assassins", pp. 387–489; ed., Mehmet Şerefeddin (Yaltkaya), in *Darülfünun Ilâhiyat Fakültesi Mecmuası* (Istanbul), 2, no. 7 (1928), pp. 45–71; ed., Muṣṭafā Ghālib, in his *Sinān Rāshid al-Dīn*, pp. 163–214. Excerpt, from another text with the same title, ed. with French trans., S. Guyard, in his *Fragments relatifs à la doctrine des Ismaélîs*, fragment I, Arabic text pp. 193–195, translation pp. 275–284; an earlier French translation of this excerpt, fragment I, may be found in Jean Baptiste L.J. Rousseau's "Extraits d'un Livre qui contient la doctrine des Ismaélis" (1812), pp. 226–234.

This hagiographic text attributed to Sinān may have been compiled by the Syrian Nizārī *dāʿī* Abū Firās Shihāb al-Dīn al-Maynaqī (d. 937/1530 or 947/1540), or possibly by another Abū Firās who lived earlier. One of the earliest Ismaili works studied by the orientalists, the manuscript of this text (dated 724/1324) was discovered in Syria by Joseph Catafago, a dragoman at the Prussian consulate in Syria; *see* his "Lettre de M. Catafago à M. Mohl", pp. 485–493.

al-Rāzī, Abū Ḥātim Aḥmad b. Ḥamdān (d. 322/934), Qarmaṭī (Ismaili) *dāʿī* in Persia

- *Aʿlām al-nubuwwa*, ed., Ṣalāḥ al-Ṣāwī and Ghulām Riḍā Aʿvānī, with an English introduction by S. Hossein Nasr. Imperial Iranian Academy of Philosophy, Publication no. 33. Tehran: Imperial Iranian Academy of Philosophy, 1397/1977. pp. xxxii + 353. Urdu trans., ʿAzīz Allāh Najīb. Karachi: Iqbal Brothers, 1998. pp. 551. Selections: Paul Kraus, in his "Raziana II", *Orientalia*, NS, 5 (1936), pp. 35–56, 358–378; also in *Rasāʾil falsafiyya li-Abī Bakr Muḥammad ibn Zakariyyāʾ al-Rāzī*, ed., P. Kraus. Universitatis Fouadi I Litterarum Facultatis Publicationum, Fasc. XXII. Cairo: n.p., 1939, pp. 291–313; and in ʿAbd al-Laṭīf al-ʿAbd, *al-Ṭibb al-rūḥanī li-Abī Bakr al-Rāzī*. Cairo: n.p., Maktabat al-Nahḍa al-Miṣriyya, 1978, pp. 125–147. Partial French trans., Fabienne Brion, in his "Philosophie et révèlation. Traduction annotée de six extraits du *Kitāb Aʿlām al-Nubuwwa* d'Abū Ḥātim al-Rāzī", *Bulletin de Philosophie Médiévale*, 28 (1986), pp. 134–162, and in Fabienne Brion, "Le temps, l'espace et la genèse du monde selon Abū Bakr al-Rāzī. Présentation et traduction des chapitres 1, 3–4 du *Kitāb Aʿlām al-Nubuwwa* d'Abū Ḥātim al-Rāzī", *Revue Philosophique de Louvain*, 87 (1989), pp. 139–164. Excerpt, English trans., Everett K. Rowson as *Aʿlām al-nubuwwah, Science of Prophecy*, in *APP*, pp. 140–172.

A work in defence of revelation and prophethood, and in refutation of the physician-philosopher Abū Bakr Muḥammad b. Zakariyyāʾ al-Rāzī (d. 313/925), the *Aʿlām* is essentially a record of the disputation (*munāẓarāt*) held between the two Rhazes in Rayy in the presence of that city's governor and other notables. This disputation is also reported in al-Kirmānī's *al-Aqwāl al-dhahabiyya*, which states (pp. 2–3) that it took place in the presence of Mardāwīj (d. 323/935), the founder of the Ziyārid dynasty of northern Persia with their capital at Rayy.

- *Kitāb al-iṣlāḥ*, ed., Ḥasan Mīnūchihr and Mahdī Muḥaqqiq, with an English introduction by Shin Nomoto. Wisdom of Persia, 42. Tehran: McGill University, Institute of Islamic Studies, Tehran Branch; Tehran University, 1377 Sh./1998. pp. 34 (English) + 49 (Persian) + 350 (Arabic). Selection, English trans., Shin Nomoto, in his "An Ismāʿīlī Thinker on the Prophets in the Cosmic Correspondence: Translation of the *Kitāb al-Iṣlāḥ* by Abū Ḥātim al-Rāzī I", in *Reports of the Keio Institute of Cultural and Linguistic Studies*, 34 (2002), pp. 97–152.

This book was composed to correct certain ideas expressed in the *Kitāb al-maḥṣūl* written by the Central Asian Qarmaṭī *dāʿī* Muḥammad b. Aḥmad al-Nasafī who was executed by the Sāmānids in 332/943. The *dāʿī* al-Kirmānī defends Abū Ḥātim al-Rāzī's corrections of al-Nasafī's views in his own *Kitāb al-riyāḍ*, which also contains fragments of al-Rāzī's *al-Iṣlāḥ*. This work deals mainly with prophethood, specifically with the *nuṭaqāʾ*, from Adam to Jesus, and the laws enunciated by them; al-Rāzī also discusses the nature of the soul (*nafs*), cosmogony, types of matter, etc. This is one of the earliest extant Ismaili works manifesting Neoplatonic influences.

- *Kitāb al-zīna fiʾl-kalimāt al-Islāmiyya al-ʿArabiyya*, part 1 (pp. 152) and part 2 (pp. 235), ed., Ḥusayn b. Fayḍ Allāh al-Hamdānī. Cairo: Dār al-Kitāb al-ʿArabī bi-Miṣr, 1956–58; part 3, ed., ʿAbd Allāh Sallūm al-Sāmarrāʾī, in his *al-Ghuluww waʾl-firaq al-ghāliya fiʾl-haḍāraʾl-Islāmiyya*. Baghdad: Dār Wāsiṭ liʾl-Nashr, 1392/1972, pp. 225–312; excerpt, French trans., in Louis Massignon, *Salmân Pâk et les prémices spirituelles de l'Islam Iranien*. Publications de la Société des Études Iraniennes, 7. Paris: G.P. Maisonneuve, 1934, pp. 43–44; reprinted in L. Massignon, *Opera Minora*, ed., Youakim Moubarac. Beirut: Dar al-Maarif, 1963, vol. 1, pp. 475–476; reprinted, Paris: Presses Universitaires de France, 1969, vol. 1, pp. 475–476.

This is a lexicographical work on religious terms for the attributes of God, rituals, etc. The final section of this dictionary of Islamic technical terms deals with Muslim sects and schools of thought. As a rare instance of its kind in Ismaili literature, *al-Zīna* is mentioned in Ibn al-Nadīm's *al-Fihrist* and in Niẓām al-Mulk's *Siyāsat-nāma*, reflecting its ready availability to non-Ismaili milieus.

Ṣadr al-Dīn, Pīr (fl. end of 8th/14th century), Satpanth Nizārī preacher-saint in India

- *Bāvan Bodh; Sō Kriyā, Sahi Samrani*, English trans., Vali Mahomed N. Hooda, in his "Some Specimens of Satpanth Literature", in W. Ivanow, ed., *Collectanea*, pp. 115–122, also in C. Shackle and Z. Moir, *Ismaili Hymns from South Asia*, pp. 63–67.
- *Būjh Nirañjan*, ed. and English trans., Ali S. Asani, in his *The Būjh Nirañjan: An Ismaili Mystical Poem*, pp. 120–193.

  Professor A. Asani has refuted the traditional attribution of this lengthy poem of the *ginān* literature on the mystical path to Pīr Ṣadr al-Dīn, considering it rather as an anonymous composition in Hindustani emanating from the Qādirī Sufi circles of South Asia.
- *Dasa Avatāra*, excerpt, covering the tenth *avatāra*, English trans., Vali Mahomed N. Hooda, in his "Some Specimens of Satpanth Literature", in W. Ivanow, ed., *Collectanea*, pp. 112–115.
- *Saloko Nāno*, selections, English trans., A. Esmail, in his *A Scent of Sandalwood*, pp. 151–179, in C. Shackle and Z. Moir, *Ismaili Hymns from South Asia*, pp. 76–79.
- *Ginān*s, selections, English trans., Vali Mahomed N. Hooda, in his "Some Specimens of Satpanth Literature", in W. Ivanow, ed., *Collectanea*, pp. 104–109; in C. Shackle and Z. Moir, *Ismaili Hymns from South Asia*, pp. 69, 71, 85, 87, 89, 91, 101, 107, 109, 111, 113, 119, 121, 123; in A. Esmail, *A Scent of Sandalwood*, pp.79, 81–82, 83, 85–86, 90–91, 92, 93–94, 95–96, 101, 104–105, 108–109, 110–112, 113, 114, 119–120, 132, 136, 137, 141–145, 146, 147, and in A.S. Asani, *Ecstasy and Enlightenment*, pp. 159–161, 167.

al-Shādilī al-Yamānī, Abū Manṣūr, Syrian Nizārī author

- *Kitāb al-bayān li-mabāḥith al-ikhwān*, ed., Muṣṭafā Ghālib. Silsilat al-dirāsāt al-Ismāʿīliyya, 4. Salamiyya: n. p., 1375/1956. pp. 112.

  Divided into seven sections (*mabāḥith*), this work deals with *tawḥīd*, the creation, imamate, ranks of the Ismaili hierarchy, etc. According to I.K. Poonawala, *Biobibliography*, p. 297, it is a plagiarized version of Abū Firās Shihāb al-Dīn al-Maynaqī's *Risālat maṭāliʿ al-shumūs*. No biographical details are available on this author.

al-Shahrastānī, Abu'l-Fatḥ Muḥammad b. ʿAbd al-Karīm (d. 548/1153), Ashʿarī (Ismaili?) theologian and heresiographer

- *Majlis-i maktūb Shahrastānī munʿaqid dar Khwārazm*, ed., Muḥammad Riḍā Jalālī Nā'īnī, in his *Sharḥ-i ḥāl va āthār-i ḥujjat al-ḥaqq Abu'l-Fatḥ Muḥammad b. ʿAbd al-Karīm b. Aḥmad Shahrastānī*. Tehran: Chāp-i Tābān, 1343 Sh./1964, pp. 1–38; also in al-Shahrastānī, *Kitāb al-milal wa'l-niḥal*, Persian trans., Afḍal al-Dīn Ṣadr Turka-yi Iṣfahānī (d. 850/1446), ed., Muḥammad Riḍā Jalālī Nā'īnī. Tehran: Iqbāl, 1350 Sh./1971, pp. 111–161. Reprinted with French trans., Diane Steigerwald as *Majlis: Discours sur l'Ordre et la création*. Saint-Nicolas, Québec: Les Presses de l'Université Laval, 1998. pp. 168.

  The *Majlis*, al-Shahrastānī's only extant treatise in Persian, was originally delivered as a sermon to a Twelver Shiʿi audience in Khwārazm around the year 540/1145. This work on the two worlds of order (*amr*) and creation (*khalq*), clearly reflects Ismaili perspectives, including the Neoplatonized Ismaili cosmology propounded by Abū Yaʿqūb al-Sijistānī and other Ismaili *dāʿīs* operating in Khurāsān and Transoxania during the Fatimid period. This brief text of some thirty printed pages is also permeated with Qur'anic verses and *ḥadīth*s for which al-Shahrastānī provides esoteric interpretations through the methodology of *ta'wīl*.

- *Kitāb al-muṣāraʿa*, ed., Suhayr Muḥammad Mukhtār as *Kitāb muṣāraʿat al-falāsifa*. Cairo, 1396/1976; ed., Ḥasan al-Muʿizzī, together with Naṣīr al-Dīn al-Ṭūsī's *Maṣāriʿ al-muṣāriʿ*. Makhṭūṭāt Maktabat Āyat Allāh al-Marʿashī al-ʿāmma, 11. Qumm: Maktabat Āyat Allāh al-Marʿashī, 1405/1984–85, pp. 1–127; ed., Muwaffaq Fawzī al-Jabr as *Muṣāraʿat al-falāsifa*. Silsilat turāthunā. Damascus: Dār al-Maʿadd and Dār al-Namīr, 1997. pp. 128, ed. and English trans., Wilferd Madelung and Toby Mayer as *Struggling with the Philosopher: A Refutation of Avicenna's Metaphysics*. Ismaili Texts and Translations Series, 2. London: I.B. Tauris in association with The Institute of Ismaili Studies, 2001. pp. 105 (English) + 135 (Arabic).

  This book represents an intellectual wrestling match (*muṣāraʿa*) with Ibn Sīnā (d. 428/1037), whose concept of the 'necessary being' (*wājib al-wujūd*) is refuted here on the basis of Ismaili ideas, especially the absolute transcendence of God beyond existence and comprehension by human reason. Al-Shahrastānī's Ismaili thought is investigated in D. Steigerwald, *La pensée philosophique et théologique de Shahrastânî*.

- *Tafsīr al-Shahrastānī al-musammā Mafātīḥ al-asrār wa-maṣābīḥ al-abrār*, facsimile edition of the unique manuscript at the Library of the Islamic Consultative Assembly, Tehran, with introduction by ʿAbd al-Ḥusayn Ḥāʾirī. Tehran: Center for the Publication of Manuscripts, 1368 Sh./1989. 2 vols; ed., Muḥammad ʿAlī Ādharshab. Tehran: Daftar-i Nashr-i Mīrath-i Maktūb and Iḥyā-i Kitāb, 1417–/1997–.

  A partial Qurʾan commentary bearing an Ismaili imprint. In this work, produced a few years before 540/1145, al-Shahrastānī fully employs the methodology of Ismaili *taʾwīl*.

Shahriyār b. al-Ḥasan (fl. 5th/11th century), Ismaili *dāʿī* in Persia and Yaman

- *Risāla fiʾl-radd ʿalā man yunkir al-ʿālam al-rūḥānī*, ed., Muṣṭafā Ghālib, in al-Kirmānī, *Majmūʿat rasāʾil*, pp. 183–189.

  This epistle on the spiritual world, written as a reply to al-Sulṭān ʿĀmir b. Sulaymān al-Zawāḥī (d. 492/1099), a tribal leader in Yaman, is commonly but wrongly included in the collection of thirteen *Rasāʾil* attributed to Ḥamīd al-Dīn al-Kirmānī. After his initial career as a *dāʿī* in Persia, Shahriyār settled in Yaman serving the Ismaili Ṣulayḥids who recognized the suzerainty of the Fatimids.

Shams al-Dīn, Pīr (fl. 7th/13th century), Satpanth Nizārī preacher-saint in India

- *Garbī*, a collection of 28 poems, English trans., Vali Mahomed N. Hooda, in his "Some Specimens of Satpanth Literature", in W. Ivanow, ed., *Collectanea*, pp. 55–85.
- *Ginān*s, selections, English trans., Vali Mahomed N. Hooda, in his "Some Specimens of Satpanth Literature", in W. Ivanow, ed., *Collectanea*, p. 103; an anthology of Pīr Shams's *Ginān*s, including the 28 *Garbī*s, translated by Tazim R. Kassam, in her *Songs of Wisdom*, pp. 165–370; selections also in C. Shackle and Z. Moir, *Ismaili Hymns from South Asia*, pp. 73, 91, 93, 103, 104, 109, 111, 113, 117, 119, 129, 131, 133; in A. Esmail, *A Scent of Sandalwood*, pp. 80, 89, 102–103, 116–117, 118, 130–131, 138, 139–140, 148–149, and in A.S. Asani, *Ecstasy and Enlightenment*, pp. 166–167.

Shams al-Dīn b. Aḥmad (or Muḥammad) al-Ṭayyibī (d. 652/1254), Nizārī poet and *dāʿī* in Syria

- *Risālat al-dustūr wa-daʿwat al-muʾminīn liʾl-ḥuḍūr*, ed., ʿĀrif Tāmir, in his *Arbaʿ rasāʾil Ismāʿīliyya*, pp. 67–101.

  A treatise on the rules for entering the Ismaili *daʿwa* and the attributes of the master (*murshid*) and disciple (*mustajīb*), dedicated to the penultimate ruler of Alamūt, ʿAlāʾ al-Dīn Muḥammad (618–653/1221–1255). The author evidently spent some time in Alamūt at the court of this Nizārī imam.

Shihāb al-Dīn Shāh al-Ḥusaynī, Pīr (d. 1302/1884), Persian Nizārī author

- *Kitāb-i khiṭābāt-i ʿāliya*, ed., Hūshang Ujāqī, with an English Foreword by W. Ivanow. Ismaili Society Series A, no. 14. Bombay: Ismaili Society, 1963. pp. xv (English) + 82 (Persian).

  The writings of Pīr Shihāb al-Dīn Shāh, the eldest son of Āqā ʿAlī Shāh (d. 1302/1885), Āghā Khān II, the forty-seventh (Qāsim-Shāhī) Nizārī imam, represent the earliest examples of a modern revival in Nizārī Ismaili literary activities in Persian. In these sixty-four *khiṭābāt* or sermons written before 1298/1881, the author discusses *tawḥīd*, the attributes of God, prophethood, imamate, the origin of the Khoja community, esoteric interpretation (*taʾwīl*) of prayer, fasting, *ḥajj*, *jihād*, etc., the Nizārī-Mustaʿlī schism, imams of the Alamūt and post-Alamūt periods, genealogy of the Nizārī imams, virtues of a true believer (*muʾmin*), etc.

- *Risāla dar ḥaqīqat-i dīn*, ed. and English trans., Wladimir Ivanow as *True Meaning of Religion (Risala dar Haqiqati Din)*. Islamic Research Association [Series], no. 3. Bombay: A.A.A. Fyzee, 1933. pp. iii + 28 (English) + 37 (Persian). Facsimile edition of the autograph copy by Wladimir Ivanow. Ismaili Society Series B, no. 1. Bombay: Published for the Ismaili Society by Thacker and Co., 1947. pp. xi + 75; reprinted, Ismaili Society Series B, no. 8, Bombay: Ismaili Society, 1955. pp. xv + 75. English trans., Wladimir Ivanow as *True Meaning of Religion, or Risala dar Haqiqat-i Din*. Ismaili Society Series B, no. 2. 2nd ed., Bombay: Published for the Ismaili Society by Thacker and Co., 1947. pp. xiv + 51; 3rd ed., Ismaili Society Series B, no. 9. Bombay: Ismaili Society, 1956. pp. xix + 52. Urdu trans., ʿAbbās Sabzavārī, *Risāla dar ḥaqīqat-i dīn*. Karachi: Ismailia Association Pakistan, [1950]. pp. 106.

Intended for the general reader, this incomplete treatise contains a summary exposition of certain Ismaili teachings, with special reference to the doctrine of the imamate as well as ethical and mystical aspects of Ismailism.

al-Sijistānī (al-Sijzī), Abū Yaʿqūb Isḥāq b. Aḥmad (d. after 361/971), Ismaili *dāʿī* in Khurāsān and Transoxania

- *Ithbāt al-nubū'āt* (or *al-nubuwwāt*), ed., ʿĀrif Tāmir. Beirut: al-Maṭbaʿa al-Kāthūlīkiyya, 1966. pp. xiv + 201.

  In this work, comprising seven sections (*maqāla*s), al-Sijistānī puts forward a variety of proofs for the necessity of prophecy (*nubuwwa*), also explaining different prophetic eras.

- *Kashf al-maḥjūb*, ed., Henry Corbin. Bibliothèque Iranienne, 1. Tehran: Institut Franco-Iranien; Paris: A. Maisonneuve, 1949. pp. 24 (French) + 114 (Persian). Excerpt, in Mahdī Bayānī, *Namūna-yi sukhan-i Fārsī*. Tehran: Shirkat-i Chāp-i Khudkār, 1317 Sh./1938, pp. 226–232. French trans., Henry Corbin as *Le dévoilement des choses cachées: Kashf al-Maḥjûb, Recherches de philosophie Ismaélienne*. Collection «Islam spirituel». Lagrasse: Verdier, 1988. pp. 139. Partial English trans., Hermann Landolt as *Kashf al-maḥjūb, Unveiling of the Hidden*, in *APP*, pp. 71–124.

  Originally written in Arabic, only this Persian paraphrase or translation of the text has survived. The Persian version, perhaps produced by Nāṣir-i Khusraw or the commentator of Abu'l-Haytham Jurjānī's *Qaṣīda*, has been dated to the 5th/11th century for linguistic reasons. The *Kashf al-maḥjūb* (*The Unveiling of the Hidden*) comprises seven chapters or discourses (*maqālāt*), each one subdivided into seven parts (*jastār*s), which are to be regarded as the most important sources of divine knowledge, or gnosis, which the book seeks to unveil. These discourses deal with *tawḥīd* and the stages of creation, namely, intellect, soul and nature as well as prophethood and resurrection (*qiyāmat*).

- *Kitāb al-iftikhār*, ed., Muṣṭafā Ghālib. Beirut: Dār al-Andalus, 1980. pp. 132; ed., Ismail K. Poonawala. Beirut: Dār al-Gharb al-Islāmī, 2000. pp. xxviii (English) + 497 (Arabic).

  Composed in 17 chapters toward the end of his life, around 361/971, this is a polemical work which also presents a summary exposition of

Ismaili doctrine and preserves remnants of the mythological cosmology propounded by the early Ismailis, including the spiritual beings called *jadd*, *fatḥ* and *khayāl* which mediated between the spiritual and the physical worlds.

- *Kitāb al-yanābīʿ*, ed. and French trans., Henry Corbin, in his *Trilogie Ismaélienne*. Bibliothèque Iranienne, 9. Tehran: Département d'Iranologie de l'Institut Franco-Iranien; Paris: A. Maisonneuve, 1961, Arabic text pp. 1–97, translation as *Le livre des sources*, pp. 5–127; ed., Muṣṭafā Ghālib. Beirut: al-Maktab al-Tijārī, 1965. pp. 174. English trans., Paul E. Walker as *The Book of Wellsprings*, in his *The Wellsprings of Wisdom*. Salt Lake City: University of Utah Press, 1994. pp. 37–111. Excerpt, English trans., Latimah Parvin Peerwani as *Kitāb al-yanābīʿ, The Book of Wellsprings*, in *APP*, pp. 124–138.

  Composed around 350/961 and later paraphrased extensively in Nāṣir-i Khusraw's *Khwān al-ikhwān*, this is an advanced text containing a corpus of philosophical and doctrinal material. It is organized as a collection of themes, each one being the subject of a separate section called *yanbūʿ* (plural, *yanābīʿ*), meaning wellspring or source. Some forty such themes are covered here, ranging from metaphysical proofs of the universal intellect and the universal soul, the transcendence of God and the nature of the creation, to religious doctrines concerning prophethood, angels, resurrection, and eternal reward and punishment. The primary theme of the *Kitāb al-yanābīʿ* is, however, the wellsprings of human knowledge and spiritual life in each era of religious history. Al-Sijistānī's metaphysical system is investigated extensively by P.E. Walker in his *Early Philosophical Shiism* and other publications.

- *al-Risāla al-bāhira fi'l-maʿād*, ed., Bustān Hīrjī (Boustan Hirji), in *Taḥqīqāt-i Islāmī*, 7 (1371 Sh./1992), pp. 21–50. Persian trans., ʿAbd Allāh Nūrānī, in *Taḥqīqāt-i Islāmī*, 7 (1371 Sh./1992), pp. 51–62. English trans., in B. Hirji's doctoral thesis "A Study of *al-Risālah al-Bāhirah*", pp. 60–75.

  A short epistle revolving around eschatology (*maʿād*) and salvation.

- *Sullam al-najāt*, ed., Muhtadī Muṣṭafā Ghālib. Salamiyya: Dār al-Ghadīr, 2002. pp. 119.

  Here, al-Sijistānī expounds in summary form the doctrines that are essential for achieving salvation, including beliefs in God, His angels, books, messengers, the Last Day, resurrection, etc.

- *Tuḥfat al-mustajībīn*, ed., ʿĀrif Tāmir, in his *Khams rasāʾil Ismāʿīliyya*, pp. 145–155; reprinted in *al-Mashriq*, 61 (March-April, 1967), pp. 136–146; reprinted in his *Thalāth rasāʾil Ismāʿīliyya*, pp. 5–20.

  A short treatise on numerous Ismaili concepts and terms such as intellect (*ʿaql*), soul (*nafs*), *jadd*, *fatḥ*, *khayāl*, preceder and followers (*sābiq* and *tālī*), the seven letters (*al-ḥurūf al-sabʿa*), etc.

al-Sijzī, Abū Yaʿqūb, *see* al-Sijistānī, Abū Yaʿqūb Isḥāq

Sinān, Rāshid al-Dīn, *see* Rāshid al-Dīn Sinān b. Salmān

Sulaymān b. Ḥaydar, al-Shaykh (d. 1210/1795), Muḥammad-Shāhī, Nizārī *dāʿī* in Syria

- *al-Qaṣīda al-Ḥaydariyya*, ed., ʿĀrif Tāmir, in his *Murājaʿāt Ismāʿīliyya*. Beirut: Dār al-Aḍwāʾ, 1415/1994, pp. 5–20.

  In this *Qaṣīda* the imams of the Muḥammad-Shāhī (Muʾminī) branch of Nizārī Ismailism are listed until Muḥammad b. Ḥaydar al-Bāqir, the last known imam of this branch who lived in Awrangābād and was contemporary with the author. Subsequently, the bulk of the Muḥammad-Shāhī Nizārīs switched their allegiance to the Qāsim-Shāhī line of Nizārī imams then represented by the Āghā Khāns. At present, the remnants of the Muḥammad-Shāhī Nizārīs living in Maṣyāf, Qadmūs and a few surrounding villages in central Syria, are evidently awaiting the reappearance of their last known imam as the Mahdi.

al-Sulṭān al-Khaṭṭāb b. al-Ḥasan b. Abiʾl-Ḥifāẓ al-Ḥajūrī al-Hamdānī (d. 533/1138), Ṭayyibī Mustaʿlī *dāʿī* and poet in Yaman

- *Dīwān al-Sulṭān al-Khaṭṭāb*, ed., Ismāʿīl Qurbān Ḥusayn (Ismail K. Poonawala), in his *al-Sulṭān al-Khaṭṭāb: ḥayātuhu wa-shiʿruhu*. Maktabat al-dirāsāt al-ʿArabiyya, 42. Cairo: Dār al-Maʿārif bi-Miṣr, 1967. pp. 97–241; 2nd ed., al-Dirāsāt al-Fāṭimiyya. Beirut: Dār al-Gharb al-Islamī, 1999, pp. 183–489.

  In two parts, of which the first contains 26 poems in praise of the Fatimid imams and high dignitaries of the Ismaili *daʿwa* as well as theological and philosophical themes. The second part of the *Dīwān*, recovered recently, has 31 poems in praise of the Ṣulayḥid queen, al-Sayyida al-Ḥurra (d. 532/1138), the Banū Hāshim and various tribes, also containing biographical details on al-Khaṭṭāb himself.

- *Risāla fī bayān iʿjāz al-Qurʾān*, ed., Ismail K. Poonawala, in his "Al-Sulṭān al-Ḫaṭṭāb's Treatise on the *Iʿǧāz al-Qurʾān*", *Arabica*, 41 (1994), pp. 84–126.

  This is the only work in Ismaili literature dealing with the important Islamic dogma of the inimitability (*iʿjāz*) of the Qurʾan, defended here primarily on the basis of the Ismaili views on prophethood. In the second part of this *Risāla* the author refutes the arguments of those who allege that the religious commandments of the *sharīʿa* are burdensome, affirming the Ismaili position of the Fatimid times that the exoteric (*ẓāhir*) and esoteric (*bāṭin*) aspects of religion and the *sharīʿa* are complementary, and that both are indispensable.

al-Ṣūrī, Muḥammad b. ʿAlī (fl. 5th/11th century), Syrian Ismaili poet

- *al-Qaṣīda al-Ṣūriyya*, ed., ʿĀrif Tāmir. Damascus: Institut Français de Damas, 1955. pp. 74.

  A poem on *tawḥīd*, the creation, spiritual hierarchies, the prophets from Ādam to Muḥammad, etc.

Ṭāhir Sayf al-Dīn b. Muḥammad Burhān al-Dīn (d. 1385/1965), Dāʾūdī Ṭayyibī *dāʿī muṭlaq* in India

- *al-Risāla al-Ramaḍāniyya*. Bombay, 1337–75/1918–55. 40 vols. The Institute of Ismaili Studies Library has various volumes, ending in vol. 40.

  In addition to the extensive corpus of the writings of Sayyidnā Ṭāhir Sayf al-Dīn, who led the Dāʾūdī Ṭayyibīs for half a century (1333–1385/1915–1965) as their fifty-first *dāʿī muṭlaq*, this vast chrestomathy contains fragments and quotations from earlier Ismaili works.

Tamīm b. al-Muʿizz li-Dīn Allāh, Amīr Abū ʿAlī (d. 375/985), Fatimid prince and poet

- *Dīwān Tamīm b. al-Muʿizz li-Dīn Allāh al-Fāṭimī*, ed., Muḥammad Ḥasan al-Aʿẓamī, Aḥmad Yūsuf Najātī, Muḥammad ʿAlī al-Najjār and Muḥammad Kāmil Ḥusayn. Cairo: Dār al-Kutub al-Miṣriyya, 1377/1957. pp. 476; 2nd ed., prepared by Muḥammad Ḥasan al-Aʿẓamī. Beirut: Dār al-Thaqāfa, 1970. pp. 63 + 476; partial edition by Muḥammad Ḥasan al-Aʿẓamī, in his *ʿAbqariyyat al-Fāṭimiyyīn*, pp. 141–209.

A collection of poems on love, gardens, enjoyments of life, etc. Many of the poems are in praise of the imams, especially the poet's father al-Muʿizz (d. 365/975) and his younger brother al-ʿAzīz (d. 386/996), who succeeded to the Ismaili imamate and Fatimid caliphate. Occasionally, Tamīm's panegyrics also contain references to Ismaili teachings under the Fatimids. Tamīm's poems belong to different genres, including *marthiya*s or elegies on the premature deaths of his brothers, and on the violent deaths of some of his ʿAlid ancestors.

al-Ṭūsī, Naṣīr al-Dīn Abū Jaʿfar Muḥammad b. Muḥammad (d. 672/1274), Shiʿi theologian, philosopher and scientist

- *Āghāz va anjām* (or *Tadhkira*), ed., Īraj Afshār. Intishārāt-i Dānishgāh-i Tehran, 301. Tehran: Dānishgāh-i Tehran, 1335 Sh./1956. pp. 50; facsimile ed., in Abu'l-Majd Muḥammad b. Masʿūd Tabrīzī (fl. 8th/14th century), *Safīna-yi Tabrīz*. Tehran: Iran University Press, 1381 Sh./2002, pp. 352–357.

Divided into 20 chapters (*faṣl*s), this is a work on eschatology and the origin and return of the human soul. Here, al-Ṭūsī elucidates the esoteric meanings and ethical underpinnings of eschatology as depicted in the Qur'an from Ismaili perspectives. The treatise was originally lithographed with some of al-Ṭūsī's other works in Tehran in 1313/1895, and again in 1324/1906.

- *Maṭlūb al-mu'minīn*, ed., Wladimir Ivanow, in his *Two Early Ismaili Treatises*. Bombay: A.A.A. Fyzee, 1933, pp. 43–55.

This short treatise was written at the fortress of Alamūt, or Maymūndiz, at the request of a noble lady (*ḥaḍrat-i ʿulyā*), from the household of the Nizārī Imam ʿAlā' al-Dīn Muḥammad (d. 653/1255), who wanted the author to compile a summary of the *Fuṣūl-i mubārak*, or epistles of an earlier Nizārī imam, and other Ismaili works. The four chapters (*faṣls*) of this brief and elementary treatise deal with eschatology, attributes of an Ismaili *mu'min* or believer, doctrine of solidarity and dissociation (*tawallā* and *tabarrā*), and the seven pillars of the *sharīʿa* and their esoteric interpretation (*ta'wīl*) for the Ismailis.

- *Rawḍat al-taslīm*, ed. and English trans., Wladimir Ivanow as *The Rawdatu't-Taslim commonly called Taṣawwurāt*. Ismaili Society Series A, no. 4. Leiden: Published for the Ismaili Society by E.J. Brill, 1950. pp. lxxxviii (English) + 249 (English) + 160 (Persian); ed. and English trans., S. Jalal Badakhchani as *Paradise of Submission*, with an introduction by Hermann Landolt and analytical commentary by Christian Jambet. Ismaili Texts and Translations Series, 5. London: I.B. Tauris in association with The Institute of Ismaili Studies, forthcoming. French trans., Christian Jambet as *La Convocation d'Alamût. Somme de philosophie Ismaélienne*. Collection 'Islam spirituel'. Lagrasse: Verdier, 1996. pp. 374. Excerpt, English trans., based on the edition of the Persian text in S.J. Hosseini Badakhchani's doctoral thesis, "The Paradise of Submission", pp. 20–33, 35–59, 46–51, by Latimah Parvin Peerwani as *Rawḍat al-taslīm or Taṣawwurāt, The Garden of Submission, or Notions*, in *APP*, pp. 357–378.

  A comprehensive treatise expounding the Nizārī teachings of the Alamūt period, especially following the declaration of *qiyāma* in 559/1164. Here, the author also elaborates the new doctrine of *satr* or concealment of the spiritual truth (*ḥaqīqa*) under the veil of the *sharīʿa*. Divided into 28 chapters or representations (*taṣawwurāt*), it deals with a variety of themes such as the Creator, cosmogony, nature of human existence, ethics, eschatology, prophethood and imamate.

- *Risāla dar tawallā wa-tabarrā*, in Naṣīr al-Dīn al-Ṭūsī, *Akhlāq-i Muḥtashamī*, ed., Muḥammad Taqī Dānishpazhūh. Silsila-yi intishārāt-i Mu'assasa-yi Vaʿẓ va Tablīgh-i Islāmī. Tehran: Dānishgāh-i Tehran, 1339 Sh./1960, pp. 561–570; 2nd ed., Intishārāt-i Dānishgāh-i Tehran, 1811. Tehran: Dānishgāh-i Tehran, 1361 Sh./1982, pp. 561–570.

  The Qur'anic concept of *tawallā wa-tabarrā*, or solidarity and dissociation, occupied an important place in the Nizārī teachings of the Alamūt period. Al-Ṭūsī elaborates the doctrine in this short treatise, composed around 633/1235 for his patron Nāṣir al-Dīn ʿAbd al-Raḥīm b. Abī Manṣūr (d. 655/1257), the Nizārī *muḥtasham* or governor in Quhistān.

- *Sayr va sulūk*, lithographed, Tehran, n.d.; also in Naṣīr al-Dīn Ṭūsī,

Majmūʿa-yi rasāʾil-i Khwāja Naṣīr al-Dīn Muḥammad b. Muḥammad al-Ṭūsī, ed., Muḥammad Taqī Mudarris Raḍavī. Intishārāt-i Dānishgāh-i Tehran, 308. Tehran: Dānishgāh-i Tehran, 1335 Sh./1956, pp. 36–55; ed. and English trans., S. Jalal Badakhchani as *Contemplation and Action: The Spiritual Autobiography of a Muslim Scholar*. London: I.B. Tauris in association with The Institute of Ismaili Studies, 1998. pp. xiii + 86 (English) + 22 (Persian). Excerpt (pp. 26–47), reprinted as *Sayr wa Sulūk, Contemplation and Action*, in *APP*, pp. 344–356; excerpt, in M.T. Dānishpazhūh's "Guftārī az Khwāja-yi Ṭūsī bi ravish-i Bāṭiniyān", pp. 82–88.

This is al-Ṭūsī's spiritual autobiography in which he explains his conversion to Ismailism as well as the Nizārī Ismaili doctrine of *taʿlīm*, or authoritative teaching by the imam. Composed in the Nizārī strongholds of Quhistān, the work takes the form of an extended letter addressed to the chief of the *dāʿī*s, a dignitary called Muẓaffar b. Muḥammad. Al-Ṭūsī spent some three decades, from around 624/1227 to 654/1256, in the Nizārī fortress communities of Persia.

al-Yamānī, Muḥammad b. Muḥammad (fl. 4th/10th century), Ismaili author

- *Sīrat al-ḥājib Jaʿfar b. ʿAlī wa-khurūj al-Mahdī min Salamiyya*, ed., Wladimir Ivanow, in *Majallat Kulliyyat al-Ādāb, al-Jāmiʿa al-Miṣriyya/Bulletin of the Faculty of Arts, University of Egypt*, 4, part 2 (1936), pp. 107–133. English trans., W. Ivanow, in his *Ismaili Tradition*, pp. 184–223. French trans., M. Canard, in his "L'autobiographie d'un chambellan du Mahdî ʿObeidallâh le Fâṭimide", *Hespéris*, 39 (1952), pp. 279–324; reprinted in his *Miscellanea Orientalia*. London: Variorum Reprints, 1973, article V.

The autobiography of Jaʿfar b. ʿAlī, chamberlain to the Fatimid caliph-imam al-Mahdī (d. 322/934) that was compiled during the caliphate of al-ʿAzīz (365–386/975–996) by a certain Muḥammad b. Muḥammad al-Yamānī. It contains valuable details on al-Mahdī's long journey (289–297/902–909) from Salamiyya in Syria to North Africa and his stay in Sijilmāsa, from where he was rescued by the *dāʿī* Abū ʿAbd Allāh al-Shīʿī and taken to Raqqāda to be installed to the Fatimid caliphate. Jaʿfar b. ʿAlī had accompanied al-Mahdī on this fateful journey. Born in 260/874–75, Jaʿfar was an eyewitness to many important events in early Ismaili history.

B. Collective Ismaili Works

- *Taʾrīkh akhbār al-Qarāmiṭa*, ed., Suhayl Zakkār. Beirut: Muʾassasat al-Risāla and Dār al-Amāna, 1391/1971. pp. 127; 2nd ed., as *Akhbār al-Qarāmiṭa*. Damascus: Dār Ḥassān, 1402/1982. pp. 77 + 483. Includes works by non-Ismaili authors, such as Thābit b. Sinān, al-Qāḍī ʿAbd al-Jabbār, Ibn Mālik al-Ḥammādī, Ibn al-Jawzī, Ibn Ẓāfir and Ibn al-ʿAdīm. Our references to this book are to the second edition.
- *An Anthology of Philosophy in Persia:* Volume II, *Ismāʿīlī and Hermetico-Pythagorean Philosophy*, ed., Seyyed Hossein Nasr with Mehdi Aminrazavi. Oxford: Oxford University Press, 2001. pp. xiii + 400.
- *Arbaʿ kutub ḥaqqāniyya*, ed., Muṣṭafā Ghālib. Beirut: al-Muʾassasa al-Jāmiʿiyya li'l-Dirāsāt wa'l-Nashr wa'l-Tawzīʿ, 1403/1983. pp. 142.
- *Arbaʿ rasāʾil Ismāʿīliyya*, ed., ʿĀrif Tāmir. Salamiyya: Dār al-Kashshāf, 1953. pp. 133.
- *Gnosis-Texte der Ismailiten*, with the Arabic title as *Arbaʿa kutub Ismāʿīliyya*, ed., Rudolf Strothmann. Abhandlungen der Akademie der Wissenschaften in Göttingen, Philologisch-historische Klasse, Dritte Folge, 28. Göttingen: Vandenhoeck & Ruprecht, 1943. pp. 61 (German) + 215 (Arabic).
- Hooda, Vali Mahomed Nanji (1889–1959) (ed. and tr.), "Some Specimens of Satpanth Literature", in W. Ivanow, ed., *Collectanea*: Vol. 1. Ismaili Society Series A, no. 2. Leiden: Published for the Ismaili Society by E.J. Brill, 1948, pp. 55–137.
- *Khams rasāʾil Ismāʿīliyya*, ed., ʿĀrif Tāmir. Salamiyya: Dār al-Inṣāf, 1375/1956. pp. 179.
- *Majmūʿat al-wathāʾiq al-Fāṭimiyya*, ed., Jamāl al-Dīn al-Shayyāl. al-Wathāʾiq al-taʾrīkhiyya li-Miṣr al-Islāmiyya, 1. Cairo: al-Jamʿīyya al-Miṣriyya li'l-Dirāsāt al-Taʾrīkhiyya, 1958. pp. 492.

  A collection of 23 documents issued by the Fatimid chancery of state (*dīwān al-inshāʾ*) on behalf of various Fatimid caliph-imams; the majority having been preserved in Aḥmad b. ʿAlī al-Qalqashandī's *Ṣubḥ al-aʿshā* (Cairo, 1332–38/1914–20). The Arabic texts and English translations of another ten Fatimid documents are contained in S.M. Stern's *Fāṭimid Decrees: Original Documents from the Fāṭimid Chancery.*
- *Muntakhabāt Ismāʿīliyya*, ed., ʿĀdil al-ʿAwwā. Damascus: Maṭbaʿat al-Jāmiʿa al-Sūriyya, 1378/1958. pp. 272.

- *Thalāth rasāʾil Ismāʿīliyya*, ed., ʿĀrif Tāmir. Beirut: Dār al-Āfāq al-Jadīda, 1403/1983. pp. 52.
- *Trilogie Ismaélienne*, with the Persian title as *Īrān va Yaman: yaʿnī sih risāla-yi Ismāʿīlī*, ed. and French trans., Henry Corbin. Bibliothèque Iranienne, 9. Tehran: Département d'Iranologie de l'Institut Franco-Iranien; Paris: A. Maisonneuve, 1340 Sh./1961. pp. 200 (French) + 196 (French) + 184 (Arabic and Persian); reprinted, without the Arabic and Persian texts and with Christian Jambet's new introduction. Collection "Islam spirituel". Lagrasse: Verdier, 1994. pp. xvi + 460.
- *Two Early Ismaili Treatises: Haft babi Baba Sayyid-na and Matlubu'l-muʾminin*, ed., Wladimir Ivanow. Islamic Research Association [Series], no. 2. Bombay: A.A.A. Fyzee, 1933. pp. 9 (English) + 64 (Persian).

C. Anonymous Ismaili and Pseudo-Ismaili Works

This section also includes a selection of non-Ismaili works preserved and used by the Ismailis of Syria, India, Central Asia and elsewhere.

- *Āfāq-nāma*, in two parts, ed., A.E. Bertel's, in *Panj risāla*, pp. 1–24.

  Contains ideas on the elements, senses, the creation, etc., attributed to Sayyid Nāṣir-i Khusraw.
- *Baʿḍī az taʾwīlāt-i gulshan-i rāz*, ed. and French trans., Henry Corbin, in his *Trilogie Ismaélienne*, Persian text pp. 131–161, translation as *Symboles choisis de la "Roseraie du Mystère"*, pp. 1–174.

  This may be identical with a work entitled *Sharḥ-i gulshan-i rāz*, attributed to Shāh Ṭāhir al-Ḥusaynī al-Dakkanī (d. ca. 956/1549), the thirty-first imam of the Muḥammad-Shāhī (or Muʾminī) Nizārī Ismailis; *see* Poonawala, *Biobibliography*, p. 274. A partial commentary, it comprises esoteric interpretations (*taʾwīlāt*) of selected passages of the celebrated Sufi *mathnawī*, *Gulshan-i rāz*, composed by Maḥmūd-i Shabistarī (d. after 740/1339).
- *Bilawhar wa-Būdhāsf*, Arabic version, lithographed by Nūr al-Dīn b. Jīwā Khān. Bombay, 1306/1888–89. pp. 288; ed., Daniel Gimaret as *Kitāb Bilawhar wa-Būdhāsf*. Recherches publiées sous la direction de l'Institut de Lettres Orientales de Beyrouth, Série 1: Pensée Arabe et Musulmane, VI. Beirut: Dar al-Mashriq, 1972. pp. xx + 202. French trans., Daniel Gimaret, *Le Livre de Bilawhar et Būdāsf selon la version*

Arabe Ismaélienne. Centre de Recherches d'Histoire et de Philosophie de la IVe section de l'École Pratique des Hautes Études, Hautes études Islamiques et orientales d'histoire comparée, 3. Paris and Geneva: Librairie Droz, 1971. pp. xii + 216. Russian trans., V. Rosen, *Povest' o Varlaame i Iosafa*, ed., Ignace Kratchkovsky (1883–1951). Leningrad, 1947. Urdu trans., Mawlavī Sayyid ʿAbd al-Ghanī, *Kitāb Bilawhar wa-Būdhāsf*. Hyderabad: Maṭbaʿ Shams, n.d. Excerpts, as preserved by Ibn Bābawayh (d. 381/991), ed. and tr., Samuel M. Stern and Sofie Walzer as *Three Unknown Buddhist Stories in an Arabic Version*. Oxford: Cassirer, 1971. pp. 38.

A form of the legendary biography of the Buddha was translated from Sanskrit into Middle Persian and then rendered into Arabic, probably in early Abbasid times. The Arabic version of Bilawhar and Būdhāsf, heroes of the story, provided the source for all other versions, including the Greek and the Christian legend of Barlaam and Joasaph (Josephat), (*see* Ernst Kuhn's *Barlaam und Joasaph. Eine bibliographisch-literargeschichtliche Studie*, in *Abhandlungen der Bayerischen Akademie der Wissenschaften*, Philosophisch-philologische Klasse, Band XX, Munich, 1893. pp. 88). The full Arabic version of this work has been preserved by the Ṭayyibī Ismaili Bohras of South Asia and used in their curriculum on ethics; *see* al-Majdūʿ, *Fihrist*, pp. 11–15.

- *Fragments relatifs à la doctrine des Ismaélîs*, ed. and French trans., Stanislas Guyard, in *Notices et Extraits des Manuscrits de la Bibliothèque Nationale et autres bibliothèques*, 22 (1874), pp. 177–428 (text pp. 193–274, translation pp. 275–428); also published separately, Paris: Imprimerie Nationale, 1874. pp. 253.

  These fragments on Ismaili doctrines contained in a manuscript recovered around 1809 from Maṣyāf in Syria by Jean Baptiste L.J. Rousseau (1780–1831), the French consul general in Aleppo, represent the earliest Ismaili source materials used by orientalists in Europe. Initially, French translations of some of the fragments were published, through the efforts of Silvestre de Sacy, in J.B.L.J. Rousseau's "Extraits d'un Livre qui contient la doctrine des Ismaélis" (1812), pp. 222–249.

- *Haft bāb-i Bābā Sayyidnā*, ed., Wladimir Ivanow, in his *Two Early Ismaili Treatises*. Islamic Research Association [Series], no. 2. Bombay: A.A.A. Fyzee, 1933, pp. 4–42. English trans., Marshall Hodgson as *The Popular Appeal of the Qiyāma*, in his *The Order of Assassins*, pp. 279–324.

A treatise on the declaration of the *qiyāma* in 559/1164 at Alamūt, evidently witnessed by the author, as well as Nizārī teachings of the *qiyāma* times, wrongly attributed to Bābā Sayyidnā, viz., Ḥasan-i Ṣabbāḥ (d. 518/1124).

- *Kitāb al-haft wa'l-aẓilla*, attributed to al-Mufaḍḍal b. ʿUmar al-Juʿfī, ed., ʿĀrif Tāmir and I.ʿA. Khalīfa. Recherches publiées sous la direction de l'Institut de Lettres Orientales de Beyrouth, Série 1: Pensée Arabe et Musulmane, XVIII. Beirut: al-Maṭbaʿa al-Kāthūlīkiyya, 1960. pp. 19 (French) + 153 (Arabic); 2nd ed., Beirut: Dār al-Mashriq, 1970. pp. 24 (French) + 220 (Arabic); 3rd ed., Beirut: Dār wa-Maktabat al-Hilāl, 1981. pp. 222; ed., Muṣṭafā Ghālib as *Kitāb al-haft al-sharīf min faḍā'il mawlānā Jaʿfar al-Ṣādiq*. Beirut: Dār al-Andalus, 1964. pp. 232; 2nd ed., Beirut: Dar al-Andalus, 1403/1983. pp. 198. Partial German trans., H. Halm, in his *Die islamische Gnosis*, pp. 240–274.

  An eminent *ghālī*, al-Mufaḍḍal was a follower of the Imam Jaʿfar al-Ṣādiq (d. 148/765) who later became an adherent of the Twelver Imāmī Imam, Mūsā al-Kāẓim (d. 183/799), during whose imamate he died. This is the most famous of the works attributed to al-Mufaḍḍal. Reporting certain views of Jaʿfar al-Ṣādiq, the *Kitāb al-haft* is essentially a Mufaḍḍalī-Nuṣayrī text which found its way to the Syrian Nizārī Ismailis who seized the Nuṣayrī fortresses of central Syria in the 6th/12th century. Subsequently, this book, also known to the Ṭayyibīs, came to be regarded by the Ismailis as belonging to their literature, even though it does not contain any Ismaili ideas.

- *Khazā'in al-adilla*, ed., Muṣṭafā Ghālib, in al-Kirmānī, *Majmūʿat rasā'il al-Kirmānī*, pp. 190–209.

  An anonymous work, on cosmology, theology and imamate that has been incorrectly attributed to al-Kirmānī and, as such, included in the collection of the thirteen *Rasā'il* by him.

- *Kitāb al-tarātīb*, ed., Suhayl Zakkār, in his *Akhbār al-Qarāmiṭa*, pp. 133–141.

  This is a chapter on early Ismaili history from an anonymous work, acquired in Syria, on seven stages of attainment in Ismailism.

- *Masā'il majmūʿa min al-ḥaqā'iq al-ʿāliya* (also as *Majmūʿ al-masā'il fi'l-ḥaqā'iq*), ed., R. Strothmann, in *Gnosis-Texte*, pp. 4–136.

  A compendium of several *masā'il* dealing with the creation, *qā'im*, eschatology, etc. Several of the *masā'il* are drawn from Muḥammad

b. Ṭāhir al-Ḥārithī's (d. 584/1188) well-known *al-Anwār al-laṭīfa*, a treatise on the Ṭayyibī *ḥaqā'iq*.

- *Mir'āt al-muḥaqqiqīn*, lithographed by Sayyid Munīr Badakhshānī, together with Nāṣir-i Khusraw's *Rawshanā'ī-nāma* and Khayrkhwāh-i Harātī's *Risāla*. Bombay, 1333/1915; ed., A.E. Bertel's, in *Panj risāla*, pp. 25–89.

  A treatise on intelligible beings, the soul (*nafs*), and the knowledge of self and God.

- *Panj risāla dar bayān-i āfāq va anfus ya'nī barābarī-yi Ādam va 'ālam*, ed., Andrey Evgen'evich Bertel's, supervised by Bobodzhon G. Gafurov and A.M. Mirzoev. Akademiya Nauk SSSR, Institut Vostokovedeniya; Akademiya Nauk Tadzhiskoy SSR, Institut Vostokovedeniya. Moscow: Nauka, Glavnaya redaktsiya vostochnoy literaturï, 1970. pp. 148 (Russian) + 511 (Persian).

  Five Persian treatises, permeated with Sufi ideas, preserved by the Nizārī Ismailis of Badakhshān in Central Asia. The manuscripts of the works, dated to the 7th/13th and later centuries and included in this collection, were for the most part acquired during 1959–63 from Tajik Badakhshān, where they are preserved in private libraries; *see* A. Bertel's and M. Bokoev, *Alfavitnïy katalog rukopisey*.

- *al-Qaṣīda al-shāfiya*, ed. and English trans., Sami Nassib Makarem as *Ash-Shâfiya (The Healer): An Ismâ'îlî Poem attributed to Shihâb ad-Dîn Abû Firâs*. American University of Beirut, Publication of the Faculty of Arts and Sciences, Oriental Series, no. 48. Beirut: American University of Beirut, 1966. pp. 260; ed., 'Ārif Tāmir. Recherches publiées sous la direction de l'Institut de Lettres Orientales de Beyrouth, Série 1: Pensée Arabe et Musulmane, XXXVI. Beirut: Dār al-Mashriq, 1967. pp. xxii (French) + 99 (Arabic).

  This versified work attributed in one of its Syrian manuscripts to Abū Firās Shihāb al-Dīn al-Maynaqī (d. 937/1530 or ten years later), may have been originally composed by a Ḥāfiẓī Musta'lī poet and then revised by a Nizārī author; *see* W. Madelung's reviews, in *ZDMG*, 118 (1968), pp. 423–427 and *Oriens*, 23–24 (1974), pp. 517–518. The *qaṣā'id* deal with *tawḥīd*, God's command (*amr*), the creation, cyclical conception of history and eras of different prophets from Ādam to Muḥammad, the hierarchy of ranks in the Ismaili *da'wa*, etc. In verses 704–733 (ed. Makarem), 617–635 (ed. Tāmir) the names of different imams recognized by the Ḥāfiẓīs and the Nizārīs are enumerated, indicating different Ismaili origins and authorships of the work.

- *Risālat al-ism al-aʿẓam*, ed., Rudolf Strothmann, in *Gnosis-Texte*, pp. 171–177.
- Salisbury, Edward E., "Translation of Two Unpublished Arabic Documents, Relating to the Doctrines of the Ismâʿilis and other Bâṭinian Sects", *JAOS*, 2 (1851), pp. 259–324.

The manuscript of these anonymous fragments on Neoplatonized cosmology and other Ismaili doctrines, preserved by the Syrian Nizārīs, was acquired by an American missionary in Syria, Dr. Henry W. de Forest, and sent to Salisbury who translated them into English for the American Oriental Society.

- *Umm al-khiṭāb*, ed., A.E. Bertel's, in *Panj risāla*, pp. 209–300.

On the creation of man, the apparent and hidden attributes and functions of various parts of the human body, and the requirements for an ethical life.

- *Umm al-kitāb*, ed., Wladimir Ivanow, in *Der Islam*, 23 (1936), pp. 132. Italian trans., Pio Filippani-Ronconi, *Ummu'l-Kitāb*. Naples: Istituto Universitario Orientale di Napoli, 1966. pp. lv + 301. Partial German trans., E.F. Tijdens, in his "Der mythologisch-gnostische Hintergrund der Umm al-Kitāb", pp. 241–526. Partial German trans., H. Halm, in his *Die islamische Gnosis*, pp. 113–198. Excerpt, English trans., Latimah Parvin Peerwani as *Umm al-kitāb, The Mother of Books*, in *APP*, pp. 17–32.

Written in archaic Persian and preserved by the Nizārī Ismailis of Central Asia, this work was originally produced in the 2nd/8th century in Arabic by the Mukhammisa, an early group of Shīʿī *ghulāt*; *see* W. Madelung's review, in *Oriens*, 25–26 (1976), pp. 352–358, and H. Halm, *Kosmologie und Heilslehre der frühen Ismāʿīlīya*, pp. 142–168. It contains the discourses of the Imam Muḥammad al-Bāqir (d. ca. 114/732) in response to questions posed by an anachronistic group of disciples, including Jābir b. ʿAbd Allāh al-Anṣārī, Jābir al-Juʿfī and Muḥammad b. al-Mufaḍḍal. The *Umm al-kitāb*, which does not contain any Ismaili doctrines, was at some point adopted into Ismaili literature and found its way into private libraries of the Nizārīs of Badakhshān.

- *Uṣūl-i ādāb*, ed., A.E. Bertel's, in *Panj risāla*, pp. 301–381.

Emphasizing the necessity of knowing the imam of the time (*imām-i zamān*) and expounding the esoteric interpretation (*ta'wīl*) of certain religious duties, this treatise contains separate sections on *tawḥīd*, prophethood (*nubuwwat*), imamate, commanding the right and forbidding the wrong, and solidarity (*tawallā*) with the prophet and the imams and dissociation (*tabarrā*) from their enemies and unbelievers.

- *Zubdat al-ḥaqāʾiq*, lithographed, Tehran, 1320/1902; ed., A.E. Bertel's, in *Panj risāla*, pp. 91–207.

  A treatise on origination (*mabdaʾ*) and destination (*maʿād*) and the hierarchies of creation written by ʿAzīz al-Dīn Nasafī (d. ca. 661/1262) who, in line with the general Sufi tendencies of the period, dealt with metaphysical and cosmological teachings of various schools of Sufism and philosophy in a popular manner. In particular, Nasafī popularized some of the esoteric teachings of his Sufi master, Saʿd al-Dīn Ḥammūʾī (d. ca. 650/1252), who himself was a disciple of Najm al-Dīn Kubrā (d. 618/1221). The treatise, in two sections (*bābs*), opens with a discussion of three categories of people, *ahl-i sharīʿat*, *ahl-i ḥikmat* or *bāṭinīs*, and *ahl-i waḥdat* who profess the unity of being (*waḥdat al-wujūd*), a central idea in this treatise. The Nizārī Ismailis of Central Asia regard this Sufi work as belonging to their literature as they consider ʿAzīz Nasafī a co-religionist.

D. *Rasāʾil Ikhwān al-Ṣafāʾ*, by an Anonymous Group of Authors

Much controversy has surrounded the identity of the authors who have become famous as the Ikhwān al-Ṣafāʾ, usually translated as the "Sincere Brethren" or "Brethren of Purity", and produced their encyclopedic work in Arabic entitled *Rasāʾil Ikhwān al-Ṣafāʾ*, comprised of fifty-two epistles as well as their abridged versions. At any rate, modern scholarship has acknowledged the Ismaili affiliation of this group of learned authors who probably lived in Baṣra in the middle of the 4th/10th century. However, Professor Abbas Hamdani dates the composition of the *Rasāʾil* to the final decades of the 3rd/9th century, shortly before the foundation of the Fatimid caliphate in 297/909. The secondary literature on the Ikhwān al-Ṣafāʾ and their *Rasāʾil* is rather extensive; *see* especially the publications of C. Baffioni, A. Hamdani, Y. Marquet, A.L. Tibawi and other relevant entries in Chapter 4: Studies.

Complete editions of the *Rasāʾil Ikhwān al-Ṣafāʾ*

- *Kitāb Ikhwān al-Ṣafāʾ wa-Khullān al-Wafāʾ*. Bombay: Maṭbaʿat Nukhbat al-Akhbār, 1305–6/1887–89. 4 vols.; *Rasāʾil Ikhwān al-Ṣafāʾ wa-Khullān al-Wafāʾ*, ed., Khayr al-Dīn al-Ziriklī, with introductions by Ṭāhā Ḥusayn and Aḥmad Zakī Pasha. Cairo: al-Maṭbaʿa al-ʿArabiyya bi-Miṣr, 1347/1928. 4 vols.; *Rasāʾil Ikhwān al-Ṣafāʾ wa-Khullān al-Wafāʾ*, with an introduction by Buṭrūs al-Bustānī. Beirut: Dār Ṣādir and Dār Beirut, 1376/1957. 4 vols; reprinted, Beirut: Dār Bayrūt, 1403/1983. 4 vols; *Rasāʾil Ikhwān al-Ṣafāʾ wa-Khullān al-Wafāʾ*, ed., ʿĀrif Tāmir. Beirut and Paris: Manshūrāt ʿUwaydāt, 1415/1995. 5 vols. See also D.R. Blumenthal, "A Comparative Table of the Bombay, Cairo and Beirut Editions of the Rasāʾil Iḫwān al-Ṣafāʾ."

  The *Rasāʾil*, numbering 52 and representing a compendium of a variety of sciences known at the time of their composition, are divided into four books or sections dealing with mathematical sciences (geometry, astronomy, music, logic, etc.), bodily and natural sciences, physical and intellectual sciences (cosmology, eschatology, etc.), and theological sciences. The authors of the *Rasāʾil* drew on diverse schools of Hellenistic wisdom, notably Neoplatonism, and a variety of other pre-Islamic sources and traditions, which they combined with Islamic teachings. The Ikhwān al-Ṣafāʾ attempted in an original manner to harmonize religion and philosophy for the ultimate purpose of guiding mankind to purify their soul and achieve salvation.

Original summaries of the *Rasāʾil Ikhwān al-Ṣafāʾ*

- *al-Risāla al-jāmiʿa, tāj Rasāʾil Ikhwān al-Ṣafāʾ wa-Khullān al-Wafāʾ*, ed., Jamīl Ṣalībā. Damascus: al-Majmaʿ al-ʿIlmī al-ʿArabī bi-Dimashq, 1949–51. 2 vols.; ed., M. Ghālib. Beirut: Dar Ṣādir, 1394/1974. pp. 551; 2nd ed., Beirut: Dār al-Andalus, 1404/1984. pp. 551.

  An abridged version of selected portions of the *Rasāʾil*, produced by the same original *Ikhwān al-Ṣafāʾ*. The *Jāmiʿa* was intended for more advanced readers.

- *Risālat Jāmiʿat al-jāmiʿa li-Ikhwān al-Ṣafāʾ wa-Khullān al-Wafāʾ*, ed., ʿĀrif Tāmir. Beirut: Dār al-Nashr liʾl-Jāmiʿīyyīn, 1378/1959, pp. 222; 2nd ed., Beirut: Dār Maktabat al-Ḥayāt, 1970, pp. 239.

  A further abridgement of *al-Risāla al-jāmiʿa* produced by the Ikhwān al-Ṣafāʾ.

Partial editions of the *Rasā'il Ikhwān al-Ṣafā'*

- *Tuḥfat Ikhwān al-Ṣafā'*, revised and edited by Schuekh Ahmud-bin-Moohummud Schurwan-ool-Yummunee. Calcutta: Hindoostanee Press, 1812. pp. viii + 442; ed., Aḥmad b. Muḥammad al-Anṣārī al-Shīrwānī. Calcutta: n. p., 1263/1847. pp. 400.
- *Ikhwān al-Ṣafā'*, ed., Ghulām Ḥaydar. Calcutta: Maṭbaʿat al-Ṭibī, 1846. pp. 400.
- *al-Ḥayawān wa'l-insān,* lithographed in Calcutta, 1263/1847; also lithographed in Lucknow, 1316/1899.
- *Ikhwān al-Ṣafā'*. Lahore: Maṭbaʿa-i Sarkārī, 1866. pp. 288.
- *The Ikhwan-us-Safa*, revised and corrected by William Nassau Lees. Calcutta: College Press, 1867. pp. 158.
- *Thier und Mensch vor dem König der Genien. Ein arabisches Märchen aus den Schriften der Lautern Brüder in Basra*, ed., Friedrich Dieterici. Leipzig: J.C. Hinrich, 1879–81. pp. 148. Reprinted, as *Die Philosophie bei den Arabern im X. Jahrhundert n. Chr.* Gesamtdarstellung und Quellenwerke, X. Hildesheim: G. Olms, 1969.
- *Khulāṣat al-Wafā' bi-ikhtiṣār Rasā'il Ikhwān al-Ṣafā': Die Abhandlungen der Ichwân es-Safâ in Auswahl. Zum ersten Mal aus arabischen Handschriften*, ed., Friedrich Dieterici. Leipzig: J.C. Hinrich, 1883–86. 3 vols. (with continous pagination) pp. xix (German) + 637 (Arabic). Reprinted, as *Die Philosophie bei den Arabern im X. Jahrhundert n. Chr.* Gesamtdarstellung und Quellenwerke, XIII, XIV. Hildesheim: G. Olms, 1969. 2 vols.
- *Rasā'il Ikhwān al-Ṣafā' wa-Khullān al-Wafā'*. Bombay: Mīrzā Muḥammad Shīrāzī, 1884. pp. 167.
- *al-Ḥayawān wa'l-insān, wa-hiya khātimat wa-zubdat Rasā'il Ikhwān al-Ṣafā'*. Cairo: Dār al-Taraqqī, 1900. pp. 168; Cairo: Maktabat al-Maʿārif, 1331/1913. pp. 176.
- *Tadāʿī al-ḥayawānāt ʿalā'l-insān*, ed., Fārūq Saʿd. Beirut: Dār al-Āfāq al-Jadīda, 1977. pp. 269; 2nd ed., Beirut: Dār al-Āfāq al-Jadīda, 1980. pp. 269.
- *Sirr al-asrār li-ta'sīs al-siyāsa wa-tartīb al-riyāsa li-Ikhwān al-Ṣafā' wa-Khullān al-Wafā'*, ed., Aḥmad al-Turaykī (Ahmed Triki). Beirut: Dār al-Kalima al-ʿArabiyya, 1983. pp. 152; ed., Sāmī Salmān al-Aʿwar as *Sirr al-asrār: al-siyāsa wa'l-farāsa fī tadbīr al-ri'āsa*. Beirut: Dār

al-Kātib al-ʿArabī, 1980. pp. 171; Beirut: Dār al-Kātib li'l-Jamīʿ, 1986. pp. 174; Beirut: Dār al-ʿUlūm al-ʿArabiyya, 1995. pp. 170 (questionable attribution).

Partial translations of the *Rasāʾil Ikhwān al-Ṣafāʾ*

Some of the following translations also include partial editions, in Arabic, of sections of the *Rasāʾil Ikhwān al-Ṣafāʾ*.

English:

- Cavendish, A. C. *Studies in Hindustanee: Ikhwan us Safa*. Cottayam: Church Missionary Society's Press, 1885. pp. vi + 193 + iii.
- Dowson, John. *Ikhwánu-s Safá; or, Brothers of Purity*. London: Trübner & Co, 1869. pp. viii + 156 (based on the Urdu rendering from the Arabic by Ikrām ʿAlī).
- Goldstein, Bernard R. "A Treatise on the Number Theory from a Tenth-century Arabic Source", *Centaurus*, 10 (1964), pp. 129–160; reprinted as *A Theory of Numbers*, in *APP*, pp. 225–245.
- Goodman, Lenn Evan. *The Case of the Animals versus Man before the King of the Jinn: A Tenth-century Ecological Fable of the Pure Brethren of Basra*. Library of Classical Arabic Literature, vol. 3. Boston: Twayne Publishers, 1978. pp. xi + 271. Excerpt, pp. 51–77, 198–202, reprinted as *Man and Animals*, in *APP*, pp. 246–278.
- Johnson-Davis, Denys. *The Island of Animals*. London: Quartet Books, 1994. pp. xix + 76.
- Manuel, Thomas Philip. *The Ikhwan-oos-suffa*. Calcutta: D'Rozario & Co, 1860. pp 42.
- Peerwani, Latimah Parvin. *Microcosm and Macrocosm*, in *APP*, pp. 202–225.
- Platts, John. *Ikhwanu-ṣ-ṣafā; or, Brothers of Purity*. London: W.H. Allen & Co, 1869. pp. xii + 234; reprinted, carried through the press by Edward B. Eastwick. London: W.H. Allen & Co, 1875. pp. xii + 234 (based on the Urdu translation of Ikrām ʿAlī).
- Shiloah, Amnon. *The Epistle on Music of the Ikhwān al-Ṣafāʾ (Baghdad, 10th Century)*. Tel-Aviv University, Documentation and Studies, 3. Tel-Aviv: Tel-Aviv University, 1978. pp. 73.

- van Reijn, Eric. *The Epistles of the Sincere Brethren (Rasa'il Ikhwan al-Safa'): An Annotated Translation of Epistles 43 to 47*. Montreux, etc.: Minerva Press, 1995. pp. 137 + x.
- Wall, Joseph. *The Ikhwan-us-suffa: A Translation into English*. Lucknow: Printed at the Oudh Gazette Press, 1863. pp. 113 (Hindustani and English on opposite pages); reprinted, Lucknow: Newul Kishore Press, 1889. pp. 141.
- Yusufji, D.H. "The Forty-third Treatise of the Ikhwān al-Ṣafā'", *MW*, 33 (1943), pp. 39–49; reprinted in *RIS*, vol. 2, pp. 225–235.

French:

- Callataÿ, Godefroid de. *Ikwān al-Ṣafā'. Les révolutions et les cycles (Épîtres des Frères de la Pureté, XXXVI)*. Sagesses Musulmanes, 3. Beirut: al-Bouraq; Louvain-la-Neuve: Academia-Bruylant, 1996. pp. 207.
- Callataÿ, Godefroid de. "Ikhwân al-Ṣafâ: des arts scientifiques et de leur objectif", *Le Muséon*, 116 (2003), pp. 231–258.
- Marquet, Yves. *La philosophie des Iḫwān al-Ṣafā'* (1975), pp. 41–584; revised ed. (1999), pp. 41–584. For Y. Marquet's other partial French translations of the *Rasā'il*; *see* his entries listed in Chapter 4: Studies.
- Michot, Jean. "L'épître de la résurrection des Ikhwān al-Ṣafā'", *Bulletin de Philosophie Médiévale*, 16–17 (1974–75), pp. 114–148.
- Shiloah, Amnon. "L'épître sur la musique des Ikhwān al-Ṣafa'", *REI*, 32 (1964), pp. 125–162; 34 (1966), pp. 159–193.
- Shiloah, Amnon (ed. and tr.) "Deux textes Arabes inédits sur la musique", in Israël Adler et al., ed., *Yuval: Studies of the Jewish Music Research Centre*. Jerusalem: Magnes Press, 1968, pp. 221–248.
- Tassy, Garcin de. *Les Animeaux: extrait du Tuhfat Ikwan Ussafa (Cadeau des Frères de la Pureté)*. Paris: Benjamin Duprat, 1864. pp. 118.

German:

- Dieterici, Friedrich. *Die Propaeldeutik der Araber im zehnten Jahrhundert*. Berlin: E.S. Mittler und Sohn, 1865. pp. ix + 201. Reprinted, as *Die Philosophie bei den Arabern im X. Jahrhundert n. Chr.* Gesamtdarstellung und Quellenwerke, III. Hildesheim: G. Olms, 1969.

- Dieterici, Friedrich. *Die Logik und Psychologie der Araber im zehnten Jahrhundert n. Chr.* Leipzig: J.C. Hinrich, 1868. pp. ix + 196. Reprinted, as *Die Philosophie bei den Arabern im X. Jahrhundert n. Chr.* Gesamtdarstellung und Quellenwerke, IV. Hildesheim: G. Olms, 1969 (translation of treatises 7–13).
- Dieterici, Friedrich. *Die Naturanschauung und Naturphilosophie der Araber im zehnten Jahrhundert.* Aus den Schriften der lautern Brüder. Berlin: Nicolai, 1861; Posen: Jagielski, 1864; Leipzig: J. C. Hinrich, 1876. pp. xvi + 216. Reprinted, as *Die Philosophie bei den Arabern im X. Jahrhundert n. Chr.* Gesamtdarstellung und Quellenwerke, V. Hildesheim: G. Olms, 1969 (translation of treatises 14–21).
- Dieterici, Friedrich. *Die Anthropologie der Araber im zehnten Jahrhundert n. Chr.* Leipzig: J.C. Hinrich, 1871. pp. viii + 221. Reprinted, as *Die Philosophie bei den Arabern im X. Jahrhundert n. Chr.* Gesamtdarstellung und Quellenwerke, VI. Hildesheim: G. Olms, 1969 (translation of treatises 22–30).
- Dieterici, Friedrich. *Die Lehre von der Weltseele bei den Arabern im X. Jahrhundert.* Leipzig: Hinrich, 1872. pp. xi + 196. Reprinted, as *Die Philosophie bei den Arabern im X. Jahrhundert n. Chr.* Gesamtdarstellung und Quellenwerke, VIII. Hildesheim: G. Olms, 1969.
- Diwald, Susanne. *Arabische Philosophie und Wissenschaft in der Enzyklopädie Kitāb Ihwān aṣ-ṣafāʾ (III): Die Lehre von Seele und Intellekt.* Akademie der Wissenschaften und der Literatur, Mainz. Wiesbaden: O. Harrassowitz, 1975. pp. xi + 641.
- Giese, Alma. *Ihwān aṣ-Ṣafāʾ: Mensch und Tier vor dem König der Dschinnen.* Philosophische Bibliothek, Band 433. Hamburg: F. Meiner, 1990. pp. xlviii + 231.
- Landsberger, Julius. *Iggereth Baale Chajim: Abhandlung über die Thiere von Kalonymos ben Kalonymos, oder Rechtsstreit zwischen Mensch und Their vor dem Gerichtshofe des Königs der Genien. Ein arabisches Märchen.* Darmstadt: G. Jonghaus, 1882. pp xxxiv + 284.
- Nauwerck, Karl. *Notiz über das arabische Buch: Tuḥfat Ikhwān al-Ṣafāʾ, d.h. Gabe der aufrichtigen Freunde, nebst Proben desselben, Arabisch und Deutsch.* Berlin: G. Reimer, 1837. pp. 99 (German) + 55 (Arabic); reprinted in *RIS*, vol. 1, pp. 35–192.

Italian:

- Baffioni, Carmela. *L'Epistola degli Ihwān al-Ṣafā' "Sulle opinioni e le religioni"*. Naples: Istituto Universitario Orientale di Napoli, Dipartimento di Studi e Ricerche su Africa e Paesi Arabi, 1989. pp. 268. For Carmela Baffioni's other partial Italian translations of the *Rasā'il*, *see* her entries listed in Chapter 4: Studies.
- Bausani, Alessandro. *L'Enciclopedia dei Fratelli della Purità*. Istituto Universitario Orientale, Seminario di Studi Asiatici, Series Minor, IV. Naples: Istituto Universitario Orientale, 1978. pp. 284.

Persian:

- Ḥalabī, ʿAlī Aṣghar. *Guzīda-yi matn-i Rasā'il Ikhwān al-Ṣafā' wa-Khullān al-Wafā'*. Tehran: Zavvār, 1360 Sh./1981. pp. viii + 223.
- *Mujmal al-ḥikma, tarjama gūna'ī kuhan az Rasā'il Ikhwān al-Ṣafā'*, ed., Muḥammad Taqī Dānishpazhūh and Īraj Afshār. Tehran: Pazhūhishgāh-i ʿUlūm-i Insānī va Muṭālaʿāt-i Farhangī, 1375 Sh./1996. pp. xxvii + 414.
- Zangī Bukharī, Muḥammad b. Maḥmūd b. Muḥammad. *Bustān al-ʿuqūl fī tarjumān al-manqūl*, ed., Muḥammad Taqī Dānishpazhūh and Īraj Afshār. Tehran: Pazhūhishgāh-i ʿUlūm-i Insānī va Muṭālaʿāt-i Farhangī, 1374 Sh./1995. pp. 235.

Spanish:

- Ricardo-Felipe, Albert Reyna. "La 'Risāla fī māhiyyat al-ʿišq' de las *Rasā'il Ijwān al-Ṣafā'*", *Anaquel de Estudios Árabes*, 6 (1995), pp. 185–207.
- Tornero Poveda, Emilio. *La Disputa de los Animales contra el Hombre (Traducción del Original Árabe de La Disputa del Asno Contra Fray Anselmo Turmeda)*. Madrid: Editorial de la Universidad Complutense, 1984. pp. 234.

Urdu:

- Abū al-Ṭayyib Afaḍ al-Dīn Aḥmad, al-Mawlawī. *Hādhihi Risāla min Rasā'il Ikhwān al-Ṣafā' wa-Khullān al-Wafā' qad ishtamalat ʿalā mā dāra bayna al-ins wa'l-ḥayawānāt*. Lithographed, Kānfūr: Maṭba'at al-Majīdiyya, 1913 (partial edition with Urdu translation).

- Ikrām 'Alī, Maulavī. *The Ikhwan-oos-safa. Hindustani text of Animals vs. Man*. Reprinted for the use of the College of Fort William by W. Nassau Lees. Calcutta: Printed at W.N. Lees' Press, 1859. pp. 153 (in Hindustani, the Hindi-Urdu of the time).
- Ikrām 'Alī, Maulavī. *Ikhwānu-ṣ-Ṣafā*, ed., Duncan Forbes and Charles Rieu. London: W.H. Allen & Co, 1861 [1873?]. pp. vi (English) + 176 (Urdu).

Other languages:

- Bauwens, Jan. "Zeventiende Zendbrief van de Rasâ'il Iḫwân aṣ-Ṣafâ'. Over de fysische lichamen", *Orientalia Gandensia*, 1 (1964), pp. 171–185 (in Dutch).
- Gautier Dalché, Patrick. "Epistola fraterum sincerorum in cosmographia: une traduction Latine inédite de la quatrième Risāla des Iḫwān al-Ṣafā'", *Revue d'Histoire des Textes*, 18 (1988), pp. 137–167 (in Latin).
- Karič, Enes. *Rasprava čovjeka sa životinjama*. Sarajevo: Mešihat Islamske Zajednice Bosne i Hercegovine, 1991. pp. 361 (in Serbo-Croatian).

E. Selected Works by Non-Ismaili Muslim Authors

'Abd al-Jabbār b. Aḥmad al-Hamadhānī al-Asadābādī, al-Qāḍī (d. 415/1024–25), Mu'tazilī theologian and chief *qāḍī* in Rayy

- *Fī aḥwāl al-Bāṭiniyya*, an excerpt from *Tathbīt dala'il nubuwwat Sayyidnā Muḥammad*, ed., Suhayl Zakkār, in his *Akhbār al-Qarāmiṭa*, pp. 143–191.

  The most prominent theologian of the late Mu'tazilī school, 'Abd al-Jabbār wrote his *Tathbīt*, on the miraculous proofs of Muḥammad's prophethood, in 385/995; it also contains polemical refutations of other religions as well as Ismaili and Imāmī Shi'ism. This section contains his refutation of the Ismailis, an extract from the *Tathbīt dalā'il nubuwwat Sayyidnā Muḥammad*, ed., 'Abd al-Karīm 'Uthmān (Beirut:Dār al-'Arabiyya, 1966–69), vol. 2, pp. 376–399, 594–609, as well as valuable information on Ismaili *dāʿīs* and their activities in the author's lifetime.

ʿAlī b. Muḥammad b. ʿUbayd Allāh al-ʿAlawī (fl. 3rd/9th century), Yamanī historian

- *Sīrat al-Hādī ilāʾl-Ḥaqq Yaḥyā b. al-Ḥusayn*, ed., Suhayl Zakkār, in his *Akhbār al-Qarāmiṭa*, pp. 85–110.

This biography of the first Zaydī imam of Yaman, the Ḥasanid Yaḥyā b. al-Ḥusayn al-Hādī ilāʾl-Ḥaqq (d. 298/911), composed by ʿAlī b. Muḥammad, contains excerpts on the Ismailis of Yaman.

al-Anṭākī, Abuʾl-Faraj Yaḥyā b. Saʿīd (d. 458/1066), Melkite Christian physician and historian

- *Taʾrīkh Yaḥyā ibn Saʿīd al-Anṭākī*, ed., Louis Cheikho, B. Carra de Vaux and Habib Zayyat. Corpus Scriptorum Orientalium, Scriptores arabici, series III, vol. VII. Paris and Beirut: Maṭbaʿat al-Ābāʾ al-Yasūʿiyyīn, 1909, pp. 91–273; partial ed. and French trans., Ignace Kratchkovsky and A. Vasiliev as *Histoire de Yahya-Ibn-Saʿïd d'Antioche, continuateur de Saʿïd-Ibn-Bitriq*, in *Patrologia Orientalis*, 18 (1924), pp. 699–833; 23 (1932), pp. 347–520 (ending with the events of the year 404/1013); ed., ʿUmar ʿAbd al-Salām Tadmurī as *Taʾrīkh al-Anṭākī, al-maʿrūf bi-ṣilat taʾrīkh Ūtīkhā*. Tripoli, Lebanon: Jarrūs Press, 1990. pp. 582. Partial ed. and French trans., *Histoire de Yaḥyā ibn Saʿīd d'Antioche*, ed., Ignace Kratchkovsky and trans. into French by Françoise Micheau and Gérard Troupeau. Turnhout: Brepols, 1997. pp. 191; being, *Patrologia Orientalis*, 47 (1997), pp. 373–559. Italian trans., Bartolomeo Pirone as *Cronache dell'Egitto Fāṭimide e dell'impero Bizantino 937–1033*. Biblioteca del Vicino Oriente. Patrimonio Culturale Arabo Cristiano, 3. Milan: Jaca Book, 1998. pp. 399.

The only extant contemporary account of the Fatimids is contained in the *Taʿrīkh* of al-Anṭākī, an Arab-Melkite Christian who spent the earlier part of his life in Fatimid Egypt and then migrated, in 405/1014 in the reign of al-Ḥākim, to Antioch where he composed his history of the Abbasid, Fatimid and Byzantine empires, covering the period 326–425/937–1033, as a continuation of Ibn al-Baṭrīq's history.

al-Baghdādī, Abū Manṣūr ʿAbd al-Qāhir b. Ṭāhir (d. 429/1037), Sunni theologian, jurist and heresiographer

- *al-Farq bayn al-firaq*, ed., Muḥammad Badr. Cairo: Maṭbaʿat al-Maʿārif, 1328/1910, pp. 265–299; ed. Muḥammad Zāhid al-Kawtharī. Cairo: Maktab Nashr al-Thaqāfa al-Islāmiyya, 1367/1948. pp. 271; ed. Muḥammad Muḥyiʾ al-Dīn ʿAbd al-Ḥamīd. Cairo: Maktabat Muḥammad ʿAlī Ṣabīḥ, [1964], pp. 281–312. English trans., Abraham S. Halkin as *Moslem Schisms and Sects (Al-Farḳ Bain al-Firaḳ); being, the History of the Various Philosophic Systems Developed in Islam*, part II. Tel-Aviv: Palestine Publishing Co., 1935, pp. 107–157. Persian trans., Muḥammad Javād Mashkūr as *Tarjama-yi al-Farq bayn al-firaq dar taʾrīkh-i madhāhib-i Islām*. Tehran: Amīr Kabīr, 1344 Sh./1965, pp. 201–225.

This chapter on the Bāṭiniyya from al-Baghdādī's well-known heresiographical work, written in the 420s/1030s, contains typical anti-Ismaili polemics. Al-Baghdādī had access to the anti-Ismaili treatises of Ibn Rizām and Akhū Muḥsin and also claims to have used an Ismaili book entitled *Kitāb al-siyāsa wa'l-balāgh*, which modern scholarship has shown to have been a cleverly produced travesty against the Ismailis. In line with a tradition established by anti-Ismaili polemicists, al-Baghdādī portrays Ismailism as a heretical movement designed to destroy Islam.

al-Bustī, Abu'l-Qāsim Ismāʿīl b. Aḥmad al-Jīlī (d. 420/1029), Muʿtazilī Zaydī author

- *Min kashf asrār al-Bāṭiniyya wa-ʿiwār* (or *ghawār*) *madhhabihim*, ed., ʿĀdil Sālim al-ʿAbd al-Jādir, in his *al-Ismāʿīliyyūn: kashf al-asrār wa-naqd al-afkār*, pp. 187–369. Extract, on the origins of Ismailism, in S.M. Stern, "Abu'l-Qasim al-Bustī and his Refutation of Ismāʿīlism", pp. 14–35; reprinted in his *Studies in Early Ismāʿīlism*, pp. 299–320.

This is only a fragment of a work devoted entirely to refutation of the Ismailis. Written around 400/1009, it contains valuable quotations from Ismaili works, notably the lost *al-Maḥṣūl* of the *dāʿī* Muḥammad b. Aḥmad al-Nasafī (d. 332/943). The author is also familiar with the writings of Abū Yaʿqūb al-Sijistānī (d. after 361/971), referred to as Khayshafūj, and several other Ismailis. A student of the Muʿtazilī al-Qāḍī ʿAbd al-Jabbār (d. 415/1024–25), al-Bustī also had access to Ibn

Rizām's anti-Ismaili polemic and argues for a Qaddāḥid ancestry for the Fatimids in addition to tracing Ismailism to Iranian dualistic and Zoroastrian origins.

al-Daylamī, Muḥammad b. al-Ḥasan (d. after 707/1308), Zaydī author in Yaman

- *Bayān madhhab al-Bāṭiniyya wa-buṭlānih, manqūl min Kitāb qawāʿid Āl Muḥammad*, with the German title as *Die Geheimlehre der Batiniten nach der Apologie Dogmatik des Hauses Muhammad*, ed., Rudolf Strothmann. Bibliotheca Islamica, 11. Istanbul: Deutsche Morgenländische Gesellschaft, 1939. pp. xiii + 137.

  A portion of a larger work, *Kitāb qawāʾid Āl Muḥammad*, written against the Ismailis.
- *Qawāʾid ʿaqāʾid Āl Muḥammad fiʾl-radd ʿalāʾl-Bāṭiniyya*, ed., Muḥammad Zāhid al-Kawtharī. Cairo: ʿIzzat al-ʿAṭṭār al-Ḥusaynī, 1950. pp. 157; reprinted, Sanaa: Maktabat al-Yaman al-Kubrā, 1987. pp. 157.

  A polemical work written in 707/1308 by this relatively unknown Zaydī author against the Ismailis. Here, the origins of Ismailism are traced to Iranian and other non-Islamic sources while the Ismaili beliefs are refuted on the basis of a travesty called *Kitāb al-balāgh*, etc.

al-Fazārī, Abu'l-Qāsim Muḥammad (d. 345/956), Sunni poet of Qayrawān

- *al-Qaṣīda al-Fazāriyya fī madḥ al-khalīfa al-Fāṭimī al-Manṣūr*, ed., Mustapha Zmerli, presented by Ḥammādī al-Saḥlī and Muḥammad al-Yaʿlāwī. Beirut: Dār al-Gharb al-Islāmī, 1995. pp. 266. This *Qaṣīda* is also found in M. al-Yaʿlāwī, *al-Adab bi-Ifrīqiya fiʾl-ʿahd al-Fāṭimī*, pp. 221–235.

  A minor Mālikī poet from Qayrawān, al-Fazārī wrote this poem in celebration of the Fatimid caliph-imam al-Manṣūr's victory over the Nukkārī Ibāḍī Khārijī leader Abū Yazīd (d. 336/947), who revolted in North Africa with much initial success against the Fatimids. On other occasions, however, al-Fazārī composed verses against the Fatimids.

al-Ghazālī, Abū Ḥāmid Muḥammad b. Muḥammad al-Ṭūsī (d. 505/1111), Sunni theologian, jurist and mystic

- *Faḍā'iḥ al-Bāṭiniyya wa-faḍā'il al-Mustaẓhiriyya*, ed., ʿAbd al-Raḥmān Badawī. al-Maktaba al-ʿArabiyya, 7. Cairo: al-Dār al-Qawmiyya, 1383/ 1964. pp. 236. Selections, in Ignaz Goldziher, *Streitschrift des Ġazālī gegen die Bāṭinijja-Sekte*. Veröffentlichungen der de Goeje-Stiftung, 3. Leiden: E.J. Brill, 1916, Arabic text pp. 1–81, German translation pp. 36–112. English trans., Richard J. McCarthy (1913–1981), in his *Freedom and Fulfillment*. Boston: Twayne Publishers, 1980, pp. 175–286. Turkish trans., Avni Ilhan, *Fedâihu'l-Bâtiniyye: Bâtinîligin iç Yüzü*. Ankara, 1993.

  This work, written shortly before 488/1095 and commonly known as *al-Mustaẓhirī* after the Abbasid caliph al-Mustaẓhir (487–512/ 1094–1118) who commissioned it, is al-Ghazālī's major polemical treatise against the Ismailis (Bāṭiniyya), especially arguing against the doctrine of *taʿlīm* propagated by Ḥasan-i Ṣabbāḥ (d. 518/1124) and the early Nizārī Ismailis. This refutation has been studied in F. Mitha, *Al-Ghazālī and the Ismailis*.

- *Kitāb qawāṣim al-Bāṭiniyya*, ed. and Turkish trans., Ahmed Ateş as "Gazâlî'nin 'Bâtinîlerin belini kıran deliller' i. 'Kitâb Ḳavâṣim al-Bâtinîya'", in *Ilâhiyat Fakültesi Dergisi, Ankara University*, 3, nos. 1–2 (1954), 23–54.

  Another short anti-Ismaili tract.

- *al-Qisṭās al-mustaqīm*, ed., Victor Chelhot. Beirut: al-Maṭbaʿa al-Kāthūlīkiyya, 1959. pp. 104. English trans., D.B. Brewster as *The Just Balance*. Lahore: Sh. Muhammd Ashraf, 1978. pp. xxiii + 142. English trans., Richard J. McCarthy, in his *Freedom and Fulfillment*. Boston: Twayne Publishers, 1980, pp. 287–332. French trans., Victor Chelhot, in his "Al-Qisṭās al-Mustaqīm et la connaissance rationnelle chez Ġazālī", pp. 43–88.

  Yet another polemical tract against the Taʿlīmiyya or Bāṭiniyya, as al-Ghazālī referred to the Ismailis.

Ḥāfiẓ-i Abrū, ʿAbd Allāh b. Luṭf Allāḥ al-Bihdādīnī (d. 833/1430), Persian historian

- *Majmaʿ al-tawārīkh al-sulṭāniyya: qismat-i khulafāʾ-i ʿAlawiyya-yi Maghrib va Miṣr va Nizāriyān va rafīqān*, ed., Muḥammad Mudarrisī Zanjānī. Tehran: Intishārāt-i Iṭṭilāʿāt, 1364 Sh./1985. pp. 288.

In the Ismaili section of his universal history to the year 830/1426, written for the Tīmūrid prince Bāysunghur (799–837/1397–1433), Ḥāfiẓ-i Abrū draws extensively on the Ismaili history of Rashīd al-Dīn, adding nothing to the account of his predecessor; see F. Daftary's review in *Nashr-i Dānish*, 6 (June–July, 1986), pp. 34–37. This edition includes parallel texts of the corresponding Ismaili sections from Rashīd al-Dīn's *Jāmiʿ al-tawārīkh* and Kāshānī's *Zubdat al-tawārīkh*.

al-Ḥammādī al-Yamānī, Muḥammad b. Mālik (d. ca. 470/1077), Yamanī Sunni jurist and historian

- *Kashf asrār al-Bāṭiniyya wa-akhbār al-Qarāmiṭa*, ed., Muḥammad Zāhid al-Kawtharī. Cairo: ʿIzzat al-ʿAṭṭār, 1357/1939. pp. 44; ed., Suhayl Zakkār, in his *Akhbār al-Qarāmiṭa*, pp. 201–251; French trans., A. Batal as *Dévoilement des secrets de la Bâtiniyya et chroniques de la Qâramita*. Aldoha: n.p., 2002. pp. 120; English trans., Muhtar Holland as *Disclosure of the Secrets of the Bâtiniyya and the Annals of the Qarâmita*. Aldoha: n.p., n.d. [2003]. pp. 128.

An anti-Ismaili polemical work written by someone, perhaps a brother of the Ismaili *dāʿī* Lamak b. Mālik (d. ca. 491/1098), who temporarily became an Ismaili, but later abjured. This work apparently served as a primary source for subsequent Yamanī Sunni historians, such as al-Janadī, writing on the Ismailis.

Ibn ʿAbd al-Ẓāhir, Muḥyiʾl-Dīn Abu'l-Faḍl ʿAbd Allāh (d. 692/1293), private secretary to Mamlūk sultans in Cairo

- *al-Rawḍa al-bahiyya al-Ẓāhira fī khiṭaṭ al-Muʿizziyya al-Qāhira*, ed., Ayman Fuʾād Sayyid. Cairo: al-Dār al-ʿArabiyya li'l-Kitāb, 1996. pp. 185.

The earliest work in the topographical *khiṭaṭ* genre specifically on Cairo as opposed to *Fusṭāṭ*, with much on the Fatimid period, *al-Rawḍa* inspired al-Maqrīzī's later work (*al-Khiṭaṭ*) on the subject.

Ibn al-ʿAdīm Kamāl al-Dīn Abu'l-Qāsim ʿUmar (d. 660/1262), historian of Aleppo and vizier to Ayyūbids

- *al-Qarmaṭī ṣāḥib al-khāl*, an excerpt from *Bughyat al-ṭalab fī ta'rīkh Ḥalab*, ed., Suhayl Zakkār, in his *Akhbār al-Qarāmiṭa*, pp. 273–300.

Part of an extensive biographical dictionary of men connected with Aleppo. This extract is devoted to al-Ḥusayn, known as Ṣāḥib al-Khāl, one of the *dāʿī* Zikrawayh b. Mihrawayh's sons who led the Qarmaṭī movement in the Syrian desert from 288/901 until 291/903.

Ibn al-Dawādārī, Abū Bakr b. ʿAbd Allāh (d. after 736/1335), Egyptian historian

- *Kanz al-durar wa-jāmiʿ al-ghurar: al-juz' al-sādis, al-durra al-muḍiyya fī akhbār al-dawla al-Fāṭimiyya*, ed., Ṣalāḥ al-Dīn al-Munjjid. Deutsches Archäologisches Institut Kairo, Quellen zur Geschichte des Islamischen Ägyptens, 1f. Cairo: In Kommission bei O. Harrassowitz, 1961, pp. 44–156.

Ibn al-Dawādārī has devoted, in this sixth volume of his universal history, completed in 736/1335, large sections to the Fatimids in addition to preserving quotations and paraphrases from the lost anti-Ismaili treatise of the Sharīf Abu'l-Ḥusayn Muḥammad b. ʿAlī, better known as Akhū Muḥsin (d. after 372/982).

Ibn Ḥammād (Ḥamādu) al-Ṣanhājī, Abū ʿAbd Allāh Muḥammad b. ʿAlī (d. 628/1231), Berber *qāḍī* and historian

- *Akhbār mulūk Banī ʿUbayd wa-sīratuhum,* ed. and French trans., M. Vonderheyden as *Histoire des Rois ʿObaïdides (Les Califes Fatimides).* Publications de la Faculté des Lettres d'Alger, IIIe série, Textes relatifs à l'histoire de l'Afrique du Nord, fascicule II. Algiers: J. Carbonel; Paris: P. Geuthner, 1927. pp. xii + 100 (French) + 64 (Arabic); ed., ʿAbd al-Ḥalīm ʿUways and al-Tihāmī Naqra. Cairo: Dār al-Saḥwa; Riyadh: Dār al-ʿUlūm, [1401/1980]. pp. 114; ed., Jallūl Aḥmad al-Badawī. [Algiers]: al-Mu'assasa al-Waṭaniyya li'l-Kitāb, 1984. pp. 137.

Ibn Ḥammād wrote this brief history of the Fatimids, referred to as the ʿUbaydids, in 617/1220.

Ibn ʿIdhārī al-Marrākushī, Abu'l-ʿAbbās Aḥmad b. Muḥammad (d. after 712/1312), Maghribī historian

- *Kitāb al-bayān al-mughrib fī akhbār al-Andalus wa'l-Maghrib*, ed., George S. Colin and Évariste Lévi-Provençal (1894–1956) as *Histoire de l'Afrique du Nord et de l'Espagne Musulmane intitulée Kitāb al-Bayān al-Mughrib*. New ed., Leiden: E.J. Brill, 1948–51. 2 vols; reprinted, Beirut: Dār al-Thaqāfa, 1400/1980. 4 vols. (vol. 4, ed., Iḥsān ʿAbbās).

  The first part of this work is a comprehensive history of Islamic Ifrīqiya from earliest times until 602/1205. A major source on the history of the Fatimids in North Africa, this work is based on a number of earlier sources, notably the chronicle of ʿArīb b. Saʿd (d. ca. 370/980), an Andalusian who wrote his own history of the Maghrib for the Umayyads of Spain.

Ibn al-Jawzī, ʿAbd al-Raḥmān b. ʿAlī (d. 597/1200), Sunni jurist and historian

- *al-Qarāmiṭa*, an excerpt from *Kitāb al-muntaẓam fī ta'rīkh al-mulūk wa'l-umam*, ed., Muḥammad al-Ṣabbāgh. Beirut: al-Maktab al-Islāmī, 1388/1968. pp. 79; ed., Suhayl Zakkār, in his *Akhbār al-Qarāmiṭa*, pp. 253–268; excerpt with English trans., in J. de Somogyi's "A Treatise on the Qarmaṭians", pp. 248–265.

  A portion of this Ḥanbalī jurist and anti-Shiʿi author's universal history. Ibn al-Jawzī, too, used the Ibn Rizām and Akhū Muḥsin anti-Ismaili accounts.

Ibn Mālik al-Ḥammādī, *see* al-Ḥammādī al-Yamānī, Muḥammad b. Mālik

Ibn al-Ma'mūn al-Baṭā'iḥī, Jamāl al-Dīn Abū ʿAlī Mūsā (d. 588/1192), Egyptian historian

- *Nuṣūṣ min Akhbār Miṣr*, ed., Ayman Fu'ād Sayyid. Textes Arabes et études Islamiques, XXI. Cairo: Institut Français d'Archéologie Orientale du Caire, 1983. pp. vii (French) + 157 (Arabic).

  Written by the son of the Fatimid vizier al-Ma'mūn (d. 519/1125), who succeeded al-Afḍal (d. 515/1121), this is a major source on the Fatimid ceremonials and the caliph-imam al-Āmir's reign (495–524/1101–1130). The fragments edited here are based mainly on later quotations of this lost history by al-Maqrīzī and al-Nuwayrī.

Ibn Munqidh, Usāma (d. 584/1188), Syrian author and poet

- *Kitāb al-iʿtibār*, ed., Hartwig Derenbourg, in vol. 2 (pp. 183) of his *Ousâma Ibn Mounḳidh. Un émir Syrien au premier siècle des Croisades (1095–1188)*. Publications de l'École des Langues Orientales Vivantes, 2e série, XII. Paris: E. Leroux, 1886–93. 2 vols.; Derenbourg's French trans. of this work originally appeared as *Autobiographie d'Ousâma*, in *Revue de l'Orient Latin*, 2 (1894), pp. 327–565; published separately, Paris: E. Leroux, 1895. pp. vi + 238; ed., Philip K. Hitti. Princeton Oriental Texts, 1. Princeton, NJ: Princeton University Press, 1930. pp. 306. English trans., Philip K. Hitti as *An Arab-Syrian Gentleman and Warrior in the Period of the Crusades: Memoirs of Usāmah Ibn-Munqidh (Kitāb al-Iʿtibār)*. Records of Civilisation: Sources and Studies. New York: Columbia University Press, 1929. pp. x + 265. English trans., George Richard Potter as *The Autobiography of Ousâma*. Broadway Medieval Library. New York: Harcourt, Brace and Co., 1929. pp. xii + 301; ed. and French trans., André Miquel as *Kitāb al-Iʿtibār. Des enseignements de la vie, souvenirs d'un gentilhomme Syrien du temps des Croisades*. Paris: Imprimerie Nationale, 1983. pp. 444. German trans., Georg Schumann as *Memoiren eines syrischen Emirs aus der Zeit der Kreuzzüge*. Innsbruck: Wagner, 1905. pp. xii + 299. German trans., Gernot Rotter as *Ein Leben im Kampf gegen Kreuzritterheere*. Bibliothek Arabischer Klassiker, 4. Tübingen and Basel: H. Erdmann, 1978. pp. 260. German trans., Holger Preissler as *Die Erlebnisse des syrischen Ritters Usāma ibn Munqid: Unterhaltsames und Belehrendes aus der Zeit der Kreuzzüge*. Orientalische Bibliothek. Munich: C.H. Beck, 1985. pp. 315. Russian trans., M.A. Sal'e, *Kniga nazidaniya*. Moscow: Izdatel'stvo Vostochnoy Literaturï, 1958. pp. 326.

The famous memoirs of Usāma Ibn Munqidh, who personally knew the Fatimid caliph-imam al-Ḥāfiẓ (d. 544/1149) and the later Fatimid viziers Ibn al-Salār and ʿAbbās, contain important details on the closing phase of the Fatimid dynasty. Composed in 579/1183, the memoirs (which were discovered by H. Derenbourg in 1880 at the Escorial Library, Madrid) contain important information on the author's stay in Fatimid Cairo during 539–549/1144–1154. In 549/1154, Usāma fled back to his native Syria in the aftermath of the Fatimid caliph al-Ẓāfir's murder.

Ibn Muyassar, Tāj al-Dīn Muḥammad b. ʿAlī (d. 677/1278), Egyptian historian

- *Akhbār Miṣr*, ed., Henri Massé as *Annales d'Égypte (Les khalifes Fâṭimides)*. Publications de l'Institut Français d'Archéologie Orientale, Textes Arabes, I.Cairo: Institut Français d'Archéologie Orientale, 1919. pp. xxxii (French) + 140 (Arabic); ed., Ayman Fu'ād Sayyid as *al-Muntaqā min Akhbār Miṣr*. Textes Arabes et études Islamiques, XVII. Cairo: Institut Français d'Archéologie Orientale du Caire, 1981. pp. vii (French) + 221 (Arabic).

A history of Egypt, covering portions of the events of the Fatimid caliphate during the period 439–553/1047–1158, with two fragments on the years 362–365 and 381–387 A.H. It is preserved in a unique and incomplete manuscript derived from a copy made by al-Maqrīzī in 814/1411 and now held at the Bibliothèque Nationale in Paris. Ibn Muyassar drew on earlier sources, like the histories of Ibn Zūlāq (d. 386/996) and al-Muḥannak (d. 549/1154), in addition to that of al-Musabbiḥī (d. 420/1030), which have not survived.

Ibn al-Nadīm, Abu'l-Faraj Muḥammad b. Isḥāq al-Warrāq al-Baghdādī (d. ca. 380/990), Imāmī Shīʿī author in Baghdad

- *Kitāb al-fihrist*, ed., Gustav Flügel. Leipzig: Vogel, 1871–72, vol. 1, pp. 139, 186–190; reprinted (with the same pagination), Rawāʾiʿ al-turāth al-ʿArabī. Beirut: Maktabat Khayyāṭ, 1964; ed., M. Riḍā Tajaddud as *Kitāb al-fihrist li'l-Nadīm*. 2nd ed., Tehran: Marvī, 1973, pp. 154, 238–241. English trans., Bayard Dodge as *The Fihrist of al-Nadīm: A Tenth-Century Survey of Muslim Culture*. New York: Columbia University Press, 1970, vol. 1, pp. 306, 462–473. Persian trans., M. Riḍā Tajaddud as *Kitāb-i fihrist*. 2nd ed., Tehran: Bānk-i Bāzargānī-yi Īrān, 1967, pp. 230, 348–355.

This famous catalogue (*fihrist*) of Arabic books, completed in 377/987–88 with much encyclopedic information on the culture of medieval Islam and Muslim literary figures, contains valuable details on early Ismaili *daʿwa* and *dāʿīs*, including direct quotations from Ibn

Rizām's lost anti-Ismaili polemical treatise, entitled perhaps *Kitāb radd ʿalāʾl-Ismāʿīliyya.*

Ibn Qalāqis, Abu'l-Fatḥ Naṣr Allāh b. ʿAbd Allāh (d. 567/1172), Egyptian author under the later Fatimids

- *Dīwān,* ed., Khalīl Muṭrān. Cairo: Maṭbaʿat al-Jawāʾib, 1905. pp. 120; ed., Sihām al-Furayḥ. Kuwait: Maktabat al-Muʿallā, 1988. pp. 730.

  Ibn Qalāqis, who travelled extensively in Sicily and Yaman, praises numerous rulers and dignitaries in his collected poems, notably the later Fatimid caliph-imams and several of their viziers such as Ibn Maṣāl and Shāwar.

- *Tarassul Ibn Qalāqis al-Iskandarī,* ed., ʿAbd al-ʿAzīz b. Naṣīr al-Māniʿ. Riyadh: Jāmiʿat al-Malik Saʿūd, 1984. pp. 171.

  Collection of letters written by Ibn Qalāqis to some of his friends and Fatimid officials in Egypt and Yaman.

Ibn Ruzzīk, Ṭalāʾiʿ, *see* Ṭalāʾiʿ b. Ruzzīk

Ibn al-Ṣayrafī, Tāj al-Riʾāsa Amīn al-Dīn Abu'l-Qāsim ʿAlī b. Munjib (d. 542/1147), Egyptian author and administrator under the Fatimids

- *al-Ishāra ilā man nāla al-wizāra,* ed., ʿAbd Allāh Mukhliṣ, in *BIFAO,* 25 (1924), pp. 49–112; 26 (1925), pp. 49–70; reprinted, Baghdad: Maktabat al-Muthannā, [1964]; ed., Ayman Fuʾād Sayyid (together with Ibn al-Ṣayrafī's *al-Qānūn).* Cairo: al-Dār al-Miṣriyya al-Lubnāniyya, 1410/1990, pp. 43–107.

  A short history of the Fatimid viziers from Ibn Killis (d. 380/991) to al-Maʾmūn al-Baṭāʾiḥī (d. 519/1125).

- *al-Qānūn,* ed., ʿAlī Bahjat. Cairo: ʿAlī Bahjat, 1905. pp. 168; ed. Ayman Fuʾād Sayyid as *al-Qānūn fī dīwān al-rasāʾil waʾl-Ishāra ilā man nāla al-wizāra.* Cairo: al-Dār al-Miṣriyya al-Lubnāniyya, 1410/1990. pp. 148. French trans., Henri Massé, in his "Ibn Çaïrafi, Code de la chancellerie d'État (Période Fāṭimide)", *BIFAO,* 11 (1914), pp. 65–120.

  A guide to chancery practices under the Fatimids dedicated to the Fatimid vizier Abū ʿAlī Aḥmad Kutayfāt (d. 526/1131). Ibn al-Ṣayrafī, who may have been an Ismaili himself, worked in the Fatimid chancery (*dīwān al-inshā'*), also heading it from 495/1102 until his death in 542/1147.

Ibn Taghrībirdī, Abu'l-Maḥāsin Jamāl al-Dīn Yūsuf (d. 874/1470), Egyptian historian

- *al-Nujūm al-zāhira fī mulūk Miṣr wa'l-Qāhira*, ed., William W. Popper as *Abû'l-Maḥâsin Ibn Taghrî Birdî's Annals*. University of California Publications in Semitic Philology. Berkeley: University Press, 1909–29, vol. 2, part 2; vol. 3, part 1, etc.; ed., Cairo: al-Mu'assasa al-Miṣriyya al-ʿĀmma, 1348–92/1929–72, vols. 4–5.

  These parts cover the Fatimids in Ibn Taghrībirdī's vast history of Egypt from 20/641 to his own times. Ibn Taghrībirdī manifests the anti-Fatimid biases of some of his sources, notably Ibn al-Athīr (d. 630/1233) and Sibṭ Ibn al-Jawzī (d. 654/1256).

Ibn al-Ṭuwayr, al-Murtaḍā ʿAbd al-Salām b. al-Ḥasan al-Qaysarānī (d. 617/1220), Egyptian historian and official under the later Fatimids

- *Nuzhat al-muqlatayn fī akhbār al-dawlatayn*, ed., Ayman Fu'ād Sayyid. Bibliotheca Islamica, 39. Stuttgart and Beirut: F. Steiner, 1412/1992. pp 290.

  This portion of Ibn al-Ṭuwayr's history of the Fatimids and the Ayyūbids, which has not survived directly, deals with aspects of Fatimid history, ceremonials and administration. It has been reconstructed by Professor Sayyid on the basis of later quotations, such as those in Ibn Khaldūn, al-Qalqashandī, al-Maqrīzī and Ibn Taghrībirdī.

Ibn Ẓāfir, Jamāl al-Dīn Abu'l-Ḥasan ʿAlī al-Azdī (d. 613/1216), Egyptian historian and administrator under the Ayyūbids

- *Akhbār al-duwal al-munqaṭiʿa*, ed., André Ferré. Textes Arabes et études Islamiques, XII. Cairo: Institut Français d'Archéologie Orientale du Caire, 1972. pp. 37 (French) + 133 (Arabic). Excerpt, as *al-Dawla al-ʿAlawiyya bi-Ifrīqiya wa-Miṣr wa'l-Shām*, ed., Suhayl Zakkār, in his *Akhbār al-Qarāmiṭa*, pp. 269–272.

This extant portion of Ibn Ẓāfir's history relates to the Fatimid dynasty, from al-Mahdī to al-ʿĀḍid.

Ibn al-Zubayr, al-Qāḍī al-Rashīd Abu'l-Ḥusayn Aḥmad (d. after 461/1069)

- *Kitāb al-hadāyā* (or *al-dhakhā'ir*) *wa'l-tuḥaf*, ed., Muḥammad Ḥamīd Allāh. Wizārat al-Iʿlām fi'l-Kuwayt, al-Turāth al-ʿArabī, 1. Kuwait: Maṭbaʿat Ḥukūmat al-Kuwayt, 1959. pp. 367+14 plates; reprinted, Kuwait, 1984. English trans., Ghāda al-Ḥijjāwī al-Qaddūmī as *Book of Gifts and Rarities* (*Kitāb al-Hadāyā wa al-Tuḥaf*): *Selections Compiled in the Fifteenth Century from an Eleventh-Century Manuscript on Gifts and Treasures*. Harvard Middle Eastern Monographs, XXIX Cambridge, MA: Harvard University Press, 1996. pp. xv+544.

A unique source on the material culture of Islamic history that contains details on gifts (*hadāyā*) and related correspondence exchanged between Muslim rulers, descriptions of celebrations, diplomatic visits and other special occasions as well as information on elaborate feasts, etc. The Fatimids of Egypt are treated extensively in this work. Most of the paragraphs on the Fatimids relate to their treasures, including especially the treasures taken from the Fatimid palace in Cairo during the rebellion of the Turkish soldiers in 460–61/1068–69 (paragraphs 372–414). The treasures of the Fatimid caliph-imam al-Muʿizz's daughters ʿAbda and Rāshida (paragraphs 355, 357), al-Mustanṣir's mother (paragraphs 96, 100, 262, 391) as well as those of other female members of the Fatimid house are also discussed. No biographical details are available on the author of this book.

al-Janadī, Bahā' al-Dīn Abū ʿAbd Allāh Muḥammad b. Yūsuf (d. 732/1332), Sunni jurist and historian of Yaman

- *Akhbār al-Qarāmiṭa bi'l-Yaman*, extract from his *Kitāb al-sulūk fī ṭabaqāt al-ʿulamā' wa'l-mulūk*, ed. and English trans., Henry C. Kay, in his *Yaman, its Early Mediaeval History*. London: E. Arnold, 1892, text pp. 139–152, translation as *Account of the Karmathians in Yaman*, pp. 191–212.

The *Kitāb al-sulūk* is al-Janadī's only known extant work, which is an important biographical dictionary of the learned men of Yaman, preceded by a long introduction on the history of Yaman from early

Islamic times until 724/1323. The *Akhbār al-Qarāmiṭa* is a portion of this historical introduction covering the activities of the Ismaili *dāʿī* Ibn Ḥawshab Manṣūr al-Yaman (d. 302/914) and his collaborator ʿAlī b. al-Faḍl (d. 303/915), who later turned against the central leadership of the Ismaili *daʿwa* and started an abortive Qarmaṭī movement in Yaman. Al-Janadī reiterates the anti-Ismaili polemics and names Maymūn al-Qaddāḥ as the progenitor of the Fatimids.

Juwaynī, ʿAlāʾ al-Dīn ʿAṭā-Malik b. Muḥammad (d. 681/1283), Persian historian and administrator under the Īlkhānid Mongols

- *Taʾrīkh-i jahān-gushā*, volume 3, facsimile ed., Edward Denison Ross (1871–1940). James G. Forlong Fund, X. London: Royal Asiatic Society, 1931. pp. ii (English) + 108 (Persian); ed., Muḥammad Qazwīnī. E.J.W. Gibb Memorial Series, Old Series, XVI, 3. Leiden: E.J. Brill; London: Luzac, 1937, vol. 3, pp. 106–278. English trans., John Andrew Boyle as*The History of the World-Conqueror*. UNESCO Collection of Representative Works, Persian Series. Manchester: Manchester University Press; Cambridge, MA: Harvard University Press, 1958, vol. 2, pp. 618–725; reprinted, with an introduction by David O. Morgan. Manchester: Manchester University Press; Paris: UNESCO Publishing, 1997, pp. 618–725; ed. and rewritten in contemporary Persian by Manṣūr Tharvat as *Taḥrīr-i nuvīn-i taʾrīkh-i jahān-gushā*. Tehran: Amīr Kabīr, 1362 Sh./1983, pp. 329–392. Partial Arabic trans., Muḥammad al-Saʿīd Jamāl al-Dīn, in his *Dawlat al-Ismāʿīliyya fī Īrān*, pp. 150–255.

Juwaynī composed his history of the Ismailis and included it in the third volume of his *Taʾrīkh-i jahān-gushā*, on the basis of the official Nizārī chronicles and other documents which he found in the famous library at Alamūt, shortly before its destruction by the Mongols in 654/1256. Juwaynī's Ismaili history comprises parts devoted to early Ismailis, the Fatimids and the "new *daʿwa*" of Ḥasan-i Ṣabbāḥ (d. 518/1124) and his successors at Alamūt, a model adopted later by Rashīd al-Dīn and Kāshānī as well. The most valuable parts of all three histories, however, relate to the Nizārī Ismaili state of Persia, as all three historians of the Īlkhānid period made independent use of contemporary Nizārī source materials which have not survived.

Kāshānī (al-Qāshānī), Jamāl al-Dīn Abu'l -Qāsim ʿAbd Allāh b. ʿAlī (d. ca. 738/1337), Persian historian and administrator under the Īlkhānid Mongols

- *Zubdat al-tawārīkh: taʾrīkh-i Ismāʿīliyya va Nizāriyya va malāḥida*, ed., Muḥammad Taqī Dānishpazhūh, in *Nashriyya-yi Dānishkada-yi Adabiyyāt, Dānishgāh-i Tabrīz, ḍamīma-yi* 9/*Revue de la Faculté des Lettres, Université de Tabriz, Supplément* no. 9 (1343 Sh./1964), pp. 1–218; 2nd ed., Muḥammad Taqī Dānishpazhūh as *Zubdat al-tawārīkh: bakhsh-i Fāṭimiyān va Nizāriyān*. Tehran: Muʾassasa-yi Muṭālaʿāt va Taḥqīqāt-i Farhangī, 1366 Sh./1987. pp. xxxi + 262 + facsimile text (Tehran University, MS 9067).

  Kāshānī, an Imāmī Shīʿī historian who participated in the compilation of Rashīd al-Dīn's *Jāmiʿ al-tawārīkh*, had independent access to the Nizārī sources of the Alamūt period which have not survived; and his account of the Nizārī Ismaili state of Persia is more detailed than those produced by Juwaynī and Rashīd al-Dīn; *see* F. Daftary's review in *Nashr-i Dānish*, 8 (February-March, 1988), pp. 28–30. Kāshānī's section on the Ismailis is contained in his *Zubdat al-tawārīkh*, a general history of the Muslim world dedicated to Öljeytü (703–716/1304–1316), the Mongol Īlkhānid ruler of Persia.

al-Khazrajī, Muwaffaq al-Dīn Abu'l-Ḥasan ʿAlī b. al-Ḥasan (d. 812/1410), Yamanī historian

- *al-ʿAsjad al-masbūk fi-man waliya al-Yaman min al-mulūk: al-faṣl al-sādis fī dhikr al-Qarāmiṭa bi'l-Yaman*, ed., Suhayl Zakkār, in his *Akhbār al-Qarāmiṭa*, pp. 411–431.

  Drawing on earlier sources such as ʿUmāra al-Yamanī and al-Janadī, al-Khazrajī produced three historical works on Yaman, including this annalistic chronicle. The sixth chapter of *al-ʿAsjad*, edited here by S. Zakkār, deals with ʿAlī b. al-Faḍl (d. 303/915) and his Qarmaṭī movement in Yaman, closely following al-Janadī's account.

al-Maqrīzī, Taqī al-Dīn Abu'l-ʿAbbās Aḥmad b. ʿAlī (d. 845/1442), Egyptian historian

- *Ittiʿāẓ al-ḥunafāʾ bi-akhbār al-aʾimma al-Fāṭimiyyīn al-khulafāʾ*, ed., Jamāl al-Dīn al-Shayyāl and Muḥammad Ḥilmī Muḥammad Aḥmad.

United Arab Republic, al-Majlis al-Aʿlā li'l-Shuʾūn al-Islāmiyya, Lajnat iḥyāʾ al-turāth al-Islāmī, al-Kitāb, 12. Cairo: Lajnat iḥyāʾ al-turāth al-Islāmī, 1387–93/1967–73. 3 vols. Partial edition of volume one by Hugo Bunz as *Kitāb Ittiʿāẓ al-ḥunafāʾ bi-akhbār al-aʾimma al-Fāṭimiyyīn al-hulafāʾ* (*Fatimidengeschichte*). Leipzig: O. Harrassowitz, 1909. pp. viii (German) + 151 (Arabic); partial edition of vol. 1, by Jamāl al-Dīn al-Shayyāl as *Ittiʿāẓ al-ḥunafāʾ bi-akhbār al-aʾimma al-Fāṭimiyyīn al-khulafāʾ*. Maktabat al-Maqrīzī al-ṣaghīra, 2. Cairo: Dār al-Fikr al-ʿArabī, 1367/1948. pp. 390 (corresponding to J. al-Shayyāl, 1967 ed., vol. 1, pp. 1–200); excerpt, *Min akhbār al-Qarāmiṭa*, ed., Suhayl Zakkār, in his *Akhbār al-Qarāmiṭa*, pp. 323–389.

This is a comprehensive and only independent history of the Fatimids by a Sunni author, who may have claimed Fatimid ancestry from Tamīm b. al-Muʿizz. Al-Maqrīzī, too, had access to the anti-Ismaili treatise of Akhū Muḥsin and identified Ibn Rizām as its source. The *Ittiʿāẓ* has survived only in the form of a *musawwada*, or first draft, in a single complete manuscript preserved in Istanbul.

- *Kitāb al-mawāʿiẓ wa'l-iʿtibār fī dhikr al-khiṭaṭ wa'l-āthār*, lithographed, Būlāq, 1270/1853–54. 2 vols.; reprinted, Baghdad: Maktabat al-Muthannā, n.d. 2 vols., and other reprints; edition of the *musawwada* (autograph copy) by Ayman Fuʾād Sayyid. London: Al-Furqān Islamic Heritage Foundation, 1416/1995. pp. 106 (introduction) + 534; critical ed., Ayman Fuʾād Sayyid. London: Al-Furqān Islamic Heritage Foundation, 1422–24/2003. 4 vols. Partial ed., Gaston Wiet (1887–1971), in Mémoires publiés par les membres de l'Institut Français d'Archéologie Orientale du Caire, 30, 33, 46, 49, 53. Cairo: Imprimerie de l'Institut Français d'Archéologie Orientale, 1911–27. 5 vols. (corresponding to vol. 1, pp. 1–322 of the Būlāq edition). Partial French trans., U. Bouriant (1849–1903) as *Description topographique et historique de l'Égypte*, in Mémoires publiés par les membres de la Mission Archéologique Français du Caire, 17, fascicules 1–2. Cairo: E. Leroux, 1895–1900. 2 vols. (covering vol. 1, pp. 2–250 of the Būlāq edition). Partial French trans., Paul Casanova (1861–1926) as *Livre des admonitions et de l'observation pour l'histoire des quartiers et des monuments ou Description historique et topographique de l'Égypte*, in Mémoires publiés par les membres de l'Institut Français d'Archéologie Orientale du Caire, 3, 4. Cairo: Imprimerie de l'Institut Français d'Archéologie Orientale, 1906–20. 2 vols. (covering vol. 1, pp. 250–397 of the Būlāq edition). This French translation was never completed.

Generally known as the *Khiṭaṭ*, this is the most important medieval text of its genre on the history and historical geography of Islamic Egypt and topography of Cairo, with its palaces, mosques, convents, town quarters (*akhṭāṭ*), baths, etc. Much of it deals with Fatimid Cairo as well as Fatimid history and institutions, in addition to containing accounts of the Ismaili *daʿwa* drawn evidently from genuine Ismaili works; *see* P. Casanova, "La doctrine secrète des Fatimides d'Égypte". In addition to personal observations, the *Khiṭaṭ* is based on a variety of sources, such as histories of al-Musabbiḥī and Ibn al-Ṭuwayr, which are otherwise lost. A comparison of the *musawwada*, or initial draft preserved at Khazīna Library attached to the Topkapı Sarayı Museum, Istanbul, with later manuscripts of the *Khiṭaṭ* reveals how al-Maqrīzī greatly expanded this work over time. Some 170 manuscript copies of the *Khiṭāṭ* are known to exist.

- *Kitāb al-muqaffā al-kabīr*, ed., Muḥammad al-Yaʿlāwī (Mohammed Yalaoui). Beirut: Dār al-Gharb al-Islāmī, 1991. 8 vols.; abridged ed., Muḥammad al-Yaʿlāwī. Beirut: Dār al-Gharb al-Islāmī, 1407/1987. pp. 486; excerpt, on *al-Ḥasan al-Aʿṣam al-Qarmaṭī*, ed., Suhayl Zakkār, in his *Akhbār al-Qarāmiṭa*, pp. 391–409.

A biographical work containing about four hundred entries on individuals connected in various ways to the Fatimid state.

Mīrkhwānd, Muḥammad b. Khwāndshāh (d. 903/1498), Persian historian

- *Histoire de la dynastie des Ismaéliens de Perse,* excerpt from *Rawḍat al-ṣafāʾ fī sīrat al-anbiyāʾ waʾl-mulūk waʾl-khulafāʾ*, ed. and French trans., Am. Jourdain, in *Notices et Extraits des Manuscripts de la Bibliothèque Impériale et autres bibliothèques*, 9 (1813), translation pp. 143–182, Persian text pp. 192–248; also in the complete edition of the Persian text of the *Rawḍat al-ṣafāʾ* (Tehran, 1338–39 Sh./1960), vol. 4, pp. 181–235.

Mīrkhwānd included a relatively detailed account of the Fatimids and the Persian Nizārīs of the Alamūt period in his history, *Rawḍat al-ṣafāʾ*. In this section, devoted to the lords of Alamūt, from Ḥasan-i Ṣabbāḥ to Rukn al-Dīn Khurshāh, the author also recounts a version of the tale of the three schoolfellows (Ḥasan-i Ṣabbāḥ, Niẓām al-Mulk and ʿUmar Khayyām), based on a spurious work, the *Waṣāya*, attributed to the Saljūq vizier Niẓām al-Mulk (d. 485/1092).

al-Musabbiḥī, al-Mukhtār ʿIzz al-Mulk Muḥammad b. ʿUbayd Allāh (d. 420/1030), Fatimid historian and official

- *Akhbār Miṣr*, ed., Ayman Fu'ād Sayyid, Thierry Bianquis and Ḥusayn Naṣṣār. Textes Arabes et études Islamiques, XIII, 1–2. Cairo: Institut Français d'Archéologie Orientale du Caire, 1978–84. 2 vols. (historical and literary parts); partial edition of part 1 (*al-qism al-ta'rīkhī*) by W.G. Millward. Cairo: General Egyptian Book Organization, 1980. pp. 16 (English) + 289 (Arabic).

The amir al-Musabbiḥī, who may have been an Ismaili, produced a major history of Fatimid Egypt, covering the period 365–415/975–1025, of which only this small portion of the 40th volume (relating to 414–415 A.H.) has survived in a unique manuscript held at the Escorial Library, Madrid. The work has separate historical and literary parts. Later historians, such as Ibn Muyassar, Ibn Ẓāfir and al-Maqrīzī, have quoted from sections of this history which have not survived directly.

Niẓām al-Mulk, Abū ʿAlī Ḥasan b. ʿAlī Ṭūsī (d. 485/1092), Saljūq vizier

- *Siyāsat-nāma,* ed. and French trans., Charles Schefer as *Siasset Namèh, traité de gouvernement.* Publications de l'École des Langues Orientales Vivantes, 3e série, VII-VIII. Paris: E. Leroux, 1891–93. 2 vols. (Persian text, vol. 1, pp. 183–199; French trans., vol. 2, pp. 268–284, 285–291); lithographed, Allahabad, 1931, pp. 184–200; ed., ʿA.R. Khalkhālī. Tehran: Mu'assasa-yi Khurshīd, 1310 Sh./1931, pp. 157–168, 169–73; ed., ʿAbbās Iqbāl. Tehran: Chāpkhāna-yi Majlis, 1320 Sh./1941, pp. 260–274, 277–282; ed., Muḥammad Qazwīnī and Murtaḍā Mudarrisī Chahārdihī. Zabān va farhang-i Īrān, 14. Tehran: Ṭahūrī, 1334 Sh./1955, pp. 215–229, 232–236; ed., Hubert Darke as *Siyar al-mulūk (Siyāsat-nāma).* Majmūʿa-yi mutūn-i Fārsī, 8. 2nd ed., Tehran: Bungāh-i Tarjama va Nashr-i Kitāb, 1347 Sh./1968, pp. 282–305, 306–311; ed., Jaʿfar Shuʿār. Majmūʿa-yi sukhan-i Pārsī, 2. Tehran: Kitābhā-yi Jībī, 1348 Sh./1969, pp. 322–358; ed., Mehmet Altay Köymen. Dil ve Tarih-Çografya Fakültesi Yayinlari, 268. Ankara: Ankara Üniversitesi, 1976, pp. 227–240, 248–252; ed., ʿAṭā Allāh Tadayyun. Tehran: Intishārāt-i Tehran, 1373 Sh./1994, pp. 219–228, 230–233. English trans., Hubert Darke as *The Book of Government; or, Rules for Kings: The Siyāsat-nāma or Siyar al-mulūk.* UNESCO Collection of Representative Works, Persian Series. London: Routledge and K. Paul, 1960, pp. 213–238; 2nd ed., Persian Heritage Series, 32. London: Routledge and K. Paul, 1978, pp. 208–231. German trans., Karl Emil Schabinger von Schowingen as *Siyāsatnāma: Gedanken und Geschichten*. Freiburg and Munich: K. Alber, 1960, pp. 306–324. Russian trans., B.N. Zakhoder as *Siaset-Name, kniga o pravlenii*. Moscow and Leningrad: Izdatel'stvo Akademii Nauk SSSR, 1949, pp. 207–224. Turkish trans., M. Şerif Çavdaroğlu as *Siyasetname*. Istanbul Üniversitesi, Hukuk Fakültesi, Idare Hukuku vie Idare Ilimleri Enstitüsü Yayinlari, 1. Istanbul: Sermet Matbaasi, 1954, pp. 219–228, 230–234.

The *Siyāsat-nāma*, also known as *Siyar al-mulūk*, completed in 484/1091 with additions of eleven chapters (including that on the Ismailis) in the following year, comprises fifty chapters of advice to the Saljūq sultan Malik Shāh (465–485/1073–1092). The last eleven chapters, added shortly before the vizier's assassination in 485/1092, focus on dangers which threatened the Saljūq state at the time, notably those emanating from certain Iranian movements and from the Ismailis in particular who are discussed in chapter 46. This chapter in the *Siyāsat-nāma* provides an important source on the history of the early Ismaili (Qarmaṭī) *da'wa* and *dā'īs* in Persia and Central Asia, even though Niẓām al-Mulk was extremely hostile toward the Ismailis.

al-Nuwayrī, Shihāb al-Dīn Aḥmad b. 'Abd al-Wahhāb (d. 733/1333), Egyptian historian

- *Nihāyat al-arab fī funūn al-adab*, volume 25, ed., Muḥammad Jābir 'Abd al-'Āl al-Ḥīnī and 'Abd al-'Azīz al-Ahwānī. Cairo: al-Maktaba al-'Arabiyya, 1404/1984, pp. 187–317; excerpts, *Dhikr akhbār al-dawla al-'Ubaydiyya*, ed., Suhayl Zakkār, in his *Akhbār al-Qarāmiṭa*, pp. 301–321. French trans., in Silvestre de Sacy, *Exposé de la religion des Druzes*, vol. 1, introduction pp. 73–238, 430–453.

  Like Ibn al-Dawādārī and al-Maqrīzī, but more extensively, al-Nuwayrī has preserved in this volume of his encyclopedic work substantial selections from the anti-Ismaili treatise of Akhū Muḥsin, who drew on Ibn Rizām.

- *Nihāyat al-arab fī funūn al-adab*, volume 28, ed., Muḥammad Muḥammad Amīn and Muḥammad Ḥilmī Muḥammad Aḥmad. Cairo: Hay'a al-Miṣriyya al-'Āmma li'l-Kitāb, 1992, pp. 63–350; excerpt, ed., Muṣṭafā Abū Ḍayf Aḥmad as *Nihāyat al-arab fī funūn al-adab: al-dawla al-Fāṭimiyya bi-bilād al-Maghrib*. Casablanca: Maṭba'at al-

Najāḥ al-Jadīda, 1988. pp. 85.

This volume of al-Nuwayrī's *Nihāyat al-arab* contains a long section on the Fatimids.

al-Qalqashandī, Shihāb al-Dīn Aḥmad b. ʿAlī (d. 821/1418), Sunni legal scholar and secretary in the Mamlūk chancery

- *Tartīb mamlakat al-Fāṭimiyyīn fī Miṣr, maʾkhūdh min Kitāb Ṣubḥ al-aʿshā fī ṣināʿat al-inshāʾ* (*al-juzʾ al-thālith*), ed., Marius Canard. Bibliothèque de l'Institut d'Études Supérieures Islamiques d'Alger, XII. Algiers: La Maison des Livres, 1957. pp. 64.

Completed in 814/1412, al-Qalqashandī has preserved in his encyclopedic secretarial manual, *Ṣubḥ al-aʿshā*, the texts of numerous Fatimid decrees of different kinds, including caliphal edicts and diplomas of investiture. As such, the *Ṣubḥ* is a major source of information on Fatimid administration, institutions and documents. This extract, on Fatimid administration, comes from the published edition of the *Ṣubḥ* (Cairo: Dār al-Kutub al-Miṣriyya, 1332–38/1914–20), vol. 3, pp. 468–528.

Rashīd al-Dīn Ṭabīb, Faḍl Allāh b. ʿImād al-Dawla (d. 718/1318), Persian historian and vizier to Īlkhānid Mongols

- *Jāmiʿ al-tawārīkh: qismat-i Ismāʿīliyān va Fāṭimiyān va Nizāriyān va dāʿīyān va rafīqān*, ed., Muḥammad Taqī Dānishpazhūh and Muḥammad Mudarrisī Zanjānī. Majmūʿa-yi mutūn-i Fārsī, 3. Tehran: Bungāh-i Tarjama va Nashr-i Kitāb, 1338 Sh./1959. pp. 16 + 241; partial ed., Muḥammad Dabīr Siyāqī as *Faṣlī az Jāmiʿ al-tawārīkh: taʾrīkh-i firqa-yi rafīqān va Ismāʿīliyān-i Alamūt*. Tehran: Ṭahūrī, 1337 Sh./1958. pp. 160.

Rashīd al-Dīn made independent use of the Nizārī sources of the Alamūt period as well as Juwaynī's history of the Ismailis. However, Rashīd al-Dīn's own history of the Ismailis is fuller than that produced by Juwaynī; he is also more objective than his predecessor. Rashīd al-Dīn's section on the Ismailis is contained in the second volume of his *Jāmiʿ al-tawārīkh* completed in 710/1310. By contrast to Dabīr Siyāqī's edition, which relates only to the history of the Nizārī Ismaili state in

Persia, Dānishpazhūh and Mudarrisī's edition covers the earlier history of the Ismailis as well.

al-Ṭabarī, Abū Jaʿfar Muḥammad b. Jarīr (d. 310/923), Sunni historian

- *Taʾrīkh al-rusul waʾl-mulūk*, ed., Michael Jan de Goeje et al., as *Annales quos scripsit Abu Djafar Mohammed ibn Djarir at-Tabari*. Leiden: E.J. Brill, 1879–1901, third series, vol. 4, pp. 2124–2130 (and in later editions). English trans., Philip M. Fields as *The History of al-Ṭabarī*: Volume XXXVII, *The ʿAbbāsid Recovery*. Albany, NY: State University of New York Press, 1987, pp. 169–175. Persian trans., Abu'l-Qāsim Pāyanda as *Taʾrīkh-i Ṭabarī yā "Taʾrīkh al-rusul waʾl mulūk"*. Majmuʿa-yi taʾrīkh-i Īrān, 20. Tehran: Intishārāt-i Asāṭīr, 1364 Sh./1985, vol. 15, pp. 6642–6648.

Al-Ṭabarī's narrative of the opening phase of the Qarmaṭī (Ismaili) *daʿwa* in Iraq, cited here, is based on information supplied by Ismaili informants. Subsequent to this section, al-Ṭabarī provides further valuable details on early Ismaili activities in Iraq, Baḥrayn and Syria, including those of the *dāʿī* Zikrawayh b. Mihrawayh (d. 294/907) and his sons.

Ṭalāʾiʿ b. Ruzzīk, al-Malik al-Ṣāliḥ (d. 556/1161), Fatimid vizier and poet of Armenian origins

- *Dīwān*, ed., Aḥmad Aḥmad Badawī. Cairo: Maktabat Nahḍat Miṣr, [1958]. pp. 116; ed., Muḥammad Hādī al-Amīnī. Najaf: al-Maktaba al-Ahliyya, 1383/1964. pp. 191.

Collection of poems in praise of the Imams ʿAlī b. Abī Ṭālib, al-Ḥusayn b. ʿAlī and their descendants by a Fatimid vizier who adhered to Twelver or possibly Nuṣayrī Shiʿism. Ṭalāʾiʿ was also a patron of poets and his retinue included ʿUmāra al-Yamanī amongst others.

Thābit b. Sinān (d. 365/975–76), Sabean historian

- *Taʾrīkh akhbār al-Qarāmiṭa*, ed., Suhayl Zakkār, in his *Akhbār al-Qarāmiṭa*, pp. 1–84.

Thābit and several of his relatives, all belonging to the learned Sabean

(Ṣābi'a) family of scholars and secretaries in the service of the Abbasids in Baghdad, produced supplementary continuations of al-Ṭabarī's history. Thābit continued the narrative until the year 362/973 in his own universal history which seems to be almost completely lost. In this extant fragment, Thābit discusses the opening phase of the Ismaili (Qarmaṭī) *daʿwa* in Kūfa, under the leadership of Ḥamdān Qarmaṭ, the activities of Zikrawayh b. Mihrawayh, as well as those of the Qarmaṭīs of Baḥrayn.

ʿUmāra al-Yamanī, Abū Ḥamza Najm al-Dīn b. ʿAlī (d. 569/1174), Yamanī historian and poet

- *Ta'rīkh al-Yaman*, ed. and English trans., Henry C. Kay, in his *Yaman, its Early Mediaeval History*. London: E. Arnold, 1892, text pp. 1–102, translation as *The History of Yaman*, pp. 1–137; reprinted (with the same pagination), Farnborough, England: Gregg International Publishers, 1968; ed., Ḥasan Sulaymān Maḥmūd. Cairo: Maktabat Miṣr, 1957, pp. 34–130; 2nd ed., Cairo: Maṭbaʿat al-Saʿāda, 1976; ed., Muḥammad b. ʿAlī al-Akwaʿ al-Ḥiwālī. Sanaa: al-Maktaba al-Yamaniyya, 1985. pp. 344.

  Produced in 563/1167–68, at the instigation of al-Qāḍī al-Fāḍil who was at the time chief secretary to the Fatimid caliph al-ʿĀḍid and subsequently a close companion of Ṣalāḥ al-Dīn (d. 589/1193), founder of the Ayyūbid dynasty, ʿUmāra's *Ta'rīkh* covers the events in both northern and southern Yaman during the Fatimid period. It is a major and the earliest source on the Ṣulayḥids, an Ismaili dynasty ruling over extensive parts of Yaman during 439–532/1047–1138, and on the south Arabian (Ḥāfiẓī) Ismaili dynasty of the Zurayʿids of ʿAdan (473–569/1080–1173). Later Yamanī historians, like al-Khazrajī (d. 812/1410), add very little to ʿUmāra's account of the Zurayʿids, some of whom were personally known to him.

- *Dīwān* and *Memoirs* entitled *al-Nukat al-ʿaṣriyya fī akhbār al-wuzarā' al-Miṣriyya*, ed., Hartwig Derenbourg, in his *ʿOumâra du Yémen, sa vie et son oeuvre*. Publications de l'École des Langues Orientales Vivantes, 4e série, X–XI. Paris: E. Leroux, 1897–1902. 2 vols.

  Much information on ʿUmāra's contemporaries, notably several Fatimid viziers, and on Fatimid court life, may be obtained from ʿUmāra's poems and *Memoirs* (*al-Nukat al-ʿaṣriyya fī akhbār al-wuzarā' al-Miṣriyya*), covering the period 558–564/1162–1169. Adhering nominally to the Shāfiʿī Sunni *madhhab*, this Yamanī historian and poet emigrated to Egypt in 552/1157 and became an ardent supporter of the Fatimids, whom he eulogizes in his poetry in addition to the *ahl-al bayt*. ʿUmāra's outward Shiʿi sympathies eventually endangered him; he was executed on Ṣalāḥ al-Dīn's order in Cairo in 569/1174, on charges of involvement in a plot to restore the Fatimids to power.

Umayya b. ʿAbd al-ʿAzīz, Abu'l-Ṣalt al-Ishbīlī (d. 528/1134), Spanish Muslim scholar at the Fatimid court

- *al-Risāla al-Miṣriyya,* ed., ʿAbd al-Salām Hārūn, in *Nawādir al-makhṭūṭāt*. Cairo: Maṭbaʿat Lajnat al-Ta'līf wa'l-Tarjama wa'l-Nashr, 1951, vol. 1, pp. 5 56. Partial French trans., Alfred Luis de Prémare as "Un Andalou en Égypte à la fin du XIe siècle: Abu l-Ṣalt Omayya de Denia et son Épître Égyptienne", in *Mélanges de l'Institut Dominicain d'Études Orientales du Caire*, 3(1964–66), pp. 179–208.

A poet and also a writer on medicine, astronomy, music, philosophy and literature, in this historical work Abu'l-Ṣalt describes his eyewitness observations for the years 489–506/1096–1112 in Fatimid Cairo, including the poets and scholars he saw there. Belonging to the circle of scholars under the Fatimid vizier al-Afḍal's patronage, Abu'l-Ṣalt later joined the Zīrid court where he dedicated his *al-Risāla al-Miṣriyya* to the Zīrid prince Yaḥyā b. Tamīm (501–509/1108–1116).

Usāma b. Munqidh, *see* Ibn Munqidh, Usāma

Yaḥyā b. Ḥamza al-Ḥasanī al-ʿAlawī, al-Mu'ayyad bi'llāh (d. 749/1348), Zaydī imam and scholar in Yaman

- *al-Ifḥām li-af'idat al-Bāṭiniyya al-ṭaghām*, ed., Fayṣal Budayr ʿAwn. Maktabat ʿilm uṣūl al-dīn, 3. Alexandria: Mansha'at al-Maʿārif, n.d. pp. 133.
- *Mishkāt al-anwār al-hādima li-qawāʿid al-Bāṭiniyya al-ashrār*, ed., Muḥammad al-Sayyid al-Julaynid. Cairo: Dār al-Fikr al-Ḥadīth, 1973. pp. 227.

Both these works are polemical tracts against the Ismailis.

4

Studies

A

- Abāẓa, Fārūq ʿUthmān. *Āghā Khān wa-muhimmatuhu fī Miṣr fī bidāyat al-ḥarb al-ʿālamiyya al-ūlā*. Cairo: Dār al-Maʿārif, 1981. pp. 215 (Arabic) + 23 (English).
- al-ʿAbbādī, Aḥmad Mukhtār. *Fi'l-taʾrīkh al-ʿAbbāsī wa'l-Fāṭimī*. Beirut: Dār al-Nahḍa al-ʿArabiyya, 1971. pp. 377.
- al-ʿAbbādī, Aḥmad Mujtar (Mukhtār). "Los Fāṭimíes en Túnez y Egipto", in María Jesús Viguera Molins, ed., *El esplendor de los Omeyas Cordobeses: la civilizacíon Musulmana de Europa Occidental; exposicíon en Madīnat al-Zahrāʾ...2001*. Granada: Fundacíon El Legado Andalusi, 2001, pp. 302–309.
- Abboud-Haggar, Soha. "El Cairo, fundacíon de los Fāṭimíes", in María Jesús Viguera Molins, ed., *El esplendor de los Omeyas Cordobeses: la civilizacíon Musulmana de Europa Occidental; exposicíon en Madīnat al-Zahrāʾ...2001*. Granada: Fundacíon El Legado Andalusi, 2001, pp. 96–101.
- al-ʿAbd, ʿAbd al-Laṭīf Muḥammad. *al-Insān fī fikr Ikhwān al-Ṣafāʾ*. Cairo: Maktabat al-Anjlū al-Miṣriyya, 1967. pp. 354.
- ʿAbd Allāh, Wajīh Aḥmad. *al-Wujūd ʿinda Ikhwān al-Ṣafāʾ*. Alexandria: Dār al-Maʿrifa al-Jāmiʿiyya, 1989. pp. 368.
- ʿAbd Allāh b. al-Murtaḍā (1895–1936). *al-Falak al-dawwār fī samāʾ*

al-a'imma al-aṭhār. Aleppo: al-Maṭbaʿa al-Mārūniyya, 1352/1933. pp. 275.

- ʿAbd al-Ghanī, ʿAbd al-Raḥmān Muḥammad. "Mawqif al-Bīzanṭiyyīn wa'l-Fāṭimiyyīn min ẓuhūr al-Atrāk al-Salājiqa bi-minṭaqat al-sharq al-adnā al-Islāmī fi'l-qarn al-khāmis al-hijrī, al-ḥādiya ʿashara al-mīlādī", *Ḥawliyyāt Kulliyyat al-Ādāb, Jāmiʿat al-Kuwayt/Annals of the Faculty of Arts, Kuwait University*, 15, no. 97 (1994–95), pp. 5–98.
- al-ʿAbd al-Jādir, ʿĀdil Sālim. *al-Ismāʿīliyyūn: al-daʿwa wa'l-dawla fi'l-Yaman*. Kuwait: n. p., 2000. pp. 269.
- al-ʿAbd al-Jādir, ʿĀdil Sālim. *al-Ismāʿīliyyūn: kashf al-asrār wa-naqd al-afkār*. Silsilat al-buḥūth wa'l-dirāsāt al-Islāmiyya, 2. Kuwait: n. p., 2002. pp. 457.
- ʿAbd al-Mawlā, Muḥammad Aḥmad. *al-Quwā al-Sunniyya fi'l-Maghrib min qiyām al-dawla al-Fāṭimiyya ilā qiyām al-dawla al-Zīriyya (296–361H/909–972M.)*. Alexandria: Dār al-Maʿrifa al-Jāmiʿiyya, 1985. 2 vols.
- ʿAbd al-Nūr, Jabbūr. *Ikhwān al-Ṣafā'*. Nawābigh al-fikr al-ʿArabī, 7. Cairo: Dār al-Maʿārif, 1961. pp. 127.
- ʿAbd al-Raḥmān, ʿĀṣim Muḥamad Rizq. "al-Maḥārīb al-Fāṭimiyya fī jawāmiʿ al-Qāhira wa-masājidihā", *Majallat Kulliyat al-Ādāb, Jāmiʿat al-Malik Saʿūd*, 11, no. 1 (1984), pp. 3–62.
- ʿAbd al-Raḥmān, ʿĀṣim Muḥamad Rizq. "al-Maḥārīb al-Fāṭimiyya fī aḍriḥat al-Qāhira wa-mashāhidihā", *Majallat Kulliyat al-Ādāb, Jāmiʿat al-Malik Saʿūd*, 11, no. 2 (1984), pp. 461–525.
- ʿAbd al-Razzāq, Maḥmūd Ismāʿīl. *Ikhwān al-Ṣafā': ruwwād al-tanwīr fi'l-fikr al-ʿArabī*. Cairo: Dār Qibā', 1998. pp. 152.
- Abdel Kader, Ali Hassan. "Aga Khan", "Fatimite Dynasty", in *The World Book Encyclopedia*. Chicago, Frankfurt, etc.: World Book-Childcraft International, 1978.
- Abdu, Abdallah Kamel Mosa. *The Fatimid Architecture in Cairo*. Cairo: General Egyptian Book Organization, 1998. pp. 161.
- ʿAbduh, ʿAbd Allāh Kāmil Mūsā. *al-Fāṭimiyyūn wa-āthāruhum al-miʿmāriyya fī Ifrīqiya wa-Miṣr wa'l-Yaman*. Cairo: Dār al-Āfāq al-ʿArabiyya, 1421/2001. pp. 296 + 38.
- Abdul Husain, Mian Bhai Mulla. *Gulzare Daudi, for the Bohras of India: A Short Note on the Bohras of India, their 21 Imams and 51 Dais,*

with their Customs and Tenets. Ahmedabad: Amarsinhji P. Press, 1920. pp. 223.

- Abdulhussein, Mustafa et al. *Al-Dai Al-Fatimi Syedna Mohammed Burhanuddin: An Illustrated Biography*. London: Al-Jamea-tus-Saifiyah Trust, 2001. pp. 180.
- Abdulhussein, Mustafa. "Bohras", "Burhānuddīn, Sayyidnā Muḥammad", "al-Jāmiʿah al-Sayfiyah", in *OE*.
- Abdul-Wahhab, H.H. and Farhat Dachraoui. "Le régime foncier en Sicile au moyen âge IXe et Xe siècle", in *Études d'Orientalisme dédiées à la mémoire de Lévi-Provençal*. Paris: G.P. Maisonneuve et Larose, 1962, pp. 401–444.
- Abel, Armand (1903–1973). "De historische betekenis van de Loutere Broeders van Basra (Bassorah), een wijsgerig gezelschap in de Islam van de Xe eeuw", *Orientalia Gandensia*, 1 (1964), pp. 157–170 (in Dutch).
- Abrahamov, Binyamin. "An Ismāʿīlī Epistemology: The Case of al-Dāʿī al-Muṭlaq ʿAlī b. Muḥammad b. al-Walīd", *JSS*, 41 (1996), pp. 263–273.
- "Abu Abd Allah Muhammad b. Ahmad an-Nasafi", in *GIH*, p. 7.
- Abū ʿAzza, ʿAbd Allāh. "al-Qarāmiṭa wa-qabāʾil al-Aʿrāb al-bādiya", *al-Muʾarrikh al-ʿArabī*, 11 (1986), pp. 56–60.
- Abū ʿAzza, ʿAbd Allāh. "Taṭawwur ʿalāqat al-Qarāmiṭa biʾl-sulṭa al-ʿAbbāsiyya", *al-Wathīqa*, 5, no. 10 (1987), pp. 97–111.
- Abū Ismāʿīl, Salīm. *al-Durūz: al-tashayyuʿ al-Fāṭimī al-Ismāʿīlī, wujuduhum wa-madhhabuhum wa-tawaṭṭunuhum*. Beirut: Muʾassasat al-Taʾrīkh al-Durzī, 1955. pp. 269.
- Abu-Izzeddin (Abū ʿIzz al-Dīn), Nejla (Najlāʾ) Mustafa (Muṣṭafā). *The Druzes: A New Study of their History, Faith and Society*. Leiden: E.J. Brill, 1984. pp. 259. Arabic trans., *al-Durūz fiʾl-taʾrīkh*, tr., Nejla M. Abu-Izzeddin. Beirut: Dār al-ʿIlm liʾl-Malāyīn, 1985. pp. 343. Persian trans., *Taḥqīqī jadīd dar taʾrīkh, madhhab va jāmiʿa-yi Durūziyān*, tr., Aḥmad Nahāʾī. Mashhad, Iran: Āstān-i Quds-i Raḍavī, 1372 Sh./1993. pp. 428.
- Abū Ṣāliḥ, ʿAbbās, in collaboration with Sāmī Nasīb Makārim. *Taʾrīkh al-muwaḥḥidīn al-Durūz al-siyāsī fiʾl-mashriq al-ʿArabī*. Beirut: Manshūrāt al-Majlis al-Durzī liʾl-Buḥūth waʾl-Inmāʾ, n.d. [1980]. pp. 432.

- Abu Zayd, Sihām Muṣṭafā. *al-Duʿāt al-mashāriqa al-Ismāʿīliyyūn wa-dawruhum fī nashr al-madhhab fī Miṣr fī fatrat min sanat 358 ilā 567 H/min 968 ilā 1171 M*. Cairo: 1991.
- Adalis, Adelina E. (1900–1969). "Khisrov Nosir o razume i prosveshchenii" [Nāṣir-i Khusraw on Reason and Enlightenment], in *Antologiya Tadzhikskoy Poézii*, ed., I.S. Braginskiy. Moscow: Goslitizdat, 1951, pp. 261–263.
- Adamec, Ludwig W. "Aga Khan, Imam", "Alamut", "Bohras", "Druzes", "Fatimids", "Hakim, Abu'l Ali al-Mansur al-", "Hasan al-Sabbah", "Ismaʿilis", "Khojas", "Nizaris", "Qarmatians (Carmatians)", "Ta'wil", in his *Historical Dictionary of Islam*. Lanham, MD and London: The Scarecrow Press, 2001.
- Adams, Charles J. "Ismailis", in *Encyclopedia Americana*. Danbury, CT: Grolier, 1991, vol. 15, p. 512.
- Adatia, A.K. and N.Q. King. "Some East African *Firmans* of H.H. Aga Khan III", *Journal of Religion in Africa*, 2 (1969), pp. 179–191.
- Adīb Pīshavarī, S. Aḥmad. *Sharḥ-i mushkillāt-i Dīwān-i Nāṣir-i Khusraw*, ed., Jamshīd Surūshyār. Isfahan, Iran: Suhrawardī, 1363 Sh./1984. pp. 174.
- Adler, Jakob Georg C. (ed. and tr.), "Beyträge zur Geschichte der Drusen", *Repertorium für Biblische und Morgenländische Litteratur*, 15 (1784), pp. 265–298.
- Afshār, Īraj. "Qaymat-i ajnās dar Safar-nāma-yi Nāṣir-i Khusraw", in *YNK*, pp. 59–70.
- "Ağa Han", in *IA*, vol. 1, p. 147.
- "Ağa Han", in *Türk Ansiklopedisi*. Ankara: Millî Eğitim Basimevi, 1946, vol. 1, pp. 219–220.
- "Āgā Jān", in *Diccionario Enciclopedico Salvat Universal*. Barcelona, Madrid, etc.: Salvat Editores, 1975, vol. 1, p. 259.
- "Aga Khan", in *Brockhaus Enzyklopädie*. Mannheim: F.A. Brockhaus, 1986, vol. 1, p. 204.
- "Aga Khan", in *Chamber's Encyclopaedia*. New rev. ed., Oxford, etc.: Pergamon Press, 1966, vol. 1, p. 150.
- "Aga Khan", in *Grote Winkler Prins Encyclopedie*. Amsterdam and Brussels: Elsevier, 1979, vol. 1, p. 410.
- "Aga Khan", in *The New Encyclopaedia Britannica*. 15th ed., Chicago,

London, etc.: Encyclopaedia Britannica, 2002, vol. 1, p. 137.

Aga Khan Case, *see* "Judgement of the Honourable Sir J. Arnould..."

- "Aga Khan", "Aga Khan Foundation", "Batin", "Bohras", "Burhanuddin, Sayyidna Muhammad", "Druze", "Fatimid Dynasty", "Ikhwan al-Safa", "Kirmani, Hamid al-Din", "Muhammad ibn Ismail", "Mustansir, al-", "Nasir-i Khusraw", "Nizaris", "Numan, al-Qadi", "Qaramita", "Sabbah, Hasan-i", in *The Oxford Dictionary of Islam*, ed., John L. Esposito. Oxford: Oxford University Press, 2003.
- *H.H. the Aga Khan: A Sketch of His Life and Career*. Madras: G.A. Natesan, 1916. pp. 40.
- Aga Khan III, Sulṭān Muḥammad Shāh (1877–1957). *India in Transition: A Study in Political Evolution*. Bombay and Calcutta: Bennett, Coleman and Co., 1918. pp. xii + 310.
- Aga Khan III, Sulṭān Muḥammad Shāh. *The Memoirs of Aga Khan: Word Enough and Time*, with a Foreword by W. Somerset Maugham. London: Cassell; New York: Simon and Schuster, 1954. pp. xviii + 350. Finnish trans., *Aga Khans Memoarer*. Helsinki: Forum, 1955. pp. 320. French trans., *Mémoires*, tr., Jane Fillion, with an additional Preface by Jean Cocteau. Paris: A. Michel, 1955. pp. xxiv + 422. German trans., *Die Memoiren des Aga Khan: Welten und Zeiten*, tr., Hans B. Wagenseil. Vienna and Munich: Kurt Desch, 1954. pp. 446. Norwegian trans., *Erindringer*, tr., Karin Holst Hemsen and Anne-Margrethe Omsted. Oslo: H. Aschehoug, 1955. pp. 294. Spanish trans., *Memorias de S.A. El Aga Khan*, tr., J. Romero de Tejada. Barcelona: Editorial Planeta, 1954. pp. 372.
- Aga Khan III, Sulṭān Muḥammad Shāh. *Aga Khan III: Selected Speeches and Writings of Sir Sultan Muhammad Shah*, ed., Khursheed Kamal Aziz. London: K. Paul International, 1997–98. 2 vols.
- Agahi, Abbas. "Some Names and Practices in the Druze System of Beliefs", *Bulletin of the British Association of Orientalists*, 9 (1977), pp. 14–21.
- "Agha Khān", in *EI*, vol. 1, p. 180.
- "Āghā Khān", in *Grande Dizionario Enciclopedico*. Turin: Unione Tipografico-Editrice Torinese, 1984, vol. 1, p. 331.
- "Āghā Khān", in *Lessico Universale Italiano*. Rome: Istituto della Enciclopedia Italiana, 1986, vol. 1, p. 257.
- "Agha Khān III", "Agha Khān IV", in *Grande Larousse Encyclopédique*.

Paris: Librairie Larousse, 1960.

- Agius, Dionisius A. "The Arab Šalandī", in *ESFAM* 3, pp. 49–60.
- Aguilar, Maravillas Aguiar. "La Recepción Árabe de la cosmología Neoplatónica a través de las epístolas de los *Ijwān al-Ṣafā'* (siglo X)", *Fortunatae: Revista Canaria de Filología, Cultura y Humanidades Clásicas*, 8 (1996), pp. 363–372.
- Aguilar, Maravillas Aguiar. "*'Ilm al-misāḥa* en las epistolas de los *Iḫwān al-Ṣafā'*", in Urbain Vermeulen and Daniel de Smet, ed., *Philosophy and Arts in the Islamic World.* Orientalia Lovaniensia Analecta, 87. Louvain: Peeters, 1998, pp. 193–200.
- Aḥmad, 'Aṭiyya Sulaymān. *al-Lahja al-Miṣriyya al-Fāṭimiyya: dirāsa ta'rīkhiyya waṣfiyya*. Fī 'ilm al-lugha al-ta'rīkhī. n.p.: n.p., 1993. pp. 218.
- Aḥmad, Ḥasan Khuḍayrī. *'Alāqāt al-Fāṭimiyyīn fī Miṣr bi-duwal al-Maghrib (362–567 H./973–1171 M.)*. Ṣafiḥāt min ta'rīkh Miṣr, 36. Cairo: Maktabat Madbūlī, 1997. pp. 344.
- Aḥrār, Aḥmad. *Shāhīn-i sipīd.* Tehran: Shabāvīz, 1364 Sh./1985. pp. 508.
- Aḥsan, 'Abd al-Shakūr. "Arzish-i akhlāqī va fikrī-yi shi'r-i Ḥakīm Nāṣir-i Khusraw", in *YNK*, pp. 341–364.
- Akbar, Faiza. "The Secular Roots of Religious Dissidence in Early Islam: The Case of the Qaramita of Sawad al-Kūfa", *JIMMA*, 12 (1991), pp. 376–390.
- Akhtar, Ahmed Mian. "Shams Tabrizi: Was he an Ismailian?", *IC*, 10 (1936), pp. 131–136.
- 'Akkāwī, Riḥāb. *al-Ḥashshāshūn, ḥukkām Alamūt.* Beirut: Dār al-Ḥarf al-'Arabī and Dār al-Manāhil, 1414/1994. pp. 206.
- Āl Dāvūd, Sayyid 'Alī. "Abu'l-Ḥasan Khān Beglerbegi Maḥallātī", in *DMBI*, vol. 5, pp. 339–341.
- 'Alā' al-Dīn, Nasīb. *al-Qarāmiṭa*. Beirut: Dār al-Hādī, 2003. pp. 147.
- 'Alām al-Dīn, Salīm. *Qarāmiṭa: nash'atuhum, 'aqā'iduhum, ḥurūbuhum.* Beirut: Nawfal, 2003. pp. 311.
- "Alamūt", in *EI*, vol. 1, pp. 249–250.
- Alamūtī, Sayyid Ḍiyā' al-Dīn. *Qiyām-i musalaḥāna-yi dihqānān-i Alamūt.* Tehran, n.p., 1359 Sh./1980. pp. 136.

- ʿAlavī Muqaddam, Muḥammad. "Balāghat dar shiʿr-i Nāṣir-i Khusraw", in *YNK*, pp. 365–382.
- Albu, J. "Der Ursitz des Alten vom Berge", *Globus*, 65 (1894), pp. 210–212.
- Algar, Hamid. "The Revolt of Āghā Khān Maḥallātī and the Transference of the Ismāʿīlī Imamate to India", *SI*, 29 (1969), pp. 55–81. Persian trans., "Shūrish-i Āqā Khān Maḥallātī va intiqāl-i imāmat-i Ismāʿīlī bi Hind", in Ḥāmid Algār, *Shūrish-i Āqā Khān Maḥallātī va chand maqāla-yi dīgar*, ed., Abu'l-Qāsim Sirrī. Tehran: Intishārāt Tūs, 1370 Sh./1991, pp. 13–43.
- Algar, Hamid. "Maḥallātī, Āghā Khān", in *EI2*, vol. 5, pp. 1221–1222.
- Algar, Hamid. "Āqā Khan .i. Āqā Khan Maḥallātī", "Āqā Khan .ii. Āqā Khan II", "Āqā Khan .iii. Āqā Khan III", in *EIR*.
- ʿAlī, Khaṭṭāb ʿAṭiyya. *al-Taʿlīm fī Miṣr fi'l-ʿaṣr al-Fāṭimī al aww al 358–465 H./968–1072 M*. Cairo: Dār al-Fikr al-ʿArabī, 1947. pp. 240.
- Ali, Othman. "The Fidāwiyya Assassins in Crusades and Counter-Crusades", *Intellectual Discourse*, 4 (1996), pp. 45–61.
- Ali, Syed Mujtaba (b. 1904). *The Origin of the Khojāhs and their Religious Life Today*. Bonn: L. Röhrscheid; Würzburg: R. Mayr, 1936. pp. 109.

ʿAlī, Zāhid, *see* Zāhid ʿAlī

- Alibhai, Mohamed A. "The Transformation of Spiritual Substance into Bodily Substance in Ismāʿīlī Neoplatonism", in Parviz Morewedge, ed., *Neoplatonism and Islamic Thought*. Studies in Neoplatonism: Ancient and Modern, 5. Albany, NY: State University of New York Press, 1992, pp. 167–177.
- Alimardonov, Amriyazdon. "Dikhālat payravān-i madhāhib dar Safar-nāma-yi Nāṣir-i Khusraw", *Nomai Pazhouhishgoh* (Dushanbe), 4 (2003), pp. 93–104.
- Allouche, Adel. "The Establishment of Four Chief Judgeships in Fāṭimid Egypt", *JAOS*, 105 (1985), pp. 317–320.
- al-ʿAlūjī, ʿAbd al-Ḥamīd. *al-Bāṭiniyya wa-tayyarātuhā al-takhrībiyya*. Baghdad: Dār al-Shu'ūn al-Thaqāfiyya al-ʿĀmma, 1989. pp. 219.
- Álvarez, Lourdes María. "Beastly Colloquies: Of Plagiarism and

Pluralism in Two Medieval Disputations Between Animals and Men", *Comparative Literature Studies*, 39 (2002), pp. 179–200.

- Alvès de Sá, R. "Les Buhrah", *Mélanges de l'Institut Dominicain d'Études Orientales du Caire*, 15 (1982), pp. 265–270.
- ʿAlyān, Muḥammad al-Fatāḥ. *Qarāmiṭat al-ʿIrāq fi'l-qarnayn al-thālith wa'l-rābiʿ al-hijriyyayn*. Cairo: al-Hay'a al-Miṣriyya al-ʿĀmma, 1970. pp. 230.
- Amari, Michele (1806–1889). *Storia dei Musulmani di Sicilia*, 2nd enlarged ed., with notes by Carlo Alfonso Nallino (1872–1938). Catania: R. Prampolini, 1933–39, vol. 2, pp. 165–490 (on Fatimids and their vassals, the Kalbids, in Sicily).
- Amiji, Hatim M. (d. 1982). "The Asian Communities", in James Kritzeck and William H. Lewis, ed., *Islam in Africa*. New York: D. Van Nostrand-Reinhold, 1969, pp. 141–181.
- Amiji, Hatim M. "Some Notes on Religious Dissent in Nineteenth-century East Africa", *African Historical Studies*, 4 (1971), pp. 603–616.
- Amiji, Hatim M. "The Bohras of East Africa", *Journal of Religion in Africa*, 7 (1975), pp. 27–61.
- Amiji, Hatim M. "Islam and Socio-Economic Development: A Case Study of a Muslim Minority in Tanzania", *JIMMA*, 4 (1982), pp. 175–187.
- Amīn, Ḥasan. "Ishtihār-i Nāṣir-i Khusraw bi ʿAlawī", *Hilāl*, 19, no. 12 (1351 Sh./1972), pp. 37–39.
- al-Amīn, Ḥasan (1908–2002). *al-Ismāʿīliyyūn wa'l-Mughūl wa-Naṣīr al-Dīn al-Ṭūsī*. Beirut: Markaz al-Ghadīr li'l-Dirāsāt al-Islāmiyya, 1997. pp. 304.
- al-Amīnī, Muḥammad Hādī. *ʿĪd al-ghadīr fī ʿahd al-Fāṭimiyyīn*. Dirāsāt fī adab Miṣr al-Fāṭimiyya, 1. Najaf: Maṭbaʿat al-Qaḍā', 1962. pp. 160; also in Tehran: Mu'assasat al-Āfāq, 1376/1956. pp. 254.
- Amir-Moezzi, Mohammad Ali. *Le guide divin dans le Shîʿisme originel: aux sources de l'ésotérisme en Islam*. Collection "Islam spirituel". Lagrasse: Verdier, 1992. pp. 378. English trans., *The Divine Guide in Early Shiʿism: The Sources of Esotericism in Islam*, tr., David Streight. Albany, NY: State University of New York Press, 1994. pp. x + 279.
- Amir-Moezzi, Mohammad Ali and Christian Jambet. *Qu'est-ce que le Shîʿisme?* Histoire de la pensée. Paris: Fayard, 2004. pp. 387.

- Amīrī, Manūchihr. "Āyā Safar-nāma-yi Nāṣir-i Khusraw talkhīṣī ast az matnī mufaṣṣaltar", in *YNK*, pp. 80–95.
- al-ʿAmrī, Ḥusayn ʿAbd Allāh. "al-Ṣulayḥiyyūn", in Aḥmad Jābir et al., ed., *al-Mawsūʿa al-Yamaniyya*. Sanaa, 1992, vol. 2, pp. 573–574.
- al-ʿAmrī, Ḥusayn ʿAbd Allāh. "The Text of an Unpublished *Fatwā* of the Scholar al-Maqbalī (d. 1108/1728) Concerning the Legal Position of the Bāṭiniyyah (Ismāʿīliyyah) of the People of Hamdān", *New Arabian Studies*, 2 (1994), pp. 165–174.
- Amīrī Fīrūzkūhī, Karīm. "Ḥakīm Nāṣir-i Khusraw", *Yaghmā*, 28, no. 1 (1354 Sh./1975), pp. 48–51.
- Anderson, James Norman D. (1908–1994). "The Personal Law of the Druze Community", *WI*, NS, 2 (1952–53), pp. 1–9, 83–94.
- Anderson, James N.D. "The Ismaʿili Khojas of East Africa: A New Constitution and Personal Law for the Community", *Middle Eastern Studies*, 1 (1964), pp. 21–39.
- Andreyev, Sergei. "Ismaili Sects – Central Asia", in *Encyclopedia of Modern Asia*: Volume 3, *Laido to Malay-Indonesian Language,* ed., David Levinson and Karen Christensen. New York: Charles Scribner's Sons – Thomson, 2002, pp. 183–184.
- Annan, David. "The Assassins and the Knights Templar", in Norman Mackenzie, ed., *Secret Societies*. London: Aldus Books, 1967, pp. 106–129.
- Anṣārī, Ḥasan. "Abu'l-Khaṭṭāb", in *DMBI*, vol. 5, pp. 432–435.
- Anūsha, Ḥasan. "Āqā Khāniyya", "Ibn Ḥawshab", "Ibn ʿAṭṭāsh", "Abū Isḥāq Quhistānī", "Abū Ḥātim Rāzī", "Abū Saʿīd Jannābī", "Abū ʿAbd Allāh Shīʿī", "Abu'l-Fawāris Ismāʿīlī", "Aḥmad al-Mastūr", "Ismāʿīl b. Jaʿfar", "Ismāʿīliyya", "Ismāʿīliyya-yi Alamūt", "Alamūt (dizh)", "Imām Mustawdaʿ", "Buzurg-Umīd", "Bahrām Ismāʿīlī", "Tamīm b. Muʿizz Fāṭimī", "Jāmiʿ al-Ḥikmatayn", "Jaʿfar b. Manṣūr al-Yaman", "Jaʿfar Muṣāddiq", "Ḥāfiẓ li-Dīn Allāh", "Ḥākim bi-Amr Allāh", "Ḥāmidī", "Ḥusayn-i Qā'inī", "Ḥamīd al-Dīn Kirmānī", in *DT*.
- Anzābī Nizhād, Riḍā. "Ibn Ṭuwayr", in *DMBI*, vol. 4, pp. 158–159.
- Āqā Ḥusaynī, Sayyid Muḥammad. "Shīvahā-yi balāghī dar shiʿr-i Nāṣir-i Khusraw", *NP*, 8, no. 2 (1382 Sh./2003), pp. 7–26.
- "Āqā Khān", in *DMBI*, vol. 1, pp. 460–465.
- Āqā Nūrī, ʿAlī. "Ismāʿīliyya va bāṭinī-garī", in *IMM*, pp. 249–307.

- al-ʿAqqād, ʿAbbās Maḥmūd (d. 1964). *Fāṭima al-Zahrāʾ wa'l-Fāṭimiyyūn*. Beirut: Dār al-Kitāb al-ʿArabī, 1967. pp. 227; reprinted, Cairo: Dār al-Hilāl, 1971. pp. 159.
- Arabzoda, Nazir. "Mafhumi zamon dar falsafai Nosiri Khusrav" [Concept of Time in Nāṣir-i Khusraw's Philosophy], *Akhboroti Akademiyai Fanhoi RSS Tojikiston* (Dushanbe), 1 (1985), pp. 34–40 (in Tajik).
- Arabzoda, Nazir. "Muhiti maʿrifat" [Atmosphere of Enlightenment], *Sadoi Sharq* (Dushanbe), 12 (1986), pp. 114–120 (in Tajik).
- Arabzoda, Nazir. "Ratsionalizmi shoirona" [Poetic Rationalism], *Maktabi Soveti* (Dushanbe), 10 (1986), pp. 35–37 (in Tajik).
- Arabzoda, Nazir. "Tavsifi kategoriyai makon dar falsafai Nosiri Khusrav" [Description of the Category of Space in Nāṣir-i Khusraw's Philosophy], *Akhboroti Akademiyai Fanhoi RSS Tojikiston. Filosofiya, ékonomika, pravovedenie* (Dushanbe), 1 (1988), pp. 15–18 (in Tajik).
- Arabzoda, Nazir. "Andarzi Hakimi Qubodieni" [Teaching of Ḥakīm Qubādiyānī], *Sadoi Sharq* (Dushanbe), 12 (1989), pp. 124–130 (in Tajik).
- Arabzoda, Nazir. "Zarurati maʿrifati olam az nazari Nosiri Khusrav" [The Requirement of the Enlightenment of the World According to Nāṣir-i Khusraw], *Akhboroti Akademiyai Fanhoi RSS Tojikiston. Filosofiya, ékonomika, pravovedenie* (Dushanbe), 4 (1989), pp. 3–8 (in Tajik).
- Arabzoda, Nazir. "Harakat az didi Nosiri Khusrav" [Movement from Nāṣir-i Khusraw's Point of View], *Ilm va hayot* (Dushanbe), 12 (1989), pp. 31–33 (in Tajik).
- Arabzoda, Nazir. "Andeshai ofarinish dar falsafai Nosiri Khusrav" [Creation in Nāṣir-i Khusraw's Philosophy], *Farhang* (Dushanbe), 7 (1991), pp. 57–61 (in Tajik).
- Arabzoda, Nazir. "Javhariyati jism, modda va surat az nazari Nosiri Khusrav" [The Value of the Body, Substance and Form from Nāṣir-i Khusraw's Point of View], *Ilm va hayot* (Dushanbe), 2 (1991), pp. 9–11 (in Tajik).
- Arabzoda, Nazir. "Sushchnost'dushi. Traktovka psikhofizickheskoy problemï v filosofii Nosiri Khusrava" [The Quintessence of Soul. The Explanation of Psychological Problems in Nāṣir-i Khusraw's Philosophy], *Akhboroti Akademiyai Fanhoi RSS Tojikiston* (Dushanbe), 1 (1991), pp. 29–39.

- Arabzoda, Nazir. "Éjodiyoti Nosiri Khusrav" [Nāṣir-i Khusraw's Creation], *Maʿrifat* (Dushanbe), 2 (1992), pp. 13–17 (in Tajik).
- Arabzoda, Nazir. "Shakkokii Nosiri Khusrav" [The Doubtfulness of Nāṣir-i Khusraw], *Adab* (Dushanbe), 5 (1992), pp. 53–59 (in Tajik).
- Arabzoda, Nazir. "Nosiri Khusrav dar borai nubuvvat va imomat" [Nāṣir-i Khusraw on Prophethood and Imamate], *Ilm va hayot* (Dushanbe), 8 (1993), pp. 29–31 (in Tajik).
- Arabzoda, Nazir. "Ta'vili Qurʾon dar ilohiyoti Nosiri Khusrav" [Qurʾanic *taʾwīl* in Nāṣir-i Khusraw's Theology], *Farhang* (Dushanbe), 1, no. 3 (1993), pp. 53–57 (in Tajik).
- Arabzoda, Nazir. *Nasir Khusrav*. Dushanbe: Maorif, 1994. pp. 176 (in Tajik).
- Arabzoda, Nazir. "Odobi sukhan guftan dar taʿlimoti akhloqii Nosiri Khusrav" [Ethics of Speech in Nāṣir-i Khusraw's Ethical Teachings], *Adab* (Dushanbe), 7 (1996), pp. 33–37 (in Tajik).
- Arabzoda, Nazir. "Fazilati neki va nakukori dar taʿlimoti akhloqii Nosiri Khusrav" [Value of Kindness in Nāṣir-i Khusraw's Ethical Teachings], *Ilm va hayot* (Dushanbe), 1 (1999), pp. 4–6 (in Tajik).
- Arabzoda, Nazir. *Mir idey i razmïshleniy Nosira Khusrava* [Nāṣir-i Khusraw's World of Ideas and Thoughts]. Dushanbe: Nodir, 2003. pp. 263.
- Āriyan Nizhād, Shāpūr. *Qiyām-i Ismāʿīliyya: Malik Shāh-i Saljūqī va Ḥasan-i Ṣabbāḥ*. Tehran: Dunyā-yi Kitāb, 1370 Sh./1991. 3 vols.
- Arnaldez, Roger. "Assassins", "Bāṭin & Bāṭiniyya", "Nāsir-e Khosraw (1004–1088)", in *EUDI*.
- Arnold, Thomas Walker (1864–1930). "Bohorā", "Imām Shāh", in *EI*.
- Arnold, Thomas W. "Bohorâ", in *IA*, vol. 2, pp. 705–707.
- Arzanda, Mihrān. "Ibn Hānī", in *DMBI*, vol. 5, pp. 93–97.
- Asʿadī, Murtaḍā. "Alamūt", in *DT*, vol. 2, pp. 318–320.
- Asani, Ali S. "The Khojkī Script: A Legacy of Ismaili Islam in the Indo-Pakistan Subcontinent", *JAOS*, 107 (1987), pp. 439–449; reprinted in his *Ecstasy and Enlightenment*, pp. 100–123.
- Asani, Ali S. "The Khojahs of Indo-Pakistan: The Quest for an Islamic Identity", *JIMMA*, 8 (1987), pp. 31–41.
- Asani, Ali S. *The Būjh Nirañjan: An Ismaili Mystical Poem*, with a

Foreword by Annemarie Schimmel. Cambridge, MA: Harvard Center for Middle Eastern Studies, 1991. pp. xix + 221.

- Asani, Ali S. "The *Ginān* Literature of the Ismailis of Indo-Pakistan: Its Origins, Characteristics, and Themes", in D.L. Eck and Françoise Mallison, ed., *Devotion Divine: Bhakti Traditions from the Regions of India: Studies in Honour of Charlotte Vaudeville.* Groningen Oriental Series, VIII. Groningen: E. Forsten; Paris: École Française d'Extrême-Orient, 1991, pp. 1–18; reprinted in slightly revised form, in his *Ecstasy and Enlightenment*, pp. 25–53.
- Asani, Ali S. *The Harvard Collection of Ismaili Literature in Indic Languages: A Descriptive Catalog and Finding Aid.* Boston: G.K. Hall and Co., 1992. pp. vii + 689.
- Asani, Ali S. "The Ismaili *ginān*s as Devotional Literature", in R.S. McGregor, ed., *Devotional Literature in South Asia: Current Research, 1985–1988*. Cambridge: Cambridge University Press, 1992, pp. 101–112.
- Asani, Ali S. "Bridal Symbolism in Ismāʿīlī Mystical Literature of Indo-Pakistan", in Robert A. Herrera, ed., *Mystics of the Book: Themes, Topics and Typologies.* New York, etc.: P. Lang, 1993, pp. 389–404; reprinted in his *Ecstasy and Enlightenment*, pp. 54–70.
- Asani, Ali S. "The Impact of Modernization on the Marriage Rites of the Khojah Ismailis of East Africa", in Maria Eva Subtelny, ed., *Annemarie Schimmel Festschrift: Essays presented to Annemarie Schimmel on the Occasion of her Retirement from Harvard University by her Colleagues, Students and Friends*; being, *Journal of Turkish Studies,* 18 (1994), pp. 17–24.
- Asani, Ali S. "A Testimony of Love: The *Gīt* Tradition of the Nizari Ismailis", in Alma Giese and Johann Christoph Bürgel, ed., *Gott ist schön und Er liebt die Schönheit/God is Beautiful and He Loves Beauty. Festschrift für Annemarie Schimmel zum 7. April, 1992 dargebracht von Schülern, Freunden und Kollegen/Festschrift in Honour of Annemarie Schimmel Presented by Students, Friends and Colleagues on April 7, 1992*. Bern, Berlin, etc: P. Lang, 1994, pp. 39–51; reprinted in his *Ecstasy and Enlightenment*, pp. 71–81.
- Asani, Ali S. "The Ismaili *ginān*s: Reflections on Authority and Authorship", in *MIHT*, pp. 265–280; reprinted in slightly revised form, in his *Ecstasy and Enlightenment*, pp. 82–99. Arabic trans., "al-Jinān al-Ismāʿīlī: ta'ammulāt fi'l-marjiʿiyya wa'l-ta'līf", in *IAW*, pp. 273–288. Persian trans., "Ginānhā-yi Ismāʿīlī: ta'amulātī dar bāra-yi marjaʿiyyat

va padīdārandagī", in *TAI*, pp. 325–344.

- Asani, Ali S. "The Khojahs of South Asia: Defining a Space of their Own", *Cultural Dynamics*, 13 (2001), pp. 155–168.
- Asani, Ali S. *Ecstasy and Enlightenment: The Ismaili Devotional Literature of South Asia*, with a Foreword by Annemarie Schimmel. Ismaili Heritage Series, 6. London: I.B. Tauris in association with The Institute of Ismaili Studies, 2002. pp. xxiii + 184.
- Asani, Ali S. "Creating Tradition through Devotional Songs and Communal Script: The Khojah Isma'ilis of South Asia", in Richard Eaton, ed., *India's Islamic Traditions 711–1750, Themes in Indian History*. New Delhi: Oxford University Press, 2003, pp. 285–310.
- Asani, Ali S. "Aga Khan", "Ginān", in *ER*.
- "Asesinos", in *Enciclopedia Universal Ilustrada Europeo-Americana*. Barcelona: J. Espasa é Hijos, n.d., vol. 6, pp. 626–627.
- Ashkivarī, Ḥasan Yūsufī. "Ta'rīkh al-khulafā' al-Fāṭimiyyīn bi'l-Maghrib", in *DT*, vol. 4, pp. 34–35.
- Ashraf Ṣādiqī, 'Alī. "Umm al-kitāb", in *DMBI*, vol. 10, pp. 232–234.
- 'Ashrī, 'Uthmān 'Abd al-Ḥamīd. *al-Ismā'īliyyūn fī bilād al-Shām 'alā 'aṣr al-ḥurūb al-Ṣalībiyya, 491–691H-1097–1291M*. Cairo: Dār al-Nahḍa al-'Arabiyya, 1983. pp. 279 + 31.
- Ashtor, Eliyahu (1914–1984). "Fatimids", in *Encyclopaedia Judaica*. Jerusalem: Encyclopaedia Judaica; Keter Publishing House, 1973, vol. 6, pp. 1196–1198.
- 'Āshūr (Âsür), Sa'īd 'Abd al-Fattāḥ (Abdülfettâh). "Shakhṣiyyat al-dawla al-Fāṭimiyya fi'l-ḥaraka al-Ṣalībiyya", *al-Majalla al-Ta'rīkhiyya al-Miṣriyya*, 16 (1969), pp. 15–66.
- 'Āshūr, Sa'īd 'Abd al-Fattāḥ. "Ibn Killis", in *IA2*, vol. 20, pp. 136–137.
- Ashurov, Gafor A. "Nosiri Khisrav i ego filosofskiy traktat Zad al-musafirin" [Nāṣir-i Khusraw and his Philosophical Treatise *Zād al-musāfirīn*], in *Tezisï nauchnoy konferentsii molodïkh uchyonïkh, posvashchyonnoy 30 – letiyu Tadzhikskoy SSR*. Akademiya Nauk Tadzhikskoy SSR. Stalinabad, 1959, pp. 82–83.
- Ashurov, Gafor A. "Filosofskiy traktat Nosiri Khisrava Zad al-musafirin" [Nāṣir-i Khusraw's Philosophical Treatise *Zād al-musāfirīn*], *Akhboroti Akademiyai Fanhoi RSS Tojikiston* (Dushanbe), 2 (1960), pp. 53–60.

- Ashurov, Gafor A. "Ob otnoshenii Nosiri Khisrava k Abu Bakru ar-Razi" [Nāṣir-i Khusraw's View of Abū Bakr al-Rāzī], *Akhboroti Akademiyai Fanhoi RSS Tojikiston* (Dushanbe), 2, 33 (1963), pp. 41–49.
- Ashurov, Gafor A. "Reshenie osnovnogo voprosa filosofii Nosiri Khisravom (na osnove analiza filosofskogo traktata Zad al-musafirin)" [Solving the Basic Question of Philosophy by Nāṣir-i Khusraw (on the basis of an analysis of the philosophical treatise *Zād al-musāfirīn*)], *Akhboroti Akademiyai Fanhoi RSS Tojikiston* (Dushanbe), 2, 33 (1963), pp. 29–40.
- Ashurov, Gafor A. *Filosofskie vzglyadï Nosiri Khisrava* (na osnove analiza traktata Zad al-musafirin)[Nāṣir-i Khusraw's Philosophical Views (based on an analysis of *Zād al-musāfirīn*)]. *Avtoreferat dissertatsıı na zvanıe kandıdata fılosofskıkh nauk*. Dushanbe, 1964. pp. 25.
- Ashurov, Gafor A. *Filosofskie vzglyadï Nosiri Khisrava* (na osnove analiza traktata Zad al-musafirin)[Nāṣir-i Khusraw's Philosophical Views (based on an analysis of *Zād al-musāfirīn*)]. Dushanbe, 1965. pp. 113.
- Ashurov, Gafor A. "Nasir Khosrov" [Nāṣir-i Khusraw], in *Filosofskaya Éntsiklopediya*. Moscow, 1964, vol. 3, pp. 555–556.
- Asín Palacios, Don Miguel (1871–1944). *El original Árabe de la Disputa del Asno: Contra Fr. Anselmo Turmeda*. Madrid: Junta para Ampliación de Estudios e Investigaciones Cientificas, Centro de Estudios Históricos, 1914. pp. 56.
- Assaad, Sadik A. [I.] *The Reign of al-Hakim bi Amr Allah (386/996–411/1021): A Political Study*. Beirut: The Arab Institute for Research and Publishing, 1974. pp. 209.
- Assaad, Sadik Ismail. "Sayyidna Hamid ad-Din al-Kirmani", in *GIH*, pp. 39–40.
- "Assassijnen", in *Grote Winkler Prins Encyclopedie*. Amsterdam and Brussels: Elsevier, 1979, vol. 2, p. 552.
- "Assassin", in *The New Encyclopaedia Britannica*. 15th ed., Chicago, London, etc.: Encyclopaedia Britannica, 2002, vol. 1, p. 640.
- "Assassinen", in *Brockhaus Enzyklopädie*. Mannheim: F.A. Brockhaus, 1987, vol. 2, p. 202.
- "Assassinen", in *HI*, pp. 60–61.
- "Assassini", in *Lessico Universale Italiano*. Rome: Istituto della

Enciclopedia Italiana, 1969, vol. 2, p. 299.

- "Assassino", in *Grande Enciclopédia Portuguesa e Brasileira*. Lisbon and Rio de Janeiro: Editorial Encilopédia, n.d., vol. 3, pp. 523–524 (in Portuguese).
- "Assassins", in *Encyclopedia Americana*. Danbury, CT: Grolier, 1991, vol. 2, p. 524.
- "Assassins", in *EI*, vol. 1, pp. 491–492.
- "Assassins", in *Grande Larousse Encyclopédique*. Paris: Librairie Larousse, 1960, vol. 1, p. 643.
- "Assassins", in *SEI*, pp. 48–49.
- Assemani, Simone (1752–1821). *Ragguaglio storico-critico sopra la setta Assissana, detta volgarmente degli Assassini*, in *Giornale dell'Italiana Letteratura*, 13 (1806), pp. 241–262; also published separately in Padua: Stamperia del Seminario, 1806. pp. 22.
- Assrauy, Nagib. *O Druzismo*. Belo Horizonte, [Brazil]: Editôra São Vicente, 1967. pp. 135 (in Portuguese).
- Ateş, Ahmed (1911–1966). "Bâtiniye", in *IA*, vol. 2, pp. 339–342.
- al-ʿAtrash, Fu'ād Yūsuf. *al-Durūz: muʾāmara wa-taʾrīkh wa-ḥaqāʾiq*. Beirut: n.p., 1975. pp. 388.
- Aucapitaine, Henri. "Étude sur les Druzes", *Nouvelles Annales des Voyages*, 1 (1862), pp. 135–156; also published separately in Paris: A. Bertrand, 1862. pp. 24.
- Awa (al-ʿAwwā), Adel (ʿĀdil) (d. 2002). *L'esprit critique des "Frères de la Pureté": Encyclopédistes Arabes du IVe/Xe siècle*. Beirut: Imprimerie Catholique, 1948. p. 342.
- Awa, Adel. "Le Contrepoint Baṭinite", in *Arabic and Islamic Garland: Historical, Educational and Literary Papers Presented to Abdul-Latif Tibawi*. London: Islamic Cultural Centre, 1397/1977, pp. 54–58.
- Awa, Adel. *Ḥaqīqat Ikhwān al-Ṣafāʾ*. Damascus: al-Ahālī, 1993. pp. 414.
- ʿAwaḍ Allāh, al-Shaykh al-Amīn. *al-Ḥayāt al-ijtimāʿiyya fi'l-ʿaṣr al-Fāṭimī*. Jeddah: Dār al-Majmaʿ al-ʿIlmī, 1979. pp. 132.
- Awfī, Muḥammad Sālim. *al-ʿAlāqāt al-siyāsiyya bayna al-dawla al-Fāṭimiyya wa'l-dawla al-ʿAbbāsiyya fi'l-ʿaṣr al-Saljūqī, 447–567 H./1055–1171 M.* [Riyadh]: n.p., 1982. pp. 418.

- Ayni, Mehmet Ali. "Karmatlara dair yazılmiş kitaplar", *DIFM*, 3, no. 11 (1929), pp. 103–109.
- al-ʿAyyāsh, Sāmī. *al-Ismāʿīliyyūn fiʾl-marḥala al-Qarmaṭiyya*. Beirut: Dār Ibn Khaldūn, 1970. pp. 254.
- Ayyūb, Ibrāhīm Rizq Allāh. "Dawr al-marʾa fiʾl-mujtamaʿ al-Fāṭimī", *Taʾrīkh al-ʿArab waʾl-ʿĀlam*, 8 (1986), pp. 16–24.
- Ayyūb, Ibrāhīm Rizq Allāh. "Maẓāhir al-tharwa fiʾl-mujtamaʿ al-Fāṭimī", *al-Fikr al-ʿArabī*, 7 (1987), pp. 168–180.
- Ayyūb, Ibrāhīm Rizq Allāh. *al-Taʾrīkh al-Fāṭimī al-ijtimāʿī*. Beirut: al-Sharika al-ʿĀlamiyya liʾl-Kitāb, 1997. pp. 301.
- Ayyūb, Ibrāhīm Rizq Allāh. *al-Taʾrīkh al-Fāṭimī al-siyāsī*. Beirut: al-Sharika al-ʿĀlamiyya liʾl-Kitāb, 1997. pp. 271.
- Aʿẓamī, Chirāgh-ʿAlī. "Sikaʾī yaktā va bī hamtā az dizh-i Alamūt", *Gawhar*, 1 (1351 Sh./1973), pp. 99–103.
- al-Aʿẓamī, Muḥammad Ḥasan (b. 1914). *ʿAbqariyyat al-Fāṭimiyyīn: aḍwāʾ ʿalāʾl-fikr waʾl-taʾrīkh al-Fāṭimiyyīn*. Beirut: Dār Maktabat al-Ḥayāt, [1960]. pp. 240.
- al-Aʿẓamī, Muḥammad Ḥasan. *Niẓām al-ṣawm ʿinda al-Fāṭimiyyīn*. Silsilat maṭbūʿāt rābiṭ-i taʾlīf va tarjama Pakistan, 79. Karachi: n.p., 1380/1960. pp. 128 (in Urdu).
- al-Aʿẓamī, Muḥammad Ḥasan. *al-Ḥaqāʾiq al-khafiyya ʿan al-Shīʿa al-Fāṭimiyya waʾl-Ithnāʿashariyya*. Cairo: al-Hayʾa al-Miṣriyya al-ʿĀmma liʾl-Kitāb, 1970. pp. 209.
- Āzhand, Yaʿqūb (ed. and tr.), *Nahḍat-i Qarāmiṭa*. Tehran: Mīrāth-i Millal, 1368 Sh./1989. pp. 116.
- Āzhand, Yaʿqūb. "Qarmaṭiyān dar Īrān", *Taʾrīkh-i Islām*, 9 (1381 Sh./2002), pp. 67–82.
- Aziz, Abualy A. (b. 1919). *A Brief History of Ismailism*. Dar-es-Salaam: Ismailia Association for Tanzania, 1974. pp. 188; reprinted, Toronto: n.p., 1985. pp. 188.
- Aziz, Abualy A. "Pir Hasan Kabiruddin", in *GIH*, pp. 91–92.
- Aziz, Philippe, in collaboration with Florence Bruneau. *Les sectes secrètes de l'Islam de l'ordre des Assassins aux Frères Musulmans*. Paris: Éditions R. Laffront, 1983. pp. 359.
- ʿAzīzī, Manṣūr. *Mubārazāt-i ḍidd-i fiʾūdālī dar Īrān (Ismāʿīliyya dar gudhargāh-i taʾrīkh)*. Tehran: Nigāh, 1359 Sh./1980. pp. 125.

- al-ʿAzzāwī, al-Sayyid Muḥammad. *Firqat al-Nizāriyya*. Cairo: Jāmiʿat ʿAyn Shams, 1392/1972. pp. 327.

B

- al-Baʿalī, Fuʾād. *Falsafat Ikhwān al-Ṣafāʾ*. Baghdad: Maṭbaʿat al-Maʿārif, 1958. pp. 171.
- Badakhchani, S. Jalal. "Nasir al-Din Tusi and his Ismaili Writings", in *Farhang, Quarterly Journal of Humanities and Cultural Studies*, 15–16, nos. 44–45 (2003), pp. 183–193.
- Baer, Eva. "Fatimid Art at the Crossroads: A Turning Point in the Artistic Concepts of Islam?", in *EF*, pp. 385–394.
- Baffioni, Carmela. "The Rasāʾil Ikhwān al-Ṣafāʾ: Recent Research and New Perspectives", in Gerhard Endress, ed., *Symposium Graeco-Arabicum, Akten des zweiten Symposium Graeco-Arabicum, Ruhr-Universität, Bochum, 3–5 März 1987*. Amsterdam: Grüner, 1989, pp. 3–9.
- Baffioni, Carmela. "Euclides in the Rasāʾil by Ikhwān al-Ṣafāʾ", *Études Orientales*, 5–6 (1990), pp. 58–68.
- Baffioni, Carmela. "Oggetti e caratteristiche del *curriculum* delle scienze nell'*Enciclopedia* dei Fratelli della Purità", in G. di Stefano, ed., *Studi Arabo-Islamici in memoria di Umberto Rizzitano*. Mazara del Vallo: Istituto di Studi Arabo-Islamici "Michele Amari", 1991, pp. 25–31.
- Baffioni, Carmela. "The Platonic Virtues of the Ruler in Islāmic Tradition", *Études Orientales*, 9–10 (1991), pp. 111–118.
- Baffioni, Carmela. "Probable Syriac Influences in the Ikhwān al-Ṣafāʾs Logical Epistles?", *ARAM*, 3 (1991), pp. 7–22.
- Baffioni, Carmela. "Traces of Aristotelian Dialogues in the *Rasāʾil* by Ikhwān al-Ṣafāʾ", in *BRISMES* [British Society for Middle Eastern Studies] *Proceedings of the 1991 International Conference on Middle Eastern Studies (SOAS, London, 10–12 July 1991)*. London: British Society for Middle Eastern Studies, 1991, pp. 439–448.
- Baffioni, Carmela. "Uso e interpretazioni di versetti coranici nell'Ep. 42 degli Ikhwān al-Ṣafāʾ", in Biancamaria Amoretti and Lucia Rostagno, ed., *Yād-nāma in memoria di Alessandro Bausani*: Vol. I, *Islamistica*. Università di Roma "La Sapienza", Studi Orientali, X. Rome: Bardi, 1991, pp. 57–70.

- Baffioni, Carmela. "Greek Ideas and Vocabulary in Arabic Philosophy: The Rasāʾil by Ikhwān al-Ṣafāʾ", in A. Harrak, ed., *Contacts Between Cultures: West Asia and North-Africa*, vol. 1. Lewiston, New York, etc.: E. Mellen Press, 1992, pp. 391–398.
- Baffioni, Carmela. "Traces of 'Secret Sects' in the *Rasāʾil* of the Ikhwān al-Ṣafāʾ", in Frederick de Jong, ed., *Shīʿa Islam, Sects and Sufism: Historical Dimensions, Religious Practice and Methodological Considerations.* Utrecht: M. Th. Houtsma Stichting, 1992, pp. 10–25.
- Baffioni, Carmela. "Il 'quarto clima' nell'Epistola sulla geografia degli Iḫwān al-Ṣafāʾ", in F. Bencardino, ed., *Oriente Occidente. Scritti in memoria di Vittorina Langella.* Naples: Istituto Universitario Orientale, 1993, pp. 45–60.
- Baffioni, Carmela. "Detti aurei di Pitagora in trasmissione Araba", in *I moderni ausili all' ecdotica.* Naples: Edizioni Scientifiche Italiane, 1994, pp. 107–131.
- Baffioni, Carmela. "Il 'Liber introductorius in artem logicae demonstrationis', problemi storici e filologici", *Studi Filosofici*, 17 (1994), pp. 69–90.
- Baffioni, Carmela. "L'Epistola sul concepimento nell'Enciclopedia degli Iḫwān al-Ṣafāʾ", *Medicina nei secoli, Arte e Scienza*, 6 (1994), pp. 365–376.
- Baffioni, Carmela. *Frammenti e testimonianze di autori antichi nelle Rasāʾil degli Iḫwān al-Ṣafāʾ*. Studi Pubblicati dall' Istituto Nazionale per la Storia Antica, 57. Rome: Istituto Nazionale per la Storia Antica, 1994. pp. 546.
- Baffioni, Carmela. "Gli Iḫwān al-Ṣafāʾ e la filosofia del Kalām", *AIUON*, 54 (1994), pp. 464–478.
- Baffioni, Carmela. "Le 'testimonianze' sulla logica di Aristotele nelle Epistole degli Ikhwān al-Ṣafāʾ", in Pier Giovanni Donini et al., ed., *Un ricordo che non si spegne. Scritti di docenti e collaboratori dell'Istituto Universitario Orientale di Napoli in memoria di Alessandro Bausani.* Istituto Universitario Orientale, Dipartimento di Studi Asiatici, Series Minor, L. Naples: Istituto Universitario Orientale, 1995, pp. 1–10.
- Baffioni, Carmela. "Valutazione, utilizzazione e sviluppi delle scienze nei primi secoli dell'Islām: il caso degli Ikhwān al-Ṣafāʾ", in Clelia Sarnelli Cerqua, Ornella Marra and Pier Giovanni Pelfer, ed., *La civiltà Islamica e le scienze.* Atti del Simposio internazionale – 23 novembre

1991. Naples: *CUEN*, 1995, pp. 23–35.

- Baffioni, Carmela. "L'Islām e la legittimazione della filosofia. I 'curricula scientiarum' del secolo X", in G. Piaia, ed., *La filosofia e l'Islam*. Padova: Gregoriana Libreria Editrice, 1996, pp. 13–34.
- Baffioni, Carmela. "Il messaggio profetico di Gesù e di Muḥammad in un passo degli Iḫwān al-Ṣafā'", in *Recueil d'articles offert à Maurice Borrmans par ses collègues et amis*. Studi Arabo-Islamici del PISAI, 8. Rome: Pontificio Istituto di Studi Arabi e d'Islamistica (P.I.S.A.I.), 1996, pp. 21–27.
- Baffioni, Carmela. "An Essay on Terminological Research in Philosophy: The 'Friends of God' in the *Rasā'il Iḫwān al-Ṣafā'*", in Carmela Baffioni et al., ed., *Scritti in onore di Giovanni Oman*; being, *Studi Magrebini*, 25 (1993–97), pp. 23–43.
- Baffioni, Carmela. "Citazioni di autori antichi nelle *Rasā'il Ikhwān al-Ṣafā'*: il caso di Nicomaco di Gerasa", in Gerhard Endress and Remke Kruk, ed., *The Ancient Tradition in Christian and Islamic Hellenism: Studies on the Transmission of Greek Philosophy and Sciences dedicated to H.J. Drossaart Lulofs on his Ninetieth Birthday*. CNWS Publications, 50. Leiden: Leiden Research School (CNWS), School of Asian, African and Amerindian Studies, 1997, pp. 3–27.
- Baffioni, Carmela. "Fragments et témoignages d'auteurs anciens dans les Rasā'il des *Ikhwān al-Ṣafā'*", in Ahmad Hasnawi et al., ed., *Perspectives Arabes et médiévales sur la tradition scientifique et philosophique Grecque*. Orientalia Lovaniensia Analecta, 79. Louvain: Peeters; Paris: Institut du Monde Arabe, 1997, pp. 319–329.
- Baffioni, Carmela. "L'influenza degli astri sul feto nell'Enciclopedia degli Iḫwān al-Ṣafā'", *Medioevo. Rivista di Storia della Filosofia Medievale*, 23 (1997), pp. 409–439.
- Baffioni, Carmela. "Sulla ricezione di due luoghi di Platone e Aristotele negli Iḫwān al-Ṣafā", in *Documenti e studi sulla tradizione filosofica medievale, International Journal on the Philosophical Tradition from Late Antiquity to the Late Middle Ages of the SISMEL*, 8 (1997), pp. 479–492.
- Baffioni, Carmela. "Textual Problems in the Iḫwān al-Ṣafā''s Quotations of Ancient Authors", in Wilferd Madelung et al., ed., *Proceedings of the 17th Congress of the UEAI* [Union Européenne des Arabisants et Islamisants]. St. Petersburg: Thesa, 1997, pp. 13–26.

- Baffioni, Carmela. "Uso e rielaborazione degli autori classici nella *Risāla al-ǧāmiʿa*", in Alfredo Valvo, ed., *La diffusione dell'eredità classica nell'età tardoantica e medievale. Forme e modi di trasmissione.* Atti del Seminario Nazionale (Trieste 19–20 settembre 1996). Alessandria: Edizioni dell'Orso, 1997, pp. 1–17.
- Baffioni, Carmela. "Bodily Resurrection in the Iḫwān al-Ṣafāʾ", in Urbain Vermeulen and Daniel de Smet, ed., *Philosophy and Arts in the Islamic World.* Orientalia Lovaniensia Analecta, 87. Louvain: Peeters, 1998, pp. 201–208.
- Baffioni, Carmela. "From Sense Perception to the Vision of God: A Path Towards Knowledge According to the Iḫwān al-Ṣafāʾ", *Arabic Sciences and Philosophy*, 8 (1998), pp. 213–231.
- Baffioni, Carmela. "La lettura di Alessandro Bausani degli Iḫwān al-Ṣafāʾ", in *In memoria di Alessandro Bausani nel decennale della morte*; being, *Oriente Moderno*, NS, 17 (1998), pp. 421–433.
- Baffioni, Carmela. "L'inizio del concepimento in scienziati Greci e Musulmani", in Luigi Cagni, ed., *Biblica et Semitica: Studi in memoria di Francesco Vattioni.* Naples: Istituto Universitario Orientale, 1999, pp. 1–15.
- Baffioni, Carmela. "The Concept of Science and its Legitimation in the Iḫwān al-Ṣafāʾ", in Carmela Baffioni, ed., *Religion versus Science in Islam: A Medieval and Modern Debate*; being, *Oriente Moderno*, NS, 19 (2000), pp. 427–441.
- Baffioni, Carmela. "Conversion in the *Epistles* of the Iḫwān al-Ṣafāʾ", in Simonetta Graziani et al., ed., *Studi sul Vicino Oriente antico dedicati alla memoria di Luigi Cagni.* Istituto Universitario Orientale, Dipartimento di Studi Asiatici, Series Minor LXI. Naples: Istituto Universitario Orientale, 2000, vol. 3, pp. 1249–1259.
- Baffioni, Carmela. "Different Conceptions of Religious Practice, Piety and God-Man Relations in the Epistles of the Ikhwān al-Ṣafāʾ", *Al-Qanṭara*, 21 (2000), pp. 381–386.
- Baffioni, Carmela. "Uso e rielaborazione degli autori classici nella *Risāla Gāmiʿa al-ǧāmiʿa*", in Carmela Baffioni, ed., *La diffusione dell' eredità classica nell' età tardoantica e medievale: Filologia, storia, dottrina.* Atti del Seminario Nazionale di Studio (Napoli-Sorrento, 29–31 ottobre, 1998). L'eredità classica nel mondo orientale, 3. Alessandria: Edizioni dell'Orso, 2000, pp. 1–10.

- Baffioni, Carmela. "Antecedenti Greci e Arabi delle dottrine degli Iḫwān al-Ṣafā' sulla sensazione", in Rosa Bianca Finazzi and Alfredo Valvo, ed., *Pensiero e istituzioni del mondo classico nelle culture del Vicino Oriente.* Atti del Seminario Nazionale di Studio (Brescia, 14–15–16 ottobre 1999). Alessandria: Edizioni dell'Orso, 2001, pp. 27–53.
- Baffioni, Carmela. "Frammenti e testimonianze platoniche nelle *Rasā'il* degli Ikhwān al-Ṣafā'" and "Aspetti della dottrina di Archimede nella tradizione Araba: nuovi testi negli Ikhwān al-Ṣafā'", in Gianfranco Fiaccadori, ed., *Autori classici in lingue del Vicino e Medio Oriente.* Atti del VI, VII e VIII Seminario sul tema: "Recupero di testi classici attraverso recezioni in lingue del Vicino e Medio Oriente". Rome: Istituto Poligrafico e Zecca dello Stato, Libreria dello Stato, 2001, pp. 163–178, 327–339.
- Baffioni, Carmela. "Antecedenti Greci del concetto di 'Natura' negli Iḫwān al-Ṣafā'", in M. Barbanti, G.R. Giardina and P. Manganaro, ed., *Enosis Kai Filia/Unione e Amicizia. Omaggio a Francesco Romano.* Catania: CUECM, 2002, pp. 545–556.
- Baffioni, Carmela. "Echi di *Meteorologica* IV nell'enciclopedia dei Fratelli della Purità", in Cristina Viano, ed., *Aristoteles Chemicus: Il IV Libro dei* Meteorologica *nella tradizione antica e medievale.* Sankt Augustin: Academia Verlag, 2002, pp. 113–131.
- Baffioni, Carmela. "*Al-Madīnah al-Fāḍilāh* in al-Fārābī and in the Ikhwān al-Ṣafā': A Comparison", in S. Leder et al., ed., *Studies in Arabic and Islam.* Proceedings of the 19th Congress, Union Européenne des Arabisants et Islamisants, Halle, 1998. Orientalia Lovaniensia Analecta, 108. Louvain: Peeters, 2002, pp. 3–12.
- Baffioni, Carmela. "Les sens chez les Ikhwān al-Ṣafā' et l'héritage aristotélicien", in Agostino Paravicini Bagliani, ed., *I Cinque Sensi/The Five Senses.* Sismel: Edizioni del Galluzzo, 2002; being, *Micrologus*, 10 (2002), pp. 463–476.
- Baffioni, Carmela. "La posizione della medicina nel *Curriculum* Ikhwaniano delle scienze", in Ugo Marazzi, ed., *Turcica et Islamica: Studi in memoria di Aldo Gallota.* Naples: Università degli Studi di Napoli "L'Orientale", Dipartimento di Studi Asiatici, 2003, pp. 1–13.
- Baffioni, Carmela and Claudio Baffioni. "Citazioni matematiche negli Iḫwān al-Ṣafā': il caso di Nicomaco di Gerasa", in Clelia Sarnelli Cerqua, Ornella Marra and Pier Giovanni Pelfer, ed., *La civiltà Islamica e le scienze.* Naples: *CUEN*, 1995, pp. 37–61.

- Bahrāmī, ʿAskar. "Dīnhā-yi Īrān-i bāstān az manẓar-i Dīwān-i Nāṣir-i Khusraw", *NP*, 8, no. 2 (1382 Sh./2003), pp. 95–104.
- Bahrāmī, Muḥammad. "Garāyish-i madhhabī-yi Shahrastānī", *Pazhūhishhā-yi Qurʾānī/Quranic Research Quarterly*, 21–22 (1379 Sh./2000), pp. 354–383; English summary, p. 8.
- Baker, Robert L. "The Aga Khan: Moslem Pontiff", *Current History*, 42 (1935), pp. 591–597.
- Bakoev, Mamadvafo. "V poiskakh vostochnïkh rukopisey" [In search of Oriental Manuscripts], *Narodï Azii i Afriki* (Moscow), 3 (1962), pp. 238–239.
- Bakoev, Mamadvafo. "Novïe nakhodki na Pamire" [New Discoveries in the Pamirs], *Narodï Azii i Afriki* (Moscow), 4 (1963), pp. 236–237.
- Bakoev, Mamadvafo. "Pyataya Pamirskaya ékspeditsiya po sboru vostochnïkh rukopisey" [The Fifth Pamirian Expedition in Search of Oriental Manuscripts], *Narodï Azii i Afriki* (Moscow), 3 (1964), p. 212.
- Balard, Michel. "Notes sur le commerce entre l'Italie et l'Égypte sous les Fatimides", in *EF*, pp. 627–633.
- Balog, Paul (1900–1982). "Apparition prématurée de l'écriture naskhy sur un dinar de l'Imam Fatimite Al Moustaly-Billah", *BIE*, 31 (1948–49), pp. 181–185.
- Balog, Paul. "Études numismatiques de l'Égypte Musulmane. Périodes Fatimite et Ayoubite, nouvelles observations sur la téchnique du monnayage", *BIE*, 33 (1950–51), pp. 1–23, 31–42.
- Balog, Paul. "Quatre dinars du khalife Fatimide al-Mountazar li-Amr-Illah ou bi-Amr-Illah (525–526 A.H.)", *BIE*, 33 (1950–51), pp. 375–378.
- Balog, Paul. "Études numismatiques de l'Égypte Musulmane III: Fatimites, Ayoubites, premiers Mamelouks, leurs téchniques monétaires", *BIE*, 35 (1952–53), pp. 401–429.
- Balog, Paul. "Monnaies Islamiques rares Fatimites et Ayoubites", *BIE*, 36 (1953–54), pp. 327–345.
- Balog, Paul. "Note sur quelques monnaies et jetons Fatimites de Sicile", *BIE*, 37 (1954–55), pp. 65–72.
- Balog, Paul. "Poids forts Fatimites en plomb", *Revue Belge de Numismatique*, 105 (1959), pp. 171–188.
- Balog, Paul. "History of the Dirhem in Egypt from the Fāṭimid

Conquest until the Collapse of the Mamlūk Empire, 358–922H/968–1517 A.D.", *Revue Numismatique*, 6 série, 3 (1961), pp. 109–146.

- Balog, Paul. "Les jetons Fatimites en verre", *Revue Belge de Numismatique*, 107 (1961), pp. 171–183.
- Balog, Paul. "Notes on Some Fāṭimid Round-flan Dirhems", *Numismatic Chronicle*, 7th series, 1 (1961), pp. 175–179.
- Balog, Paul. "Poids en plomb du khalife Fâṭimite al-Ḥâkim Biamr-il-lâh frappé à Miṣr en l'an 389H", *JESHO*, 6 (1963), pp. 216–218.
- Balog, Paul. "The Fatimid Glass Jeton", *Annali, Istituto Italiano di Numismatico*, 17–19 (1971–72), pp. 175–264; 20 (1973), pp. 121–212.
- Balog, Paul. "Fatimid and Post-Fatimid Glass Jetons from Sicily", *Studi Magrebini*, 7 (1975), pp. 125–148.
- Balog, Paul. "The Fāṭimid Glass Jetons: Token Currency or Coin Weights?", *JESHO*, 24 (1981), pp. 93–109.
- Banu, Zenab. "Muslim Women's Right to Inheritance: Shari'a Law and its Practice among the Dawoodi Bohras of Udaipur, Rajasthan", in Asghar Ali Engineer, ed., *Problems of Muslim Women in India*. Hyderabad: Orient Longman, 1995, pp. 34–39.
- Bar-Asher, Meir Mikhael and Aryeh Kofsky. "A Druze – Nuṣayrī Debate in the 'Epistles of Wisdom'", *Quaderni di Studi Arabi*, 17 (1999), pp. 95–103.
- Baradin, Chingiz G. "Ḥakīm Nizārī Quhistānī", *Farhang-i Īrān Zamīn*, 6 (1337 Sh./1958), pp. 178–203.
- Bareket, Elinoar. "Personal Adversities of Jews during the Period of the Fatimid Wars in Eleventh Century Palestine", in Yaacov Lev, ed., *War and Society in the Eastern Mediterranean, 7th-15th Centuries*. The Medieval Mediterranean Peoples, Economies and Cultures, 400–1453, vol. 9. Leiden: E.J. Brill, 1997, pp. 153–162.
- Barghuthy, Omar Saleh. "A Ministry of Propaganda under the Fatimids", *Journal of the Middle East Society*, 2 (1947), pp. 57–59.
- Bariani, Laura. "Parentela e potere: uso ed abuso. Indagine sulle 'madri' del califfo al-Ḥākim bi-Amr Allāh al-Fāṭimī", *Al-Qanṭara*, 16 (1995), pp. 357–367.
- al-Barrāwī, Rāshid. *Ḥālat Miṣr al-iqtiṣādiyya fī 'ahd al-Fāṭimiyyīn*. Dirāsāt fī ta'rīkh Miṣr al-iqtiṣādī. Cairo: Maktabat al-Nahḍa al-Miṣriyya, 1948. pp. 402.

- Barrucand, Marianne. "L'architecture Fatimide et son rayonnement en Afrique du Nord", *Dossiers d'Archéologie*; special issue *Égypte: L'Âge d'or des Fatimides*, 233 (May, 1998), pp. 42–49.
- Barrucand, Marianne (ed.), *L'Égypte Fatimide, son art et son histoire.* Actes du colloque organisé à Paris les 28, 29 et 30 mai 1998. Paris: Presses de l'Université de Paris-Sorbonne, 1999. pp. 704.
- Bartlett, Wayne B. *The Assassins: The Story of Medieval Islam's Secret Sect.* Stroud, Gloucestershire: Sutton Publishing, 2001. pp. xviii + 270.
- Bartol, Vladimir (1903–1967). *Alamut, roman*, tr., from Slovak into French by Claude Vincenot. Paris: Éditions Phébus, 1988. pp. 582. Arabic trans., *Alamūt*, tr., Hāla Ṣalāḥ al-Dīn Lūlū. Beirut: Dār Amwāj and Ward, 2001. pp. 565. Persian trans., *Alamūt*, tr., Muḥammad Majlisī. Tehran: Nashr-i Dunyā-yi Naw, 1373 Sh./1994. pp. 472.
- Basaj, Aḥmad Ḥasan. *Ibn Hāniʾ al-Andalusī: ʿaṣruhu wa-bīʿatuhu wa-ḥayātuhu wa-shiʿruhu.* al-Aʿlām min al-udabāʾ waʾl-shuʿarāʾ. Beirut: Dār al-Kutub al-ʿIlmiyya, 1994. pp. 110.
- "al-Basāsīrī", in *EI*, vol. 1, p. 669.
- al-Bāshā, Ḥasan Maḥmūd Ḥasan. "Ṭabaq min al-khazaf biʾism Ghabn mawlā al-Ḥākim bi-Amr Allāh", *Majallat Kulliyat al-Ādāb, Jāmiʿat al-Qāhira/Bulletin of the Faculty of Arts, Cairo University*, 18, no. 1 (1956), pp. 71–85.
- al-Bāshā, Muḥammad Khalīl. *Muʿjam aʿlām al-Durūz.* al-Mukhtāra, Lebanon: al-Dār al-Taqaddumiyya, 1990. 2 vols.
- Bashardūst, Mujtabā. "Farāsū-yi tanzīl", *NP*, 8, no. 2 (1382 Sh./2003), pp. 71–94.
- Basset, René (1855–1924). "Abū Yazīd", "Bulukkīn", in *EI*.
- Bāstānī Pārīzī, Muḥammad Ibrāhīm. "Jādhiba-yi siyāsī-yi Qāhira va Ismāʿīliyān-i Īrān", *Rāhnamā-yi Kitāb*, 18 (1354 Sh./1975), pp. 252–273, 532–548, 807–826.
- Bates, Michael L. "Notes on Some Ismāʿīlī Coins from Yemen", *American Numismatic Society Museum Notes*, 18 (1972), pp. 149–162.
- Bates, Michael L. "The Chapter on the Fāṭimid Dāʿīs in Yemen in the *Taʾrīkh* of ʿUmāra al-Ḥakamī (d. 569/1174): An Interpolation", in Abdelgadir Mahmoud Abdallah et al., ed., *Studies in the History of Arabia*, I: *Sources for the History of Arabia.* Riyadh: Riyadh University Press, 1979, part 2, pp. 51–61.

- Bates, Michael L. "The Function of Fāṭimid and Ayyūbid Glass Weights", *JESHO*, 24 (1981), pp. 63–92.
- Bates, Michael, L. "Coinage in Egypt: Islamic Period", in Aziz Sourial Atiya, ed., *The Coptic Encyclopedia*. New York: Macmillan, 1989, pp. 575–577.
- Bates, Michael L. "How Egyptian Glass Coin Weights were used", *Rivista Italiana di Numismatica e Scienze Affini*, 95 (1993), pp. 539–545.
- Baumstark, A. "Zu den Schriftzitaten al-Kirmānīs", *Der Islam*, 20 (1932), pp. 308–313.
- Bausani, Alessandro (1921–1988). "Scientific Elements in Ismā'īlī Thought: The Epistles of the Brethren of Purity (*Ikhwān al-Ṣafā'*)", in *ICIC*, pp. 121–140.
- Bausani, Alessandro. "Le dimensioni dell' universo nel *Kitāb Iḫwān al-Ṣafā'*", in *La signification du bas moyen âges dans l'histoire et la culture du monde Musulman*. Actes du VIIIe congrès de l'Union Européenne des Arabistants et Islamisants, Aix-en-Provence, septembre 1976. Aix-en-Provence: EDISUD, 1978, pp. 23–29.
- Bausani, Alessandro. "Aspetti scientifici delle Epistole dei *Fratelli della Purezza*", in *Convegno sugli Ikhwān*, pp. 27–47.
- Bausani, Alessandro. "Die Bewegungen der Erde im *Kitāb Ikhwān aṣ-Ṣafā'*: Ein vor-philolaïsch-pythagoraïsches System?", *Zeitschrift für Geschichte der Arabisch-Islamischen Wissenschaften*, 1 (1984), pp. 88–99.
- Bausani, Alessandro. "L'enciclopedia e il mondo Arabo-Islamico medievale", *Rivista di Storia della Filosofia*, 40 (1985), pp. 137–146.
- Bauwens, Jan. "Les Épîtres des Frères Sincères: une *imago mundi*", *Acta Orientalia Belgica*, 10 (1966), pp. 7–18.
- Bayburdi, Chingiz Gulam-Ali. "Srednevekoviy persidskiy poét Nizari v Zakavkaz'e" [Medieval Persian Poet Nizārī in the Trans-Caucasis], *Istoriko-filologicheskiy Zhurnal, Erevan*, 4 (1959), pp. 233–243.
- Bayburdi, Chingiz G.A. "Zhizn' i tvorchestvo Nizari-Persidskogo poéta" [Life and Works of the Persian Poet Nizārī]. *Avtoreferat dissertatsii na zvanie kandidata filologicheskikh nauk*. Leningrad, 1963. pp. 18.
- Bayburdi, Chingiz G.A. "Rukopisi proizvedeniy Nizārī" [Manuscript of Nizārī's Works], *Kratkie Soobshcheniya Instituta Narodov Azii*

(Moscow), 65 (1964), pp. 13–24.

- Bayburdi, Chingiz G.A. *Zhizn' i tvorchestvo Nizārī-Persidskogo poéta XIII–XIV vv.* [Life and Works of Nizārī-Persian Poet of the XIII–XIV Centuries]. Moscow: Nauka, 1966. pp. 272. Persian trans., *Zindigī va āthār-i Nizārī*, tr., Mahnāz Ṣadrī. Tehran: Intishārāt-i ʿIlmī, 1370 Sh./ 1991. pp. 290.
- Bayburdi, Chingiz G.A. "O perepiske Malik-shakha s Khasanom ibn Sabbakhom" [About the Correspondence of Malik-Shāh with Ḥasan ibn Ṣabbāḥ], in *Iranskaya filologiya. Kratkoe izlozhenie dokladov nauchnoy konferentsii*. Moscow, 1969, pp. 9–12.
- Bayburdi, Chingiz G.A. "Ob ideologicheskoy obshchnosti nekotorïkh doktrin ismailizma i babizma" [About the Ideological Commonness of Some Doctrines of Ismailism and Babism], in *Filologiya i istoriya stran zarubezhnoy Azii i Afriki. Tezisï dokladov nauchnoy konferentsii, posvyashchyonnoy 120-letiyu osnovaniya Vostfaka LGU*. Leningrad, 1974, pp. 58–61.
- Baykov, A.A. "Pechat' fatimidskogo khalifa Ẓāhira" [The Stamp of the Fatimid Caliph Ẓāhir], *Zapiski Kollegii Vostokovedov* (Leningrad), 5 (1930), pp. 201–219.
- Bazzūn, Ḥasan. *al-Qarmaṭiyya bayna al-dīn wa'l-thawra*. Beirut: Dār al-Ḥaqīqa, 1988. pp. 208; 2nd ed., Beirut: Mu'assasat al-Intishār al-ʿArabī, 1997. pp. 295.
- Becker, Carl Heinrich (1876–1933). *Beiträge zur Geschichte Ägyptens unter dem Islam*. Strassburg: K.J. Trübner, 1902–1903. 2 vols. in 1; reprinted, *Studies in Islamic History*, 5. Philadelphia: Porcupine, 1977. 2 vols. in 1.
- Becker, Carl H. "Das Reich der Ismaeliten im koptischen Danielbuch", *Nachrichten von der königlichen Gesellschaft der Wissenschaften zu Göttingen, Philologisch-historische Klasse* (1916), pp. 7–57.
- Becker, Carl H. "Badr al-Jamālī", in *DDI*, vol. 2, pp. 485–486.
- Becker, Carl H. "ʿAbbās b. Abi'l-Futūḥ", "al-ʿĀḍid li-Dīn Allāh", "al-Afḍal", "Badr al-Djamālī", "Ibn Killis", in *EI*.
- Becker, Carl H. "Badr al-Djamālī", in *EI2*, vol. 1, pp. 869–870.
- Becker, Carl H. and Samuel M. Stern. "ʿAbbās b. Abi'l-Futūḥ", in *EI2*, vol. 1, p. 9.
- Beeston, Alfred Felix L. (1911–1995). "An Ancient Druze Manuscript",

The Bodleian Library Record, 5 (1954–56), pp. 286–290.

- Behrens-Abouseif, Doris. "The Citadel of Cairo: Stage for Mamluk Ceremonial", *AI*, 24 (1988), pp. 25–79.
- Behrens-Abouseif, Doris. "The Façade of the Aqmar Mosque in the Context of Fatimid Ceremonial", *Muqarnas*, 9 (1992), pp. 29–38.
- Beksaç, A. Engin. "Fâtimîlir. III. Sanat", in *IA2*, vol. 12, pp. 237–240.
- Bekzoda, Komil. "Nāṣir-i Khusraw va mawḍūʿ-i falsafa-yi millī", *Nomai Pazhouhishgoh* (Dushanbe), 4 (2003), pp. 131–136.
- Bello, Iysa Ade. "The Qarmaṭians", *IC*, 54 (1980), pp. 229–241.
- Ben-Cheneb, Moh. "Ibn Hānī", in *EI*, vol. 2, p. 383.
- Ben Milad, Mahjoub. "La contribution des Fāṭimides à la philosophie Islamique (Résumé)", in *Colloque international sur l'histoire du Caire*, pp. 325–326.
- Berchem, Max van (1863–1921). "Une mosquée du temps des Fatimites au Caire: Notice sur le Gâmiʿ El Goyûshi", *Mémoire de l'Institut Egyptien*, 2 (1889), pp. 605–619; reprinted in Max van Berchem, *Opera Minora*. Geneva: Éditions Slatkine, 1978, vol. 1, pp. 61–75.
- Berchem, Max van. "Notes d'archéologie Arabe. Monuments et inscriptions Fatimites", *JA*, 8 série, 17 (1891), pp. 411–495; 18 (1891), pp. 46–86; reprinted in Max van Berchem, *Opera Minora*. Geneva: Éditions Slatkine, 1978, vol. 1, pp. 77–201.
- Berchem, Max van. "Notes d'archéologie Arabe. Deuxième article. Toulounides et Fatimites", *JA*, 8 série, 19 (1892), pp. 377–407; reprinted in Max van Berchem, *Opera Minora*. Geneva: Éditions Slatkine, 1978, vol. 1, pp. 203–233.
- Berchem, Max van. "Épigraphie des Assassins de Syrie", *JA*, 9 série, 9 (1897), pp. 453–501; reprinted in Max van Berchem, *Opera Minora*. Geneva: Éditions Slatkine, 1978, vol. 1, pp. 453–501; reprinted in Bryan S. Turner, ed., *Orientalism: Early Sources*, Volume I, *Readings in Orientalism*. London: Routledge, 2000, pp. 279–309.
- Berezin, Il'ya Nikolaevich (1818-1896). "Vostochnïe reformatorï-assassinï" [Eastern Reformers – The Assassins], *Sovremennik* (St. Petersburg), 10 (1857), pp. 93–122.
- Berman, Lawrence V. "Brethren of Sincerity, Epistles of", in *Encyclopaedia Judaica*. Jerusalem: Keter Publishing House, 1971, vol. 4, p. 1364.

- Berque, J. "Du nouveau sur les Banu Hilāl?", *SI*, 36 (1972), pp. 99–113.
- Bertel's, Andrey Evgen'evich (1926–1995). "Nasir-i Khosrov i ego vremya" [Nāṣir-i Khusraw and his Time]. *Avtoreferat dissertatsii na zvanie kandidata filologicheskikh nauk*. Moscow, 1952. pp. 15.
- Bertel's, Andrey E. "Rūdakī i karmatï" [Rūdakī and the Qarmaṭīs], in *Rudaki i ego épokha*. Stalinabad, 1958, pp. 63–78.
- Bertel's, Andrey E. "Nakhodki novïkh rukopisey v Tadzhikistane" [Discoveries of New Manuscripts in Tajikistan], *Problemï vostokovedeniya* (Moscow), 6 (1959), pp. 222–223.
- Bertel's, Andrey E. *Nasir-i Khosrov i ismailizm* [Nāṣir-i Khusraw and Ismailism]. Akademiya Nauk SSSR, Institut Vostokovedeniya. Moscow: Izdatel'stvo Vostochnoy Literaturï, 1959. pp. 289. Persian trans., *Nāṣir-i Khusraw va Ismāʿīliyān*, tr., Yaḥyā Āriyanpūr. Intishārāt-i Bunyād-i Farhang-i Īrān, 34. Tehran: Bunyād-i Farhang-i Īrān, 1346 Sh./1967. pp. 323.
- Bertel's, Andrey E. "Nakhodki rukopisey na Pamire" [Discoveries of Manuscripts in the Pamirs], *Narodï Azii i Afriki* (Moscow), 2 (1961), pp. 234–236.
- Bertel's, Andrey E. "Otchyot o rabote Pamirskoy ékspeditsii Otdela vostokovedeniya i pis'mennogo naslediya Akademii Nauk Tadzhikskoy SSR (avgust 1959)" [Report on the Work of the Pamirian Expedition of the Department of Oriental Studies and Written Heritage of the Tajikistan Academy of Science (August 1959)], *Izvestiya Akademii Nauk Tadzhikskoy SSR* (Dushanbe), no. 2 (29) (1962), pp. 11–16.
- Bertel's, Andrey E. "Arzish-i mīrāth-i adabī-yi Nāṣir-i Khusraw", *Sophia Perennis*, 1 (1975), pp. 31–42.
- Bertel's, Andrey E. "Naẓariyāt-i barkhī az ʿurafā va Shīʿayān-i Ithnāʿasharī rājiʿ bi arzish-i mīrāth-i adabī-yi Nāṣir-i Khusraw", in *YNK*, pp. 96–121.
- Bertel's, Andrey E. "Poéticheskiy kommentariy shakha Niʿmatullakha Vali na filosofskuyu kasïdu Nasir-i Khusrau" [Poetic Commentary of Shāh Niʿmatullāh Valī on Philosophical *qaṣīda* by Nāṣir-i Khusraw], in *Sad odnogo tsvetka*. Moscow: Nauka, Glavnaya redaktsiya vostochnoy literaturï, 1991, pp. 7–30.
- Bertel's, Andrey E. "Nasir Khosrov", in *Bolshaya Sovetskaya Éntsiklopediya*. Moscow: Bolshaya Sovetskaya Éntsiklopediya, 1974, vol, 17, p. 880; also as "Naser-e Khosrow", in *Great Soviet Encyclopedia*, New

York: Macmillan; London: Collier Macmillan, 1978, vol. 17, p. 349.

- Bertel's, Andrey E. and Mamadvafo Bakoev. *Alfavitnïy katalog rukopisey obnaruzhennïkh v Gorno-Badakhshanskoy Avtonomnoy Oblasti ékspeditsiey 1959–1963* gg./*Alphabetic Catalogue of Manuscripts found by 1959–1963 Expedition in Gorno-Badakhshan Autonomous Region*, ed., Bobodzhon G. Gafurov and A.M. Mirzoev. Moscow: Nauka, 1967. pp. 119. Persian trans., *Fihrist-i nuskhahā-yi khaṭṭī-yi mawjūd dar vilāyat-i Badakhshān-i Tājikistān*, tr., Qodrat-Beg Īlchī and Sayyid Anvar Shāh Khomarof. Qom, Iran: Kitābkhāna-yi Buzurg-i Āyat Allāh al-ʿUẓmā Marʿashī Najafī, 1376/1997. pp. 140.
- Bertel's (Berthels), Evgeniy Éduardovich (1890–1957). "Nasir-i Khusrau i ego vzglyad na poéziyu" [Nāṣir-i Khusraw's Views on Poetry], *Izvestiya Akademii Nauk Tadzhikskoy SSR, otdelenie obshchestvennïkh nauk*, 4 (1953), pp. 139–153; also in *Izbrannïe trudï*, Moscow: Nauka, Glavnaya redaktsiya vostochnoy literaturï, 1988, pp. 314–332.
- Bertel's, Evgeniy É. "Nāṣir-i Khusraw", in *EI*, vol. 3, pp. 869–870.
- Beshir, Beshir Ibrahim. "New Light on Nubian Fāṭimid Relations", *Arabica*, 22 (1975), pp. 15–24.
- Beshir, Beshir Ibrahim. "Fatimid Military Organization", *Der Islam*, 55 (1978), pp. 37–56.
- Beshir (Bashīr), Beshir (Bashīr)Ibrahim (Ibrāhīm). "al-Fāṭimiyyīn wa'l-Baḥr al-Aḥmar", *Ādāb Jāmiʿat al-Kharṭūm*, 1 (1982), pp. 142–152.
- Beshir, Beshir Ibrahim. "Abu ʿAbd Allah al-Shiʿi", in *GIH*, pp. 6–7.
- Besterman, Thedore. "The Belief in Rebirth of the Druses and Other Syrian Sects", *Folk-Lore*, 39 (1928), pp. 133–148.
- Betts, Robert Brenton. *The Druze*. New Haven: Yale University Press, 1988. pp. xiv + 161.
- Betts, Robert B. "Druze", in *OE*, vol. I, pp. 388–389.
- Bhownagree, Mancherjee Merwanjee. "Aga Khan I", in *Encyclopaedia Britannica*. 11th ed., Cambridge: Cambridge University Press, 1910, vol. 1, pp. 362–363.
- Bianquis, Thierry. "La prise du pouvoir par les Fatimides en Égypte (357–363/968–974)", *AI*, 11 (1972), pp. 49–108.
- Bianquis, Thierry. "La transmission du Hadith en Syrie à l'époque Fatimide: cinq notices tirées de *l'Histoire de la ville de Damas* d'Ibn ʿAsākir", *BEO*, 25 (1972), pp. 85–95.

- Bianquis, Thierry. “Notables ou malandrins d’origine rurale à Damas à l’époque Fatimide”, *BEO*, 26 (1973), pp. 185–207.
- Bianquis, Thierry. “L’acte de succession de Kāfūr d’après Maqrīzī”, *AI*, 12 (1974), pp. 263–269.
- Bianquis, Thierry. “Ibn al-Nābulusī, un martyr Sunnite au IVe siècle de l’hégire”, *AI*, 12 (1974), pp. 45–65.
- Bianquis, Thierry. “ʿAbd al-Ġanī Ibn Saʿīd, un savant Sunnite au service des Fatimides”, in *Études Arabes et Islamiques*, I, *Histoire et Civilisation. Actes du XXIXe Congrès international des Orientalistes*. Paris: L’Asiathèque, 1975, pp. 39–47.
- Bianquis, Thierry. “Al-H’ākim bi Amr Allāh ou la folie de l’unité chez un souverain Fāt’imide”, *Les Africains*, 11 (1978), pp. 107–133
- Bianquis, Thierry. “Une crise frumentaire dans l’Égypte Fatimide”, *JESHO*, 23 (1980), pp. 67–101.
- Bianquis, Thierry. *Damas et la Syrie sous la domination Fatimide (359–468/969–1076). Essai d’interprétation de chroniques Arabes médiévales*. Damascus: Institut Français de Damas, 1986–89. 2 vols.
- Bianquis, Thierry. “Egypt from the Arab Conquest until the end of the Fāṭimid State (1171)”, in M. El Fasi and I. Hrbek, ed., *General History of Africa:* Volume III, *Africa from the Seventh to the Eleventh Century*. Paris: UNESCO, 1988, pp. 163–193.
- Bianquis, Thierry. “Le fonctionnement des *Dīwān* financièrs d’aprés al-Musabbiḥī”, *AI*, 26 (1992), pp. 47–61.
- Bianquis, Thierry. “Les pouvoirs de l’espace Ismaïlien”, in Jean Claude Garcin et al., *États, sociétés et cultures du monde Musulman médiéval, Xe–XVe siècle*: Tome I, *L’évolution politique et sociale*. Nouvelle Clio, l’histoire et ses problèmes. Paris: Presses Universitaires de France, 1995, pp. 81–117.
- Bianquis, Thierry. “L’espace politique des Fāṭimides”, in *EF*, pp. 21–28.
- Bianquis, Thierry. “al-Musabbiḥī”, “Ruzzīk b. Ṭalāʾiʿ”, “Ṭalāʾiʿ b. Ruzzīk”, “Wazīr .I. In the Arab World .2. The Fāṭimid Caliphate”, “al-Yāzūrī”, “al-Ẓāfir bi-Aʿdāʾ Allāh”, “al-Ẓāhir li-Iʿzāz Dīn Allah”, in *EI2*.
- Bierman, Irene A. “The Art of the Public Text: Medieval Islamic Rule”, in Irving Lavin, ed., *World Art: Themes of Unity in Diversity*. Acts of the XXXVIth International Congress of the History of Art. University

Park, PA: Pennsylvania State University Press, 1989, vol. 2, pp. 283–290.

- Bierman, Irene A. "Inscribing the City: Fatimid Cairo", in *Islamische Textilkunst des Mittelalters: Aktuelle Probleme*. Riggisberger Berichte, 5. Riggisberg: Abegg-Stiftung, 1997, pp. 105–114.
- Bierman, Irene A. *Writing Signs: The Fatimid Public Text*. Berkeley: University of California Press, 1998. pp. xvi + 214.
- Biliński, Janusz. "The Concept of Time in the Ismaelitic Gnosis", *Folia Orientalia*, 23 (1985–86), pp. 69–110.
- Bin ʿAmmū, Samīra. *"Āl-Mūt" aw īdiyūlūjiyā al-irhāb al-fidāʾī*. Beirut: al-Muʾassasa al-Jāmiʿiyya liʾl-Dirāsāt waʾl-Nashr waʾl-Tawzīʿ, 1992. pp. 207.
- Bīnish, Taqī. "Du Nāṣir-i Khusraw", in *YNK*, pp. 122–133.
- "Biographies (with portraits) of Their Highnesses, the Present and the Two Preceding 'Aga Sahibs' of Bombay, the Chiefs of the Khojas and Other Ismailians, the Disciples of the 'Old Man of the Mountain', the So-called 'Assassins' of the Crusades", *Imperial and Asiatic Quarterly Review*, NS, 8 (1894), pp. 150–163.
- Blair, Sheila S. "Floriated Kufic and the Fatimids", in *EF*, pp. 107–116.
- Blake, H., A. Hutt and D. Whitehouse. "Ajdābīyah and the Earliest Fāṭimid Architecture", *Libya Antiqua*, 8 (1971), pp. 105–120.
- Blank, Jonah. "Annual Rites of the Daudi Bohras: Islamic Identity as Universal and Unique", *Eastern Anthropologist*, 53 (2000), pp. 457–480. Rejoinder by Rehana Ghadially, in *Eastern Anthropologist*, 55 (2002), pp. 109–110.
- Blank, Jonah. *Mullahs on the Mainframe: Islam and Modernity among the Daudi Bohras*. Chicago: University of Chicago Press, 2001. pp. viii + 408.
- Blois, François de. "The Abu Saʿidis or so-called 'Qarmatians' of Bahrayn", in *Proceedings of the Seminar for Arabian Studies*, 16 (1986), pp. 13–21.
- Blois, François de. "Abū Ṭāhir's Epistle to the Caliph al-Muqtadir: Studies on the History of Baḥrayn and the Yemen", in *Proceedings of the Seminar for Arabian Studies*, 17 (1987), pp. 21–35.

  See also under Abbas Hamdani
- Bloom, Jonathan Max. "The Mosque of al-Ḥākim in Cairo", *Muqarnas*,

1 (1983), pp. 15–36.

- Bloom, Jonathan M. "Five Fatimid Minarets in Upper Egypt", *Journal of the Society of Architectural Historians*, 43 (1984), pp. 162–167.
- Bloom, Jonathan M. "The Origins of Fatimid Art", *Muqarnas*, 3 (1985), pp. 20–38.
- Bloom, Jonathan M. "Al-Ma'mun's Blue Koran?", *REI*, 54 (1986), pp. 59–65.
- Bloom, Jonathan M. "The Mosque of the Qarāfa in Cairo", *Muqarnas*, 4 (1987), pp. 7–20.
- Bloom, Jonathan M. "The Introduction of Muqarnas into Egypt", *Muqarnas*, 5 (1988), pp. 21–28.
- Bloom, Jonathan M. "The Blue Koran: An Early Fatimid Kufic Mansucript from the Maghrib", in François Déroche, ed., *Les manuscrits du Moyen-Orient. Essais de codicologie et paléographie*. Actes du colloque d'Istanbul, 26–29 mai 1986. Istanbul and Paris: L'Institut d'Études Anatoliennes d'Istanbul; Bibliothèque Nationale, 1989, pp. 95–99.
- Bloom, Jonathan M. "The Early Fatimid Blue Koran Manuscript", *Graeco-Arabica*, 4 (1991), pp. 171–178.
- Bloom, Jonathan M. "The Fatimids (909–1171): Their Ideology and Their Art", in *Islamische Textilkunst des Mittelalters: Aktuelle Probleme*. Riggisberger Berichte, 5. Riggisberg: Abegg-Stiftung, 1997, pp. 15–26.
- Bloom, Jonathan M. "L'iconographie figurative dans les arts décoratifs", and "Les techniques des arts décoratifs", *Dossiers d'Archéologie* ; special issue *Égypte: L'Âge d'or des Fatimides*, 233 (May, 1998), pp. 58–65, 66–71.
- Bloom, Jonathan M. "Paper in Fatimid Egypt", in *EF*, pp. 395–401.
- Blumenthal, David R. "A Comparative Table of the Bombay, Cairo, and Beirut Editions of the Rasā'il Iḫwān al-Ṣafā'", *Arabica*, 21 (1974), pp. 186–203.
- Blumenthal, David R. "An Illustration of the Concept of 'Philosophic Mysticism' from Fifteenth Century Yemen", in Gérard Nahon and Charles Touati, ed., *Hommage à Georges Vajda. Études d'histoire et de pensée juives*. Louvain: Peeters, 1980, pp. 291–308.
- Blumenthal, David R. "On the Theories of Ibdāʿ and Ta'thīr", *WI*, 20 (1980), pp. 162–177.

- Blumenthal, David R. "An Example of Ismaili Influence in Post-Maimonidean Yemen", in Shelomo Morag et al., ed., *Studies in Judaism and Islam Presented to Shelomo Dov Goitein*. Jerusalem: Magnes Press – The Hebrew University, 1981, pp. 155–174.
- Bobrinskiy, Aleksey Aleksandrovich (1852–1927). "Sekta Ismailiya v Russkikh i Bukharskikh predelakh Sredney Azii" [The Ismaili Sect in Russian and Bukharan Central Asia], *Étnograficheskoe Obozrenie*, 2 (1902), pp. 1–20; also published separately, Moscow, 1902. pp. 18.
- Bobrinskiy, Aleksey A. *Gortsï verkhov'ev Pyandzha (vakhantsï i ishkashimtsï)* [The Mountainers of the Upper Panj (The Wakhis and Ishkashimis)]. Moscow: n.p., 1908. pp. viii + 150.
- Bocock, Robert J. "The Ismailis in Tanzania: A Weberian Analysis", *British Journal of Sociology*, 22 (1971), pp. 365–380.
- Boer, T.J. de. "Ikhwān al-Ṣafā", in *EI*, vol. 2, pp. 459–460.
- Bogoutdinov, Alautdin Mukhmudovich (1911–1970). "Nasir Khisrau" [Nāṣir-i Khusraw], in *Obshchestvenno-politicheskaya i filosofskaya mïsl tadzhikskogo naroda v period XI–XV vekov. Izbrannïe proizvedeniya*. Dushanbe: Donish, 1980, pp. 277–285.
- Bohas, Georges. "Ḥākim Bi-Amr Allāh al-(985–1025) Calife Fāṭimide (996–1021)", in *EUDI*, p. 347.
- "Bohra", in *The New Encyclopaedia Britannica*. 15th ed., Chicago, London, etc.: Encyclopaedia Britannica, 2002, vol. 2, p. 331.
- Boivin, Michel. "Islam, nationalisme et avenir de l'Inde d'après Sultan Muhammad Shah Aga Khan (1877–1957)", *Cahiers d'Histoire*, 38 (1993), pp. 55–73.
- Boivin, Michel. "Sulṭān Muḥammad Shāh Aga Khan et le modernisme Musulman en Inde (1902–1936)", in *Lettre d'information – La transmission du savoir dans le monde Musulman péripherique*, 13 (1993), pp. 44–54.
- Boivin, Michel. "The Reform of Islam in Ismaili Shīʿism from 1885 to 1957", in Françoise 'Nalini' Delvoye, ed., *Confluences of Cultures: French Contributions to Indo-Persian Studies*. New Delhi: Manohar, 1994, pp. 197–216.
- Boivin, Michel. "Contestation et identité chez les Khojas Indo-Pakistanais (1866–1986)", in *Lettre d'information – La transmission du savoir dans le monde Musulman péripherique*, 17 (1997), pp. 4–23.

- Boivin, Michel. "L'Inde ou le Pakistan? Les procédures de choix nationaux chez les Musulmans de Bombay. Le cas de Khojas et des Bohras", *Les Cahiers du Sahib* (1997), pp. 27–52.
- Boivin, Michel. "Quelques problèmes relatifs à l'histoire et à la tradition religieuse des Khojas Aghakhanis de Karachi et du Sindh", *JA*, 285 (1997), pp. 411–472.
- Boivin, Michel. "Institutions & production normative chez les Ismaéliens d'Asie du Sud", *SI*, 88 (1998), pp. 141–179.
- Boivin, Michel. *Les Ismaéliens, des communautés d'Asie du Sud entre Islamisation et Indianisation.* Fils d'Abraham. Turnhout: Éditions Brepols, 1998. pp. 223.
- Boivin, Michel. "New Problems related to the History and to the Tradition of the Āghākhānī Khojāhs in Karachi and Sindh", *Journal of the Pakistan Historical Society*, 46 (1998), pp. 5–33.
- Boivin, Michel. "Satpanth, Daryāpanth et Shaktīpanth. Notes sur quelques rituels du Sindh", in *Lettre d'information – La transmission du savoir dans le monde Musulman péripherique*, 19 (1999), pp. 1–16.
- Boivin, Michel. "Ghulât et Chiʿisme Salmanien chez Louis Massignon", in Ève Pierunek and Yann Richard, ed., *Louis Massignon et l'Iran*. Travaux et mémoires de l'Institut d'Études Iraniennes, 5. Paris: Institut d'Études Iraniennes; Louvain: Peeters, 2000, pp. 61–75.
- Boivin, Michel. "Hiérophanie et sotériologie dans les traditions Ismaéliennes du sous-continent Indo-Pakistanais", in Mercedes García-Arenal, ed., *Mahdisme et millénarisme en Islam*; being, *Revue des Mondes Musulmans et de la Méditerranée*, 91–94 (2000), pp. 275–296.
- Boivin, Michel. "A Persian treatise for the Ismāʿīlī Shīʿīs of India: Introduction to the *Pandiyāt-i Jawānmardī* (end of XVth C.)", in Muzaffar Alam et al., ed., *The Evolution of Medieval Indian Culture: The Indo-Persian Context.* New Delhi: Manohar, 2000, pp. 117–128.
- Boivin, Michel. "Sindhi et Gujarati: figures emblematiques et diversité regionale chez les Khoja du Pakistan", in V. Bouiller and C. Le Blanc, ed., *L'usage des heros. Tradition narratives et affirmations identitaires dans le monde Indien.* Paris: Champion, 2002, pp. 53–83.
- Boivin, Michel. *La rénovation du Shîʿisme Ismaélien en Inde et au Pakistan. D'après les Ecrits et les Discours de Sulṭān Muḥammad Shah Aga Khan (1902–1954).* London and New York: Routledge Curzon, 2003. pp. xxv + 475.

- Bokti, Giuseppe. "Notizie sull' origine della religione dei Drusi, raccolte da vari istorici Arabi", *Fundgruben des Orients*, 1 (1809), pp. 27–31.

- Boldïrev, Aleksander N. (b. 1909). "Bïl li Rudaki ismailitom?" [Was Rudaki an Ismaili?], *Archiv Orientalny*, 30 (1962), pp. 541–542.

- Bol'shakov, Oleg G. "Al-Fatimiyun", in *Islam: Éntsiklopedicheskiy slovar'* [Islam: A Concise Dictionary]. Moscow: Nauka, Glavnaya redaktsiya vostochnoy literaturï, 1991, pp. 253–254.

- Bonebakker, S.A. "A Fatimid Manual for Secretaries", *AION*, 37 (1977), pp. 295–337.

- Bosworth, Clifford Edmund. *The Islamic Dynasties: A Chronological and Genealogical Handbook*. Islamic Surveys, 5. Edinburgh: Edinburgh University Press, 1967, pp. 46–48 (Fāṭimids), 60–70 (Qarāmiṭa), 74–75 (Ṣulayḥids), 127–128 (Ismāʿīlīs or Assassins). Arabic trans., *al-Usar al-ḥākima fi'l-Islām: dirāsa fi'l-ta'rīkh wa'l-ansāb*. Kuwait: Mu'assasat al-Shirāʿ al-ʿArabī, 1994. Persian trans., *Silsilahā-yi Islāmī*, tr. Farīdūn Badra'ī. Tehran: Bunyād-i Farhang-i Īrān, 1349 Sh./1970; reprinted, Tehran: Mu'assasa-yi Muṭālaʿāt va Taḥqīqāt-i Farhangī, 1371 Sh./1992. Russian trans., *Musulmanskie dynastii. Spravochnik po khronologii i genealogii*, tr., P.A. Gryaznevich. Moscow: Nauka, Glavnaya redaktsiya vostochnoy literaturï, 1971. Turkish trans., *Islâm devletleri tarihi (kronoloji ve soykütüğü elketabı)*, tr., Eredoğan Merçil and Mehmet İpširli. Istanbul: Oğuz Press, 1980.

- Bosworth, C. Edmund. "Ṣanawbarī's Elegy on the Pilgrims Slain in the Carmathian Attack on Mecca (317/930): A Literary-historical Study", *Arabica*, 19 (1972), pp. 222–239; reprinted in C. Edmund Bosworth, *Medieval Arabic Culture and Administration*. Variorum Collected Studies Series, CS 165. London: Variorum Reprints, 1982, article IV.

- Bosworth, C. Edmund. "A Mediaeval Islamic Prototype of the Fountain Pen?", *JSS*, 26 (1981), pp. 229–234.

- Bosworth, C. Edmund. "The Ismaʿilis of Quhistān and the Maliks of Nīmrūz or Sīstān", in *MIHT*, pp. 221–229. Arabic trans., "Ismāʿīliyyat Qūhistān wa-mulūk Nīmrūz aw Sīstān", in *IAW*, pp. 228–237. Persian trans., "Ismāʿīliyān-i Quhistān va mulūk-i Nīmrūz yā Sīstān", in *TAI*, pp. 275–285.

- Bosworth, C. Edmund. *The New Islamic Dynasties: A Chronological and Genealogical Manual.* Edinburgh: Edinburgh University Press; New York: Columbia University Press, 1996, pp. 63–65 (Fāṭimids), 68–69 (chief *dāʿīs* of the Nizārī Ismāʿīlīs in Syria), 94–95 (Carmathian or Qarmaṭī rulers), 102–103 (Ṣulayḥids), 104–105 (Zurayʿids), 203–204 (Nizārī Ismāʿīlīs in Persia). Persian trans., *Silsilahā-yi Islāmī-yi jadīd*, tr., Farīdūn Badra'ī. Tehran: Markaz-i Bāzshināsī-yi Islām va Īrān, 1381 Sh./1992, pp. 139–142, 146–148, 193–195, 207–208, 209–211, 391–393.
- Bosworth, C. Edmund. "Alamūt", in *Dictionary of the Middle Ages.* New York: Charles Scribner's Sons, 1982, vol. 1, pp. 118–119.
- Bosworth, C. Edmund. "al-Qāḍī al-Nuʿmān (d. 363/974)", in *EAL*, vol. 2, p. 627.
- Bosworth, C. Edmund. "Lanbasar", "Maymūn-Diz", "Shughnān", in *EI2*.
- Bosworth, C. Edmund. "Druzes", "Ismaʿilis", in *The Penguin Dictionary of Religions*, ed., John R. Hinnells. Harmondsworth, Middlesex, New York, etc.: Penguin Books, 1984.
- Bouron, Narcisse. *Les Druzes: Histoire du Liban et de la montagne haouranaise.* Paris: Éditions Berger-Levrault, 1930. pp. 423. English trans., *Druze History*, tr. and ed., Fred Massey. Detroit: n. p., 1952. pp. 164.
- Bouthoul, Betty. *Le grand maître des Assassins.* Ames et visages. Paris: A. Colin, 1936. pp. 230; reprinted, as *Le Vieux de la Montagne*. Paris: Gallimard, 1958. pp. 308.
- Bouthoul, Betty. *Le calife Hakim, Dieu de l'an mille.* Paris: Le Sagittaire, 1950. pp. 227.
- Bowen, Harold. "The *sar-gudhasht-i sayyidnā*, the 'Tale of the Three Schoolfellows' and the *wasaya* of the Niẓām al-Mulk", *JRAS* (1931), pp. 771–782.
- Boyle, John Andrew (1916–1978). "The Ismāʿīlīs and the Mongol Invasion", in *ICIC*, pp. 5–22.
- Braginskiy, Iosif S. "Tragediya pravdoiskatelya" [The Tragedy of the

Truth Seeker], *Zvezda Vostoka*, 10 (1966), pp. 158–168.

- Branca, Paolo. *Un "catechismo" Druso della Biblioteca Reale di Torino*. Studi Camito-Semitici, 3. Milan: Centro Studi Camito-Semitici, 1996. pp. vi + 121.
- Branca, Paolo. "Some Druze Catechisms in Italian Libraries", *Quaderni di Studi Arabi*, 15 (1997), pp. 151–164.
- Branca, Paolo. "The Druze Manuscripts in the Biblioteca Reale of Turin", *AI*, 34 (2000), pp. 47–80.
- Brentjes, Sonja. "Die erste Risâla der Rasâ'il Ihwân as-Safâ' über elementare Zahlentheorie – ihr mathematischer Gehalt und ihre Beziehungen zu spätantiken arithmetischen Schriften", *Janus*, 71 (1984), pp. 181–274.
- Brett, Michael. "Ifrīqiya as a Market for Saharan Trade from the Tenth to the Twelfth Century A.D.", *Journal of African History*, 10 (1969), pp. 343–364; reprinted in his *Ibn Khaldun and the Medieval Maghrib*, article II.
- Brett, Michael. "The Zughba at Tripoli, 429 H (1037–8 A.D.)", in Society for Libyan Studies, *Sixth Annual Report* (1974–75), pp. 41–47.
- Brett, Michael. "The Military Interest of the Battle of Ḥaydarān", in V. J. Parry and M.E. Yapp, ed., *War, Technology and Society in the Middle East*. London, etc.: Oxford University Press, 1975, pp. 78–88.
- Brett, Michael. "The Fatimid revolution (861–973) and its Aftermath in North Africa", in *The Cambridge History of Africa:* Volume 2, *From c. 500 BC to AD 1050*, ed., J.D. Fage. Cambridge: Cambridge University Press, 1978, pp. 589–636.
- Brett, Michael. "Sijill al-Mustansir", in *Actes du premier congrès d'histoire et de la civilisation du Maghreb, Tunis, December, 1974*. Publications de la Faculté des Lettres de la Manouba, série histoire, 1. Tunis: Université de Tunis, Centre d'Études et des Recherches Économiques et Sociales, 1979, vol. 1, pp. 101–110.
- Brett, Michael. "Fatimid Historiography: A Case Study – The Quarrel with the Zirids, 1048–58", in David O. Morgan, ed., *Medieval Historical Writing in the Christian and Islamic Worlds*. London: School of Oriental and African Studies, University of London, 1982, pp. 47–59; reprinted in his *Ibn Khaldun and the Medieval Maghrib*, article VIII.
- Brett, Michael. "Ibn Khaldun and the Invasion of Ifriqiya by the Banu Hilal, 5th Century A.H./11th Century A.D.", in *Actes du colloque*

internationale sur Ibn Khaldoun, Alger, 21–26 juin 1978. Algiers: Société Nationale d'Édition et de Diffusion, 1982, pp. 289–298.

- Brett, Michael. "The Way of the Peasant", *BSOAS*, 47 (1984), pp. 44–56.
- Brett, Michael. "The Flood of the Dam and the Sons of the New Moon", in *Mélanges offerts à Mohamed Talbi à l'occasion de son 70e anniversaire*. Manouba: Faculté des Lettres, 1993, pp. 55–67; reprinted in his *Ibn Khaldun and the Medieval Maghrib*, article IX.
- Brett, Michael. "The Mīm, the ʿAyn, and the Making of Ismāʿīlism", *BSOAS*, 57 (1994), pp. 25–39; reprinted in his *Ibn Khaldun and the Medieval Maghrib*, article III.
- Brett, Michael. "The Battles of Ramla (1099–1105)", in *ESFAM*, pp. 17–37.
- Brett, Michael. "The Origins of the Mamluk Military System in the Fatimid Period", in *ESFAM*, pp. 39–52.
- Brett, Michael. "The Realm of the Imām: The Fāṭimids in the Tenth Century", *BSOAS*, 59 (1996), pp. 431–449; reprinted in his *Ibn Khaldun and the Medieval Maghrib*, article IV.
- Brett, Michael. "The Near East on the Eve of the Crusades", in Luis García-Guijarro Ramos, ed., *La primera Cruzada, novecientos años después: El Concilio de Clermont y los orígenes del movimiento Cruzado*. Madrid: Universidad Autónoma de Madrid, 1997, pp. 119–136.
- Brett, Michael. "The Execution of al-Yāzūrī", in *ESFAM2*, pp. 15–27.
- Brett, Michael. *Ibn Khaldun and the Medieval Maghrib*. Variorum Collected Studies Series, CS 627. Aldershot: Ashgate, 1999. pp. x + 300.
- Brett, Michael. "Le Mahdi dans le Maghreb médiéval", in Mercedes García-Arenal, ed., *Mahdisme et millénarisme en Islam*; being, *Revue des Mondes Musulmans et de la Méditerranée*, 91–94 (2000), pp. 93–105.
- Brett, Michael. "Lingua Franca in the Mediterranean: John Wansbrough and the Historiography of Medieval Egypt", in Hugh Kennedy, ed., *The Historiography of Islamic Egypt (c. 950–1800)*. The Medieval Mediterranean Peoples, Economies and Cultures, 400–1453, vol. 31. Leiden: E.J. Brill, 2001, pp. 1–11.
- Brett, Michael. *The Rise of the Fatimids: The World of the Mediterranean*

and the Middle East in the Fourth Century of the Hijra, Tenth Century CE. The Medieval Mediterranean Peoples, Economies and Cultures, 400–1453, vol. 30. Leiden: E.J. Brill, 2001. pp. xi + 497.

- Briggs, Martin S. "The Fatimite Architecture of Cairo (A.D. 969–1171)", *Burlington Magazine*, 37 (1920), pp. 137–147, 190–195.
- Brinner, W.M. "Geniza", in *EAL*, vol. 1, pp. 242–243.
- Browne, Edward Granville (1862–1926). "Nasir-i-Khusraw: Poet, Traveller, and Propagandist", *JRAS* (1905), pp. 313–352. Persian trans., in S. Ḥasan Taqīzāda (1878–1970), *Maqālāt-i Taqīzāda*, ed., Īraj Afshār. Tehran: Intishārāt-i Shikūfān, 1353 Sh./1974, vol. 4, pp. 223–230.
- Browne, Edward G. *A Literary History of Persia, from the Earliest Times until Firdawsí.* London: T. Fisher Unwin, 1902, pp. 391–415; reprinted as *A Literary History of Persia*: Volume I, *From the Earliest Times until Firdawsí.* Cambridge: At the University Press, 1928, pp. 391–415. Persian trans., *Ta'rīkh-i adabī-yi Īrān*, tr., ʿAlī Pāshā Ṣāliḥ. Tehran: Bank Melli Iran Press, 1333 Sh./1954, vol. 1, pp. 568–606.
- Browne, Edward G. *A Literary History of Persia, from Firdawsí to Saʿdí.* London: T. Fisher Unwin, 1906, pp. 190–211, 310–316, 453–460; reprinted as *A Literary History of Persia*: Volume II, *From Firdawsí to Saʿdí.* Cambridge: At the University Press, 1928, pp. 190–211, 453–460. Persian trans., *Ta'rīkh-i adabī-yi Īrān*, vol. 2, part 1, tr., Fatḥ Allāh Mujtabā'ī. Tehran: Murvārīd, 1341 Sh./1962, pp. 280–314; vol. 2, part 2, tr., Ghulām Ḥusayn Ṣadrī Afshār. Tehran: Murvārīd, 1351 Sh./1972, pp. 14–20, 140–147.
- Bruijn, J.T.P. de. "al-Kirmānī", "Nizārī Ḳuhistānī", in *EI2*.
- Bruns, Paul Jacob. "Von Hakem, Caliphen in Egypten, aus der syrischen Chronik", *Repertorium für Biblische und Morgenländische Litteratur*, 14 (1784), pp. 1–30.
- Brunschvig, Robert (1901–1990). "Fiqh Fatimide et histoire de l'Ifriqiya", in *Mélanges d'histoire et d'archéologie de l'occident Musulman: II, Hommage à Georges Marçais.* Algiers: Imprimerie Officielle, 1957, pp. 13–20; reprinted in R. Brunschvig, *Études d'Islamologie.* Paris: G.P. Maisonneuve et Larose, 1976, vol. 1, pp. 63–70.
- Brunschvig, Robert. "Argumentation Fāṭimide contre le raisonnement juridique par analogie (*qiyās*)", in Roger Arnaldez and S. van Riet, ed., *Recherches d'Islamologie. Recueil d'articles offerts à Georges C. Anawa-*

ti et Louis Gardet par leur collègues et amis. Louvain: Peeters, 1977, pp. 75–84.

- Bryer, David R.W. "The Origins of the Druze Religion", *Der Islam*, 52 (1975), pp. 47–84, 239–262; 53 (1976), pp. 5–27.
- Bryer, David R.W. "An Analysis of Samuel M. Stern's Writings on Ismāʿīlism", in S.M. Stern, *Studies in Early Ismāʿīlism*, pp. ix–xii.
- Brzezinski, Steven J. and Sami G. Hajjar. "The Nizārī Ismāʿīlī Imām and Plato's Philosopher King", *Islamic Studies*, 16 (1977), pp. 303–316.
- Būbakr, al-Tawānī. "al-Usṭūl al-Fāṭimī", *al-Turāth al-ʿArabī*, 7 (1986–87), pp. 158–170.
- Buchanan, J. Robertson. "The Druzes: Their Origins and Development to the Zenith of their Power under Fakhr-al-Din II", *Glasgow University Oriental Society Transactions*, 19 (1961–62), pp. 41–51.
- Buckley, Jorunn J. "The Nizārī Ismāʿīlites' Abolishment of the Sharīʿa during the 'Great Resurrection' of 1164 A.D./559 A.H.", *SI*, 60 (1984), pp. 137–165.
- Buniyatov, Jamil Ziya-Oglï. *Vosstaniya karmatov (IX–Xv.v.)* [The Rebellion of the Qarmatians (IX–X Centuries)]. Baku: "Elm", 1988. pp. 124.
- Burman, Edward. *The Assassins*. London: Crucible, 1987. pp. 208. Italian trans., *Gli Assassini: La setta segreta dei sacri killers dell' Islam*, tr., Silvana Vassallo. Documentaria. Florence: Convivio, 1988, pp. 251. Spanish trans., *Los Asesinos: La secta de los Guerreros Santos del Islam*, tr., Luis Racionero. Barcelona: Edicíones Martinez Roca, 2002. pp. xx + 236.
- Buschhausen, Helmut. "Les Coptes dans l'Égypte Fatimide", *Dossiers d'Archéologie* ; special issue *Égypte: L'Âge d'or des Fatimides*, 233 (May, 1998), pp. 20–27.
- Buschhausen, Helmut. "The Coptic Art under the Fatimids", in *EF*, pp. 549–568.
- Busse, Heribert. "Abu'l-Ḥasan Khan Maḥallātī", in *EIR*, vol. 1, p. 310.
- Bustān Shīrīn, Kubrā. "Tanavvuʿ-i vāzhigān dar Dīwān-i Nāṣir-i Khusraw", *NP*, 8 no. 2 (1382 Sh./2003), pp. 49–70.

C

- Cahen, Claude (1909–1991). “Quelques chroniques anciennes relatives aux derniers Fatimides”, *BIFAO*, 37 (1937–38), pp. 1–27.
- Cahen, Claude. “Quelques aspects de l’administration Égyptienne médiévale vus par un de ses fonctionnaires”, *Bulletin de la Faculté des Lettres de Strasbourg*, 26 (1948), pp. 98–118.
- Cahen, Claude. “Un texte peu connu relatif au commerce oriental d’Amalfi au Xe siècle” in *Archivio Storico per le province Napoletane*, NS, 34 (1953–54), pp. 61–66.
- Cahen, Claude. “Histoires Coptes d’un Cadi médiéval. Extraits du *Kitāb Tadjrīd Saïf al-Himma Li’stikhrādj mā fī Dhimmat al-Dhimma* de ʿUthmān b. Ibrāhīm an-Nābulusī”, *BIFAO*, 59 (1960), pp. 133–150.
- Cahen, Claude. “Un traité financier inédit d’époque Fatimide-Ayyubide”, *JESHO*, 5 (1962), pp. 139–159; reprinted in C. Cahen, *Makhzūmiyyāt. Études sur l’histoire économique et financière de l’Égypte médiévale*. Leiden: E.J. Brill, 1977, pp. 1–21.
- Cahen, Claude. “Quelques notes sur les Hilaliens et le nomadisme”, *JESHO*, 11 (1968), pp. 130–133.
- Cahen, Claude. “Un récit inédit du vizirat de Dirghām”, *AI*, 8 (1969), pp. 27–46.
- Cahen, Claude. “L’administration financière de l’armée Fatimide d’après al-Makhzūmī”, *JESHO*, 15 (1972), pp. 163–182; reprinted in his *Makhzūmiyyāt*, pp. 155–174.
- Cahen, Claude. “Al-Makhzūmī et Ibn Mammāṭī sur l’agriculture Égyptienne médiévale”, *AI*, 11 (1972), pp. 141–151; reprinted in his *Makhzūmiyyāt*, pp. 179–189.
- Cahen, Claude. “Les marchands étrangers au Caire sous les Fatimides et les Ayyubides”, in *Colloque international sur l’histoire du Caire*, pp. 97–101.
- Cahen, Claude. “La circulation monétaire en Égypte des Fatimides aux Ayyubides”, *Revue Numismatique*, 6 série, 26 (1984), pp. 208–217.
- Cahen, Claude and M. Adda. “Les éditions de l’Ittiʿāẓ al-ḥunafā’ (histoire Fatimide) de Maqrīzī par Aḥmad Hilmy, Sadok Hunī (Khounī), Fātiḥa Dib et Peter Kessler”, *Arabica*, 22 (1975), pp. 302–320.
- Cahen, Claude, Yūsuf Rāġib and Muṣṭafā Anouar Taher. “L’achat et le waqf d’un grand domaine Égyptien par le vizir Fatimide Ṭalāʾiʿ b.

Ruzzīk", *AI*, 14 (1978), pp. 59–126.

- Calderini, Simonetta. "'*Ālam al-dīn* in Ismāʿīlism: World of Obedience or World of Immobility?", *BSOAS*, 56 (1993), pp. 459–469.
- Callataÿ, Godefroid de. "L'épître XXXVI ('Sur les révolutions et les cycles') des Ikhwân al-Ṣafâ'", *Acta Orientalia Belgica*, 12 (1999), pp. 161–166.
- Callebeaut, Paul Jacques. *Les mystérieux Druzes du Mont-Liban*. Collection l'esprit des lieux. Tournai: La Renaissance du Libre, 2000. pp. 128.
- Calverley, Edwin Elliott (1882–1971). "The Priest in Ismailism", *MW*, 37 (1947), pp. 80–81.
- Campanini, Massimo. "L'eresia nell'Islàm e nel Cristianesimo: Ismailiti Assassini e Catari Albigesi", *Islàm Storia e Civiltà*, 8 (1989), pp. 165–175.
- Canard, Marius (1888–1982). "L'impérialisme des Fatimides et leur propagande", *AIEO*, 6 (1942–47), pp. 156–193; reprinted in his *Miscellanea Orientalia*, article II.
- Canard, Marius. "Le cérémonial Fatimite et le cérémonial Byzantin: essai de comparison", *Byzantion*, 21 (1951), pp. 355–420; reprinted in M. Canard, *Byzance et les Musulmans du Proche Orient*. Variorum Reprint Series, CS18. London: Variorum Reprints, 1973, article XIV.
- Canard, Marius. "La procession du Nouvel An chez les Fatimides", *AIEO*, 10 (1952), pp. 364–398; reprinted in his *Miscellanea Orientalia*, article IV.
- Canard, Marius. "Un vizir chrétien à l'époque Fâṭimite: l'Arménien Bahrâm", *AIEO*, 12 (1954), pp. 84–113; reprinted in his *Miscellanea Orientalia*, article VI.
- Canard, Marius. "Notes sur les Arméniens en Égypte à l'époque Faṭimite", *AIEO*, 13 (1955), pp. 143–157; reprinted in his *Miscellanea Orientalia*, article VIII.
- Canard, Marius. "Une lettre du calife Fâṭimite al-Ḥâfiẓ (524–544/1130–1149) à Roger II", in *Atti del Convegno Internazionale di Studi Ruggeriani (21–25 aprile 1954)*. Palermo: Società Siciliana di Storia Patria, 1955, vol. 1, pp. 125–146; reprinted in his *Miscellanea Orientalia*, article VII.
- Canard, Marius. "Quelques notes relatives à la Sicile sous les premiers califes Fatimites", in *Studi Medievali in onore di Antonino de Stefano*.

Palermo: Società Siciliana per la Storia Patria, 1956, pp. 569–576; reprinted in M. Canard, *L'expansion Arabo-Islamique et ses repércussions*. Variorum Reprint Series, CS31. London: Variorum Reprints, 1974, article IV.

- Canard, Marius. "Une famille de partisans, puis d'adversaires, des Fatimides en Afrique du Nord", in *Mélanges d'histoire et d'archéologie de l'occident Musulman: II, Hommage à Georges Marçais*. Algiers: Imprimerie officielle du Gouvernement Général de l'Algérie, 1957, pp. 33–49; reprinted in M. Canard, *L'expansion Arabo-Islamique et ses repércussions*. Variorum Reprint Series, CS31. London: Variorum Reprints, 1974, article V.
- Canard, Marius. "La destruction de l'Église de la Résurrection par le calife Ḥākim et l'histoire de la descente du feu sacré", *Byzantion*, 35 (1965), pp. 16–43; reprinted in his *Byzance et les Musulmans du Proche Orient*, article XX.
- Canard, Marius. "Fāṭimides et Būrides à l'époque du calife al-Ḥāfiẓ li-Dīn-Illāh", *REI*, 35 (1967), pp. 103–117; reprinted in his *Miscellanea Orientalia*, article XVII.
- Canard, Marius. *Miscellanea Orientalia*. Variorum Reprint Series, CS19. London: Variorum Reprints, 1973.
- Canard, Marius. "al-ʿAzīz Bi'llāh", "Bahrām", "al-Basāsīrī", "Daʿwa", "Ḍirghām", "Djawdhar", "al-Djannābī, Abū Ṭāhir", "Fāṭimids", "al-Ḥākim bi-Amr Allāh", "al-Ḥasan al-Aʿṣam", "Ibn Killis", "Ibn Maṣāl", in *EI2*.
- Cannuyer, Christian. "L'intérêt pour l'Égypte pharaonique à l'époque Fatimide. Étude sur *L'Abrégé des Merveilles (Mukhtaṣar al-ʿajā'ib)*", in *EF*, pp. 483–496.
- Cantineau, Jean (1899–1956). "Le parler des Drūz de la montagne Horānaise", *AIEO*, 4 (1938), pp. 157–184.
- Carali (Qarʿalī), Paul (Būlus). *Fakhr al-Dīn al-Maʿnī al-thānī, amīr Lubnān: idārātuhu wa-siyāsatahu 1590–1635/Fakhr ad-Dīn II Prince du Liban*. Ḥarīṣā, Lebanon: Maṭbaʿat al-Qiddīs Būlus, 1938. 3 vols. Italian trans., *Fakhr ad-Din II, principe del Libano e la Corte di Toscana, 1605–1635*. Rome: Reale Accademia d'Italia, 1936–38. 2 vols.
- Carali, Paul. *Fakhr al-Dīn al-Maʿnī al-thānī, amīr Lubnān wa-Fardinandū al-thānī amīr Tuskānā 1621–1635*. Ḥarīṣā, Lebanon: Maṭbaʿat al-Qiddīs Būlus, 1938. pp. 424.

- Carboni, Stefano. "Glass Production in the Fatimid Lands and Beyond", in *EF*, pp. 169–177.
- "Cármates", in *Enciclopedia Universal Ilustrada Europeo-Americana*. Barcelona: J. Espasa é Hijos, n.d., vol. 11, pp. 1116–1117.
- "Carmati", in *Grande Dizionario Enciclopedico*. Turin: Unione Tipografico-Editrice Torinese, 1986, vol. 4, p. 306.
- "Càrmati", in *Lessico Universale Italiano*. Rome: Istituto della Enciclopedia Italiana, 1970, vol. 4, p. 237.
- Carnarvon, Henry Howard Molyneux Herbert (4th Earl of Carnarvon) (1831–1890). *Recollections of the Druses of the Lebanon and Notes on their Religion*. London: J. Murray, 1860. pp. viii + 122.
- Carra de Vaux, Bernard (1867–1953). "Ousama, un émir Syrien au 1er siècle des Croisades", *Revue des Questions Historiques*, 58 (1895), pp. 367–390.
- Carra de Vaux, Bernard. "Bāṭinīya", "Dāʿī", "Darazī", "Djannābī, Abū Saʿīd", "Druzes", in *EI*.
- Carra de Vaux, Bernard. "Bāṭinīya", "Dāʿī", "Darazī", "Drusen", in *HI*.
- Carra de Vaux, Bernard. "Bāṭinīya", "Dāʿī", "Darazī", "Druzes", in *SEI*.
- Carra de Vaux, Bernard and Marshall G.S. Hodgson. "al-Djannābī, Abū Saʿīd", in *EI2*, vol. 2, p. 452.
- Casamar, Manuel and Fernando Valdés Fernandez. "Les objects Égyptiens en cristal de roche dans Al-Andalus, éléments pour une reflexion archéologique", in *EF*, pp. 367–382.
- Casanova, Paul (1861–1926). "Notice sur une coupe Arabe", *JA*, 8 série, 17 (1891), pp. 323–330.
- Casanova, Paul. "Monnaie des Assassins de Perse", *Revue Numismatique*, 3 série, 11 (1893), pp. 343–352.
- Casanova, Paul. "Les derniers Fāṭimides", *Mémoires de la Mission Archéologique Française du Caire*, 6 (1897), pp. 415–445.
- Casanova, Paul. "Notice sur un manuscrit de la secte des Assassins", *JA*, 9 série, 11 (1898), pp. 151–159.
- Casanova, Paul. "Une date astronomique dans les Épîtres des Ikhwân aṣ Ṣafâ", *JA*, 11 série, 5 (1915), pp. 5–17.
- Casanova, Paul. "La doctrine secrète des Fatimides d'Égypte", *BIFAO*, 18 (1921), pp. 121–165. A portion, pp. 130–154, of this article entitled

"Description de l'enseignement et de son ordonnance", is the translation of a section of Taqī al-Dīn al-Maqrīzī's *Kitāb al-mawāʿiẓ wa'l-iʿtibār fī dhikr al-khiṭaṭ wa'l-āthār* (Būlāq, 1270/1853–54), vol. 1, pp. 391–397, which appeared originally in P. Casanova's partial French translation of the *Khiṭaṭ* as *Description historique et topographique de l'Égypte*, in Mémoires publiés par les membres de l'Institut Français d'Archéologie Orientale du Caire, 4. Cairo: Imprimerie de l'Institut Français d'Archéologie Orientale, 1920, pp. 122–144; *see also under* al-Maqrīzī in Chapter 3: Primary Sources.

- Casanova, Paul. "Alphabets magiques Arabes", *JA*, 11 série, 18 (1921), pp. 37–55; 19 (1922), pp. 250–262.
- Casanova, Paul. "Un nouveau manuscrit de la secte des Assassins", *JA*, 11 série, 19 (1922), pp. 126–135.
- Casanova, Paul. "Carmath", in *La Grande Encyclopédie*. Paris: H. Lamirault, n.d., vol. 9, pp. 450–451.
- Castro, F. "Su *ġaṣb* e *taʿaddī* nel *fiqh* Fatimida", *Annali di Ca'Foscari*, serie orientale, 6 (1975), pp. 95–100.
- Catafago, Joseph. "Lettre de M. Catafago à M. Mohl", *JA*, 4 série, 12 (1848), pp. 72–78, 485–493.
- Catafago, Joseph. "Anecdote Druze: extrait du manuscrit Arabe du *British Museum*, no 22, 486", *JA*, 5 série, 17 (1861), pp. 269–275.
- Cerbella, Gino. "Ǧawhar al-Siqilī (Il Siciliano) fondo nel' 969 al-Qāhira (Il Cairo), construendovi nel 971 la Moschea al-Azhar", *Levante*, 24 (1977), pp. 37–45.
- Chahārdihī (Mudarrisī), Nūr al-Dīn. *Ismāʿīliyya dar gudhashta va ḥāl*. Tehran: Mīr (Gutinbirg), 1363 Sh./1984. pp. 179.
- Chambers, Frank M. "The Troubadours and the Assassins", *Modern Language Notes*, 64 (1949), pp. 245–251.
- Chasseaud, George Washington. *The Druzes of the Lebanon: Their Manners, Customs, and History, with a Translation of their Religious Code*. London: R. Bentley, 1855. pp. xv + 422.
- Chatterji, Miniya. "The Shiʿa Imami Ismaʿili Community in Canada", International Institute for the Study of Islam in the Modern World, *ISIM Newsletter*, 11 (December, 2002), p. 14.
- Chelhot, Victor. "Al-Qisṭās al-Mustaqīm et la connaissance rationnelle chez Ġazālī", *BEO*, 15 (1955–57), pp. 7–90; includes French trans. of al-

Ghazālī's *al-Qisṭās al-mustaqīm*, pp. 43–88.

- Cherbonneau, Jacques Auguste (1813–1882). "Documents inédits sur Obeïd Allah, fondateur de la dynastie Fatimite, traduits de la chronique d'Ibn Hammâd", *JA*, 5 série, 5 (1855), pp. 529–547.
- Cherbonneau, Jacques A. "Documents inédits sur Obeïd-Allah, fondateur de la dynastie Fatimite. Extraits de la chronique d'Ibn-Hammad, *Ta'rīkh ibn Ḥammād*", *Revue Africaine*, 12 (1868), pp. 464–477.
- Christie, A.H. "Fatimid Wood-Carvings in the Victoria and Albert Museum", *Burlington Magazine*, 46 (1925), pp. 184–187.
- Christie, A.H. "Two Rock-Crystal Carvings of the Fatimid Period", *Ars Islamica*, 9 (1942), pp. 166–168.
- Chunara (Chunāra), Alimahomed ('Alī Muḥammad) Janmahomed (Jān Muḥammad) (1881–1966). *Nūrūm Mobīn athva Allāhnī pavītra rasī = Noorum Mobin or the Sacred Cord of God: A Glorious History of Ismaili Imams*. Bombay: Ismailia Association for India, 1935, pp. 823 (in Gujarati); 3rd ed., revised by Jafferali Mahomed Sufi. Bombay: Ismailia Association for India, 1951. 2 vols.; 4th ed., Bombay: Ismailia Association for India, 1961. Urdu trans., *Nūr-i Mubīn ḥabl Allāh al-matīn*. Bombay: Ismailia Association for India, 1937. pp. 760.
- Churchill, Charles Henry Spencer (1828–1877). *Mount Lebanon: A Ten Years' Residence from 1842 to 1852 Describing the Manners, Customs and Religion of its Inhabitants with a Full & Correct Account of the Druse Religion and Containing Historical Records of the Mountain Tribes from Personal Intercourse with their Chiefs and other Authentic Sources*. London: Saunders and Otley, 1853. 3 vols.
- Churchill, Charles H.S. *The Druzes and the Maronites under the Turkish Rule from 1840 to 1860*. London: B. Quaritch, 1862. pp. viii + 300; reprinted in the Middle East Collection. New York: Arno Press, 1973. pp. viii + 300. Arabic trans., *Bayna al-Durūz wa'l-Mawārina*, tr., Fandī al-Sha'ār. Reading, UK: Garnet Publishing, 1994. pp. 152.
- Cilardo, Agostino. *Diritto ereditario Islamico delle scuole giuridiche Ismailita e Imamita*. Rome: Istituto per l'Oriente C.A. Nallino; Naples: Istituto Universitario Orientale, 1993. pp. 275.
- Clarke, Peter B. "The Imam of the Ismailis", *A Sociological Yearbook of Religion in Britain*, 8 (1975), pp. 125–138.
- Clarke, Peter B. "The Ismailis: A Study of Community", *British Journal of Sociology*, 27 (1976), pp. 484–494.

- Clarke, Peter B. "The Ismaili Sect in London: Religious Institutions and Social Change", *Religion*, 8 (1978), pp. 68–84.
- Cohen, Mark R. *Jewish Self-Government in Medieval Egypt: The Origins of the Office of Head of the Jews, ca. 1065–1126*. Princeton: Princeton University Press, 1980. pp. xxi + 385.
- Cohen, Mark R. "Administrative Relations Between Palestinian and Egyptian Jewry during the Fatimid Period", in Amnon Bohen and Gabriel Baer, ed., *Egypt and Palestine: A Millennium of Association (868–1948)*. New York: St. Martin's Press, 1984, pp. 113–135.
- Cohen, Mark R. "The Burdensome Life of a Jewish Physician and Communal Leader: A Geniza Fragment from the Alliance Israélite Universelle Collection", *Jerusalem Studies in Arabic and Islam*, 16 (1993), pp. 125–136.
- Cohen, Mark R. and Sasson Somekh. "In the Court of Yaʿqūb ibn Killis: A Fragment from the Cairo Genizah", *Jewish Quarterly Review*, NS, 80 (1990), pp. 283–314.
- Cohen, Mark R. and Sasson Somekh. "Interreligious Majālis in Early Fatimid Egypt", in Hava Lazarus-Yafeh et al., ed., *The Majlis: Interreligious Encounters in Medieval Islam*. Studies in Arabic Language and Literature, 4. Wiesbaden: O. Harrassowitz, 1999, pp. 128–136.
- Colebrooke, Henry T. "On the Origin and Peculiar Tenets of Certain Muhammedan Sects", *Asiatic Researches*, 7 (1803), pp. 336–342.
- *Colloque international sur l'histoire du Caire*, sponsored by the Ministry of Culture of the Arab Republic of Egypt. Cairo: Ministry of Culture of the Arab Republic of Egypt, General Egyptian Book Organisation, 1972. pp. 474.
- Combe, É. "Tissus Fāṭimides du Musée Benaki", in *Mélanges Maspero*, III: *Orient Islamique*. Cairo: Imprimerie de l'Institut Français d'Archéologie Orientale, 1940; being, Mémoires publiés par les membres de l'Institut Français d'Archéologie Orientale du Caire, 68 (1935–40), pp. 259–272.
- Contadini, Anna. *Fatimid Art at the Victoria and Albert Museum*. London: V&A Publications, 1998. pp. 138.
- Contadini, Anna. "The Cutting Edge: Problems of History, Identification and Technique of Fatimid Rock Crystals", in *EF*, pp. 319–329.
- Contractor, Norman L. "The History of the Dawoodi Bohras", *New Quest*, 7 (1978), pp. 47–51.

- Contractor, Norman L., et al. *The Dawoodi Bohras*. New Quest Pamphlets, 2. Pune: New Quest Publications, 1980. pp. 47.
- *Convegno sugli Ikhwān aṣ-Ṣafā'*. Rome: Accademia Nazionale dei Lincei, 1981. pp. 96.
- Corbin, Henry (1903–1978). "Le Livre du Glorieux de Jâbir Ibn Ḥayyân (alchimie et archétypes)", *EJ*, 18 (1950), pp. 47–114; reprinted in H. Corbin, *L'alchimie comme art hiératique*, ed., Pierre Lory. Paris: L'Herne, 1986, pp. 145–219.
- Corbin, Henry. "Ritual Sabéen et exégèse Ismaélienne du rituel", *EJ*, 19 (1950), pp. 181–246; reprinted in his *Temple et Contemplation*. Paris: Flammarion, 1980, pp. 143–196. English trans., "Sabian Temple and Ismailism", in H. Corbin, *Temple and Contemplation*, tr., Philip Sherrard. Islamic Texts and Contexts. London: KPI in association with Islamic Publications, 1986, pp. 132–182.
- Corbin, Henry. "Le temps cyclique dans le Mazdéisme et dans l'Ismaélisme", *EJ*, 20 (1951), pp. 149–217; reprinted in his *Temps cyclique*, pp. 9–69. English trans. by Ralph Manheim, "Cyclical Time in Mazdaism and Ismailism", in Joseph Campbell, ed., *Man and Time: Papers from the Eranos Yearbooks*, vol. 3. Bollingen Series, XXX–3. Princeton: Princeton University Press, 1957, pp. 115–172; reprinted in his *Cyclical Time*, pp. 1–58.
- Corbin, Henry. *Étude préliminaire pour le "Livre réunissant les deux sagesses" (Kitâb-e Jâmi' al-Ḥikmatain) de Nasir-e Khosraw*. Bibliothèque Iranienne, 3a. Tehran: Département d'Iranologie de l'Institut Franco-Iranien; Paris: A. Maisonneuve, 1953. pp. 144.
- Corbin, Henry. "Épiphanie divine et naissance spirituelle dans la gnose Ismaélienne", *EJ*, 23 (1954), pp. 141–249; reprinted in his *Temps cyclique*, pp. 70–166. English trans. by Ralph Manheim, "Divine Epiphany and Spiritual Birth in Ismailian Gnosis", in Joseph Campbell, ed., *Man and Transformation: Papers from the Eranos Yearbooks*, vol. 5. Bollingen Series XXX–5. Princeton: Princeton University Press, 1964, pp. 69–160; reprinted in his *Cyclical Time*, pp. 59–150.
- Corbin, Henry. "L'Ismaélisme et le symbole de la Croix", *La Table Ronde*, 120 (December, 1957), pp. 122–134.
- Corbin, Henry. "De la gnose antique à la gnose Ismaélienne", in *XII Convegno "Volta", Classe di Scienze Morali, Storiche e Filologiche: Oriente ed Occidente nel Medioevo*. Accademia Nazionale dei Lincei,

Fondazione Alessandro Volta, Atti dei convegni, 12. Rome: Accademia Nazionale dei Lincei, 1957, pp. 105–143; reprinted in his *Temps cyclique*, pp. 167–208. English trans. by James W. Morris, "From the Gnosis of Antiquity to Ismaili Gnosis", in his *Cyclical Time*, pp. 151–193.

- Corbin, Henry. "Le Kitāb Jāmiʿ al-Ḥikmatain de Nāṣir-e Khosraw (Summary)", in Zeki Velidi Togan, ed., *Proceedings of the Twenty-second Congress of Orientalists*: Vol. II, *Communications*. Leiden: E.J. Brill, 1957, pp. 241–242.
- Corbin, Henry. "Le combat spirituel du Shîʿisme", *EJ*, 30 (1961), pp. 69–125.
- Corbin, Henry. "De la philosophie prophétique en Islam Shîʿite", *EJ*, 31 (1962), pp. 49–116.
- Corbin, Henry. "Herméneutique spirituelle comparée: I. Swedenborg–II. Gnose Ismaélienne", *EJ*, 33 (1964), pp. 71–176; reprinted in H. Corbin, *Face de Dieu, Face de l'homme. Herméneutique et Soufisme*. Paris: Flammarion, 1983, pp. 41–162. English trans., in H. Corbin, *Swedenborg and Esoteric Islam*, tr., Leonard Fox. Swedenborg Studies, 4. West Chester, PA: Swedenborg Foundation, 1995, pp. 35–149.
- Corbin, Henry, in collaboration with Seyyed Hossein Nasr and Osman Yahya (1919–1997). *Histoire de la philosophie Islamique: I, Des origines jusqu'à la mort d'Averroës (1198)*. Collection idées. Paris: Gallimard, 1964, pp. 110–151, 351–352. Arabic trans., *Ta'rīkh al-falsafa al-Islāmiyya*, tr., Naṣīr Muruwwa and Ḥasan Qubaysī. Beirut: Manshūrāt ʿUwaydāt, 1966, pp. 132–168. Italian trans., *Storia della filosofia Islamica: I. Dalle origini alla morte di Averroè*, tr., Vanna Calasso. Milan: Adelphi, 1973, pp. 85–112, 258–259. Persian trans., *Ta'rīkh-i falsafa-yi Islāmī*, tr., Asad Allāh Mubashirī. Tehran: Amīr Kabīr, 1352 Sh./1973, pp. 98–135, 349–350. Turkish trans., *Islam Felsefesi Tarihi*, tr., Hüseyin Hatemi. Istanbul, 1986, pp. 85–112. This book was reproduced, together with Corbin's section entitled "La philosophie Islamique depuis la mort d'Averroës jusqu'à nos jours", in *Encyclopédie de la Pléiade, Histoire de la Philosophie: III, du XIXe siècle à nos jours*. Paris: Gallimard, 1974, pp. 1067–1188, as *Histoire de la philosophie Islamique*. Collection folio/essais. Paris: Gallimard, 1986, pp. 115–154, 444–448, with revised bibliography, pp. 505–506. English trans., *History of Islamic Philosophy*, tr., Liadain Sherrard assisted by Philip Sherrard. London: K. Paul International in association with Islamic Publications for The Institute of Ismaili Studies, 1993, pp. 74–104, 324–327, 371–373.

- Corbin, Henry. "Huitième centenaire d'Alamût", *Mercure de France* (February, 1965), pp. 285–304.
- Corbin, Henry. "L'initiation Ismaélienne ou l'ésotérisme et le Verbe", *EJ*, 39 (1970), pp. 41–142; reprinted in H. Corbin, *L'homme et son ange. Initiation et chevalerie spirituelle.* L'espace intérieur, 29. Paris: Fayard, 1983, pp. 81–205. English trans., *Ismaili Initiation or Esotericism and the Word.* London: Press of Pembridge Design Studio, 1981. pp. 91.
- Corbin, Henry. *En Islam Iranien. Aspects spirituels et philosophiques.* Paris: Gallimard, 1971, vol. 1.
- Corbin, Henry. "Un roman initiatique Ismaélien du Xe siècle", *Cahiers de Civilisation Médiévale*, 15, no. 2 (1972), pp. 1–25, 121–142; reprinted in Jean Claude Frère, *L'ordre des Assassins.* Paris: Culture, Art, Loisirs, 1973, pp. 228–260.
- Corbin, Henry. "Une liturgie Shî'ite du Graal", in *Mélanges d'histoire des religions offerts à Henri Charles Puech.* Paris: Presses Universitaires de France, 1974, pp. 81–99; reprinted in H. Corbin, *L'Iran et la philosophie.* L'espace intérieur, 39. Paris: Fayard, 1990, pp. 185–217. English trans., H. Corbin, *The Voyage and the Messenger: Iran and Philosophy*, tr., Joseph Rowe. Berkeley: North Atlantic Books, 1998, pp. 173–204.
- Corbin, Henry. "Nāṣir-i Khusrau and Iranian Ismāʿīlism", in *The Cambridge History of Iran*: Volume 4, *The Period from the Arab Invasion to the Saljuqs*, ed., Richard N. Fryee. Cambridge: Cambridge University Press, 1975, pp. 520–542, 689–690. Persian trans., "Nāṣir-i Khusraw va Ismāʿīliyya-yi Īrān", in *Ta'rīkh-i Īrān-i Kimbirīj: ta'rīkh-i Īrān az Islām tā Salājiqa*, ed., Richard N. Frye, tr., Ḥasan Anūsha. Tehran: Amīr Kabīr, 1363 Sh./1984, pp. 449–466, 593–594.
- Corbin, Henry. "The Ismāʿīlī Response to the Polemic of Ghazālī" [translated from the French by James W. Morris], in *ICIC*, pp. 67–98. Persian trans., "Pāsukh-i Ismāʿīliyya bi daʿāvī-yi Ghazālī", tr., Ḥātim Qādirī, in *DKGI*, vol. 2, pp. 349–388.
- Corbin, Henry. "La prophétologie Ismaélienne", in Christian Jambet, ed., *Les cahiers de l'Herne: Henry Corbin.* Paris: Éditions de l'Herne, 1981, pp. 138–149; reprinted in H. Corbin, *L'imâm caché*, ed., Christian Jambet. Paris: L'Herne, 2003, pp. 47–77.
- Corbin, Henry. *Temps cyclique et gnose Ismaélienne.* Paris: Berg International, 1982. pp. 208. English trans., *Cyclical Time and Ismaili Gnosis*, tr., Ralph Manheim and James W. Morris. Islamic Texts and

Contexts. London: K. Paul in association with Islamic Publications, 1983. pp. x + 212.

- Corbin, Henry. *Itinéraire d'un enseignement. Résumé des conférences à l'École Pratique des Hautes Études (Section des Sciences Religieuses) 1955–1979*, ed., Christian Jambet. Bibliothèque Iranienne, 38. Tehran: Institut Français de Recherche en Iran; Paris: École Pratique des Hautes Études, 1993. pp. 197.
- Corbin, Henry. "Abu'l-Hayṯam Gorgānī", in *EIR*, vol. 1, pp. 316–317.

See also under Sayyid Muḥammad Ḥusayn Ṭabāṭabā'ī

- Corbin, Henry and Wladimir Ivanow. *Correspondence Corbin-Ivanow: Lettres échangées entre Henry Corbin et Vladimir Ivanow de 1947 à 1966*, ed., Sabine Schmidtke, with Preface by Christian Jambet. Travaux et mémoires de l'Institut d'Études Iraniennes, 4. Paris: Institut des Études Iraniennes and Peeters, 1999. pp. 235. Persian trans., *Mukātabāt-i Henry Corbin va Vladimir Ivanov*, tr., 'Abd al-Muḥammad Rūḥbakhshān. Tehran: Mūza va Markaz-i Asnād-i Majlis-i Shūrā-yi Islāmī, 1382 Sh./2003. pp. 336.
- Cornu, Georgette. "Les tissus d'apparat Fatimides, parmi les plus somptueux le 'voile de Saint Anne' d'Apt", in *EF*, pp. 331–337.
- Cortese, Delia. "*Imāmat* and *Qiyāmat* in the *Haft Bāb-e Bābā Sayyidnā*", *AION*, 46 (1986), pp. 403–417.
- Cortese, Delia. *Ismaili and Other Arabic Manuscripts: A Descriptive Catalogue of Manuscripts in the Library of The Institute of Ismaili Studies*. London: I.B. Tauris in association with The Institute of Ismaili Studies, 2000. pp. xviii + 170.
- Cortese, Delia. *Arabic Ismaili Manuscripts: The Zāhid 'Alī Collection in the Library of The Institute of Ismaili Studies*. London: I.B. Tauris in association with The Institute of Ismaili Studies, 2003. pp. xxii + 215.
- Creswell, Keppel Archibald Cameron (1879–1974). "The Great Salients of the Mosque of al-Hakim at Cairo", *JRAS* (1923), pp. 573–584.
- Creswell, Keppel A.C. "The Foundation of Cairo", *Majallat Kulliyyat al-Ādāb, al-Jāmi'a al-Miṣriyya/Bulletin of the Faculty of Arts, University of Egypt*, 1 (1933), pp. 258–281.
- Creswell, Keppel A.C. *The Muslim Architecture of Egypt:* Volume I, *Ikhshīds and Fāṭimids, A.D. 939–1171*. Oxford: Clarendon Press, 1952. pp. xxvi + 292 + 125 plates; reprinted, New York: Hacker Art Books, 1978. pp. xxvi + 292 + 125 plates.

- Creswell, Keppel A.C. "The Founding of Cairo", in *Colloque international sur l'histoire du Caire*, pp. 125–130.
- Crone, Patricia and W. Luke Treadwell. "A New Text on Ismailism at the Samanid Court", in Chase F. Robinson, ed., *Texts, Documents and Artefacts: Islamic Studies in Honour of D.S. Richards*. Islamic History and Civilization, Studies and Texts, 45. Leiden: E.J. Brill, 2003, pp. 37–67.
- Cserneky, A. "Die Ismaeliten in Ungarn", *Ungarische Revue*, 1 (1881), pp. 658–675.
- Cutler, Anthony. "The Parallel Universes of Arab and Byzantine Art (with Special Reference to the Fatimid Era)", in *EF*, pp. 635–648.

D

- Dabashi, Hamid. "The Philosopher/Vizier: Khwāja Naṣīr al-Dīn al-Ṭūsī and the Isma'ilis", in *MIHT*, pp. 231–245. Arabic trans., "al-Wazīr/al-faylasūf: Khwāja Naṣīr al-Dīn al-Ṭūsī wa'l-Ismā'īliyyūn", in *IAW*, pp. 239–254. Persian trans., "Fīlsūf/vazīr: Khwāja Naṣīr al-Dīn Ṭūsī va Ismā'īliyān", in *TAI*, pp. 286–303.
- Dabīr Siyāqī, Muḥammad (b. 1919). "Nukta'ī chand dar bāra-yi Safar-nāma va masīr-i Nāṣir-i Khusraw", in *YNK*, pp. 180–193.
- Dabrowski, Leszek Marcin. "Zaginione miasta Muzulmańskie środkowego Maghrebu z czasów Fatymidów" [The Lost Muslim Cities in the Middle Maghrib at the Time of the Fatimids], *Przeglad Orientalistyczny*, 102 (1977), pp. 131–135 (in Polish).
- Dachraoui (al-Dashrāwī), Farhat (Farḥāt). "La captivité d'Ibn Wāsūl, le rebelle de Sidjilmassa, d'après le Cadi an-Nu'mān", *CT*, 4 (1956), pp. 295–299.
- Dachraoui, Farhat. "Tentative d'infiltration Šhī'ite en Espagne Musulmane sous le règne d'al-Ḥakim II", *al-Andalus*, 23 (1958), pp. 97–106.
- Dachraoui, Farhat. "La Crète dans le confit entre Byzance et al-Mu'izz", *CT*, 7 (1959), pp. 307–318.
- Dachraoui, Farhat. "Contribution à l'histoire des Fāṭimides en Ifrīqiya", *Arabica*, 8 (1961), pp. 189–203.
- Dachraoui, Farhat. "Les commencements de la prédication Ismā'īlienne en Ifrīqiya", *SI*, 20 (1964), pp. 89–102.

- Dachraoui, Farhat. *Le califat Fatimide au Maghreb (296–365 H./909–975 Jc.): histoire politique et institutions*. Tunis: S.T.D., 1981. pp. 579. Arabic trans., *al-Khilāfa al-Fāṭimiyya bi'l-Maghrib (296–365 H./909–975 M.): al-ta'rīkh al-siyāsī wa'l-mu'assasāt*, tr., Ḥammādī al-Sāḥilī. Beirut: Dār al-Gharb al-Islāmī, 1994. pp. 681.
- Dachraoui, Farhat. "Ibn Hāni' al-Andalusī", "al-Ḳā'im", "al-Mahdī 'Ubayd Allāh", "al-Manṣūr Bi'llāh", "al-Mu'izz li-Dīn Allāh", "al-Nu'mān", in *EI2*.

  See also under H.H. Abdul-Wahhab
- Dādbih, Aṣghar. "Nigāhī bi Ismā'īliyya va naẓariyahā-yi kalāmī-falsafī dar maktab-i Ismā'īlī", *Majalla-yi Dānishkada-yi Adabiyyāt va 'Ulūm-i Insānī, Dānishgāh-i Tarbiyat-i Mu'allim*, 3, nos. 9–11 (1374 Sh./1995–96).
- Dādbih, Aṣghar. "Nāṣir-i Khusraw va ḥikāyat-i Īrān-garā'ī", *NP*, 8, no. 2 (1382 Sh./2003), pp. 105–114.
- Dādbih, Aṣghar. "Bāṭiniyya", in *DMBI*, vol. 11, pp. 196–198.
- Dadkhwāh, 'Abbās 'Alī. "Du'āt-i Ismā'īliyya dar Īrān pīsh az Ḥasan-i Ṣabbāḥ", *Dānish-i Imrūz*, 1, no. 4 (1352 Sh./1973), pp. 317–319.
- Dadoyan, Seta B. "A Thirteenth Century Armenian Summary of the Epistles of the Brethren of Purity", *Al-Abḥāth*, 40 (1992), pp. 3–18.
- Dadoyan, Seta B. "The Phenomenon of the Fāṭimid Armenians", *Medieval Encounters*, 2 (1996), pp. 193–213.
- Dadoyan, Seta B. *The Fatimid Armenians: Cultural and Political Interaction in the Near East*. Islamic History and Civilization, Studies and Texts, 18. Leiden: E.J. Brill, 1997, pp. viii + 214.
- Dadoyan, Seta B. "Yānis", in *EI2*, vol. 11, pp. 281–282.
- Daftary, Farhad. "Bibliography of the Publications of the late W. Ivanow", *IC*, 45 (1971), pp. 55–67; reprinted in abridged form, in *Ilm*, 3 (1978), pp. 35–40.
- Daftary, Farhad. "W. Ivanow: A Biographical Notice", *Middle Eastern Studies*, 8 (1972), pp. 241–244.
- Daftary, Farhad. "Bibliography of W. Ivanow: Addenda and Corrigenda", *IC*, 56 (1982), pp. 239–240.
- Daftary, Farhad. "Taḥqīqāt-i Ismā'īlī va Ismā'īliyān-i nakhustīn", in *Kitāb-i Āgāh: majmū'a-yi maqālāt dar bāra-yi Īrān va Khāvar-i Miyāna*. Tehran: Āgāh, 1362 Sh./1983, pp. 105–139.

- Daftary, Farhad. "Vilādīmīr Īvānuf, ustādī dar Ismāʿīliyya shināsī", *Ayandeh*, 9 (1362 Sh./1983), pp. 665–674.
- Daftary, Farhad. "The Bibliography of Asaf A.A. Fyzee", *Indo-Iranica*, 37 (1984), pp. 49–63.
- Daftary, Farhad. "Professor Asaf A.A. Fyzee (1899–1981)", *Arabica*, 31 (1984), pp. 327–330.
- Daftary, Farhad. "Ghazālī va Ismāʿīliyya", *Maʿārif*, 1 (1363 Sh./1985); special issue on Ghazālī, pp. 179–198; English summary, p. 5; reprinted in *DKGI*, vol. 1, pp. 193–220.
- Daftary, Farhad. "Marius Canard (1888–1982): A Bio-bibliographical Notice", *Arabica*, 33 (1986), pp. 251–262.
- Daftary, Farhad. "Nukātī dar bara-yi aghaz-i nahḍat-i Ismāʿīliyya", *Iran Nameh*, 7 (1989), pp. 430–442; English summary, pp. 28–29.
- Daftary, Farhad. "Avvalīn rahbarān-i Ismāʿīliyya", in Yaḥyā Mahdavī and Īraj Afshār, ed., *Haftād maqāla. Armaghān-i farhangī bi Duktur Ghulām Ḥusayn Ṣadīqī*. Tehran: Asāṭīr, 1369 Sh./1990, vol. 1, pp. 113–124.
- Daftary, Farhad. *The Ismāʿīlīs: Their History and Doctrines*, with a Foreword by Wilferd Madelung. Cambridge: Cambridge University Press, 1990. pp. xviii + 804. Arabic trans., *al-Ismāʿīliyyūn: taʾrīkhuhum wa-ʿaqāʾiduhum*, tr., Sayf al-Dīn al-Qaṣīr. Damascus: Dār al-Yanābīʿ li'l-Nashr wa'l-Tawzīʿ, 1994–95. 3 vols; reprinted in one volume, Salamiyya: Dār al-Ghadīr, 1997. pp. 790. Persian trans., *Taʾrīkh va ʿaqāʾid-i Ismāʿīliyya*, tr., Farīdūn Badraʾī. Tehran: Farzān, 1375 Sh./1996. pp. xxii + 949. Tajik trans., in Cyrillic transcription, *Ismoiliyan: Tarikh va aqoid*, tr., Abdusalom Makhmadnazar. Moscow: Ladomir, 1999. pp. 816. Urdu trans., *Ismāʿīlī taʾrīkh va ʿaqāʾid*, tr., ʿAzīz Allāh Najīb, ed., Shaykh Muḥammad Iqbāl. Karachi: Iqbal Brothers, 1997. pp. xiv + 991.
- Daftary, Farhad. "The Earliest Ismāʿīlīs", *Arabica*, 38 (1991), pp. 214–245; reprinted in Etan Kohlberg, ed., *Shīʿism*. The Formation of the Classical Islamic World, 33. Aldershot: Ashgate, 2003, pp. 235–266.
- Daftary, Farhad. "Persian Historiography of the Early Nizārī Ismāʿīlīs", *Iran, Journal of the British Institute of Persian Studies*, 30 (1992), pp. 91–97.
- Daftary, Farhad. "A Major Schism in the Early Ismāʿīlī Movement", *SI*, 77 (1993), pp. 123–139.

- Daftary, Farhad. *The Assassin Legends: Myths of the Isma'ilis*. London: I.B. Tauris, 1994. pp. viii + 213; includes A.I. Silvestre de Sacy's *Memoir on the Dynasty of the Assassins, and on the Etymology of their Name*, translated from the French by Azizeh Azodi, edited and introduced by F. Daftary, pp. 129–188. Arabic trans., *Khurāfāt al-ḥashshāshīn wa-asāṭīr al-Ismāʿīliyyīn*, tr., Sayf al-Dīn al-Qaṣīr. Damascus and Beirut: Dār al-Madā, 1996. pp. 302. Hungarian trans., *Aszaszin legendák: Az iszmá'iliták mítoszai*, tr., István Hajnal. Budapest: Osiris Kiado, 2000. pp. 195. Persian trans., *Afsānahā-yi ḥashshāshīn, yā usṭūrihā-yi fidāʾīyān-i Ismāʿīlī*, tr., Farīdūn Badraʾī. Tehran: Farzān, 1376 Sh./1997. pp. xviii + 361.
- Daftary, Farhad. "Guftigū bā Farhād Daftarī", text of an interview on Ismāʿīlī studies, in *Kelk*, 49–50 (1373 Sh./1994), pp. 191–214; reprinted in ʿAlī Dihbāshī, ed., *Guftigūhā*. Tehran: Ṣidā-yi Muʿāṣir, 1379 Sh./ 2000, pp. 137–158.
- Daftary, Farhad (ed.), *Mediaeval Isma'ili History and Thought*. Cambridge: Cambridge University Press, 1996. pp. xviii + 331. Arabic trans., *al-Ismāʿīliyyūn fi'l-ʿaṣr al-wasīṭ: taʾrīkhuhum wa-fikruhum*, tr., Sayf al-Dīn al-Qaṣīr. Damascus and Beirut: Dār al-Madā, 1998. pp. 328. Persian trans., *Taʾrīkh va andīshahā-yi Ismāʿīlī dar sadahā-yi miyāna*, tr., Farīdūn Badraʾī. Tehran: Farzān, 1382 Sh./2003. pp. 403.
- Daftary, Farhad. "Introduction: Isma'ilis and Isma'ili Studies", in *MIHT*, pp. 1–18. Arabic trans., "al-Ismāʿīliyyūn wa'l-dirāsāt al-Ismāʿīliyya", in *IAW*, pp. 11–31. Persian trans., "Muqaddima: Ismāʿīliyān va muṭālaʿāt-i Ismāʿīlī", in *TAI*, pp. 12–34.
- Daftary, Farhad. "Ḥasan-i Ṣabbāḥ and the Origins of the Nizārī Isma'ili Movement", in *MIHT*, pp. 181–204. Arabic trans., "Ḥasan al-Ṣabbāḥ wa-uṣūl al-ḥaraka al-Ismāʿīliyya al-Nizāriyya", in *IAW*, pp. 185–209. Persian trans., "Ḥasan-i Ṣabbāḥ va sarāghāz-i junbish-i Ismāʿīlī Nizārī", in *TAI*, pp. 225–253.
- Daftary, Farhad. *A Short History of the Ismailis: Traditions of a Muslim Community*. Islamic Surveys. Edinburgh: Edinburgh University Press; Princeton: Markus Wiener Publishers, 1998. pp. viii + 248. Arabic trans., *Mukhtaṣar taʾrīkh al-Ismāʿīliyyīn*, tr., Sayf al-Dīn al-Qaṣīr. Damascus: Dār al-Madā, 2001. pp. 392. French trans., *Les Ismaéliens. Histoire d'une communauté Musulmane*, tr., Zarien Rajan-Badouraly, with a Foreword by Mohammed Ali Amir-Moezzi. Paris: Fayard, 2003. pp. 371. German trans., *Kurze Geschichte der Ismailiten: Traditionen einer*

muslimischen Gemeinschaft, tr., Kurt Maier, with a Foreword by Heinz Halm. Kultur, Recht und Politik in muslimischen Gesellschaften, 4. Würzburg: Ergon, 2003. pp. xvii + 286. Persian trans., *Mukhtaṣarī dar ta'rīkh-i Ismā'īliyya: sunnathā-yi yak jamā'at-i Musalmān*, tr., Farīdūn Badra'ī. Tehran: Farzān, 1378 Sh./1999. pp. vii + 334. Portuguese trans., *Breve história dos Ismaelitas: Tradições de uma comunidade Muçulmana*, tr., Paulo Jorge de Sousa Pinto. Colecção estudos e documentos, 8. Lisbon: Universidade Católica Portuguesa, 2003. pp. 258. Russian trans., *Kratkaya istoriya isma'ilizma: Traditsii musul'manskoy obshchini*, tr., Leila R. Dodikhudoeva and Lola N. Dodkhudoeva, with a Foreword by Oleg F. Akimushkin. Moscow: Ladomir, 2003. pp. 274. Tajik trans., in Cyrillic transcription, *Mukhtasare dar ta'rikhi Ismoilia*, tr., Amriyazdon Alimardonov. Dushanbe: Nodir, 2003. pp. 368.

- Daftary, Farhad. "Sayyida Ḥurra: The Ismā'īlī Ṣulayḥid Queen of Yemen", in Gavin R.G. Hambly, ed., *Women in the Medieval Islamic World: Power, Patronage and Piety*. The New Middle Ages, 6. New York: St. Martin's Press, 1998, pp. 117–130.
- Daftary, Farhad. "The Ismaili *Da'wa* outside the Fatimid *Dawla*", in *EF*, pp. 29–43.
- Daftary, Farhad. "Ismā'īlī-Sufi Relations in Early Post-Alamūt and Safavid Persia", in Leonard Lewisohn and David Morgan, ed., *The Heritage of Sufism*: Volume III, *Late Classical Persianate Sufism (1501–1750)*. Oxford: Oneworld, 1999, pp. 275–289.
- Daftary, Farhad. "Intellectual Life among the Ismailis: An Overview", in F. Daftary, ed., *Intellectual Traditions in Islam*. London: I.B. Tauris in association with The Institute of Ismaili Studies, 2000, pp. 87–111. Arabic trans., "al-Ḥayāt al-fikriyya bayna al-Ismā'īliyyīn: naẓarat 'āmma", in F. Daftary, ed., *al-Manāhij wa'l-a'rāf al-'aqlāniyya fi'l-Islām*, tr., Nāṣiḥ Mīrzā. Beirut and London: Dār al-Sāqī in association with The Institute of Ismaili Studies, 2004, pp.141–174. Persian trans., "Zindigī-yi 'aqlānī dar miyān-i Ismā'īliyān: yak chashmandāz-i kullī", in F. Daftary, ed., *Sunnathā-yi 'aqlānī dar Islām*, tr., Farīdūn Badra'ī. Tehran: Farzān, 1380 Sh./2001, pp. 99–126. Tajik trans., in Cyrillic transcription, in F. Daftary, ed., *Sunnathoi aqloni dar Islom*, tr., Muso Dinorshoev. Dushanbe: Nodir, 2002, pp. 128–157.
- Daftary, Farhad. "The Medieval Ismā'īlīs of the Iranian Lands", in Carole Hillenbrand, ed., *Studies in Honour of Clifford Edmund Bosworth*, Volume II, *The Sultan's Turret: Studies in Persian and Turkish*

Culture. Leiden: E.J. Brill, 2000, pp. 43–81; reprinted in Reza Rezazadeh Langaroudi, ed., *Payandeh Memorial Volume: Forty-six Papers in Memory of the late Mahmud Payandeh Langarudi*. Tehran: Sālī Publications, 2001, pp. 25–60.

- Daftary, Farhad. "Muṭālaʿāt-i Ismāʿīlī: pīshīna-yi taʾrīkhī va ravandhā-yi jadīd", *Iran Nameh*, 18 (2000), pp. 257–271; English summary, pp. 12–13.
- Daftary, Farhad. "Naṣīr al-Dīn al-Ṭūsī and the Ismailis of the Alamūt Period", in Nasrollah Pourjavady and Živa Vesel, ed., *Naṣīr al-Dīn Ṭūsī, philosophe et savant de XIIIe siècle*. Bibliothèque Iranienne, 54. Tehran: Presses Universitaires d'Iran and Institut Français de Recherche en Iran, 2000, pp. 59–67.
- Daftary, Farhad. "The Ismailis: A Religious Community in Islam", *Bulletin of the Royal Institute for Inter-Faith Studies*, 3 (Spring-Summer, 2001), pp. 1–15. Abstract in *Bulletin of the Royal Institute for Inter-Faith Studies*, 1 (1999), pp. 199–200.
- Daftary, Farhad. "The Ismaʿilis and the Crusaders: History and Myth", in Zsolt Hunyadi and József Laszlovszky, ed., *The Crusaders and the Military Orders: Expanding the Frontiers of Medieval Latin Christianity*. Budapest: Department of Medieval Studies, Central European University, 2001, pp. 21–41.
- Daftary, Farhad. "Pīsh-guftār", in *IMM*, pp. 11–35.
- Daftary, Farhad. "Ismaili Studies: Antecedents and Modern Developments", International Institute for the Study of Islam in the Modern World, *ISIM Newsletter*, 9 (January, 2002), p. 37.
- Daftary, Farhad. "ʿAqāʾid va muṭālaʿāt-i Ismāʿīlī", *Haft Āsmān*, 16 (1381 Sh./2003), pp. 11–46.
- Daftary, Farhad. "Bāṭiniyya" (with Marshall G.S. Hodgson), "Badakhshānī, Sayyid Suhrāb Valī", "Burhānpūrī, Quṭb al-Dīn", "Buzurg-Umīd, Kiyā", "Bharūchī, Ḥasan ibn Nūḥ", "Bohra", "Bīrjandī, Raʾīs Ḥasan", "Pandiyāt-i jawānmardī", "Pīr Shams", "Pīr Ṣadr al-Dīn", "Taʾrīkh/Taʾrīkh-nigārī: 5. Taʾrīkh-nigārī-yi Ismāʿīliyān", "Jalāl al-Dīn Ḥasan", "Ḥasan-i Ṣabbāḥ", in *DDI*.
- Daftary, Farhad. "Ismāʿīliyya", "Bāb", "Badakhshānī, Sayyid Suhrāb Valī", "Buzurg-Umīd, Kiyā", "Bohra", in *DMBI*.
- Daftary, Farhad. "Ismāʿīliyya", in *Dānishnāma-yi Zabān va Adab-i Fārsī*, ed., Gh. R. Ḥadād ʿĀdil. Tehran: Farhangistān-i Zabān va Adab-

i Fārsī, forthcoming.

- Daftary, Farhad. "Egypt: The Later Fatimids (1073–1171): Historical Outline", in *Encyclopedia of African History*, ed., Kevin Shillington. London: Routledge, Taylor and Francis, 2004.
- Daftary, Farhad. "Bāṭiniyya va Qur'ān", in *The Encyclopedia of the Holy Qur'an* (*Dānishnāma-yi Qur'ān va Qur'ān Pazhūhī*), ed., B. Khorramshāhī. Tehran: Dūstān-Nāhīd, 1377 Sh./1999, vol. 1, pp. 349–350.
- Daftary, Farhad. "Nūr al-Dīn Muḥammad II", "Rāshid al-Dīn Sinān", "Rukn al-Dīn Khurshāh", "Salamiyya" (with Johannes H. Kramers), "Shams al-Dīn Muḥammad", "Shihāb al-Dīn al-Ḥusaynī", "al-Ṭayyibiyya", "Umm al-Kitāb: 2. Among the Shī'a", in *EI2*.
- Daftary, Farhad. "Khayrkhwāh-i Harātī", "Muḥammad III 'Alā' al-Dīn", "Muḥammad b. Ismā'īl", "Satr", in *EI2*, Supplement.
- Daftary, Farhad. "Anjedān", "Anjoman-e Esmā'īlī", "Carmatians", "Dā'ī", "Dawr", "Dezkūh", "Esmā'īl b. Ja'far al-Ṣādeq", "Fatimids, relations with Persia", "Fedā'ī", "Fedā'ī Ḵorāsānī", "Freewill: ii. In Isma'ili Shi'ism" (with F.M. Hunzai), "Gerdkūh", "Ḥākem be-Amr-Allāh", "Ḥamid-al-Din Kermāni", "Ḥasan II", "Ḥasan Ṣabbāḥ", "Isma'ilism: i. Isma'ili Studies", "Isma'ilism: ii. History", "Isma'ilism: iii. Historiography", "Ivanow, Wladimir", in *EIR*.
- Daftary, Farhad. "Assassins", "Shi'a: Isma'ili", in *Encyclopedia of Islam and the Muslim World*, ed., Richard C. Martin. New York: Macmillan Reference USA/Thomson-Gale, 2004.
- Daftary, Farhad. "Aga Khan", "Ismailis", in *Encyclopaedia of the World's Minorities*, ed., Carl Skutsch. Chicago and London: Fitzroy Dearborn Publishers, 2004.
- Daftary, Farhad. "Assassins", "Fatimids", "Hasan-i Sabbah", "Isma'ilis", in *Medieval Islamic Civilization: An Encyclopedia*, ed., Josef W. Meri. London: Routledge, forthcoming.
- Daftary, Farhad. "Alamut", "Ismailis", "Sijistani, Abu Ya'qub ibn Ishaq al-", "Sinan, Rashid al-Din", in *The Oxford Dictionary of Islam*, ed., John L. Esposito. Oxford: Oxford University Press, 2003.
- Daftary, Farhad and Azim Nanji. "Ismaili Sects – South Asia", in *Encyclopedia of Modern Asia*: Volume 3, *Laido to Malay-Indonesian Language*, ed., David Levinson and Karen Christensen. New York: Charles Scribner's Sons-Thomson, 2002, pp. 185–187.

- Daghfous, Radhi. "De l'origine des Banu Hilal et des Banu Sulaym", *CT*, 23, nos. 91–92 (1975), pp. 41–68.
- Daghfous, Radhi. "Aspects de la situation économique de l'Égypte au milieu du Ve siècle/milieu du XIe siècle: contribution à l'étude des conditions de l'immigration des tribus Arabes (Hilāl et Sulaym) en Ifrīqiya", *CT*, 25, nos. 97–98 (1977), pp. 23–50.
- Dagorn, René. "Al-Baladi: un medecin obstetricien et pediatre à l'époque des prèmiers Fatimides du Caire", in *Mélanges de l'Institut Dominicain d'Études Orientales du Caire*, 9 (1967), pp. 73–118.
- Ḍāhir, Sulaymān. *al-Shīʿa al-Ismāʿīliyya*. Beirut: al-Dār al-Islāmiyya, 2002. pp. 163.
- Daiber, Hans. "Abū Ḥātim ar-Rāzī (10th century A.D.) on the Unity and Diversity of Religions", in Jerald Gort et al., ed., *Dialogue and Syncretism: An Interdisciplinary Approach*. Grand Rapids, MI: William B. Eerdmans; Amsterdam: Rodopi, 1989, pp. 87–104.
- Daiber, Hans. "The Ismaili Background of Fārābī's Political Philosophy – Abū Ḥātim ar-Rāzī as a Forerunner of Fārābī", in Udo Tworuschka, ed., *Gottes ist der Orient, Gottes ist der Okzident: Festschrift für Abdoljavad Falaturi zum 65. Geburtstag*. Kölner Veröffentlichungen zur Religionsgeschichte, 21. Köln and Vienna: Böhlau, 1991, pp. 143–150.
- al-Dālī, Muḥammad. "Makānat al-ʿaql fi'l-fikr al-Ismāʿīlī", *al-Mawsim*, 43–44 (1999), pp. 241–249.
- Dalū, Burhān al-Dīn. "al-Qarāmiṭa: thawra ijtimāʿiyya wa-mujtamaʿ dimuqrāṭī", *al-Fikr al-Dimuqrāṭī*, 1 (1988), pp. 97–109.
- al-Ḍamān, Fāyiz (d. 1994). *Salamiyya umm al-Qāhira fi'l-mīzān*. Damascus: Dār al-Ṣafaḥāt al-Zarqā', n.d. pp. 494.
- Dānishpazhūh, Muḥammad Taqī (1911–1996). "Ikhwān al-Ṣafā', barādarān-i rawshan", *Mihr*, 8, no. 6 (1331 Sh./1952), pp. 353–357; no. 10 (1331 Sh./1953), pp. 605–610; no. 12 (1331 Sh./1953), pp. 709–714; reprinted in *Mujmal al-ḥikma, tarjama gūna'ī kuhan az Rasā'il Ikhwān al-Ṣafā'*, ed., Muḥammad Taqī Dānishpazhūh and Īraj Afshār. Tehran: Pazhūhishgāh-i ʿUlūm-i Insānī va Muṭālaʿāt-i Farhangī, 1375 Sh./1996, pp. i–xxvii.
- Dānishpazhūh, Muḥammad Taqī. "Guftārī az Khwāja-yi Ṭūsī bi ravish-i Bāṭiniyān", *Majalla-yi Dānishkada-yi Adabiyyāt, Dānishgāh-i Tehran/Revue de la Faculté des Lettres, Université de Tehran*, 3, no. 4 (1335 Sh./1956), pp. 82–88.

- Dānishpazhūh, Muḥammad Taqī. "Dhaylī bar ta'rīkh-i Ismā'īliyya: sanadī chand dar bāra-yi aṣl-i ta'līm va ta'rīkh-i Ismā'īliyān", *Majalla-yi Dānishkada-yi Adabiyyāt, Dānishgāh-i Tabrīz/Revue de la Faculté des Lettres, Université de Tabriz*, 17 (1344 Sh./1965), pp. 289–330, 440–465; 18 (1345 Sh./1966), pp. 18–32, 213–228.
- Dānishpazhūh, Muḥammad Taqī. "Dā'ī al-du'āt Tāj al-Dīn Shahrastāna", *Nāma-yi Āstān-i Quds*, 7, nos. 2–3 (1346 Sh./1967), pp. 71–80; 8, no. 4 (1347 Sh./1968), pp. 59–71.
- Dānishpazhūh, Muḥammad Taqī. "Manṭiq nazd-i Nāṣir-i Khusraw Qubādiyānī", in *YNK*, pp. 172–179.
- Dānishpazhūh, Muḥammad Taqī. "Satīhandigī-yi Ghazālī", in Chingīz Pahlavān and Vaḥīd Nawshīrvānī, ed., *Zamīna-yi Īrān shināsī*. Tehran: Farāz, 1364 Sh./1985, pp. 190–221; reprinted in *DKGI*, vol. 1, pp. 151–192.
- Darakhshān, Mahdī. "Sabk-i nathr-i Nāṣir-i Khusraw dar Safar-nāma", in *YNK*, pp. 194–214.
- Dargāhī, Maḥmūd. *Surūd-i bīdārī: barrasī va tafsīr-i sukhan, andīsha va ā'īn-i Ḥakīm Nāṣir-i Khusraw Qubādiyānī*. Tehran: Amīr Kabīr, 1378 Sh./1999. pp. 309.
- Dargāhī, Maḥmūd. "Nāṣir-i Khusraw niyā-yi naw-andīshī-yi dīnī", *NP*, 8, no. 2 (1382 Sh./2003), pp. 115–127.
- Dashtī, 'Alī. *Taṣvīrī az Nāṣir-i Khusraw*, ed., Mahdī Māḥūzī. Tehran: Jāvīdān, 1362 Sh./1983. pp. 353.
- Dastghayb, 'Abd al-'Alī. "Shā'ir-i Yumgān-dara", *Payām-i Nuvīn*, 6, no. 8 (1343 Sh./1964), pp. 51–64; no. 9 (1343 Sh./1964), pp. 30–48.
- al-Dasūqī, 'Umar. *Ikhwān al-Ṣafā'*. Mu'allafāt al-Jam'iyya al-Falsafiyya al-Miṣriyya. Cairo: Dār Iḥyā' al-Kutub al-'Arabiyya, 'Īsā al-Bābī al-Ḥalabī, [1947]. pp. 237; 3rd ed., Cairo: Dār Nahḍat Miṣr, n.d. pp. 292.
- Davidson, Thomas. "The Brothers of Sincerity", *International Journal of Ethics*, 8 (1898), pp. 439–460; reprinted in *RIS*, vol. 2, pp. 77–98.
- Dāvūdī, Taqī. *Nahḍat-i Ḥasan-i Ṣabbāḥ*. Zanjān, Iran: Zangān, 1377 Sh./1998. pp. 140.
- Dāwūd (Daoud), Māysa Maḥmūd (Mayssa Mahmoud). *al-Maskūkāt al-Fāṭimiyya bi-majmū'āt matḥaf al-fann al-Islāmī bi'l-Qāhira: dirāsa athariyya wa-fanniyya*. Cairo: Dār al-Fikr al-'Arabī, 1991. pp. 550.
- Dāyah, Jān. *al-Āghā Khān bayna Fāris al-Khūrī wa-'Abd al-Ḥamīd:*

wathīqa Barīṭāniyya tunshar li-awwal marra. Beirut: Fajr al-Nahḍa, 2000. pp. 64.

de la Ravalière, P.A., *see* Lévesque de la Ravalière, P.A.

de Sacy, Silvestre, *see* Silvestre de Sacy, Antoine Isaac

De Smet, Daniel, *see* Smet, Daniel de

- Deedarali (Dīdar ʿAlī), Muḥammad Iqbāl and Ẓawāhir Mu'ir (Moir). *Ta'rīkh-i a'imma-i Ismāʿīliyya*. Karachi: Prince Aga Khan Shia Imami Ismailia Association for Pakistan, 1978–83. 4 vols.
- Deedarali, Alijah. "Yaqub Bin Killis", in *GIH*, pp. 21–22.
- Defrémery, Charles François (1822–1883). "Nouvelles recherches sur les Ismaéliens ou Bathiniens de Syrie, plus connus sous le nom d'Assassins, et principalement sur leur rapports avec les états chrétiens d'Orient", *JA*, 5 série, 3 (1854), pp. 373–421; 5 (1855), pp. 5–76.
- Defrémery, Charles F. "Essai sur l'histoire des Ismaéliens ou Batiniens de la Perse, plus connus sous le nom d'Assassins", *JA*, 5 série, 8 (1856), pp. 353–387; 15 (1860), pp. 130–210. This article was never completed.

Den Heijir, J., *see* Heijer, Johannes den

- The Department of Islamic Denominations [Gurūh-i Madhāhib-i Islāmī], The Center for Religious Studies [Markaz-i Muṭālaʿāt va Taḥqīqāt-i Adiyān va Madhāhib], *Ismāʿīliyya: majmūʿa-yi maqālāt*. Qom, Iran: The Center for Religious Studies, 1381 Sh./2002. pp. 696.
- Derenbourg, Hartwig (1844–1908). *ʿOumâra du Yémen, sa vie et son oeuvre*. Publications de l'École des Langues Orientale Vivantes, 4e série, X–XI. Paris: E. Leroux, 1897–1904. 2 vols. in 3 parts; *see also under* ʿUmāra in Chapter 3: Primary Sources.
- Dewhurst, R.P. (1869–1935). "Abu Tammam and Ibn Hani", *JRAS* (1926), pp. 629–642.
- Dhakāvatī Qarāguzlū, ʿAlī Riḍā. "Abu Tammām Nīshābūrī", "Abu'l-Ḥasan ʿAlī b. Qāsim ʿAlī", "Abu'l-Khaṭṭāb", "Aḥmad b. Kayyāl", "Ismāʿīliyya va Ṣūfiyya", "Ismāʿīliyya va Nuqṭawiyya", "Ḥasan-i Ṣabbāḥ", in *DT*.
- "Die Drusen", *Preußische Jahrbücher*, 15 (1865), pp. 188–211.
- "Die Drusen des Libanon", *Das Ausland*, 28 (1855), p. 88.
- "Die Druzen", *Das Ausland*, 7 (1834), pp. 407–408, 411–412, 416; 17 (1844), pp. 999–1000, 1004, 1007–1008.

- Diem, W. "Zwei arabische Privatbriefe aus dem Ägyptischen Museum in Kairo", *Zeitschrift für Arabische Linguistik*, 25 (1993), pp. 148–153.
- Dieterici, Friedrich Heinrich (1821–1903). "Die philosophischen Bestrebungen der lautern Brüder", *ZDMG*, 15 (1861), pp. 577–614; reprinted in *RIS*, vol. 1, pp. 273–310.
- Dihgān, Ibrāhīm. *Kārnāma yā du bakhsh-i dīgar az ta'rīkh-i Arāk*. Tehran: Mūsavī, 1345 Sh./1966. pp. 323.
- Dinorshoev, Muso. *Filosofiya Nasiriddina Tusi* [Philosophy of Naṣīr al-Dīn al-Ṭūsī]. Dushanbe: Donish, 1968. pp. 157.
- Diwald, Susanne. "Die Seele und ihre 'geistigen' Kräfte: Darstellung und philosophiegeschichtlicher Hintergrund im K. Ikhwān Aṣ-Ṣafā", in Samuel M. Stern et al., ed., *Islamic Philosophy and the Classical Tradition: Essays Presented by his Friends and Pupils to Richard Walzer on his Seventieth Birthday*. Oxford: B. Cassirer, 1972, pp. 49–61.
- Diwald, Susanne. "Die Bedeutung des Kitāb Iẖwān aṣ-Ṣafā' für das islamische Denken", in *Convegno sugli Ikhwan*, pp. 5–25.
- Ḍiyā' Nūr, Faḍl Allāh. "Andīshahā-yi falsafī-yi Nāṣir-i Khusraw", *Majalla-yi Dānishkada-yi Adabiyyāt va 'Ulūm-i Insānī, Dānishgāh-i Iṣfahān*, 1 (1362 Sh./1983), pp. 262–280.
- Diyāb, Muḥammad Aḥmad. *al-Qarāmiṭa: ṭā'ifa munāhiḍa li'l-Islām*. Cairo: al-Amāna, 1990. pp. 55.
- Döbeln, Ernst von. "Ein Traktat aus den Schriften der Drusen", *Monde Oriental*, 3 (1909), pp. 89–126.
- Dobrovol'skiy, I. "O monetakh ismailitov Alamuta" [On the Coins of the Ismailis of Alamūt], *Soobshcheniya Gosudarstvennogo Érmitazha* (Leningrad), 45 (1980), pp. 66–68.
- Doctor, Max. *Die Philosophie des Josef (Ibn) Zaddik, nach ihren Quellen, insbesondere nach ihren Beziehungen zu den Lautern Brüdern und zu Gabirol untersucht*. Beiträge zur Geschichte der Philosophie des Mittelalters. Texte und Untersuchungen, 2,2. Münster: Druck und Verlag der Aschendorffschen Buchhandlung, 1895. pp. 52; reprinted in *RIS*, vol. 2, pp. 1–58.
- Dodd, Erica C. "On a Bronze Rabbit from Fatimid Egypt", *Kunst des Orients*, 8 (1972), pp. 60–76.
- Dodge, Bayard. "Al-Ismā'īliyyah and the Origin of the Fāṭimids", *MW*, 49 (1959), pp. 296–305.

- Dodge, Bayard. "Aspects of the Fāṭimid Philosophy", *MW*, 50 (1960), pp. 182–192.
- Dodge, Bayard. "The Fāṭimid Hierarchy and Exegesis", *MW*, 50 (1960), pp. 130–141.
- Dodge, Bayard. "The Fāṭimid Legal Code", *MW*, 50 (1960), pp. 30–38.
- Dodikhudoev, Khaelbek. *Mazhabi Ismoiliya va mohiyati ijtimoii on* [The Ismaili Faith and its Social Meaning]. Dushanbe: Donish, 1967. pp. 48 (in Tajik).
- Dodikhudoev, Khaelbek. *Filosofiya ismailizma. Kharakteristika osnovnïkh printsipov doktrinï* [Ismaili Philosophy. A Sketch of the Main Principles of the Doctrine]. *Avtoreferat dissertatsii na zvanie kandidata filosofskikh nauk*. Dushanbe, 1969. pp. 22.
- Dodikhudoev, Khaelbek. *Ocherki filosofii ismailizma. Obshchaya kharakteristika filosofskoy doktrinï* [Essays on Ismaili Philosophy. A Sketch of Doctrinal Philosophy]. Dushanbe: Donish, 1976. pp. 143.
- Dodikhudoev, Khaelbek. *Filosofiya krest'yanskogo bunta (O roli srednevekovogo Ismailizma v razvitii svobodomïsliya na musul'manskom Vostoke* [The Role of Medieval Ismailism in the Development of Thought in Muslim East]. Dushanbe: Irfon, 1987. pp. 430.
- Dodikhudoev, Khaelbek. *Ismoiliya va ozodandeshii Sharq* [Ismailism and the Freedom of Thought in the East]. Dushanbe: Irfon, 1989. pp. 285 (in Tajik).
- Dodikhudoev, Khaelbek. "Razum ne mozhet predstavit' tvortsa (Koran s tochki zreniya Nosir-i Khusrava)" [Reason cannot conceive the Creator (The Qur'an from the Viewpoint of Nāṣir-i Khusraw)], in *Shyolkovïy put', Al'manakh*. Dushanbe: Irfon, 1990, pp. 149–164.
- Dodkhudoeva, Larisa N. "Svadebnïe obryadï ismailitov Pamira" [Wedding Rites of the Pamiri Ismailis], *Problemï istorii, kul'turï, filologii stran Azii* (Leningrad), vol. 1 (6) (1973), pp. 31–39.
- Donaldson, Dwight Martin (1884–1976). *The Shi'ite Religion: A History of Islam in Persia and Irak*. Luzac's Oriental Religions Series, VI. London: Luzac, 1933. pp. xxvi + 393.
- Doorninck, Jr., Frederick H. van. "The Medieval Shipwreck at Serçe Limani: An Early 11th-century Fatimid-Byzantine Commercial Voyage", *Graeco-Arabica*, 4 (1991), pp. 45–52.

- Dorjahn, Vernon Robert. "Druses", in *The World Book Encyclopaedia*. Chicago, Frankfurt, etc.: World Book-Childcraft International, 1978, vol. 5, p. 291.
- Dorri, Jahangir. "Baʿze maʿlumot dar borai Nizori" [Some Information on Nizārī], *Sharqi Surkh* (Stalinobod), 9 (1958), pp. 140–154 (in Tajik).
- Dorri, Jahangir. "Stalinabadskiy ékzemplyar 'Kulliyata' Nizārī" [The Stalinabad Version of Nizārī's *Kulliyyāt*], *Izvestiya Akademii Nauk Tadzhikskoy SSR, otdelenie obshchestvennïkh nauk* (Stalinabad), 1 (1958), pp. 117–122.
- Dossa, Parin Aziz. "Women's Space and Time: An Anthropological Perspective on Ismaili Immigrant Women in Calgary and Vancouver", *Canadian Ethnic Studies*, 20 (1988), pp. 45–65.
- Dossa, Parin A. "Critical Anthropology and Life Stories: Case Study of Elderly Ismaili Canadians", *Journal of Cross-Cultural Gerontology*, 9 (1994), pp. 335–354.
- Dossa, Parin A. "Reconstruction of the Ethnographic Field Site: Mediating Identities, Case Study of a Bohra Muslim Woman in Lamu (Kenya)", *Women's Studies International Forum*, 20 (1997), pp. 505–515.
- Dossa, Parin A. "(Re)imagining Aging Lives: Ethnographic Narratives of Muslim Women in Diaspora", *Journal of Cross-Cultural Gerontology*, 14 (1999), pp. 245–272.
- Douwes, Dick and Norman N. Lewis. "The Trials of Syrian Ismaʿilis in the First Decade of the 20th Century", *IJMES*, 21 (1989), pp. 215–232.
- al-Dubaysī, ʿUmar. *Ikhwān al-Ṣafāʾ*. al-Muʾallafāt al-Jamʿiyya al-Falsafiyya al-Miṣriyya. Cairo: Dār Iḥyāʾ al-Kutub al-ʿArabiyya, 1947. pp. 237.
- al-Dubaysī, Yūsuf Salīm. *Ahl al-tawḥīd "al-Durūz" wa-khaṣāʾiṣ madhhabihim al-dīniyya waʾl-ijtimāʿiyya*. [Beirut]: n.p., 1413/1992. 5 vols.
- Dufourcq, Charles Emmanuel. "La coexistence des Chrétiens et des Musulmans dans *al-Andalus* et dans le Maghrib au Xe siècle", in *Occident et Orient au Xe siècle. Actes du IXe Congrès de la Société des Historiens Médiévistes de l'Enseignement Supérieur Public (Dijon, 2–4 juin 1978)*. Publications de l'Université de Dijon, 57. Paris: Société les Belles Lettres, 1979, pp. 209–234.
- Dumasia, Naoroji M. *A Brief History of the Aga Khan, with an Account of his Predecessors, the Ismailian Princes or Benefatimite Caliphs of*

Egypt. Bombay: Times of India Press, 1903. pp. x + 221.

- Dumasia, Naoroji M. *The Aga Khan and His Ancestors: A Biographical and Historical Sketch*, with a Foreword by Maharajah of Bikaner. Bombay: Times of India Press, 1939. pp. xv + 375.
- Dumasia, Naoroji M. "H.H. the Aga Khan, Great Indian Leader and World Statesman", in L.F. Rushbrook Williams, ed., *Great Men of India*. [London]: Home Library Club, [1939], pp. 401–413.
- Dunlop, D.M. "al-Baṭā'iḥī", in *EI2*, vol. 1, pp. 1091–1092.
- Dupont, Marie. *Les Druzes*. Fils d'Abraham. Paris: Éditions Brepols, 1994. pp. 217.
- Dussaud, René (1868–1958). "Influence de la religion Noṣairî sur la doctrine de Râchid ad-Dîn Sinân", *JA*, 9 série, 16 (1900), pp. 61–69.
- Dzhonboboev, Sunatullo. "Problema universaliy v filosofii Nosira Khisrava" [Universal Problems in Nāṣir-i Khusraw's Philosophy], *Izvestiya Akademii Nauk Tadzhikskoy SSR, otdelenie obshchestvennïkh nauk*, 3–4 (1996), pp. 83–88.

E

- Eboo Jamal, Nadia. *Surviving the Mongols: Nizārī Quhistānī and the Continuity of Ismaili Tradition in Persia*, with a Foreword by F. Daftary. Ismaili Heritage Series, 8. London: I.B. Tauris in association with The Institute of Ismaili Studies, 2002. pp. xvi + 190. Persian trans., *Baqā-yi ba'd az Mughūl: Nizārī Quhistānī va tadāvum-i sunnat-i Ismā'īlī dar Īrān*, tr., Farīdūn Badrā'i. Tehran: Farzan, 1382 Sh./2003. pp. 207. Persian trans., *Ismā'īliyān pas az Mughūl: Nizārī Quhistānī va tadāvum-i sunnat-i Ismā'īlī dar Īrān*, tr., Maḥmūd Rafī'ī. Tehran: Hīrmand, 1382 Sh./2003. pp. 244.
- Édel'man, A. "Shoir, mutifakkir, sayyoh va khodimi buzurgi jam'iyati Tojik dar asari XI Nosir Khisrav" [A Prominent Tajik Poet, Thinker, Traveller and Public Figure of the 11th Century, Nāṣir-i Khusraw], *Maktabi Soveti*, (Stalinobod), 12 (1952), pp. 32–44 (in Tajik).
- Édel'man, A. "Nekotorïe dannïe o nauchnïkh i filosofskikh vzglyadakh Noseri Khisrau" [Some Data on the Scientific and Philosophical Views of Nāṣir-i Khusraw], *Izvestiya Akademii Nauk Tadzhikskoy SSR, otdelenie obshchestvennïkh nauk*, 4 (1953), pp. 153–159.
- Édel'man, A. "Nosiri Khisrau i ego mirovozzrenie" [Nāṣir-i Khusraw

and his Views]. *Avtoreferat dissertatsii na zvanie kandidata filosofskikh nauk*. Stalinabad, 1955. pp. 24.

- Edwards, Anne. *Throne of Gold: The Lives of the Aga Khans*. London: Harper Collins, 1995. pp. 346.
- Ehrenkreutz, Andrew Stefan. "Saladin's Coup d'État in Egypt", in Sami A. Hanna, ed., *Medieval and Middle Eastern Studies in Honor of Aziz Suryal Atiya*. Leiden: E.J. Brill, 1972, pp. 144–157.
- Ehrenkreutz, Andrew S. "The Fatimids in Palestine – The Unwitting Promoters of the Crusade", in Amnon Bohen and Gabriel Baer, ed., *Egypt and Palestine: A Millennium of Association, 868–1948*. New York: St. Martin's Press 1984, pp. 66–72.
- Ehrenkreutz, Andrew S. and Gene W. Heck. "Additional Evidence of the Fāṭimid Use of Dīnārs for Propaganda Purposes", in M. Sharon, ed., *Studies in Islamic History and Civilization in Honour of Professor David Ayalon*. Jerusalem: Cana; Leiden: E.J. Brill, 1986, pp. 145–151; reprinted in A.S. Ehrenkreutz, *Monetary Change and Economic History in the Medieval Muslim World*, ed., J.L. Bacharach. Variorum Collected Studies Series, CS371. Hampshire: Variorum, 1992, article XI.
- Eichhorn, Johann G. "Von der Religion der Drusen", *Repertorium für Biblische und Morgenländische Litteratur*, 12 (1783), pp. 108–224.
- Eisenstein, Herbert. "Die Wezire Ägyptens unter al-Mustanṣir A.H. 452–466", *Wiener Zeitschrift für die Kunde des Morgenlandes*, 77 (1987), pp. 37–50.
- Él'chibekov, Kudratbek. "Obshchie religiozno-filosofskie i fol'klorno-mifologicheskie osnovï ierarkhii dukhovenstva v sufizme i ismailizme" [Common Religio-Philosophical and Folklore-Mythological Foundations of the Hierarchy of Clergy in Sufism and Ismailism], in *Religiya i obshchestvennaya mïsl' stran Vostoka* [Religion and Social Thought of the Countries of the Orient]. Moscow: Nauka, 1974, pp. 299–319.
- Él'chibekov, Kudratbek. "Pirï i ikh rol' v ismailizme" [*Pīrs* and their Role in Ismailism], *Trudï respublikanskoy konferentsii molodïkh uchyonïkh Tadzhikskoy SSR, posvyashchyonnoy XXV s'ezdu KPSS*. Dushanbe, 1977, pp. 73–74.
- Él'chibekov, Qudratbek (Kudratbek). "Mansha'-i rivāyāt dar bāra-yi Nāṣir-i Khusraw", *Nomai Pazhouhishgoh* (Dushanbe), 4 (2003), pp. 157–164.

- Emadi, Hafizullah. "Minority Group Politics: The Role of Ismailis in Afghanistan's Politics", *Central Asian Survey*, 12 (1993), pp. 379–392.
- Emadi, Hafizullah. "The End of *Taqiyya*: Reaffirming the Religious Identity of Ismailis in Shughnan, Badakhshan and Political Ramifications for Afghanistan", *Middle Eastern Studies*, 34, (1998), pp. 103–120.
- Emadi, Hafizullah. "Politics of Transformation and Ismailis in Gorno-Badakhshan, Tajikistan", *Internationales Asienforum*, 29 (1998), pp. 5–22.
- Emadi, Hafizullah. "Praxis of *Taqiyya*: Perseverance of Pashaye Ismaili Enclave, Nangarhar, Afghanistan", *Central Asian Survey*, 19 (2000), pp. 253–264.
- Emadi, Hafizullah. "Struggle for Recognition: Hazara Isma'ili Women and their Role in the Public Arena in Afghanistan", *Asian Journal of Women's Studies*, 8 (2002), pp. 76–103.
- Enayat, Hamid (1932–1982). "An Outline of the Political Philosophy of the *Rasā'il* of the Ikhwān al-Ṣafā'", in *ICIC*, pp. 23–49.
- Engineer, Asghar Ali. *The Bohras*. New Delhi: Vikas Publishing House, 1980. pp. ix + 332; rev. ed., New Delhi: Vikas Publishing House, 1993. pp. ix + 335.
- Engineer, Asghar Ali. *The Muslim Communities of Gujarat: An Exploratory Study of Bohras, Khojas and Memons*. Delhi: Ajanta Publications, 1989. pp. 275.
- Epalza, Míkel de. "El esplendor de al-Andalus, reflejo del esplendor Fatimi en el siglo XI/V", in Manuela Marin, ed., *Actas del IV Coloquio Hispano-Tunecino (Palma de Mallorca, 1979)*. Madrid: Instituto Hispano-Árabe de Cultura, 1983, pp. 79–82.
- Erdmann, Kurt (1901–1964). "Fatimid Rock Crystals", *Oriental Art*, 3 (1951), pp. 142–146.
- Erdmann, Kurt. "Die Fatimidischen Bergkristallkannen", in *Wandlungen Christlicher Kunst im Mittelalter* (1953), pp. 189–205.
- Esmail, Aziz. *A Scent of Sandalwood: Indo-Ismaili Religious Lyrics (Ginans)* Volume 1. Richmond, Surrey: Curzon, 2002. pp. xi + 227.
- Esmail, Aziz and Azim Nanji. "The Ismā'īlīs in History", in *ICIC*, pp. 225–265.
- Espéronnier, Maryta. "Les fêtes civiles et les cérémonies d'origine

antique sous les Fatimides d'Égypte", *Der Islam*, 65 (1988), pp. 46–59.

- Espéronnier, Maryta. "Faste des costumes et insignes sous les Fatimides d'Égypte (Xè-XIIè ss.), d'après le *Ṣubḥ al-A'šā* d'al-Qalqašandī", *Der Islam*, 70 (1993), pp. 301–310.
- Ess, Josef van. "Neuere arabisch-sprachige Literatur über die Drusen", *WI*, 12 (1969–70), pp. 111–125.
- Ess, Josef van. *Chiliastische Erwartungen und die Versuchung der Göttlichkeit: Der Kalif al-Ḥākim* (386–411 H.). Abhandlungen der Heidelberger Akademie der Wissenschaften, Philosophisch-historische Klasse; Jahrgang 1977, Abhandlung 2. Heidelberg: C. Winter, 1977. pp. 85.
- Ess, Josef van. "Biobibliographische Notizen zur islamischen Theologie. I. Zur Chronologie der Werke des Ḥamīdaddīn al-Kirmānī", *WO*, 9 (1977–78), pp. 255–261.
- Ess, Josef van. "'Aṭṭāš (or Ebn 'Aṭṭāš)", in *EIR*, vol. 3, p. 26.
- Ethé, Hermann (1844–1917). "Auswahl aus Nāṣir Chusrau's Ḳaṣīden", *ZDMG*, 36 (1882), pp. 478–508.
- Ethé, Hermann. "Kürzere Lieder und poetische Fragmente aus Nâçir Khusrau's Dîwân", in *Nachrichten von der Königlichen Gesellschaft der Wissenschaften und der Georg-Augusts-Universität zu Göttingen* (1882), pp. 124–152.
- Ethé, Hermann. "Nāsir Khosrau", in *Encyclopaedia Britannica*. 11th ed., Cambridge: Cambridge University Press, 1911, vol. 19, p. 248.
- Ettinghausen, Richard (1906–1979). "Painting in the Fāṭimid Period: A Reconstruction", *Ars Islamica*, 9 (1942), pp. 112–124.

F

- Fackenheim, Emil L. "The Conception of Substance in the Philosophy of the Ikhwan as-Safa' (*Brethren of Purity*)", *Mediaeval Studies* (Toronto), 5 (1943), pp. 115–122; reprinted in *RIS*, vol. 2, pp. 217–224.
- Faḍā'ī, Yūsuf. *Madhhab-i Ismā'īlī va nahḍat-i Ḥasan-i Ṣabbāḥ*. Farhang-i Islāmī, 32. Tehran: 'Aṭā'ī, 1363 Sh./1984. pp. 215; 2nd ed., Tehran: 'Aṭā'ī, 1374 Sh./1995. pp. 240.
- Fagnan, Edmond (1846–1931). "Note sur Nāçir ibn Khosroū", *JA*, 7 série, 13 (1879), pp. 164–168.

- Fagnan, Edmond. "Nouveaux textes historiques relatifs à l'Afrique du Nord et à la Sicile: I, Traduction de la biographie d''Obeyd Allāh contenu dans le "Moḳaffa" de Maḳrīzī", in *Centenario della nascita di Michele Amari*. Palermo: Stabilimento Tipografico Virzi, 1910, vol. 2, pp. 35–85.
- Fahmī, 'Abd al-Raḥmān Muḥammad. "Iḍāfāt jadīda fī maskūkāt al-Fāṭimiyyīn", *Majallat al-Majma' al-'Ilmī al-Miṣrī*, 52 (1970–71), pp. 3–24.
- Fakhr, H.M. "*At-Tarajamatu'z-zāhira*: An Anonymous Tract on the History of the Bohoras", *JBBRAS*, NS, 16 (1940), pp. 87–98.
- al-Fakhrānī, Abu'l-Sa'ūd Aḥmad. *al-Baḥth al-lughawī 'inda Ikhwān al-Ṣafā'*. Cairo: Maṭba'at al-Amāna, 1991. pp. 226.
- al-Fākhūrī al-Bulusī, Yūḥanna. *Ikhwān al-Ṣafā'*. Falāsifat al-'Arab, 2. Ḥarīṣā, Lebanon: Maṭba'at al-Qiddīs Būlus, 1947. pp. 46.
- Falconet, Camille (1671–1762). "Dissertation sur les Assassins, peuple d'Asie", *Mémoires de Littérature, tirés des registres de l'Académie Royale des Inscriptions et Belles Lettres*, 17 (1751), pp. 127–170. English trans., "A Dissertation on the Assassins, a People of Asia", as an appendix in John of Joinville (d. 1317), *Memoirs of John Lord de Joinville*, tr., Thomas Johnes. Hafod: At the Hafod Press, 1807, vol. 2, pp. 287–328.
- Falke, O. von. "Gotisch oder Fatimidisch?", *Pantheon*, 5 (1930), pp. 120–129.
- Fallāḥ Rastigār, Gītī. "Āzād-andishī dar shi'r-i Nāṣir-i Khusraw", in *YNK*, pp. 423–436.
- Fandi, Talal and Ziyad Abi-Shakra. *The Druze Heritage: An Annotated Bibliography*. Amman: Published for the Druze Heritage Foundation by Royal Institute for Inter-Faith Studies, 2001. pp. xii + 212.
- Faqīdī Nīshābūrī, Muḥammad Karīm. *Ta'rīkh va 'aqā'id-i firqa-yi Āqā Khāniyya*, ed., Ḥusayn Ḥusaynī Bīrjandī. Tehran: Nimūna, 1377 Sh./1998. pp. 140.
- al-Faraḥ, Muḥammad Ḥusayn. "Abu'l-Fatḥ 'Alī b. al-Faḍl al-Ḥimyarī: dirāsa ta'rīkhiyya li-'ahd al-da'wa al-Yamaniyya wa-zu'amā'ihā bi'l-Yaman 290–390 H.", *Dirāsāt Yamaniyya*, 13 (1983), pp. 109–188; 14 (1983), pp. 265–373.
- Farhan, Mohd Jalub. "Philosophy of Mathematics of Ikhwan al-Safa", *Journal of Islamic Science*, 15 (1999), pp. 25–51.

- Farīdūnī, Barātʿalī. "Falsafa-yi siyāsī-yi Ikhwān al-Ṣafāʾ", *ʿUlūm-i Siyāsī*, 6 (1378 Sh./1999), pp. 160–188.
- Farīdūnī, Barātʿalī. *Andīsha-yi siyāsī-yi Ikhwān al-Ṣafāʾ*. Qom, Iran: Bustān-i Kitāb-i Qom, Daftar-i Tablīghāt-ī Islāmī, Ḥawza-yi ʿIlmiyya-yi Qom, Markaz-i Intishārāt, 1380 Sh./2001.
- Farmand, Ḥusayn (ed.), *Dānā-yi Yumgān: majmūʿ-yi maqālāt-i simīnār-i bayn al-millalī-yi Nāṣir-i Khusraw*. [Kabul]: Ākadimī-yi ʿUlūm, 1366 Sh./1987. pp. 347.
- Farmāniyān, Mahdī. "Shahrastānī: Sunnī-yi Ashʿarī yā Shīʿī-yi bāṭinī", *Haft Āsmān*, 2 (1379 Sh./2000), pp. 135–180; reprinted in *IMM*. 449–503.
- Farmāniyān, Mahdī. "Khudā va ṣifāt-i ū dar nigāh-i Ismāʿīliyān", in *IMM*, pp. 33–73.
- Farmer, Henry G. "An Early Arabic Treatise on Calligraphy", *Transactions of the Glasgow University Oriental Society*, 10 (1940–41), pp. 21–26.
- Farrugia de Candia, J. "Les Monnaies Fāṭimites du Musée du Bardo", *Revue Tunisienne*, NS, 7 (1936), pp. 334–372; 8 (1937), pp. 89–136.
- Farrugia de Candia, J. "Monnaies Fāṭimites du Musée du Bardo (Premier Supplément)", *Revue Tunisienne*, 3rd series, nos. 3–4 (1948), pp. 103–130.
- Farrukh, ʿUmar (1908–1987). *Ikhwān al-Ṣafāʾ*. Dirāsāt qaṣīra fiʾl-adab waʾl-taʾrīkh waʾl-falsafa, 15. Beirut: Maktabat Munaymina, 1945. pp. 136; 2nd ed., Beirut: Maktabat Munaymina, 1953. pp. 165; 3rd ed., Beirut: Dār al-Kitāb al-ʿArabī, 1981. pp. 192.
- Farrukh, ʿUmar. "Ikhwān al-Ṣafa", in M.M. Sharif, ed., *A History of Muslim Philosophy*. Wiesbaden: O. Harrassowitz, 1963–66, vol. 1, pp. 289–310.
- Farsi, Mustapha. "Le Qarmatisme: révolte des esclaves contre les maîtres", *Institut des Belles Lettres Arabes*, 23 (1960), pp. 7–50.
- al-Fārūqī, Ismāʿīl Rāgī. "On the Ethics of the Brethren of Purity (Ikhwān al-Ṣafāʾ wa Khillān al-Wafā)", *MW*, 50 (1960), pp. 109–121, 193–198, 252–258; 51 (1961), pp. 18–24; reprinted in *RIS*, vol. 2, pp. 321–356.
- Farzād, Masʿūd. "Muṭālaʿa-yi ʿarūḍī dar awzān-i shiʿrī-yi Nāṣir-i Khusraw", in *YNK*, pp. 399–422.

- Farzānpūr, Ḥusayn. "Barrasī-yi andīshahā-yi Ikhwān al-Ṣafā", *Nāma-yi Farhang*, 32–33 (1378 Sh./1999), pp. 168–183.
- "Fátima", in *Enciclopedia Universal Ilustrada Europeo-Americana*. Barcelona: Hijos de J. Espasa, 1924, vol. 23, pp. 281–282.
- "Fāṭimī", in *Diccionario Enciclopedico Salvat Universal*. Barcelona, Madrid, etc.: Salvat Editores, 1976, vol. 11, pp. 55–56.
- "Fāṭimid", in *The New Encyclopaedia Britannica*. 15th ed., Chicago, London, etc.: Encyclopaedia Britannica, 2002, vol. 4, pp. 697–698.
- "Fatimiden", in *Brockhaus Enzyklopädie*. Mannheim: F.A. Brockhaus, 1988, vol. 7, p. 138.
- "Fatimiden", in *Grote Winkler Prins Encyclopedie*. Amsterdam and Brussels: Elsevier, 1980, vol. 8, pp. 489–490.
- "Fatìmidi", in *Lessico Universale Italiano*. Rome: Istituto della Enciclopedia Italiana, 1971, vol. 7, p. 503.
- "Fatimites", in *La Grande Encyclopédie*. Paris: H. Lamirault, n.d., vol. 17, p. 34.
- "Fatimiti", in *Grande Dizionario Enciclopedico*. Turin: Unione Tipografico-Editrice Torinese, 1987, vol. 8, pp. 46–47.
- Fayyāḍ, Nabīl. "al-Ṭā'ifa al-Ismā'īliyya jisr yarbuṭ al-dīn bi'l-'aql", *al-Mawsim*, 43–44 (1999), pp. 139–174.
- Feghali, M. "Texte Druse", in *Mélanges Maspero*, III: *Orient Islamique*. Cairo: Imprimerie de l'Institut Français d'Archéologie Orientale, 1940; being, Mémoires publiés par les membres de l'Institut Français d'Archéologie Orientale du Caire, 68 (1935–40), pp. 83–96.
- Féhervári, Géza. "Bayṭār: Enigma of a Fāṭimid Potter", in *Essays in Honour of Alexander Fodor on his Sixtieth Birthday*; being, *The Arabist, Budapest Studies in Arabic*, 23 (2001), pp. 65–72.
- Feki (al-Faqī), Habib (al-Ḥabīb). *Les idées religieuses et philosophiques de l'Ismaélisme Fatimide (organisation et doctrine)*. Université de Tunis, Faculté des Lettres et Sciences Humaines de Tunis, 6e série, philosophie-littérature, XIII. Tunis: L'Université de Tunis, 1978. pp. 334.
- Feki, Habib. *al-Ta'wīl, ususuh wa-ma'ānīh fi'l-madhhab al-Ismā'īlī*. (1) *al-Qāḍī al-Nu'mān (dirāsa wa-nuṣūṣ)*. Tunis: al-Jāmi'a al-Tūnusiyya, Markaz al-Dirāsāt wa'l-Abḥāth al-Iqtiṣādiyya wa'l-Ijtimā'iyya, [1980]. pp. 158.
- Fenton, Paul B. "La communauté Juive dans l'Égypte Fatimide",

Dossiers d'Archéologie ; special issue *Égypte: L'Âge d'or des Fatimides*, 233 (May, 1998), pp. 28–33.

- Fernandez-Puertas, Antonio. "Dos ventanas decoradas en la mezquita de al-Ḥākim en El Cairo", *al-Andalus*, 42 (1977), pp. 421–445.
- Fernando, T. "East African Asians in Western Canada: The Ismaili Community", *New Community*, 7 (1979), pp. 361–368.
- Fierro, Maribel I. "On *al-Fāṭimī* and *al-Fāṭimiyyūn*", *Jerusalem Studies in Arabic and Islam*, 20 (1996), pp. 130–161.
- Fierro, Maribel I. "Bāṭinism in al-Andalus. Maslama b. Qāsim al-Qurṭubī (d. 353/964), Author of the *Rutbat al-Ḥakīm* and the *Ghāyat al-Ḥakīm* (Picatrix)", *SI*, 84 (1996), pp. 87–112.
- Fierro, Maribel I. "Espacio Sunni y espacio Šīʿī", in María Jesús Viguera Molins, ed., *El esplendor de los Omeyas Cordobeses: la civilizacíon Musulmana de Europa Occidental; exposicíon en Madīnat al-Zahrāʾ...2001*. Granada: Fundacíon El Legado Andalusi, 2001, pp. 168–177.
- Fikrī, Aḥmad. *Masājid al-Qāhira wa-madārisuhā: al-juzʾ al-awwal, al-ʿaṣr al-Fāṭimī*. Cairo: Dār al-Maʿārif, 1965. pp. 224 + 80 plates.
- Filippani-Ronconi, Pio (b. 1920). "Note sulla soteriologia e sul simbolismo cosmico dell' Umm'ul-Kitāb", in *Scritti in onore di Laura Veccia Vaglieri*; being, *AIUON*, NS, 14 (1964), pp. 111–134.
- Filippani-Ronconi, Pio. "Quelques influences Indiennes dans la rédaction de *l'Ummu'l-Kitāb*", in *XVII. Deutscher Orientalistentag vom 21. bis 27. Juli 1968 in Würzburg: Vorträge*. Wiesbaden: F. Steiner, 1969, vol. 3, pp. 885–893.
- Filippani-Ronconi, Pio. *Ismaeliti ed "Assassini"*. Basilea: Fondazione L. Keimer; Milan: Thoth, 1973. pp. 353.
- Filippani-Ronconi, Pio. "Nukātī chand dar bāra-yi iṣṭilāḥāt-i falsafī-yi Kitāb-i gushāʾish va rahāʾish-i Nāṣir-i Khusraw", in *YNK*, pp. 437–443.
- Filippani-Ronconi, Pio. "The Soteriologial Cosmology of Central-Asiatic Ismāʿīlism", in *ICIC*, pp. 99–120.
- Filippani-Ronconi, Pio. "Ai margini dell'Islām. Note sugli Ismaeliti *satpanthī*", in Clelia Sarnelli Cerqua, ed., *Studi Arabo-Islamici in onore di Roberto Rubinacci nel suo settantesimo compleanno*. Naples: Istituto Universitario Orientale, 1985, vol. 1, pp. 269–277.
- Filippani-Ronconi, Pio. "La concezione del tempo nel *Kitāb-i Gošayeš*

wa Rahāyeš di Nāṣir-i Khosrow", in Pier Giovanni Donini et al., ed., *Un ricordo che non si spegne. Scritti di docenti e collaboratori dell' Istituto Universitario Orientale di Napoli in memoria di Alessandro Bausani*. Istituto Universitario Orientale, Dipartimento di Studi Asiatici, Series Minor, L. Naples: Istituto Universitario Orientale, 1995, pp. 47–57.

- Firro, Kais M. *A History of the Druzes*. Handbuch der Orientalistik, Abteilung I, Ergänzungsband 9. Leiden: E.J. Brill, 1992. pp. xiv + 395.
- Firro, Kais M. "The Attitude of the Druzes and ʿAlawis vis-à-vis Islam and Nationalism in Syria and Lebanon", in Krisztina Kehl-Bodrogi et al, ed., *Syncretistic Religious Communities in the Near East*. Leiden: E.J. Brill, 1997, pp. 87–100.
- Fīrūz, Shīrzamān. *Falsafa-yi akhlāqī-yi Nāṣir-i Khusraw va rīshahā-yi ān*. Islamabad: Iran Pakistan Institute of Persian Studies, 1371 Sh./1992. pp. 360.
- Fīrūzī, Javād. "Ivanow, Vladimir A.", in *DMBI*, vol. 10, pp. 721–722.
- Fīrūzkūhī, Amīrī. "Ḥakīm Nāṣir-i Khusraw", *Yaghmā*, 28 (1354 Sh./ 1975), pp. 48–51.
- Fischel, Walter Joseph (b. 1902). *Jews in the Economic and Political Life of Mediaeval Islam*. Royal Asiatic Society Monographs, XXII. London: Royal Asiatic Society of Great Britain and Ireland, 1937, pp. 45–89 (under the Fāṭimid Caliphate).
- Fleischhauer, Wolfgang. "The Old Man of the Mountain: The Growth of a Legend", *Symposium*, 9, no. 1 (1955), pp. 79–90.
- Flügel, Gustav Leberecht (1802–1870). "Ueber Inhalt und Verfasser der arabischen Encyclopädie Rasā'il Ikhwān al-Ṣafā' wa Khillān al-Wafā d. i. die Abhandlungen der aufrichtigen Brüder und treuen Freunde", *ZDMG*, 13 (1859), pp. 1–43; reprinted in *RIS*, vol. 1, pp. 229–271.
- Flury, Samuel. *Die Ornamente der Hakim - und Ashar-Moschee*. Materialien zur Geschichte der älteren Kunst des Islam. Heidelberg: Carl Winters Universitätsbuchhandlung, 1912. pp. 52 + 34 plates.
- Flury, Samuel. "Le décor épigraphique des monuments Fatimides du Caire", *Syria*, 17 (1936), pp. 365–376.
- Foy, Danièle. "Lampes de verre Fatimides à Fostat: Le mobilier des fouilles de Istabl ʿAntar", in *EF*, pp. 179–196.
- Frank, Richard M. "Ismailis", in *Encyclopedic Dictionary of Religion*.

Washington, DC: Corpus Publications, 1979, vol. F-N [2], p. 1848.

- Frantz-Murphy, Gladys. "A New Interpretation of the Economic History of Mediaeval Egypt: The Role of the Textile Industry, 254–567/868–1171", *JESHO*, 24 (1981), pp. 274–297.
- Franzius, Enno (b. 1901). *History of the Order of Assassins*. New York: Funk and Wagnalls, 1969. pp. xviii + 261.
- Fraschery, Samy-Bey Ch. "Ismāʿīliyya", "Fāṭimiyyūn", "Qarmaṭī", in his *Dictionnaire universel d'histoire et de géographie*. Istanbul: Mihran, 1889–1896.
- Frenkel, Yehoshu'a. "The *Ketubba* (Marriage Document) as a Source for the Study of the Economic History of the Fatimid Period", in *ESFAM* 3, pp. 33–48.
- Frere, H. Bartle E. "The Khojas: The Disciples of the Old Man of the Mountain", *Macmillan's Magazine*, 34 (1876), pp. 342–350, 430–438.
- Frère, Jean Claude. *L'ordre des Assassins: Hasan Sabbah, le Vieux de la Montagne et l'Ismaélisme*. Histoire des personnages mystérieux et des sociétés secrètes. Paris: Culture, Art, Loisirs, 1973. pp. 284.
- Frischauer, Willi (b. 1906). *The Aga Khans*. London: Bodley Head, 1970. pp. 286.

Fuʾād Sayyid, A., *see* Sayyid, Ayman F.

- Furqānī, Muḥammad Fārūq. *Ta'rīkh-i Ismāʿīliyān-i Quhistān*. Silsila intishārāt-i Anjuman-i Āthār va Mafākhir-i Farhangī, 262. Tehran: Anjuman-i Āthār va Mafākhir-i Farhangī, 1381 Sh./2002. pp. 507.
- Fyzee (Fayḍī), Asaf Ali Asghar (Āṣaf b. ʿAlī Aṣghar) (1899–1981). "Bequests to Heirs: Shia Ismāʿīlī Law", *Bombay Law Reporter, Journal*, 31 (1929), pp. 84–87.
- Fyzee, Asaf A.A. "Bequests to Heirs: Ismāʿīlī Shīʿa Law", *JBBRAS*, NS, 5 (1929), pp. 141–145.
- Fyzee, Asaf A.A. "Studies in Ismāʿīlī Law", *Bombay Law Reporter, Journal*, 33 (1931), pp. 30–32; 34 (1932), pp. 89–92; 38 (1936), pp. 41–43.
- Fyzee, Asaf A.A. "Notes on Mutʿa or Temporary Marriage in Islam: II, The Ismaili Law of Mutʿa", *JBBRAS*, NS, 8 (1932), pp. 85–92.
- Fyzee, Asaf A.A. "An Ancient Copy of the Daʿāʾimu'l-Islām", *Journal of the University of Bombay*, 2 (1934), pp. 127–133.
- Fyzee, Asaf A.A. "A Chronological List of the Imams and Daʿis of the Mustaʿlian Ismailis", *JBBRAS*, NS, 10 (1934), pp. 8–16.

- Fyzee, Asaf A.A. "Qadi an-Nuʿman, The Fatimid Jurist and Author", *JRAS* (1934), pp. 1–32.
- Fyzee, Asaf A.A. "Ismaʿili Law and its Founder", *IC*, 9 (1935), pp. 107–112.
- Fyzee, Asaf A.A. "Materials for an Ismaili Bibliography: 1920–1934", *JBBRAS*, NS, 11 (1935), pp. 59–65.
- Fyzee, Asaf A.A. "Additional Notes for an Ismaili Bibliography", *JBBRAS*, NS, 12 (1936), pp. 107–109.
- Fyzee, Asaf A.A. "Materials for an Ismaili Bibliography: 1936–1938", *JBBRAS*, NS, 16 (1940), pp. 99–101.
- Fyzee, Asaf A.A. "Three Sulaymani Daʿis: 1936–1939", *JBBRAS*, NS, 16 (1940), pp. 101–104.
- Fyzee, Asaf A.A. "A Note on the Fatimid Jurist Nuʿman and his Book: The Pillars of Islam (Summary)", in Zeki Velidi Togan, ed., *Proceedings of the Twenty-second Congress of Orientalists*: Volume II, *Communications*. Leiden: E.J. Brill, 1957, pp. 245–247.
- Fyzee, Asaf A.A. "The Fatimid Law of Inheritance", *SI*, 9 (1958), pp. 61–69.
- Fyzee, Asaf A.A. "The Fatimid Law of Inheritance", *University of Malaya Law Review*, 1 (1959), pp. 245–265; reprinted in *Studies in Law: Patna Law College Golden Jubilee Commemoration Volume*. Bombay, Calcutta, etc.: Asia Publishing House, 1960, pp. 444–471.
- Fyzee, Asaf A.A. "The Study of the Literature of the Fatimid *Daʿwa*", in George Makdisi, ed., *Arabic and Islamic Studies in Honor of Hamilton A.R. Gibb*. Leiden: E.J. Brill; Cambridge, MA: Department of Near Eastern Languages and Literatures, Harvard University, 1965, pp. 232–249. Persian trans., "Adabiyyāt-i daʿwat-i Fāṭimī", tr., Farīdūn Badraʾī, in *Rāhnamā-yi Kitāb*, 11 (1347 Sh./1968), pp. 246–251, 304–310, 362–368.
- Fyzee, Asaf A.A. *Compendium of Fatimid Law*. Simla: Indian Institute of Advanced Study, 1969. pp. l + 160.
- Fyzee, Asaf A.A. "The Ismāʿīlīs", in Arthur J. Arberry, ed., *Religion in the Middle East: Three Religions in Concord and Conflict*: Volume 2, *Islam*. Cambridge: Cambridge University Press, 1969, pp. 318–329, 684–685.
- Fyzee, Asaf A.A. "Aspects of Fāṭimid Law", in *Voluminis memoriae J.*

Schacht dedicati, pars prior; being, *SI*, 31 (1970), pp. 81–91.

- Fyzee, Asaf A.A. “W. Ivanow (1886–1970)”, *Indo-Iranica*, 23 (1970), pp. 22–27; also in *Journal of the Asiatic Society of Bombay*, NS, 45–46 (1970–71), pp. 92–97.
- Fyzee, Asaf A.A. “The Religion of the Ismailis”, in S.T. Lokhandwalla, ed., *India and Contemporary Islam: Proceedings of a Seminar*. Transactions of the Indian Institute of Advanced Study, 6. Simla: Indian Institute of Advanced Study, 1971, pp. 70–87.
- Fyzee, Asaf A.A. “A Collection of Fatimid Manuscripts”, in N.N. Gidwani, ed., *Comparative Librarianship: Essays in Honour of Professor D.N. Marshall*. Delhi: Vikas Publishing House, 1973, pp. 209–220.
- Fyzee, Asaf A.A. “al-Nuʿmān”, in *EI*, vol. 3, pp. 953–954.
- Fyzee, Asaf A.A. “Bohorās”, *EI2*, vol. 1, pp. 1254–1255. Persian trans., “Firqa-yi Buhra”, tr., Yaʿqūb Āzhand, in B. Lewis et al., *Ismāʿīliyān dar taʾrīkh*, pp. 389–396.
- Fyzee, Asaf A.A. “Imām Shāh”, in *EI2*, vol. 3, p. 1163.
- Fyzee, Asaf A.A. “Qadi an-Nuʿman”, in *GIH*, pp. 18–20.

See also under M. Goriawala

G

- Gabrieli, Francesco. “Il ‘Sefer-nāmeh’ e la crisi religiosa di Nāṣir-i Ḫusraw”, in *Atti del XIX Congresso internazionale degli Orientalisti, Roma, 23–29 settembre, 1935*. Rome: Tipografia del Santo, 1938, pp. 556–559.
- Gabrieli, Francesco. “Le Caire de Nāṣir-i Khusrev”, in *Colloque international sur l’histoire du Caire*, pp. 155–157; also in *Revue de l’Occident Musulman et de la Mediterranée*, 13–14 (1973), pp. 357–360.
- Gabrieli, Francesco. “Il ‘Sefer-nāme’ e i Fatimidi d’Egitto”, *Studi Iranici: 17 Saggi di Iranisti Italiani*. Rome: Centro Culturale Italo-Iraniano, 1977, pp. 209–212.
- Gabrieli, Francesco. “Nāṣir-i Khusraw”, in *Enciclopedia Italiana*. Rome: Istituto della Enciclopedia Italiana, 1934, vol. 24, pp. 286–287.
- Gacek, Adam. *Catalogue of Arabic Manuscripts in the Library of The Institute of Ismaili Studies*. London: Islamic Publications, 1984. vol. 1 (pp. xvii + 180).

- Gacek, Adam. "Library Resources at the Institute of Ismaili Studies, London", *British Society for Middle Eastern Studies Bulletin*, 11 (1984), pp. 63–64.
- García Gómez, Emilio (1905–1995). "Alusiones a los 'Ijwān al-Ṣafā'' en la poesía arábigoandaluza", *al-Andalus*, 4 (1936–39), pp. 462–465; reprinted in *RIS*, vol. 2, pp. 212–215.
- García Gómez, Emilio. "Mutanabbī et Ibn Hānī'", in *Mélanges offerts à William Marçais par l'Institut d'Études Islamiques de l'Université de Paris*. Paris: G.P. Maisonneuve, 1950, pp. 147–153.
- Gateau, Albert (1902–1949). "Sur un dinār Fatimide", *Hespéris*, 32 (1945), pp. 69–74.
- Gateau, Albert. "La *Sīrat* Ja'far al-Ḥajib, contribution à l'histoire des Fatimides", *Hespéris*, 34 (1947), pp. 375–396.
- Gatti, Daniela. "Assassini", in *Grande Dizionario Enciclopedico*. Turin: Unione Tipografico-Editrice Torinese, 1985, vol. 2, p. 413.
- Gaube, Heinz. "Arrajān", in *EIR*, vol. 2, pp. 519–520.
- Gayraud, Roland Pierre. "La nécropole des Fatimides à Fostat", *Dossiers d'Archéologie* ; special issue *Égypte: L'Âge d'or des Fatimides*, 233 (May, 1998), pp. 34–41.
- Gayraud, Roland P. "Le Qarāfa al-Kubrā, dernière demeure des Fatimides", in *EF*, pp. 443–464.

  See also under Ayman F. Sayyid
- Geddes, C.L. "The Apostasy of 'Alī b. al-Faḍl", in Robin L. Bidwell and Gerald R. Smith, ed., *Arabian and Islamic Studies: Articles Presented to R.B. Serjeant on the Occasion of his Retirement from the Sir Thomas Adams's Chair of Arabic at the University of Cambridge*. London: Longman, 1983, pp. 80–85.
- Geddes, C.L. "Bilāl b. Djarīr al-Muḥammadī", in *EI2*, vol. 1, pp. 1214–1215.
- Gelpke, R. "Der Geheimbund von Alamut: Legende und Wirklichkeit", *Antaios*, 8 (1966–67), pp. 269–293.
- Ghadially, Rehana. "Daudi Bohra Muslim Women and Modern Education: A Beginning", *Indian Journal of Gender Studies*, 1 (1994), pp. 195–213.
- Ghadially, Rehana. "Women and Personal Law in an Ismā'īlī Shī'ah (Dā'ūdī Bohra) Sect of Indian Muslims", *IC*, 70 (1996), pp. 27–51.

- Ghadially, Rehana. "Women's Vows, Roles and Household Ritual in a South Asian Muslim Sect", *Asian Journal of Women's Studies*, 4 (1998), pp. 27–52.
- Ghadially, Rehana. "A Muslim Widow: The Practice of *Idda*, Seclusion and Mourning in a South Asian Sect", *Asian Women*, 8 (1999), pp. 209–224.
- Ghadially, Rehana. "Women's Religious Gatherings in a South Asian Muslim Sect", *Thamyris*, 6 (1999), pp. 43–63.
- Ghadially, Rehana. "Women Pilgrims: Boons and Bonds in an Ismaili Sect", International Institute for the Study of Islam in the Modern World, *ISIM Newsletter*, 8 (2001), pp. 22–25.
- Ghālib, Muṣṭafā (1923–1981). *Taʾrīkh al-daʿwa al-Ismāʿīliyya*. Damascus: Dār al-Yaqẓā al-ʿArabiyya, [1953]. pp. 336; 2nd ed., Beirut: Dār al-Andalus, 1965. pp. 404.
- Ghālib, Muṣṭafā. *Aʿlām al-Ismāʿīliyya*. Beirut: Dār al-Yaqẓā al-ʿArabiyya, 1964. pp. 624.
- Ghālib, Muṣṭafā. *al-Ḥarakāt al-bāṭiniyya fi'l-Islām*. Beirut: Dār al-Kātib al-ʿArabī, [1965]; 3rd ed., Beirut: Dār al-Andalus, 1402/1982. pp. 303.
- Ghālib, Muṣṭafā. *al-Thāʾir al-Ḥimyarī al-Ḥasan ibn al-Ṣabbāḥ*. Beirut: Dār al-Andalus, 1386/1966. pp. 139.
- Ghālib, Muṣṭafā. *Sinān Rāshid al-Dīn, shaykh al-jabal al-thālith*. Beirut: Dār al-Yaqẓā al-ʿArabiyya wa-Manshūrāt Ḥamad, 1967. pp. 214.
- Ghālib, Muṣṭafā. *Fī riḥāb Ikhwān al-Ṣafāʾ wa-Khullān al-Wafāʾ*. Beirut: Manshūrāt Ḥamad, 1969. pp. 446.
- Ghālib, Muṣṭafā. *The Ismailis of Syria*. Beirut: Intersales Enterprises, 1970. pp. 173.
- Ghālib, Muṣṭafā. *al-Qarāmiṭa bayna al-madd wa'l-jazr*. Beirut: Dār al-Andalus, 1979. pp. 447; 2nd ed., Beirut: Dār al-Andalus, 1983. pp. 447.
- Ghālib, Muṣṭafā. *al-Imāma wa-qāʾim al-qiyāma*. Beirut: Dār wa-Maktabat al-Hilāl, 1981. pp. 334.
- Ghālib, Muṣṭafā. *Mafātīḥ al-maʿrifa*. Beirut: Muʾassasat ʿIzz al-Dīn, 1402/1982. pp. 403.
- Ghālib, Muṣṭafā. "al-Ismāʿīliyya madhhab min al-madhāhib al-Islāmiyya al-mutakāmila", *al-Bāḥith*, 9 (1987), pp. 101–112.
- Ghawānma, Yūsuf Darwīsh. "al-Afḍal b. Badr al-Jamālī wa-mawqi-

fuhu min al-ḥamla al-Ṣalībiyya al-ūlā", *Majallat Kulliyyat al-Ādāb, Jāmiʿat al-Malik Saʿūd*, 10 (1983), pp. 71–90.

- Ghulāmī, Yad Allāh. "al-Aqmar", in *DMBI*, vol. 9, pp. 692–694.
- Gibb, Hamilton Alexander Rosskeen (1895–1971). "al-Muʿizz li-Dīn Allāh", "al-Mustaʿlī Bi'llāh", "al-Mustanṣir Bi'llāh" (with Paul Kraus), "Nizār b. al-Mustanṣir", "Ruzzīk b. Ṭalā'iʿ", in *EI*.
- Gibb, Hamilton A.R. "Agha Khān", "al-Mustaʿlī Bi'llāh", "al-Mustanṣir Bi'llāh" (with Paul Kraus), "Nizār b. al-Mustanṣir" in *EI2*.
- Gibb, Hamilton A.R. "Nizâr", in *IA*, vol. 9, p. 335.
- Gibb, Hamilton A.R. and Charles F. Beckingham. "Fatimids", in *Chamber's Encyclopaedia*. New rev. ed., Oxford, etc.: Pergamon Press, 1966, vol. 5, p. 572.
- Giese, Alma. "Zur Erlösungsfunktion des Traumes bei den Iḫwān aṣ-Ṣafā'", in Alma Giese and Johann Christoph Bürgel, ed., *Gott ist schön und Er liebt die Schönheit/God is Beautiful and He Loves Beauty. Festschrift für Annemarie Schimmel zum 7. April 1992 dargebracht von Schülern, Freunden und Kollegen/Festschrift in Honour of Annemarie Schimmel Presented by Students, Friends and Colleagues on April 7, 1992*. Bern, Berlin, etc.: P. Lang, 1994, pp. 191–207.
- Gil, Moshe. *Documents of the Jewish Pious Foundation from the Cairo Geniza*. Publications of the Diaspora Research Institute, 12. Leiden: E.J. Brill, 1976. pp. xiv + 611.
- Gil, Moshe. *A History of Palestine, 634–1099*, translated from the Hebrew by Ethel Broido. Cambridge: Cambridge University Press, 1992, pp. 335–429 (on the Fatimid conquest).
- Glassé, Cyril. "ʿAbd Allāh ibn Maymūn al-Qaddāḥ", "Aga Khan", "Assassins", "Bohoras", "Brotherhood of Purity", "Dāʿī", "Druzes", "Fāṭimids", "Ismāʿīlīs", "Khojas", "Khusraw, Nāṣir-i", "Mukhī", "Qarmatians", "Rashid ad-Dīn Sinān", "Seveners", "Ta'wīl", "Umm al-Kitāb", in his *The Concise Encyclopedia of Islam*. London: Stacey International, 1989; 2nd ed., London: Stacey International, 1991.
- Glidden, Harold W. "Fatimid Carved-wood Inscriptions in the Collections of the University of Michigan", *Ars Islamica*, 6 (1939), pp. 94–95.
- Gnoli, Gherardo. "Note sul 'Kitāb-e gošāyeš wa rahāyeš' di Nāṣir-e Ḫosraw in relazione ad alcune analogie con la letteratura religiosa pahlavica", in *Scritti in onore di Laura Veccia Vaglieri*; being, *AIUON*, NS, 14 (1964), pp. 191–202.

- Gobillot, Geneviève. *Les Chiites*. Fils d'Abraham. Turnhout: Éditions Brepols, 1998. pp. 224.
- Goeje, Michael Jan de (1836–1909). *Mémoire sur les Carmathes du Bahraïn et les Fatimides*. Mémoires d'histoire et de géographie orientales, 1. Leiden: E.J. Brill, 1862; 2nd ed., Leiden: E.J. Brill, 1886. pp. 232; reprinted, Osnabrück: Biblio Verlag, 1977. pp. 232. Arabic trans., *al-Qarāmiṭa*, tr., Ḥusnī Zayna. Beirut: Dār Ibn Khaldūn, 1978. pp. 223. Persian trans., *Qarāmiṭa-yi Baḥrayn va Fāṭimiyyūn*, tr., Muḥammad Bāqir Amīr Khānī, in *Nashriyya-yi Dānishkada-yi Adabiyyāt-i Tabrīz/Revue de la Faculté des Lettres, Université de Tabriz*, 16, no. 3 (1343 Sh./1964), pp. 321–336; 16, no. 4 (1343 Sh./1965), pp. 471–486; 17, no. 4 (1344 Sh./1965), pp. 508–521; 18, no. 3 (1345 Sh./1966), pp. 339–355; 18, no. 4 (1345 Sh./1967), pp. 476–490; 19, no. 1 (1346 Sh./1967), pp. 60–72; 19, no. 2 (1346 Sh./1967), pp. 226–238; this translation remained incomplete. Complete Persian translation was published separately as *Qarmaṭiyān-i Baḥrayn va Fāṭimiyān*, tr., Muḥammad Bāqir Amīr Khānī. Tehran: Surūsh, 1371 Sh./1992. pp. 188.
- Goeje, Michael Jan de. "La fin de l'empire des Carmathes du Bahraïn", *JA*, 9 série, 5 (1895), pp. 5–30; reprinted in Bryan S. Turner, ed., *Orientalism: Early Sources*, Volume I, *Readings in Orientalism*. London: Routledge, 2000, pp. 263–278.
- Goeje, Michael Jan de. "Carmaṭians", in *ERE*, vol. 3, pp. 222–225. Persian trans., "Qarmaṭiyān", in Y. Āzhand, *Nahḍat-i Qarāmiṭa*, pp. 61–74.
- Goitein, Solomon (Shelomo) Dov (1900–1985). "Petitions to Fatimid Caliphs from the Cairo Geniza", *Jewish Quarterly Review*, NS, 45–46 (1954–56), pp. 30–38.
- Goitein, Solomon D. "A Caliph's Decree in Favour of the Rabbinite Jews of Palestine", *Journal of Jewish Studies*, 5 (1954), pp. 118–125.
- Goitein, Solomon D. "The Cairo Geniza as a Source for the History of Muslim Civilization", *SI*, 3 (1955), pp. 75–91.
- Goitein, Solomon D. "New Light on the Beginnings of the Kārim Merchants", *JESHO*, 1 (1957–58), pp. 175–184.
- Goitein, Solomon D. "L'état actuel de la recherche sur les documents de la Geniza du Caire", *Revue des Études Juives*, 3 série, 118 (1959–60), pp. 9–27.
- Goitein, Solomon D. "The Documents of the Cairo Geniza as a Source

for Mediterranean Social History", *JAOS*, 80 (1960), pp. 91–100.

- Goitein, Solomon D. "La Tunisie du XIe siècle à la lumière des documents de la *Geniza* du Caire", in *Études d'Orientalisme dédiées à la mémoire de Lévi-Provençal*. Paris: G.P. Maisonneuve et Larose, 1962, pp. 559–579.
- Goitein, Solomon D. "The Exchange Rate of Gold and Silver Money in Fatimid and Ayyubid Times: A Preliminary Study of the Relevant Geniza Material", *JESHO*, 8 (1965), pp. 1–46; 9 (1966), pp. 67–68; 12 (1969), p. 112 (Erratum).
- Goitein, Solomon D. "Bankers' Account from the Eleventh Century A.D.", *JESHO*, 9 (1966), pp. 28–68.
- Goitein, Solomon D. *A Mediterranean Society: The Jewish Communities of the Arab World as Portrayed in the Documents of the Cairo Geniza*. Berkeley: University of California Press, 1967–93. 6 vols.
- Goitein, Solomon D. "Cairo: An Islamic City in the Light of the Geniza Documents", in Ira M. Lapidus, ed., *Middle Eastern Cities*. Berkeley: University of California Press, 1969, pp. 80–96.
- Goitein, Solomon D. "A Mansion in Fustat: A Twelfth-century Description of a Domestic Compound in the Ancient Capital of Egypt", in Harry A. Miskimin, David Herlihy and A. L. Udovitch, ed., *The Medieval City*. New Haven: Yale University Press, 1977, pp. 163–178; reprinted in David Waines, ed., *Patterns of Everyday Life*. The Formation of the Classical Islamic World, 10. Aldershot: Ashgate, 2002.
- Goitein, Solomon D. "Urban Housing in Fatimid and Ayyubid Times (as Illustrated by the Cairo Geniza Documents)", *SI*, 47 (1978), pp. 5–23.
- Goitein, Solomon D. "Prayers from the Geniza for Fatimid Caliphs, the Head of the Jerusalem Yeshiva, the Jewish Community and the Local Congregation", in Sheldon R. Brunswick, ed., *Studies in Judaica, Karaitica and Islamica Presented to Leon Nemoy on his Eightieth Birthday*. Ramat-Gan: Bar-Ilan University Press, 1982, pp. 47–57.
- Goitein, Solomon D. "Geniza", in *EI2*, vol. 2, pp. 987–989.
- Goldziher, Ignaz (1850–1921). "Polemik der Drusen gegen den Pentateuch", *Jüdische Zeitschrift für Wissenschaft und Leben*, 11 (1874–75), pp. 68–79.
- Goldziher, Ignaz. "Über die Benennung der 'Ichwān al-ṣafā'", *Der Islam*, 1 (1910), pp. 22–26; reprinted in *RIS*, vol. 2, pp. 122–126.

- Goldziher, Ignaz. "Asās", in *EI*, vol. 1, pp. 476–477.
- Gölpinarli, Abdülbaki. "Ismâilî'ler", in Türk Ansiklopedisi. Ankara: Millî Eğitim Basimevi, 1972, vol. 20, pp. 314–316.
- Golvin, Lucien. "Mahdiya à l'époque Fātimide", *Revue de l'Occident Musulman et de la Mediterranée*, 27 (1979), pp. 75–98.
- Golvin, Lucien. "Buluggîn fils de Zîri, prince Berbère", *Revue de l'Occident Musulman et de la Mediterranée*, 35 (1983), pp. 93–113.
- Gonzalez, Valérie. "Pratique d'une technique d'art Byzantine chez les Fatimides: l'émaillerie sur métal", in *EF*, pp. 197–217.
- Goodman, L.E. "Rāzī vs Rāzī-Philosophy in the *Majlis*", in Hava Lazarus-Yafeh et al., ed., *The Majlis: Interreligious Encounters in Medieval Islam*. Studies in Arabic Language and Literature, 4. Wiesbaden: O. Harrassowitz, 1999, pp. 84–107.
- Goriawala, Muʿizz. *A Descriptive Catalogue of the Fyzee Collection of Ismaili Manuscripts*. Bombay: University of Bombay, 1965. pp. v + 172.
- Gottheil, Richard J.H. "A Distinguished Family of Fatimide Cadis (al-Nuʿmān) in the Tenth Century", *JAOS*, 27 (1906), pp. 217–296.
- Gottheil, Richard J.H. "An Eleventh-century Document Concerning a Cairo Synagogue", *Jewish Quarterly Review*, 19 (1906–7), pp. 467–539.
- Gottheil, Richard J.H. "Al-Hasan ibn Ibrāhīm ibn Zūlāḳ", *JAOS*, 28 (1907), pp. 254–270.
- Gottheil, Richard J.H. "A Decree in Favour of the Karaites of Cairo dated 1024", in D. von Günzburg and I. Markon, ed., *Festschrift zu Ehren des Dr. A. Harkavy*. St. Petersburg: n. p., 1908, pp. 115–125.
- Grabar, Oleg. "Imperial and Urban Art in Islam: The Subject Matter of Fāṭimid Art", in *Colloque international sur l'histoire du Caire*, pp. 173–189; reprinted in his *Studies in Medieval Islamic Art*. London: Variorum Reprints, 1976, article VII.
- Grabar, Oleg. "Fāṭimid Art, Precursor or Culmination", in *ICIC*, pp. 207–224.
- Grabar, Oleg. "Qu'est-ce que l'art Fatimide?", in *EF*, pp. 11–18.
- Graefe, E. "Ḍirghām", "Djawhar", "Fāṭimids", "al-Ḥāfiẓ", "al-Ḥākim Bi Amri'llāh", in *EI*.
- Graefe, E. "Fâtimîler", in *IA*, vol. 4, pp. 521–526.

- Gray, Basil (1904–1989). "A Fātimid Drawing", *The British Museum Quarterly*, 12 (1938), pp. 91–96.
- *The Great Ismaili Heroes: Contains the Life Sketches and the Works of Thirty Great Ismaili Figures*, with Preface by Abdul Rehman Kanji. Karachi: Prince Aly S. Khan Colony Religious Night School, 1973. pp. 107.
- Greif, Avner. "Contract Enforceability and Economic Institutions in Early Trade: The Maghribi Traders' Coalition", *American Economic Review*, 83, no. 3 (1993), pp. 525–548.
- Grelou, G. "Fāṭimides", "Ismaéliens", in *Grande Larousse Encyclopédique*. Paris: Librairie Larousse, 1961–62.
- Griffini, Eugenio (1878–1925). "Die jüngste ambrosianische Sammlung arabischer Handschriften", *ZDMG*, 69 (1915), pp. 63–88.
- Grigor'ev, Sergey E. "Ismailitï Afganistana: nekotorïe zamechaniya i nablyudeniya" [The Ismailis of Afghanistan: Some Notes and Observations]. *Vestnik Vostochnogo Instituta* (St. Petersburg), 3 (1996), pp. 88–107.
- Grigor'ev, Sergey E. "K voprosu o rodoslovnoy ismailitskikh pirov Afganistana" [On the Genealogy of the Ismaili Pirs of Afghanistan], *Stranï i narodï Vostoka*, 30 (1998), pp. 242–251.
- Grohmann, Adolf. "Ṭirāz", "Yām", in *EI*.
- Grohmann, Adolf A. and Pahor Labib. "Ein Fāṭimidenerlass vom Jahre 415 A.H. (1024 A.D.) im Koptischen Museum in Alt-Kairo", *RSO*, 32 (1957), pp. 641–654.
- Grube, Ernst J. "The Earliest Known Paintings from Islamic Cairo", in *Colloque international sur l'histoire du Caire*, pp. 195–198.
- Grube, Ernst J. "Realism or Formalism: Notes on Some Fatimid Lustre-painted Ceramic Vessels", in Renato Traini, ed., *Studi in onore di Francesco Gabrieli nel suo ottantesimo compleanno*. Rome: Universitá di Roma "La Sapienza", Dipartimento di Studi Orientali, 1984, vol. 1, pp. 423–432.
- Grube, Ernst J. "A Coloured Drawing of the Fatimid Period in the Keir Collection", *RSO*, 59 (1985), pp. 147–174.

- Grube, Ernst J. "Il periodo Fatimide in Egitto dal 297/909 al 567/1171", in G. Curatola, ed., *Eredità dell' Islam. Arte Islamica in Italia*. Milan: Cinisello Balsamo, 1993, pp. 133–160.
- Grube, Ernst J. "Fatimid Pottery", in *Cobalt and Lustre: The First Centuries of Islamic Pottery*. London: Nour Foundation, 1994, pp. 137–146.
- Grube, Ernst J. "La Pittura Islamica nella Sicilia Normanna del XII secolo", in Carlo Bertelli, ed., *La Pittura in Italia. L'Altomedioevo*. Milan: Electa, 1994, pp. 416–431.
- Grunebaum, Gustave Edmund von (1909–1972). "The Nature of the Fāṭimid Achievement", in *Colloque international sur l'histoire du Caire*, pp. 199–215.
- Guichard, Pierre. "Omeyyades et Fatimides au Maghreb. Problématique d'un conflit politico-idéologique (vers 929–vers 980)", in *EF*, pp. 55–67.
- Guillaume, Jean Patrick. "Les Ismaéliens dans le *Roman de Baybarṣ*: genèse d'un type littéraire", *SI*, 84 (1996), pp. 145–179.
- Gulchīn Maʿānī, Aḥmad. "Taṣḥīḥ-i yak qaṣīda az Dīwān-i Ḥakīm Nāṣir-i Khusraw", in *YNK*, pp. 444–450.
- Güner, Ahmet. "Hâfiz-Lidînallâh", "Kaim-Biemrillâh el-Fâtemî", in *IA2*.
- Guyard, Stanislas (1824–1884). "Un grand maître des Assassins au temps de Saladin", JA, 7 série, 9 (1877), pp. 324–489.
- Guys, Ch. Ed., "Considérations sur les Maronites et sur les Druses", *Revue de l'Orient*, NS, 8 (1858), pp. 222–235.
- Guys, Henri (1823–1884). *La nation Druse, son histoire, sa religion, ses moeurs et son état politique avec la vie de Darazi, de Hamzé et des autres fondateurs de la religion Druse*. Paris: Chez France, 1863. pp. 248; reprinted, Amsterdam: APA-Philo Press, 1979. pp. 248.
- Guys, Henri. *Théogonie des Druses, ou abrégé de leur système religieux*. Traduit de l'Arabe. Paris: Imprimerie Impériale, 1863. pp. xxxii + 141.

H

- Haase, Claus Peter. "Some Aspects of Fatimid Calligraphy on Textiles", in *EF*, pp. 339–347.

- Habib, Muhammad. "Lord of the Assassins", *Muslim Review*, 3, no. 2 (1928–29), pp. 11–19; no. 4 (1928–29), pp. 10–19.
- el Habib, Mustapha. "Notes sur un tiraz au nom d'Abī l-Mansūr al ʿAziz bi l-Lāh, le Fatimide (365–386 H./975–996 ap. J.-C.)", *Revue du Louvre*, 23 (1973), pp. 299–302.
- Ḥabīb Allāhī "Navīd", Abu'l-Qāsim. "al-Mu'ayyad fi Dīn Allāh ustād-i Nāṣir-i Khusraw", in *YNK*, pp. 134–154.
- Ḥabībī, ʿAbd al-Ḥayy. "ʿAlī b. Asad", in *EIR*, vol. 1, p. 848
- Ḥabībī Maẓāhirī, Masʿūd. "Abū ʿAbd Allāh Shīʿī", "Aḥmad b. ʿAbd Allāh Mastūr", "Idrīs b. Ḥasan", "Ismāʿīl b. Jaʿfar", "Amīnjī", in *DMBI*.
- Habibullah, Abdul Qaiyum. *His Holiness Doctor Syedna Taher Saifuddin Saheb Dai-ul-Mutlaq of Dawoodi Bohra*. Bombay: Dawoodi Bohra Book Dcpot., n.d. [1947?]. pp. 23.
- Haji, Amin (Hamid). "Institutions of Justice in Fatimid Egypt (358–567/969–1171)", in A. Al-Azmeh, ed., *Islamic Law: Social and Historical Contexts*. London and New York: Routledge, 1988, pp. 198–214.
- Haji, Hamid. *A Distinguished Dāʿī under the Shade of the Fāṭimids: Ḥamīd al-Dīn al-Kirmānī (d. circa 411/1020) and his Epistles*. London: H. Haji, 1419/1998. pp. 87.
- Haji, S.G. *Genealogical Table of H. H. the Hon'ble Sir Aga Sultan Muhammad Shah Aga Khan, G.C.I.E., K.C.I.E., &c.* Karachi: "Mercantile" Steam Press, 1905.
- Hajnal, István. "The Background Motives of the Qarmaṭī Policy in Baḥrayn", *The Arabist, Budapest Studies in Arabic*, 8 (1994), pp. 9–31.
- Hajnal, István. "The Pseudo-Mahdī Intermezzo of the Qarāmiṭa in Baḥrayn", in K. Dévényi and T. Iványi, ed., *Proceedings of the Arabic and Islamic Sections of the 35th International Congress of Asian and North African Studies*, Part One; being, *The Arabist, Budapest Studies in Arabic*, 19–20 (1998), pp. 187–201.
- Hajnal, István. "On the History of the Ismāʿīlī 'Hidden Imāms' as Reflected in the Kitāb at-tarātīb as-sabʿa", in *Essays in Honour of Alexander Fodor on his Sixtieth Birthday*; being, *The Arabist, Budapest Studies in Arabic*, 23 (2001), pp. 101–116.
- Hakkı, Izmirli Ismail (1897–1960). *Dürzi Mezhebi*. Istanbul: Evkaf-i Islamiye Matbaasi, 1926. pp. 124 (in Ottoman Turkish).

- Hakkı, Izmirli Ismail. "Dürzi mezhebi", *DIFM*, 1, no. 2 (1926), pp. 36–99; 1, no. 3 (1926), pp. 177–234 (in Ottoman Turkish).
- Hakkı, Izmirli Ismail. *Ihvan-i Safa felsefeti ve Islam ʿda tekamül nazariyesi*. Istanbul: Hilmi Kitabevi, 1949.
- Ḥalabī, ʿAlī Aṣghar. "*Ikhwān al-Ṣafā*", in *DT*, vol. 2, pp. 29–30.
- Ḥalīm, Asmāʾ. *Ikhwān al-Ṣafāʾ wa-Khullān al-Wafāʾ: riwāya Miṣriyya*. Cairo: Dār al-Shaʿb, [1990]. pp. 171.
- Halit, Halil. "Ismailîyeler, Aga Han, Hint Müslümanlare", *DIFM*, 4, no. 14 (1930), pp. 53–60.
- Hallam, Roger. "The Ismailis in Britain", *New Community*, 1 (1971–72), pp. 383–388.
- Halm, Heinz. "Die Sieben und die Zwölf: Die ismāʿīlitische Kosmogonie und das Mazdak-Fragment des Šahrastānī", *ZDMG*, Supplement II (1974), pp. 170–177.
- Halm, Heinz. "Zur Datierung des ismāʿīlitischen 'Buches der Zwischenzeiten und der zehn Konjunktionen' (*Kitāb al-fatarāt waʾl-qirānāt al-ʿaṣara*) HS Tübingen Ma VI 297", *WO*, 8 (1975), pp. 91–107.
- Halm, Heinz. *Kosmologie und Heilslehre der frühen Ismāʿīlīya: Eine Studie zur islamischen Gnosis*. Deutsche Morgenländische Gesellschaft, Abhandlungen für die Kunde des Morgenlandes, XLIV, 1. Wiesbaden: F. Steiner, 1978. pp. 240.
- Halm, Heinz. "Die Söhne Zikrawaihs und das erste fatimidische Kalifat (290/903)", *WO*, 10 (1979), pp. 30–53.
- Halm, Heinz. "Methoden und Formen der frühesten ismailitischen *daʿwa*", in Hans R. Roemer and Albrecht Noth, ed., *Studien zur Geschichte und Kultur des Vorderen Orients. Festschrift für Bertold Spuler zum siebzigsten Geburtstag*. Leiden: E.J. Brill, 1981, pp. 123–136. English trans., "Methods and Forms of the Earliest Ismāʿīlī Daʿwa", in Etan Kohlberg, ed., *Shīʿism*. The Formation of the Classical Islamic World, 33. Aldershot: Ashgate, 2003, pp. 277–290.
- Halm, Heinz. "Die *Sīrat Ibn Ḥaušab*: Die ismailitische *daʿwa* im Jemen und die Fatimiden", *WO*, 12 (1981), pp. 107–135.
- Halm, Heinz. *Die islamische Gnosis: Die extreme Schia und die ʿAlawiten*. Die Bibliothek des Morgenlandes. Zürich and Munich: Artemis, 1982. pp. 406.
- Halm, Heinz. "Der Mann auf dem Esel: Der Aufstand des Abū Yazīd

gegen die Fatimiden nach einem Augenzeugenbericht", *WO*, 15 (1984), pp. 144–204.

- Halm, Heinz. "Les Fatimides à Salamya", in *Mélanges offerts au Professeur Dominique Sourdel*; being, *REI*, 54 (1986), pp. 133–149.
- Halm, Heinz. "Der Treuhänder Gottes: Die Edikte des Kalifen al-Ḥākim", *Der Islam*, 63 (1986), pp. 11–72.
- Halm, Heinz. "Eine Inschrift des *magister militum* Solomon in arabischer Überlieferung zur Restitution der Mauretania Caesariensis unter Justinian", *Historia*, 36 (1987), pp. 250–256.
- Halm, Heinz. *Die Schia*. Darmstadt: Wissenschaftliche Buchgesellschaft, 1988. pp. xiii+261. English trans., *Shi'ism*, tr., Janet Watson. Islamic Surveys, 18. Edinburgh: Edinburgh University Press, 1991. pp. 218.
- Halm, Heinz. "Zwei fāṭimidische Quellen aus der Zeit des Kalifen al-Mahdī (909–934)", *WO*, 19 (1988), pp. 102–117.
- Halm, Heinz. "Die Fatimiden", in Ulrich Haarmann, ed., *Geschichte der arabischen Welt*. Munich: C.H. Beck, 1991, pp. 166–199, 605–606, 635–638.
- Halm, Heinz. *Das Reich des Mahdi: Der Aufstieg der Fatimiden (875–973)*. Munich: C.H. Beck, 1991. pp. 470. English trans., *The Empire of the Mahdi: The Rise of the Fatimids*, tr., M. Bonner. Handbuch der Orientalistik, Abteilung I, Band 26. Leiden: E.J. Brill, 1996. pp. xiii + 452.
- Halm, Heinz. "Nachrichten zu Bauten der Aglabiden und Fāṭimiden in Libyen und Tunesien", *WO*, 23 (1992), pp. 129–157.
- Halm, Heinz. "Die Bekehrung der Berber der kleinen Kabylei zum ismailitischen Islam im 9. Jahrhundert", in Andre Gingrich et al., ed., *Studies in Oriental Culture and History: Festschrift for Walter Dostal*. Frankfurt am Main, Berlin, etc.: P. Lang, 1993, pp. 120–126.
- Halm, Heinz. "La refutation d'une note diplomatique du calife 'Abdarraḥmān III par la cour du calife Fatimide al-Mu'izz", in *Saber religioso y poder político en el Islam*. Actas del Simposio Internacional (Granada, 15–18 Octobre 1991). Madrid: Agencia Española de Cooperación Internacional, 1994, pp. 117–125.
- Halm, Heinz. "Al-Azhar, Dār al-'Ilm, al-Raṣad. Forschungs-und Lehranstalten der Fatimiden in Kairo", in *ESFAM*, pp. 99–109.

- Halm, Heinz. "Al-Šamsa. Hängekronen als Herrschaftszeichen der Abbasiden und Fatimiden", in *ESFAM*, pp. 125–138.
- Halm, Heinz. "Die Zeremonien der Salbung des Nilometers und der Kanalöffnung in fatimidischer Zeit", in *ESFAM*, pp. 111–123.
- Halm, Heinz. "Die Assassinen 1092 bis 1273", in Alexander Demandt, ed., *Das Attentat in der Geschichte*. Köln, etc.: Böhau, 1996, pp. 61–73.
- Halm, Heinz. "The Cosmology of the Pre-Fatimid Ismāʿīliyya", in *MIHT*, pp. 75–83. Arabic trans., "Kūzmūlūjiyya al-Ismāʿīliyyīn min al-ʿahd mā qabla al-Fāṭimī", in *IAW*, pp. 83–92. Persian trans., "Jahānshināsī-yi Ismāʿīliyya pīsh az Fāṭimiyān", in *TAI*, pp. 102–112.
- Halm, Heinz. "The Ismaʿili Oath of Allegiance (*ʿahd*) and the 'Sessions of Wisdom' (*majālis al-ḥikma*) in Fatimid Times", in *MIHT*, pp. 91–115. Arabic trans., "al-ʿahd al-Ismāʿīlī wa-majālis al-ḥikma zamana al-Fāṭimiyyīn", in *IAW*, pp. 99–124. Persian trans., "Sawgand-i ʿahd-i Ismāʿīlī va majālis al-ḥikma dar rūzigār-i Fāṭimiyān", in *TAI*, pp. 119–150.
- Halm, Heinz. *The Fatimids and their Traditions of Learning*. Ismaili Heritage Series, 2. London: I.B. Tauris in association with The Institute of Ismaili Studies, 1997, pp. xv + 112. Arabic trans., *al-Fāṭimiyyūn wa-taqālīduhum fi'l-taʿlīm*, tr., Sayf al-Dīn al-Qaṣīr. Damascus: al-Madā, 1999. pp. 155. Persian trans., *Fāṭimiyān va sunnathā-yi taʿlīmī va ʿilmī-yi ānān*, tr., Farīdūn Badra'ī. Tehran: Farzān, 1377 Sh./1998. pp. ix + 148.
- Halm, Heinz. "Les Fatimides, califes du Caire", *Dossiers d'Archéologie*; special issue *Égypte: L'Âge d'or des Fatimides*, 233 (May, 1998), pp. 4–11.
- Halm, Heinz. "Der nubische *baqṭ*", in *ESFAM2*, pp. 63–103.
- Halm, Heinz. "Der Tod Ḥamzas, des Begründers der drusischen Religion", in *ESFAM2*, pp. 105–113.
- Halm, Heinz. "Le destin de la princesse Sitt al-Mulk", in *EF*, pp. 69–72.
- Halm, Heinz. "Fatimiden und Ghaznawiden", in Ian R. Netton, ed., *Studies in Honour of Clifford Edmund Bosworth*, Volume I, *Hunter of the East: Arabic and Semitic Studies*. Leiden: E.J. Brill, 2000, pp. 209–221.
- Halm, Heinz. *Die Kaliefen von Kairo. Die Fatimiden in Ägypten 973–1074*. Munich: C.H. Beck, 2003. pp. 508.

- Halm, Heinz. "Miṣr: D. History of the Islamic Province. 3. The Fāṭimid Period, 969–1171", "Sabʿiyya", "Shamsa", "Sitt al-Mulk", "Zakrawayh b. Mihrawayh", "al-Walīd b. Hishām", in *EI2*.
- Halm, Heinz. "Dawr", "Djaʿfar b. Manṣūr al-Yaman", in *EI2*, Supplement.
- Halm, Heinz. "ʿAbdallāh b. Maymūn al-Qaddāḥ", "Abū Ḥātem Rāzī", "Aḥmad b. ʿAbdallāh", "Asās", "Bāṭenīya", "Ebn Ḥawšab", in *EIR*.
- Halm, Heinz. "Fātimiden", "Ismailiten", in *Lexikon des Mittelalters*. Munich and Zürich: Artemis and LexMA. 1977–1998.
- Halm, Heinz. "Ismaeliten", in *Lexikon für Theologie und Kirche*. Freiburg, Basel, etc.: Herden, 1996, vol. 5, p. 634.
- al-Ḥamad, ʿĀdila ʿAlī. *Qiyām al-dawla al-Fāṭimiyya bi-bilād al-Maghrib*. Cairo: Dār wa-Maṭābiʿ al-Mustaqbal, 1980. pp. 299.
- al-Ḥamad, Muḥammad ʿAbd al-Ḥamīd. *Ṣābi'at Ḥarrān wa-Ikhwān al-Ṣafā'*. Damascus: al-Ahālī, 1998. pp. 236.
- al-Ḥamad, Muḥammad ʿAbd al-Ḥamīd. *Ikhwān al-Ṣafā' wa'l-tawḥīd al-ʿAlawī*. Damascus: Dār Ārām li'l-Thaqāfa wa'l-Kutub, 1999. pp. 324.
- al-Ḥamad, Muḥammad ʿAbd al-Ḥamīd. *Ṣābi'at Ḥarrān wa'l-tawḥīd al-Durzī*. Damascus: Dār al-Ṭalīʿa al-Jadīda, 1999. pp. 215.
- Ḥamāda, Muḥammad Māhir. *al-Wathā'iq al-siyāsiyya wa'l-idāriyya li'l-ʿuhūd al-Fāṭimiyya wa'l-Atābakiyya wa'l-Ayyūbiyya*. Silsilat wathā'iq al-Islām, 4. Beirut: Mu'assasat al-Risāla, 1980. pp. 446.
- Hamadanizadeh, Javad. "Interpolation Schemes in Dastūr al-Munajjimīn", *Centaurus*, 22 (1978–79), pp. 44–52.
- Hamarneh, Sami K. "Medicine and Pharmacy under the Fāṭimids", in *ICIC*, pp. 141–185.
- Hamarneh, Sami K. "Medical Sciences under the Fatimiyy Dynasty", in *Hamdard Medicus*, 22 (1979), pp. 33–69; reprinted in Sami K. Hamarneh, *Health Sciences in Early Islam: Collected Papers*, ed., Munawar A. Anees. Blanco, TX: Noor Health Foundation and Zahra Publications, 1983, vol. 1, pp. 61–93.
- Hamawi, Khodr. *Introduction of Ismailism*. Beirut: n.p., 1970. pp. 108.
- Hamblin, William James. "The Fatimid Navy during the Early Crusades: 1099–1124", *The American Neptune*, 46 (1986), pp. 77–83.
- Hamblin, William J. "To Wage *Jihād* or not: Fatimid Egypt during the

Early Crusades", in Hadia Dajani-Shakeel and Ronald A. Messier, ed., *The Jihād and its Times*. Michigan Series on the Middle East. Ann Arbor, MI: University of Michigan, 1991, pp. 31–39.

- Hamdani (al-Hamdani), Abbas. "Kitāb az-zīnat of Abū Ḥātim ar-Rāzī", in *Actes du XXIe Congrès International des Orientalistes, Paris-23–31 juillet 1948*. Paris: Société Asiatique de Paris, 1949, pp. 291–294.
- Hamdani, Abbas. *The Beginnings of the Ismāʿīlī Daʿwa in Northern India*. The Hamdani Institute of Islamic Studies, Surat, Islamic Studies Series, 1. Cairo: Sirovic Bookshop. 1956. pp. 16.
- Hamdani, Abbas. "The Discovery of a Lost Literature (Fāṭimid)", *Proceedings of the Pakistan History Conference*, 8 (1958), pp. 61–73.
- Hamdani, Abbas. *The Fatimids*. Karachi: Pakistan Publishing House, 1962. pp. 84. Persian trans., *Dawlat-i Fāṭimiyān*, tr., Yaʿqūb Āzhand, in B. Lewis et al., *Ismāʿīliyān dar taʾrīkh*, pp. 151–254.
- Hamdani, Abbas. "The Fāṭimid-ʿAbbāsid Conflict in India", *IC*, 41 (1967), pp. 185–191.
- Hamdani, Abbas. "Some Considerations on the Fāṭimid Caliphate as a Mediterranean Power", in *Atti del terzo congresso di studi Arabi e Islamici (Ravello, 1–6 Settembre 1966)*. Naples: Istituto Universitario Orientale, 1967, pp. 385–396.
- Hamdani, Abbas. "A Possible Fāṭimid Background to the Battle of Manzikert", in *Ankara Üniv. D.T.C. Fakültesi Tarih Araştırmaları Dergisi*, 6, no. 10–11 (1968), pp. 1–39.
- Hamdani, Abbas. "The Dāʿī Ḥātim Ibn Ibrāhīm al-Ḥāmidī (d. 596 H./ 1199 A.D.) and his Book *Tuḥfat al-Qulūb*", *Oriens*, 23–24 (1970–71), pp. 258–300.
- Hamdani, Abbas. "Some Aspects of the History of Libya during the Fāṭimid Period", in Fawzi F. Gadallah, ed., *Libya in History*. Beirut and Benghazi: al-Jāmiʿa al-Lībiyya, Kulliyyat al-Ādāb, 1970, pp. 321–348.
- Hamdani, Abbas. "Byzantine-Fāṭimid Relations before the Battle of Manzikert", *Byzantine Studies*, 1(1974), pp. 169–179.
- Hamdani, Abbas. "Evolution of the Organisational Structure of the Fāṭimī Daʿwah: The Yemeni and Persian Contribution", *Arabian Studies*, 3 (1976), pp. 85–114.
- Hamdani, Abbas. "Abū Ḥayyān al-Tawḥīdī and the Brethren of Purity", *IJMES*, 9 (1978), pp. 345–353.

- Hamdani, Abbas. "An Early Fāṭimid Source on the Time and Authorship of the *Rasā'il Iḫwān al-Ṣafā'*", *Arabica*, 26 (1979), pp. 62–75.
- Hamdani, Abbas. "Shades of Shī'ism in the Tracts of the Brethren of Purity", in Peter Slater and Donald Wiebe, ed., *Traditions in Contact and Change*. Selected Proceedings of the XIVth Congress of the International Association for the History of Religions. Waterloo, Ontario: Published for the Canadian Corporation for Studies in Religion by W. Laurier University Press, 1983, pp. 447–460, 726–728.
- Hamdani, Abbas. "The Arrangement of the *Rasā'il Ikhwān al-Ṣafā'* and the Problem of Interpolations", *JSS*, 29 (1984), pp. 97–110.
- Hamdani, Abbas. "The Ṭayyibī-Fāṭimid Community of the Yaman at the Time of the Ayyūbid Conquest of Southern Arabia", *Arabian Studies*, 7 (1985), pp. 151–160.
- Hamdani, Abbas. "Al-Hamdānī [at] the Outset of the Domination of the Hamdān over Yaman", in Yusuf Mohammad Abdallah, ed., *al-Hamdānī: A Great Yemeni Scholar, Studies on the Occasion of his Millennial Anniversary*. Sanaa: Sanaa University, 1986, pp. 159–167.
- Hamdani, Abbas. "Time According to the Brethren of Purity", *Journal of Comparative Poetics*, 9 (1989), pp. 98–104.
- Hamdani, Abbas. "Fāṭimid History and Historians", in M.J.L. Young et al., ed., *Religion, Learning and Science in the 'Abbasid Period*. The Cambridge History of Arabic Literature. Cambridge: Cambridge University Press, 1990, pp. 234–247, 535–536.
- Hamdani, Abbas. "Surt: The City and its History", *The Maghreb Review*, 16 (1991), pp. 2–17.
- Hamdani, Abbas. "A Critique of Paul Casanova's Dating of the *Rasā'il Ikhwān al-Ṣafā'*", in *MIHT*, pp. 145–152. Arabic trans., "Dirāsa naqdiyya li-ta'rīkh Paul Casanova li-Rasā'il Ikhwān al-Ṣafā'", in *IAW*, pp. 147–154. Persian trans., "Naqd-i ta'rīkh-gudhārī-yi Paul Casanova bar Rasā'il Ikhwān al-Ṣafā'", in *TAI*, pp. 182–191.
- Hamdani, Abbas. "Examples of Fatimid Realpolitik", *DOMES, Digest of Middle East Studies*, 7 (1998), pp. 1–12.
- Hamdani, Abbas. "Brethren of Purity, a Secret Society for the Establishment of Fāṭimid Caliphate: New Evidence for the Early Dating of their Encyclopaedia", in *EF*, pp. 73–82.
- Hamdani, Abbas. "Did the Turkicization of Asia Minor lead to the Arabization of North Africa?", *The Maghreb Review*, 24 (1999), pp.

34–41.

- Hamdani, Abbas. "The Name Ikhwan al-Safa", *DOMES, Digest of Middle East Studies*, 8 (1999), pp. 1–11.
- Hamdani, Abbas "The *Rasa'il Ikhwan al-Safa'* and the Controversy about the Origin of Craft Guilds in Early Medieval Islam", in Nelly Hanna, ed., *Money, Land and Trade: An Economic History of the Muslim Mediterranean*. London: I.B. Tauris in association with The European Science Foundation, Strasbourg, 2002, pp. 157–173.
- Hamdani, Abbas. "Surt", in *EI2*, vol. 9, pp. 894–895.
- Hamdani, Abbas. "The Da'i Jalam b. Shayban and the Ismaili State of Multan", in *GIH*, pp. 14–15.
- Hamdani, Abbas. "The Fatimid Da'i al-Mu'ayyad: His Life and Work", in *GIH*, pp. 41–47.
- Hamdani, Abbas and François de Blois. "A Re-examination of al-Mahdī's Letter to the Yemenites on the Genealogy of the Fatimid Caliphs", *JRAS* (1983), pp. 173–207.
- al-Hamdānī, Ḥusain F. (Ḥusayn b. Fayḍ Allāh)(1901–1962). "The Life and Times of Queen Saiyidah Arwā the Ṣulaiḥid of the Yemen", *JRCA*, 18 (1931), pp. 505–517.
- al-Hamdānī, Ḥusain F. "The History of the Ismā'īlī Da'wat and its Literature during the Last Phase of the Fāṭimid Empire", *JRAS* (1932), pp. 126–136.
- al-Hamdānī, Ḥusain F. "Rasā'il Ikhwān aṣ-Ṣafā in the Literature of the Ismā'īlī Ṭaiyibī Da'wat", *Der Islam*, 20 (1932), pp. 281–300; reprinted in *RIS*, vol. 2, pp. 129–148.
- al-Hamdānī, Ḥusain F. "Some Unknown Ismā'īlī Authors and their Works", *JRAS* (1933), pp. 359–378.
- al-Hamdānī, Ḥusain F. "The Letters of al-Mustanṣir Bi'llāh", *BSOS*, 7 (1934), pp. 307–324.
- al-Hamdānī, Ḥusain F. *Baḥth ta'rīkhī fī Rasā'il Ikhwān al-Ṣafā' wa-'aqā'id al-Ismā'īliyya fīhā*. Bombay: Maktaba al-'Arabiyya al-Kubrā, 1354/1935. pp. 32; reprinted in *RIS*, vol. 2, pp. 149–180.
- al-Hamdānī, Ḥusain F. "A Compendium of Ismā'īlī Esoterics", *IC*, 11 (1937), pp. 210–220.
- al-Hamdānī, Ḥusain F. "al-Mu'aiyad fi'l-Dīn", in *EI*, vol. 3, p. 615.
- al-Hamdānī, Ḥusayn b. Fayḍ Allāh (Ḥusain F.) with Ḥasan Sulaymān

Maḥmūd al-Juhanī. *al-Ṣulayḥiyyūn wa'l-ḥaraka al-Fāṭimiyya fi'l-Yaman (min sanat 268 H. ilā sanat 626 H.)*. al-Maʿhad al-Hamdānī li'l-Dirāsāt al-Islāmiyya, Silsilat al-buḥūth al-Yamaniyya, 1. Cairo: Makṭabat Miṣr, 1955. pp. 402.

- Hamdani, Sumaiya. "The *Kitāb al-Majālis wa'l-Musāyarāt* and Fatimid *daʿwa-dawla* Relations", *The Maghreb Review*, 19 (1994), pp. 266–276.
- Hamdani, Sumaiya. "The Dialectic of Power: Sunni-Shiʿi Debates in Tenth-century North Africa", *SI*, 90 (2000), pp. 5–21.
- Ḥamīd, Ḥamīd. "Ta'thīrāt-i Ismāʿīlī bar tafakkur-i falsafi-yi Mūsā ibn Maymūn Yahūdī", *Iranshenāsī*, 9 (1997), pp. 285–303.
- Ḥamīdī, Sayyid Jaʿfar. *Nahḍat-i Abū Saʿīd-i Ganāva'ī*. Tehran: Rasā, 1360 Sh./1981. pp. 175.
- Hammer (-Purgstall), Joseph Freiherr von (1774–1856). "Sur le paradis du Vieux de la Montagne", *Fundgruben des Orients*, 3 (1813), pp. 201–206.
- Hammer (-Purgstall), Joseph von. *Die Geschichte der Assassinen aus Morgenländischen Quellen*. Stuttgart and Tübingen: F.G. Cotta'schen Buchhandlung, 1818. pp. viii + 341. French trans., *Histoire de l'ordre des Assassins*, tr., J.J. Hellert and P.A. de la Nourais. Paris: Paulin, 1833. pp. 365; reprinted, Paris: Le Club Français du Livre, 1961. pp. 316. English trans., *The History of the Assassins, derived from Oriental Sources*, tr., Oswald Charles Wood. London: Smith and Elder, Cornhill, 1835. pp. [x] + 240; reprinted, Burt Franklin Research and Source Works Series, 311. New York: B. Franklin, 1968. pp. [x] + 240; reprinted, with an introduction by Swami Shraddhanand Sanyasi. Benares: Gyanmandal Press, 1926. pp. xxxviii + 304.
- Hammer-Purgstall, Giuseppe de (Joseph von). *Origine potenza e caduta degli Assassini*. Opera interessantissima attinta alle fonti orientali ed occidentali dal Barone Giuseppe de Hammer-Purgstall consiglice aulico, interprete per le lingue orientali. Prima traduzione Italiana di Samuele Romanini con moltissime aggiunte e speciale approvazione dell'autore. Tomo I. Padova: Tipografia Penada Editrice, 1838. pp. 90 + 80 + 72 + 79. This may be an Italian trans. of von Hammer's *Die Geschichte der Assassinen*.
- Hammer-Purgstall, Joseph von. "Sur les Druzes", *JA*, 3 série, 4 (1837), pp. 483–491.

- Hammer-Purgstall, Joseph von. "Inscription coufique de la mosquée de Hakim bi-Emrillah", *JA*, 3 série, 5 (1838), pp. 388–391.
- Hampikian, Nairy and Monica Cyran. "Recent Discoveries Concerning the Fatimid Palaces Uncovered during the Conservation Works on Parts of al-Ṣāliḥiyya Complex", in *EF*, pp. 649–663.
- Ḥamza, Muḥammad Ḥabīb. "Madīnat al-Mahdiyya: risāla taʾrīkhiyya", *Mujtamaʿ wa-ʿImrān*, 3 (1983), pp. 64–70.
- "Ḥamza b. ʿAlī", in *EI*, vol. 2, p. 255.
- "Ḥamza b. ʿAlī", in *HI*, p. 164.
- "Ḥamza b. ʿAlī", in *SEI*, p. 131.
- Haneberg, Daniel Bonifacius. "Ali Abulhasan Schadeli. Zur Geschichte der nordafrikanischen Fatimiden und Sufis", *ZDMG*, 7 (1853), pp. 13–27.
- Haneberg, Daniel B. "Ueber das Verhältniss von Ibn Gabirol zur der Encyklopädie der Ichwān uç çafa", *Sitzungsberichte der königlich bayerischen Akademie der Wissenschaften zu München*, 2 (1866), pp. 73–102; reprinted in *RIS*, vol. 1, pp. 333–362.
- Hanlon, Don. "The Plan of al-Qahira", *Journal of Urban Design*, 1 (1996), pp. 299–314.
- Hanrath, J.J. "De Ismailis in Oost-Afrika" [The Ismailis of East Africa], *Tijdschrift voor Economische en Sociale Geographie*, 48 (1957), pp. 263–264 (in Dutch).
- Hans, Raj Kumar. "The Legitimisation of the Aga Khan's Authority over the Khojas of Western India under Colonial Dispensation in the Nineteenth Century", *IC*, 71 (1997), pp. 19–35.
- Ḥaqīqat, ʿAbd al-Rafīʿ. "Nahḍathā-yi millī-yi Īrān: nahḍat-i Bāṭiniyān", *Armaghān*, 42, no. 6 (1352 Sh./1973), pp. 376–385.
- Ḥaqīqat, ʿAbd al-Rafīʿ. "Nahḍathā-yi millī-yi Īrān: faʿʿāliyat-i Bāṭiniyān dar Khurāsān", *Armaghān*, 42, no. 7 (1352 Sh./1973), pp. 448–458.
- Ḥaqīqat, ʿAbd al-Rafīʿ. "Nahḍathā-yi millī-yi Īrān: ahammiyyat-i siyāsī-yi firqa-yi Ismāʿīliyya", *Armaghān*, 44, nos. 8–9 (1354 Sh./1975), pp. 469–473.
- Ḥaqīqat, ʿAbd al-Rafīʿ. "Nahḍathā-yi millī-yi Īrān: ẓuhūr-i Nāṣir-i Khusraw shāʿir-i mutifakkir-i buzurg-i Īrānī", *Armaghān*, 44, no. 10 (1354 Sh./1975), pp. 567–576; also in *Talāsh*, 10, no. 48 (1354 Sh./1975), pp. 12–16.

- Ḥaqīqat, ʿAbd al-Rafīʿ. "Nahḍathā-yi millī-yi Īrān: tabʿīd-i Nāṣir-i Khusraw", *Armaghān*, 44, nos. 11–12 (1354 Sh./1976), pp. 629–639.
- Ḥaqīqat, ʿAbd al-Rafīʿ. "Kushtārhā-yi vaḥshatnāk-i Ismāʿīliyān", *Armaghān*, 45, nos. 7–8 (2535 [1355 Sh.] /1976), pp. 375–382.
- Ḥaqīqat, ʿAbd al-Rafīʿ. "Nahḍathā-yi millī-yi Īrān: gustarish-i nufūdh-i Ḥasan-i Ṣabbāḥ dar Īrān", *Armaghān*, 45, no. 3 (2535 [1355 Sh.] /1976), pp. 149–157.
- Ḥaqīqat, ʿAbd al-Rafīʿ. "Nahḍathā-yi millī-yi Īrān: Ḥasan-i Ṣabbāḥ rahbar-i inqilābī va purqudrat-i firqa-yi Ismāʿīliyya dar Īrān", *Armaghān*, 45, no. 1 (1355 Sh./1976), pp. 23–30.
- Ḥaqīqat, ʿAbd al-Rafīʿ. "Nahḍathā-yi millī-yi Īrān: iṭāʿat-i bī chūn va charā-yi fidāʾīyān az dāʿī", *Armaghān*, 45, no. 4 (2535 [1355 Sh.] /1976), pp. 204–211.
- Ḥaqīqat, ʿAbd al-Rafīʿ. "Nahḍathā-yi millī-yi Īrān: majara-yi kushta shudan-i Niẓām al-Mulk", *Armaghān*, 45, nos. 5–6 (2535 [1355 Sh.] /1976), pp. 272–278.
- Ḥaqīqat, ʿAbd al-Rafīʿ. "Nahḍathā-yi millī-yi Īrān: taskhīr-i Alamūt yā pāytakht-i rafīʿ-i Ḥasan-i Ṣabbāḥ", *Armaghān*, 45, no. 2 (2535 [1355 Sh.]/1976), pp. 71–76.
- Ḥaqīqat, ʿAbd al-Rafīʿ. "Nahḍathā-yi millī-yi Īrān: dawra-yi farmānravāʾī-yi Muḥammad pisar-i Buzurg-Umīd", *Armaghān*, 46, nos. 4–5(2536 [1356 Sh.] /1977), pp. 216–222.
- Ḥaqīqat, ʿAbd al-Rafīʿ. "Nahḍathā-yi millī-yi Īrān: farmānravāʾī-yi Ḥasan-i duvvum dāʿī va imām-i Ismāʿīliyān-i Īrān", *Armaghān*, 46, nos. 8–9 (2536 [1356 Sh.] /1977), pp. 427–437.
- Ḥaqīqat, ʿAbd al-Rafīʿ. "Nahḍathā-yi millī-yi Īrān: ikhtilāf-i Ismāʿīliyān-i Īrān va Bāvandiyān (Āl-i Bāvand)", *Armaghān*, 46, no. 3 (2536 [1356 Sh.]/1977), pp. 143–150.
- Ḥaqīqat, ʿAbd al-Rafīʿ. "Nahḍathā-yi millī-yi Īrān: irtibāṭ-i Ismāʿīliyān-i Shām bā Alamūt", *Armaghān*, 46, no. 10 (2536 [1356 Sh.]/1977), pp. 527–536.
- Ḥaqīqat, ʿAbd al-Rafīʿ. "Nahḍathā-yi millī-yi Īrān: barkhurd va muqābala-yi Ismāʿīliyān va Ghūriyān", *Armaghān*, 47, nos. 7–8 (1357 Sh./1978), pp. 369–378.
- al-Ḥarīr, Idrīs Ṣāliḥ. "al-Fāṭimiyyūn fī Tūnis, 296–362 H./909–973 A.D.: dirāsa ḥawla aṣlihim wa-siyāsatihim al-dākhiliyya wa'l-

khārijiyya", *Majallat al-Buḥūth al-Ta'rīkhiyya*, 10, no. 1 (1988), 74–94.

- Hartmann, Angelika. "Ismâ'îlitische Theologie bei sunnitischen 'Ulamâ' des Mittelalters?", in Ludwig Hagemann and Ernst Pulsfort, ed., *"Ihr alle aber seid Brüder". Festschrift für A. Th. Khoury zum 60. Geburtstag*. Würzburg: Echter; Altenberge: Telos-Verlag, 1990, pp. 190–206.
- Ḥasan, 'Alī Ḥasan. "al-Ghazw al-hilālī li'l-Maghrib asbābuhu wa-natā'ijuhu", *al-Majalla al-Ta'rīkhiyya al-Miṣriyya*, 24 (1977), pp. 103–153.
- Ḥasan, 'Alī Ibrāhīm. *Ta'rīkh Jawhar al-Ṣiqillī, qā'id al-Mu'izz li-Dīn Allāh al-Fāṭimī*. Cairo: al-Maktaba al-Tijāriyya, 1933. pp. 128; 2nd ed., Cairo: Dār al-Nahḍa al-Miṣriyya, 1963. pp. 152. Urdu trans., *Jawhar Ṣiqillī*, tr., Jūn Īliyā. Karachi: Ismailia Association [for] Pakistan, 1966. pp. 147.
- Ḥasan (Hassan), Ḥasan Ibrāhīm (1892–1968). *al-Fāṭimiyyūn fī Miṣr*. Cairo: al-Maṭba'a al-Amīriyya, 1932. pp. 367; 2nd ed., Cairo: Maktabat al-Nahḍa al-Miṣriyya, 1958; 3rd ed., as *Ta'rīkh al-dawla al-Fāṭimiyya fi'l-Maghrib wa-Miṣr wa-Sūriyā wa-bilād al-'Arab*. Cairo: Maktabat al-Nahḍa al-Miṣriyya, 1964. pp. 739.
- Ḥasan, Ḥasan Ibrāhīm. "Relations Between the Fâṭimids in North Africa and Egypt and the Umayyads in Spain during the 4th Century A.H. (10th Century A.D.)", *Majallat Kulliyyat al-Ādāb, Jāmi'at Fu'ād al-Awwal/Bulletin of the Faculty of Arts, Fouad I University*, 10 (1948), pp. 39–83.
- Ḥasan, Ḥasan Ibrāhīm. "The Fatimids and the Umayyads in the IV cent. of the Hijra (Xth cent. A.D.)", in *Actes du XXIe Congrès International des Orientalistes, Paris-23–31 juillet 1948*. Paris: Société Asiatique de Paris, 1949, pp. 284–285.
- Ḥasan, Ḥasan Ibrāhīm. "Contributions to the Study of Fāṭimid History in Egypt during the last 12 Years", *Majallat Kulliyyat al-Ādāb, Jāmi'at Fu'ād al-Awwal/Bulletin of the Faculty of Arts, Fouad I University*, 13 (1951), pp. 129–140.
- Ḥasan, Ḥasan Ibrāhīm and Ṭāhā Aḥmad Sharaf. *'Ubayd Allāh al-Mahdī: imām al-Shī'a al-Ismā'īliyya wa-mu'assis al-dawla al-Fāṭimiyya fī bilād al-Maghrib*. Cairo: Maktabat al-Nahḍa al-Miṣriyya, 1366/1947. pp. 367.
- Ḥasan, Ḥasan Ibrāhīm and Ṭāhā Aḥmad Sharaf. *al-Mu'izz li-Dīn*

Allāh: imām al-Shīʿa al-Ismāʿīliyya wa-muʾassis al-dawla al-Fāṭimiyya fī Miṣr. Cairo: Maktabat al-Nahḍa al-Miṣriyya, 1948. pp. 371; 2nd ed., Cairo: Maktabat al-Nahḍa al-Miṣriyya, 1963. pp. 341.

- Ḥasan, Muḥammad ʿAbd al-Ghanī. *Miṣr al-shāʿira fiʾl-ʿaṣr al-Fāṭimī*. Cairo: al-Majlis al-Aʿlā liʾl-Thaqāfa; al-Hayʾa al-Miṣriyya al-ʿĀmma liʾl-Kitāb, 1983. pp. 328.
- Ḥasan, Zakī Muḥammad. *Kunūz al-Fāṭimiyyīn*. Cairo: Dār al-Kutub al-Miṣriyya, 1356/1937. pp. 291 + 64 plates.
- "al-Ḥasan b. al-Ṣabbāḥ", in *EI*, vol. 2, p. 276.
- "al-Ḥasan b. al-Ṣabbāḥ", in *HI*, pp. 170–171.
- "al-Ḥasan b. al-Ṣabbāḥ", in *SEI*, pp. 136–137.
- al-Hāshimī, Muḥammad Yaḥyā. "al-ʿUlūm al-ṭabīʿiyya ʿinda Ikhwān al-Ṣafāʾ", *Majallat al-Majmaʿ al-ʿIlmī al-ʿArabī* (Damascus), 12 (1932), pp. 513–520; reprinted in *RIS*, vol. 2, pp. 182–189.
- "Haşşâsîn", in *IA*, vol. 5, pp. 355–357.
- Ḥatāmila, ʿAbd al-Karīm ʿAbduh. "Ṣalāḥ al-Dīn wa-mawqifuhu min al-qiwā al-munāwiʾa fī bilād al-Shām 570–589 H./1174–1193 M.", *al-Dāra*, 12 (1986), pp. 159–172,
- Hauziński, Jerzy. "On Alleged Attempts at Converting the Assassins to Christianity in the Light of William of Tyre's Account", *Folia Orientalia*, 15 (1974), pp. 229–246.
- Hauziński, Jerzy. "Fryderik II Hohenstauf i Asasyni. Malo znany epizod w relacji Muhammada al-Hamawi", *Ars Historica*, 71 (1976), pp. 229–239 (in Polish).
- Hauziński, Jerzy. *Muzulmańska sekta asasynów w europejskim piśmiennictwie wieków średnich* [Islamic Sect of the Assassins in the European Writings of Middle Ages]. Uniwersytet Im. Adama Mickiewicza w Poznaniu, Seria historia, 74. Poznan: Wydawnictwo Naukowe Uniwersytetu Im. Adama Mickiewicza w Poznaniu, 1978. pp. 184 (in Polish); English summary, pp. 180–184.
- Hauziński, Jerzy. "Zródla arabskie do dziejów asasynóow", *Studia Zrodlozaucze*, 24 (1979), pp. 157–166 (in Polish).
- al-Hawwary, Hasan Mohamed., "Trois minarets Fatimides à la frontière Nubienne", *BIE*, 17 (1934–35), pp. 141–153.
- al-Hayyārī, Muṣṭafā. *al-Quds fī zamān al-Fāṭimiyyīn waʾl-Faranja*. Amman: Maktabat ʿAmmān, 1994. pp. 208.

- Heijer, Johannes den. "Apologetic Elements in Coptic-Arabic Historiography: The Life of Afrahām ibn Zurʿah, 62nd Patriarch of Alexandria", in Samir Khalil Samir and Jorgen S. Nielsen, ed., *Christian Arabic Apologetics during the Abbasid Period (750–1258)*. Studies in the History of Religions, 63. Leiden: E.J. Brill, 1994, pp. 192–202.
- Heijer, Johannes den. "Coptic Historiography in the Fāṭimid, Ayyūbid and Early Mamlūk Periods", *Medieval Encounters*, 2 (1996), pp. 67–98.
- Heijer, Johannes den. "Considérations sur les communautés chrétiennes en Égypte Fatimide: l'État et l'Église sous le vizirat de Badr al-Jamālī (1074–1094)", in *EF*, pp. 569–578.
- Heinen, Anton M. "The Notion of Taʾwīl in Abū Yaʿqūb al-Sijistānī's Book of the Sources: (*Kitāb al-Yanābīʿ*)", *Hamdard Islamicus*, 2 (1979), pp. 35–45.
- Heller Wilensky, S.O. "The 'First Created Being' in Early Kabbalah: Philosophical and Ismailian Sources", in Joseph Dan, ed., *Jewish Intellectual History in the Middle Ages*. Binah, 3. West Port, CT; London: Praeger, 1994, pp. 65–77.
- Hellmann, Gustav. *Denkmäler Mittelalterlicher Meteorologie. Ichwân eṣ Ṣafâ. Meteorologie der "Lauteren Brüder" (X. Jahrhundert)*. Neudrucke von Schriften und Karten über Meteorologie und Erdmagnetismus, 15. Berlin: A. Asher, 1904, pp. 23–41; reprinted in *RIS*, vol. 2, pp. 99–121.
- Hellmuth, Leopold. *Die Assassinenlegende in der österreichischen Geschichtsdichtung des Mittelalters*. Archiv für österreichische Geschichte, Band 134. Vienna: Österreichische Akademie der Wissenschaften, 1988. pp. 182.
- d'Herbelot de Molainville, Barthélemy (1625–1695). "Bathania", "Carmath", "Fathemiah", "Ismaélioun", "Molhedoun", in his *Bibliothèque orientale, ou Dictionnaire universel, contenant généralement tout ce qui regarde la connoissance des peuples de l'Orient*. Paris: Compagnie des Libraires, 1697; reprinted, Maestricht: J.E. Dufour & Ph. Roux, 1776, with later editions.
- Hermosilla, María José. "Asesino", in *Diccionario Enciclopedico Salvat Universal*. Barcelona, Madrid, etc.: Salvat Editores, 1975, vol. 3, p. 214.
- Hermosilla (Llisterri), María José "Siete tipos humanos (según los Ijwān al-Ṣafāʾ)", *Anuario de Filología*, 10 (1984), pp. 109–126.

- Hervás Jávega, Isabel. "Los Ismāʿīliyyūn Nizāriyyūn Sirios: un epilogo a su historia", in Aly Tawfik, Mohamed Essawy and J.M. Carabaza Bravo, ed., *El saber en al-Andalus: textos y studios*, II. Serie literatura, 38. Seville: Universidad de Sevilla & Fundación El Monte, 1999, pp. 239–256.
- Herz-Pacha, Max. "Boiseries Fatimites aux sculptures figurales", *Orientalisches Archiv*, 3 (1912–13), pp. 169–174.
- Hichi (Hishshī), Selim Hassan (Salīm Ḥasan). *al-Ismāʿīliyyūn ʿabra al-taʾrīkh*. Beirut: n.p., 1969. pp. 189.
- Hichi, Selim Hassan. *La communauté des Ismaʿilites de l'époque des Mamaliques à nos jours*. Beirut: n. p., 1972. pp. 111.
- Hichi, Selim H. *La communauté Druze, son Origine et son histoire*. Beirut: Imprimerie Numnon, 1973. pp. 79.
- Hichi, Selim H. *La lutte des Ismaʿilites (Assassins) à l'époque de Saladin*. Beirut: Direction Générale des Antiquités, Section des Études Historiques, 1974. pp. 157.
- Hichi, Selim H. *Fi'l-Ismāʿīliyya*. 2nd ed., Beirut: Maṭbaʿat Namnam, 1975. pp. 168.
- Hichi, Selim H. *Fi'l-Ismāʿīliyyūn wa'l-Durūz*. al-Khazāna al-taʾrīkhiyya, 5. 2nd ed., Beirut: Dār Laḥd Khāṭir, 1985. pp. 162.
- Ḥijāb, Muḥammad Farīd. *al-Falsafa al-siyāsiyya ʿinda Ikhwān al-Ṣafāʾ*. Cairo: al-Hayʾa al-Miṣriyya al-ʿĀmma li'l-Kitāb, 1982. pp. 494.
- Hillenbrand, Carole. "Islamic Orthodoxy or Realpolitik? Al-Ghazālī's Views on Government", *Iran, Journal of the British Institute of Persian Studies*, 26 (1988), pp. 81–94.
- Hillenbrand, Carole. "1092: A Murderous Year", in Alexander Fodor, ed., *Proceedings of the 14th Congress of the Union Européenne des Arabisants et Islamisants*; being, *The Arabist, Budapest Studies in Arabic*, 15–16 (1995), pp. 281–296.
- Hillenbrand, Carole. "The Power Struggle Between the Saljuqs and the Ismaʿilis of Alamūt, 487–518/1094–1124: The Saljuq Perspective", in *MIHT*, pp. 205–220. Arabic trans., "Ṣirāʿ al-sulṭa bayna al-Salājiqa wa-Ismāʿīliyyat Alamūt, 487–518/1094–1124: manẓūr Saljūqī", in *IAW*, pp. 211–227. Persian trans., "Jang-i qudrat miyān-i Saljūqiyān va Ismāʿīliyān-i Alamūt, 487–518/1094–1124: az chashmandāz-i Saljūqiyān", in *TAI*, pp. 254–274.

- Hirschberg, H.Z. (J.W.). "The Druzes", in Arthur J. Arberry, ed., *Religion in the Middle East: Three Religions in Concord and Conflict*. Cambridge: Cambridge University Press, 1969, vol. 2, pp. 330–348, 685.
- Hirschfeld, Yizhar, Oren Gutfeld, Elias Khamis and Roni Amir. "A Hoard of Fatimid Bronze Vessels from Tiberias", *al-ʿUṣūr al-Wusṭā*, 12 (2000), pp. 1–7, 27.
- Hitti, Philip Khuri (1886–1978). *The Origins of the Druze People and Religion, with Extracts from their Sacred Writings*. Columbia University Oriental Studies, XXVIII. New York: Columbia University Press, 1928. pp. viii + 80; reprinted, New York: AMS Press, 1966. pp. viii+80.
- Hizmetli, Sabri. "Karmatîler", in *IA*2, vol. 25, pp. 510–514.
- Hodgson, Marshall Goodwin Simms (1922–1968). "How Did the Early Shîʿa Become Sectarian?", *JAOS*, 75 (1955), pp. 1–13; reprinted in Etan Kohlberg, ed., *Shīʿism*. The Formation of the Classical Islamic World, 33. Aldershot: Ashgate, 2003, pp. 3–15.
- Hodgson, Marshall G.S. *The Order of Assassins: The Struggle of the Early Nizārī Ismāʿīlīs against the Islamic World*. The Hague: Mouton, 1955. pp. xi + 352; reprinted, New York: AMS Press, 1980. pp. xi + 352. Persian trans., *Firqa-yi Ismāʿīliyya*, tr., Farīdūn Badraʾī. Tabrīz: Kitābfurūshī-yi Tehran, 1343 Sh./1964. pp. xiv + 612; 2nd ed., Tehran: Sāzimān-i Intishārāt va Āmūzish-i Inqilāb-i Islāmī, 1369 Sh./1990. pp. xxxix + 461. A major part of this book was written in 1949–51 as a doctoral thesis submitted to the University of Chicago.
- Hodgson, Marshall G.S. "Al-Darazī and Ḥamza in the Origin of the Druze Religion", *JAOS*, 82 (1962), pp. 5–20.
- Hodgson, Marshall G.S. "The Ismāʿīlī State", in *The Cambridge History of Iran:* Volume 5, *The Saljuq and Mongol Periods*, ed., John A. Boyle. Cambridge: Cambridge University Press, 1968, pp. 422–482, 695. Persian trans., "Dawlat-i Ismāʿīliyya", tr., Yaʿqūb Āzhand, in B. Lewis et al., *Ismāʿīliyān dar taʾrīkh*, pp. 255–340. Persian trans., "Dawlat-i Ismāʿīlī", in *Taʾrīkh-i Īrān-i Kīmbirīj: az āmadan-i Saljūqiyān tā furūpāshī-yi dawlat-i Īlkhāniyān (jild-i panjum)*, ed., John A. Boyle, tr., Ḥasan Anūsha. Tehran: Amīr Kabīr, 1366 Sh./1987, pp. 397–453.
- Hodgson, Marshall G.S. "Ismaʿili Piety: Esotericism and Hierarchy", in S. Hossein Nasr et al., ed., *Shiʿism: Doctrines, Thought and Spirituality*. Albany, NY: State University of New York Press, 1988, pp. 88–91. Originally published in M.G.S. Hodgson, *The Venture of Islam: Conscience*

and History in a World Civilization. Chicago: University of Chicago Press, 1974, vol.1, pp. 378–381.

- Hodgson, Marshall G.S. "Alamūt: (II)The Dynasty", "Bāṭiniyya", "Buzurg-Ummīd, Kiyā", "Dā'ī", "al-Darazī", "Durūz", "Ḥasan-i Ṣabbāḥ", "Ḥudjdja: In Shī'ī Terminology", in *EI2*.
- Hoffmann, Eva R. "A Fatimid Book Cover: Framing and Re-framing Cultural Identity in the Medieval Mediterranean World", in *EF*, pp. 403–419.
- Hoffmann, Gerhard. "An Ismā'īlī/Fatimid Stronghold in Iraq? The Case of al-Basāsīrī", in Frederick de Jong, ed., *Shī'a Islam, Sects and Sufism: Historical Dimensions, Religious Practice and Methodological Considerations.* Utrecht: M. Th. Houtsma Stichting, 1992, pp. 26–34.
- Hoffmann, Gerhard. "Al-Maqrīzī als militärhistorische Quelle für die Fatimidenära", in *Ibn an-Nadim und die mittelalterliche arabische Literatur.* Beiträge zum 1. Johann Wilhelm Fück-Kolloquium (Halle 1987). Wiesbaden: O. Harrassowitz, 1996, pp. 96–102.
- Hollenberg, David. "Disrobing Judges with Veiled Truths: An Early Ismā'īlī Torah Interpretation (*ta'wīl*) in Service of the Fāṭimid Mission", *Religion*, 33 (2003), pp. 127–145.
- Hollister, John Norman. *The Shi'a of India.* Luzac's Oriental Religion Series, VIII. London: Luzac, 1953. pp. xiv + 440; reprinted, New Delhi: Oriental Books Reprint Corporation, 1979. pp. xiv + 440. Persian trans., *Tashayyu' dar Hind*, tr., Ādharmīdukht Mashāyikh Farīdanī. Tehran: Markaz-i Nashr-i Dānishgāhī, 1373 Sh./1994. pp. 539.
- Holt, Peter M. "al-Darazī", in *EI2*, vol. 2, pp. 136–137.
- Holzwarth, Wolfgang. *Die Ismailiten in Nordpakistan. Zur Entwicklung einer religiösen Minderheit im Kontext neuer Aussenbeziehungen.* Ethnizität und Gesellschaft, Occasional Papers, 21. Berlin: Das arabische Buch, 1994. pp. 136.
- Honigmann, E. "Maṣyād", in *EI*, vol. 3, pp. 404–406.
- Hosain, M. Hidayet. "The Druzes, their Origin, Manners and Customs", in Jal Dastur Cursetji Pavry, ed., *Oriental Studies in Honour of Cursetji Erachji Pavry*. London: Oxford University Press, 1933, pp. 156–162.
- Hosain, M. Hidayat. "Conquest of Sholāpūr by Burhān Niẓām Shāh I (914–961 A.H., 1508–1553 A.D.) as Described by Shāh Ṭāhir", *JASB*, 3 series, 5 (1939), pp. 133–153.

- Hosain, M. Hidayat. "Shāh Ṭāhir of the Deccan", *New Indian Antiquary*, 2 (1939), pp. 460–473; reprinted in S.M. Katre and P.K. Gode, ed., *A Volume of Indian and Iranian Studies Presented to Sir E. Denison Ross*. Bombay: Karnatak Publishing House, 1939, pp. 147–160.
- Houdas, O. "Ismaéliens", in *La Grande Encyclopédie*. Paris: H. Lamirault, n.d., vol. 20, p. 1016.
- Hourcade, Bernard. "Alamūt", in *EIR*, vol. 1, pp. 797–801.
- Houssen, Dilavard. "Note sur la communauté des Khoja Shiites de Tananarive", *Archipel*, 17 (1979), pp. 71–79.
- Houtsma, Martinus Theodorus (1851–1943). "ʿAbd Allāh b. Maimūn", in *EI*, vol. 1, p. 26.
- Houtsma, M. Th. "ʿAbd Allāh b. Maimūn", in *HI*, pp. 2–3.
- Houtsma, M. Th. "ʿAbd Allāh b. Maimūn", in *SEI*, pp. 4–5.
- Houtum-Schindler, Albert (1868–1916). "Alamût, Ámût", *JRAS* (1909), pp. 162–164.
- Howard, E.I. *The Shia School of Islam and its Branches, especially that of the Imamee-Ismailies*. A Speech delivered by E.I. Howard in the Bombay High Court, in June, 1866. Bombay: Oriental Press, 1866. pp. 101. The author was one of the Counsels for defence in the "Aga Khan Case", 1866.
- Hrbek, Ivan. "Die Slawen im Dienste der Fāṭimiden", *Archiv Orientální*, 21 (1953), pp. 543–581.
- Huart, Clément (1854–1926). "La forteresse d'Alamut", *Mémoire de la Société de Linguistique de Paris*, 15 (1908–9), pp. 130–132.
- Huart, Clément. "Buzurgummīd", "Fidāʾī", "Ḥamdān Ḳarmaṭ", "Ismāʿīlīya", in *EI*.
- Huart, Clément. "Fidāʾī" (with M.G.S. Hodgson), in *EI2*, vol. 2, p. 882.
- Huart, Clément. "Fidāʾī", "Ḥamdān Ḳarmaṭ", in *HI*.
- Huart, Clément. "Fidāʾī", "Ḥamdān Ḳarmaṭ", in *SEI*.
- Hughes, Thomas Patrick (1838–1911). "Al-Fatimiyah", in *A Dictionary of Islam*. London: W.H. Allen & Co., 1885, pp. 125–127.
- Humāʾī, Jalāl al-Dīn. "Muqaddima-yi qadīm-i Akhlāq-i Nāṣirī", *Majalla-yi Dānishkada-yi Adabiyyāt, Dānishgāh-i Tehran*, 3, no. 3 (1335 Sh./1956), pp. 17–25.

- Ḥumaysh, Sālim. *Majnūn al-ḥukm: riwāya*. al-Silsila al-riwā'iyya. London: Riad El-Rayyes Books, 1990. pp. 271.
- Hungerford, Edward. "The Arabian Brother of Purity", *The Andover Review*, 12 (1889), pp. 490–506; reprinted in *RIS*, vol. 2, pp. 60–76.
- Hunsberger, Alice C. "Nasir Khusraw: Fatimid Intellectual", in Farhad Daftary, ed., *Intellectual Traditions in Islam*. London: I.B. Tauris in association with The Institute of Ismaili Studies, 2000, pp. 112–129. Arabic trans., "Nāṣir Khusraw: mufakkir Fāṭimī", in F. Daftary, ed., *al-Manāhij wa'l-a'rāf al-'aqlāniyya fi'l-Islām*, tr., Nāṣiḥ Mīrzā. Beirut and London: Dār al-Sāqī in association with The Institute of Ismaili Studies, 2004, pp. 175–198. Persian trans., "Nāṣir-i Khusraw: mutifakkir-i Fāṭimī" in F. Daftary, ed., *Sunnathā-yi 'aqlānī dar Islām*, tr., Farīdūn Badra'ī. Tehran: Farzān, 1380 Sh./2001, pp. 127–147. Tajik trans., in Cyrillic transcription, in F. Daftary, ed., *Sunnathoi aqloni dar Islom*, tr., Muso Dinorshoev. Dushanbe: Nodir, 2002, pp. 158–180.
- Hunsberger, Alice C. *Nasir Khusraw, The Ruby of Badakhshan: A Portrait of the Persian Poet, Traveller and Philosopher*. Ismaili Heritage Series, 4. London: I.B. Tauris in association with The Institute of Ismaili Studies, 2000. pp. xxiii + 292. Persian trans., *Nāṣir-i Khusraw, la'l-i Badakhshān: taṣvīrī az shā'ir, jahāngard va fīlsūf-i Īrānī*, tr., Farīdūn Badra'ī. Tehran: Farzān, 1380 Sh./2001. pp. 340. Tajik trans., in Cyrillic transcription, *Nosiri Khusrav, la'li Badakhshon*, tr. from the Persian trans. of F. Badra'ī by Noyobshoi Zurobek. Dushanbe: Nodir, 2003. pp. 328.
- Hunt, Lucy-Anne. "Churchs of Old Cairo and Mosques of al-Qāhira: A Case of Christian-Muslim Interchange", *Medieval Encounters*, 2 (1996), pp. 43–66.
- Hunzai, Fakquir Muhammad. "Famous Ismaili Poet and Intellect Rodaki", in *GIH*, pp. 4–5.
- Hunzai, Fakquir Muhammad. "Hakim Nizari Birjindi Kohistani", in *GIH*, pp. 81–82.
- Hunzai, Fakquir Muhammad. "Hazrat Abu Yaqub as-Sijistani", in *GIH*, pp. 10–13.
- Hunzai, Fakquir Muhammad. "Sayyidna Abu Hatim ar-Razi", in *GIH*, pp. 8–9.
- Ḥusayn, 'Āshiq and Muḥammad Shākir. *'Ahd-i Fāṭimī min 'ilm va adab*. Bombay: D.B. Book Depot, [1950]. pp. 207 (in Urdu).

- Ḥusayn, Muḥammad Kāmil (1901–1961). "Ismaili Ideas in the Egyptian Poetry of the Fatimid Period", in *Actes du XXIe Congrès International des Orientalistes, Paris-23–31 juillet 1948*. Paris: Société Asiatique de Paris, 1949, pp. 294–295.
- Ḥusayn, Muḥammad Kāmil. *Fī adab Miṣr al-Fāṭimiyya*. al-Alf kitāb, 455. Cairo: Dār al-Fikr al-ʿArabī, [1950]. pp. 381.
- Ḥusayn, Muḥammad Kāmil. "Theory of 'Matter' and 'Spirit' and its Influence on the Egyptian Poetry of the Fatimide Period, tr., Jawad Masqati", *IC*, 24 (1950), pp. 108–116.
- Ḥusayn, Muḥammad Kāmil. *al-Ḥayāt al-fikriyya wa'l-adabiyya bi-Miṣr mina al-fatḥ al-ʿArabī ḥattā ākhir al-dawla al-Fāṭimiyya*. al-Alf kitāb, 244. Cairo: Maktabat al-Nahḍa al-Miṣriyya, 1959. pp. 243.
- Ḥusayn, Muḥammad Kāmil. *Ṭāʾifat al-Ismāʿīliyya, taʾrīkhuhā, nuẓumuhā, ʿaqāʾiduhā*. al-Maktaba al-taʾrīkhiyya, 4. Cairo: Maktabat al-Nahḍa al-Miṣriyya, 1959. pp. 190.
- Ḥusayn, Muḥammad Kāmil. *Ṭāʾifat al-Durūz, taʾrīkhuhā wa-ʿaqāʾiduhā*. Maktabat al-dirāsāt al-taʾrīkhiyya. Cairo: Dār al-Maʿārif, 1962. pp. 130.
- Ḥusaynī Isfīd Vajānī, Mahdī. "Āqā Khān va Ismāʿīliyya-yi Badakhshān va Tājikistān", *Muṭālaʿāt-i Āsiyā-yi Markazī va Qafqāz*, 5 (1373 Sh./1994), pp. 49–67.
- Ḥusaynī Ṭabāṭabāʾī, Sayyid Muṣṭafā. "Henry Corbin va bāṭinīgarī", *Taḥqīqāt-i Islāmī*, 9, nos. 1–2 (1373 Sh./1994), pp. 35–43.
- Hussein, Mahmoud Ibrahim. *Die Vergnügungen des Hofes und Alltagsleben: Eine ikonographische Untersuchung der Darstellungen in der Malerei der Fatimidenzeit und deren Wirkung auf die nachfolgenden Epochen in Ägypten*. Schriften zur Literatur, Kunst und Sozialgeschichte, 1. Berlin: Edition Orient, n. d. pp. 343 + plates.
- Hutt, Antony. "Ajdabiyah and the Development of Early Fatimid Architecture", *Azure*, 7 (1980), pp. 6–9.

I

- Ibn ʿĪsā, ʿAbd Allāh Ṣāliḥ. "al-Maktabāt al-Islāmiyya fī Miṣr fi'l-ʿaṣr al-Fāṭimī", *ʿĀlam al-Kutub*, 6 (1985), pp. 504–507.
- Ibn Mīlād, Maḥjūb. "Ishām al-Fāṭimiyyīn fi'l-falsafa al-Ismāʿīliyya", in *Abḥāth al-nadwa al-dawliyya li-taʾrīkh al-Qāhira*. Cairo: Wizārat al-

Thaqāfa wa'l-I'lām, 1971, vol. 3, pp. 889–904.

- Ibrāhīm, ʿAfīfī Maḥmūd. "al-ʿAlāqāt al-siyāsiyya wa'l-madhhabiyya bayna Banī Zīrī wa'l-khulafā' al-Fāṭimiyyīn fī Miṣr (362–443H)", in *Dirāsāt fī ta'rīkh bilād al-Maghrib*. Cairo: Dār al-Thaqāfa, 1986, pp. 1–32.
- Ibrāhīm, Sunūsī Yūsuf. *Zanāta wa'l-khilāfa al-Fāṭimiyya*. Qabā'il al-Maghrib, 1. Cairo: Maktabat Saʿīd Ra'fat, 1986. pp. 342.
- Ibrāhīmī Dinānī, Ghulām Ḥusayn. "Naqd va barrasī-yi barkhī az āthār va naẓariyāt-i Ḥamīd al-Dīn Kirmānī", in *Yādnāma-yi ʿAllāma Ṭabāṭabā'ī*. Tehran: Mu'assasa-yi Muṭālaʿāt va Taḥqīqāt-i Farhangī, 1362 Sh./1983, pp. 341–370.
- Idhkā'ī, Parvīz. "Nukātī chand az tafsīr-i Shahrastānī", *Maʿārif*, 5, no. 3 (1367 Sh./1989), pp. 405–414.
- Idhkā'ī, Parvīz. "Ḥakīm Rāzī va Nāṣir-i Khusraw", *NP*, 8, no. 2 (1382 Sh./2003), pp. 27–48.
- Idris, Hady Roger (1912–1978). "Contribution à l'histoire de l'Ifriḳiya. Tableau de la vie intellectuelle et administrative à Kairouan sous les Aġlabites et les Fatimites", *REI*, 9 (1935), pp. 105–178, 273–305; 10 (1936), pp. 45–104.
- Idris, Hady R. "Sur le retour des Zîrîdes à l'obédience Fâṭimide", *AIEO*, 11 (1953), pp. 25–39.
- Idris, Hady R. "Une des phases de la lutte du Mālikisme contre le Šiʿisme sous les Zirides (XIe siècle): al-Tūnisī, juriste Kairouanais et sa célèbre fatwa sur les Šīʿites", CT, 4 (1956), pp. 508–517.
- Idris, Hady R. "Contribution à l'histoire de la vie religieuse en Ifrīqiya Zīrīde (Xème-XIème siècles)", in *Mélanges Louis Massignon*. Publiés sous le patronage de l'Institut d'Études Islamiques de l'Université de Paris et de l'Institut Français de Damas. Damascus: Institut Français de Damas, 1957, vol. 2, pp. 327–359.
- Idris, Hady R. "Problématique de l'épopée Ṣanhādjienne en Berbérie Orientale (X–XIIe siècles)", *AIEO*, 17 (1959), pp. 243–255.
- Idris, Hady R. "Commerce maritime et ḳirāḍ en Berbérie Orientale d'après un recueil inédit de fatwās médiévales", *JESHO*, 4 (1961), pp. 225–239.
- Idris, Hady R. *La Berbérie orientale sous les Zīrīdes, X[e]–XIIe siècles*. Publications de l'Institut d'Études Orientales, Faculté des Lettres et

Sciences Humains d'Alger, XXII. Paris: A. Maisonneuve, 1962. 2 vols.

- Idris, Hady R. "Glanes sur les Zīrides d'Ifrīqiya dans le manuscrit d'Istanbul de l'*Itti'āẓ al-Ḥunafā*", *Arabica*, 11 (1964), pp. 286–305.
- Idris, Hady R. "De la réalité de la catastrophe Hilâlienne", *Annales: Économies, Sociétés, Civilisations*, 23 (1968), pp. 390–396.
- Idris, Hady R. "L'invasion Hilālienne et ses conséquences", *Cahiers de Civilisation Médiévale*, 11 (1968), pp. 353–369.
- Idris, Hady R. "D'al-Dabbāġ, hagiographe et chroniqueur Kairouanais de XIIIe siècle et de son jugement sur les Fāṭimides", *BEO*, 29 (1977), pp. 243–249.
- Idris, Hady R. "Buluggīn b. Zīrī", "Hilāl", in *EI2*.
- Idrīs, Muḥammad Maḥmūd. *Ta'rıkh al-ḥaḍāra al-Islāmiyyu fī Miṣr: al-'aṣr al-Fāṭimī*. Cairo: Maktabat Nahḍat al-Sharq, [1986]. pp. 328.
- Ilhāmī, Dāvūd. "Paydāyish-i Shī'a-yi Ismā'īliyya", *Kalām-i Islām*, 4 (1374 Sh./1995), pp. 46–52.
- Ilhāmī, Dāvūd. "Ismā'īliyān dar pusht-i parda-yi istitār va ikhtifā", *Kalām-i Islām*, 5 (1375 Sh./1996), pp. 34–44.
- Ilhāmī, Dāvūd. "Naẓarī kullī bi bāvarhā-yi Ismā'īliyān", *Kalām-i Islāmī*, 5 (1375 Sh./1996), pp. 44–53.
- Ilhāmī, Dāvūd. "Taḥqīqī jāmi' dar bāra-yi Maymūn-i Qaddāḥ va pisarash 'Abd Allāh", *Kalām-i Islāmī*, 5 (1375 Sh./1996), pp. 37–44.
- Ilhāmī, Dāvūd. "Nizāriyya va Musta'liyya", *Kalām-i Islāmī*, 6 (1376 Sh./1997), pp. 94–105.
- Ilhāmī, Dāvūd. "Ta'sīs-i dawlat-i Fāṭimī dar Miṣr", *Kalām-i Islāmī*, 6 (1376 Sh./1997), pp. 51–63.
- Ilhan, Avni. "Bâtiniyye", "Ebû Ya'kûb es-Sicistânî", "Fedâihu'l-Bâtiniyye", "Keşfü Esrâri'l-Bâtiniyye", in *IA2*.
- al-Imad, Leila Sami. *The Fatimid Vizierate, 969–1172*. Islamkundliche Untersuchungen, Band 133. Berlin: K. Schwarz, 1990. pp. vii + 229.
- al-Imad, Leila S. "Women and Religion in the Fatimid Caliphate: The Case of al-Sayyidah al-Hurrah, Queen of Yemen", in Michel M. Mazzaoui and Vera B. Moreen, ed., *Intellectual Studies on Islam: Essays Written in Honor of Martin B. Dickson*. Salt Lake City: University of Utah Press, 1990, pp. 137–144.
- 'Imādī, 'Abd al-Raḥmān. "'Aqā'id-i nujūmī dar āthār-i Nāṣir-i

Khusraw", in *YNK*, pp. 383–398.

- ʿImādī, ʿAbd al-Raḥmān. "Asāsīn va Ismāʿīliyān", *Ayandeh*, 5 (1358 Sh./1979), pp. 280–290; 6 (1359 Sh./1980), pp. 41–47.
- ʿImādī Ḥāʾirī, Sayyid Muḥammad. "Firqa-yi Nāṣiriyya", *Maʿārif*, 20 (1382 Sh./2003), pp. 58–73; also in *NP*, 8, no. 2 (1382 Sh./2003), pp. 190–206.
- Imāmī, Naṣr Allāh. "Tawṣīfhā-yi hunarī-yi Nāṣir-i Khusraw dar Safar-nāma", *Majalla-yi Dānishkada-yi Adabiyyāt va ʿUlūm-i Insānī, Dānishgāh-i Firdawsī* (Mashhad), 25, no. 3 (1371 Sh./1992), pp. 603–631.
- Imamuddin, S.M. "Commercial Relations of Spain with Ifriqiyah and Egypt in the Tenth Century A.C.", *IC*, 38 (1964), pp. 9–14.
- Imamuddin, S.M. "Administration under the Fatimids", *Journal of the Asiatic Society of Pakistan*, 14 (1969), pp. 253–269.
- Imamuddin, S.M. "Diwan al-Inshā (Chancery in later Medieval Egypt) with Special Reference to later Fatimid, Ayyubid and Mamluk Decrees dated 528–894 H./1134–1489 A.C.", *Journal of the Pakistan Historical Society*, 28 (1980), pp. 63–77.
- Īmānī, ʿAlī Riḍā. "Taʾrīkh va andīsha-yi Durūziyya", in *IMM*, pp. 537–595.
- ʿImāra, Muḥammad. *ʿIndamā aṣbaḥat Miṣr ʿArabiyya: dirāsa ʿan al-mujtamaʿ al-Miṣrī fiʾl-ʿaṣr al-Fāṭimī*. Beirut: al-Muʿassasa al-ʿArabiyya liʾl-Dirāsāt waʾl-Nashr, 1974. pp. 208.
- ʿInān, Muḥammad ʿAbd Allāh (b. 1896). *al-Ḥākim bi-Amr Allāh wa-asrār al-daʿwa al-Fāṭimiyya*. Cairo: Dār al-Nashr al-Ḥadīth, [1356/1937]. pp. 277; 2nd ed., Cairo: Maṭbaʿat Lajnat al-Taʾlīf waʾl-Tarjama waʾl-Nashr, 1379/1959. pp. 423.
- Inostrantsev, Konstantin Aleksandrovich (1876–1941). "Torzhestvennïy vïezd fatimidskikh khalifov" [Ceremonial Procession of the Fatimid Caliphs], *Zapiski Vostochnogo otdeleniya Imperatorskogo Russkogo Arkheologicheskogo obschestva* (St. Petersburg), 17 (1906), pp. 1–113.
- Institut du Monde Arabe, Paris. *Trésors Fatimides du Caire*. Exposition présentée à l'Institut du Monde Arabe du 28 avril au 30 août 1998. Paris: Institut du Monde Arabe, 1998. pp. 239.

- Iqbāl, Shaykh Muḥammad. *Sayyidnā Ḥasan bin Ṣabbāḥ*. Karachi: The Aga Khan Ismailia Association for Pakistan, 1972. pp. 64 (in Urdu).
- Iqbāl, Shaykh Muḥammad. "Abdul Malik Bin Attash", in *GIH*, pp. 56–57.
- Iqbāl, Shaykh Muḥammad. "Sayyidna Hasan Bin Sabbah", in *GIH*, pp. 63–66.
- Iqtidārī, Aḥmad. "Naẓarī bi safarhā-yi Nāṣir-i Khusraw dar junūb-i Īrān va savāḥil-i Khalīj-i Fārs", in *YNK*, pp. 71–79.
- Īrānbān, Nigīn. *Ḥasan-i Ṣabbāḥ va fidāʾīyān-i ū*. Tehran: Intishārāt-i ʿIlmī, 1376 Sh./1997. pp. 242.
- Islāmī Nadūshan, Muḥammad ʿAlī. "Payvand-i fikr va shiʿr dar nazd-i Nāṣir-i Khusraw", in *YNK*, pp. 31–58.
- "Ismaelita", in *Enciclopedia Universal Ilustrada Europeo-Americana*. Barcelona: Hijos de J. Espasa, 1926, vol. 28, pp. 2115–2116.
- Ismāʿīl, Maḥmūd. "al-Mālikiyya wa'l-Shīʿa bi-Ifrīqiya ibbāna qiyām al-dawla al-Fāṭimiyya", *al-Majalla al-Taʾrīkhiyya al-Miṣriyya*, 23 (1976), pp. 73–105.
- Ismāʿīl, Maḥmūd. *Ikhwān al-Ṣafāʾ: ruwwād al-tanwīr fi'l-fikr al-ʿArabī*. al-Manṣūra: ʿĀmir li'l-Ṭibāʿa wa'l-Nashr, 1996. pp. 148.
- "Ismāʿīlī", in *Diccionario Enciclopedico Salvat Universal*. Barcelona, Madrid, etc.: Salvat Editores, 1976, vol. 13, p. 336.
- "Ismāʿīlīte", in *The New Encyclopaedia Britannica*. 15th ed., Chicago, London, etc.: Encyclopaedia Britannica, 2002, vol. 6, p. 415.
- "Ismailiten", in *Brockhaus Enzyklopädie*. Mannheim: F.A. Brockhaus, 1989, vol. 10, p. 677.
- "Ismáiliten", in *Grote Winkler Prins Encyclopedie*. Amsterdam and Brussels: Elsevier, 1981, vol. 12, p. 123.
- "Ismailiti", in *Lessico Universale Italiano*. Rome: Istituto della Enciclopedia Italiana, 1972, vol. 10, p. 695.
- *Ismāʿīliyān dar taʾrīkh*, tr., Yaʿqūb Āzhand, *see* Lewis, Bernard et al., *Ismāʿīliyān dar taʾrīkh*
- Israeli, Raphael. "Is There Shiʿa in Chinese Islam?", *JIMMA*, 9 (1988), pp. 49–66.

  Ivanov, Vladimir Alekseevich, *see* Ivanow, Wladimir
- Ivanow (Ivanov), Wladimir (Vladimir) (1886–1970). "Ismailitskie

rukopisi Aziatskago Muzeya. Sobranie I. Zarubina, 1916 g." [Ismaili Manuscripts of the Asiatic Museum. I. Zarubin's Collection, 1916], *Izvestiya Rossiyskoy Akademii Nauk* (Petrograd)/*Bulletin de l'Académie Impériale des Sciences de Russie*, 6 série, 11 (1917), pp. 359–386. English summary, in E. Denison Ross, "W. Ivanow, Ismaili MSS in the Asiatic Museum, Petrograd 1917", *JRAS* (1919), pp. 429–435.

- Ivanow, Wladimir. "An Ismailitic Pedigree", *JASB*, NS, 18 (1922), pp. 403–406.
- Ivanow, Wladimir. *Ismailitica*, in *Memoirs of the Asiatic Society of Bengal*, 8 (1922), pp. 1–76.
- Ivanow, Wladimir. "Notes on the Ismailis in Persia", in his *Ismailitica*, pp. 50–76.
- Ivanow, Wladimir. "Imam Ismail", *JASB*, NS, 19 (1923), pp. 305–310.
- Ivanow, Wladimir. "Alamut", *Geographical Journal*, 77 (1931), pp. 38–45.
- Ivanow, Wladimir. "An Ismailitic Work by Nasiru'd-din Tusi", *JRAS* (1931), pp. 527–564.
- Ivanow, Wladimir. "An Ismaili Interpretation of the Gulshani Raz", *JBBRAS*, NS, 8 (1932), pp. 69–78.
- Ivanow, Wladimir. "Notes sur l'Ummu'l-kitab des Ismaëliens de l'Asie Centrale", *REI*, 6 (1932), pp. 419–481.
- Ivanow, Wladimir. *A Guide to Ismaili Literature*. Royal Asiatic Society, Prize Publication Fund, XIII. London: Royal Asiatic Society, 1933. pp. xii + 138.
- Ivanow, Wladimir. "The Sect of Imam Shah in Gujrat", *JBBRAS*, NS, 12 (1936), pp. 19–70.
- Ivanow, Wladimir. "Some Muhammadan Shrines in Western India", *Ismaili*, Golden Jubilee Number (21 January, 1936), pp. 16–23.
- Ivanow, Wladimir. "A Forgotten Branch of the Ismailis", *JRAS* (1938), pp. 57–79.
- Ivanow, Wladimir. "Some Ismaili Strongholds in Persia", *IC*, 12 (1938), pp. 383–396.
- Ivanow, Wladimir. "Tombs of Some Persian Ismaili Imams", *JBBRAS*, NS, 14, (1938), pp. 49–62.
- Ivanow, Wladimir. "The Organization of the Fatimid Propaganda", *JBBRAS*, NS, 15 (1939), pp. 1–35; reprinted in Bryan S. Turner, ed., *Ori-*

entalism: Early Sources, Volume I, *Readings in Orientalism*. London: Routledge, 2000, pp. 531–571.

- Ivanow, Wladimir. "Ismailis and Qarmatians", *JBBRAS*, NS, 16 (1940), pp. 43–85.
- Ivanow, Wladimir. "Early Shiʿite Movements", *JBBRAS*, NS, 17 (1941), pp. 1–23.
- Ivanow, Wladimir. *Ismaili Tradition Concerning the Rise of the Fatimids*. Islamic Research Association Series, 10. London, etc.: Published for the Islamic Research Association by H. Milford, Oxford University Press, 1942. pp. xxii + 337 (English) + 113 (Arabic).
- Ivanow, Wladimir. *The Alleged Founder of Ismailism*. Ismaili Society Series A, no. 1. Bombay: Published for the Ismaili Society by Thacker and Co., 1946. pp. xv + 197; 2nd revised edition as *Ibn al-Qaddah* (*The Alleged Founder of Ismailism*). Ismaili Society Series A, no. 9. Bombay: Ismaili Society, 1957. pp. 159.
- Ivanow, Wladimir (ed.), *Collectanea:* Vol. 1. Ismaili Society Series A, no. 2. Leiden: Published for the Ismaili Society by E.J. Brill, 1948. pp. xii + 242.
- Ivanow, Wladimir. *Nasir-i Khusraw and Ismailism*. Ismaili Society series B, no. 5. Bombay: Ismaili Society, 1948. pp. 78. Persian trans., *Nāṣir-i Khusraw va Ismāʿīliyān*, tr., Yaʿqūb Āzhand, in B. Lewis et al., *Ismāʿīliyān dar taʾrīkh*, pp. 403–463.
- Ivanow, Wladimir. "Satpanth", in Ivanow, ed., *Collectanea*: Vol. 1, pp. 1–54.
- Ivanow, Wladimir. *Studies in Early Persian Ismailism*. Ismaili Society Series A, no. 3. Leiden: Published for the Ismaili Society by E.J. Brill, 1948. pp. 202; 2nd ed., Ismaili Society Series A, no. 8. Bombay: Ismaili Society, 1955. pp. 157.
- Ivanow, Wladimir. "Noms bibliques dans la mythologie Ismaélienne", *JA*, 237 (1949), pp. 249–255.
- Ivanow, Wladimir. *Brief Survey of the Evolution of Ismailism*. Ismaili Society Series B, no. 7. Leiden: Published for the Ismaili Society by E.J. Brill, 1952. pp. 92.
- Ivanow, Wladimir. "Abū ʿAlī Sīnā va Ismāʿīliyān-i makhfī", in *Jashn-nāma-yi Ibn Sīnā/Le livre du millénaire d'Avicenne*, vol. 2. Anjuman-i Āthār-i Millī, Tehran, Silsila-yi intishārāt, 31. Tehran: Anjuman-i Āthār-i Millī, 1334 Sh./1955, pp. 450–454.

- Ivanow, Wladimir. "Shums Tabrez of Multan", in S.M. Abdullah, ed., *Professor Muḥammad Shafiʿ Presentation Volume*. Lahore: Majlis-e-Armughān-e-ʿIlmi, 1955, pp. 109–118.
- Ivanow, Wladimir. "Ismaili Mission in Indo-Pakistan", *Imamat*, 1, no. 2 (November, 1956), pp. 19–24.
- Ivanow, Wladimir. *The Ismaili Society of Bombay: The Tenth Anniversary (16–2–1946/16–2–1956)*. Bombay: Ismaili Printing Press, 1956. pp. 13.
- Ivanow, Wladimir. "Ismailis in Russia", *Imamat*, 1, no. 2 (November, 1956), pp. 39–41; reprinted in *Read and Know*, 1, no. 12 (1967), pp. 11–15.
- Ivanow, Wladimir. *Problems in Nasir-i Khusraw's Biography*. Ismaili Society Series B, no. 10. Bombay: Ismaili Society, 1956. pp. xiv + 88.
- Ivanow, Wladimir. "Study Ismailism", *Imamat*, 1, no. 3 (October, 1957), pp. 15–18; reprinted as "The Importance of Studying Ismailism", *Ilm*, 1, no. 3 (1975), pp. 8–9, 20, and as "Why Should we Study Ismailism", *Ismaili Bulletin*, 4, no. 9 (May, 1978), pp. 13–15.
- Ivanow, Wladimir. "Sufism and Ismailism: *Chiragh-nama*", *Majalla-yi Mardum-shināsī/Revue Iranienne d'Anthropologie*, 3 (1338 Sh./1959), pp. 13–17 (English summary), 53–70 (Persian text).
- Ivanow, Wladimir. *Alamut and Lamasar: Two Mediaeval Ismaili Strongholds in Iran – An Archaeological Study*. Ismaili Society Series C, no. 2. Tehran: Ismaili Society, 1960. pp. xiv + 105. Persian trans. of chapter four as "Nukātī taʾrīkhī dar bāra-yi Alamūt", tr., Masʿūd Rajab Niyā, in Riḍā Riḍāzāda Langarūdī, ed., *Yādigār-nāma: majmūʿa-yi taḥqīqī taqdīm shuda bi ustād Ibrāhīm Fakhrāʾī*. Tehran: Nashr-i Naw, 1363 Sh./1984, pp. 465–484.
- Ivanow, Wladimir. *Ismaili Literature: A Bibliographical Survey*. Ismaili Society Series A, no. 15. Tehran: Ismaili Society, 1963. pp. 245.
- Ivanow, Wladimir. "My First Meeting with Ismailis of Persia", *Read and Know*, 1 (1966), pp. 11–14; reprinted in *Ilm*, 3, no. 3 (December, 1977), pp. 16–17.
- Ivanow, Wladimir. "Hakim Nizari Kohistani", *African Ismaili*, 2, no. 7 (September, 1969), pp. 6–7.
- Ivanow, Wladimir. "Ismailism and Sufism", *Ismaili Bulletin*, 1, no. 12 (September, 1975), pp. 3–6.

- Ivanow, Wladimir. "al-ʿIrq al-mansī fi'l-Ismāʿīliyya", abridged and translated by ʿĀrif Tāmir, *al-Bāḥith*, 7, no. 1 (1985), pp. 75–81.
- Ivanow, Wladimir. "Rāshid al-Dīn Sinān", in *EI*, vol. 3, pp. 1123–1124.
- Ivanow, Wladimir. "Ismāʿīlīya", in *EI*, Supplement, pp. 98–102.
- Ivanow, Wladimir. "Bohoras", "Imām-Shāh", "Ismāʿīlīya", "Khodja", "Ṭāhir", in *HI*.
- Ivanow, Wladimir. "Bohoras", "Imām-Shāh", "Ismāʿīlīya", "Khodja", "Ṭāhir", in *SEI*.

  See also under Henry Corbin
- Ivry, Alfred L. "Ismāʿīlī Theology and Maimonides' Philosophy", in Daniel Frank, ed., *The Jews of Medieval Islam: Community, Society and Identity*. Études sur le Judaïsme Médiéval, XVI. Leiden: E.J. Brill, 1995, pp. 271–299.
- Īzadī, Ḥasan. "Nāṣir-i Khusraw va Ismāʿīliyya", *Kayhān-i Andīsha*, 43 (1371 Sh./1992), pp. 149–157.
- Īzadī, Ḥusayn. *Ḥasan-i Ṣabbāḥ*. Tehran: Muʾassasa-yi Kitāb-i Hamrāh, 1377 Sh./1998. pp. 74.

J

- Jād al-Rabb, Ibrāhīm al-Dasūqī. *Shāʿir al-dawla al-Fāṭimiyya, Tamīm ibn al-Muʿizz*. Cairo: Markaz al-Nashr li-Jāmiʿat al-Qāhira, 1991. pp. 250.
- Jaʿfarī Nadavī, Sayyid Raʾīs Aḥmad. *Taʾrīkh-i dawlat Fāṭimiyya*. Lahore: Idāra-i Thaqāfat Islāmiyya, 1965. pp. 530 + 32 plates (in Urdu).
- Jafferali (Haji), Zaibunisa. "Khaki Khorasani", in *GIH*, pp. 95–97.
- Jafri, Syed Husain M. *Origins and Early Development of Shīʿa Islam*. London and New York: Longman; Beirut: Librairie du Liban, 1979. pp. xii + 332.
- Jahānbakhsh, Jūyā. "Gudharī bar yak taʾrīkh-nāma-yi Ismāʿīlī", *Āyana-yi Pazhūhish*, 9 (1377 Sh./1998), pp. 47–49.
- Jakobsdottir, Gudrun S. "Nāṣir-i Khosro's beretning om Jerusalem i Safarnāmeh, Rejsedagbog", in Egon Kock et al., ed., *Living Waters: Scandinavian Orientalistic Studies Presented to Dr. Frede Løkkegaard*. Copenhagen: Museum Tusculanum Press, 1990, pp. 129–146 (in Danish).

- Jalāl, Ibrāhīm. *al-Muʿizz li-Dīn Allāh*. Aʿlām al-Islām, 4. [Cairo]: Dār Iḥyāʾ al-Kutub al-ʿArabiyya, ʿĪsā al-Bābī al-Ḥalabī wa-Shurakāʾuhu, 1944. pp. 126; 2nd ed., as *al-Muʿizz li-Dīn Allāh al-Fāṭimī wa-tashyīd madīnat al-Qāhira*. al-Alf kitāb, 483. Cairo: Dār al-Fikr al-ʿArabī, 1963. pp. 141.
- Jalālī Muqaddam, Masʿūd. "Abī Ḥātim Rāzī", "Ibn Ḥawshab", in *DMBI*.
- Jamal, Arif A. "Principles in the Development of Ismaili Law", *Yearbook of Islamic and Middle Eastern Law*, 7 (2002), pp. 115–126.
- Jamāl al-Dīn, ʿAbd Allāh Muḥammad. *al-Dawla al-Fāṭimiyya: qiyāmuhā bi-bilād al-Maghrib wa-intiqāluhā ilā Miṣr ilā nihāyat al-qarn al-rābiʿ al-hijrī maʿa ʿināya khāṣṣa biʾl-jaysh*. Cairo: Dār al-Thaqāfa, 1411/1991. pp. 307.
- Jamāl al-Dīn, Muḥammad al-Saʿīd. *Dawlat al-Ismāʿīliyya fī Īrān: baḥth fī taṭawwur al-daʿwa al-Ismāʿīliyya ilā qiyām al-dawla*. Cairo: Muʾassasat Sijill al-ʿArab, 1975. pp. 274; 2nd ed., Cairo: al-Dār al-Thaqāfiyya, 1999. pp. 236.
- Jamāl al-Dīn, Nādiya. *Falsafat al-tarbiya ʿinda Ikhwān al-Ṣafāʾ*. Cairo: al-Markaz al-ʿArabī liʾl-Ṣiḥāfa, 1983. pp. 445.
- Jambet, Christian. "Bibliographie générale", in Christian Jambet, ed., *Les cahiers de l'Herne: Henry Corbin*. Paris: Éditions de l'Herne, 1981, pp. 345–360.
- Jambet, Christian. "La grande résurrection d'Alamût d'après quelques textes Ismaéliens", in *Apocalypse et sens de l'histoire*. Paris: Berg International, 1983; being, *Cahiers de l'Université Saint Jean de Jerusalem*, 9 (1983), pp. 113–131.
- Jambet, Christian. "Le messianisme Ismaélien d'Alamût", *Mi-Dit*, 2, no. 4 (1985), pp. 92–101.
- Jambet, Christian. *La grande résurrection d'Alamût. Les formes de la liberté dans le Shîʿisme Ismaélien*. Lagrasse: Verdier, 1990. pp. 418.
- Jambet, Christian. "Aperçus philosophiques de la morale de Naṣir al-din Ṭusi dans les Taṣavvorât", in Christophe Balaÿ, Claire Kappler and ŽivaVesel, ed., *Pand-o Sokhan. Mélanges offerts à Charles-Henri de Fouchécour*. Bibliothèque Iranienne, 44. Tehran: Institut Français de Recherche en Iran, 1995, pp. 117–131.
- al-Janḥānī, al-Ḥabīb. "al-Ṣirāʿ al-Fāṭimī al-Umawī fiʾl-Maghrib khilāla al-qarn al-rābiʿ al-hijrī", *CT*, 26, nos. 103–104 (1978), pp. 17–32.

- al-Jārim, ʿAlī. *Sayyidat al-quṣūr: ākhir ayyām al-Fāṭimiyyīn bi-Miṣr.* Iqraʾ, 19. Cairo: Dār al-Maʿārif, 1955. pp. 152.
- Javān Ārāstah, Amīr. "Qāḍī Nuʿmān va madhhab-i ū", *Haft Āsmān*, 3 (1380 Sh./2001), pp. 47–82; reprinted in *IMM*, pp. 309–355.
- Jāvdān, Muḥammad. "Zindigī va andīshahā-yi Abū Ḥātim Rāzī", in *IMM*, pp. 357–399.
- Jaydar-Pūr, Farībā. "Ibn Mālik, Abū ʿAbd Allāh Muḥammad b. Mālik Ḥammādī Yamānī", in *DMBI*, vol. 4, pp. 572–573.
- Jenkins, Marilyn. "Muslim: An Early Fatimid Ceramist", *Bulletin of the Metropolitan Museum of Art*, NS, 26 (1968), pp. 359–369.
- Jenkins, Marilyn. "Western Influences on Fatimid Egyptian Iconography", *Kunst des Orients*, 10 (1975), pp. 91–107.
- Jenkins, Marilyn. "Fatimid Jewelry: Its Subtypes and Influences", *Ars Orientalia*, 18 (1988), pp. 39–57.
- Jenkins (-Madina), Marilyn. "Fatimid Decorative Arts: The Picture the Sources Paint", in *EF*, pp. 421–427.
- Jettmar, Karl von. "Die Ismaeliten Nordpakistans", *Indo-Asia*, 18 (1976), pp. 333–338.
- Jhaveri, Krishnalal Mohanlal. "A Legendary History of the Bohoras", *JBBRAS*, NS, 9 (1933), pp. 37–52 (contains English translation of an Arabic *Risāla* entitled *al-Tarjama al-zāhira li-firqat Buhrat al-bāhira*).
- Jiwa, Shainool. "The Initial Destination of the Fatimid Caliphate: The Yemen or the Maghrib?", *British Society for Middle Eastern Studies Bulletin*, 13 (1986), pp. 15–26.
- Jiwa, Shainool. "The Genesis of Ismāʿīlī Daʿwa Activities in the Yemen", *British Society for Middle Eastern Studies Bulletin*, 15 (1988), pp. 50–63.
- Jiwa, Shainool. "Fāṭimid-Būyid Diplomacy during the Reign of al-ʿAzīz Billāh (365/975–386/996)", *JIS*, 3 (1992), pp. 57–71.
- Johns, Jeremy. "Malik Ifrīqiyah: The Norman Kingdom of Africa and the Fāṭimids", *Libyan Studies*, 18 (1987), pp. 89–101.
- Johns, Jeremy. "The Norman Kings of Sicily and the Fatimid Caliphate", *Anglo-Norman Studies*, 15 (1993), pp. 133–159.
- Johns, Jeremy. "I re Normanni e i califfi Fāṭimiti: Nuove prospettive su vecchi materiali", in *Giornata di Studio del Nuovo sulla Sicilia Musulmana (Roma, 3 maggio 1993)*. Accademia Nazionale dei Lincei-Fon-

dazione Leone Caetani, 26. Rome: Accademia Nazionale dei Lincei, 1995, pp. 9–50.

- Jourdain, Am. "Lettre à M. Michaud sur les Assassins", in Joseph François Michaud (1767–1839), *Histoire des Croisades*. 4th ed., Paris: Ponthieu, 1825, vol. 2, pp. 549–577; reprinted in the enlarged new edition of this work prepared by M. Huillard Bréholles. Paris: Furne, Jouvet et Cie, 1849, vol. 1, pp. 472–488. English trans., "Letter to M. Michaud upon the Assassins", in J.F. Michaud, *Michaud's History of the Crusades*, tr., William Robson. London: G. Routledge, 1852, vol. 3, pp. 413–431.
- Jourdain, Am. "Haçan-ben-Sabbah", in *Biografia Universale antica e moderna ossia storia per alfabeto della vita pubblica e privata di tutte le persone che si distinsero per opere, azioni, talenti, virtù e delitti*. Venice: Gio.-Battista Missiaglia, 1826, vol. 27, pp. 241–244.
- "Judgement of the Honourable Sir Joseph Arnould in the Khojah Case, otherwise known as the Aga Khan Case, heard in the High Court of Bombay, during April and June 1866; Judgement delivered 12th November, 1866". Bombay, 1867; also in *Bombay High Court Reports*, 12 (1866), pp. 323–363. Summarized, in Abdus Salam Picklay, *History of the Ismailis*, pp. 113–170; also in Asaf A.A. Fyzee, *Cases in the Muhammadan Law of India and Pakistan*. Oxford: At the Clarendon Press, 1965, pp. 504–549; analyzed in Amrita Shodan, *A Question of Community: Religious Groups and Colonial Law*. Calcutta: Samya, 1999, pp. 82–116.

  See also under E.I. Howard
- "Judgement of the Honourable Mr. Justice Russell in the Aga Khan Case heard in the High Court of Bombay, from 3rd February to 7th August 1908; Judgement delivered 1st September 1908". Bombay: Times Press, 1908. pp. 139.
- al-Jundī, Salīm. "Abu'l-ʿAlāʾ al-Maʿarrī wa-Ikhwān al-Ṣafāʾ", *Majallat al-Majmaʿ al-ʿIlmī al-ʿArabī* (Damascus), 16 (1941), pp. 346–351; reprinted in *RIS*, vol. 2, pp. 205–210.
- Jungfleisch, Marcel. "Un poids Fatimite en plomb", *BIE*, 9 (1927), pp. 115–128.
- Jungfleisch, Marcel. "Poids Fatimites en verre polychrome", *BIE*, 10 (1929), pp. 19–31.
- Jungfleisch, Marcel. "Jetons (ou Poids?) en verre de l'Imam El

Montazer", *BIE*, 33 (1950–51), pp. 359–374.

- Justi, Ferdinand (1837–1907). *Iranisches Namenbuch*. Marburg: N.G. Elwert, 1895, p. 457; reprinted, Hildesheim: G. Olms, 1963, p. 457.

K

- Kabir, Mafizullah. "The Relation of the Bawayhids with the Fatimids", *Indo-Iranica*, 8 (1955), pp. 28–33.
- Kadende-Kaiser, R.M. and Paul J. Kaiser. "Identity, Citizenship, and Transnationalism: Ismailism in Tanzania and Burundians in the Diaspora", *Africa Today*, 45, nos. 3–4 (1998), pp. 461–480.
- Kahhāla, ʿUmar Riḍā. "al-Ḥurra bint Aḥmad b. Jaʿfar b. Mūsā al-Ṣulayḥiyya", in his *Aʿlām al-nisāʾ*. Beirut: Muʾassasat al-Risāla, 1977, vol. 1, pp. 253–254.
- Kahle, Paul Ernst (1875–1964). "Die Schätze der Fatimiden", *ZDMG*, NS, 14 (1935), pp. 329–362.
- Kahle, Paul E. *The Cairo Geniza*. London: Oxford University Press, 1947. pp. ix + 240.
- Kaiser, Paul J. *Culture, Transnationalism, and Civil Society: Aga Khan Social Service Initiative in Tanzania*. Westport, CT: Praeger, 1996. pp. xvi + 133.
- Kakar, Hassan Kawun. "Shighnan and Roshan in the Nineteenth Century", *Afghanistan*, 31, no. 1 (1978), pp. 43–48.
- Kamada, Shigeru. "The First Being: Intellect (*ʿaql/khiradh*) as the Link Between God's Command and Creation According to Abū Yaʿqūb al-Sijistānī", *The Memoirs of the Institute of Oriental Culture, University of Tokyo*, 106 (March, 1988), pp. 1–33.
- Kaplony, Andreas. "Die fatimidische 'Moschee der Wiege Jesu' in Jerusalem", *Zeitschrift des Deutschen Palästina-Vereins*, 113 (1997), pp. 123–132.
- Karam, J. "Las ideas filosóficas de los Hermanos de la Pureza (Ikhuan es-safa)", *La Ciencia Tomista*, 56 (1937), pp. 398–412; reprinted in *RIS*, vol. 2, pp. 190–204.
- Karamshoev, Dodikhudo. "Duʿāhā va fātaḥahā-yi mardum-i Badakhshān", *Nomai Pazhouhishgoh* (Dushanbe), 4 (2003), pp. 139–156.

- Karič, Enes. *Neki aspekti Enciklopedije Ihvanus-Safa*. Sarajevo: Islamski Teološki Fakultet Sarajevo, 1986. pp. 130 (in Serbo-Croatian).
- Karīmān, Ḥusayn. "Māzandarān va Nāṣir-i Khusraw", *Nomai Pazhouhishgoh* (Dushanbe), 4 (2003), pp. 107–116.
- Karīmī Zanjānī Aṣl, Muḥammad. "Ibn Sīnā va manṭiq-i al-Mashriqiyyīn: ḥikmat-i Mashriqī va khāstgāh-i Ismā'īlī-yi ān", *Miras Shahab: Journal of the Grand Library of Ayat Allah Marashi Najafi*, 7, nos. 3–4 (1380/2001), pp. 124–135.
- Karīmī Zanjānī Aṣl, Muḥammad. *Suhrawardī, ḥikmat-i Ishrāqī va pāsukh-i Ismā'īlī bi Ghazālī*. Tehran: Nashr-i Shahīd Sa'īd Muḥibbī, 1382 Sh./2003. pp. 240.
- "Karmaten", in *Brockhaus Enzyklopädie*. Mannheim: F.A. Brockhaus, 1990, vol. 11, p. 482.
- "Karmaten", in *Grote Winkler Prins Encyclopedie*. Amsterdam and Brussels: Elsevier, 1981, vo. 12, p. 517.
- "Karmatî'ler", in *Türk Ansiklopedisi*. Ankara: Millî Eğitim Basimevi, 1974, vol. 21, pp. 351–353.
- Kassam, Tazim Rahim. "Syncretism on the Model of the Figure-ground: A Study of Pīr Shams' Brahma Prakāśa", in Katherine K. Young, ed., *Hermeneutical Paths to the Sacred Worlds of India: Essays in Honour of Robert W. Stevenson*. Atlanta, GA: Scholars Press, 1994, pp. 231–242.
- Kassam, Tazim R. *Songs of Wisdom and Circles of Dance: Hymns of the Satpanth Ismā'īlī Muslim Saint, Pīr Shams*. McGill Studies in the History of Religions. Albany, NY: State University of New York Press, 1995. pp. xvi + 424.
- Kassim Ali, Muhammad. *Ever Living Guide*. Karachi: Ismailia Association [for] Pakistan, 1955. pp. viii + 52.
- Kay, Henry Cassels (1827–1903). "al Ḳāhirah and its Gates", *JRAS*, NS, 14 (1882), pp. 229–245.
- Kay, Henry C. "Inscriptions at Cairo and the Burju-ẓ Ẓafar", *JRAS*, NS, 18 (1886), pp. 82–88.
- Kay, Henry C. "'Omārah's History of Yemen", *JRAS* (1893), pp. 218–236.
- Kaya, Mahmut. "Dârülhikme", in *IA2*, vol. 8, pp. 67–69.
- Kāẓim Bigī, Muḥammad 'Alī. "Ibn 'Aṭṭāsh", "Ibn Killis", in *DMBI*.

- Kazimi, Masoom Raza. "Shah Tahir-ul-Hussaini", *Indo-Iranica*, 18 (1965), pp. 41–49.
- Kedar, Benjamin. "Mercanti genovesi in Alessandria d'Egitto negli anni sessanta del secolo XI", in *Miscellanea di studi storici II*. Collana storica di fonti e studi, 38. Genova: Università di Genova, Istituto di Medievistica, 1983, pp. 19–30.
- Kerlau, Yann. *Les Aga Khans*. Paris: Perrin, 1990. pp. 425.
- Kervran, Monique. "Une forteresse d'Azerbaidjan: Samīrān", *REI*, 41 (1973), pp. 71–93.
- Keshavjee, Habib V. *The Aga Khan and Africa: His Leadership and Inspiration*. Durban, South Africa: Designed and Printed by the Mercantile Printing Works, [1946]. pp. 200.
- Keshavjee, Rafique H. *Mysticism and the Plurality of Meaning: The Case of the Ismailis of Rural Iran*. The Institute of Ismaili Studies, Occasional Papers, 2. London: I.B. Tauris in association with The Institute of Ismaili Studies, 1998. pp. vii + 47.
- Khaḍḍūr, Ḥusām. *Ahamm al-qilāʿ al-Ismāʿīliyya fī Sūriyā*. Salamiyya: Dār al-Ghadīr, 2000. pp. 209.
- Khaḍḍūr, Ḥusām. *Lamasāt naqdiyya li-shuʿarāʾ Salamiyya*. Salamiyya: Dār al-Ghadīr, 2000. pp. 176.
- Khaḍḍūr, Ḥusām. *al-Madhhab al-Islāmī al-Shīʿī al-Ismāʿīlī: wijhat naẓar muʿāṣira*. Salamiyya: Dār al-Ghadīr, 2000. pp. 163.
- Khaḍḍūr, Ḥusām. *Ziyārat sumuww al-amīr Karīm Āghā Khān li-Sūriyā*. Salamiyya: Dār al-Ghadīr, 2002. pp. 55.
- Khakee, Gulshan. "Note on the Imām Shāhī Ms at the Deccan College, Poona", *JASB*, 45–46 (1970–71), pp. 143–155.
- Khakee, Gulshan. "The Dasa Avatara of Pir Shams as Linguistic and Literary Evidence of the Early Development of Ismailism in Sind", in Hamida Khuhro, ed., *Sind through the Centuries*. Karachi: Oxford University Press, 1981, pp. 143–155; summary in *Sind Quarterly*, 8 (1980), pp. 44–47.
- Khalʿatbarī, Allāhyār. "Ismāʿīliyān-i Nizārī dar taʾrīkh-i Īrān", *Majalla-yi Dānishkada-yi Adabiyyāt va ʿUlūm-i Insānī, Dānishgāh-i Shahīd Bihishtī*, nos. 1–2 (1369 Sh./1990), pp. 56–70.
- Khalʿatbarī, Allāhyār. "Ismāʿīliyān-i Quhistān", *Pazhūhishnāma-yi Dānishkada-yi Adabiyyāt va ʿUlūm-i Insānī, Dānishgāh-i Shahīd*

Bihishtī, nos. 3–4 (1370 Sh./1991), pp. 69–82.

- Khalʿatbarī, Allāhyār. "Ismāʿīliyān va Qazwīn", *Pazhūhishnāma-yi Dānishkada-yi Adabiyyāt va ʿUlūm-i Insānī, Dānishgāh-i Shahīd Bihishtī/Revue de la Faculté des Lettres et des Sciences Humaines, Université Chahid Beheshti*, 14 (1372 Sh./1993), pp. 80–109.
- Khalʿatbarī, Allāhyār. "Ismāʿīliyān-i Nizārī va shahr-i Rayy", *Pazhūhishnāma-yi Dānishkada-yi Adabiyyāt va ʿUlūm-i Insānī, Dānishgāh-i Shahīd Bihishtī/Revue de la Faculté des Lettres et des Sciences Humaines, Université Chahid Beheshti*, 19 (1375 Sh./1996), pp. 111–130.
- Khalīfa, ʿAbd al-Karīm. *Ikhwān al-Ṣafāʾ wa-Khullān al-Wafāʾ*. Aleppo: ʿAbd al-Wadūd al-Kayyālī wa-awlāduh, 1949. pp. 86.
- *al-Khalīfa al-Muʿizz li-Dīn Allāh bānī al-Qāhira wa-munshiʾ al-jāmiʿ al-Azhar mā kāna murtaddan wa-lā Naṣrāniyyan*. [Cairo]: n.p., [1931]. pp. 80.
- Khalil, J. and L. Ronzevalle. "L'épître à Constantin, traité religieux Druse", in *Mélanges de la Faculté Orientale, Université Saint-Joseph, Beyrouth*, 3 (1909), pp. 493–534.
- Khalīlī, Khalīl Allāh. "Mazār-i Nāṣir-i Khusraw", *Yaghmā*, 20, no. 9 (1346 Sh./1967), pp. 472–476.
- Khalīlī, Khalīl Allāh. "Yumgān va vathāʾiq-i taʾrīkhī dar bāra-yi Nāṣir-i Khusraw", *Yaghmā*, 20, no. 8 (1346 Sh./1967), pp. 438–442, 472–476; also in *Āriyānā*, 33, no. 2 (1354 Sh./1975), pp. 1–22.
- Khan, Ansar Zahid. "Ismaʿilism in Multan and Sind", *Journal of the Pakistan Historical Society*, 23 (1975), pp. 36–57.
- Khan, Dominique-Sila. "L'origine Ismaélienne du culte Hindou de Rāmdeo Pīr", *Revue de l'Histoire des Religions*, 210 (1993), pp. 27–47.
- Khan, Dominique-Sila. "Ramdeo Pir and the Kamaḍiya Panth", in N.K. Singhi and R. Joshi, ed., *Folk, Faith and Feudalism*. Rajasthan Studies. Jaipur and New Delhi: Rawat Publishers, 1995, pp. 295–327.
- Khan, Dominique-Sila. "The Kāmaḍ of Rajasthan – Priests of a Forgotten Tradition", *JRAS*, 3rd series, 6 (1996), pp. 29–56.
- Khan, Dominique-Sila. "The Coming of Nikalank Avatar: A Messianic Theme in Some Sectarian Traditions of North-western India", *Journal of Indian Philosophy*, 25 (1997), pp. 401–426.
- Khan, Dominique-Sila. *Conversions and Shifting Identities: Ramdev*

Pir and the Ismailis in Rajasthan, with a Foreword by Zawahir Moir. New Delhi: Manohar, 1997. pp. 294.

- Khan, Dominique-Sila. "La tradition de Rāmdev Pīr au Rajasthan: acculturation et syncrétisme", in Jackie Assayag and Gilles Tarabout, ed., *Altérité et identité, Islam et Christianisme en Inde/Alterity and Identity, Islam and Christianism in India*. Collection Puruṣārtha, 19. Paris: École des Hautes Études en Sciences Sociales, 1997, pp. 121–140.
- Khan, Dominique-Sila. "Conversations Between Guru Hasan Kabīruddīn and Jogī Kāniphā: Tantra Revisited by the Isma'ili Preachers", in David Gordon White, ed., *Tantra in Practice*. Princeton Readings in Religions. Princeton: Princeton University Press, 2000, pp. 285–295.
- Khan, Dominique-Sila. "Jāmbhā, fondateur de la secte des Biśnoï au Rajasthan: de l'Islam Ismaélien à la dévotion Hindoue", in Françoise Mallison, ed., *Contructions hagiographiques dans le monde Indien. Entre mythe et histoire*. Bibliothèque de l'École des Hautes Études, Sciences Historiques et Philologiques, 338. Paris: Librairie Honoré Champion, 2001, pp. 337–364.
- Khan, Dominique-Sila. "The Prannathis of Rajasthan: Bhakti and Irfan", in L.A. Babb et al., ed., *Multiple Histories: Culture and Society in the History of Rajasthan*. Jaipur and New Delhi: Rawat Publishers, 2002, pp. 209–231.
- Khan, Dominique-Sila. "The Tale of the Hidden Pir", International Institute for the Study of Islam in the Modern World, *ISIM Newsletter*, 11 (December, 2002), p. 26.
- Khan, Dominique-Sila. "Diverting the Ganges: The Nizari Ismaili Model of Conversion in South Asia", in R. Robinson and S. Clarkes, ed., *Religious Conversions in India*. Delhi: Oxford University Press, 2003, pp. 29–53.
- Khan, Dominique-Sila and Zawahir Moir. "Coexistence and Communalism, the Shrine of Pirana in Gujarat", *South Asia: Journal of South Asian Studies*, 22 (1999), pp. 133–154.
- Khan, Dominique-Sila and Zawahir Moir. "The Lord will Marry the Virgin Earth: Songs of the Time to Come", *Journal of Indian Philosophy*, 28 (2000), pp. 99–115.
- Khan, Geoffrey A. "The Arabic Fragments in the Cambridge Genizah Collections", *Manuscripts of the Middle East*, 1 (1986), pp. 54–60.

- Khan, Geoffrey A. "A Copy of a Decree from the Archives of the Fatimid Chancery in Egypt", *BSOAS*, 49 (1986), pp. 439–453.
- Khan, Geoffrey A. "A Petition to the Fāṭimid Caliph al-Āmir", *JRAS* (1990), pp. 44–54.
- Khan, Geoffrey A. *Arabic Legal and Administrative Documents in the Cambridge Genizah Collections*. Cambridge University Library Genizah Series, 10. Cambridge: Cambridge University Press, 1993. pp. xviii + 567.
- Khan, Mahmood Hasan and Shoaib Sultan Khan. *Rural Change in the Third World: Pakistan and the Aga Khan Rural Support Program*. Contributions in Economics and Economic History, 129. New York, etc.: Greenwood Press, 1992. pp. xiv + 179.
- Khan, Quadrat Allāh. *Fāṭimī khilāfat-i Miṣr*. Karachi: Khurshīd Akīdimī, 1962. pp. 320 (in Urdu).
- Khānlū, Manṣūr. *ʿUqāb-i safīd: pazhūhishī dar zindigī-yi Ḥasan-i Ṣabbāḥ va firqa-yi Ismāʿīliyya*. Tabrīz, Iran: Intishārāt-i Talāsh, 1363 Sh./1984. pp. 160.
- Khansa, Samīr Aḥmad. "Qilāʿ al-Fāṭimiyyīn fī jibāl al-Buhra", *Al-ʿArabī*, 524 (2002), pp. 166–168.
- al-Kharbūṭlī, ʿAlī Ḥusnī. *al-ʿAzīz bi'llāh al-Fāṭimī*. Aʿlām al-ʿArab, 73. Cairo: Dār al-Kātib al-ʿArabī, 1968. pp. 181.
- al-Kharbūṭlī, ʿAlī Ḥusnī. *al-Daʿwa al-Fāṭimiyya: daʿwat al-ḥaqq wa'l-ḥaḍāra*. Bombay: Hizbul Iman, n. d. pp. 225.
- al-Kharbūṭlī, ʿAlī Ḥusnī. *ʿImād al-Dīn Idrīs, al-dāʿī wa'l-mu'arrikh al-Fāṭimī (794–872h.) maʿa dirāsa li'l-daʿwa wa'l-maktaba al-Fāṭimiyya fī bilād al-Yaman wa'l-Hind*. Cairo: n.p., [1973]. pp. 137
- Kharyukov, L. N. *Anglo-russkoe sopernichestvo v Tsentral'noy Azii i ismailizm* [The Anglo-Russian Rivalry in Central Asia and Ismailism]. Moscow: Izdatel'stvo Moskovskogo Universiteta, 1995. pp. 237.
- al-Khashshāb (El-Khachab), Yaḥyā. *Nāṣir è Ḫosraw, son voyage, sa pensée religieuse, sa philosophie et sa poésie*. Cairo: Imprimerie P. Barbey, 1940. pp. 347.
- al-Khashshāb, Yaḥyā. "Waṣf Miṣr min Kitāb al-Safarnāma li-Nāṣir Khusraw", *Abḥāth al-nadwa al-dawliyya li-ta'rīkh al-Qāhira*. Cairo: Wizārat al-Thaqāfa wa'l-Iʿlām, 1971, vol. 3, pp. 1307–1312. French summary, Yaḥyā al-Khashshāb, "Description de l'Égypte d'après le Safar-

nāmah de Nāṣir-e Khosraw (Résumé)", in *Colloque international sur l'histoire du Caire*, pp. 277–278.

- al-Khashshāb, Yaḥyā. "Nāṣir Khusraw, al-rajul wa'l-ḥaqīqa", in *YNK*, pp. 641–667.
- al-Khaṭīb, Muḥammad Aḥmad. *al-Ḥarakāt al-bāṭiniyya fi'l-ʿālam al-Islāmī, ʿaqā'iduhā wa-ḥukm al-Islām fīhā*. Amman: Maktabat al-Aqṣā; Riyadh: Dār ʿĀlam al-Kutub, 1404/1984. pp. 480.
- Khaṭīb Rahbar, Khalīl. "Pīshnahād barā-yi taṣḥīḥ-i chand bayt az ashʿār-i Ḥakīm Nāṣir-i Khusraw", in *YNK*, pp. 155–171.
- Khoury, R.G. "Une description fantastique des fonds de la bibliothèque Royale, Ḫizānat al-Kutub, au Caire, sous le règne du calife Fatimide al-ʿAziz bi-lāh (365–86/975–97)", in Rudolph Peters, ed., *Proceedings of the Ninth Congress of the Union Européenne des Arabisants et Islamisants (Amsterdam, 1–7 September 1978)*. Publications of the Netherlands Institute of Archaeology and Arabic Studies in Cairo, 4. Leiden: E.J. Brill, 1981, pp. 123–140.
- Khurāsānī (Sharaf), Sharaf al-Dīn (1927–2003). "Ikhwān al-Ṣafā'", in *DMBI*, vol. 7, pp. 242–269.
- Khusht, Muḥammad ʿUthmān. *Ḥarakat al-Ḥashshāshīn: ta'rīkh wa-ʿaqā'id akhṭar firqa sirriyya fi'l-ʿālam al-Islāmī*. Cairo: Maktabat Ibn Sīnā, [1988]. pp. 208.
- Kiener, Ronald C. "Jewish Ismāʿīlism in Twelfth Century Yemen: R. Nathanel ben al-Fayyūmī", *Jewish Quarterly Review*, 74 (1983–84), pp. 249–266.
- Kikuchi, Tatsuya. "Ḥamīd al-Dīn al-Kirmānī's Theory of Intellect", *Bulletin of the Society for Near Eastern Studies in Japan*, 38, no. 1 (1995), pp. 45–60.
- Kikuchi, Tatsuya. "The Transformation of Ismāʿīlī Eschatology in the Fāṭimid Period: The Role and Meaning of Ḥamīd al-Dīn al-Kirmānī", *Bulletin of the Society for Near Eastern Studies in Japan*, 41, no. 1 (1998), pp. 95–109.
- Kikuchi, Tatsuya. "Some Problems in D. De Smet's Understanding of the Development of Ismāʿīlism: A Re-examination of the Fallen Existent in al-Kirmānī's Cosmology", *Orient: Report of the Society for Near Eastern Studies in Japan*, 34 (1999), pp. 106–120.
- Kinānī, Muṣṭafā Ḥasan M. *al-ʿAlāqāt bayna Jinuwa wa'l-Fāṭimiyyīn fi'l-sharq al-adnā 1095–1171 M/484–567 H., aḍwa' jadīda ʿalā'lḥaraka*

al-Ṣalībiyya. Alexandria: al-Hayʾa al-Miṣriyya al-ʿĀmma liʾl-Kitāb, 1981. 2 vols.

- King, David A. "Aspects of Fatimid Astronomy: From Hard-core Mathematical Astronomy to Architectural Orientations in Cairo", in *EF*, pp. 497–517.
- King, James Roy. "The Restoration of the al-Ḥākim Mosque in Cairo", *Islamic Studies*, 23 (1984), pp. 325–335.
- King, Noel. "Toward a History of the Ismāʿīlīs in East Africa", in Ismāʿīl Raji [Rāgī] al-Fārūqī, ed., *Essays in Islāmic and Comparative Studies*. Washington, DC: International Institute of Islāmic Thought, 1402/1982, pp. 67–83.
- Kishāvarz, Karīm (1900–1986). *Ḥasan-i Ṣabbāḥ*. Kitāb-i javānān, 2. Tehran: Ibn Sīnā, 1344 Sh./1965. pp. 232.
- Kleiss, Wolfram. "Assassin Castles in Iran", in Robert Hillenbrand, ed., *The Art of the Saljūqs in Iran and Anatolia*. Costa Mesa, CA: Mazda Publishers, 1994, pp. 315–319.
- Klemm, Verena. *Die Mission des fāṭimidischen Agenten al-Muʾayyad fī d-dīn in Šīrāz*. Europäische Hochschulschriften, Reihe XXVII. Asiatische und Afrikanische Studien, Band 24. Frankfurt am Main: P. Lang, 1989. pp. xxvii + 290.
- Klemm, Verena. *Memoirs of a Mission: The Ismaili Scholar, Statesman and Poet al-Muʾayyad fiʾl-Dīn al-Shīrāzī*. Ismaili Heritage Series, 9. London: I.B. Tauris in association with The Institute of Ismaili Studies, 2003. pp. xx + 160.
- Knapp, Bettina L. "The Kaliph Hakim and History as a Cyclical Happening", *Nineteenth-century French Studies*, 5 (1976–77), pp. 79–93.
- Koenig, N.A. "al-Āmir bi-Aḥkām Allāh", "al-ʿAzīz Biʾllāh", in *EI*.
- Koenig, N.A. "Azîz Billâh", in *IA*, vol. 2, pp. 152–154.
- Kohlberg, Etan. "Some Imāmī-Shīʿī Views on *taqiyya*", JAOS, 95 (1975), pp. 395–402; reprinted in Etan Kohlberg, *Belief and Law in Imāmī Shīʿism*. Variorum Collected Studies Series, CS 339. Aldershot: Variorum, 1991, article III.
- Kohlberg, Etan. "Muḥammad b. ʿAlī al-Bāḳir", in *EI2*, vol. 7, p. 397–400.
- Köhler, Bärbel. *Die Wissenschaft unter den ägyptischen Fatimiden*.

Arabistische Texte und Studien, Band 6. Hildesheim: G. Olms, 1994. pp. 194.

- Köhler, Michael A. "Al-Afḍal und Jerusalem – was versprach sich Ägypten vom ersten Kreuzzug", *Saeculum*, 37 (1986), pp. 228–239.
- Kohlhaussen, Heinrich. "al-Zujāja al-Fāṭimiyya: Ka's Hedwig", *Fikrun wa Fann*, 9 (1967), pp. 20–22.
- Kraemer, Joel. "A Jewish Cult of the Saints in Fāṭimid Egypt", in *EF*, pp. 579–601.
- Kraus, Paul (1904–1944). "Dschābir ibn Ḥajjān und die Isma'īlijja", in *Der Zusammenbruch der Dschābir-Legende, Dritter Jahresbericht des Forschungs-Institut für Geschichte der Naturwissenschaften in Berlin*. Berlin: J. Springer, 1930, pp. 23–42; reprinted in his *Alchemie, Ketzerei*, pp. 27–46.
- Kraus, Paul. "Hebräische und syrische Zitate in ismā'īlitischen Schriften", *Der Islam*, 19 (1931), pp. 243–263; reprinted in his *Alchemie, Ketzerei*, pp. 3–23.
- Kraus, Paul. "La bibliographie Ismaëlienne de W. Ivanow", *REI*, 6 (1932), pp. 483–490.
- Kraus, Paul. "Beiträge zur islamischen Ketzergeschichte: Das Kitāb az-Zumurruḏ des Ibn ar-Rāwandī", *RSO*, 14 (1933–34), pp. 93–129, 335–379; reprinted in his *Alchemie, Ketzerei*, pp. 109–190.
- Kraus, Paul. "Raziana II. Extraits du *Kitāb a'lām al-nubuwwa d'Abū Ḥātim al-Rāzī*", *Orientalia*, NS, 5 (1936), pp. 35–56, 358–378; reprinted in his *Alchemie, Ketzerei*, pp. 256–298.
- Kraus, Paul. "Les 'controverses' de Fakhr al-Dīn Rāzī", *BIE*, 19 (1936–37), pp. 187–214; reprinted in his *Alchemie, Ketzerei*, pp. 191–218. Partial English trans., "The Controversies of Fakhr al-Dīn Rāzī", *IC*, 12 (1938), pp. 131–153.
- Kraus, Paul. "Les dignitaires de la hiérarchie religieuse selon Ǵābir Ibn Ḥayyān", *BIFAO*, 41 (1942), pp. 83–97; reprinted in his *Alchemie, Ketzerei*, pp. 71–85.
- Kraus, Paul. *Alchemie, Ketzerei, Apokryphen im frühen Islam*, ed., Rémi Brague. Hildesheim: G. Olms, 1994. pp. xiii + 346.

See also under Hamilton A.R. Gibb

- Kremer, Alfred von (1828–1889). "Über den shī'ītischen Dichter Abū'l-Ḳāsim Muḥammed ibn Hāni'", *ZDMG*, 24 (1870), pp. 481–494.

- Krenkow, F. "Ṣulaiḥī", in *EI*, vol. 4, pp. 515–517.
- Kritzeck, James. "Ismailis", in *New Catholic Encyclopedia*. New York, St. Louis, etc.: McGraw-Hill Book Company, 1967, vol. 7, pp. 690–691.
- Kröger, Jens. "Fusṭāṭ and Nishapur. Questions about Fatimid Cut Glass", in *EF*, pp. 219–232.
- Kubiak, W. "The Burning of Miṣr al-Fusṭāṭ in 1168: A Reconsideration of Historical Evidence", *Africana Bulletin* (Warsaw), 25 (1976), pp. 51–64.
- Kühnel, Ernst (1882–1964). "Zur Tirāz-Epigraphik der Abbasiden und Fatimiden", in Ernst F. Weidner, ed., *Festschrift Max Freiherrn von Oppenheim zum 70. Geburtstage gewidmet von Freunden und Mitarbeitern*. Archiv für Orientforschung, Beiband I. Aus fünf Jahrtausenden Morgenländischer Kultur. Berlin, 1933, pp. 59–65.
- Kühnel, Ernst. "Fatimidi", in *Enciclopedia Italiana*. Rome: Istituto della Enciclopedia Italiana, 1932, vol. 14, pp. 895–897.
- Kühnel, Ernst and Louisa Bellinger. *Catalogue of Dated Tiraz Fabrics: Umayyad, Abbasid, Fatimid*. Washington, DC: The Textile Museum, 1952. pp. 137 + 52 plates.
- Kunitzsch, Paul von. "Zur Namengebung Kairos (al-Qahir Mars?)", *Der Islam*, 52 (1975), pp. 209–225.
- Kurrū, Abu'l-Qāsim Muḥammad. *Ibn Hāni', Mutanabbī al-Maghrib*. Aʿlām al-Maghrib al-ʿArabī, 2. Tunis: Dār al-Maghrib al-ʿArabī, 1967. pp. 79.

L

- Labbād, Mīshīl. *al-Ismāʿīliyyūn wa'l-dawla al-Ismāʿīliyya bi-Maṣyāf, 535–670 H.* [Damascus]: Maṭbaʿat al-Ittiḥād, 1381/1962. pp. 114.
- Ladak, Akbar H. "Daʿi Ali Ibn Muhammad al-Sulayhi (b. ca. 410–1020 d. 459–1067)", in *GIH*, pp. 59, 62.
- al-Lādhiqānī, Muḥyī al-Dīn. *Thulāthiyyat al-ḥulm al-Qarmaṭī, dirāsa fī adab al-Qarāmiṭa*. Silsilat al-dirāsāt al-adabiyya wa'l-lughawiyya. Syria: Dār al-Ḥiwār, 1987. pp. 400; reprinted, Cairo: Maktabat Madbūlī, 1413/1993. pp. 400.
- Laithwaite, Gilbert. "The Aga Khan", in E.T. Williams and Helen M. Palmer, ed., *The Dictionary of National Biography*, 1951–1960. Oxford:

Oxford University Press, 1971, pp. 7–10.

- Lakhani, J.H. "Pir Sadar Din", in *GIH*, pp. 87–90.
- Lalani, Arzina R. *Early Shīʿī Thought: The Teachings of Imam Muḥammad al-Bāqir*. London: I.B. Tauris in association with The Institute of Ismaili Studies, 2000. pp. xv + 192. Arabic trans., *al-Fikr al-Shīʿī al-mubkir: taʿālīm al-imām Muḥammad al-Bāqir*, tr., Sayf al-Dīn al-Qaṣīr. Beirut and London: Dār al-Sāqī in association with The Institute of Ismaili Studies, 2004. pp. 214. Persian trans., *Nakhustīn andīshahā-yi Shīʿī: taʿālīm-i imām Muḥammad Bāqir*, tr., Farīdūn Badra'ī. Tehran: Farzān, 1381 Sh./2002. pp. 201.
- Lamm, Carl J. "Fatimid Woodwork, its Style and Chronology", *BIE*, 18 (1935–36), pp. 59–91 + 12 plates.
- Landolt, Hermann. "Khwāja Naṣīr al-Dīn al-Ṭūsī (597/1201–672/1274), Ismāʿīlism and Ishrāqī Philosophy", in Nasrollah Pourjavady and Živa Vesel, ed., *Naṣīr al-Dīn Ṭūsī, philosophe et savant de XIIIe siècle*. Bibliothèque Iranienne, 54. Tehran: Presses Universitaires d'Iran and Institut Français de Recherche en Iran, 2000, pp. 13–30.
- Landolt, Hermann. "Suhrawardī Between Philosophy, Sufism and Ismailism: A Re-appraisal", *Dāneshnāmeh: The Bilingual Quarterly of the Shahīd Beheshtī University*, 1 (1381 Sh./2003), pp. 13–29; Persian summary pp. 203–205.
- Landolt, Hermann. "Abū Ḥātim al-Rāzī, Aḥmad ibn Ḥamdān (d. 322/933–34?)", "Abū Yaʿqūb al-Sijzī, Isḥāq ibn Aḥmad (fourth/tenth century)", in *EAL*.
- Lane-Poole, Stanley (1854–1931). *The Coinage of Egypt (AH. 358–922) under the Fatimee Khaleefehs, the Ayyoobees and the Mamlook Sultans*, ed., Reginal Stuart Poole. Catalogue of Oriental Coins in the British Museum, IV. London: British Museum, 1879. pp. xxx + 279; reprinted, Bologna: Forni, 1967. pp. xxx + 279.
- Lane-Poole, Stanley. *The Mohammadan Dynasties: Chronological and Genealogical Tables with Historical Introductions*. Westminster, UK: Archibald Constable and Co., 1894, pp. 70–73 (Fāṭimids), 94 (Ṣulayḥids), 97 (Zurayʿids); reprinted, New York: F. Ungar Publishing Co., 1965, pp. 70–73, 94, 97. Persian trans., *Ṭabaqāt-i salāṭīn-i Islām*, tr., ʿAbbās Iqbāl. Tehran: Kitābkhāna-yi Mihr, 1312 Sh./1933, pp. 59–61 (Fāṭimids), 84 (Ṣulayḥids), 85–86 (Zurayʿids). Arabic trans., from the Persian trans. of ʿAbbās Iqbāl, *Ṭabaqāt salāṭīn al-Islām*, tr., Makī Ṭāhir

al-Kaʿabī [Baghdad]: Dār Manshūrāt al-Baṣrī, 1388/1968, pp. 68–71 (Fāṭimids), 90–91 (Ṣulayḥids), 93–95 (Zurayʿids). Persian trans., together with other genealogical works, as *Ta'rīkh-i dawlathā-yi Islāmī va khānidānhā-yi ḥukūmatgar*, tr., Ṣādiq Sajjādī. Nashr-i ta'rīkh-i Īrān, 22; Majmūʿa-yi pazhūhishhā-yi ta'rīkhī, 4. Tehran: Nashr-i Ta'rīkh-i Īrān, 1363 Sh./1984, pp. 110–115 (Fāṭimids), 171 (Ṣulayḥids), 172–173 (Zurayʿids), 252–253 (Ismailis in Alamūt).

- Lane-Poole, Stanley. *A History of Egypt in the Middle Ages*. London: Methuen, 1901. pp. xv + 382; 4th ed., London: Methuen, 1925. pp. xiv + 382; new impression, Cass Library of African Studies, General Studies, 66. London: F. Cass, 1968. pp. xviii + 382.
- Lane-Poole, Stanley. *The Brotherhood of Purity*. Lahore: Orientalia, 1954. pp. 46; reprinted, Lahore: National Book Society, 1960. pp. 36.
- Lapidus, Ira Marvin. "Carmathian", in *Encyclopedia Americana*. Danbury, CT: Grolier, 1991, vol. 5, p. 674.
- Laqbāl, Mūsā. *Dawr Kutāma fī ta'rīkh al-khilāfa al-Fāṭimiyya mundhu ta'sīsihā ilā muntaṣaf al-qarn al-khāmis al-hijrī (11M.)* Algiers: al-Sharika al-Waṭaniyya li'l-Nashr wa'l-Tawzīʿ, 1979. pp. 734.
- Laqbāl, Mūsā. "Ḥarakat al-ṣirāʿ bayna al-Umawiyyīn wa'l-Fāṭimiyyīn fi'l-qarn al-rābiʿ al-hijrī/al-ʿāshir al-mīlādī", *al-Mu'arrikh al-ʿArabī*, 21 (1982), pp. 33–50.
- Lashi'ī, Ḥusayn. "Ibāḥiyya: Ismāʿīliyya", in *DMBI*, vol. 2, pp. 302–303.
- Latham, J. Derek and Helen W. Mitchell. "The Bibliography of S. M. Stern", *JSS*, 15 (1970), pp. 226–238; reprinted, with additions, in Samuel M. Stern, *Hispano-Arabic Strophic Poetry: Studies by Samuel Miklos Stern*, ed., L.P. Harvey. Oxford: At the Clarendon, Press, 1974, pp. 231–245.
- Launois, Aimée. "Catalogue des monnaies Fatimites entrées au Cabinet des Médailles depuis 1896", *BEO*, 24 (1971), pp. 19–53.
- Layish, Aharon. *Marriage, Divorce and Succession in the Druze Family*. Social, Economic and Political Studies of the Middle East, 31. Leiden: E.J. Brill, 1982. pp. xxv + 474.
- Layish, Aharon. "*Taqiyya* among the Druzes", *Asian and African Studies*, 19 (1985), pp. 245–281.
- Le Chatelier, A. "Aga Khan", *Revue du Monde Musulman*, 1 (1906), pp. 48–85.

- Le Tourneau, Roger (1907–1971). "La révolte d'Abū-Yazīd au Xme siècle", CT, 1 (1953), pp. 103–125.
- Leaman, Oliver. "al-Ḥāmidī (d. 557/1162)", in *EAL*, vol.1, p. 269.
- Leaman, Oliver. "Ikhwan al-Safa'", in *Encyclopedia of Asian Philosophy*, ed., Oliver Leaman. London and New York: Routledge, 2001, p. 255.
- Lebey de Batilly, Denis. *Traicté de l'origine des anciens Assasins porte-couteaux. Avec quelques exemples de leurs attentats & homicides és personnes d'aucuns Roys, Princes, & Seigneurs de la Chrestienté.* Lyon: Vincent Vaspaze, 1603. pp. 64; reprinted in *Collection des meilleurs dissertations, notices et traités particuliers relatifs à l'Histoire de France*, ed., C. Leber. Paris: G.A. Dentu, 1838, vol. 20, pp. 453–501.
- Leiser, Gary. "Muslims from al-Andalus in the Madrasas of Late Fāṭimid and Early Ayyūbid Egypt", *al-Qanṭara*, 20 (1999), pp. 137–159.
- Leist, A. "Gefangene Drusenhäuptlinge in Belgrad", *Globus Illustrierte: Zeitschrift für Länder und Völkerkunde*, 8 (1865), pp. 120–122.
- Leisten, Thomas. "Dynastic Tomb or Private Mausolea: Observations on the Concept of Funerary Structures of the Fāṭimid and ʿAbbāsid Caliphs", in *EF*, pp. 465–479.
- Leitner, G.W. "A Secret Religion in the Hindukush [the Pamir Region] and in the Lebanon", *Imperial and Asiatic Quarterly Review*, NS, 5 (1893), pp. 417–430.
- Lester, Ayala, Yael D. Arnon and Rachel Polak. "The Fatimid Hoard from Caesarea: A Preliminary Report", in *EF*, pp. 233–248.
- Leuthold, Enrico Jr. "Di alcune monete Fatimidi inedite", *Notizie dal Chiostro del Monastero Maggiore*, 11–14 (1971–74), pp. 43–49.
- Lev, Yaacov. "The Fāṭimid Conquest of Egypt-Military, Political and Social Aspects", *Israel Oriental Studies*, 9 (1979), pp. 315–328.
- Lev, Yaacov. "The Fatimid Army, A.H. 358–427/968–1036 C.E.: Military and Social Aspects", *Asian and African Studies*, 14 (1980), pp. 165–192.
- Lev, Yaacov. "The Fatimid Vizier Yaʿqub Ibn Killis and the Beginning of the Fatimid Administration in Egypt", *Der Islam*, 58 (1981), pp. 237–249.
- Lev, Yaacov. "Fāṭimid Policy towards Damascus (358/968–386/996):

Military, Political and Social Aspects", *Jerusalem Studies in Arabic and Islam*, 3 (1981–82), pp. 165–183.

- Lev, Yaacov. "The Fāṭimids and the Aḥdāth of Damascus 386/996–411/1021", *WO*, 13 (1982), pp. 97–106.
- Lev, Yaacov. "The Fatimid Navy, Byzantium and the Mediterranean Sea, 909–1036 C.E./297–427 A.H.", *Byzantion*, 54 (1984), pp. 220–252.
- Lev, Yaacov. "Army, Regime, and Society in Fatimid Egypt, 358–487/968–1094", *IJMES*, 19 (1987), pp. 337–365.
- Lev, Yaacov. "The Fāṭimid Princess Sitt al-Mulk", *JSS*, 32 (1987), pp. 319–328.
- Lev, Yaacov. "The Fāṭimid Imposition of Ismāʿīlism on Egypt (358–386/969–996)", *ZDMG*, 138 (1988), pp. 313–325.
- Lev, Yaacov. "The Fāṭimids and Egypt 301–358/914–969", *Arabica*, 35 (1988), pp. 186–196.
- Lev, Yaacov. "Persecutions and Conversion to Islam in Eleventh-century Egypt", *The Medieval Levant: Studies in Memory of Eliyahu Ashtor* ; being, *Asian and African Studies*, 22 (1988), pp. 73–91.
- Lev, Yaacov. "The Suppression of Crime, the Supervision of Markets, and Urban Society in the Egyptian Capital during the Tenth and Eleventh Centuries", *Mediterranean Historical Review*, 3, no. 2 (1988), pp. 71–95.
- Lev, Yaacov. *State and Society in Fatimid Egypt*. Arab History and Civilization, Studies and Texts, 1. Leiden: E.J. Brill, 1991. pp. xi + 217.
- Lev, Yaacov. "The Fatimids and Byzantium, 10th-12th Centuries", *Graeco-Arabica*, 6 (1995), pp. 190–208; 7–8 (1999–2000), pp. 273–281.
- Lev, Yaacov. "Regime, Army and Society in Medieval Egypt, 9th-12th Centuries", in Y. Lev, ed., *War and Society in the Eastern Mediterranean, 7th-15th Centuries*. The Medieval Mediterranean Peoples, Economies and Cultures, 400–1453, vol. 9. Leiden: E.J. Brill, 1997, pp. 115–152.
- Lev, Yaacov. *Saladin in Egypt*. The Medieval Mediterranean Peoples, Economies and Cultures, 400–1453, vol. 21. Leiden: E.J. Brill, 1999. pp. xv + 214.
- Lev, Yaacov. "Tinnīs: An Industrial Medieval Town", in *EF*, pp. 83–96.
- Lev, Yaacov. "Charity and Social Practice: Egypt and Syria in the Ninth-Twelfth Centuries", *Jerusalem Studies in Arabic and Islam*, 24

(2000), pp. 472–507.

- Lev, Yaacov. "Human Cost of Warfare: War in the Medieval Middle East, 9th-12th Centuries", in Giulio Cipollone, ed., *La liberazione dei captivi tra Christianita e Islam*. Collectanea Archivi Vaticani, 46. Vatican City: Archivio Segreto Vaticano, 2000, pp. 635–648.
- Lev, Yaacov. "Aspects of the Egyptian Society in the Fatimid Period", in *ESFAM* 3, pp. 1–31.
- Lev, Yaacov. "Prisoners of War during the Fatimid-Ayyubid Wars with the Crusaders", in Michael Gervers and James M. Powell, ed.,*Tolerance and Intolerance: Social Conflict in the Age of the Crusades*. Syracuse, NY: Syracuse University Press, 2001, pp. 11–27.
- Lévesque de la Ravalière, Pierre Alexandre (1697–1762). "Éclaircissemens sur quelques circonstances de l'histoire du Vieux de la Montagne, Prince des Assassins", *Histoire de l'Académie Royale des Inscriptions et Belles Lettres*, 16 (1751), pp. 155–164. English trans., "Explanations Relative to Some Circumstances of the History of the Old Man of the Mountain, Prince of the Assassins", as an appendix in John of Joinville (d. 1317), *Memoirs of John Lord de Joinville*, tr., Thomas Johnes. Hafod: At the Hafod Press, 1807, vol. 2, pp. 275–285.
- Levi Della Vida, Giorgio (1886–1967). "A Marriage Contract on Parchment from Fāṭimite Egypt", in M. Avi-Yonah et al., ed., *L.A. Mayer Memorial Volume (1895–1959)*; being, *Eretz-Israel*, 7 (1964), pp. 64–69.
- Levi Della Vida, Giorgio. "Assassini", "Ismā'īlīti", in *Enciclopedia Italiana*. Milan and Rome: Istituto della Enciclopedia Italiana, 1929–1933.
- Levin, S.F. "Reformatorskoe dvizhenie v indiyskoy torgovoy obshchine khodzha v 1825–1866" [The Reformist Movement in the Indian Khoja Trading Community in 1825–1866], *Kratkie soobshcheniya Instituta narodov Azii* (Moscow), 51 (1962), pp. 151–166.
- Levin, S.F. "Organizatsiya ismailitskoy burzhuazii v Pakistane" [The Organization of the Ismaili Bourgeoisie in Pakistan], *Kratkie soobshcheniya Instituta narodov Azii* (Moscow), 71(1964), pp. 72–87.
- Levin, S.F. "Torgovaya kasta khodzha (Iz istorii musul'manskoy burzhuazii Indii i Pakistana)" [The Trading Caste of Khoja. Toward the History of the Muslim Bourgeoisie in India and Pakistan]. *Avtoreferat skoy dissertatsii na zvanie kandidata istoricheskikh nauk*. Moscow, 1964. pp. 24.

- Levin, S.F. "Ob évolyutsii musul'manskikh torgovïkh kast v svyazi s razvitiem kapitalizma (na primere bokhra, memanov i khodzha)" [On the Evolution of Muslim Trading Castes in Connection with the Development of Capitalism (Bohras, Momnas and Khojas)], in *Kastï v Indii* [Castes in India]. Moscow: Nauka, 1965, pp. 233–261.
- Levin, S.F. "Finansovaya imperiya Aga-Khana IV" [The Financial Empire of Aga Khan IV], *Nauka i religiya* (Moscow), 8 (1971), pp. 58–59.
- Levin, S.F. "Étapï i osobennosti formirovaniya musul'manskoy burzhuazii iz obshchinï ismailitov khodzha" [Stages and Peculiarities of the Transformation of the Ismaili-Khoja Community into Muslim Bourgeoisie], in *Islam i sotsial'nïe strukturï stran Blizhnego i Srednego Vostoka* [Islam and Social Structures of the Countries of the Near and Middle East]. Moscow: Nauka, 1990, pp. 39–50.
- Levin, S.F. "Aga Khan III", in *Bolshaya Sovetskaya Éntsiklopediya.* Moscow: Bolshaya Sovetskaya Éntsiklopediya, 1970, vol. 1, p. 503; also in *Great Soviet Encyclopedia.* New York: Macmillan; London: Collier Macmillan, 1973, vol. 1, pp. 128–129.
- Levonian, Lootfy. "The Ikhwān al-Ṣafā' and Christ", *MW*, 35 (1945), pp. 27–31; reprinted in *RIS*, vol. 2, pp. 237–241.
- Levy, Reuben (1891–1966). "The Account of the Isma'ili Doctrines in the *Jami' al-Tawarikh* of Rashid al-Din Fadlallah", *JRAS* (1930), pp. 509–536.
- Lewin, Bernhard. "Le grand fauconnier de 'Azīz-billāh al-Fāṭimī et son Kitāb al-Baizara", *Orientalia Suecana*, 7 (1958), pp. 110–121.
- Lewis, Bernard (b. 1916). "An Ismaili Interpretation of the Fall of Adam", *BSOS*, 9 (1938), pp. 691–704.
- Lewis, Bernard. *The Origins of Ismā'īlism: A Study of the Historical Background of the Fāṭimid Caliphate.* Cambridge: W. Heffer and Sons, 1940. pp. vi + 114; reprinted, New York: AMS Press, 1975. pp. vi + 114. Arabic trans., *Uṣūl al-Ismā'īliyya: baḥth ta'rīkhī fī nash'at al-khilāfa al-Fāṭimiyya,* tr., Khalīl Aḥmad Jullū and Jāsim Muḥammad al-Rajab. Cairo, 1947; reprinted, Baghdad: Maktabat al-Muthanabbī, n.d. [1965]. pp. 217. Arabic trans., *Uṣūl al-Ismā'īliyya wa'l-Fāṭimiyya wa'l-Qarmaṭiyya,* tr., Ḥikmat Talḥūq. al-Silsila al-ta'rīkhiyya. Beirut: Dār al-Ḥadātha, 1980. pp. 175. Persian trans., *Paydāyish-i Ismā'īliyya,* tr., Ya'qūb Azhand, in B. Lewis et al., *Ismā'īliyān dar ta'rīkh,* pp. 1–130. Persian trans., *Āghāz-i kār-i Ismā'īliyān,* in B. Lewis, *Ta'rīkh-i*

Ismāʿīliyān, tr., Farīdūn Badra'ī. Tehran: Intishārāt-i Tūs, 1362 Sh./ 1984, pp. 29–133. Persian trans., *Bunyādhā-yi kīsh-i Ismāʿīliyān*, tr., Abu'l-Qāsim Sirrī. Tehran: Vīsman, 1370 Sh./1991. pp. 184.

- Lewis, Bernard. "An Epistle on Manual Crafts", *IC*, 17 (1943), pp. 141–151; reprinted in B. Lewis, *Studies in Classical and Ottoman Islam (7th-16th Centuries)*. Variorum Reprints Series, CS 54. London: Variorum Reprints, 1976, article XII; reprinted in Bryan S. Turner, ed., *Orientalism: Early Sources*, Volume I, *Readings in Orientalism*. London: Routledge, 2000, pp. 520–530.
- Lewis, Bernard. "Ismāʿīlī Notes", *BSOAS*, 12 (1948), pp. 597–600.
- Lewis, Bernard. "The Fatimids and the Route to India", *Revue de la Faculté des Sciences Économiques de l'Université d'Istanbul*, 11 (1949–50), pp. 50–54. Turkish trans., "Fatımiler ve Hindistan yolu", in *60. doğum yılı münasebetiyle Prof. Dr. Fuad Köprülü'ye*; being, *Iktisat Fakültesi Mecmuası, Istanbul Universitesi*, 11 (1952), pp. 355–360.
- Lewis, Bernard. "The Legend of the Jewish Origin of the Fatimid Caliphs", *Melilah*, 3–4 (1950), pp. 185–187.
- Lewis, Bernard. "The Sources for the History of the Syrian Assassins", *Speculum*, 27 (1952), pp. 475–489; reprinted in B. Lewis, *Studies in Classical and Ottoman Islam (7th-16th Centuries)*. London: Variorum Reprints, 1976, article VIII.
- Lewis, Bernard. "Saladin and the Assassins", *BSOAS*, 15 (1953), pp. 239–245; reprinted in B. Lewis, *Studies in Classical and Ottoman Islam (7th-16th Centuries)*. London: Variorum Reprints, 1976, article IX.
- Lewis, Bernard. "Three Biographies from Kamāl ad-Dīn", in *60. doğum yılı münasebetiyle Fuad Köprülü Aramağani. Mélanges Fuad Köprülü*. Ankara: Faculté des Lettres d'Ankara, 1953, pp. 325–344.
- Lewis, Bernard. "The Ismāʿīlites and the Assassins", in Kenneth M. Setton, ed., *A History of the Crusades*: Volume I, *The First Hundred Years*, ed., Marshall W. Baldwin. Philadelphia: University of Pennsylvania Press, 1955, pp. 99–132; 2nd ed., Madison, WI: University of Wisconsin Press, 1969, pp. 99–132. Persian trans., "*Ismāʿīliyān-i Sūriyya*", tr., Yaʿqūb Āzhand, in B. Lewis et al., *Ismāʿīliyān dar ta'rīkh*, pp. 341–388.
- Lewis, Bernard. "Government, Society and Economic Life under the Abbasids and Fatimids", in *The Cambridge Medieval History*: Volume 4, *The Byzantine Empire*, Part 1, *Byzantium and its Neighbours*, ed.,

J.M. Hussey. Cambridge: Cambridge University Press, 1966, pp. 638–661, 1009–1013.

- Lewis, Bernard. "Kamāl al-Dīn's Biography of Rāšid al-Dīn Sinān", *Arabica*, 13 (1966), pp. 225–267; reprinted in B. Lewis, *Studies in Classical and Ottoman Islam (7th-16th Centuries).* London: Variorum Reprints, 1976, article X.
- Lewis, Bernard. *The Assassins: A Radical Sect in Islam*. London: Weidenfeld and Nicholson, 1967. pp. x + 166, with several reprints. Arabic trans., *al-Daʿwa al-Ismāʿīliyya al-jadīda: al-ḥashīshiyya*, tr., Suhayl Zakkār. Beirut: Dār al-Fikr, 1971. pp. 191. Arabic trans., *al-Hashshāshūn: firqa thawriyya fī taʾrīkh al-Islām*, tr., Muḥammad al-ʿAzab Mūsā. Beirut: Dār al-Mashriq al-ʿArabī al-Kabīr, 1400/1980. pp. 252. Arabic trans., *Firqat al-ḥashshāshīn*, tr., al-Muqaddam al-Rukn Ilyās Farḥāt. n.p.: Muʾassasat Aḥmad Manṣūr Ḥusayn; Rawḍat al-Maʿārif liʾl-Tawzīʿ, 1414/1993. pp. 171. French trans., *Les Assassins: terrorisme et politique dans l'Islam médiéval*, tr., Annick Pélissier, with Preface by Maxime Rodinson. Collection "Stratégies". Paris: Berger-Levrault, 1982. pp. 208; also in Brussels: Éditions Complexe, 1984. pp. 208. German trans., *Die Assassinen: Zur Tradition des religiösen Mordes im radikalen Islam*, tr., Kurt Jürgen Huch. Die Andere Bibliothek. Frankfurt am Main: Eichborn, 1989. pp. 260. Italian trans., *Gli assassini: una setta radicale Islamica, i primi terroristi della storia*, tr., Marco Lunari. Milan: A. Mondadori, 1992. pp. 194. Japanese trans., Tokyo: Shinsen-sha co., 1973. Persian trans., *Fidāʾīyān-i Ismāʿīlī*, tr., Farīdūn Badraʾī. Intishārāt-i Bunyād-i Farhang-i Īrān, 59. Tehran: Bunyād-i Farhang-i Īrān, 1348 Sh./1969. pp. 250; reprinted, with some revisions, under the title of *Ismāʿīliyān-i Nizārī*, in B. Lewis, *Taʾrīkh-i Ismāʿīliyān*, tr., Farīdūn Badraʾī. Tehran: Intishārāt-i Tūs, pp. 135–319. Spanish trans., *Los asesinos: una secta radical del Islam*, tr., Lorenzo Díaz. Madrid: Biblioteca Mondadori, 1990. pp. 176. Turkish trans., *Haşîşîler*, tr., Ali Aktan. Istanbul, 1995.
- Lewis, Bernard. "Palṭiel: A Note", *BSOAS*, 30 (1967), pp. 177–181; reprinted in B. Lewis, *Studies in Classical and Ottoman Islam (7th-16th Centuries).* London: Variorum Reprints, 1976, article VII.
- Lewis, Bernard. "Assassins of Syria and Ismāʿīlīs of Persia", in Accademia Nazionale dei Lincei, *Atti del convegno internazionale sul tema: La Persia nel medioevo*. Rome: Accademia Nazionale dei Lincei, 1971, pp. 573–580; reprinted in B. Lewis, *Studies in Classical and Ottoman*

Islam (7th-16th Centuries). London: Variorum Reprints, 1976, article XI.

- Lewis, Bernard. "An Interpretation of Fāṭimid History", in *Colloque international sur l'histoire du Caire*, pp. 287–295.
- Lewis, Bernard. *Ta'rīkh-i Ismā'īliyān*, tr., Farīdūn Badra'ī. Tehran: Intishārāt-i Tūs, 1362 Sh./1984. pp. xvi + 348. Persian translations of B. Lewis's *The Origins of Ismā'īlism* (pp. 29–133) and *The Assassins* (pp. 135–319).
- Lewis, Bernard. "Isma'ilis", in *Chamber's Encyclopaedia*. New rev. ed., Oxford, etc.: Pergamon Press, 1966, vol. 7, pp. 780–781.
- Lewis, Bernard. "Assassins", in *Dictionary of the Middle Ages*. New York. Charles Scribner's Sons, 1982, vol. 1, pp. 589–593.
- Lewis, Bernard. "Bāb", "Bardjawān", "Dindān", "Ḥashīshiyya", "Ibn 'Aṭṭāsh", in *EI2*.
- Lewis, Bernard. "'Alā'-al-Dīn Moḥammad", in *EIR*, vol. 1, p. 780.
- Lewis, Bernard. "Ismâilîler", in *IA*, vol. 2, pp. 1120–1124.
- Lewis, Bernard. "Fāṭimids", in *The New Encyclopaedia Britannica*. 15th ed., Chicago, etc.: Encyclopaedia Britannica, 1982, vol. 4, pp. 193–195.
- Lewis, Bernard, et al. *Ismā'īliyān dar ta'rīkh*, tr., Ya'qūb Āzhand. Tehran: Intishārāt-i Mawlā, 1363 Sh./1984. pp. xv + 492. Includes translation of B. Lewis's *The Origins of Ismā'īlism*, pp. 1–130.
- Lewis, Norman N. "The Isma'ilis of Syria Today", *JRCA*, 39 (1952), pp. 69–77.
- Lewisohn, Leonard. "Sufism and Ismā'īlī Doctrine in the Persian Poetry of Nizārī Quhistānī (645–721/1247–1321)", *Iran, Journal of the British Institute of Persian Studies*, 41 (2003), pp. 229–251.
- Lézine, Alexandre. *Mahdiya. Recherches d'archéologie Islamique*. [Paris]: C. Klincksieck, 1965. pp. 149 + 120 plates.
- Lézine, Alexandre. "Notes d'archéologie Ifriqiyenne, IV: Mahdiya, quelques précisions sur la 'ville' des premiers Fatimides", *REI*, 35 (1967), pp. 82–101.
- Light, Henry. "Nachrichten über die Drusen", *Ethnographisches Archiv*, 6 (1820), pp. 432–444.
- Lindsay, James E. "Prophetic Parallels in Abu 'Abd Allah al-Shi'i's Mission among the Kutama Berbers, 893–910", *IJMES*, 24 (1992), pp. 39–56.

- Lindsay, James E. "Damascene Scholars during the Fāṭimid Period: An Examination of ʿAlī b. ʿAsākir's *Taʾrīkh Madīnat Dimashq*", *Al-Masāq: Studia Arabo-Islamica Mediterranea*, 7 (1994), pp. 35–75.
- Lindsay, James E. "The Fatimid *daʿwa* in North Africa", *Graeco-Arabica*, 7–8 (1999–2000), pp. 283–309.
- Literary Section, H.S.H. Prince Aly S. Khan Colony Religious Night School. "Jaʿfar bin Mansur al-Yaman", in *GIH*, pp. 16–17.
- Literary Section, H.S.H. Prince Aly S. Khan Colony Religious Night School. "Missionary Kara Ruda" in *GIH*, pp. 102–103.
- Literary Section, H.S.H. Prince Aly S. Khan Colony Religious Night School. "Pir Ismailbhai Gangji", in *GIH*, pp. 98–99.
- Literary Section, H.S.H. Prince Aly S. Khan Colony Religious Night School. "Pir Sabzali", in *GIH*, pp. 104–105.
- Literary Section, H.S.H. Prince Aly S. Khan Colony Religious Night School. "Pir Satgur Noor", in *GIH*, pp. 60–62.
- Literary Section, H.S.H. Prince Aly S. Khan Colony Religious Night School. "Sayyidna Nasir Khusraw", in *GIH*, pp. 48–51.
- Littmann, Enno (1875–1958). "Der Messias als Drusenheiliger", *Zeitschrift für Assyriologie*, 19 (1905–6), pp. 148–150.
- Lo Jacono, Claudio. "ʿAṭāyā, waṣāyā e farāʾiḍ nel *Kitāb al-iqtiṣār* del Qāḍī an-Nuʿmān", in *Studi in memoria di Paola Maria Arcari*. Milan: A. Giuffre, 1978, pp. 445–457.
- Lo Jacono, Claudio. "Su un caso di istiqsām nel fiqh Imamita e Ismailita-Fatimide: il ricorso alla Qurʿah nelle Farāʾiḍ", in *La Bisaccia dello Sheikh, Omaggio ad Alessandro Bausani, Islamista nel sessantesimo compleanno;* being, *Quaderni del seminario di Iranistica, Uralo-Altaistico e Caucasologia, Universita di Venezia*, 19 (1981), pp. 221–224.
- Lockhart, Laurence (1890–1975). "Hasan-i-Sabbah and the Assassins", *BSOS*, 5 (1929–30), pp 675–696.
- Lockhart, Laurence. "Some Notes on Alamut", *Geographical Journal*, 77 (1931), pp. 46–48.
- Lockhart, Laurence. "Alamūt: (I) The Fortress", in *EI2*, vol. 1, pp. 352–353.
- Loewe, Louis. *Observations on a Unique Cufic Gold Coin, Issued by al-Âmir beâkhcam Allah, Abû Ali Manzour ben Mustali, Tenth Caliph of the Fatimite Dynasty*. London: D. Nutt, J.R. Smith; Brighton: H.S.

King; Paris: M. Rollin, 1849. pp. 17.

- Lokhandwalla, Sh. (Shamoon) T. (Tayyib Ali). "The Bohras, a Muslim Community of Gujarat", *SI*, 3 (1955), pp. 117–135.
- Lokhandwalla, Sh. T. "Islamic Law and Ismaili Communities (Khojas and Bohras)", *Indian Economic and Social History Review*, 4 (1967), pp. 155–176; reprinted in S.T. Lokhandwalla, ed., *India and Contemporary Islam: Proceedings of a Seminar.* Transactions of the Indian Institute of Advanced Study, 6. Simla: Indian Institute of Advanced Study, 1971, pp. 379–397.
- Longhurst, M.H. "Some Crystals of the Fatimid Period", *Burlington Magazine*, 48 (1926), pp. 149–155.
- Lory, Pierre. "La magie chez les Iḫwān al-Ṣafā'", *BEO*, 44 (1992), pp. 147–159.
- Lowe, John D. "A Medieval Instance of Gresham's Law: The Fatimid Monetary System and the Decline of Bimetallism", *Jusūr*, 2 (1986), pp. 1–24.
- Lowick, Nicholas M. (1940–1986). "Some Unpublished Dinars of the Ṣulayḥids and Zurayʿids", *Numismatic Chronicle*, 7th series, 4 (1964), pp. 261–270; reprinted in N.M. Lowick, *Coinage and History of the Islamic World*, ed., Joe Cribb. Variorum Collected Studies Series, CS 311. Aldershot: Variorum, 1990, article III.
- Lowick, Nicholas M. "Fātimid Coins of Multān", *Numismatic Digest*, 7, parts 1–2 (1983), pp. 62–69; reprinted in N.M. Lowick, *Islamic Coins and Trade in the Medieval World.* Aldershot: Variorum, 1990, article XIX.
- Luke, H.C. "The Old Man of the Mountains", *JRCA*, 13 (1926), pp. 331–349.
- Lung, Haha. *Assassin! The Deadly Art of the Cult of the Assassins.* Boulder, CO: Paladin Press, 1997. pp. xi + 191.
- Lyons, M.C. "Assassinen", in *Lexikon des Mittelalters.* Munich and Zürich: Artemis, 1979, vol. 1, pp. 1118–1119.

M

- MacEoin, Dennis. "al-Ḥasan ibn al-Ṣabbāḥ", in *Who's Who of World Religions*, ed., John R. Hinnells. London and Basingstoke: Macmillan Press, 1991, pp. 148–149.

- Maʿāḍīdī, Khāshiʿ. *al-Ḥayāt al-siyāsiyya fī bilād al-Shām khilāla al-ʿaṣr al-Fāṭimī, 359–567h/969–1171n*. Baghdad: Dār al-Ḥurriyya li'l-Ṭibāʿa, 1975–76. pp. 225.
- Madelung, Wilferd. "Fatimiden und Baḥrainqarmaṭen", *Der Islam*, 34 (1959), pp. 34–88. English trans. (slightly revised), "The Fatimids and the Qarmaṭīs of Baḥrayn", in *MIHT*, pp. 21–73. Arabic trans., "al-Fāṭimiyyūn wa-Qarāmiṭat al-Baḥrayn", in *IAW*, pp. 35–82. Persian trans., "Fāṭimiyān va Qarmaṭiyān-i Baḥrayn", in *TAI*, pp. 37–101.
- Madelung, Wilferd. "Das Imamat in der frühen ismailitischen Lehre", *Der Islam*, 37 (1961), pp. 43–135.
- Madelung, Wilferd. "Aš-Šahrastānīs Streitschrift gegen Avicenna und ihre Widerlegung durch Naṣīr ad-Dīn aṭ-Ṭūsī", in Albert Dietrich, ed., *Akten des VII. Kongresses für Arabistik und Islamwissenschaft*. Abhandlungen der Akademie der Wissenschaften in Göttingen, Philologisch-historische Klasse, Folge 3, nr. 98. Göttingen: Vandenhoeck & Ruprecht, 1976, pp. 250–259; reprinted in his *Religious Schools*, article XVI.
- Madelung, Wilferd. "The Sources of Ismāʿīlī Law", *Journal of Near Eastern Studies*, 35 (1976), pp. 29–40; reprinted in his *Religious Schools*, article XVIII. Persian trans., "Manābiʿ-i fiqh-i Ismāʿīlī", in his *Maktabhā*, pp. 252–269.
- Madelung, Wilferd. "Aspects of Ismāʿīlī Theology: The Prophetic Chain and the God Beyond Being", in *ICIC*, pp. 51–65; reprinted in his *Religious Schools*, article XVII. Persian trans., "Barkhī az janbihā-yi kalām-i Ismāʿīlī: silsila-yi nubuvvat va khudā-yi māvarā-yi hastī", in his *Maktabhā*, pp. 240–251. Persian trans., "Naẓargāhhā-yi kalām-i Ismāʿīliyya", *Kayhān-i Andīsha*, 49 (Murdād 1372 Sh./August 1993), pp. 97–105.
- Madelung, Wilferd. "The Account of the Ismāʿīlīs in *Firaq al-Shīʿa*: A Note", in Samuel M. Stern, *Studies in Early Ismāʿīlism*. Jerusalem: The Magnes Press – The Hebrew University; Leiden, E.J. Brill, 1983, pp. 47–48.
- Madelung, Wilferd. "Naṣīr ad-Dīn Ṭūsī's Ethics Between Philosophy, Shiʿism, and Sufism", in Richard G. Hovannisian, ed., *Ethics in Islam*. Ninth Giorgio Levi della Vida Biennial Conference. Malibu, CA: Undena Publications, 1985, pp. 85–101.
- Madelung, Wilferd. *Religious Schools and Sects in Medieval Islam*.

Variorum Collected Studies Series, CS 213. London: Variorum Reprints, 1985. pp. x + 352. Persian trans., *Maktabhā va firqahā-yi Islāmī dar sadahā-yi miyāna*, tr., Javād Qāsimī. Mashhad: Āstān-i Quds-i Raḍavī, Bunyād-i Pazhūhishhā-yi Islāmī/Islamic Research Foundation, 1375 Sh./1986. pp. 318.

- Madelung, Wilferd. "Abū Ya'qūb al-Sijistānī and Metempsychosis", in *Textes et Mémoires*, Volume XVI. *Iranica Varia: Papers in Honor of Professor Ehsan Yarshater*. Leiden: E.J. Brill, 1990, pp. 131–143.
- Madelung, Wilferd. "Abū Ya'qūb al-Sijistānī and the Seven Faculties of the Intellect", in *MIHT*, pp. 85–89. Arabic trans., "Abū Ya'qūb al-Sijistānī wa-quwa'l-'aql al-sab'", in *IAW*, pp. 93–98. Persian trans., "Abū Ya'qūb Sijistānī va quvā'i haftgāna-yi 'aql", in *TAI*, pp. 113–118.
- Madelung, Wilferd. "Ḥamdān Qarmaṭ and the Dā'ī Abū 'Alī", in W. Madelung et al., ed., *Proceedings of the 17th Congress of the UEAI* [Union Européenne des Arabisants et Islamisants]. St. Petersburg: Thesa, 1997, pp. 115–124.
- Madelung, Wilferd. "The Religious Policy of the Fatimids toward their Sunnī Subjects in the Maghrib", in *EF*, pp. 97–104.
- Madelung, Wilferd. "A Treatise on the Imamate of the Fatimid Caliph al-Manṣūr Bi-Allāh", in Chase F. Robinson, ed., *Texts, Documents and Artefacts: Islamic Studies in Honour of D.S. Richards*. Islamic History and Civilization, Studies and Texts, 45. Leiden: E.J. Brill, 2003, pp. 69–77.
- Madelung, Wilferd. "Die Šī'a: Die Ismā'īlīya", in Helmut Gätje, ed., *Grundriß der Arabischen Philologie: Band II, Literaturwissenschaft*. Wiesbaden: Dr. L. Reichert, 1987, pp. 368–373.
- Madelung, Wilferd. "Ḥaḳā'iḳ", "Ḥamdān Ḳarmaṭ", "al-Ḥāmidī", "Ḥamza b. 'Alī", "Ibāḥa (II)", "Ismā'īliyya", "Ḳarmaṭī", Persian trans., "Qarmaṭī", in Y. Āzhand, *Nahḍat-i Qarāmiṭa*, pp. 35–56, "Khodja", "Madjlis: 2. In Ismā'īlī Usage", "Makramids", "Malā'ika: 2. In Shī'ism", "Manṣūr al-Yaman", "Maymūn b. al-Aswad al-Ḳaddāḥ", "Mulḥid", in *EI2*.
- Madelung, Wilferd. "'Abdān b. al-Rabīṭ", "Abū Sa'īd Jannābī", "'Alī b. Ḥosayn", "al-Bāqer, Abū Ja'far Moḥammad", "Bozorg-Omīd, Kīā", "Cosmogony and Cosmology: vi. In Isma'ilism", "Ḡazālī: vii. Ḡazālī and the Bāṭenīs", "Ḥamdān Qarmaṭ", "Ḥasan b. 'Alī", in *EIR*.
- Madelung, Wilferd. "Shiism: Ismā'īlīyah", in *ER*, vol. 13, pp. 247–260.

- Madkour, Ibrahim. "La vie culturelle entre le Caire et Baghdad (Résumé)", in *Colloque international sur l'histoire du Caire*, pp. 297–298.
- Magfale, Haldane. *Three Students*. Persian trans., *Sih yār-i dabistānī, Khayyām,Niẓām al-Mulk, Ḥasan-i Ṣabbāḥ*, tr., ʿAbd Allāh Vazīrī and Asad Allāh Ṭāhirī. Tehran: Furūghī, 1347 Sh./1968. pp. 283.
- Maḥāmīd, Ḥātim Muḥammad. *al-Taṭawwūrāt fī niẓām al-ḥukm wa'l-idāra fī Miṣr al-Fāṭimī*. Jerusalem: n.p., 1422/2001. pp. 248.
- Maḥāsina, Muḥammad Ḥusayn. *Ta'rīkh madīnat Dimashq khilāla al-ḥukm al-Fāṭimī*. Damascus: al-Awā'il, 2001. pp. 383.
- Maḥbūbī Ardakānī, Ḥusayn. "Āqā Khān Maḥallātī", in *EII*, vol. 1, pp. 111–113.
- Mahfoudh, Faouzi. "La grande mosquée de Mahdiya et son influence sur l'architecture médiévale Ifriqiyenne", in *EF*, pp. 127–140.
- Māhir, Suʿād. "Athar al-funūn al-tashkīliyya al-waṭaniyya al-qadīma ʿalā fann al-Qāhira fi'l-ʿaṣr al-Fāṭimī" in *Abḥāth al-nadwa al-dawliyya li-ta'rīkh al-Qāhira*. Cairo: Wizārat al-Thaqāfa wa'l-Iʿlām, 1971, vol. 3, pp. 519–551.
- Māhir (Maher), Suʿād (Soad). "Influence de l'art traditionnel sur l'art figuratif du Caire durant le periode Fāṭimide (Résumé)", in *Colloque international sur l'histoire du Caire*, p. 299.
- Maḥjūb, Muḥammad Jaʿfar. "Ghazālī va Ismāʿīliyān", *Iran Nameh*, 4 (1986), pp. 616–678, English summary, pp. 29–30; reprinted in *DKGI*, vol. 2, pp. 545–630.
- Mahjubi, Ali. "Fāṭimides", in *La Grande Encyclopédie*. Paris: Librairie Larousse, 1973, vol. 8, pp. 4799–4801.
- Maḥmūd, Sallām Shāfiʿī. *Ahl al-dhimma fī Miṣr fi'l-ʿaṣr al-Fāṭimī al-thānī wa'l-ʿaṣr al-Ayyūbī*. Cairo: Dār al-Maʿārif, 1982. pp. 350.
- Maḥmūd, Sallām Shāfiʿī. *Ahl al-dhimma fī Miṣr fi'l-ʿaṣr al-Fāṭimī al-awwal*. Ta'rīkh al-Miṣriyyīn, 75. Cairo: al-Hay'a al-Miṣriyya al-ʿĀmma li'l-Kitāb, 1995. pp. 327.
- Māḥūzī, Mahdī. "Ḥakīm Nāṣir-i Khusraw ʿAlawī Qubādiyānī", *NP*, 8, no. 2 (1382 Sh./2003), pp. 207–220.
- Majerczak, R. "Les Ismaéliens de Choughnan", *Revue du Monde Musulman*, 24 (1913), pp. 202–218.
- Mājid (Magued), ʿAbd al-Munʿim (1920–1999). "al-Nuqūd al-Fāṭimiyya fī Miṣr", *Majallat Kulliyyat al-Ādāb, Jāmiʿat Ibrāhīm/Annales de la*

Faculté des Arts, Université Ibrahim, 2 (1953), pp. 223–228. French trans., as "La monnaie Fatimide en Égypte", *Annales de la Faculté des Arts, Université Ibrahim Pacha,* 1 (1951), pp. 170–174.

- Mājid, ʿAbd al-Munʿim. *Nuẓum al-Fāṭimiyyīn wa-rusūmuhum fī Miṣr (Institutions et cérémonial des Fatimides en Égypte).* Cairo: Maktabat al-Anjlū al-Miṣriyya, 1953–55. 2 vols; 2nd ed., Cairo: Maktabat al-Anjlū al-Miṣriyya, 1973–78. 2 vols.
- Mājid, ʿAbd al-Munʿim. "Aṣl ḥafalāt al-Fāṭimiyyīn fī Miṣr (358–567/ 969–1171)", *Rivista del Instituto Egipcio de Estudios Islámicos en Madrid/Ṣaḥīfat al-Maʿhad al-Miṣrī li'l-Dirāsāt al-Islāmiyya fī Mādrīd,* 2 (1954), pp. 253–257.
- Mājid, ʿAbd al-Munʿim. "Le personnel de la cour Fatimide en Égypte", *Ḥawliyyāt Kulliyyat al-Ādāb, Jāmiʿat ʿAyn Shams/Annals of the Faculty of Arts, Ain Shams University,* 3 (1955), pp. 147–159.
- Mājid, ʿAbd al-Munʿim. *al-Ḥākim bi-Amr Allāh al-khalīfa al-muftarā ʿalayh.* Cairo: Maktabat al-Anjlū al-Miṣriyya, 1959. pp. 245; 2nd ed., Cairo: Maktabāt al-Anjlū al-Miṣriyya, 1982. pp. 245.
- Mājid, ʿAbd al-Munʿim. "La fonction de juge suprême dans l'état Fatimide en Égypte", *L'Égypte Contemporaine*, 50 (1960), pp. 45–56.
- Mājid, ʿAbd al-Munʿim. "De quelques juridictions Fatimides en Égypte", *L'Égypte Contemporaine*, 52 (1961), pp. 47–60.
- Mājid, ʿAbd al-Munʿim. *al-Imām al-Mustanṣir Bi'llāh al-Fāṭimī.* Cairo: Maktabat al-Anjlū al-Miṣriyya, 1961. pp. 304.
- Mājid, ʿAbd al-Munʿim. "Mā allafahu al-muʾarrikhūn al-ʿArab fī mi'at al-sana al-akhīra min dirāsāt fi'l-ta'rīkh al-ʿArabī: al-fatra al-Fāṭimiyya 358–567/696–1171", *Ḥawliyyāt Kulliyyat al-Ādāb, Jāmiʿat ʿAyn Shams/Annals of the Faculty of Arts, Ain Shams University,* 6 (1961), pp. 11–35.
- Mājid, ʿAbd al-Munʿim. "L'organisation financière en Égypte sous les Fatimides", *L'Égypte Contemporaine*, 53 (1962), pp. 47–57.
- Mājid, ʿAbd al-Munʿim. *Ẓuhūr khilāfat al-Fāṭimiyyīn wa-suqūṭuhā fī Miṣr: al-ta'rīkh al-siyāsī.* al-Maktaba al-ta'rīkhiyya. Alexandria: Dār al-Maʿārif, 1968. pp. 553.
- Mājid, ʿAbd al-Munʿim. "Imra'a Miṣriyya, tatazaʿʿamu muẓāhara fī ʿahd al-khalīfa al-Mustanṣir Bi'llāh al-Fāṭimī", *al-Majalla al-Ta'rīkhiyya al-Miṣriyya*, 24 (1977), pp. 33–38.

- Mājid, ʿAbd al-Munʿim. "al-Ḥāfiẓ", in *EI2*, vol. 3, pp. 54–55.
- Majīdī, ʿInāyat Allāh. "Maymūndizh-i Alamūt", *Nāma-yi Anjuman: Quarterly Journal of the Society for the Appreciation of Cultural Works and Dignitaries*, 2, no. 4 (1381 Sh./2003), pp. 76–79.
- Mājidzāda, Yūsuf. "Barrasī-yi chand manbaʿ-i taʾrīkhī-yi Ismāʿīliyya az dīdgāh-i bāstān-shināsī", *Majalla-yi Bāstān-shināsī va Taʾrīkh/Iranian Journal of Archaeology and History*, 2 (1367 Sh./1988), pp. 28–40.
- Makarem (Makārim), Sami Nasib (Sāmī Nasīb). *Aḍwāʾ ʿalā maslak al-tawḥīd "al-Durziyya"*. Beirut: Dār Ṣādir, 1966. pp. 173.
- Makarem, Sami N. "al-Amr al-ilāhī wa-mafhūmuhu fiʾl-ʿaqīda al-Ismāʿīliyya", *al-Abḥāth*, 20 (1967), pp. 3–16.
- Makarem, Sami N. "The Philosophical Significance of the Imām in Ismāʿīlism", *SI*, 27 (1967), pp. 41–53.
- Makarem, Sami N. "The Hidden Imāms of the Ismāʿīlīs", *al-Abḥāth*, 22 (1969), pp. 23–37.
- Makarem, Sami N. "Al-Ḥākim bi-Amrillāh's Appointment of his Successors", *al-Abḥāth*, 23 (1970), pp. 319–324.
- Makarem, Sami N. "Al-Ḥākim bi-Amrillāh, an Essay in Historical Interpretation", in Denis Sinor, ed., *Proceedings of the Twenty-seventh International Congress of Orientalists (Ann Arbor, Michigan, 13th-19th August 1967)*. Wiesbaden: O. Harrassowitz, 1971, pp. 229–230.
- Makarem, Sami N. *The Doctrine of the Ismailis*. Beirut: The Arab Institute for Research and Publishing, 1972. pp. 85.
- Makarem, Sami N. *The Druze Faith*. Delmar, NY: Caravan Books, 1974. pp. xi + 153.
- Makarem, Sami N. "Ismaʿili and Druze Cosmogony in Relation to Plotinus and Aristotle", in Michael E. Marmura, ed., *Islamic Theology and Philosophy: Studies in Honor of George F. Hourani*. Albany, NY: State University of New York Press, 1984, pp. 81–91.
- Makarem, Sami N. "Banū Jarrāḥ umarāʾ al-Ramla", *Taʾrīkh al-ʿArab waʾl-ʿĀlam*, 8 (1986), pp. 14–28.

  See also under ʿAbbās Abū Ṣāliḥ
- al-Makkī, Maḥmūd ʿAlī. "Maẓhar min maẓāhir al-ʿalāqāt bayna Miṣr al-Fāṭimiyya waʾl-Andalus khilāl al-qarn al-hādī ʿashar al-mīlādī ṭibqan li-wathāʾiq jadīda makhṭūṭa", in *Abḥāth al-nadwa al-dawliyya li-taʾrīkh al-Qāhira*. Cairo: Wizārat al-Thaqāfa waʾl-Iʿlām, 1971, vol. 2,

pp. 1237–1262.

- Malick, Qayyum A. *His Royal Highness Prince Aga Khan, Guide, Philosopher and Friend of the World of Islam*. Karachi: Ismailia Association for Pakistan, 1954. pp. 171; 2nd ed., Karachi: Ismaili Association for Pakistan, 1969. pp. 266.
- Malik Makān, Ḥamīd. "Khawāja Naṣīr al-Dīn Ṭūsī va Ismā'īliyān", *Haft Āsmān*, 3 (1380 Sh./2001), pp. 94–120; reprinted in *IMM*, pp. 505–536.
- al-Mallāḥ, Maḥmūd. *Ḥaqīqat Ikhwān al-Ṣafā'*. Baghdad: Maṭba'at Dār al-Ma'rifa, 1954. pp. 96.
- Mallison, Françoise. "Hinduism as Seen by the Nizārī Ismā'īlī Missionaries of Western India: The Evidence of the *Ginān*", in Günther D. Sontheimer and Hermann Kulke, ed., *Hinduism Reconsidered*. Heidelberg University, South Asian Studies, 24. New Delhi: Manohar and South Asia Institute, New Delhi Branch, 1989, pp. 93–103; revised ed., New Delhi: Manohar, 1997, pp. 189–201.
- Mallison, Françoise. "Les chants *Garabī* de Pīr Shams", in Françoise Mallison, ed., *Littératures médiévales de l'Inde du Nord*. Publications de l'École Française d'Extrême-Orient, 165. Paris: École Française d'Extrême-Orient, 1991, pp. 115–138.
- Mallison, Françoise. "La secte Ismaélienne des Nizārī ou Satpanthī en Inde. Hétérodoxie Hindoue ou Musulmane?", in Serge Bouez, ed., *Ascèse et renoncement en Inde ou la solitude bien ordonnée*. Paris: L'Harmattan, 1992, pp. 105–113.
- Mallison, Françoise. "Muslim Devotional Literature in Gujarati: Islam and Bhakti", in R.S. McGregor, ed., *Devotional Literature in South Asia: Current Research, 1985–1988*. Cambridge: Cambridge University Press, 1992, pp. 89–100.
- Mallison, Françoise. "Sant-vānī and Harijan, Mahāmārgī Bhajan and Ismaili *Ginān*: A New Appraisal of Popular Devotion in Saurashtra", in Mariola Offredi, ed., *The Banyan Tree: Essays on Early Literature in New Indo-Aryan Languages*. New Delhi: Manohar, 2000, pp. 235–243.
- Mallison, Françoise. "Resistant Ginān s and the Quest for an Ismaili and Islamic Identity among the Khojas", in Vasudha Dalmia et al., ed., *Charisma and Canon: Essays on the Religious History of the Indian Subcontinent*. New Delhi: Oxford University Press, 2001, pp. 360–375.

- Mallison, Françoise and Zawahir Moir. "Recontrer l'Absolu, ô Ami…(Sakhī! Mahā pada kerī vāta). Un hymne commun aux Hindous Tantriques et aux Musulmans Ismaéliens du Saurashtra (Gujarat)", in Jackie Assayag and Gilles Tarabout, ed., *Altérité et identité, Islam et Christianisme en Inde/Alterity and Identity, Islam and Christianism in India.* Collection Puruṣārtha, 19. Paris: École des Hautes Études en Sciences Sociales, 1997, pp. 265–276.
- Mamour, Prince P.H. [Peter Hagop]. *Polemics on the Origin of the Fatimi Caliphs.* London: Luzac, 1934. pp. 230; reprinted, Karachi: Indus Publications, 1979. pp. 230.
- al-Manāwī, Muḥammad Ḥamdī. *al-Wizāra wa'l-wuzarā' fi'l-'aṣr al-Fāṭimī.* Maktabat al-dirāsāt al-ta'rīkhiyya. Cairo: Dār al-Ma'ārif, 1970. pp. 332.
- Mann, Jacob (1888–1940). *The Jews in Egypt and in Palestine under the Fāṭimid Caliphs. A Contribution to their Political and Communal History, based chiefly on Genizah Material hitherto Unpublished.* Oxford: Oxford University Press, 1920–22. 2 vols.; reprinted, with Preface and Reader's Guide by Shelomo D. Goitein. Library of Jewish Classics. New York: KTAV Publishing House, 1970. 2 vols.
- Mansouri, Mohammed-Tahar. "Juifs et Chrétiens dans le Maghreb Fatimide (909–969)", in *EF*, pp. 603–611.
- Manṣūrī, Dhabīḥ Allāh. *Khudāvand-i Alamūt.* Tehran: Jāvīdān, 1356 Sh./1977. pp. 776, with many reprints.
- Manṣūrī, Fīrūz. *Nigāhī naw bi Safar-nāma-yi Nāṣir-i Khusraw.* Tehran: Intishārāt-i Chāpakhsh, 1372 Sh./1993. pp. 243.
- Mantran, Robert (d. 1999). "Druzes", in *Encyclopaedia Universalis.* Paris: Encyclopaedia Universalis, 1996, vol. 7, pp. 723–725.
- Mantran, Robert. "Druzes", in *EUDI*, pp. 248–249.
- Manuel, Thomas Philip. *A Complete Vocabulary to the Ikhwan-oos-Suffa.* Calcutta: Thacker, Spink and Co., R.C. Lepage and Co., G.C. Hay and Co., P.S. D'Rozario, 1862. pp. 23.
- Marçais, Georges (1876–1962). "Les figures d'hommes et de bêtes dans les bois sculptés d'époque Fâṭimide conservés au Musée Arabe du Caire: étude d'iconographie Musulmane", in *Mélanges Maspero, III: Orient Islamique.* Cairo: Institut Français d'Archéologie Orientale, 1940; being, Mémoires publiés par les membres de l'Institut Français d'Archéologie Orientale du Caire, 68 (1935–40), pp. 241–257.

- Marçais, Georges. *La Berbérie Musulmane et l'Orient au moyen âge*. Les grandes crises de l'histoire. Paris: Éditions Montaigne, 1946. pp. 310.
- Marçais, Georges. "al-Manṣūr Ismāʿīl", in *EI*, vol. 3, p. 257.
- Margoliouth, David Samuel. (1858–1940). "Abu'l-ʿAlā al-Maʿarrī's Correspondence on Vegetarianism", *JRAS* (1902), pp. 289–332.
- Margoliouth, David S. "Fatimites", in *Encyclopaedia Britannica*. 11th ed., Cambridge: Cambridge University Press, 1910, vol. 10, p. 202–204.
- Margoliouth, David S. "Assassins", in *ERE*, vol. 2, pp. 138–141.
- Mariti, Giovanni Filippo. *Istoria di Faccardino Grand-Emir dei Drusi*. Livorno: Stamperia di Tommaso Masi, 1787. pp. viii + 291. German trans., *Geschichte Fakkardin's, Gross-Emirs der Drusen: Wie auch der übrigen Gross-Emir bis auf das Jahr 1773*. Gotha: Ettinger, 1790. pp. 322. Arabic trans., *Ta'rīkh Fakhr al-Dīn, amīr al-Durūz al-kabīr*, tr., Buṭrus Shalfūn. Beirut: al-Dār al-Lubnāniyya li'l-Nashr al-Jāmiʿī, 1985.
- Mariti, Giovanni Filippo. *Memorie istoriche del popolo degli Assassini e del Vecchio della Montagna, loro capo-signore*. Leghorn, 1807.
- Marquet, Yves. "La place du travail dans la hiérarchie Ismāʿīlienne d'après *l'Encyclopédie des Frères de la Pureté*", *Arabica*, 8 (1961), pp. 225–237.
- Marquet, Yves. "Imamat, résurrection et hiérarchie selon les Ikhwan as-Safa", *REI*, 30 (1962), pp. 49–142.
- Marquet, Yves. "Coran et création. Traduction et commentaire de deux extraits des Iḫwān al-Ṣafā'", *Arabica*, 11 (1964), pp. 279–285.
- Marquet, Yves. "Révélation et vision véridique chez les Ikhwān al-Safā'", *REI*, 32 (1964), pp. 27–44.
- Marquet, Yves. "Sabéens et Iḫwān al-Ṣafā'", *SI*, 24 (1966), pp. 35–80; 25 (1966), pp. 77–109.
- Marquet, Yves. "Des Iḫwān al-Ṣafā' à al-Ḥāǧǧ 'Umar (b. Saʿīd Tall), marabout et conquérant Toucouleur", *Arabica*, 15 (1968), pp. 6–47; 16 (1969), pp. 88–90.
- Marquet, Yves. "Les cycles de la souveraineté selon les Épîtres des Iḫwān al-Ṣafā'", *SI*, 36 (1972), pp. 47–69.
- Marquet, Yves. *La Philosophie des Iḫwān al-Ṣafā'*. Algiers: Société

Nationale d'Édition et de Diffusion, 1975, pp. 604. New enlarged ed., Textes et travaux de Chrysopoeia, 5. Paris: S.É.H.A.; Milan: Archè, 1999. pp. xv + 620.

- Marquet, Yves. "Iḫwān al-Ṣafā', Ismaïliens et Qarmaṭes", *Arabica*, 24 (1977), pp. 233–257.
- Marquet, Yves. "Le Qāḍī Nu'mān à propos des heptades d'imāms", *Arabica*, 25 (1978), pp. 225–232.
- Marquet, Yves. "910 en Ifrīqiyā: une épître des Iḫwān aṣ-Ṣafā'", *BEO*, 30 (1978), pp. 61–73.
- Marquet, Yves. "Les Iḫwān aṣ-Ṣafā' et l'Ismaïlisme", in *Convegno sugli Ikhwān*, pp. 69–96.
- Marquet, Yves. "La pensée d'Abū Ya'qūb as-Sijistānī à travers le 'Iṯbāt an-Nubuwwāt' et le 'Tuḥfat al-Mustajībīn'", *SI*, 54 (1981), pp. 95–128.
- Marquet, Yves. "Un poème Ismaïlien dans les Epîtres des Ikhwān al-Ṣafā': traduction et commentaire", *REI*, 49 (1981), pp. 123–153.
- Marquet, Yves. "À propos d'un poème Ismaïlien dans les Épîtres des Iḫwān aṣ-Ṣafā'", *SI*, 55 (1982), pp. 137–142.
- Marquet, Yves. "Les Iḫwān al-Ṣafā' et le Christianisme", *Islamochristiana*, 8 (1982), pp. 129–158.
- Marquet, Yves. "Quelques remarques à propos de *Kosmologie und Heilslehre der frühen Ismā'īliyya* de Heinz Halm", *SI*, 55 (1982), pp. 115–135.
- Marquet, Yves. "Les Épîtres des Ikhwān as-Safā', oeuvre Ismaïlienne", *SI*, 61 (1985), pp. 57–79.
- Marquet, Yves. "Grades et heptades d'Imāms dans la *Risāla Kāfiya*, traité Ismaïlien Nizārite du 8e/14e siècle", *JA*, 273 (1985), pp. 139–160.
- Marquet, Yves. "Note rectificative concernant les conjonctions de Saturne et de Jupiter", *SI*, 64 (1986), pp. 158–159.
- Marquet, Yves. "Quelles furent les relations entre 'Jâbir ibn Ḥayyân' et les Iḫwān aṣ-Ṣafâ'?", *SI*, 64 (1986), pp. 39–51.
- Marquet, Yves. "La pensée philosophique et religieuse du Qāḍī al-Nu'mān, à travers La *Risāla Muḏhiba*", *BEO*, 39–40 (1987–88), pp. 141–181.
- Marquet, Yves. *La philosophie des alchimistes et l'alchimie des philosophes: Jâbir ibn Ḥayyân et les "Frères de la Pureté"*. Islam d'hier et d'aujourd'hui, 31. Paris: Maisonneuve et Larose, 1988, pp. 139.

- Marquet, Yves. "Les références à Aristote dans les Épîtres des *Iḫwān aṣ-Ṣafā*", in Thierry Zarcone, ed., *Individu et Société: l'influence d'Aristote dans le monde Méditerranéen.* Actes du colloque d'Istabul, Palais de France, 5–9 janvier 1986. Varia Turcica, X. Istanbul, Paris, etc.: Isis, 1988, pp. 159–164.
- Marquet, Yves. "À propos de la secte des auteurs Jâbiriens", *SI*, 73 (1991), pp. 127–135.
- Marquet, Yves. "L'Encyclopédie des 'Frères de la pureté' (Iḫwān aṣ-Ṣafā')", in Annie Becq, ed., *L'Encyclopédisme.* Actes du colloque de Caen 12–16 janvier 1987. Paris: Klincksieck, 1991, pp. 47–56.
- Marquet, Yves. "La détermination astrale de l'évolution selon les Frères de la Pureté", *BEO*, 44 (1992), pp. 127–146.
- Marquet, Yves. "Philosophe et poète de talent, ʿĀmir al-Baṣrī, missionnaire", *Arabica*, 40 (1993), pp. 1–31.
- Marquet, Yves. "La révélation par l'astrologie selon Abū Yaʿqūb as-Sijistānī et les Iḫwān aṣ-Ṣafā'", *SI*, 80 (1994), pp. 5–28.
- Marquet, Yves. "L'ascension spirituelle chez quelques auteurs Ismailïens", in Mohammad Ali Amir-Moezzi, ed., *Le voyage initiatique en terre d'Islam. Ascensions célestes et itinéraires spirituels.* Bibliothèque de l'École des Hautes Études, Section des Sciences Religieuses, 103. Louvain and Paris: Peeters, 1996, pp. 117–132.
- Marquet, Yves. "À propos du poème Ismaïlien *al-Qaṣīda al-Šāfiya (Le poème qui guérit [de la maladie de l'ignorance])*", *Arabica*, 46 (1998), pp. 119–121.
- Marquet, Yves. "La réponse Ismaïlienne au schisme Qarmate", *Arabica*, 45 (1998), pp. 1–21.
- Marquet, Yves. "La tolérance dans l'Ismailisme médiéval", in Urbain Vermeulen and Daniel de Smet, ed., *Philosophy and Arts in the Islamic World.* Proceedings of the Congress of the Union Européenne des Arabisants et Islamisants held at the Katholieke Universiteit Leuven (September 3– September 9, 1996). Orientalia Lovaniensia Analecta, 87. Louvain: Peeters, 1998, pp. 209–218.
- Marquet, Yves. "Socrate et les Iḫwān aṣ-Ṣafā'", *JA*, 286 (1998), pp. 409–449.
- Marquet, Yves. "Ibn al-Rūmī et les Iḫwān al-Ṣafā'", *Arabica*, 47 (2000), pp. 121–123.

- Marquet, Yves. "Ikhwān al-Ṣafā'", in *EI2*, vol. 3, pp. 1071–1076.
- Marquet, Yves. "Iḫwān al-Ṣafā'", in *Encyclopaedia Universalis*. Paris: Encyclopaedia Universalis, France, 1977, vol. 8, pp. 724–725.
- Marquet, Yves. "Ihwān al-Ṣafā' (Frères de la pureté)", in *EUDI*, pp. 406–409.
- Marzūq (Marzouk), Muḥammad ʿAbd al-ʿAzīz. *al-Zakhrafa al-mansūja fi'l-aqmisha al-Fāṭimiyya*. Cairo: Dār al-Kutub al-Miṣriyya, 1942. pp. 199 + 24 plates.
- Marzūq, Muḥammad ʿAbd al-ʿAzīz. "The Evolution of Inscriptions on Fatimid Textiles", *Ars Islamica*, 10 (1943), pp. 164–166.
- Marzūq, Muḥammad ʿAbd al-ʿAzīz. "Four Dated Tiraz Fabrics of the Fatimid Khalif aẓ-Ẓāhir", *Kunst des Orients*, 2 (1955), pp. 45–55.
- Marzūq, Muḥammad ʿAbd al-ʿAzīz. "The Earliest Fatimid Textile (Tiraz Al Mansuriya)", *Majallat Kulliyyat al-Ādāb, Jāmiʿat al-Iskandariyya/Bulletin of the Faculty of Arts, Alexandria University*, 11 (1957), pp. 37–56.
- Mashāyikh Farīdanī, Muḥammad Ḥusayn. "Ibn Hānī al-Andalusī", "Ismāʿīliyya-yi Hind", "Bohra", in *DT*.
- Mashkūr, Muḥammad Jawād (d. 1995). "Abu'l-Khaṭṭāb va firqa-yi Ismāʿīliyya", in *YNK*, pp. 553–561.

Masqatī, Jawād, *see* Muscati, Jawad

- Massé, Henri (1886–1969). "Le poème d'Ibn Hani al-Andalusi sur la conquête de l'Égypte (969)", in *Mélanges d'histoire et d'archéologie de l'occident Musulman: II, Hommage à Georges Marçais*. Algiers: Imprimerie officielle du Gouvernement Général de l'Algérie, 1957, pp. 121–127.
- Masselos, James C. "The Khojas of Bombay: The Defining of Formal Membership Criteria during the Nineteenth Century", in Imtiaz Ahmad, ed., *Caste and Social Stratification among Muslims in India*. New Delhi: Manohar, 1973, pp. 1–20; 2nd revised ed., New Delhi: Manohar, 1978, pp. 97–116.
- Massignon, Louis (1883–1962). "Sur la date de la composition des Rasāïl Ikhwān al ṣafā", *Der Islam*, 4 (1913), p. 324; reprinted in *RIS*, vol. 2, p. 128.

- Massignon, Louis. "Esquisse d'une bibliographie Qarmaṭe", in Thomas W. Arnold and Reynold A. Nicholson, ed., *A Volume of Oriental Studies Presented to Edward G. Browne on his 60th Birthday (7 February 1922)*. Cambridge: At the University Press, 1922, pp. 329–338; reprinted in L. Massignon, *Opera Minora*, ed., Youakim Moubarac. Beirut: Dar al-Maaref, 1963, vol. 1, pp. 627–639; reprinted, Paris: Presses Universitaires de France, 1969, vol. 1, pp. 627–639.
- Massignon, Louis. "Mutanabbi, devant le siècle Ismaélien de l'Islam", in *Al Mutanabbi. Recueil publié à l'occasion de son millénaire*. Mémoires de l'Institut Français de Damas. Beirut: Institut Français de Damas, 1936, pp. 1–17; reprinted in L. Massignon, *Opera Minora*, ed., Youakim Moubarac. Beirut: Dar al-Maaref, 1963, vol. 1, pp. 488–498; reprinted, Paris: Presses Universitaires de France, 1969, vol. 1, pp. 488–498.
- Massignon, Louis. "Eléments Ismaëliens dans la poétique d'al Mutanabbi", in *Atti del XIX congresso internazionale degli Orientalisti, 23–29 settembre, 1935*. Rome: Tipografia del Senato del Dott. G. Bardi, 1938, pp. 527–528.
- Massignon, Louis. "Ḳarmaṭians", in *EI*, vol. 2, pp. 767–772. Persian trans., "Dawlat-i Qarāmiṭa", tr., Yaʿqūb Āzhand, in B. Lewis et al., *Ismāʿīliyān dar taʾrīkh*, pp. 131–150; also as "Qarāmiṭa", in Y. Āzhand, *Nahḍat-i Qarāmiṭa*, pp. 79–96.
- Massignon, Louis. "Ḳarmaṭen", in *HI*, pp. 269–275.
- Massignon, Louis. "Karmatîler", in *IA*, vol. 6, pp. 352–359.
- Massignon, Louis. "Ḳarmaṭians", in *SEI*, pp. 218–223.
- Maʿṣūm, Fuʾād. *Ikhwān al-Ṣafāʾ: falsafatuhum wa-ghāyatuhum*. Damascus and Beirut: Dār al-Madā, 1998. pp. 358.
- al-Masumi, M. "Ikhwan al-Safa", *Islamic Literature*, 2 (1950), pp. 5–13.
- Matīnī, Jalāl. "Nāṣir-i Khusraw va madīḥa sarāʾī", *Majalla-yi Dānishkada-yi Adabiyyāt va ʿUlūm-i Insānī, Dānishgāh-i Firdawsī* (Mashhad), 10, no. 2 (1353 Sh./1974), pp. 165–192; also in *YNK*, pp. 465–492.
- Mawani, Rizwan. "The Nizari Ismaili Community and the Internet", International Institute for the Study of Islam in the Modern World, *ISIM Newsletter*, 12 (June, 2003), pp. 44–45.
- May, Burkhard. *Die Religionspolitik der ägyptischen Fāṭimiden, 969–1171*. Hamburg: Universität Hamburg, 1975. pp. 331.

- Mayer, L.A. (1895–1959). "A Fatimid Coin-die", *Quarterly of the Department of Antiquities of Palestine*, 1 (1932), pp. 34–35.
- Mayerson, Philip. "The Role of Flax in Roman and Fatimid Egypt", *Journal of Near Eastern Studies*, 56 (1997), pp. 201–207.
- Māyil Haravī, Najīb and Akbar ʿAshīq Kābulī. *Nāma-yi Alamūt*. Mashhad: Bungāh-i Kitāb-i Mashhad, 1360 Sh./1981. pp. 103 + 260.
- Māyil Haravī, Riḍā. "Afsānahā va qiṣṣahā dar bāra-yi Ḥakīm Nāṣir-i Khusraw Qubādiyānī Balkhī", in *YNK*, pp. 451–464.
- Mayskiy, P.M. "Ischislenie polevogo perioda sel'skokhozyaystvennïkh rabot u gortsev Pamira i verkhnego Vancha" [Calculation of the Period of Fieldworks in Agricultural Activity of the Mountain People of the Pamirs and the Upper Wanch], *Sovetskaya étnografiya* (Moscow and Leningrad), 4 (1934), pp. 102–107.
- Mayskiy, P.M. "Sledï drevnikh verovaniy v pamirskom ismailizme" [The Traces of Ancient Beliefs in the Pamirian Ismailism], *Sovetskaya étnografiya* (Moscow and Leningrad), 3 (1935), pp. 50–58.
- Mazot, Sibylle, "L'architecture d'influence Fatimide en Sicile", *Dossiers d'Archéologie* ; special issue *Égypte: L'Âge d'or des Fatimides*, 233 (May, 1998), pp. 50–57.
- Mazot, Sibylle. "L'architecture d'influence nord-africaine à Palerme", in *EF*, pp. 665–679.
- McHaffie, J. *Family Safari: H.H. the Aga Khan and Family on Kenya Tour*. Nairobi: Chaudry, 1981. pp. 104.
- Meck, Bruno. *Die Assassinen: Die Mördersekte der Haschischesser*. Vienna and Düsseldorf: Econ Verlag, 1981. pp. 356..
- Meier, Fritz (1912–1998). "Ismailiten und Mystik im 12. und 13. Jahrhundert", *Persica*, 16 (2000), pp. 9–29. Persian trans., "Ismāʿīliyya va ʿirfān dar qurūn-i shashum va haftum-i hijrī", tr., Mihr Āfāq Bāyburdī, in *Maʿārif*, 18 (1380 Sh./2001), pp. 84–113.
- Meinecke-Berg, Viktoria. "Materialien zu fatimidischen Holzdekorationen in Kairo I: Holzdecken aus dem fatimidischen Westpalast in Kairo", *Mitteilungen des Deutschen Archäologischen Instituts, Abteilung Kairo*, 47 (1991), pp. 227–233.
- Meinecke-Berg, Viktoria. "Fatimid Painting: On Tradition and Style. The Workshop of Muslim", in *EF*, pp. 349–358.
- Meinecke-Berg, Viktoria. "Das Giraffenbild des fatimidischen

Keramikmalers Muslim", *Damaszener Mitteilungen*, 11 (1999), pp. 331–344.

- Meisami, Julie Scott. "Symbolic Structure in a Poem by Nāṣir-i Khusraw", *Iran, Journal of the British Institute of Persian Studies*, 31 (1993), pp. 103–117.
- Meisami, Julie Scott. "Ibn Hāni' al-Andalusī, Muḥammad (d.c. 362/973)", in *EAL*, vol. 1, p. 331.

See also under Ian R. Netton

- Mekky, Mahmoud Aly. "Un aspect des relations entre l'Égypte Fāṭimide et l'Espagne Musulmane au cours du XIème siècle de notre ère, d'après de nouveaux documents manuscrits (Résumé)", in *Colloque international sur l'histoire du Caire*, pp. 323–324.
- Melville, Charles. "Sometimes by the Sword, Sometimes by the Dagger: The Role of the Isma'ilis in Mamlūk-Mongol Relations in the 8th/14th Century", in *MIHT*, pp. 247–263. Arabic trans., "Aḥyānan bi'l-sayf wa-aḥyānan bi'l-khanjar: dawr al-Ismā'īliyyīn fi'l-'alāqāt al-Mughūliyya-al-Mamlūkiyya fi'l-qarn 8/14, in *IAW*, pp. 255–271. Persian trans., "Gāhī bā shamshīr, gāhī bā khanjar: naqsh-i Ismā'īliyān dar rābiṭa-yi miyān-i Mamlūkān va Mughūlān dar qarn-i hashtum/chahārdahum", in *TAI*, pp. 304–324.
- Menant, Dominique. "Les Bohoras du Guzarate", *Revue du Monde Musulman*, 10 (1910), pp. 465–493.
- Menant, Dominique. "Les Khodjas du Guzarate", *Revue du Monde Musulman*, 12 (1910), pp. 214–232, 406–424.
- Mercier, E. "Chute de la dynastie des gouverneurs ar'lebites en Afrique. Établissement de l'Empire Obeïdite (886–912)", *Revue Africaine*, 15 (1871), pp. 112–137.
- Meskoob, Shahrokh. "Mansha' va ma'nā-yi 'aql dar andīsha-yi Nāṣir-i Khusraw", *Iran Nameh*, 7 (1989), pp. 239–257, 405–429.
- Meyer, E. "Die Isagoge in der Wissenschaftsenzyklopädie der Lauteren Brüder von Baṣrah", in Udo Tworuschka, ed., *Gottes ist der Orient, Gottes ist der Okzident: Festschrift für Abdoljavad Falaturi zum 65. Geburtstag*. Kölner Veröffentlichungen zur Religionsgeschichte, 21. Köln and Vienna: Böhlau, 1991, pp. 182–206.
- Meyerhof, Max (1874–1945). "Über einige Privatbibliotheken im fatimidischen Ägypten", *RSO*, 12 (1929–30), pp. 286–290.

- Meyerhof, Max. "Ḥashīsh", in *EI*, Supplement, pp. 85–86.
- Michot, Jean (Yaḥyā). "Le pèlerinage à la Mecque (*ḥajj*) dans la pensée des Ikhwân al-Ṣafâ' (Xe siècle)", *Revue Philosophique de Louvain*, 81 (1983), pp. 708–710.
- Mihryār, Muḥammad. "Shāhdiz kujāst?", *Majalla-yi Dānishkada-yi Adabiyyāt, Dānishgāh-i Iṣfahān/Revue de la Faculté des Lèttres d'Isfahan*, 1 (1343 Sh./1965), pp. 87–157.
- Miles, George Carpenter (1904–1975). *Fāṭimid Coins in the Collections of the University Museum, Philadelphia, and the American Numismatic Society*. Numismatic Notes and Monographs, 121. New York: American Numismatic Society, 1951. pp. 51 + 6 plates.
- Miles, George C. "Coins of the Assassins of Alamūt", *Orientalia Lovaniensia Periodica*, 3 (1972), pp. 155–162.
- Milstein, Rachel. "Hebrew Book Illumination in the Fatimid Era", in *EF*, pp. 429–440.
- Minasian, Caro Owen (1897–1972). *Shah Diz of Isma'ili Fame, its Siege and Destruction*, with a Foreword by Laurence Lockhart. London: Luzac, 1971. pp. xvii + 74 + 52 plates.
- Minorsky, Vladimir Fedorovich. (1877–1966). "Shughnān", in *EI*, vol. 4, pp. 389–391.
- Mīnuvī, Mujtabā (1903–1977). "Bāṭiniyya Ismā'īliyya", *Nashriyya-i Dānishkada-yi Ilāhiyāt va Ma'ārif-i Islāmī, Mashhad*, 3 (1351 Sh./ 1972), pp. 1–40; reprinted in M. Mīnuvī, *Ta'rīkh va farhang*. Tehran: Khwārazmī, 1352 Sh./1973, pp. 170–225.
- Mīnuvī, Mujtabā. "Nāṣir-i Khusraw", *Majalla-yi Dānishkada-yi Adabiyyāt-i Mashhad*, 8, no. 2 (1351 Sh./1972), pp. 272–304.
- Mīnuvī, Mujtabā. "Rawshanā'ī-nāma-yi Nāṣir-i Khusraw va Rawshanā'ī-nāma-yi manẓūm-i mansūb bi ū", in *YNK*, pp. 574–580.
- Miquel, André. "L'Égypte vue par un géographe Arabe du IVe/Xe siècle: Al-Muqaddasī", *AI*, 11 (1972), pp. 109–139.
- al-Mīr 'Alī, Ismā'īl. *al-Qarāmiṭa wa'l-ḥaraka al-Qarmaṭiyya fi'l-ta'rīkh*. Beirut: Dār wa-Maktabat al-Hilāl, 1403/1983. pp. 252; 2nd ed., Damascus: Dār al-Yanābī', 1994. pp. 254.
- al-Mīr 'Alī, Ismā'īl. *al-Qarāmiṭa 'alā ma'idat al-tashrīḥ al-ta'rīkhī*. Salamiyya: Dār al-Ghadīr, 1997. pp. 165.

- Mīr Anṣārī, ʿAlī. *Kitābshināsī-yi Ḥakīm Nāṣir-i Khusraw Qubādiyānī*. Tehran: Sāzimān-i Chāp va Intishārāt-i Vizārat-i Farhang va Irshād-i Islāmī, 1372 Sh./1994. pp. 150.
- Mīrbāqirī Fard, Sayyid ʿAlī Aṣghar. "Shiʿr va shāʿirān dar Dīwān-i Nāṣir-i Khusraw", *NP*, 8, no. 2 (1382 Sh./2003), pp. 243–255.
- Mirboboev, Aziz. "Ta'wīl bar pāya-yi raqam va ḥarf dar Wajh-i dīn", *Nomai Pazhouhishgoh* (Dushanbe), 4 (2003), pp. 119–130.
- al-Mīr Sulaymān, Ismāʿīl. *Salamiyya, ta'rīkh wa-munjazāt*. Salamiyya: Dār al-Ghadīr, 2001. pp. 177.
- Miret y Sans, Joaquín. "Vida de Fray Anselmo Turmeda", *Revue Hispanique*, 24 (1911), pp. 261–296.
- Mīrshāhī, Masʿud. "Dastur al-Munajjimīn, yak dānish-nāma-yi nujūmī-yi mutaʿalliq bi sada-yi panjum-i hijrī", *Kārnāma* (Paris), 6 (2000), pp. 45–50.
- Mirza, Nasseh Ahmad. "The Ismāʿīlīs and their Belief in the Universal Divine Order", *Glasgow University Oriental Society Transactions*, 20 (1963–64), pp. 10–22.
- Mirza, Nasseh Ahmad. "The Syrian Ismaʿilis and the Doctrine of Metempsychosis", *Milla wa-Milla, Australian Bulletin of Comparative Religion*, 4 (1964), pp. 48–51.
- Mirza, Nasseh Ahmad. "Notes on a Syrian Ismaili Manuscript", *Milla wa-Milla, Australian Bulletin of Comparative Religion*, 9 (1969), pp. 59–60.
- Mirza, Nasseh Ahmad. "Syria's Ismaili Muslims during the Crusades", *Islam and the Modern Age*, 24 (1993), pp. 183–210.
- Mirza, Nasseh Ahmad. *Syrian Ismailism: The Ever Living Line of the Imamate, AD 1100–1260*. Richmond, Surrey: Curzon Press, 1997. pp. xiv + 150.
- Mirza, Nasseh Ahmad. "Rashid al-Din Sinan", in *GIH*, pp. 72–80.
- Mirzoev, Abd al-Ghanī. "Mawḍūʿ-i nashr-i intiqādī-yi Wajh-i dīn va nusakh-i mawjūda-yi ān", in *YNK*, pp. 562–573.
- al-Misāwī, al-Ṣādiq. "al-Ḥashīshiyya: al-irhāb wa'l-siyāsa fi'l-Islām al-wasīṭ", *Ḥawliyyāt al-Jāmiʿa al-Tūnusiyya*, 22 (1983), pp. 285–292.
- Mishkat al-Dīnī, ʿAbd al-Muḥsin. "Rābiṭa mābayn-i sharʿ va ʿaql dar kutub-i Nāṣir-i Khusraw", in *YNK*, pp. 533–552.
- Misra, Satish Chandra. *Muslim Communities in Gujarat: Preliminary*

Studies in their History and Social Organization. New York: Asia Publishing House, 1964. pp. xvi + 207.

- Mistry, K. "Women and the Dawoodi Bohra Reform Movement: An Overview with a Case History", in Asghar Ali Engineer, ed., *Problems of Muslim Women in India*. Hyderabad: Orient Longman, 1995, pp. 40–51.
- Mitha, Farouk. *Al-Ghazālī and the Ismailis: A Debate on Reason and Authority in Medieval Islam*, with a Foreword by Wael B. Hallaq. Ismaili Heritage Series, 5. London: I.B. Tauris in association with The Institute of Ismaili Studies, 2001. pp. xxiv + 128. Persian trans., *Ghazālī va Ismāʿīliyān*, tr., Farīdūn Badra'ī. Tehran: Farzān, 1382 Sh./2003. pp. 157.
- Mohamed, Yasien. "The Cosmology of the Ikhwān al-Ṣafā', Miskawayh and al-Iṣfahānī", *Islamic Studies*, 39 (2000), pp. 657–679.
- Moir (Noorally), Zawahir. "Bībī Imām Begam and the End of the Ismaili Ginānic Tradition", in Alan W. Entwistle and Carol Salomon, ed., *Studies in Early Modern Indo-Aryan Languages, Literature and Culture*. Research Papers, 1992–1994, Presented at the Sixth Conference on Devotional Literature in New Indo-Aryan Languages, held at Seattle, University of Washington, 7–9 July 1994. New Delhi: Manohar, 1999, pp. 249–265.
- Moir, Zawahir. "Historical and Religious Debates amongst Indian Ismailis 1840–1920", in Mariola Offredi, ed., *The Banyan Tree: Essays on Early Literature in New Indo-Aryan Languages*. New Delhi: Manohar, 2000, vol. 1, pp. 131–153.
- Moir, Zawahir. "The Life and Legends of Pir Shams as Reflected in the Ismaili Ginans: A Critical Review" in Françoise Mallison, ed., *Constructions hagiographiques dans le monde Indien. Entre mythe et histoire*. Bibliothèque de l'École des Hautes Études, Sciences Historiques et Philologiques, 338. Paris: Librairie Honoré Champion, 2001, pp. 365–384.
- Moir, Zawahir. "Hazrat Pir Shamsuddin Sabzwari Multani", in *GIH*, pp. 83–86.
- Moir, Zawahir. "Jawhar as-Siqilli", in *GIH*, pp. 23–30.

  See also under M.I. Deedarali, Dominique-Sila Khan, F. Mallison and C. Shackle
- Momen, Moojan. *An Introduction to Shiʿi Islam: The History and*

Doctrines of Twelver Shiʿism, with a Foreword by Alessandro Bausani. New Haven and London: Yale University Press, 1985. pp. xxii + 397.

- Moncelon, Jean. "La daʿwa Fatimide au Yémén", *Chroniques Yéménites*, 3 (1995), pp. 26–37.
- Monès, H. "Le Malékisme et l'échec des Fatimides en Ifriqiya", in *Études d'Orientalisme dédiées à la mémoire de Lévi-Provençal*. Paris: G.P. Maisonneuve et Larose, 1962, pp. 197–220.
- Monès, H. "Djawhar al-Ṣiḳillī", in *EI2*, vol. 2, pp. 494–495.
- Monneret de Villard, Ugo (1881–1954). *Le pitture Musulmane al soffitto della Cappella Palatina in Palermo*. Rome: La Libreria dello Stato, 1950. pp. 82 + 250 plates.
- Monnot, Guy. "al-Shahrastānī, Abu'l-Fatḥ Muḥammad b. ʿAbd al-Karīm", in *EI2*, vol. 9, pp. 214–216.
- Monogarova, Lidiya Fedorovna. "Pamirtsï" [The Pamiris], *Voprosï istorii* (Moscow), 2 (1973), pp. 213–219.
- Monogarova, Lidiya F. "Yazïcheskie élementï v musul'manskikh obryadakh ismailitov Zapadnogo Pamira" [Pagan Elements in the Muslim Rites of the Ismailis of the Western Pamirs], in *Islam i problemï mezhtsivilizatsionnogo obshcheniya* [Islam and the Problems of Inter-Civilizational Interaction]. Moscow: Institut Islamskoy Tsivilizatsii, 1992, pp. 124–127.
- Morelon, Régis. "Un aspect de l'astronomie sous les Fatimides: l'importance d'Ibn al-Haytham dans l'histoire de l'astronomie Arabe", in *EF*, pp. 519–526.
- Morgan, Mostafa Ibrahim. "Karmānī al-(mort. apr. 1021)", in *EUDI*, p. 459.
- Morris, Harold Stephen. "The Divine Kingship of the Aga Khan: A Study of Theocracy in East Africa", *Southwestern Journal of Anthropology*, 14 (1958), pp. 454–472.
- Morris, Harold S. *The Indians in Uganda: Caste and Sect in a Plural Society*. London: Weidenfeld and Nicolson, 1968. pp. xi + 230.
- Mouton, Jean Michel. "La presénce Chrétienne au Sinaï à l'époque Fatimide", in *EF*, pp. 613–624.
- Muḥammad, Aḥmad Sayyid. *al-Shakhṣiyya al-Miṣriyya fi'l-adabayn al-Fāṭimī wa'l-Ayyūbī*. Cairo: Dār al-Maʿārif, 1979. pp. 375.
- Muḥammad, Ṣābir ʿAbduh Abā Zayd. *Fikrat al-zaman ʿinda Ikhwān*

al-Ṣafāʾ: dirāsa taḥlīliyya muqārina. Cairo: Maktabat Madbūlī, 1999. pp. 483.

- Muḥammad, Ṣubḥī ʿAbd al-Munʿim. *al-ʿAlāqāt bayna Miṣr waʾl-Ḥijāz zaman al-Fāṭimiyyīn waʾl-Ayyūbīn*. Cairo: al-ʿArabī, n.d. [1990s]. pp. 488.
- Muḥaqqiq (Mohaghegh), Mahdī (Mehdi). "Ismāʿīliyya", *Yaghmā*, 11, nos. 1–7 (1337 Sh./1958), pp. 18–26, 73–78, 124–129, 175–182, 209–211, 270–276, 306–312; reprinted in M. Muḥaqqiq, *Bīst guftār*. Wisdom of Persia Series, 17. Tehran: McGill University, Institute of Islamic Studies, Tehran Branch, 2535 [1355 Sh.]/1976, pp. 229–276; reprinted as *Ismāʿīliyya*. Tehran: Asāṭīr, 1382 Sh./2003. pp. 87.
- Muḥaqqiq, Mahdī. "Taʾthīr-i Qurʾān dar ashʿār-i Nāṣir-i Khusraw", *Majalla-yi Dānishkada-yi Adabiyyāt, Dānishgāh-i Tehran*, 8, no. 2 (1339 Sh./1961), pp. 30–57.
- Muḥaqqiq, Mahdī. "ʿAlawī būdan-i Nāṣir-i Khusraw", *Yaghmā*, 14, no. 1 (1340 Sh./1961), pp. 35–41.
- Muḥaqqiq, Mahdī. "Justijū-yi maḍāmīn va taʿbīrāt-i Nāṣir-i Khusraw dar aḥādīth va amthāl va ashʿār-i ʿArab", *Majalla-yi Dānishkada-yi Adabiyyāt, Dānishgāh-i Tehran*, 9, no. 1 (1340 Sh./1961), pp. 32–93.
- Muḥaqqiq, Mahdī. *Taḥlīl-i ashʿār-i Nāṣir-i Khusraw*. Intishārāt-i Dānishgāh-i Tehran, 987. Tehran: Dānishgāh-i Tehran, 1344 Sh./1965. pp. 326, with several reprints.
- Muḥaqqiq, Mahdī. "Nisbat-i rūḥānī-yi Nāṣir-i Khusraw", *Vaḥīd*, 6, no. 1 (1347 Sh./1968), pp. 39–46; reprinted in M. Muḥaqqiq, *Bīst guftār*. Wisdom of Persia Series, 17. Tehran: McGill University, Institute of Islamic Studies, Tehran Branch, 2535 [1355 Sh.]/1976, pp. 357–364.
- Muḥaqqiq, Mahdī. "Nāṣir-i Khusraw and his Spiritual *nisbah*", in Mujtabā Mīnuvī and Īraj Afshār, ed., *Yādnāma-yi Īrānī-yi Minorsky*. Intishārāt-i Dānishgāh-i Tehran, 1241. Tehran: Dānishgāh-i Tehran, 1348 Sh./1969, pp. 143–148.
- Muḥaqqiq, Mahdī. "Taṣḥīḥ-i Dīwān-i Nāṣir-i Khusraw", in Ḥabīb Yaghmāʾī and Īraj Afshār, ed., *Nāma-yi Mīnuvī*. Tehran: Kāviyān, 1350 Sh./1971, pp. 405–444.
- Muḥaqqiq, Mahdī. "Chihra-yi dīnī va madhhabī-yi Nāṣir-i Khusraw dar Dīwān", in *YNK*, pp. 493–519; reprinted in M. Muḥaqqiq, *Bīst guftār*. Wisdom of Persia Series, 17. Tehran: McGill University, Institute of Islamic Studies, Tehran Branch, 2535 [1355 Sh.]/1976, pp.

277–300.

- Muḥaqqiq, Mahdī. “Faḍā’iḥ al-Bāṭiniyya-yi Ghazālī va Dāmigh al-bāṭil ʿAlī b. Walīd”, in M. Muḥaqqiq, *Duvvumīn bīst guftār*. Wisdom of Persia Series. Tehran: McGill University, Institute of Islamic Studies, Tehran Branch, 1369 Sh./1980, pp. 116–127; reprinted in *DKGI*, vol. 2, pp. 631–643.
- Muḥaqqiq, Mahdī. “Imām Ḥusayn dar ashʿār-i Nāṣir-i Khusraw”, in M. Muḥaqqiq, *Duvvumīn bīst guftār*. Wisdom of Persia Series. Tehran: McGill University, Institute of Islamic Studies, Tehran Branch, 1369 Sh./1980, pp. 267–277.
- Muḥaqqiq, Mahdī. *Sharḥ-i sī qaṣīda az Ḥakīm Nāṣir-i Khusraw Qubādiyānī*. Intishārāt-i Tūs, 366. Tehran: Tūs, 1369 Sh./1990. pp. 345; 2nd ed., Tehran: Tūs, 1375 Sh./1996. pp. 278, with later reprints.
- Muḥaqqiq, Mahdī. “Maqām-i ʿilmī va falsafī-yi Ḥamīd al-Dīn al-Kirmānī”, in M. Muḥaqqiq, *Chahārumīn bīst guftār*. Tehran: Institute of Islamic Studies, University of Tehran, 1376 Sh./1997, pp. 151–157.
- Muḥaqqiq, Mahdī. “Taḥqīq dar Dīwān-i Nāṣir-i Khusraw”, in M. Muḥaqqiq, *Chahārumīn bīst guftār*. Tehran: Institute of Islamic Studies, University of Tehran, 1376 Sh./1997, pp. 197–223.
- Muḥaqqiq, Mahdī. “Sharḥ-i qaṣīda’ī az Dīwān-i Nāṣir-i Khusraw”, *Dāneshnāmeh: The Bilingual Quarterly of the Shahīd Beheshtī University*, 1 (1381 Sh./2003), pp. 93–112.
- Muḥaqqiq, Mahdī. “Taʿlīqāt bar Dīwān-i Nāṣir-i Khusraw”, *NP*, 8, no. 2 (1382 Sh./2003), pp. 221–241.
- Muḥaqqiq, Sīmīn. “Ibn Ṣayrafī”, in *DMBI*, vol. 4, pp. 125–126.
- Muʿizzī, Maryam. “Risāla-yi Ḥusayn b. Yaʿqūb Shāh”, *Faṣlnāma-yi Muṭālaʿāt-i Ta’rīkhī/Historical Research Quarterly*, 3, nos. 3–4 (1370 Sh./1992), pp. 403–425.
- Mujtabavī, Sayyid Jalāl al-Dīn. “Ikhwān al-Ṣafā’”, in *Mahdavī-nāma: jashn-nāma-yi ustād duktur Yaḥyā Mahdavī*. Tehran: Hermes, 1378 Sh./1999, pp. 609–635.
- Mujtahidzāda, Sayyid ʿAlī Riḍā. “Saʿd al-milla wa’l-dīn Ḥakīm Nizārī Quhistānī”, *Majalla-yi Dānishkada-yi Adabiyyāt-i, Dānishgāh-i Mashhad/Revue de la Faculté des Lettres de Meched*, 2, nos. 2–3 (1345 Sh./1966), pp. 71–100, 298–315.
- Mujtahidzāda Bīrjandī, Murtaḍā. *Nasīm-i bahārī dar aḥvāl-i Ḥakīm*

Nizārī. Mashhad, 1344/1925. pp. 140.

- Mukhiddinov, Ikrom M. "Religioznïe verovaniya, svyazannïe s zhilishchem u pamirskikh tadzhikov" [Religious Beliefs Related to Housing among the Pamiri Tajiks], *Vsesoyuznaya sessiya, posvyashchyonnaya itogam polevïkh étnograficheskikh i antropologicheskikh issledovaniy 1976–1977* g. *Tezisï dokladov*. Erevan, 1978, pp. 166–168.
- Mukhiddinov, Ikrom M. "Obïchai i obryadï pamirskikh tadzhikov, svyazannïe s zhilishchem: Konets XIX-nachalo XX v. (Materialï k istoriko-étnograficheskomu atlasu narodov Sredney Azii i Kasakhstana)" [Rites and Customs of the Pamiri Tajiks dealing with Dwellings: End of the 19th – Beginning of the 20th Centuries (Materials for the Historical and Ethnographic Atlas of the Peoples of Central Asia and Kazakhstan)]. *Sovetskaya étnografiya* (Moscow), no. 2 (1982), pp. 76–83.
- Mukhiddinov, Ikrom M. "Obïchai i obryadï, svyazannïe so stroitel'stvom zhilishcha u pripamirskikh narodnostey v XIX-nachale XX v." [Rites and Customs of the Pamiri Ethnic Groups dealing with Building of Dwellings in the end of the 19th – Beginning of the 20th Centuries], *Étnografiya Tadzhikistana*. Dushanbe: Donish, 1985, pp. 24–29.
- Mukhiddinov, Ikrom M. "Otrazhenie astral'nïkh verovaniy v povsednevnoy zhizni ismailitov Zapadnogo Pamira" [Astral Beliefs as Mirrored in the Everyday Life of the Ismailis of Western Pamir], in *Islam i problemï mezhtsivilizatsionnogo obshcheniya* [Islam and the Problems of Inter-Civilizational Interaction]. Moscow: Institut Islamskoy Tsivilizatsii, 1992, pp. 130–134.
- Mumtaḥan, Ḥusayn ʿAlī. *Nahḍat-i Qarmaṭiyān va baḥthī dar bāb-i anjuman-i Ikhwān al-Ṣafāʾ wa-Khullān al-Wafāʾ dar irtibāṭ bā ān*. Tehran: Dānishgāh-i Shahīd Bihishtī, 1371 Sh./1992. pp. 382.
- Mumtaz, Ali. "Ramdev Pir, a Forgotten Ismaili Saint", *Sind Review*, 32 (1995), pp. 24–29.
- Muqbil, Fahmī Tawfīq. *al-Fāṭimiyyūn wa'l-Ṣalībiyyūn*. Beirut: al-Dār al-Jāmiʿiyya, 1980. pp. 189.
- Muqīmī, Qahār. "Ibn Maṣāl", in *DMBI*, vol. 4, p. 626.
- Muradova, T.O. "O nekotorïkh aspektakh teorii émanatsii Avitsennï i Nosir-i Khisrava" [On Some Aspects of Nāṣir-i Khusraw's Theory of Emanation], *Izvestiya Akademii Nauk Tadzhikskoy SSR, otdelenie*

obshchestvennïkh nauk (Dushanbe), 1 (1982), pp. 61–64.

- Muradova, T.O. "O nekotorïkh aspektakh naturfilosofii Nosir-i Khisrava" [On Some Aspects of Nāṣir-i Khusraw's Philosophy], *Izvestiya Akademii Nauk Tadzhikskoy SSR, otdelenie obshchestvennïkh nauk* (Dushanbe), 2 (1984), pp. 28–33.
- Muradova, T.O. *"Jomeʿ ul-Khikmatayn" Nosir-i Khisrava kak filosofskiy trud* [Nāṣir-i Khusraw's *Jāmiʿ al-ḥikmatayn* as a Philosophical Work]. *Avtoreferat dissertatsii na zvanie kandidata filosofskikh nauk*. Alma-Ata, 1985. pp. 18.
- Muradova, T.O. "Kategorii dvizheniya, prostranstva i vremeni v filosofii Nosir-i Khisrava" [Categories of Movement, Space and Time in Nāṣir-i Khusraw's Philosophy], *Izvestiya Akademii Nauk Tadzhikskoy SSR, Filosofiya, ékonomika, pravovedenie* (Dushanbe), 4 (1986), pp. 14–19.
- Muradova, T.O. "K kharakteristike chuvstvennogo i ratsional'nogo poznaniya v filosofskoy kontseptii Nosir-i Khisrava" [To the Characteristic Features of Sensual and Rational Knowledge in Nāṣir-i Khusraw's Philosophical Concept], *Izvestiya Akademii Nauk Tadzhikskoy SSR, Filosofiya, ékonomika, pravovedenie* (Dushanbe), 1 (1988), pp. 3–8.
- Muradova, T.O. "Osnovnïe polozheniya filosofii Nosir-i Khisrava" [The Main Hypothesis of Nāṣir-i Khusraw's Philosophy], *Izvestiya Akademii Nauk Tadzhikskoy SSR, Filosofiya, ékonomika, pravovedenie* (Dushanbe), 4 (1989), pp. 9–14.
- Muradova, T.O. *Filosofiya Nosir-i Khisrava* [Nāṣir-i Khusraw's Philosophy]. Dushanbe: Donish, 1994. pp. 88.
- Muradova, T.O. "Nosir-i Khisrav" [Nāṣir-i Khusraw], in *Éntsiklopediyai Sovetii Tojik*. Dushanbe: Sarredaktsiyai ilmii Éntsiklopediyai Sovetii Tojik, 1984, vol. 5, pp. 235–237 (in Tajik).
- Muscati (al-Masqaṭī), Jawad. *Hasan bin Sabbah*, translated into English by Abbas H. Hamdani. Ismailia Association [for] Pakistan Series, no. 4. 2nd ed., Karachi: Ismailia Association [for] Pakistan, 1953. pp. 152. Urdu trans., *Ḥasan bin Ṣabbāh*, tr., Jūn Īliya. Karachi: Ismailia Association [for] Pakistan, 1983. pp. 160.
- Muscati, Jawad and Khan Bahadur A.M. Moulvi. *Life and Lectures of the Grand Missionary al-Muayyad-fid-Din al-Shirazi*. Ismailia Association [W] Pakistan Series, no. 2. Karachi: Ismailia Association [W]

Pakistan, 1950. pp. 183, with later reprints.

- Musharrafa, ʿAṭiyya Muṣṭafā. *Nuẓum al-ḥukm bi-Miṣr fī ʿaṣr al-Fāṭimiyyīn 358–567H./968–1171M.* Cairo: Dar al-Fikr al-ʿArabī, 1948. pp. 438.
- Muṣṭafa, Shākir. *al-Ḥarakāt al-shaʿbiyya wa-zuʿamāʾuhā fī Dimashq fi'l-ʿahd al-Fāṭimī.* [Damascus]: n.p., n.d. pp. 50.
- Muʾtamin, Zayn al-ʿĀbidīn. *Āshiyāna-yi ʿuqāb: dāstān-i taʾrīkhī.* Tehran: Bungāh-i Maṭbūʿātī-yi Afshārī, 1316 Sh./1937. 2 vols; 2nd ed., Tehran: Bungāh-i Afshārī, 1348 Sh./1969. pp. 900; 10th reprint, Tehran: ʿIlmī, 1375 Sh./1996. pp. 903.
- Muʿtazid, Wali-ur-Reḥmān. "The Psychology of Nāṣir-i Khusrow", *Journal of the Osmania University College*, 1 (1933), pp. 61–86.
- Muwaḥḥid, Ṣamad. "Abu'l-Haytham, Aḥmad b. Ḥasan Jurjānī", in *DMBI*, vol. 6, pp. 409–410.
- Muzhdih, ʿAlī Muḥammad. "Ḥakīm Nāṣir-i Khusraw va falsafa-yi ū", in *YNK*, pp. 520–532.

N

- Nabarāwī, Raʿfat Muḥammad. *al-Sinaj al-zujājiyya li'l-sikka al-Fāṭimiyya al-maḥfūẓa bi-Matḥaf al-Fann al-Islāmī bi'l-Qāhira.* Cairo: Maktabat Zahrāʾ al-Sharq, 1997. pp. 525 + 32.
- Naby, Eben. "Ethnicity and Islam in Central Asia", *Central Asian Survey*, 12 (1993), pp. 151–167.
- al-Naddāf, Ziyād. *al-Tawḥīd fi iqlīm al-Qāhira.* Baqʿātā, Lebanon: Maʿriḍ al-Shuf al-Dāʾim li'l-Kitāb, n.d. pp. 182.
- Nadiranze, L.I. and Lidiya A. Semenova. "Tri egipetski zhalovannye gramoty XIIv" [Three Egyptian Payment Bills from the 12th Century], *Pamyatriki pis'mennosti Vostoka* (1979), pp. 146–150.
- Nadvī, Syed Abū Ẓafar. "The Origin of the Bohras", *IC*, 9 (1935), pp. 638–644.
- Nadvī, Syed Abū Ẓafar. *ʿIqd al-javāhir fī aḥvāl al-bavāhir.* Karachi: A.M.N. Rājkūt Vālā, 1936. pp. 384 (in Urdu).
- Nagel, Tilman. *Frühe Ismailiya und Fatimiden im Lichte der Risālat Iftitāḥ ad-Daʿwa: Eine religionsgeschichtliche Studie.* Bonner orientalistische Studien, Neue Serie, 23. Bonn: Selbstverlag des orientalischen

Seminars der Universität, 1972. pp. 78.

- Nagel, Tilman. "Die 'Urǧūza al-Muḫtāra' des Qāḍī an-Nu'mān", *WI*, NS, 15 (1974), pp. 96–128.
- Najafali, 'Abbasali. *Law of Marriage Governing Dawoodi Bohra Muslims*. Bombay: The Times of India Press, 1943. pp. xiii + 74.
- Najāt, 'Abd al-Sattār. *Az bi'that tā raḥlat, Ismā'īliyān dar guzargāh-i ta'rīkh*. Karachi: n.p., 1380/1960. pp. 589.
- Nājī, 'Abd al-Jabbār. "Ta'rīkh akhbār al-Qarāmiṭa", *Majallat al-'Arab*, 6 (1971–72), pp. 466–470.
- Nājī, Ḥāmid. "Tusha-yi rahravān dar Zād al-musāfirīn", *NP*, 8, no. 2 (1382 Sh./2003), pp. 257–278.
- Nājī, Munīr. *Ibn Hānī' al-Andalusī, dars wa-naqd*. Beirut: Dār al-Nashr li'l-Jāmi'iyyīn, [1962]. pp. 287.
- Najīb, 'Azīz Allāh. *Ḥasan Ṣabbāḥ, ḥaqīqat aur afsānī*. Karachi: Prince Aga Khan Shia Imami Ismailia Association for Pakistan, n.d. pp. 128 (in Urdu).
- Najima, Susumu. *Pir, Waiz, and Imam: The Transformation of Socio-Religious Leadership among the Ismailis in Northern Pakistan*. Area Studies Working Paper Series, 23. Tokyo: Islamic Area Studies Project, 2001. pp. 32.
- al-Najjār, 'Abd Allāh. *Madhhab al-Durūz wa'l-tawḥīd*. Cairo: Dār al-Ma'ārif, 1965. pp. 161. English trans., *The Druze: Millennium Scrolls Revealed*, tr., Fred I. Massey. Atlanta, GA: American Druze Society, 1973.
- Najmī, Nāṣir. *Farmānravā-yi Alamūt*. Tehran: Intishārāt-i 'Aṭṭār, 1363 Sh./1984. pp. 200.
- Najmī, Nāṣir. *Sargudhasht-i Ḥasan-i Ṣabbāḥ va qal'a-yi Alamūt*. Tehran: Intishārāt-i Arghavān, 1369 Sh./1990. pp. 472.
- "Nakhodki starinnïkh rukopisey" [Discoveries of ancient manuscripts], *Vestnik Akademii Nauk SSSR* (Moscow), 1 (1960), p. 54.
- Nallino, Carlo Alfonso (1872–1938). "Carmati", in *Enciclopedia Italiana*. Rome: Istituto della Enciclopedia Italiana, 1931, vol. 9, pp. 82–83.

  See also under Michele Amari
- Nanjee, Abdul Hussain al-Waiz Alibhai. "Syed Imamshah", in *GIH*, pp. 93–94.

- Nanji, Azim. "Modernization and Change in the Nizari Ismaili Community in East Africa – A Perspective", *Journal of Religion in Africa*, 6 (1974), pp. 123–139.
- Nanji, Azim. "The Ginān Tradition among the Nizārī Ismāʿīlīs: Its Value as a Source of their History", in *Études Arabes et Islamiques: I. Histoire et civilisation*, vol. 3. Actes du XXIXe congrès international des Orientalistes. Paris: L'Asiathèque, 1975, pp. 143–146.
- Nanji, Azim. "An Ismāʿīlī Theory of *Walāyah* in the *Daʿāʾim al-Islām* of Qāḍī al-Nuʿmān", in Donald P. Little, ed., *Essays on Islamic Civilization Presented to Niyazi Berkes*. Leiden: E.J. Brill, 1976, pp. 260–273.
- Nanji, Azim. "On the Acquisition of Knowledge: A Theory of Learning in the *Rasāʾil Ikhwān al-Ṣafā*", *MW*, 66 (1976), pp. 263–271.
- Nanji, Azim. *The Nizārī Ismāʿīlī Tradition in the Indo-Pakistan Subcontinent*. Monographs in Islamic Religion and Theology. Delmar, NY: Caravan Books, 1978. pp. xii + 216.
- Nanji, Azim. "Shīʿī Ismāʿīlī Interpretations of the Qurʾan", in *Selected Proceedings of the International Congress for the Study of the Qurʾan*. Canberra: Australian National University, Faculty of Asian Studies, [1980], pp. 39–49.
- Nanji, Azim. "A Khojki Version of the Nizari Ismaili Work: The Pandiyat-i-Jawanmardi", in Graciela de la Lama, ed., *Middle East 1. 30th International Congress of Human Sciences in Asia and North Africa 1976*. Mexico City: El Colegio de Mexico, 1982, pp. 122–125.
- Nanji, Azim. "Ritual and Symbolic Aspects of Islam in African Contexts", in Richard C. Martin, ed., *Islam in Local Contexts*. Contributions to Asian Studies, 17. Leiden: E.J. Brill, 1982, pp. 102–109.
- Nanji, Azim. "The Nizari Ismaili Muslim Community in North America: Background and Development", in Earle H. Waugh et al., ed., *The Muslim Community in North America*. Edmonton, Alberta: University of Alberta Press, 1983, pp. 149–164.
- Nanji, Azim. "Towards a Hermeneutic of Qurʾānic and Other Narratives in Ismaʿili Thought", in Richard C. Martin, ed., *Approaches to Islam in Religious Studies*. Tucson, AZ: University of Arizona Press, 1985, pp. 164–173.
- Nanji, Azim. "The Ismaili Muslim Identity and Changing Contexts", in Victor C. Hayes, ed., *Identity Issues and World Religions*. Bedford Park, South Australia: Australian Association for the Study of

Religions, 1986, pp. 119–124.

- Nanji, Azim. "Early Ismāʿīlism Reconsidered", *JAOS*, 107 (1987), pp. 741–743.
- Nanji, Azim. "Ismāʿīlism", in Seyyed Hossein Nasr, ed., *Islamic Spirituality: Foundations*. World Spirituality, 19. London: Routledge and K. Paul, 1987, pp. 179–198.
- Nanji, Azim. "*Sharīʿat* and *Ḥaqīqat*: Continuity and Synthesis in the Nizārī Ismāʿīlī Muslim Tradition", in Katherine P. Ewing, ed., *Sharīʿat and Ambiguity in South Asian Islam*. Berkeley: University of California Press, 1988, pp. 63–76.
- Nanji, Azim. "Between Metaphor and Context: The Nature of the Faṭimid Ismāʿīlī Discourse on Justice and Injustice", *Arabica*, 37 (1990), pp. 234–239.
- Nanji, Azim. "Transcendence and Distinction: Metaphoric Process in Ismāʿīlī Muslim Thought", in David B. Burrell and Bernard McGinn, ed., *God and Creation: An Ecumenical Symposium*. Notre Dame, IN: University of Notre Dame Press, 1990, pp. 304–315.
- Nanji, Azim. "Ismāʿīlī Philosophy", in Seyyed Hossein Nasr and Oliver Leaman, ed., *History of Islamic Philosophy*. Routledge History of World Philosophies, 1. London: Routledge, 1996, vol. 1, pp. 144–154.
- Nanji, Azim. "Portraits of Self and Others: Ismaʿili Perspectives on the History of Religions", in *MIHT*, pp. 153–160. Arabic trans., "Rasm li'l-dhāt wa-li'l-ākharīn: manẓūr Ismāʿīlī li-ta'rīkh al-adyān", in *IAW*, pp. 155–163. Persian trans., "Khud-nigarī va dīgar-nigarī: chashm-andāzhā-yi Ismāʿīlī dar ta'rīkh-i adyān", in *TAI*, pp. 192–201.
- Nanji, Azim. "Imāmat: iii. Imāmat nazd-i Ismāʿīliyya", in *DMBI*, vol. 10, pp. 142–145.
- Nanji, Azim. "Ismaili Philosophy", in Oliver Leaman, ed., *Encyclopedia of Asian Philosophy*. London and New York: Routledge, 2001, pp. 267–269.
- Nanji, Azim. "Nāṣir-i Khusraw", "Nizāriyya", "Sabz ʿAlī", in *EI2*.
- Nanji, Azim. "Aga Khan", Ikhwan al-Safa", "Khojas", "Nizari", in *Encyclopedia of Islam and the Muslim World*, ed., Richard C. Martin. New York: Macmillan Reference USA/Thompson-Gale, 2004.
- Nanji, Azim. "Assassins", in *ER*, vol. 1, pp. 469–471.
- Nanji, Azim. "Aga Khan Award for Architecture", "Ginan", "Khojki

Script", in *The Oxford Dictionary of Islam*, ed., John L. Esposito. Oxford: Oxford University Press, 2003.

- Nanji, Azim. "Aga Khan", "Aga Khan Foundation", in *OE*.

See also under F. Daftary, Aziz Esmail and F. Ross-Sheriff

- Nantet, Bernard and Édith Ochs. *Les fils de la sagesse. Les Ismaéliens et l'Aga Khan*. Paris: J.C. Lattès, 1998. pp. 348.
- Narkiss, M. "A Jewish Bread or Cheese Stamp of the Fatimid Period", *Bulletin of the Jewish Palestine Exploration Society*, 12 (1945–46), pp. 72–74.
- Naṣīrī (Raḍī), Muḥammad. "Imāmat az dīdgāh-i Ismāʿīliyān", in *IMM*, pp. 111–187.
- Nāṣirī Ṭāhirī, ʿAbd Allāh. *Fāṭimiyān dar Miṣr*. Qom, Iran: Pazhūhishkada-yi Ḥawza va Dānishgāh, 1379 Sh./2000. pp. 195.
- Nāṣirī Ṭāhirī, ʿAbd Allāh. "Ismāʿīliyān va mukhālifānishān", *Taʾrīkh-i Islām*, 3 (1379 Sh./2000), pp. 161–180.
- Nāṣirī Ṭāhirī, ʿAbd Allāh. *Muqaddimaʾī bar andīsha-yi siyāsī-yi Ismāʿīliyya*. Tehran: Khāna-yi Andīsha-yi Javān, 1379 Sh./2000. pp. 142.
- Nāṣirī Ṭāhirī, ʿAbd Allāh. "Naqsh-i Shīʿayān-i Fāṭimī dar janghā-yi Ṣalībī", *Taʾrīkh-i Islām*, 5 (1380 Sh./2001), pp. 99–132.
- Nāṣirī Ṭāhirī, ʿAbd Allāh. "Rāshid al-Dīn Sinān, pīshvāʾ-i buzurg-i Ismāʿīliyān-i Shām dar ʿaṣr-i Ṣalībī", *Taʾrīkh-i Islām*, 7 (1380 Sh./2001), pp. 137–168.
- al-Naṣr, ʿAbd al-Munʿim ʿAzīz. *Judhūr ḥarakat al-Qarāmiṭa: taʾrīkhuhum wa-taʾrīkh daʿwatihim*. Baghdad: Maṭbaʿat Asʿad, 1986. pp. 136.
- Naṣr, Mursal and Taqī al-Dīn Ḥalīm. *al-Muwaḥḥidūn "al-Durūz" fi'l-Islām*. Beirut: al-Dār al-Islāmiyya, 1996. pp. 192.
- Nasr, Seyyed Hossein. *An Introduction to Islamic Cosmological Doctrines: Conceptions of Nature and Methods used for its Study by the Ikhwān al-Ṣafāʾ, al-Bīrūnī, and Ibn Sīnā*. Cambridge, MA: The Belknap Press of Harvard University Press, 1964. pp. xxi + 312; revised ed., London: Thames and Hudson, 1978. pp. xxiii + 318. Persian trans., *Naẓar-i mutifakkirān-i Islāmī dar bāra-yi ṭabīʿat*. Tehran: Dihkhudā, 1342 Sh./1964. pp. 444.
- Nasr, S. Hossein. "The Immutable Principles of Islam and Western

Education: Reflections on the Aga Khan Chair of Islamic Studies at the American University of Beirut", *MW*, 56 (1966), pp. 4–9.

- Nasr, S. Hossein. "Henry Corbin, the Life and Works of the Occidental Exile in Quest of the Orient of Light", *Sophia Perennis*, 3 (1977), pp. 88–127; also in French as "Henry Corbin 'l'exil occidental': une vie et une oeuvre en quête de l'Orient des Lumières", in S. Hossein Nasr, ed., *Mélanges offerts à Henry Corbin*. Wisdom of Persia Series, 9. Tehran: McGill University, Institute of Islamic Studies, Tehran Branch, 1977, pp. 3–27.
- Nasr, S. Hossein (ed.), *Ismāʿīlī Contributions to Islamic Culture*. Imperial Iranian Academy of Philosophy, Publication no. 35. Tehran: Imperial Iranian Academy of Philosophy, 1398/1977. pp. xii + 265.
- Nasr, S. Hossein. "Nāṣir-i Khusraw", in *ER*, vol. 10, pp. 312–313.

See also under Henry Corbin

- Nasr-ul-Mulk, Shahzada. "The Ismailis or Maulais of the Hindu Kush", *JRCA*, 22 (1935), pp. 641–645.
- Nazariev, Ramazon. *Allegoricheskaya interpretatsiya filosofsko-teologicheskikh problem v ismailizme* [Allegorical Interpretation of Philosophical and Theological Problems in Ismailism]. *Avtoreferat dissertatsii na zvanie kandidata filosofskikh nauk*. Dushanbe, 2000. pp. 24.
- Nègre, Arlette. "À propos d'une expédition Fatimide à Wargilan (Ouargla) d'après Abu Zakariyya al-Wargilani", *Revue d'Histoire et de Civilisation du Maghreb*, 10 (1973), pp. 37–39.
- Nejima, Susumu. "The Ismaili Imam and NGOs – A Case Study of Islamic Civil Society", *Bulletin of Asia-Pacific Studies*, 10 (2000), pp. 149–163.
- Nerval, Gérard de. "Les Druses: scènes de la vie Orientale", *Revue des Deux Mondes*, NS, 19 (1847), pp. 577–626.
- Naṣṣār, Ḥusayn. *Ẓāfir al-Ḥaddād, shāʿir Miṣrī mina al-ʿaṣr al-Fāṭimī*. Cairo: al-Hayʾa al-Miṣriyya al-ʿĀmma liʾl-Kitāb, 1975. pp. 291.
- Netton, Ian Richard. "Brotherhood versus Imāmate: Ikhwān al-Ṣafāʾ and the Ismāʿīlīs", *Jerusalem Studies in Arabic and Islam*, 2 (1980), pp. 253–262.
- Netton, Ian R. "Foreign Influences and Recurring Ismāʿīlī Motifs in the *Rasāʾil* of the Brethren of Purity", in *Convegno sugli Ikhwān*, pp.

49–67; reprinted in Ian R. Netton, *Seek Knowledge: Thought and Travel in the House of Islam*. Richmond, Surrey: Curzon Press, 1996, pp. 27–41.

- Netton, Ian R. *Muslim Neoplatonists: An Introduction to the Thought of the Brethren of Purity (Ikhwān al-Ṣafā')*. London: G. Allen and Unwin, 1982. pp. xii + 146.
- Netton, Ian R. "The Brethren of Purity (Ikhwān al-Ṣafā')", in Seyyed Hossein Nasr and Oliver Leaman, ed., *History of Islamic Philosophy*. London and New York: Routledge, 1996, vol. 1, pp. 222–230.
- Netton, Ian R. "Carmathians", "al-Kirmānī, Ḥamīd al-Dīn Aḥmad ibn ʿAbd Allāh (d. c. 411–12/1021)", in *EAL*.
- Netton, Ian R. "Āghā Khān", "Alamūt", "Assassins", "Bāṭin", "Bohorās", "Dāʿī", "Druze", "Fāṭimids", "al-Ḥākim Bi-Amr Allāh", "al-Ḥāmidī, Ibrāhīm b. al-Ḥusayn", "Ḥasan-i Ṣabbāḥ", "Ibn Killis", "Ikhwān al-Ṣafā'", "Ismāʿīlīs (Ismāʿīliyya)", "Khojas", "al-Kirmānī, Ḥamīd al-Dīn Aḥmad", "Muḥammad b. Ismāʿīl", "Mustaʿlians", "al-Mustanṣir", "Nizārīs", "al-Nuʿmān, al-Qāḍī", "Qarāmiṭa", "al-Sijistānī", "Ẓāhir", in his *A Popular Dictionary of Islam*. London: Curzon Press, 1992.
- Netton, Ian R. and Julie Scott Meisami. "Ikhwān al-Ṣafā'", "Ismāʿīlīs, Ismāʿīlī Literature", "al-Mu'ayyad fī al-Dīn al-Shīrāzī (c. 390–470/c.1000–78)", in *EAL*.
- Nicholson, John. *An Account of the Establishment of the Fatemite Dynasty in Africa*. Tübingen: L. Friedrich Fues; Bristol: William Strong, 1840. pp. 138.
- Nicholson, Reynold Alleyne(1868–1945). "Nāṣir ibn Khusrau", in *ERE*, vol. 9, pp. 186–187.
- Nicol, Norman D. "Islamic Coinage in Imitation of Fāṭimid Types", *Israel Numismatic Journal*, 10 (1988–89), pp. 58–70 + plates.
- Nīkjū, Mahvash. "Chihra-yi ta'rīkh-i ijtimāʿī va siyāsī-yi Īrān dar ā'īna-yi Safar-nāma-yi Nāṣir-i Khusraw", in *YNK*, pp. 591–618.
- Niʿmat Allāhī, Jalāl. *Ḥasan-i Ṣabbāḥ*. Tehran: ʿIlmī, 1333 Sh./1954. pp. 129.
- Niẓāmī, Ḥasan. *Fāṭimī daʿwat-i Islām*. Delhi: Barqī Prīs, 1344/1925. pp. 8 + 240 + 4 (in Urdu).
- Nola, Alfonso M. di. "Assassini", in *Enciclopedia delle Religioni*. Florence: Vallecchi Editore, 1970–71, pp. 642–643.

- Nomoto, Shin. "Qāḍī al-Nuʿmān's (d. 363/974) Concept of the Imamate", *Reports of the Keio Institute of Cultural and Linguistic Studies*, 23 (1991), pp. 101–122 (in Japanese with English abstract).
- Nomoto, Shin. "The Prophetic Figure of Jesus in Fatimid Ismaʿilism", *Reports of the Keio Institute of Cultural and Linguistic Studies*, 24 (1992), pp. 281–313 (in Japanese with English abstract).
- Nomoto, Shin. "An Early Ismāʿīlī View of Other Religions Based on a Chapter from the *Book of Correction* (*Kitāb al-Iṣlāḥ*) by Abū Ḥātim al-Rāzī (d. 322/934–5)", *Reports of the Keio Institute of Cultural and Linguistic Studies*, 25 (1993), pp. 231–252 (in Japanese with English abstract).
- Nomoto, Shin. "An Early Ismāʿīlī Theory of Belief (*Imān*): The Case of al-Qāḍī al-Nuʿmān (d. 363/974)", *Reports of the Keio Institute of Cultural and Linguistic Studies*, 26 (1994), pp. 149–168.
- Nomoto, Shin. "The Prophet's Encounter with the Angelic Beings According to al-Rāzī, an Early Ismāʿīlī Thinker", in Shigeru Kamada and H. Mori, ed., *Transcendence and Mystery: The Gedankenwelten of China, India and Islam*. Tokyo, 1994, pp. 231–252 (in Japanese).
- Nomoto, Shin. "The Cosmos and the Prophets: The Prophetology in the *Book of Correction* by Abū Ḥātim al-Rāzī", *Orient*, 38 (1995), pp. 271–283 (in Japanese with English abstract).
- Nomoto, Shin. "Notes on Early Ismāʿīlī Speculation on Numbers", *Reports of the Keio Institute of Cultural and Linguistic Studies*, 27 (1995), pp. 203–224.
- Nomoto, Shin. "The Place of Abū Ḥātim al-Rāzī's *Kitāb al-Iṣlāḥ* in the History of Early Ismāʿīlī Thought (1): The Theory of the Prophets and Qāʾim", *Reports of the Keio Institute of Cultural and Linguistic Studies*, 28 (1996), pp. 223–241 (in Japanese with English abstract).
- Nomoto, Shin. "The Place of Abū Ḥātim al-Rāzī's *Kitāb al-Iṣlāḥ* in the History of Early Ismāʿīlī Thought (2): Some Problems in the Study of al-Rāzī's Life", *Reports of the Keio Institute of Cultural and Linguistic Studies*, 29 (1997), pp. 135–154 (in Japanese with English abstract).
- Nomoto, Shin. "The Place of Abū Ḥātim al-Rāzī's *Kitāb al-Iṣlāḥ* in the History of Early Ismāʿīlī Thought (3): Survey of its Contents", *Reports of the Keio Institute of Cultural and Linguistic Studies*, 32 (2000), pp. 229–253 (in Japanese).
- Nomoto, Shin. "The Place of Missionary Thinker al-Rāzī (d. ca. 322/

933–4) in the Ismāʿīlī Movement of the Early Fāṭimid Era as Viewed from his *Kitāb al-Iṣlāḥ*", *Orient*, 44 (2001), pp. 148–162 (in Japanese with English abstract).

Noorally, Zawahir, *see* Moir (Noorally), Zawahir

- Nowell, Charles E. "The Old Man of the Mountain", *Speculum*, 22 (1947), pp. 497–519.
- Nūḥ, ʿAlī. *al-Khiṭāb al-Ismāʿīlī fi'l-tajdīd al-fikr al-Islāmī al-muʿāṣir*. Damascus: Dār al-Yanābīʿ, 1994. pp. 240.
- Nūḥ, ʿAlī. *al-Ismāʿīliyya bayna khuṣūmihā wa-anṣārihā*. Homs: Dār al-Tawḥīdī, 2000. pp. 229.
- al-Nukhaylī, Darwīsh. *Fatḥ al-Fāṭimiyyīn li'l-Shām fī marḥalatihi al-ūlā: min 358H. ilā 362H. (dirāsa fi'l-maṣādir wa'l-marājiʿ)*. Alexandria: Mu'assasat al-Thaqāfa al-Jāmiʿiyya, 1979. pp. 440.
- Nūrānī Wiṣāl, ʿAbd al-Wahhāb. "Tawḍīhātī dar bāra-yi chand bayt-i Nāṣir-i Khusraw", in *YNK*, pp. 581–590.
- Nūriyān, Mahdī. "Barkhī dushvārīhā-yi matn-i Dīwān-i Nāṣir-i Khusraw", *NP*, 8, no. 2 (1382 Sh./2003), pp. 279–287.

O

- Oddy, W.A. "The Gold Content of Fāṭimid Coins Reconsidered", *Metallurgy in Numismatics*, 1 (1980), pp. 99–118.
- O'Kane, Bernard. "The *Ziyāda* of the Mosque of al-Ḥākim and the Development of the *Ziyāda* in Islamic Architecture", in *EF*, pp. 141–158.
- O'Leary, De Lacy Evans (b. 1872). *A Short History of the Fatimid Khalifate*. Trubner's Oriental Series. London: K. Paul, Trench, Trubner; New York: E.P. Dutton, 1923. pp. viii + 267; reprinted, Delhi: Renaissance Publishing House, 1987. pp. viii + 267.
- Omran, Mahmoud Said. "King Amalric and the Siege of Alexandria, 1167", in Peter W. Edbury, ed., *Crusade and Settlement: Papers read at the First Conference of the Society for the Study of the Crusades and the Latin East and Presented to R.C. Smail*. Cardiff: University College Cardiff Press, 1985, pp. 191–196.
- Onat, Hasan. "Habîb el-Mektûm", in *IA2*, vol. 14, p. 372.
- Orak, A. "Les Arméniens en Égypte à l'époque des Fatimites", *Cahiers d'Histoire Egyptienne*, 9 série, 3 (1958), pp. 117–137.

- Ormsby, Eric L. "Ismāʿīliya", in *Dictionary of the Middle Ages*. New York: Charles Scribner's Sons, 1985, vol. 6, pp. 614–619.
- Ory, Solange. "Un tissu au nom du calife al-Mustaʿlī bi-llāh", in *Hommages à la mémoire de Serge Sauneron, 1927–1976: II, Égypte post-pharaonique*. Bibliothèque d'étude, 82. Cairo: Institut Français d'Archéologie Orientale du Caire, 1979, pp. 383–393.
- Öz, Mustafa. "Aga Han", "Beyânü Mezhebi'i-Bâtiniyye", "Bohrâ", "Caʿfer b. Mansûrü'l-Yemen", "Cennâbî, Ebû Said", "Cennâbî, Ebû Tâhir", "Dürzîlik", "Ebû Abdullah es-Sîî", "Hâkim-Biemrillâh", "Hasîsiyye", "Imam, Šah", Ismâil b. Caʿfer es-Sâdik", "Ismâiliyye" (with Mustafa Muhammed eş-Şekʿa), "Ivanow, Wladimir", in *IA2*.
- Özaydin, Abdülkerim. "Sultan Berkyaruk Devrinde (1092–1104) Bâtinîlerle Yapilan Mücadeleler", in *Prof. Dr. Fikret Işiltan'a 80. Doğum Yili Armağani*. Istanbul: Istanbul Üniversitesi Edebiyat Fakültesi Ortaçağ Tarih, 1995, pp. 177–185.
- Özaydin, Abdülkerim. "Alamut", "Aziz-Billâh", "Azîzüddevle", "Efdal b. Badr el-Cemâlî", "Hasan Sabbâh", in *IA2*.
- Özcan, Azmi. "Feyzî, Âsaf Ali Asgar (1899–1981)", in *IA2*, vol. 12, pp. 522–523.

P

- Pachniak, Katarzyna. "Listy kalifów al-Mahdiego i al-Muizza o genealogii Fatymidów", *Studia Arabistyczne i Islamistyczne*, 3 (1995), pp. 61–82 (in Polish).
- Pachniak, Katarzyna. "Al-Ǧazālī's Critique of the Ismaili Doctrine", *Studia Arabistyczne i Islamistyczne*, 6 (1998), pp. 58–79.
- Pachniak, Katarzyna. "Wczesna kosmologia ismāʿīlicka", *Studia Arabistyczne i Islamistyczne*, 7 (1999), pp. 107–120 (in Polish).
- Pachniak, Katarzyna. "Dzieje nizarytów", *Albo albo*, 3 (2002), pp. 97–105 (in Polish).
- Pachniak, Katarzyna. "Koncepcja czlowieka w ismāʿīlizmie", *The Peculiarity of Man*, 7 (2002), pp. 653–669 (in Polish).
- Pachniak, Katarzyna. "Porzadek świata duchowego w filozofi Hamida ad-Dina al-Kirmaniego. Intelekt i dziesieć inteligencji", *The Peculiarity of Man*, 8 (2003), pp. 145–153 (in Polish).

- Panāhī (Simnānī), Muḥammad Aḥmad. *Ḥasan-i Ṣabbāḥ*. Khwāndanīhā-yi ta'rīkh, 3. Tehran: Kitābfurūshī-yi Ḥāfiẓ, 1365 Sh./ 1986. pp. 240.
- Paret, Rudi (1901–1983). "Ta'wīl", in *EI*, vol. 4, pp. 704–705.
- Parmaksizoğlu, I. "Nâsir-i Husrev", "Nizâr", "Nizâriye", in Türk Ansiklopedisi. Ankara: Millî Eğitim Basimevi, 1977.
- Pauty, Edmond. *Bois sculptés d'églises Coptes (époque Fatimide)*. Cairo: Institut Français d'Archéologie Orientale, 1930. pp. vii + 38 + 45 plates.
- Pauty, Edmond. "Le pavillon du Nilomètre de l'Île de Rôdah au Vieux Caire", *BIFAO*, 31 (1931), pp. 113–120.
- Pauty, Edmond. "Un dispositif de plafond Fatimite", *BIE*, 15 (1932–33), pp. 99–107.
- Peerwani, (Latimah-) Parvin. "Ismā'īlī Exegesis of the Qur'ān in *al-Majālis al-Mu'ayyadiyya* of al-Mu'ayyad fī al-Dīn al-Shīrāzī", in *BRISMES, Proceedings of the 1988 International Conference on Middle Eastern Studies*, held at the University of Leeds between 10–13 July 1988. Oxford: *BRISMES*, 1988, pp. 118–127.
- Peerwani, Latimah-Parvin. "Abū Ḥātim Rāzī on the Essential Unity of Religions", in Muhammad H. Faghfoory, ed., *Beacon of Knowledge: Essays in Honor of Seyyed Hossein Nasr*. Louisville, KY: Fons Vitae, 2003, pp. 269–287.
- Pellitteri, Antonino. "The Historical-Ideological Framework of Islamic Fāṭimid Sicily (Fourth/Tenth Century) with Reference to the Works of the Qāḍī l-Nu'mān", *Al-Masāq: Studia Arabo-Islamica Mediterranea*, 7 (1994), pp. 111–163.
- Pellitteri, Antonino. "Qualche nota relativa ai *Banū Abī'l-Ḥusayn*", in Antonino Pellitteri and Giovanni Montaina, ed., *Azhàr, Studi Arabo-Islamici in memoria di Umberto Rizzitano (1913–1980)*. Annali della Facoltà di Lettere e Filosofia dell'Università di Palermo, Studi e ricerche, 23. Palermo: Università di Palermo, 1995, pp. 157–175.
- Pellitteri, Antonino. *I Fatimiti e la Sicilia (Sec. X)*, with Preface by B. Scarcia Amoretti. Collana Sicilia Islamica. Palermo: Centro Culturale Al-Farabi, 1997. pp. 124.
- Penrad, Jean Claude. "La présence Isma'ilienne en Afrique de l'Est: note sur l'histoire commerciale et l'organisation communautaire", in Denys Lombard and Jean Aubin, ed., *Marchands et hommes d'affaires*

Asiatiques dans l'Océan Indien et la Mer de Chine 13e-20e siècles. Ports, routes, trafics, 29. Paris: École des Hautes Études en Sciences Sociales, 1988, pp. 221–236.

- Peri, P. Hiram. *Der Religionsdisput der Barlaam-Legende, ein Motiv Abendländischer Dichtung.* Salamanca: University of Salamanca, 1959. pp. 274.
- Périllier, Louis. *Les Druzes.* Collection courants universels. Paris: Publisud, 1986. pp. 90.
- Peterson, Daniel Carl. "Ḥamīd al-Dīn al-Kirmānī on Creation", in Ahmad Hasnawi et al., ed., *Perspectives Arabes et médiévales sur la tradition scientifique et philosophique Grecque.* Orientalia Lovaniensia Analecta, 79. Louvain: Peeters; Paris: Institut du Monde Arabe, 1997, pp. 555–567.
- Peterson, Daniel C. "Al-Kirmani on the Divine *tawḥīd*", in Charles Melville, ed., *Proceedings of the Third European Conference of Iranian Studies:* Part 2, *Mediaeval and Modern Persian Studies.* Wiesbaden: L.R. Verlag, 1999, pp. 179–194.
- Peterson, Daniel C. "Ismāʿīlīyah", in *OE*, vol. 2, pp. 341–342.
- Petrushevskii, Ilya P. (1898–1977). "Ismailians", "Karmathians", in *Bolshaya Sovetskaya Éntsiklopediya.* Moscow: Bolshaya Sovetskaya Éntsiklopediya, 1972; also in *Great Soviet Encyclopedia.* New York: Macmillan; London: Collier Macmillan, 1976–77.
- Pfister, R. "Toiles à inscriptions Abbasides et Fatimides", *BEO*, 11 (1945–46), pp. 47–90.
- Phillips, John. "Assassin Castles in Syria", *Connoisseur*, 191, no. 770 (1976), pp. 286–289.
- Phillips, John. "A Thirteenth-century Ismāʿīlī Ḥammām at Qalʿat al-Kahf", *Antiquaries Journal*, 63 (1983), pp. 64–78.
- Phillips, John. "Mashhad Rāshid al-Dīn Sinān: A 13th-century Ismāʿīlī Monument in the Syrian Jabal Anṣarīya", *JRAS* (1984), pp. 19–37.
- Philon, Helen. *Early Islamic Ceramics: Ninth to Late Twelfth Centuries.* Benaki Museum Athens, Catalogue of Islamic Art, I. [Athens]: Islamic Art Publications, 1980. pp. xviii + 323.
- Picklay, Abdus Salam. *History of the Ismailis.* Bombay: A.S. Picklay, 1940. pp. x + 175.
- Picklay, Abdus Salam. *Rise and Fall of the Fatimid Empire.* Bombay:

A.S. Picklay, 1944. pp. + ii + 122.

- Pinder-Wilson, Ralph. “An Early Fatimid Bowl Decorated in Lustre”, in Richard Ettinghausen, ed., *Aus der Welt der islamischen Kunst: Festschrift für Ernst Kühnel*. Berlin: Gebr. Mann, 1959, pp. 139–143.
- Pines, Shlomo (Salomon) (1908–1989). “Nathanaël ben al-Fayyûmî et la théologie Ismaëlienne”, *Revue de l’Histoire Juive en Égypte*, 1 (1947), pp. 5–22.
- Pines, Shlomo (Salomon). “La longue récension de la Théologie d’Aristote dans ses rapports avec la doctrine Ismaélienne”, *REI*, 22 (1954), pp. 7–20.
- Pines, Shlomo (Salomon). “Une encyclopédie Arabe du 10ᵉ siècle. Les Épîtres des Frères de la Pureté, Rasāʾil Ikhwān al-Ṣafāʾ”, *Rivista di Storia della Filosofia*, 40 (1985), pp. 131–136.
- Pivati, Gianfrancesco F. “Assassini”, in *Nuovo dizionario scientifico e curioso sacro-profano di Gianfrancesco Pivati*. Venice: Benedetto Miloco, 1746, vol. 1, pp. 448–449.
- Pivati, Gianfrancesco F. “Vecchio della Montagna”, in *Nuovo dizionario scientifico e curioso sacro-profano di Gianfrancesco Pivati*. Venice: Benedetto Miloco, 1751, vol. 10, pp. 53–56.
- Pizishk, Manūchihr. “Aʿlām al-nubuwwa”, in *DMBI*, vol. 9, pp. 396–398.
- Plessner, Martin Meir. “Beiträge zur islamischen Literaturgeschichte IV: *Samuel Miklos Stern, die Ikhwān aṣ-Ṣafāʾ und die Encyclopaedia of Islam*”, *Israel Oriental Studies*, 2 (1972), pp. 353–361.
- Poggi, Vincenzo. “I Drusi di Padre Nacchi. Edizione di lettera del 25 gennaio 1699”, in *La Bisaccia dello Sheikh: omaggio ad Alessandro Bausani Islamista nel Sessantesimo Compleanno*. Quaderni del Seminario di Iranistica, Uralo-Altaistica, e Caucasologia dell’Universita degli Studi di Venezia, 19. Venice: Universita di Venezia, 1981, pp. 141–152.
- Poncet, Jean (1912–1980). “Le mythe de la ‘catastrophe’ Hilalienne”, *Annales: Économies, Sociétés, Civilisations*, 22 (1967), pp. 1099–1120.
- Poncet, Jean. “Encore à propos des Hilaliens. La ‘mise au point’ de R. Idris”, *Annales: Économies, Sociétés, Civilisations*, 23 (1968), pp. 660–662.
- Poonawala, Ismail K. “Al-Qāḍī al-Nuʿmān’s Works and the Sources”, *BSOAS*, 36 (1973), pp. 109–115.

- Poonawala, Ismail K. "A Reconsideration of al-Qāḍī al-Nuʿmān's *Madhhab*", *BSOAS*, 37 (1974), pp. 572–579.
- Poonawala, Ismail K. "Al-Sijistānī and his *Kitāb al-Maqālīd*", in Donald P. Little, ed., *Essays on Islamic Civilization Presented to Niyazi Berkes*. Leiden: E.J. Brill, 1976, pp. 274–283.
- Poonawala, Ismail K. *Biobibliography of Ismāʿīlī Literature*. G.E. von Grunebaum Center, University of California, Los Angeles, Studies in Near Eastern Culture and Society. Malibu, CA: Undena Publications, 1977. pp. xix + 533.
- Poonawala, Ismail K. "Ismāʿīlī Sources for the History of South-west Arabia", in *Studies in the History of Arabia*, I: *Sources for the History of Arabia*. Riyadh: Riyadh University Press, 1979, part 1, pp. 151–159.
- Poonawala, Ismail K. "The Qur'an in the *Rasāʾil Ikhwān al-Ṣafāʾ*", in *Selected Proceedings of the International Congress for the Study of the Qurʾan*. Canberra: Australian National University, Faculty of Asian Studies, [1980], pp. 51–67.
- Poonawala, Ismail K. "An Ismāʿīlī Refutation of al-Ghazālī", in Graciela de la Lama, ed., *Middle East 1. 30th International Congress of Human Sciences in Asia and North Africa 1976*. Mexico City: El Colegio de Mexico, 1982, pp. 131–134.
- Poonawala, Ismail K. "Ismāʿīlī *taʾwīl* of the Qurʾān", in Andrew Rippin, ed., *Approaches to the History of the Interpretation of the Qurʾān*. Oxford: Clarendon Press, 1988, pp. 199–222.
- Poonawala, Ismail K. "An Ismāʿīlī Treatise on the Iʿjāz al-Qurʾān", *JAOS*, 108 (1988), pp. 379–385.
- Poonawala, Ismail K. "Al-Qāḍī al-Nuʿmān and Ismaʿili Jurisprudence", in *MIHT*, pp. 117–143. Arabic trans., "al-Qāḍī al-Nuʿmān wa'l-fiqh al-Ismāʿīlī", in *IAW*, pp. 125–145. Persian trans., "Qāḍī Nuʿmān va fiqh-i Ismāʿīlī", in *TAI*, pp. 151–181.
- Poonawala, Ismail K. "Hamid al-Din al-Kirmani and the Proto-Druze", *Journal of Druze Studies*, 1 (2000), pp. 71–94.
- Poonawala, Ismail K. "The Beginning of the Ismaili *Daʿwa* and the Establishment of the Fatimid Dynasty as Commemorated by al-Qāḍī al-Nuʿmān", in Farhad Daftary and Josef W. Meri, ed., *Culture and Memory in Medieval Islam: Essays in Honour of Wilferd Madelung*. London: I.B. Tauris in association with The Institute of Ismaili Studies, 2003, pp. 338–363.

- Poonawala, Ismail K. "Luķmāndjī", "al-Makramī", "al-Mu'ayyad fi'l-Dīn", "Muḥammad b. Ṭāhir al-Ḥārithī", "al-Nasafī", "Nūr Satgur", "Pīr Ṣadr al-Dīn", "Pīr Shams or Shams al-Dīn", "Shāh Ṭāhir", "Shahriyār b. al-Ḥasan", "Shaykh Ādam", "Sulaymān b. Ḥasan", "Sulaymānīs", "Ta'wīl", "al-Ẓāhir wa'l-Bāṭin", in *EI2*.
- Poonawala, Ismail K. "ʿAlī b. Ḥanẓala b. Abī Sālim", "ʿAlī b. Muḥammad b. Djaʿfar", "Amīndjī b. Djalāl b. Ḥasan", "Ḥasan b. Nūḥ al-Bharūčī", "Idrīs b. al-Ḥasan", in *EI2*, Supplement.
- Poonawala, Ismail K. "ʿAlī b. Abī Ṭāleb: i. Life", "Amīnjī b. Jalāl", "Amrī", "Hadith. iii. Hadith in Ismaʿilism", "Ḥasan Bharuči Hendi", in *EIR*.
- Poonawala, Ismail K. "Ikhwān al-Ṣafā'", "Qarāmiṭa", in *ER*.
- Posner, Ernst. "Twelfth Century 'Job Descriptions' for the Registrar and the Archivist of the Fāṭimid State Chancery in Egypt", *Mitteilungen des österreichischen Staatsarchivs*, 25 (1972), pp. 25–31.
- Pourjavady, Nasrollah and Peter Lamborn Wilson. "Ismāʿīlīs and Niʿmatullāhīs", *SI*, 41 (1975), pp. 113–135.
- Pouzet, Louis. "Activités Ismaéliennes en Syrie aux XIIe–XIIIe/VIe–VIIe siècles", in Frederick de Jong, ed., *Shīʿa Islam, Sects and Sufism: Historical Dimensions, Religious Practice and Methodological Considerations.* Utrecht: M. Th. Houtsma Stichting, 1992, pp. 35–49.
- Preux, J. "Assassins", in *La Grande Encyclopédie.* Paris: H. Lamirault, n.d., vol. 4, p. 179.
- Prozorov, Stanislav Mikhaylovich. "Al-Ismaʿiliya", "Al-Qaramiṭa", in *Islam: Éntsiklopedicheskiy slovar'* [Islam: A Concise Dictionary]. Moscow: Nauka, Glavnaya redaktsiya vostochnoy literaturï, 1991.

Q

- al-Qāḍī, Aḥmad ʿArafāt. *al-Fikr al-siyāsī ʿinda al-Bāṭiniyya wa-mawqif al-Ghazālī minhu*. Cairo: al-Hay'a al-Miṣriyya al-ʿĀmma li'l-Kitāb, 1993. pp. 284.
- al-Qāḍī, Wadād. "An Early Fāṭimid Political Document", *SI*, 48 (1978), pp. 71–108.
- al-Qāḍī, Wadād. "Druzes", "al-Ḥākim bi-Amr Allāh", in *Dictionary of*

the Middle Ages. New York: Charles Scribner's Sons, 1984–85.

- Qādīrī, Ḥātim. "Sāz va kār-i imāmat dar *Faḍā'iḥ al-Bāṭiniyya-yi* Ghazālī", in *DKGI*, vol. 1, pp. 323–348.
- Qarachānlū, Ḥusayn. "Anjidān", in *DT*, vol. 2, p. 540.

Qar'alī, Būlus, *see* Carali, Paul

- "Qarmaṭa", in *Diccionario Enciclopedico Salvat Universal*. Barcelona, Madrid, etc.: Salvat Editores, 1976, vol. 17, p. 360.
- "Qarmates", in *Grande Larousse Encyclopédique*. Paris: Librairie Larousse, 1963, vol. 8, p. 933.
- "Qarmatian", in *The New Encyclopaedia Britannica*. 15th ed., Chicago, London, etc.: Encyclopaedia Britannica, 2002, vol. 9, p. 832.
- Qāsim, 'Alī Balḥajj. *Ikhwān al-Ṣafā' fi'l-mīzān*. Susa, [Tunis]: Mu'assasat Saydān, 1985. pp. 90.
- Qāsimī, Mas'ūd. "Pīrāmūn-i chand lughat va bayt-i Nāṣir-i Khusraw", *Nomai Pazhouhishgoh* (Dushanbe), 4 (2003), pp. 7–18.
- Qāsimī, Mas'ūd. "Taṣvīr-i khirad dar shi'r-i Nāṣir-i Khusraw", *Nomai Pazhouhishgoh* (Dushanbe), 4 (2003), pp. 81–92.
- al-Qaṣīr (Qassir), Sayf al-Dīn. *Ibn Ḥawshab wa'l-ḥaraka al-Fāṭimiyya fi'l-Yaman*. Damascus: Dār al-Yanābī', 1994. pp. 138.
- al-Qaṣīr, Sayf al-Dīn. "Mansuru'l-Yaman (Ibn Hawshab)", in *GIH*, pp. 1–3.
- Qazwīnī, Muḥammad (1877–1949). "Nāṣir-i Khusraw", in M. Qazwīnī, *Yāddāshthā-yi Qazwīnī*, ed., Īraj Afshār. Tehran: Intishārāt-i 'Ilmī, 1363 Sh./1984, vol. 7, pp. 187–189.
- Quatremère, Étienne Marc (1782–1857). "Mémoire historique sur la vie du khalife Fatimite Mostanser-Billah", in his *Mémoires géographiques et historiques sur l'Égypte et sur quelques contrées voisines*. Paris: F. Schoell, 1811, vol. 2, pp. 296–485; reprinted, as Publications of the Institute for the History of Arabic-Islamic Science, ed., Fuat Sezgin. Islamic Geography, vol. 253. Frankfurt am Main: Institute for the History of Arabic-Islamic Science at the Johann Wolfgang Goethe University, 1996, vol. 2, pp. 296–485.
- Quatremère, Étienne M. "Notice historique sur les Ismaëliens", *Fundgruben des Orients*, 4 (1814), pp. 339–376.
- Quatremère, Étienne M. "Mémoires historiques sur la dynastie des khalifes Fatimites", *JA*, 3 série, 2 (1836), pp. 97–142, 400–459; (1837), pp.

45–93, 165–208. Abridged English trans., "The Dynasty of the Fatimid Caliphs", *Asiatic Journal*, NS, 23 (1837), pp. 123–129, 285–288.

- Quatremère, Étienne M. "Vie du khalife Fatimite Möezz-li-din-Allāh", *JA*, 3 série, 2 (1836), pp. 401–439; 3 (1837), pp. 44–93, 165–208. English trans., "Life of the Fatimite Caliph Moezz-li-Din-Allah", *Asiatic Journal*, NS, 24 (1837), pp. 79–85, 147–153, 217–224, 294–303; 25 (1838), pp. 30–40.
- Quddūsī, Irshād al-Ḥaqq. *Sir Āghākhān*. Lahore, etc.: Fīrūz Sanz, 1969. pp. 100.
- Qumayr, Yūḥannā. *Ikhwān al-Ṣafā': dirāsa, mukhtārāt*. Beirut: al-Maṭbaʿa al-Kāthūlīkiyya, 1950. pp. 69; 2nd ed., Beirut: al-Maṭbaʿa al-Kāthūlīkiyya, 1954. pp. 76; 3rd ed., Beirut: Dār al-Mashriq, 1982. pp. 89; Persian trans., *Ikhwān al-Ṣafā' yā rawshanfikrān-i Shīʿa madhhab*, tr., Muḥammad Ṣādiq Sajjādī. Falsafa dar jahān-i Islām, 4. Tehran: Intishārāt-i Falsafa, 1363 Sh./1984. pp. 100.

R

- Rabbat, Nasser. "Al-Azhar Mosque: An Architectural Chronicle of Cairo's History", *Muqarnas*, 13 (1996), pp. 45–67.
- Radtke, Bernd. "Bāṭen", in *EIR*, vol. 3, pp. 859–861.
- Raḍwān, Yumna. *al-Usra al-jamāliyya wa-dawruhā fi'l-ḥayāt al-siyāsiyya wa'l-ḥaḍāra fī ʿahd al-dawla al-Fāṭimiyya*. Cairo, n.p., 1994. pp. 227.
- Rafīʿī, ʿAlī. "Tawḥīdiyya", in *DT*, vol. 4, p. 139.
- Rāghib (Rāġib), Yūsuf. "Le mausolée de Yūnus al-Saʿdī est-il celui de Badr al-Ǧamālī?", *Arabica*, 20 (1973), pp. 305–307.
- Rāghib, Yūsuf. "Sur deux monuments funéraires du cimetière d'al-Qarāfa al-Kubrā au Caire", *AI*, 12 (1974), pp. 67–83.
- Rāghib, Yūsuf. "Al-Sayyida Nafisa, sa légende, son culte et son cimetière", *SI*, 44 (1976), pp. 61–86; 45 (1977), pp. 27–55.
- Rāghib, Yūsuf. "Deux monuments Fatimides au pied du Muqaṭṭam", *REI*, 46 (1978), pp. 91–155.
- Rāghib, Yūsuf. "Un épisode obscur d'histoire Fatimide", *SI*, 48 (1978), pp. 125–132.
- Rāghib, Yūsuf. "Un contrat de mariage sur soie d'Égypte Fatimide", *AI*,

16 (1980), pp. 31–37.

- Rāghib, Yūsuf. "Les mausolées Fatimides du quartier d'al-Mašāhid", *AI*, 17 (1981), pp. 1–30.
- Rāghib, Yūsuf. "Un oratoire Fatimide au sommet du Muqaṭṭam", *SI*, 65 (1987), pp. 51–67.
- Rāghib, Yūsuf. "La Mosquée d'al-Qarāfa et Jonathan M. Bloom", *Arabica*, 41 (1994), pp. 419–421.

See also under Claude Cahen

- Rajabī, Muḥammad Riḍa. "Zindigī va andīshahā-yi Nāṣir-i Khusraw", in *IMM*, pp. 401–448.
- Rajput, Ali Muhamad. "Kiya Buzurg Ummid", in *GIH*, pp. 67–69.
- Rānā, ʿAbd al-Ḥamīd. *Prins Āghākhān aur Pākistān*. Lahore: Khidr, 1976. pp. 224.
- Rashed, Roshdi. "Ibn al-Haytham, mathématicien de l'époque Fatimide", in *EF*, pp. 527–535.
- Raslān, ʿAbd al-Munʿim ʿAbd al-ʿAzīz. "Dirāsa li'l-nasīj al-Islāmī al-mudhahhab fī Ṣiqilliya", *al-Dāra*, 9 (1984), pp. 9–32.
- Ravāqī, ʿAlī. "Nāṣir-i Khusraw: rūzigār va ʿawāmm", *NP*, 8, no. 2 (1382 Sh./2003), pp. 145–170.
- Raymond, André. "Le Caire à l'époque Fatimide", *Dossiers d'Archéologie* ; special issue *Égypte: L'Âge d'or des Fatimides*, 233 (May, 1998), pp. 12–19.
- Regnault, C. "Catéchisme à l'usage des Druzes *Djahels* qui veulent être initiés", *Bulletin de la Société de Géographie*, 7 (1827), pp. 22–30.
- Regnault, C. "Recherches sur les Druzes et sur leur religion", *Bulletin de la Société de Géographie*, 7 (1827), 5–21.
- "Religion des Druses", *Revue de l'Orient*, 10 (1846), pp. 235–246.
- Rice, David S. "A Drawing of the Fatimid Period", *BSOAS*, 21 (1958), pp. 31–39.
- Richards, Donald Sidney. "A Fāṭimid Petition and 'Small Decree' from Sinai", *Israel Oriental Studies*, 3 (1973), pp. 140–158.
- Richards, Donald S. "Shāwar", "Shīrkūh", in *EI2*.
- Richards, Donald S. "Fāṭimid Dynasty", in *OE*, vol. 2, pp. 7–8.
- Richards, J. "Les bases maritimes des Fatimides, leurs corsaires et l'occupation franque en Syrie", in *ESFAM2*, pp. 115–129.

- Riḍā'ī, Laylā. "Zamān va makān dar Safar-nāma-yi Nāṣir-i Khusraw", *NP*, 8, no. 2 (1382 Sh./2003), pp. 129–144.
- Riḍāzāda Langarūdī (Rezazadeh Langroudi), Riḍā (Reza). "Kitābshināsī-yi taḥlīlī-yi junbish-i Qarmaṭī", in Riḍā Riḍāzāda Langarūdī, ed., *Yādigār-nāma: majmū'a-yi taḥqīqī taqdīm shuda bi ustād Ibrāhīm Fakhrā'ī*. Tehran: Nashr-i Naw, 1363 Sh./1984, pp. 485–543.
- Riḍāzāda Langarūdī, Riḍā. "Junbish-i Qarmaṭiyān-i Baḥrayn", *Taḥqīqāt-i Islāmī*, 11 (1375 Sh./1997), pp. 11–58.
- Riḍāzāda Langarūdī, Riḍā. "Nakhshabī va junbish-i Qarmaṭiyān-i Khurāsān dar sada-yi chahārum-i hijrī", in Reza Rezazadeh Langroudi (Riḍā Riḍāzāda Langarūdī), ed., *Payandeh Memorial Volume: Forty-six Papers in Memory of the late Mahmud Payandeh Langarudi*. Tehran: Sālī Publications, 1380 Sh./2001, pp. 503–520.
- Riḍāzāda Langarūdī, Riḍā. "Abū Sa'īd Jannābī", "Abū Ṭāhir Jannābī", in *DMBI*.
- Ridley, F.A. *The Assassins*. London: F.A. Ridley, [1936]. pp. 210; 2nd ed., London: Socialist Platform, 1988. pp. vii + 271.
- Rilli, Nicola. "Terre sconosciute. Alamut, la terra patria degli Aga Khan", *L'Universo*, 33 (1953), pp. 51–64, 199–220.
- Rippe, Karl. "Über den Sturz Nizām-ul-Mulks", in *60. doğum yılı münasebetiyle Fuad Köprülü Armağani. Mélanges Fuad Köprülü*. Ankara: Faculté des Lettres d'Ankara, 1953, pp. 423–435.
- Riter, Carl F. "The Early Fatimid Mosque of al-Hakim, 990–1010, 1087", *Oriental Art*, 27 (1981–82), pp. 303–315.
- Riyāḥī, Muḥammad Amīn. "Kasā'ī, pishru-i Nāṣir-i Khusraw", in *YNK*, pp. 234–245; also in *Yaghmā*, 27, no. 1 (1353 Sh./1974), pp. 561–571.
- Rizvi, S. Rizwan Ali. "Houtsma and the Story of the Three School-Fellows: Niẓām al-Mulk, Ḥasan b. Ṣabbāḥ and 'Umar Khayyām", *Journal of the Pakistan Historial Society*, 28 (1980), pp. 229–234.
- Rizvi, Seyyid Saeed Akhtar. "The Khoja Shia Ithna-Asheriya Community in East Africa (1840–1967)", *MW*, 64 (1974), pp. 194–204.
- Rizzitano, Umberto (1913–1980). "Musāhamat ba'ḍ Muslimī Ṣiqilliya fī thaqāfat Miṣr al-Fāṭimiyya", in *Abḥāth al-nadwa al-dawliyya li-ta'rīkh al-Qāhira*. Cairo: Wizārat al-Thaqāfa wa'l-I'lām, 1970, vol. 1, pp. 219–242. French summary, "Les Arabes de Sicile et l'influence qu'ils

ont exercée sur le mouvement culturel qui a fleuri en Égypte sous les Fāṭimides (Résumé)", in *Colloque international sur l'histoire du Caire*, p. 383.

- Robertson Smith, W. "Remarks on Mr. Kay's Edition of ʿOmārah's History of Yemen", *JRAS* (1893), pp. 181–217.
- Röder, Kurt. "Das Mīnā im Bericht über die Schätze der Fatimiden", *ZDMG*, NS, 14 (1935), pp. 363–371.
- Rodinson, Maxime (1915–2004). "Ismaéliens", in *La Grande Encyclopédie*. Paris: Librairie Larousse, 1974, vol. 11, pp. 6496–6497.
- Rodionov, Mikhail Anatol'evich "Uchenie druzov v izlozhenii Sami Nasiba Makarima" [The Druze Teachings as Described by Sami Nasib Makarim], in *Islam, religiya, obshchestvo, gosudarstvo* [Islam: Religion, Society, State]. Moscow: Nauka, 1984, pp. 111–116.
- Rodionov, M.A. "Ad-Duruziya", in *Islam: Éntsiklopedicheskiy slovar'* [Islam: A Concise Dictionary]. Moscow: Nauka, 1991, p. 71.
- Romanov, A. "Pamirskie startsï" [The Pamiri Elders], *Nauka i religiya* (Moscow), no. 7 (1969), pp. 36–39.
- Ronart, Stephan and Nandy. "al-Afdal", "Assassins", "Badr al-Jamālī", "Bātinites", "Brethren of Purity", "Druzes", "Fātimids", "Fidā'ī", "al-Hākim", "Ismāʿīlites", "Jawhar al-Siqilli", in *Concise Encyclopaedia of Arabic Civilization*. Amsterdam: Djambatan, 1959.
- Roshchin, M.I. "Khalif al-Khākim i ustanovlenie teokratii v Fatimidskom Egipte" [Caliph al-Ḥākim and the Establishment of Theocracy in Fatimid Egypt], *Stranï i narodï Azii i Afriki* (Moscow), 5 (1978), pp. 132–140.
- Ross-Sheriff, Fariyal and Azim Nanji. "Islamic Identity, Family and Community: The Case of the Nizari Ismaili Muslims", in Earle H. Waugh et al., ed., *Muslim Families in North America*. Edmonton, Alberta: University of Alberta Press, 1991, pp. 101–117.
- Rossi, Ettore. "Āghā Khān", in *Enciclopedia Italiana*. Rome: Istituto della Enciclopedia Italiana, 1929, vol. 1, p. 888.
- Rousseau, Jean Baptiste L.J. (1780–1831). "Mémoire sur les Ismaélis et les Nosaïris de Syrie, adressé à M. Silvestre de Sacy", *Annales des Voyages*, 14 (1811), pp. 271–303.
- Rousseau, Jean Baptiste L.J. "Extraits d'un Livre qui contient la doctrine des Ismaélis, faisant suite à la Notice sur les Nosaïris et les

Ismaélis", *Annales des Voyages*, 18 (1812), pp. 222–249.

- Rousseau, Jean Baptiste L. J. *Mémoire sur les trois plus fameuses sectes du Musulmanisme, les Wahabis, les Nosaïris et les Ismaélis.* Paris: A. Nepveu; Marseille: Masvert, 1818. pp. 75.
- Rousset, Marie-Odile. "La céramique des XIe et XIIe siècles en Égypte et au Bilād al-Shām. État de la question", in *EF*, pp. 249–264.
- Roy, Shibani. *The Dawoodi Bohras: An Anthropological Perspective.* Delhi: B.R. Publishing Corporation, 1984. pp. xv + 191.
- Rudolph, Kurt. "Das Problem der 'islamischen Gnosis'", *Bibliotheca Orientalis*, 38 (1981), pp. 551–557.
- Ruete, Said. "Der Aufstand der Drusen", *Globus Illustrierte: Zeitschrift für Länder und Völkerkunde*, 70 (1896), pp. 117–119.
- Rūḥānī, Muḥammad Ḥusayn. "Bāṭiniyān", *Taḥqīq va Barrasī-yi Ṭūs* (1369 Sh./1990), pp. 91–134.
- Rūḥānī, Muḥammad Ḥusayn. "Bāṭiniyya", "Ḥashīshiyya", in *DT.*
- al-Ruḥaylī, Sulaymān. *al-Sifārat al-Islāmiyya ilā al-duwal al-Bīzānṭiyya: sifārat al-duwal al-ʿAbbāsiyya wa'l-Fāṭimiyya wa'l-Umawiyya fi'l-Andalus.* Riyadh: S. al-Ruḥaylī, 1414/1993. pp. 296.
- Ruhi, Figali Ethem. "Abdullah b. Meymûn el-Kaddah", in *IA*2, vol. 1, pp. 117–118.
- Ruknī, Muḥammad Mahdī. "Ḥadd bayn-i jabr va ikhtiyār dar shiʿr-i Nāṣir-i Khusraw", *Nashriyya-yi Dānishkada-yi Ilāhiyāt va Maʿārif-i Islāmī-yi Mashhad*, 15 (1354 Sh./1975), pp. 61–65.
- Ruknī, Muḥammad Mahdī. "Nāṣir-i Khusraw, shāʿir-i andarz gū", in *YNK*, pp. 215–233.
- Runte, Hans R. "A Forgotten Old French Version of the Old Man of the Mountain", *Speculum*, 49 (1974), pp. 542–545.
- Russell, Dorothea. "Are there any Remains of the Fātimid Palaces of Cairo?", *Journal of the American Research Center in Egypt*, 3 (1964), pp. 115–121.
- Russell, Justice. "Haji Bibi v. H.H. Sir Sultan Mahomed Shah, the Aga Khan", *Bombay Law Reporter*, 11 (1909), pp. 409–495.
- Ruthven, Malise. "Nasir-i Khusraw and the Ismaʿilis of Gorno-Badakhshan", *University Lectures in Islamic Studies*, 2 (1998), pp. 151–166.

S

- Sabra, ʿAbd al-Ḥamīd. "Ibn al-Haytham and the Visual-Ray Hypothesis", in *ICIC*, pp. 187–205.
- Sachedina, Abdulaziz. "Khojas", in *OE*, vol. 2, pp. 423–427.

Sadik Ali, Mumtaz Ali Tajddin, *see* Tajddin Sadik Ali, Mumtaz Ali

- Ṣādiqī, ʿAlī Ashraf. "Umm al-kitāb", in *DMBI*, vol. 10, pp. 232–234.
- Ṣafā, Dhabīḥ Allāh (1911–1999). *Ikhwān al-Ṣafā*. Tehran: Dānishgāh-i, Tehran, 1330 Sh./1951. pp. 26.
- al-Ṣaghīr, Ajfān. *al-Ḥayāt al-iqtiṣādiyya waʾl-ijtimāʿiyya waʾl-idāriyya ʿinda al-jamāʿāt al-Ismāʿīliyya fī Sūriyā baʿda talāshī al-khilāfa al-Fāṭimiyya*. Homs: Dār al-Tawḥīdī, 2002. pp. 144.
- Sahebjam, Freidoune. *Le Vieux de la Montagne*. Paris: B. Grasset, 1995. pp. 363. Spanish trans., *Hasan Sabbah y la secta de los Asesinos*, tr., Alejandro Domaica. Barcelona: Edhasa, 1996. pp. 351.
- Sāʿī, Muḥsin. *Āqā Khān Maḥallātī va firqa-yi Ismāʿīliyya*. Tehran: n.p., 1329 Sh./1950. pp. 148.
- Saʿīd, Khayr Allāh. "Asāsiyyāt al-ikhtilāf al-Qarmaṭī al-Ismāʿīlī", *Dirāsāt ʿArabiyya*, 25, no. 2 (1988), pp. 87–99.
- Saʿīd, Khayr Allāh. *al-Niẓām al-dākhilī li-ḥarakat Ikhwān al-Ṣafāʾ*. Nicosia: Muʾassasat ʿĪbāl, 1992. pp. 255.
- Saʿīd, Khayr Allāh. *ʿAmal al-duʿāt al-Islāmiyyīn fiʾl-ʿaṣr al-ʿAbbāsī*. Damascus: Dār al-Ḥaṣād, 1993. pp. 398.
- Saʿīd Rāzī, ʿAbd al-ʿAlī. "Maʿād az dīdgāh-i Ismāʿīliyān", in *IMM*, pp. 189–247.
- al-Saʿīdī, ʿUmar. "Intiqāl al-Fāṭimiyyīn ilā Miṣr", in *Multaqā al-Qāḍī al-Nuʿmān liʾl-dirāsāt al-Fāṭimiyya* (2nd series, al-Mahdiyya, 4–7 August 1977). Tunis: Wizārat al-Shuʾūn al-Thaqāfiyya, 1981, pp. 139–149.
- al-Saʿīdī, ʿUmar. "Muḥāwalāt al-Fāṭimiyyīn al-istīlāʾ ʿalā Miṣr", *Dirāsāt Taʾrīkhiyya*, 7 (1982), pp. 74–82.
- Saifuddin, Jaʿfar us Sadiq M. *Al Aqmar: A Living Testimony to the Fatemiyeen*. Croydon, Surrey: Graphico, 2000. pp. 166.
- Saifuddin, Jaʿfar us Sadiq M. *Al Juyushi: A Vision of the Fatemiyeen*. Croydon, Surrey: Graphico, 2002. pp. 180.
- Saint Pierre, Puget de. *Histoire des Druses, peuple du Liban, formé par une colonie de François*. Paris: Cailleau, 1762. pp. xii + 358. Arabic

trans., *al-Dawla al-Durziyya*, tr., Ḥāfiẓ Abū Muṣliḥ. Beirut: al-Maktaba al-Ḥadītha, 1967. pp. 147.

- Sainte-Croix, Fl. de. *Le Vieux de la Montagne, prince des Assassins.* Toulon: Promothéa, 1995.
- Sajjādī, Ḍiyā' al-Dīn. "Taḥqīq dar Rawshanā'ī-nāma-yi Nāṣir-i Khusraw", in *YNK*, pp. 263–272.
- Sajjādī, Ṣādiq. "Nāṣir-i Khusraw va ta'rīkh-nigarī", *NP*, 8, no. 2 (1382 Sh./2003), pp. 171–174.
- Sajjādī, Ṣādiq. "al-Āmir bi-Aḥkām Allāh", "Ibn Afḍal, Abū 'Alī Aḥmad", "Ibn Sallār", "Afḍal b. Badr al-Jamālī", "Afḍal Kutayfāt", "Alamūt" (with 'Ināyat Allāh Majīdī), "Badr al-Jamālī", in *DMBI*.
- Sajjādī, Sayyid Ja'far. "Ta'thīr-i Ikhwān al-Ṣafā' va Ḥamīd al-Dīn Kirmānī dar Ṣadr al-Dīn Shīrāzī", *Majalla-yi Dānishkada-yi Adabiyyāt, Dānishgāh-i Tehrun/Revue de la Faculté des Lettres, Université de Tehran*, 9, no. 3 (1341 Sh./1962), pp. 89–96.
- Sajjādī, Sayyid Ja'far. "Naqdī bar naẓariya-pardāzān-i madhhab-i Bāṭiniyya (I): Ḥamīd al-Dīn al-Kirmānī", *Taḥqīqāt-i Islāmī*, 13 (1378 Sh./1999), pp. 95–112.
- Sajjādī, Sayyid Ja'far and Sayyid Ḥasan 'Arab. "Ta'iyya-yi Ibn 'Āmir", in *DDI*, vol. 6, pp. 346–347.
- Sākit, Muḥammad Ḥusayn. "Zindānī-yi Yumgān, zindānī-yi Shīlān" in *Kitāb-i Pāz*, 2: *yādvāra-yi Mahdī Akhavān-i Thālith*. Mashhad: Intishārāt-i Pāz, 1370 Sh./1991, pp. 71–90.
- Sākit, Muḥammad Ḥusayn. "Ghazālī: digarandīshī va digarandīshān, nigāhī bi pāsukhnāma-yi Ghazālī bi Ismā'īliyān-i Hamadān", in *DKGI*, vol. 1, pp. 221–322.
- al-Ṣalābī, 'Alī Muḥammad. *al-Dawla al-'Ubaydiyya fī Libya*. Oman: Dār al-Biyāriq, 1998. pp. 211.
- Saleh, Abdel Hamid. "Le rôle des bédouins d'Égypte à l'époque Fatimide", *RSO*, 54 (1980), pp. 51–65.
- Saleh, Marlis J. "Government Intervention in the Coptic Church in Egypt during the Fatimid period", *MW*, 91 (2001), pp. 381–397.
- Saleh, Shakib. "The Use of Bāṭinī, Fidā'ī and Ḥashīshī", *SI*, 82 (1995), pp. 35–43.
- Salem, Sahar Abdel Aziz. "Commerce and One Faith", in Saryu Doshi and Mostafa El Abbadi, ed., *India and Egypt: Influences and*

Interactions. Bombay: Marg, 1993, pp. 92–111.

- Ṣāliḥ, Muḥammad Amīn. "al-ʿAlāqa bayna dawlat al-Ṣulayḥiyyīn wa'l-khilāfa al-Fāṭimiyya", *al-Majalla al-Ta'rīkhiyya al-Miṣriyya*, 26 (1979), pp. 61–84.
- Salīm, ʿAbd al-Amīr. "Dahr dar āthār-i Nāṣir-i Khusraw", in *YNK*, pp. 273–292.
- Sallām, Ḥuriyya ʿAbduh. *al-Niẓām al-mālī fī Miṣr zaman al-Fāṭimiyyīn, 358–567H./968–1171H.* Cairo: Dār al-Fikr al-ʿArabī, 1980. pp. 113.
- Sallām, Ḥuriyya ʿAbduh. *al-Nuẓum al-ḥarbiyya fī Miṣr zaman al-Fāṭimiyyīn, 359–567H./968–1171M.* Cairo: Dār al-Fikr al-ʿArabī, 1980. pp. 110.
- Sallām, Muḥammad Zaghlūl. *al-Adab fi'l-ʿaṣr al-Fāṭimī: al-kitāba wa'l-kuttāb*. Alexandria: Mansha'at al-Maʿārif, [1988]. pp. 522.
- al-Sallūmī, Sulaymān b. ʿAbd Allāh. *Uṣūl al-Ismāʿīliyya: dirāsa, taḥlīl, naqd*. Silsilat al-rasā'il al-jāmiʿiyya, 11. Riyadh: Dār al-Fāḍila, 1422/2001. 2 vols.
- Salt, Jeremy. "The Military Exploits of the Qarmatians (al-Qarāmiṭah)", *Abr-Nahrain*, 17 (1976–77), pp. 43–51.
- Samīʿī, Majīd. "Anjidān", in *DMBI*, vol. 10, pp. 314–315.
- Samir, Samir Khalil. "The Role of Christians in the Fāṭimid Government Services of Egypt to the Reign of al-Ḥāfiẓ", in David Thomas, ed., *Second Woodbrooke-Mingana Symposium on Arab Christianity and Islam;* being, *Medieval Encounters*, 2 (1996), pp. 177–192.
- Sanders, Paula. "From Court Ceremony to Urban Language: Cermonial in Fatimid Cairo and Fusṭāṭ", in C. Edmund Bosworth et al., ed., *The Islamic World: From Classical to Modern Times (Essays in Honor of Bernard Lewis)*. Princeton: The Darwin Press, 1989, pp. 311–321.
- Sanders, Paula. "A New Source for the History of Fāṭimid Ceremonial: The *Rasā'il al-ʿAmīdī*", *AI*, 25 (1991), pp. 127–131.
- Sanders, Paula. "Claiming the Past: Ghadīr Khumm and the Rise of Ḥāfiẓī Historiography in late Fāṭimid Egypt", *SI*, 75 (1992), pp. 81–104.
- Sanders, Paula. *Ritual, Politics, and the City in Fatimid Egypt*. SUNY Series in Medieval Middle East History. Albany, NY: State University of New York Press, 1994. pp. xii + 231.

- Sanders, Paula. "The Fāṭimid State, 969–1171", in M.W. Daly, ed., *The Cambridge History of Egypt*: Volume 1, *Islamic Egypt*, 640–1517, ed., Carl F. Petry. Cambridge: Cambridge University Press, 1998, pp. 151–174, 560–561.
- Sanders, Paula. "Bohra Architecture and the Restoration of Fatimid Culture", in *EF*, pp. 159–165.
- Sanders, Paula. "Fatimids", in *Dictionary of the Middle Ages.* New York: Charles Scribner's Sons, 1985, vol. 5, pp. 24–30.

See also under Yedida K. Stillman

- Ṣaqr, Muḥammad ʿAbd al-Salām Ibrāhīm. *al-Shiʿr al-ʿArabī bi-Miṣr fī ẓilāl al-Fāṭimiyyīn, dirāsatan wa-naqdan.* Cairo: al-Amāna, 1991. pp. 207.
- Sarkārātī, Bahman. "Murvārīd pīsh-i khūk afshāndan", *Nomai Pazhouhishgoh* (Dushanbe), 4 (2003), pp. 19–36.
- Sauvaire, H. and Stanley Lane-Poole. "The Name of the Twelfth Imam on the Coinage of Egypt", *JRAS*, NS, 7 (1875), pp. 140–151.
- al-Ṣāwī, Aḥmad al-Sayyid. *Majāʿāt Miṣr al-Fāṭimiyya: asbāb wa-natāʾij.* Beirut: Dār al-Taḍāmun, 1988. pp. 311.
- Sayf Āzād, ʿAbd al-Raḥmān. *Taʾrīkh-i khulafā-yi Fāṭimī.* Tehran: Idāra-yi Majalla-yi Īrān-i Bāstān, 1341 Sh./1962. pp. 242.
- Sayyid, Ayman Fuʾād. "Lumières nouvelles sur quelques sources de l'histoire Fatimide en Égypte", *AI*, 13 (1977), pp. 1–41.
- Sayyid, Ayman F. "Dirāsāt naqdiyya li-baʿḍ maṣādir janūb gharb al-jazīra al-ʿArabiyya fiʾl-ʿaṣr al-Fāṭimī", in *Studies in the History of Arabia, I: Sources for the History of Arabia.* Riyadh: Riyadh University Press, 1979, part 1, pp. 245–252.
- Sayyid, Ayman F. "Nuṣūṣ ḍāʾiʿa min Akhbār Miṣr liʾl-Musabbiḥī", *AI*, 17 (1981), pp. 1–54.
- Sayyid, Ayman F. "Dirāsāt naqdiyya li-maṣādir taʾrīkh al-Fāṭimiyyīn fī Miṣr", in *Dirāsāt ʿArabiyya wa-Islāmiyya muhdā ilā... Maḥmūd Muḥammad Shākir.* Cairo, 1982, pp. 129–179.
- Sayyid, Ayman F. "Tanẓīm al-ʿāṣima al-Miṣriyya wa-idārātuhā fī zaman al-Fāṭimiyyīn", *AI*, 23 (1987), pp. 1–13.
- Sayyid, Ayman F. *al-Dawla al-Fāṭimiyya fī Miṣr: tafsīr jadīd.* Cairo: al-Dār al-Miṣriyya al-Lubnāniyya, 1413/1992. pp. 478; 2nd ed., Cairo: al-Dār al-Miṣriyya al-Lubnāniyya, 2000. pp. ix + 817.

- Sayyid, Ayman F. "al-Madāris fī Miṣr qabla al-ʿaṣr al-Ayyūbī", in ʿAbd al-ʿAẓīm Ramaḍān, ed., *Taʾrīkh al-madāris fī Miṣr al-Islāmiyya*. Taʾrīkh al-Miṣriyyīn, 51. Cairo: al-Hayʾa al-Miṣriyya al-ʿĀmma liʾl-Kitāb, 1992, pp. 87–136.
- Sayyid, Ayman F. *La capitale de l'Égypte jusqu'à l'époque Fatimide, al-Qāhira et al-Fusṭāṭ. Essai de reconstitution topographique*. Beiruter Texte und Studien, 48. Stuttgart: F. Steiner, 1998. pp. xl + 754 (French) + 26. (Arabic)
- Sayyid, Ayman F. "L'art du Livre", *Dossiers d'Archéologie* ; special issue *Égypte: L'Âge d'or des Fatimides*, 233 (May, 1998), pp. 80–83.
- Sayyid, Ayman F. "Khizānat kutub al-Fāṭimiyyīn: hal baqiya minhā shayʾ?", *Majallat Maʿhad al-Makhṭūṭāt al-ʿArabiyya*, 42, no. 1 (1998), pp. 7–32.
- Sayyid, Ayman F. "Le grand palais Fatimide au Caire", in *EF*, pp. 117–125.
- Sayyid, Ayman F. "Ṭabīʿat al-iqṭāʿ al-Fāṭimī", *AI*, 33 (1999), pp. 1–16.
- Sayyid, Ayman F. "Transformation du Caire en centre économique à la fin de l'époque des Fatimides et du temps des Ayyoubides", in Sylvie Denoix et al, ed., *Le Khan al-Khalili et ses environs. Un centre commercial et artisanal au Caire du XIIIe au XXe siècle*. Études urbaines, 4. Cairo: Institut Français d'Archéologie Orientale, 1999, pp. 155–160.
- Sayyid [Seyyid], Ayman Fuʾād [Eyman Fuâd]. "Fâtimîler: I. Siyasi Tarih. II. Medeniylt Tarihi", "Ibn Havseb", "Ibnü's-Sayrafi, Ebü'l-Kâsim", in *IA2*.
- Sayyid [Sayyed], Ayman Fuʾād and Roland Pierre Gayraud. "Fustāt-Le Caire à l'époque Fatimide", in Jean Claude Garlin, ed., *Grandes villesMéditerranéennes du monde Musulman médiéval*. Collection de l'École Française de Rome, 269. Rome: École Française de Rome, 2000, pp. 135–156.
- Scanlon, George T. "Leadership in the Qarmaṭian Sect", *BIFAO*, 59 (1960), pp. 29–48.
- Scanlon, George T. "Fāṭimid Filters: Archaeology and Olmer's Typology", *AI*, 9 (1970), pp. 37–51 + 13 plates.
- Scanlon, George T. "A Note on Fatimid-Saljūq Trade", in Donald S. Richards, ed., *Islamic Civilisation, 950–1150*. A Colloquium published under the auspices of the Near Eastern History Group, Oxford; The Near East Center, University of Pennsylvania. Papers on Islamic

History, 3. Oxford: Bruno Cassirer, 1973, pp. 265–274.

- Scanlon, George T. "Fatimid Underglaze Painted Wares: A Chronological Readjustment", in Farhad Kazemi and Robert D. McChesney, ed., *A Way Prepared: Essays in Islamic Culture in Honor of Richard Bayly Winder*. New York: New York University Press, 1988, pp. 185–195.
- Scanlon, George T. "Fustat Fatimid Sgraffiato: Less than Lustre", in *EF*, pp. 265–283.
- Scarcia Amoretti, Biancamaria. *Sciiti nel mondo*. Storia, 32. Rome: Jouvence, 1994. pp. 345.
- Scarcia Amoretti, Biancamaria. "Controcorrente? Il Caso della comunità Khogia di Zanzibar", *Oriente Moderno*, NS, 14 (1995), pp. 153–170.
- Scarcia Amoretti, Biancamaria. "Note sull'Ismailismo contemporaneo: il caso del ʿAllāma Naṣīr al-Dīn Naṣīr Hūnzā'ī", in Daniela Bredi and Gianroberto Scarcia, ed., *Ex libris Franco Coslovi*. Eurasiatica, 40. Venice: Poligrafo, 1996, pp. 401–421.
- Schaller, Hans M. "König Manfred und die Assassinen", *Deutsches Archiv für Erforschung des Mittelalters*, 21 (1965), pp. 173–193.
- Scheffler, Thomas. "Survival and Leadership at an Interface Periphery: The Druzes in Lebanon", in Krisztina Kehl-Bodrogi et al., ed., *Syncretistic Religious Communities in the Near East*. Studies in the History of Religions (Numen Book Series), 76. Leiden: E.J. Brill, 1997, pp. 227–246.
- Scheiber, Alexander. *Genizah Studies*. Collectanea, 17. Hildesheim and New York: G. Olms, 1981. pp. 570 (English) + 116 (Hebrew).
- Schimmel, Annemarie (1922–2003). "Some Notes on Nâṣer-e Xosrow as a Poet", in Christophe Balaÿ, Claire Kappler and Živa Vesel, ed., *Pand-o Sokhan. Mélanges offerts à Charles-Henri de Fouchécour*. Bibliothèque Iranienne, 44. Tehran: Institut Français de Recherche en Iran, 1995, pp. 259–264.
- Schlumberger, Gustave. *Campagnes du Roi Amaury Ier de Jérusalem en Égypte au XIIe siècle*. Paris: Librairie Plon, 1906. pp. 352.
- Schmidt, Heinrich. "Islamische Seidenstoffe der Fatimidenzeit", *Zeitschrift für bildende Kunst*, 64 (1930–31), pp. 185–191.
- Schmidt, Robert. "Die Hedwigsgläser und die verwandten fatimidischen Glas- und Kristallschnittarbeiten", *Schlesiens Vorzeit in Bild und*

Schrift, NS, 6 (1912), pp. 53–78.

- *Secret Societies of the Middle Ages*. London: M.A. Nattali, 1846, pp. 13–168 (on 'The Assassins').
- Seipel, Wilfried (ed.), *Schätze der Kalifen: Islamische Kunst zur Fatimidenzeit. Eine Ausstellung des Kunsthistorischen Museums Wien*. Vienna: Kunsthistorisches Museum; Milan: Skira, 1998. pp. 256.
- Sell, Canon Edward. *The Druses*. The Islam Series, 12. London, etc.: The Christian Literature Society for India, 1910. pp. 65.
- Semenov, Aleksandr Aleksandrovich (1873–1958). "Iz oblasti religioznïkh verovaniy gornïkh tadzhikov" [On the Religious Beliefs of the Mountain Tajiks], *Étnograficheskoe obozrenie* (Moscow), 47, no. 4 (1900), pp. 81 88.
- Semenov, Aleksandr A. "Iz oblasti religioznïkh verovaniy shugnanskikh ismailitov" [On the Religious Beliefs of the Ismailis of Shughnān], *Mir Islama* (St. Petersburg), 1 (44), (1912), pp. 523–561.
- Semenov, Aleksandr A. "Rasskaz shugnanskikh ismailitov o bukharskom sheykhe Bekha-ud-Dine" [The Tale of the Shughnī Ismailis on the Bukharan Shaykh Bahā' al-Dīn], *Zapiski Vostochnogo otdeleniya Imperatorskogo Russkogo Arkheologicheskogo obshchestva* (Petrograd), 22 (1915), pp. 321–326.
- Semenov, Aleksandr A. "Sheikh Dzelal-ud-Din-Rumi po predstavleniyam shugnanskikh ismailitov" [The Shughnī Ismailis' Views of Shaykh Jalāl al-Dīn Rūmī], *Zapiski Vostochnogo otdeleniya Imperatorskogo Russkogo Arkheologicheskogo obshchestva* (Petrograd), 22 (1915), pp. 247–256.
- Semenov, Aleksandr A. "Istoriya Shugnana" [History of Shughnān], *Protokolï Turkestanskogo kruzhka lyubiteley arkheologii* (Tashkent), 21 (1917), pp. 1–24.
- Semenov, Aleksandr A. "Opisanie ismailitskikh rukopisey, sobrannïkh A.A. Semyonovïm", [Description of Ismaili Manuscripts, A.A. Semenov's Collection], *Izvestiya Rossiyskoy Akademii Nauk/Bulletin de l'Académie des Sciences de Russie* (Petrograd), 6 série, 12 (1918), pp. 2171–2202.
- Semenov, Aleksandr A. "Nasïri Khosrov o mire dukhovnom i material'nom" [Nāṣir-i Khusraw on Spiritual and Material Worlds], in *Sbornik Turkestanskogo vostochnogo instituta v chest' A.É. Shmidta* [Collected Essays of Turkestan Oriental Institute in Honour of A.E.

Schmidt]. Tashkent, 1923, pp. 124–133.

- Semenov, Aleksandr A. "K biografii Nasïri-Khosrova" [Toward the Biography of Nāṣir-i Khusraw], *Byulleten' Sredneaziatskogo gosudarstvennogo universiteta* (Tashkent)/*Bulletin de l'Université de Asie Centrale*, 3 (1924), pp. 64–66.
- Semenov, Aleksandr A. "Protivorechiya vo vzglyadakh na pereselenie dush u pamirskikh ismailitov i u Nasïr-i-Khosrova" [Contradictions in the Views on Metemphsychosis in the Works of Nāṣir-i Khusraw and Pamiri Ismailis], *Byulleten' Sredneaziatskogo gosudarstvennogo universiteta* (Tashkent)/*Bulletin de l'Université de Asie Centrale*, 9 (1925), pp. 103–117. A Turkish translation of this study was published in *The Proceedings of the Istanbul University*, vol. 7 (1926).
- Semenov, Aleksandr A. *K dogmatike pamirskogo ismailizma XI glava "Litsa veri" Nasïr-i Khosrova* [On the Dogmatics of Pamiri Ismailism: The XIth Chapter of the *Wajh-i dīn* of Nāṣir-i Khusraw]. Tashkent, 1926. pp. xiv + 52.
- Semenov, Aleksandr A. "Vzglyad na Koran v vostochnom ismailizme" [The Qur'an from the Viewpoint of Oriental Ismailism], *Iran* (Leningrad), 1 (1926), pp. 59–72.
- Semenov, Aleksandr A. "Pamir Ismaililer akidelerine ait, tr., Abdülkadir", *DIFM*, 2, no. 7 (1928), PP. 81–88.
- Semenov, Aleksandr A. "Shugnansko-ismailitskaya redaktsiya 'Knigi sveta' (Roushanaéinama) Nasïr-i Khosrova" [The Shughnānī-Ismaili Edition of the 'Book of Light' (*Rawshanā'ī-nāma*) of Nāṣir-i Khusraw], *Zapiski kollegii vostokovedov pri Aziatskom muzee* AN SSSR (Leningrad), 5 (1930), pp. 589–610.
- Semenova, Lidiya Andreevna. *Iz istorii fatimidskogo Egipta. Ocherki i materialï* [From the History of Fatimid Egypt. Essays and Sources]. Moscow: Nauka, 1974. pp. 264.
- Semenova, Lidiya A. *Egipet pri Fatimidakh* [Egypt under Fatimid Dynasty]. *Avtoreferat doktorskoy dissertatsii na zvanie doktora istoricheskikh nauk*. Moscow, 1980. pp. 38.
- Semenova, Lidiya A. "Fatimidï", in *Bolshaya Sovetskaya Éntsiklopediya*. Moscow: Bolshaya Sovetskaya Éntsiklopediya, 1977, vol, 27, p. 218; also in *Great Soviet Encyclopedia*. New York: Macmillan; London: Collier Macmillan, 1981, vol. 27, pp. 112–113.
- Serauky, Eberhard. "Zur Stellung der Ismāʿīlija in der frühfeudalen

Entwicklung des Jemen", in Burchard Brentjes, ed., *Avicenna/Ibn Sina (980/1036). II. Wissenschaftsgeschichte.* Martin-Luther-Universität, Hallen-Wittenberg, Wissenschaftliche Beiträge 1980/17(112). Halle (Saale), 1980, pp. 43–50.

- Şerefeddin, Mehmet. "Fâtimîler ve Hasan Sabbâh", *DIFM*, 1, no. 4 (1926), pp. 1–44.
- Şerefeddin, Mehmet. "Nâsir-ı Hüsrev", *DIFM*, 2, nos. 5–6 (1927), pp. 1–21.
- Şerefeddin, Mehmet. "Batinîlik tarihi", *DIFM*, 2, no. 8 (1928), pp. 1–27.
- Şerefeddin, Mehmet. "Karâmeta ve Sinân-Râshid al-Dîn", *DIFM*, 2, no. 7 (1928), pp. 26–80.
- Sesen, Ramazan. "Cevher es-Sikillî", in *IA2*, vol. 7, pp. 456–457.
- Şevki Yavuz, Yusuf. "A'lâmü'n-Nübüvve", "Ebû Hâtim er-Râzî", in *IA2*.
- Sezgin, Fuat et al. (ed.), *Rasāʾil Ikhwān aṣ-Ṣafāʾ wa-Khillān al-Wafāʾ (2nd half 4th/10th cent.). Texts and Studies, I–II, Collected and Reprinted.* Institute for the History of Arabic-Islamic Science, Islamic Philosophy, 21–22. Frankfurt am Main: Institute for the History of Arabic-Islamic Science at the Johann Wolfgang Goethe University, 1999. 2 vols.
- al-Shābī, Muḥammad. "Muḥāwala fī iʿādat taḥdīd taʾrīkh al-ghazwa al-Hilāliyya al-Ifrīqiya", *Taʾrīkh al-ʿArab waʾl-ʿĀlam*, 4 (1982), pp. 58–69.
- Shackle, Christopher and Zawahir Moir. *Ismaili Hymns from South Asia: An Introduction to the Ginans.* SOAS South Asian Texts, 3. London: School of Oriental and African Studies, University of London, 1992. pp. xv + 258.
- Shāfiʿī (Shāfeʿī), Farīd. "An Early Fāṭimid Miḥrab in the Mosque of Ibn Ṭūlūn", *Majallat Kulliyyat al-Ādāb, Jāmiʿat Fuʾād al-Awwal/Bulletin of the Faculty of Arts, Fouad I University*, 15 (1953), pp. 67–81.
- Shāfiʿī, Farīd. "Mumayyizāt al-akhshāb al-muzakhrafa fiʾl-ṭirāzayn al-ʿAbbāsī waʾl-Fāṭimī fī Miṣr", *Majallat Kulliyyat al-Ādāb, Jāmiʿat al-Qāhira/Bulletin of the Faculty of Arts, Cairo University*, 16, no. 1 (1954), pp. 57–94.
- Shāfiʿī, Farīd. "The Mashhad al-Juyūshī (Archaeological Notes and

Studies)", in *Studies in Islamic Art and Architecture in Honour of Professor K.A.C. Creswell*. Cairo: Published for The Arabic Center for Arabic Studies by The American University in Cairo Press, 1965, pp. 237–252.

- Shāh, Mīr Ḥusayn. "Ismāʿīlīhā-yi qalʿa-yi Alamūt", *Āriyānā*, 16, no. 9 (1338 Sh./1959), pp. 41–48; no. 10 (1338 Sh./1959), pp. 45–52.
- Shah, Sirdar Ikbal Ali. *The Prince Aga Khan: An Authentic Life Story*. London: J. Long, 1933. pp. ix + 249.
- Shah, Sirdar Ikbal Ali. "The Aga Khan", in his *The Controlling Minds of Asia*. London: H. Jenkins, 1937, pp. 85–124.
- Shāh-Ḥusaynī, Nāṣir al-Dīn. "Tajziya va taḥlīl-i qaṣāʾid-i Nāṣir-i Khusraw", in *YNK*, pp. 293–315.
- Shahīdī, Sayyid Jaʿfar. "Afkār va ʿaqāʾid-i kalāmī-yi Nāṣir-i Khusraw", in *YNK*, pp. 316–340; also in *Yaghmā*, 27, no. 11 (1353 Sh./1974), pp. 638–645; no. 12 (1353 Sh./1974), pp. 705–711.
- Shahīdī Ṣāliḥī, ʿAbd al-Ḥusayn. "Ḥurra Ṣulayḥī", in *DT*, vol. 6, p. 207.
- Shahrī Barābādī, Muḥammad. "Qarāmiṭa dar taʾrīkh-i Islām", *Mishkāt*, 18–19 (1367/1988), pp. 58–72.
- Shahrūzī, ʿAlī. *Taʾrīkh-i Alamūt*. Qazwīn, Iran: Ṭāhā, 1376 Sh./1997. pp. 95.
- Shaked, Shaul. *A Tentative Bibliography of Geniza Documents*. Études Juives, 5. Paris and The Hague: Mouton, 1964. pp. 355.
- Shākir, Maḥmūd. *al-Lawḥa al-tidhkāriyya li'l-Jāmiʿ al-Anwar*. Croydon, Surrey: Graphico, n.d. pp. 76.
- Shalem, Avinoam. "A Note on the Shield-shaped Ornamental Bosses on the Façade of Bāb al-Naṣr in Cairo", *Ars Orientalis*, 26 (1996), pp. 55–64.
- Shalem, Avinoam. "L'origine de quelques objects Fatimides", *Dossiers d'Archéologie* ; special issue *Égypte: L'Âge d'or des Fatimides*, 233 (May, 1998), pp. 72–79.
- Shalem, Avinoam. "The Rock-Crystal Lionhead in the Badisches Landesmuseum in Karlsruhe", in *EF*, pp. 359–366.
- Shámi, Abdullah. "The Druse Rising in the Hauran", *Imperial and Asiatic Quarterly Review*, 3rd series, 2 (1896), pp. 306–314; 3 (1897), pp. 180–197.
- Shamma, Samir. "The Fāṭimid Coins of Filasṭīn", *Al-Abḥāth*, 29 (1981),

pp. 37–50.

- Shams al-Dīn, ʿAbd al-Amīr Z. *al-Falsafa al-tarbawiyya ʿinda Ikhwān al-Ṣafāʾ min khilāl rasāʾilihim*. Mawsūʿat al-tarbiya waʾl-taʿlīm al-Islāmiyya, qiṭāʿ al-falāsifa. Beirut: al-Sharika al-ʿĀlamiyya liʾl-Kitāb, 1988. pp. 272.
- Sharaf, Ḥifnī Muḥammad. *Tamīm b. al-Muʿizz, shāʿir al-Fāṭimiyyīn*. [Cairo]: al-Majlis al-Aʿlā liʾl-Shuʾūn al-Islāmiyya, 1967. pp. 211.
- Sharaf, Ṭāhā Aḥmad. *Dawlat al-Nizāriyya ajdād Āghā Khān kamā assasahā al-Ḥasan al-Ṣabbāḥ*. Cairo: Maṭbaʿat al-Shibukshī, 1369/ 1950. pp. 248.

  See also under Ḥasan Ibrāhīm Ḥasan
- Sharīʿatmadārī, Ḥamīd Riḍā. "Rahnamā-yi muṭālaʿāt-i Qarmaṭī", in *IMM*, pp. 597–644.
- Sharon, Moshe. "A New Fâṭimid Inscription from Ascalon and its Historical Setting", *ʿAtiqot*, 26 (1995), pp. 61–86.
- al-Sharqāwī, Ḥasan Muḥammad. *al-Ḥukūma al-Bāṭiniyya*. Alexandria: Dār al-Kutub al-Jāmiʿiyya, 1975. pp. 306 + 8; 2nd ed., Cairo: Dār al-Maʿārif, 1982. pp. 306 + 12.
- Shayegan, Daryush. "Le sens du Taʾwîl", in Christian Jambet, ed., *Les cahiers de l'Herne: Henry Corbin*. Paris: Éditions de l'Herne, 1981, pp. 84–87.
- Shayegan, Daryush. "Corbin, Henry", in *EIR*, vol. 6, pp. 268–272.
- al-Shayyāl (el-Shayyal), Jamāl al-Dīn (Gamal el-Din) (1911–1967). "al-ʿAlāqāt bayna Miṣr waʾl-Yaman fiʾl-ʿaṣr al-Fāṭimī", *al-Kitāb*, 5 (1948), pp. 550–561.
- al-Shayyāl, Jamāl al-Dīn. "al-Yaman fiʾl-ʿaṣr al-Fāṭimī: ṣafḥa majhūla min al-taʾrīkh al-ʿArabī", *Levante*, 1, no. 2 (1953), pp. 20–32.
- al-Shayyāl, Jamāl al-Dīn. "The Faṭimid Documents as a Source for the History of the Faṭimids and their Institutions", *Majallat Kulliyyat al-Ādāb, Jāmiʿat al-Iskandariyya/Bulletin of the Faculty of Arts, Alexandria University*, 8 (1954), pp. 3–12.
- al-Shayyāl, Jamāl al-Dīn. *Taʾrīkh Miṣr al-Islāmiyya*. Alexandria: Dār al-Maʿārif, 1967, vol. 1, pp. 181–290 (on Fatimid Egypt).
- Sheikh, M. Saeed. "Philosophy of the Ikhwan-us-Safa", *Iqbal*, 6, no. 3 (1958), pp. 19–27.
- Shepherd, Dorothy G. "Two Fatimid Tapestry Roundels", *Bulletin of*

the Cleveland Museum of Art, 39 (1952), pp. 215–217.

- Shiel, Justus. "Itinerary from Tehrān to Alamūt and Khurremābād in May 1837", *Journal of the Royal Geographical Society*, 8 (1838), pp. 430–434. The account of the first Westerner in modern times who correctly identified the site of the fortress of Alamūt.
- Shīftahfar, Afsāna. "Amthāl va ḥakam dar ash'ār-i Nāṣir-i Khusraw", *Nomai Pazhouhishgoh* (Dushanbe), 4 (2003), pp. 39–80.
- Shirley, James R. "Aga Khan", in *Encyclopedia Americana*. New York: Americana Corporation, 1977, vol. 1, p. 327.
- Shodan, Amrita. "Legal Formulation of the Question of Community: Defining the Khoja Collective", *Indian Social Science Review*, 1 (1999), pp. 137–151.
- Shokhumorov, Abusaid (1955–1999). "Otritsatel'naya teologiya kak predposïlka filosofskikh i politicheskikh vsglyadov Nosir-i Khusrava" [Negative Theology as an Argument in Nāṣir-i Khusraw's Philosophical and Political Views], in *The History of Philosophy and Contemporary Situation. Tezisï IV regional'nïkh filosofskikh chteniy molodïkh uchyonïkh respublik Sredney Azii i Kazakhstana*. Dushanbe, 1988, pp. 89–91.
- Shokhumorov, Abusaid. *Kontseptsiya poznaniya Nosir-i Khusrava* [Nāṣir-i Khusraw's Concept of Knowledge]. *Avtoreferat dissertatsii na zvanie kandidata filosofskikh nauk*. Dushanbe, 1990. pp. 19.
- Shokhumorov, Saidanvar. "Ismailism: Traditions and the Present Day", *Central Asia and the Caucasus*, 2 (2000), pp. 130–138.
- Shoshan, Boaz. "Fāṭimid Grain Policy and the Post of the Muḥtasib", *IJMES*, 13 (1981), pp. 181–189.
- al-Shurbajī, Amīna Aḥmad Imām. *Ru'yat al-raḥḥāla al-Muslimīn li'l-aḥwāl al-māliyya wa'l-iqtiṣādiyya li-Miṣr fi'l-'aṣr al-Fāṭimī (358–567H./969–1171M)*. Ta'rīkh al-Miṣriyyīn, 72. Cairo: al-Hay'a al-Miṣriyya al-'Āmma li'l-Kitāb, 1994. pp. 536.
- Silvestre de Sacy, Antoine Isaac. (1758–1838). "Mémoire sur la dynastie des Assassins et sur l'origine de leur nom", *Annales des Voyages*, 8 (1809), pp. 325–343; shorter version in *Moniteur*, 210 (July, 1809), pp. 828–830. English trans., in J. von Hammer-Purgstall, *The History of the Assassins*, pp. 227–235.
- Silvestre de Sacy, Antoine I. "Mémoire sur l'origine du culte que les Druzes rendent à la figure d'un veau", *Mémoires de l'Institut Royal de*

France, 3 (1818), pp. 74–128.

- Silvestre de Sacy, Antoine I. "Mémoire sur la dynastie des Assassins, et sur l'étymologie de leur nom", *Mémoires de l'Institut Royal de France*, 4 (1818), pp. 1–84; also in *Mémoires d'Histoire et de Litérature Orientales*. Paris, 1818, pp. 322–403; reprinted in Bryan S. Turner, ed., *Orientalism: Early Sources,* Volume I, *Readings in Orientalism*. London: Routledge, 2000, pp. 118–169. English trans., "Memoir on the Dynasty of the Assassins, and on the Etymology of their Name", tr., Azizeh Azodi, ed. F. Daftary, in F. Daftary, *The Assassin Legends: Myths of the Isma'ilis*. London: I.B. Tauris, 1994, pp. 129–188. Arabic trans., "Dirāsa fī salālat al-ḥashshashīn wa'l-aṣl al-lughawī li-ismihim", tr., S. al-Qaṣīr, in F. Daftary, *Khurāfāt al-ḥashshāshīn wa-asāṭīr al-Ismā'īliyya*, tr., S. al-Qaṣīr. Damascus and Beirut: Dār al-Madā, 1996, pp. 195–274. Hungarian trans., "Értekezés az aszaszinok dinasztiájáról és nevük étimológiájáról", tr. I. Hajnal, in F. Daftary, *Aszaszin legendák: Az iszmá'iliták mítoszai*, tr., István Hajnal. Budapest: Orisis Kiado, 2000, pp. 111–154. Persian trans., "Tadkhira dar bāra-yi silsila-yi Asāsīnhā va rīsha-shināsī-yi nām-i ānhā", tr., F. Badra'ī, in F. Daftary, *Afsānahā-yi ḥashshāshīn, yā usṭūrihā-yi fidā'īyān-i Ismā'īlī*, tr., F. Badra'ī. Tehran: Farzān, 1376 Sh./1997, pp. 221–314.
- Silvestre de Sacy, Antoine I. "Recherches sur l'initiation à la secte des Ismaéliens", *JA*, 1 série, 4 (1824), pp. 298–311, 321–331; reprinted in Jean Claude Frère, *L'ordre des Assassins*, pp. 261–274.
- Silvestre de Sacy, Antoine I. "Notice des manuscrits des livres sacrés des Druzes, qui se trouvent dans diverses bibliothèques de l'Europe", *JA*, 1 série, 5 (1824), pp. 3–18; reprinted in his "Premier mémoire sur les livres religieuse des Druzes", pp. 31–45.
- Silvestre de Sacy, Antoine I. "Observations sur une pratique superstitieuse attribuée aux Druzes, et sur la doctrine des Nosaïriens", *JA*, 1 série, 10 (1827), pp. 321–351.
- Silvestre de Sacy, Antoine I. "Mémoire sur une médaille Arabe inédite, de l'an 525 de l'hégire", *Histoire et Mémoires de l'Institut Royal de France, Académie des Inscriptions et Belles Lettres*, 9 (1831), pp. 284–316.
- Silvestre de Sacy, Antoine I. "Premier mémoire sur les livres religieux des Druzes", *Histoire et Mémoires de l'Institut Royal de France, Académie des Inscriptions et Belles Lettres*, 9 (1831), pp. 31–65.
- Silvestre de Sacy, Antoine I. "Second mémoire sur les livres religieux

des Druzes", *Histoire et Mémoires de l'Institut Royal de France, Académie des Inscriptions et Belles Lettres*, 10 (1833), pp. 89–115.

- Silvestre de Sacy, Antoine I. *Exposé de la religion des Druzes, tiré des livres religieux de cette secte, et précédé d'une Introduction et de la Vie du Khalife Hakem-Biamr-Allah.* Paris: Imprimerie Royale, 1838, 2 vols; reprinted, Paris: Librairie Orient; Amsterdam: Adolf M. Hakkert, 1964. 2 vols. Partial German trans., *Die Drusen und ihre Vorläufer*, tr., Philipp Wolff. Leipzig: F.C.W. Vogel, 1845. pp. xvi + 471.
- Simon, G. "The Agha Khan", *MW*, 20 (1930), pp. 407–408.

Sirdar Iqbal Ali Shah, *see* Shah, Sirdar Ikbal Ali

- Smet, Daniel de. "Le concept de la ġayba chez les Druzes, à la lumière de la 'Risāla al-Ġayba' de Ḥamza b. 'Alī", *Orientalia Lovaniensia Periodica*, 17 (1986), pp. 141–158. Contains a critical edition of the *Risālat al-ghayba*, epistle no. 35 of the Druze Canon.
- Smet, Daniel de. "Le verbe-impératif dans le système cosmologique de l'Ismaélisme", *Revue des Sciences Philosophiques et Théologiques*, 73 (1989), pp. 397–412.
- Smet, Daniel de. "*Le Kitâb Râḥat al-'Aql* de Ḥamîd ad-Dîn al-Kirmânî et la cosmologie Ismaélienne à l'époque Fatimide", *Acta Orientalia Belgica*, 7 (1992), pp. 81–91.
- Smet, Daniel de. "*Mīzān al-diyāna* ou l'équilibre entre science et religion dans la pensée Ismaélienne", *Acta Orientalia Belgica*, 8 (1993), pp. 247–254.
- Smet, Daniel de. "Au-delà de l'apparent: les notions de *ẓāhir* et *bāṭin* dans l'ésotérisme Musulman", *Orientalia Lovaniensia Periodica*, 25 (1994), pp. 197–220.
- Smet, Daniel de. "La fonction du Noûs dans le système religieux des Druzes: une synthèse entre Ismaélisme et *ġulūw*", in Alois van Tongerloo and Johannes van Oort, ed., *The Manichaean Nous*. Proceedings of the International Symposium organized in Louvain from 31 July to 3 August 1991. Manichaean Studies, 2. Louvain: International Association of Manichaean Studies and Center of the History of Religions – BCMS, 1995, pp. 79–102.
- Smet, Daniel de. "Comment déterminer le début et la fin du jeûne

de Ramadan? Un point de discorde entre Sunnites et Ismaéliens en Égypte Fatimide", in *ESFAM* pp. 71–84.

- Smet, Daniel de. "Les fêtes Chiites en Égypte Fatimide", *Acta Orientalia Belgica*, 10 (1995), pp. 187–196.
- Smet, Daniel de. "Les interdictions alimentaires du calife Fatimide al-Ḥākim: marques de folie ou annonce d'un règne messianique?", in *ESFAM*, pp. 53–69.
- Smet, Daniel de. "Al-Mu'ayyad fī d-Dīn aš-Šīrāzī et la polémique Ismaélienne contre les 'Brahmanes' d'Ibn ar-Rāwandī", in *ESFAM*, pp. 85–97.
- Smet, Daniel de. *La Quiétude de l'intellect: Néoplatonisme et gnose Ismaélienne dans l'oeuvre de Ḥamîd ad-Dîn al Kirmânî (Xe/XIes).* Orientalia Lovaniensia Analecta, 67. Louvain: Peeters and Departement Oosterse Studies, 1995. pp. 429.
- Smet, Daniel de. "The Influence of the Arabic Pseudo-Empedocles on Medieval Latin Philosophy: Myth or Reality?", in Dionisius A. Agius and Ian R. Netton, ed., *Across Mediterranean Frontiers: Trade, Politics and Religion, 650–1450*. Selected Proceedings of the International Medieval Congress. University of Leeds, 10–13 July 1995, 8–11 July 1996. International Medieval Research, 1. Turnhout: Brepols, 1997, pp. 225–234.
- Smet, Daniel de. "Le culte du Veau d'Or chez les Druzes", in *ESFAM2*, pp. 45–61.
- Smet, Daniel de. "La translation du *Ra's al-Husayn* au Caire Fatimide", in *ESFAM2*, pp. 29–44.
- Smet, Daniel de. "Éléments chrétiens dans l'Ismaélisme Yéménite sous les derniers Fatimides. Le problème de la gnose Ṭayyibite", in *EF*, pp. 45–53.
- Smet, Daniel de. "Le soleil, roi du ciel, dans la théologie astrale des Frères de la Pureté (Iḫwān aṣ-Ṣafā')", *Acta Orientalia Belgica*, 12 (1999), pp. 151–160.
- Smet, Daniel de. "Perfectio prima – perfectio secunda, ou les vicissitudes d'une notion, de S. Thomas aux Ismaéliens Ṭayyibites du Yémen", *Recherches de Théologie et Philosophie Médiévales*, 66 (1999), pp. 254–288.
- Smet, Daniel de. "Les jeux, les sports et l'humour, témoins d'une sagesse divine. Réhabilitation du *hazl* dans un texte Druze d'époque

Fatimide", *Acta Orientalia Belgica*, 16 (2000).

- Smet, Daniel de. "La doctrine Avicennienne des deux faces de l'âme et ses racines Ismaéliennes", *SI*, 93 (2001), pp. 77–89.
- Smet, Daniel de. "Une femme Musulmane ministre de Dieu sur terre? La réponse du *dāʿī* Ismaélien al-Ḫaṭṭāb (ob. 1138)", *Acta Orientalia Belgica*, 15 (2001), pp. 155–164.
- Smet, Daniel de. "Avicenne et l'Ismaélisme post-Fatimide, selon la *Risāla al-Mufīda fī īḍāḥ mulġaz al-Qaṣīda* de ʿAlī b. Muḥammad b. al-Walīd (*ob.* 1215)", in Jules Janssens and Daniel de Smet, ed., *Avicenna and his Heritage*. Acts of the International Colloquium, Leuven, Louvain-La-Neuve, September 8 –September 11, 1999. Ancient and Medieval Philosophy, De Wulf-Mansion Centre, Series 1, XXVIII. Louvain: Leuven University Press, 2002, pp. 1–20.
- Smet, Daniel de. "L'alphabet secret des Ismaéliens ou la force magique de l'écriture", *Res Orientales*, 14 (2002), pp. 51–60.
- Smet, Daniel de. "L'arbre de la connaissance du bien et du mal. Transformation d'un thème biblique dans l'Ismaélisme Ṭayyibite", in S. Leder et al., ed., *Studies in Arabic and Islam*. Proceedings of the 19th Congress, Union Européenne des Arabisants et Islamisants, Halle, 1998. Orientalia Lovaniensia Analecta, 108. Louvain: Peeters, 2002, pp. 513–521.
- Smet, Daniel de. "L'élaboration de l'élixir selon as-Siǧistānī. Alchimie et cosmogonie dans l'Ismaélisme Ṭayyibite", in *Proceedings of the 20th Congress of the Union Européenne des Arabistants et Islamisants*, part 1, Budapest, 10–17 September 2000; being, *The Arabist, Budapest Studies in Arabic*, 24–25 (2002).
- Smet, Daniel de. "Les climats du monde et l'inégalité des races humaines. Une approche Ismaélienne", *Acta Orientalia Belgica*, 16 (2002), pp. 69–80.
- Smet, Daniel de. "Druzisme", "Ismaélisme", "Ẓāhir et bāṭin", in J. Servier, ed., *Dictionnaire critique de l'ésotérisme*. Paris: Presses Universitaires de France, 1998.
- Smet, Daniel de. "al-Ḥâmidî", "al-Kirmânî", "Nâṣir-i Khosraw", "al-Râzî, Abû Ḥâtim", "al-Sijistânî", in *Encyclopédie Philosophique Universelle*, III: *Les Oeuvres philosophiques: Dictionnaire*, ed., Jean François Mattéi, vol. 1. Paris: Presses Universitaires de France, 1992.

See also under U. Vermeulen

- Smet, Daniel de and J.M.F. Van Reeth. "Les citations bibliques dans l'oeuvre du *dā'ī* Ismaélien Ḥamīd ad-Dīn al-Kirmānī", in Urbain Vermeulen and J.M.F. Van Reeth, ed., *Law, Christianity and Modernism in Islamic Society*. Proceedings of the Eighteenth Congress of the Union Européenne des Arabistants et Islamisants. Orientalia Lovaniensia Analecta, 86. Louvain: Peeters, 1998, pp. 147–160.
- Smirnov, A. "O raskole shiitov voobshche, i raskole izmaélitov v osobennosti" [Shi'i Schism in General and Ismaili Schism in Particular], *Uchyonïe zapiski Kazanskogo universiteta* (Kazan), 1 (1846), pp.79–180.
- Smirnov, A.V. "Khristianskie motivï v religiozno-filosofskikh kontseptsiyakh sufizma i ismailizma" [Christian Motives in the Religious and Philosophical Concepts of Sufism and Ismailism], *Vostok* (Moscow), 6 (1993), pp. 12–18.
- Smirnov, A.V. "Ismailizm", "al-Kirmani", in *Novaya filosofskaya Éntsiklopediya* [The New Philosophical Encyclopaedia]. Moscow: Mïsl', 2000–2001.
- Smirnov, A.V. "Ismailizm", in *Éntsiklopedicheskiy slovar' Étika* [The Encyclopaedic Dictionary "Ethics"]. Moscow: Gardariki, 2001, pp. 181–184.
- Smith, Bernard. "L'Aga Khan discende dal 'Vecchio della Montagna'", *Historia*, 17 (1973), pp. 50–59.
- Smith, Clive K. "The Suleihid Dynasty in the Yemen", *Asian Affairs*, 68 (1981), pp. 19–28.
- Smith, G. Rex. "Ṣulayḥids", "Yām", in *EI2*.
- Smoor, Pieter. "Fāṭimid Poets and the 'Takhalluṣ' that Bridges the Nights of Time to the Imām of Time", *Der Islam*, 68 (1991), pp. 232–262.
- Smoor, Pieter. "Palace and Ruin, a Theme for Fāṭimid Poets?", *WO*, 22 (1991), pp. 94–104.
- Smoor, Pieter. "The Poet's House: Fiction and Reality in the Works of the Fāṭimid Poets", *Quaderni di Studi Arabi*, 10 (1992), pp. 45–62.
- Smoor, Pieter. "Wine, Love and Praise for the Fāṭimid Imāms, The Enlightened of God", *ZDMG*, 142 (1992), pp. 90–104.

- Smoor, Pieter. "The Master of the Century: Fāṭimid Poets in Cairo", in *ESFAM*, pp. 139–162.
- Smoor, Pieter. "The Kaʿba of the Good and the Pure, *ṣāḥib al-ʿaṣr*", in A.M. Menara, ed., 1[er] Colloque universitaire Amsterdam, Tunis/ Amsterdam 20, 21–22 novembre 1995. Amsterdam: Universiteit van Amsterdam, n.d. [1996], pp. 125–136.
- Smoor, Pieter. "Al-Mahdī's Tears: Impressions of Fāṭimid Court Poetry", in *ESFAM2*, pp. 131–170.
- Smoor, Pieter. "ʿUmāra's Elegies and the Lamp of Loyalty", *AI*, 34 (2000), pp. 467–564.
- Smoor, Pieter. "ʿUmāra's Odes Describing the Imam", *AI*, 35 (2001), pp. 549–626.
- Smoor, Pieter. "Murder in the Palace, Poetical Reflections", *AI*, 37 (2003), pp. 383–442.
- Smoor, Pieter. "ʿUmāra's Poetical Views of Shāwar, Ḍirghām, Shīrkūh and Ṣalāḥ al-Dīn as Viziers of the Fatimid Caliphs", in Farhad Daftary and Josef W. Meri, ed., *Culture and Memory in Medieval Islam: Essays in Honour of Wilferd Madelung*. London: I.B. Tauris in association with The Institute of Ismaili Studies, 2003, pp. 410–432.
- Smoor, Pieter. "Bahāʾ al-Dīn Zuhayr (581–656/1186–1258)", "Fāṭimids", "Ibn al-Dāya, Aḥmad ibn Yūsuf ibn Ibrāhīm, Abū Jaʿfar (245 or 50–330 or 40/859 or 64–941 or 51)", "al-Sharīf al-ʿAqīlī (c. 350–450/960–1060)", "Tamīm ibn al-Muʿizz li-Dīn Allāh al-Fāṭimī (337–74/948–84)", "ʿUmāra al-Yamanī (515–69/1121–74)", "Ẓāfir al-Ḥaddād (d. 529/1135)", in *EAL*.
- Smoor, Pieter. "al-Sharīf al-ʿAḳīlī", "Tamīm b. al-Muʿizz li-Dīn Allāh", "ʿUmāra al-Yamanī", in *EI2*.
- Snesarev, Andrey Evgen'evich (1865–1937). "O prirode Pamira, religii i nravakh ego obitateley" [On the Nature of the Pamirs, Religion and Character of its Inhabitants], *Turkestanskie vedomosti* (Tashkent), 90–91 (1904).
- Snesarev, Andrey E. "Religiya i obïchai gortsev Zapadnogo Pamira" [Religion and Customs of the Mountaineers of Western Pamirs], *Turkestanskie vedomosti* (Tashkent), 89–93 (1904).
- Sobernheim. M. "al-Ḳāʾim bi-Amr Allāh", in *EI*, vol. 2, p. 643.

Sobhani, Jaʿfar, *see* Subḥānī, Jaʿfar

- Somogyi, Joseph de (1899–1976). "A Treatise on the Qarmaṭians in the 'Kitāb al-Muntaẓam' of Ibn al-Jauzī", *RSO*, 13 (1932), pp. 248–265.
- Soua, Khalifa. "Sejestānī, Abū Ya'qūb al-(X^{e}s.)", in *EUDI*, p. 766.
- Sourdel, Dominique. "Dār al-Ḥikma", in *EI2*, vol. 2, pp. 126–127.
- Sourdel, Dominique and Janine Sourdel-Thomine. "Biens fonciers constitués waqf en Syrie Fatimide pour une famille de Šarīfs Damascains", *JESHO*, 15 (1972), pp. 269–296.
- Sourdel-Thomine, Janine and Dominique Sourdel. "al-Afḍal", "Aga Khan", "Alamut", "Assassins", "Badr al-Jamâli", "Da'wa", "Fatimides", "al-Ḥâkim bi-amrillâh", "Ḥasan-i Ṣabbâḥ", "Ibn Hâni al-Andalusi", "Ibn Killîs", "Ikhwân al-Ṣafâ, Frères de la pureté", "Ismaélisme", "Jawhar al-Ṣaqalabi", "Khojas", "al-Kirmâni, Ḥamîd al-dîn Aḥmad", "al Mahdi ou 'Ubayd Allâh al-Mahdi", "Masyaf", "al-Mu'izz li-dînillâh", "al-Mustanṣir bi-llâh", "Nizaris ou nizariens", "Qarmates", "Râshid al-Dîn al-Sinân", "Salamiya", in their *Dictionnaire historique de l'Islam*. Paris: Presses Universitaires de France, 1996.
- Sprenger, Aloys (1813–1893). "Notices of Some Copies of the Arabic Work entitled Rasáyil Ikhwán al-Çafâ", *Journal of the Asiatic Society of Bengal*, 17, no. 1 (1848), pp. 501–507; 17, no. 2 (1848), pp. 183–202; reprinted in *RIS*, vol. 1, pp. 201–228.
- Sprengling, M. "The Berlin Druze Lexicon", *American Journal of Semitic Languages and Literatures*, 56 (1939), pp. 388–414; 57 (1940), pp. 75–94; 58 (1941), pp. 91–98; 60 (1943), p. 211.
- Stanishevskiy, Andrey Vladimirovich. *Sbornik arkhivnïkh documentov i materialov po istorii Pamira i ismailizmu* [Collected Archival Documents and Materials on the History of the Pamirs and Ismailism]. Moscow and Leningrad, 1933. pp. 453 (remains unpublished).
- Stark, Freya Madeline (1893–1993). "The Assassins' Valley and the Salambar Pass", *Geographical Journal*, 77 (1931), pp. 48–60.
- Stark, Freya M. "The Assassins' Castle of Lambesar", *Geographical Journal*, 80 (1932), pp. 47–56.
- Stark, Freya M. *The Valleys of the Assassins and other Persian Travels*. London: J. Murray, 1934. pp. 365. French trans., *La vallée des Assassins (The Valleys of the Assassins)*, tr., M. Metzger. Bibliothèque des voyages, 11. Paris: Éditions "Je Sers", 1946. pp. 357. German trans., *Das Tal der Mörder*. Hamburg, etc.: Rowohlt, 1949. pp. 381. Persian trans., *Safarī bi diyār-i Alamūt*, tr., 'Alī Muḥammad Sākī. Tehran: 'Ilmī, 1364

Sh./1985. pp. 431. Spanish trans., *Los Valles de los Asesinos*, tr., Carme Camps. Barcelona: Edicíones Península, 2001. pp. 299.

- Steigerwald, Diane. "L'Ordre (*amr*) et le création (*khalq*) chez Shahrastānī", *Folia Orientalia*, 31 (1995), pp. 163–175.
- Steigerwald, Diane. "L'apport Avicennien à la cosmologie à la lumière de la critique d'al-Shahrastānī et d'Averroès", *Laval Théologique et Philosophique*, 52 (1996), pp. 735–759.
- Steigerwald, Diane. "The Divine Word (*Kalima*) in Shahrastānī's *Majlis*", *Studies in Religion/Sciences Religieuses*, 25, (1996), pp. 335–352.
- Steigerwald, Diane. *La pensée philosophique et théologique de Shahrastânî (m. 548/1153)*. Saint-Nicolas, Québec: Les Presses de l'Université Laval. 1997. pp. viii + 381.
- Steigerwald, Diane. "La dissimulation (*taqiyya*) de la foi dans le Shīʿisme Ismaélien", *Studies in Religion/Sciences Religieuses*, 27 (1998), pp. 39–59.
- Steigerwald, Diane. "Le *Logos*: clef de l'ascension spirituelle dans l'Ismaélisme", *Studies in Religion/Sciences Religieuses*, 28 (1999), pp. 175–196.
- Steigerwald, Diane. "La pensée d'al-Fārābī (259/872–339/950) son rapport avec la philosophie Ismaélienne", *Laval Théologique et Philosophique*, 55 (1999), pp. 455–476.
- Steigerwald, Diane. "Faith (*īmān*) and Intellect (*ʿaql*) in Shīʿite Tradition", *Religious Studies and Theology*, 19 (2000), pp. 26–39.
- Steigerwald, Diane. "The Multiple Facets of Ismāʿīlism", *Sacred Web: A Journal of Tradition and Modernity*, 9 (2002), pp. 77–87.
- Steigerwald, Diane. "Shiʿism", "Ismaʿilism", in *The Harper Collins Encyclopedia of Religions in Canada*, ed., A. Beverley et al. Toronto: Harper Collins Canada, 2004.
- Steinschneider, Moritz. "Die lautern Brüder (Ikhwān al-Ṣafā'), ein Freimaurerorden des XI. Jahrhunderts", *Hebräische Bibliographie*, 2 (1858), pp. 91–92; reprinted in *RIS*, vol. 1, pp. 311–312.
- Steinschneider, Moritz. "Die Lauteren Brüder", *Hebräische Bibliographie*, 13 (1873), pp. 8–16, 29–37; reprinted in *RIS*, vol. 1, pp. 314–331.
- Steinschneider, Moritz. "Drusische Literatur", *Abhandlungen für die Kunde des Morgenlandes*, 6, no. 3 (1877), pp. 192–200.
- Stern, Samuel Miklos (1920–1969). "The Authorship of the Epistles of

the Ikhwān-aṣ-Ṣafā", *IC*, 20 (1946), pp. 367–372; reprinted in *RIS*, vol. 2, pp. 243–248.

- Stern, Samuel M. "Additional Notes to the Article: The Authorship of the Epistles of the Ikhwān aṣ-Ṣafā", *IC*, 21 (1947), pp. 403–404; reprinted in *RIS*, vol. 2, pp. 249–250.
- Stern, Samuel M. "Ismāʿīlī Propaganda and Fatimid Rule in Sind", *IC*, 23 (1949), pp. 298–307; reprinted in his *Studies in Early Ismāʿīlism*, pp. 177–188.
- Stern, Samuel M. "An Embassy of the Byzantine Emperor to the Fatimid Caliph al-Muʿizz", *Byzantion*, 20 (1950), pp. 239–258; reprinted in S.M. Stern, *History and Culture in the Medieval Muslim World*. Variorum Collected Studies Series, CS 200. London: Variorum Reprints, 1984, article IX.
- Stern, Samuel M. "The Epistle of the Fatimid Caliph al-Āmir (al-Hidāya al-Āmiriyya) – its Date and its Purpose", *JRAS* (1950), pp. 20–31; reprinted in S.M. Stern, *History and Culture in the Medieval Muslim World*. Variorum Collected Studies Series, CS 200. London: Variorum Reprints, 1984, article X.
- Stern, Samuel M. "The Succession to the Fatimid Imam al-Āmir, the Claims of the later Fatimids to the Imamate, and the Rise of Ṭayyibī Ismailism", *Oriens*, 4 (1951), pp. 193–255; reprinted in S.M. Stern, *History and Culture in the Medieval Muslim World*. Variorum Collected Studies Series, CS 200. London: Variorum Reprints, 1984, article XI.
- Stern, Samuel M. "Three North-African Topographical Notes (Islamic-Roman)", *Arabica*, 1 (1954), pp. 343–345.
- Stern, Samuel M. "Heterodox Ismāʿīlism at the Time of al-Muʿizz", *BSOAS*, 17 (1955), pp. 10–33; reprinted in his *Studies in Early Ismāʿīlism*, pp. 257–288.
- Stern, Samuel M. "An Original Document from the Fāṭimid Chancery Concerning Italian Merchants", in *Studi Orientalistici in onore di Giorgio Levi Della Vida*. Publicazioni dell'Istituto per l'Oriente, 52. Rome: Istituto per l'Oriente, 1956, vol. 2, pp. 529–538; reprinted in S.M. Stern, *Coins and Documents from the Medieval Middle East*. Variorum Collected Studies Series, CS 238. London: Variorum Reprints, 1986, article V.
- Stern, Samuel M. "The Early Ismāʿīlī Missionaries in North-West Persia and in Khurāsān and Transoxania", *BSOAS*, 23 (1960), pp. 56–90;

reprinted in his *Studies in Early Ismāʿīlism*, pp. 189–233. Persian trans., "Nakhustīn dāʿīyān-i Ismāʿīlī dar shumāl-i gharbī-yi Īrān va Khurāsān va Māwarā' al-Nahr, tr., Farīdūn Badra'ī", *Majalla-yi Dānishkada-yi Adabiyyāt, Dānishgāh-i Tehran/Revue de la Faculté des Lettres, Université de Tehran*, 14, no. 1 (1345 Sh./1966), pp. 23–69.

- Stern, Samuel M. "A Fāṭimid Decree of the Year 524/1130", *BSOAS*, 23 (1960), pp. 439–455.
- Stern, Samuel M. "Abu'l-Qasim al-Bustī and his Refutation of Ismāʿīlism", *JRAS* (1961), pp. 14–35; reprinted in his *Studies in Early Ismāʿīlism*, pp. 299–320.
- Stern, Samuel M. *Avvalīn ẓuhūr-i Ismāʿīliyya dar Īrān (The First Appearance of Ismailism in Iran)*, tr., S. Hossein Nasr. Text of a lecture in English and Persian, given at the Faculty of Letters of the University of Tehran on May 15, 1961, and published in *Majalla-yi Dānishkada-yi Adabiyyāt, Dānishgāh-i Tehran/Revue de la Faculté des Lettres, Université de Tehran*, 9, no. 1 (1340 Sh./1961), English text pp. 1–12, Persian translation pp. 1–13.
- Stern, Samuel M. "Ismāʿīlīs and Qarmaṭians", in *L'Élaboration de l'Islam*. Colloque de Strasbourg 12–13–14 juin 1959. Travaux du Centre d'Études Supérieures Spécialisé d'Histoire des Religions de Strasbourg. Paris: Presses Universitaires de France, 1961, pp. 99–108; reprinted in his *Studies in Early Ismāʿīlism*, pp. 289–298; reprinted in Etan Kohlberg, ed., *Shīʿism*. The Formation of the Classical Islamic World, 33. Aldershot: Ashgate, 2003, pp. 267–276. Persian trans., "Qarāmiṭa va Ismāʿīliyān", in Y. Āzhand, *Nahḍat-i Qarāmiṭa*, pp. 23–34.
- Stern, Samuel M. "Three Petitions of the Fāṭimid Period", *Oriens*, 15 (1962), pp. 172–209; reprinted in S.M. Stern, *Coins and Documents from the Medieval Middle East*. Variorum Collected Studies Series, CS 238. London: Variorum Reprints, 1986, article VI.
- Stern, Samuel M. *Fāṭimid Decrees: Original Documents from the Fāṭimid Chancery*. All Souls Studies, III. London: Faber and Faber, 1964. pp. 188.
- Stern, Samuel M. "New Information about the Authors of the 'Epistles of the Sincere Brethren'", *Islamic Studies*, 3 (1964), pp. 405–428; reprinted in his *Studies in Early Ismāʿīlism*, pp. 155–176; reprinted in *RIS*, vol. 2, pp. 357–380.
- Stern, Samuel M. "A Petition to the Fāṭimid Caliph al-Mustanṣir

Concerning a Conflict within the Jewish Community", *Revue des Études Juives*, 128 (1969), pp. 203–222; reprinted in S.M. Stern, *Coins and Documents from the Medieval Middle East*. Variorum Collected Studies Series, CS 238. London: Variorum Reprints, 1986, article VII.

- Stern, Samuel M. "Arabico-Persica", in Mary Boyce and Ilya Gershevitch, ed., *W.B. Henning Memorial Volume*. London: Lund Humphries, 1970, pp. 409–416; reprinted in S.M. Stern, *History and Culture in the Medieval Muslim World*. Variorum Collected Studies Series, CS 200. London: Variorum Reprints, 1984, article V.
- Stern, Samuel M. "Cairo as the Centre of the Ismāʿīlī Movement", in *Colloque international sur l'histoire du Caire*, pp. 437–450; reprinted in his *Studies in Early Ismāʿīlism*, pp. 234–256.
- Stern, Samuel M. *Studies in Early Ismāʿīlism*. The Max Schloessinger Memorial Series, Monographs 1. Jerusalem: Magnes Press-The Hebrew University; Leiden: E.J. Brill, 1983. pp. xxii + 340.
- Stern, Samuel M. "Abū Ḥātim al-Rāzī on Persian Religion", in his *Studies in Early Ismāʿīlism*, pp. 30–46.
- Stern, Samuel M. "The Account of the Ismāʿīlīs in *Firaq al-Shīʿa*", in his *Studies in Early Ismāʿīlism*, pp. 47–55.
- Stern, Samuel M. "The 'Book of the Highest Initiation' and Other Anti-Ismāʿīlī Travesties", in his *Studies in Early Ismāʿīlism*, pp. 56–83.
- Stern, Samuel M. "The Earliest Cosmological Doctrines of Ismāʿīlism", in his *Studies in Early Ismāʿīlism*, pp. 3–29.
- Stern, Samuel M. "Fāṭimid Propaganda among Jews According to the Testimony of Yefet b. ʿAlī the Karaite", in his *Studies in Early Ismāʿīlism*, pp. 84–95.
- Stern, Samuel M. "Jaʿfar ibn Manṣūr al-Yaman's Poems on the Rebellion of Abū Yazīd", in his *Studies in Early Ismāʿīlism*, pp. 146–152.
- Stern, Samuel M. "Al-Mahdī's Reign According to the *ʿUyūn al-Akhbār*", in his *Studies in Early Ismāʿīlism*, pp. 96–145.
- Stern, Samuel M. "Fatimids", "Hakim, al-", "Ismaʿilism", "Karmatians", in *Encyclopaedia Britannica*. Chicago, London, etc.: W. Benton, Encyclopaedia Britannica, 1968.
- Stern, Samuel M. "ʿAbd Allāh b. Maymūn", "ʿAbdān", "Abū ʿAbd Allāh al-Shīʿī", "Abū Ḥātim al-Rāzī", "Abū Yaʿḳūb al-Sidjzī", "Abū Yazīd al-Nukkārī", "al-Afḍal, Kutayfāt", "al-Āmir bi-Aḥkām Allāh", in *EI2*.

- Stern, Samuel M., E. Beazley and A. Dobson. "The Fortress of Khān Lanjān", *Iran, Journal of the British Institute of Persian Studies*, 9 (1971), pp. 45–57.
- Stewart, Devin J. "Popular Shiism in Medieval Egypt: Vestiges of Islamic Sectarian Polemics in Egyptian Arabic", *SI*, 84 (1996), pp. 35–66.
- Stillman, Norman A. "The Eleventh-century Merchant House of Ibn ʿAwkal (a Geniza Study)", *JESHO*, 16 (1973), pp. 15–88.
- Stillman, Norman A. "A Case of Labor Problems in Medieval Egypt", *IJMES*, 5 (1974), pp. 194–201.
- Stillman, Norman A. "Joseph Ibn ʿAwkal: A Jewish Communal Leader in Eleventh-century Egypt", in Stanley Ferber and Sandro Sticca, ed., *The Eleventh Century*. Acta, 1. Binghamton: Center for Medieval and Early Renaissance Studies, State University of New York at Binghamton, 1974, pp. 39–50.
- Stillman, Yedida K. "The Importance of the Cairo Geniza Manuscripts for the History of Medieval Female Attire", *IJMES*, 7 (1976), pp. 579–589.
- Stillman, Yedida K. "Textiles and Patterns Come to Life through the Cairo Geniza", in *Islamische Textilkunst des Mittelalters: Aktuelle Probleme*. Riggisberger Berichte, 5. Riggisberg: Abegg-Stiftung, 1997, pp. 35–52.
- Stillman, Yedida K. and Paula Sanders. "Ṭirāz", in *EI2*, vol. 10, pp. 534–538.
- Straface, Antonella. "Testimonianze pitagoriche alla luce di una filosofia profetica: la numerologia pitagorica negli Iḫwān al-Ṣafāʾ", *AIUON*, 47 (1987), pp. 225–241.
- Straface, Antonella. *L'origine del mondo nel pensiero Islamico dei secc. X–XI*. Naples: Istituto Universitario Orientale, Dipartimento di Studi e Ricerche su Africa e Paesi Arabi, 1996. pp. 147.
- Stroeva, Lyudmila Vladimirovna (1910–1993). "K istorii osnovaniya gosudarstva Ilkhanov v Irane" [Toward the History of the Creation of the Īlkhānid State in Iran], *Nauchnaya sessiya Leningradskogo gosudarstvennogo universiteta* (Leningrad), (1948), pp. 54–56.
- Stroeva, Lyudmila, V. "Unichtozhenie mongolami gosudarstva ismailitov v Irane" [The Mongol Destruction of the Ismaili State in Iran], *Uchyonïe zapiski Leningradskogo gosudarstvennogo universiteta*

(Leningrad), 4, no. 179 (1954), pp. 192–214.

- Stroeva, Lyudmila V. "Ismailitï v Irane" [Ismailis of Iran], in N.V. Pigulevskaya et al., *Istoriya Irana s drevneyshikh vremyon do kontsa XIII veka*. Leningrad: Izdatel'stvo Leningradskogo Universiteta, 1958, pp. 151–152. Persian trans., "Ismāʿīliyya dar Īrān", in N.V. Pigulevskaya et al., *Taʾrīkh-i Īrān*, tr., Karīm Kishāvarz. Tehran: Payām, 1354 Sh./1975, pp. 276–278.
- Stroeva, Lyudmila V. "Den' voskreseniya iz myortvïkh i ego sotsial'naya sushchnost'. Iz istorii Ismailitskogo gosudarstva v Irane XIIv." [The Day of Resurrection from the Dead and its Social Essence. From the History of the Ismaili State in the 12th-century Iran], *Kratkie soobshcheniya Instituta Vostokovedeniya* AN SSSR (Moscow), 38 (1960), pp. 19–25.
- Stroeva, Lyudmila V. "Posledniy khorezmshakh i ismailitï Alamuta" [The last Khwārazmshāh and the Ismailis of Alamūt], in *Issledovaniya po istorii kul'turï narodov Vostoka. Sbornik v chest' akademika I.A. Orbeli* [The Study of Cultural History of the Peoples of the East. Collected Articles in Honour of Academician I.A. Orbeli]. Moscow and Leningrad, 1960, pp. 451–463.
- Stroeva, Lyudmila V. "Dvizhenie ismailitov v Isfakhane v 1101–1107 gg." [The Ismaili Movement in Iṣfahān in 1101–1107], *Vestnik Leningradskogo gosudarstvennogo universiteta* (Leningard), 14, 3 (1962), pp. 60–73.
- Stroeva, Lyudmila V. "Ismailitï Irana i Sirii v zarubezhnoy i sovetskoy istoriografii" [Soviet and Foreign Historiographical Literature on the Ismailis of Iran and Syria], in *Mezhvuzovskaya nauchnaya konferentsiya po istoriografii i istochnikovedeniyu istorii stran Azii i Afriki.Tezisï dokladov*. Leningrad, 1963, pp. 46–51.
- Stroeva, Lyudmila V. "K voprosu o sotsial'noy prirode ismailitskogo dvizheniya v Irane XI–XIII vv." [On the Problem of the Social Nature of the Ismaili Movement in Iran in the 11–13th Centuries], *Vestnik Leningradskogo gosudarstvennogo universiteta* (Leningrad), 20, 4 (1963), pp. 46–51.
- Stroeva, Lyudmila V. "Vosstanie ismailitov v Irane v kontse XI – nachale XII v." [The Ismaili Rebellion in Iran at the end of the 11th-Beginning of the 12th Century], in *Issledovaniya po istorii stran Vostoka*. Leningrad, 1964, pp. 41–59.

- Stroeva, Lyudmila V. "Ismailitï Irana i Sirii v zarubezhnoy i sovetskoy istoriografii" [Soviet and Foreign Historiographical Literature on the Ismailis of Iran and Syria], in *Istoriografiya i istochnikovedenie istorii stran Azii*. Leningrad, 1965, pp. 138–148.
- Stroeva, Lyudmila V. "Rashid-ad-din kak istochnik po istorii ismailitov Alamuta" [Rashīd al-Dīn's Work as a Source on the History of the Ismailis of Alamūt], in *Voprosï istorii stran Azii*. Leningrad, 1965, pp. 123–142.
- Stroeva, Lyudmila V. "Vïstuplenie ismailitov v Sirii na grani XI–XII vv. (1090–1113 gg.)" [The Ismaili Uprising in Syria at the turn of the 11–12th Centuries], *Kratkie soobshcheniya Instituta narodov Azii AN SSSR* (Moscow), 86 (1965), pp. 189–195.
- Stroeva, Lyudmila V. "Vnutrennee polozhenie ismailitskogo gosudarstva v 20–50-kh gg. XII v." [Internal Situation in the Ismaili State in 1120–1150], in *Filologiya i istoriya stran zarubezhnoy Azii i Afriki. Tezisï nauchnoy konferentsii vostochnogo fakul'teta Leningradskogo gosudarstvennogo universiteta* [Philology and History of Asian and African Countries. Proceedings of the Conference of the Faculty of Oriental Studies of the State University of Leningrad]. Leningrad, 1965, pp. 84–86.
- Stroeva, Lyudmila V. "Shakhdiz – krepost' ismailitov" [The Ismaili Fortress of Shāhdiz], in *Iranskaya filologiya*. Moscow, 1969, pp. 43–46.
- Stroeva, Lyudmila V. "'Novïy prizïv' ismailitov kak ideologiya narodnogo dvizheniya v Irane v XI–XII vv." [The Ismaili "New Call" as the Ideology of the Popular Movement in Iran in the 11–12th Centuries], *Palestinskiy sbornik* (Leningrad), 21 (84), *Blizhniy Vostok i Iran* (1970), pp. 199–213.
- Stroeva, Lyudmila V. "Izuchenie istorii ismailizma na Pamire i v Irane v sovetskoy istoriografii za 50 let" [The Study of Ismaili History in the Pamirs and Iran in Soviet Historiography during the last 50 Years], in *Filologiya i istoriya stran Azii i Afriki. Kratkie tezisï nauchnoy konferentsii vostochnogo fakul'teta Leningradskogo gosudarstvennogo universiteta, 11–18 dekabrya 1972 g.* [Philology and History of Asian and African Countries. Proceedings of the Conference of the Faculty of Oriental Studies of the State University of Leningrad, 11–18 December 1972]. Leningrad, 1972, pp. 85–88.
- Stroeva, Lyudmila V. "Provozglashenie 'Dnya Voskresen'ya' (iz istorii

gosudarstva ismailitov v Irane v XI–XII vv.)" [The Declaration of "The Day of Resurrection" (From the History of Ismaili State in Iran in the 11–12th Centuries)], in *Iran: Sbornik Statey*. Moscow: Nauka, Glavnaya redaktsiya vostochnoy literaturï, 1973, pp. 133–165.

- Stroeva, Lyudmila V. *Gosudarstvo ismailitov v Irane v XI–XIII vv*. [The Ismaili State in Iran in the 11–13th Centuries]. *Avtoreferat doktorskoy dissertatsii*. Moscow, 1974. pp. 42.
- Stroeva, Lyudmila V. *Gosudarstvo ismailitov v Irane v XI–XIII vv*. [The Ismaili State in Iran in 11–13th Centuries]. Moscow: Nauka, Glavnaya redaktsiya vostochnoy literaturï, 1978. pp. 274. Persian trans., *Ta'rīkh-i Ismā'īliyān dar Īrān*, tr., Parvīn Munzavī. Tehran: Nashr-i Ishāra, 1371 Sh./1992. pp. 372.
- Stroeva, Lyudmila V. "Ismailitov gosudarstvo" [The State of the Ismailis], "Ismailitï" [The Ismailis], in *Sovetskaya istoricheskaya éntsiklopediya* [The Soviet Encyclopaedia of History]. Moscow, 1965.
- Strothmann, Rudolf (1877–1960). "Drusen-Antwort auf Nuṣairī-Angriff", *Der Islam*, 25 (1939), pp. 269–281.
- Strothmann, Rudolf. "Kleinere ismailitische Schriften", in Asaf A.A. Fyzee, ed., *Islamic Research Association Miscellany: Volume one 1948*. Islamic Research Association Series, 11. London, etc.: G. Cumberledge, Oxford University Press, 1949, pp. 121–163.
- Strothmann, Rudolf. "Recht der Ismailiten: Kadi Nu'mān und Da'ā'im al-Islām", *Der Islam*, 31 (1954), pp. 131–146.
- Strothmann, Rudolf. "Sab'īya", "al-Ṭūsī, Naṣīr al-Dīn", in *EI*.
- Strothmann, Rudolf. "Sab'īya", in *HI*, pp. 621–623.
- Strothmann, Rudolf. "Sab'īya", in *SEI*, pp. 478–480.
- Subḥānī (Sobhani), Ja'far. *Manshūr-i 'aqā'id-i Imāmiyya*. Qom, Iran: Mu'assasa-yi al-Imām al-Ṣādiq, 1376 Sh./1997. pp. 346. English trans., *Doctrines of Shi'i Islam: A Compendium of Imami Beliefs and Practices*, tr. and ed., Reza Shah-Kazemi. London: I.B. Tauris in association with The Institute of Ismaili Studies, 2001. pp. xxi + 240.
- Subḥānī, Ja'far. *Ta'rīkh al-Ismā'īliyya wa-firaq al-Faṭḥiyya, al-Wāqifiyya, al-Qarāmiṭa, al-Durūz wa'l-Nuṣayriyya*. Beirut: Dār al-Aḍwā', 1999. pp. 452.
- Sufian, H. Yegiptosi. *Ḥay Memlukneren u Ishkhannere Faṭimiyakan Sherjanin* [The Armenian Mamluks and Princes in Fatimid Period].

Cairo, 1928 (in Armenian).

- Sulṭān, ʿAbd al-Munʿim ʿAbd al-Ḥamīd. *al-Mujtamaʿ al-Miṣrī fiʾl-ʿaṣr al-Fāṭimī: dirāsa taʾrīkhiyya wathāʾiqiyya*. Cairo: Dār al-Maʿārif, 1985. pp. 312.
- Sulṭān, ʿAbd al-Munʿim ʿAbd al-Ḥamīd. *al-Aswāq fiʾl-ʿaṣr al-Fāṭimī: dirāsa wathāʾiqiyya, 358–567H/969–1171M*. Alexandria: Muʾassasat Shabāb al-Jāmiʿa, 1997. pp. 220.
- Sulṭān, ʿAbd al-Munʿim ʿAbd al-Ḥamīd. *al-Shurṭa waʾl-amn al-dākhilī fiʾl-ʿaṣr al-Fāṭimī*. Alexandria: Markaz al-Iskandariyya liʾl-Kitāb, 1998. pp. 111.
- Sulṭān, ʿAbd al-Munʿim ʿAbd al-Ḥamīd. *al-Ḥayāt al-ijtimāʿiyya fiʾl-ʿaṣr al-Fāṭimī: dirāsa taʾrīkhiyya wathāʾiqiyya*. Alexandria: Dār al-Thaqāfa al-ʿIlmiyya, 1999. pp. 399.
- Sulṭānī, Muṣṭafā. "Nubuwwat az dīdgāh-i Ismāʿīliyān", in *IMM*, pp. 75–109.
- Sulṭānī, Sulṭān ʿAlī. "Mukhtaṣarī az taʾrīkh-i zindigī-yi al-Muʾayyad fiʾl-Dīn dāʿī al-duʿāt Shīrāzī", *Mihr*, 10, no. 4 (1343 Sh./1964), pp. 454–458.
- Sulṭānī, Sulṭān ʿAlī. "Nasab-i Abuʾl-Muʾayyad", *Mihr*, 11, no. 1 (1344 Sh./1965), pp. 46–49.
- Surani, Iqbal. *Explication des vertus de la connaissance dans le Kalâm-i Maulâ, un texte Ismaélien fondamental*. Paris: J. Maisonneuve successeur, 2003. pp.89.
- Surūr, Muḥammad Jamāl al-Dīn (1911–1992). *al-Nufūdh al-Fāṭimī fī jazīrat al-ʿArab*. Cairo: n.p., 1950. pp. 114; 2nd ed., Cairo: Dār al-Fikr al-ʿArabī, 1957. pp. 114.
- Surūr, Muḥammad Jamāl al-Dīn. *al-Nufūdh al-Fāṭimī fī bilād al-Shām waʾl-ʿIrāq fiʾl-qarnayn al-rābiʿ waʾl-khāmis baʿda al-hijra*. Cairo: Dār al-Fikr al-ʿArabī, 1957. pp. 160.
- Surūr, Muḥammad Jamāl al-Dīn. *Miṣr fī ʿaṣr al-dawla al-Fāṭimiyya*. al-Alf kitāb, 274. Cairo: Maktabat al-Nahḍa al-Miṣriyya, 1960. pp. 13 + 251.
- Surūr, Muḥammad Jamāl al-Dīn. *al-Dawla al-Fāṭimiyya fī Miṣr: siyāsatuhā al-dākhiliyya wa-maẓāhir al-ḥaḍāra fī ʿahdihā*. Cairo: Dār al-Fikr al-ʿArabī, 1965–66. pp. 208; 2nd ed., Cairo: Dār al-Fikr al-ʿArabī, 1979. pp. 207.

- Surūr, Muḥammad Jamāl al-Dīn. *Siyāsat al-Fāṭimiyyīn al-khārijiyya*. Cairo: Dār al-Fikr al-ʿArabī, 1386 Sh./1967. pp. 291.
- Surūr, Muḥammad Jamāl al-Dīn. *Taʾrīkh al-dawla al-Fāṭimiyya*. Cairo: Dār al-Fikr al-ʿArabī, 1994. 2 vols.
- Sutūda, Manūchihr. "Qalʿa-yi Girdkūh", *Mihr*, 8 (1331 Sh./1952), pp. 339–343, 484–490.
- Sutūda, Manūchihr. "Qalʿa-yi Alamūt baldat al-iqbāl", *Farhang-i Īrān Zamīn*, 3 (1334 Sh./1955), pp. 5–21.
- Sutūda, Manūchihr. *Qilāʿ-i Ismāʿīliyya dar rishta kūhhā-yi Alburz*. Intishārāt-i Dānishgāh-i Tehran, 1090; Ganjīna-yi taḥqīqāt-i Īrānī, 45. Tehran: Dānishgāh-i Tehran, 1345 Sh./1966. pp. 8 + 196 + 70 plates; reprinted, Zabān va farhang-i Īrān, 99. Tehran: Ṭahūrī, 1362 Sh./1983. pp. 8 + 196 + 70 plates.
- Sutūda, Manūchihr. "Shamīrān, dizhī ki Nāṣir-i Khusraw dah shabānarūz dar ān mānda ast", in *YNK*, pp. 253–262.
- Swayd, Samy S. *The Druzes: An Annotated Bibliography*. Kirkland, WA: ISES Publications, 1998. pp. 199.

T

- Ṭabarī, Iḥsān. "Shimaʾī dar bāra-yi junbish-i Ismāʿīliyya", *Dunyā*, 2 (1345 Sh./1966), pp. 85–91.
- Ṭabāṭabāʾī, Sayyid Muḥammad Ḥusayn (1903–1981). *Shīʿa dar Islām*. Qom, Iran: Kitābkhāna-yi Buzurg-i Islāmī, n.d. pp. 328. English trans., *Shiʿite Islam*, tr. and ed., S. Hossein Nasr. Persian Studies Series, 5. Albany, NY: State University of New York Press, 1975. pp. xiv + 253.
- Ṭabāṭabāʾī, Sayyid Muḥammad Ḥusayn. *Shīʿa: majmūʿa-yi mudhākirāt bā Professor Henry Corbin*. Qom, Iran: Intishārāt-i Risālat, 1397/1977. pp. 502, and other editions.
- Ṭabāṭabāʾī, Sayyid Muḥammad Ḥusayn. *Ẓuhūr-i Shīʿa, bi ḍamīma-yi muṣāḥiba-yi Professor Henry Corbin*. Tehran, n.p., 1360 Sh./1981. pp. 160.
- al-Tabrīzī, Maḥmūd. *Fī taʾrīkh firqat al-Āghākhāniyya waʾl-Buhra*. Najaf: Maṭbaʿat al-Murtaḍawī, 1351/1932–33. pp. 364.
- Tadayyun, ʿAṭā Allāh. *Naqshāfarīnān-i Alamūt*. Tehran: Intishārāt-i Tehran, 1378 Sh./1999. pp. 557.

- Tadmūrī, ʿUmar ʿAbd al-Salām. "al-Shiʿr ka-maṣdar li'l-ta'rīkh: ṣafaḥāt min ta'rīkh sāḥil al-Shām min khilāl Dīwān Abi'l-Ḥasan al-Tihāmī", *Ta'rīkh al-ʿArab wa'l-ʿĀlam*, 9 (1987), pp. 16–29.
- Taherali, Y.S. "Kitab-al-Majalis wa al-Musairat of Qadi al-Nuʿman", *Sind University Research Journal*, Arts Series, Humanities & Social Sciences, 1 (1961), pp. 5–15.
- "Ṭā'ifat al-Buhra al-Ismāʿīliyya: lamia ta'rīkhiyya", *al-Mawsim*, 43–44 (1999), pp. 7–66.
- "al-Ṭā'ifa al-Ismāʿīliyya 'Āghā Khāniyya': nabdha ta'rīkhiyya", *al-Mawsim*, 43–44 (1999), pp. 67–84.
- "al-Ṭā'ifa al-Ismāʿīliyya (al-Buhra) fī dawlat al-Baḥrayn", *al-Mawsim*, 43–44 (1999), pp. 135–137.
- Tajddin Sadik Ali, Mumtaz Ali. *Genealogy of the Aga Khan*. Karachi: Islamic Book Publisher, 1990. pp. 125.
- Tajddin Sadik Ali, Mumtaz Ali. "Ramdeo Pir: A Forgotten Ismaili Saint", *Sind Review*, 32 (April, 1995), pp. 24–29.
- Tajddin Sadik Ali, Mumtaz Ali. *Ismailis through History*, with a Foreword by Michel Boivin. Karachi: Islamic Book Publisher, 1997. pp. 775.
- Tajddin Sadik Ali, Mumtaz Ali. *101–Ismaili Heroes (late 19th century to present age)*, vol. 1. Karachi: Islamic Book Publisher, 2003. pp. 438.
- Tajddin Sadik Ali, Mumtaz Ali. "Pir Shahabu'd Din Shah al-Husayni", in *GIH*, pp. 100–101.
- Tajdin, Nagib. *A Bibliography of Ismailism*, with a Foreword by Donald P. Little. Delmar, NY: Caravan Books, 1985. pp. 180.
- Tajrubahkār, Nuṣrat. "Safar-nāma-yi Ḥakīm Nāṣir-i Khusraw", *Yaghmā*, 20, no. 6 (1346 Sh./1967), pp. 281–286.
- Talbi, Mohamed., *L'émirat Aghlabide, 184–296/800–901: histoire politique*. Paris: A. Maisonneuve, 1966. pp. 767.
- Talbi, Mohamed., "al-Mahdiyya", "Sabra or al-Manṣūriyya", in *EI2*.
- Ṭalīʿ, Amīn. *Aṣl al-muwaḥḥidīn al-Durūz wa-uṣūluhum*. Beirut and Paris: Manshūrāt ʿUwaydāt, 1961. pp. 199.
- Ṭalīʿ, Amīn. *Mashyakhat al-ʿaql wa'l-qaḍā' al-madhhabī al-Durzī ʿabra al-ta'rīkh*. Beirut: Maṭbaʿat al-Ānṭūniyya, 1971. pp. 175.
- Tāmir, ʿĀrif (1921–1998). "Lamḥa min al-ta'rīkh al-Ismāʿīlī: Sinān

Rāshid al-Dīn aw Shaykh al-Jabal", *al-Adīb*, 12, no. 5 (1953), pp. 43–45.

- Tāmir, ʿĀrif. "al-Amīr Mazyad al-Ḥillī al-Asadī, shāʿir ʿSinānʾ Shaykh al-Jabal", *al-Adīb*, 12, no. 8 (1953), pp. 53–56.
- Tāmir, ʿĀrif. "al-Shāʿir al-maghmūr al-Amīr Mazyad al-Ḥillī al-Asadī", *al-Ḥikma*, 4 (1955), pp. 49–55.
- Tāmir, ʿĀrif. "Athar al-ʿaqīda fī shiʿr Mazyad al-Ḥillī al-Asadī", *al-Mashriq*, 50 (1956), pp. 466–484.
- Tāmir, ʿĀrif. "Bahrām bin Mūsā qāʾid ḥarbī shujāʿ wa-siyāsī ʿabqarī muḥannak wa-dāʿī Ismāʿīlī muṭlaq", *al-Abḥāth*, 9, no. 1 (1956), pp. 71–78.
- Tāmir, ʿĀrif. "al-Ghazal fī shiʿr Mazyad al-Ḥillī al-Asadī", *al-Mashriq*, 50 (1956), pp. 449–465.
- Tāmir, ʿĀrif. "al-Ismāʿīliyya fiʾl-Yaman", *al-Ḥikma*, 5 (1956), pp. 20–24.
- Tāmir, ʿĀrif. "al-Ismāʿīliyya", *al-Ḥikma*, 5 (1956), pp. 27–31.
- Tāmir, ʿĀrif. "Nāṣir Khusraw, shāʿir wa-raḥḥāla wa-faylasūf", *al-Mashriq*, 50 (1956), pp. 275–282.
- Tāmir, ʿĀrif. "Shihāb al-Dīn Abī Firās al-dāʿī al-Ismāʿīlī al-Sūrī", *al-Ḥikma*, 5 (1956), pp. 38–44.
- Tāmir, ʿĀrif. *Sinān wa-Ṣalāḥ al-Dīn: qiṣṣa taʾrīkhiyya*. Beirut: Dār Bayrūt, 1956. pp. 158; 2nd ed., Beirut: Dār al-Aḍwāʾ, 1415/1994. pp. 172.
- Tāmir, ʿĀrif. "Furūʿ al-shajara al-Ismāʿīliyya al-Imāmiyya", *al-Mashriq*, 51 (1957), pp. 581–612.
- Tāmir, ʿĀrif. "Ḥaqīqat Ikhwān al-Ṣafāʾ wa-Khullān al-Wafāʾ", *al-Mashriq*, 51 (1957), pp. 129–172; reprinted in *RIS*, vol. 2, pp. 277–320; 2nd ed., Nuṣūs wa-durūs, 3. Beirut: al-Maṭbaʿa al-Kāthūlīkiyya, 1957. pp. 50, with later reprints.
- Tāmir, ʿĀrif. *ʿAlā abwāb Alamūt: qiṣṣa taʾrīkhiyya*. Ḥarīṣā, Lebanon: Dār al-Shimālī, 1959. pp. 171.
- Tāmir, ʿĀrif. "al-Ismāʿīliyya waʾl-Qarāmiṭa", *al-Mashriq*, 53 (1959), pp. 557–578.
- Tāmir, ʿĀrif. *Min al-mashriq ilā al-maghrib*. [Beirut]: Maktabat al-Madrasa, 1959. pp. 138.

- Tāmir, ʿĀrif. "Ṭāhir Shāh al-Nizārī al-Alamūtī", *al-Dirāsāt al-Adabiyya*, 1 (1959), pp. 83–93.
- Tāmir, ʿĀrif. *Ibn Hāniʾ al-Andalusī, Mutanabbī al-gharb*. Aʿlām al-fikr al-ʿArabī, 16. Beirut: Dār al-Sharq al-Jadīd, 1961. pp. 157.
- Tāmir, ʿĀrif. *al-Qarāmiṭa: aṣluhum, nashʾatuhum, taʾrīkhuhum, ḥurūbuhum*. Beirut: Dār al-Kātib al-ʿArabī; Baghdad: Maktabat al-Nahḍa, [1960s]. pp. 172; 2nd ed., Beirut: Dār Maktabat al-Ḥayāt, 1979. pp. 216. Persian trans., *Ismāʿīliyya va Qarāmiṭa dar taʾrīkh*, tr., Ḥumayrā Zumurrudī. Tehran: Jāmī, 1377 Sh./1998. pp. 224.
- Tāmir, ʿĀrif. *al-Imāma fiʾl-Islām*. Beirut: Dār al-Kātib al-ʿArabī; Baghdad: Maktabat al-Nahḍa, [1964]. pp. 242; 2nd ed., Beirut: Dār al-Aḍwāʾ, 1419/1998. pp. 232.
- Tāmir, ʿĀrif. *Arwā bint al-Yaman*. Silsilat iqraʾ, 330. Cairo: Dār al-Maʿārif, 1970. pp. 160; 2nd ed., as *Arwā malikat al-Yaman*. Beirut: Dār al-Aḍwāʾ, 1418/1998. pp. 100.
- Tāmir, ʿĀrif. *al-Mawsūʿa al-taʾrīkhiyya liʾl-khulafāʾ al-Fāṭimiyyīn*. Beirut: Dār al-Jalīl and Dār Dimashq, 1980. 10 vols.
- Tāmir, ʿĀrif. *al-Qāʾid Jawhar al-Ṣiqillī*. Beirut: Dār al-Andalus, 1981.
- Tāmir, ʿĀrif. *al-Ḥākim bi-Amr Allāh, khalīfa wa-imām wa-muṣliḥ*. Beirut: Dār al-Āfāq al-Jadīda, 1402/1982. pp. 176.
- Tāmir, ʿĀrif. *al-Khalīfa al-Fāṭimī al-khāmis al-ʿAzīz Biʾllāh, qāhir al-Qarāmiṭa wa-Aftikīn*. Beirut: Dār al-Āfāq al-Jadīda, 1402/1982. pp. 147.
- Tāmir, ʿĀrif. *al-Muʿizz li-Dīn Allāh al-Fāṭimī, wāḍiʿ usus al-waḥda al-ʿArabiyya al-kubrā*. Beirut: Dār al-Āfāq al-Jadīda, 1402/1982. pp. 247.
- Tāmir, ʿĀrif. *al-Qāʾim waʾl-Manṣūr al-Fāṭimiyān*. Beirut: Dār al-Āfāq al-Jadīda, 1402/1982. pp. 140.
- Tāmir, ʿĀrif. *Tamīm al-Fāṭimī, Ibn al-imām al-Muʿizz li-Dīn Allāh al-Fāṭimī*. Beirut: Muʾassasat ʿIzz al-Dīn, 1402/1982. pp. 211.
- Tāmir, ʿĀrif. *Ibn Sīnā fī marābiʿ Ikhwān al-Ṣafāʾ*. Beirut: Muʾassasat ʿIzz al-Dīn, 1403/1983. pp. 264.
- Tāmir, ʿĀrif. *Naṣīr al-Dīn al-Ṭūsī fī marābiʿ Ibn Sīnā*. Beirut: Muʾassasat ʿIzz al-Dīn, 1403/1983. pp. 150.
- Tāmir, ʿĀrif. "Riḥla maʿa Yaʿqūb bin Killis", *al-Turāth al-ʿArabī*, 8 (1988), pp. 83–89.
- Tāmir, ʿĀrif. *al-Mustanṣir Biʾllāh al-Fāṭimī*. Beirut: Dār al-Masīra,

1410/1990. pp. 224.

- Tāmir, ʿĀrif. *ʿUbayd Allāh al-Mahdī*. Beirut: Dār al-Masīra, 1410/1990. pp. 249.
- Tāmir, ʿĀrif. *Taʾrīkh al-Ismāʿīliyya, al-daʿwa waʾl-ʿaqīda*. London: Riad El-Rayyes, 1991. 4 vols.
- Tāmir, ʿĀrif. "al-Maṣādir al-taʾrīkhiyya li-dawlat 'Alamūt' al-Ismāʿīliyya al-Nizāriyya fī bilād Fāris", *al-Bāḥith*, 13, no. 1 (1994), pp. 109–117.
- Tāmir, ʿĀrif. *Murājaʿāt Ismāʿīliyya*. Beirut: Dār al-Aḍwāʾ, 1415/1994. pp. 152.
- Tāmir, ʿĀrif. *al-Taʿrīf bi-kitābay. Daʿāʾim al-Islām wa-taʾwīl al-daʿāʾim*. Beirut: Dār al-Aḍwāʾ, 1416/1995. pp. 107.
- Tāmir, ʿĀrif. *al-Qarāmiṭa bayna al-iltizām waʾl-inkār*. Damascus: Dār al-Ṭalīʿa al-Jadīda, 1996. pp. 144.
- Tāmir, ʿĀrif. "Dirāsāt al-Ismāʿīliyya", *al-Mawsim*, 43–44 (1999), pp. 190–232.
- Taqi, Syed Mohammad. "Ismailites – Their Contribution in History", in *Proceedings of the Pakistan History Conference*, 8th Session (1958), pp. 87–90.
- Taqī al-Dīn, Ḥalīm. *Qaḍāʾ al-muwaḥḥidīn "al-Durūz" fī maḍīhi wa-ḥāḍirihi*. [Beirut: Maṭābiʿ Lubnān al-Jadīd], 1979. pp. 446.
- Taqqūsh, Muḥammad Suhayl. *Taʾrīkh al-Fāṭimiyyīn fī Shamālī Ifrīqiya wa-Miṣr wa-bilād al-Shām 297–567H./910–1171M*. Beirut: Dār al-Nafāʾis, 2001. pp. 560.
- Ṭarād, Ṭādrūs. *al-Ḥaraka al-Qarmaṭiyya fiʾl-ʿIrāq waʾl-Shām waʾl-Baḥrayn wa-ahammiyatuhā al-taʾrīkhiyya*. Damascus: Dār ʿAshtarūt, n.d. [2002]. pp. 425.
- Tarum, Maytham. *Taʾrīkh va ʿaqāʾid-i Ismāʿīliyya-yi Āqā Khāniyya*. Kirmān, Iran: Markaz-i Kirmān-shināsī, 1381 Sh./2002. pp. 224.
- Tārwā, Jīrūm. *Āghā Khān huwa Sulṭān Muḥammad Shāh al-Ḥusaynī (al-Āghā Khān al-thālith) al-imām al-rāḥil liʾl-ṭāʾifa al-Ismāʿīliyya*. Salamiyya: Dār al-Ghadīr, 2002. pp. 108.
- Ṭarzī, ʿAbd al-Wahhāb Maḥmūd. *Nāṣir Khusraw-i Balkhī*. Kabul: Bayhaqī, 1355 Sh./1976. pp. 152.
- Tengour, Habib. *Le Vieux de la Montagne*. La Bibliothèque Arabe. Paris: Sindbad, 1983. pp. 113.

- Teufel, Franz. "Zu Nâṣir Chusrau's Rušanâinâma und zu Le Livre de la Félicité", *ZDMG*, 36 (1882), pp. 206–221.
- Thatcher, Griffithes Wheeler. "Assassin", in *Encyclopaedia Britannica*. 11th ed., Cambridge: Cambridge University Press, 1910, vol. 2, pp. 774–775.
- Thobhani, Akbarali. *Islam's Quiet Revolutionary: The Story of Aga Khan IV*. New York: Vantage Press, 1993. pp. xix + 167.
- Thompson, D. "A Fatimid Textile of Coptic Tradition with Arabic Inscription", *Journal of the American Research Center in Egypt*, 4 (1965), pp. 145–150.
- Thompson, Gardner. "The Ismailis in Uganda", in Michael Twaddle, ed., *Expulsion of a Minority: Essays on Ugandan Asians*. Commonwealth Papers, 18. London: University of London, Institute of Commonwealth Studies, 1975, pp. 30–52, 211–215.
- Thorau, Peter. "Die Burgen der Assassinen in Syrien und ihre Einnahme durch Sultan Baibars", *WO*, 18 (1987), pp. 132–158.
- Thubūt, Akbar. "ʿAbd Allāh Maymūn va Ismāʿīliyān", *Haft Āsmān*, 1 (1378 Sh./1999), pp. 104–121. Arabic trans., "ʿAbd Allāh bin Maymūn wa'l-Ismāʿīliyyūn", *Riḥāb al-Maʿrifa* (Tunis), 5, no. 28 (2002), pp. 290–305.
- Tibawi (al-Ṭībāwī), Abdul-Latif (ʿAbd al-Laṭīf) (1910–1981). *Jamāʿat Ikhwān al-Ṣafāʾ*. Beirut: al-Maṭbaʿa al-Adabiyya, 1931. pp. 80.
- Tibawi, Abdul-Latif. "Ikhwān aṣ-Ṣafā and their *Rasāʾil*: A Critical Review of a Century and a Half of Research", *Islamic Quarterly*, 2 (1955), pp. 28–46; reprinted in *RIS*, vol. 2, pp. 252–270.
- Tibawi, Abdul-Latif. "Some Educational Terms in *Rasāʾil Ikhwān aṣ-Ṣafā*" *Islamic Quarterly*, 5 (1959–60), pp. 55–60; reprinted in *RIS*, vol. 2, pp. 271–276.
- Tibawi, Abdul-Latif. "Further Studies on Ikhwān aṣ-Ṣafā", *Islamic Quarterly*, 20–22 (1978), pp. 57–67.
- Tibi, Amin. "Byzantine-Fatimid Relations in the Reign of al-Muʿizz li-Din Allah (R. 953–975 A.D.) as Reflected in Primary Arabic Sources", *Graeco-Arabica*, 4 (1991), pp. 91–107.
- Tijdens, E. F. "Der mythologisch-gnostische Hintergrund des Umm al-Kitāb", in *Textes et Mémoires*: Volume VII, *Varia 1977*; being, *Acta Iranica*, 16 (1977), pp. 241–526.

- Togan, Ahmed Zeki Velidi (1890–1970). "Alamut", in *IA*, vol. 1, p. 289–290.
- Tonghini, Cristina. "Fatimid Ceramics from Italy: The Archaeological Evidence", in *EF*, pp. 285–297.
- Toorawa, Shawkat M. "Dār al-Ḥikma", in *EAL*, vol. 1, p. 182.
- Toorawa, Shawkat M. "Ṭāhir Sayf al-Dīn", in *EI2*, vol. 10, pp. 103–104.
- Toprak, M. Faruk. "Ibn Hânî", in *IA2*, vol. 20, pp. 27–29.
- Traboulsi, Samer. "Lamak ibn Mālik al-Ḥammādī and Sulayhid-Fatimid Relations", *Proceedings of the Seminar for Arabic Studies*, 30 (2000), pp. 221–227.
- Traboulsi, Samer. "The Queen was Actually a Man: Arwā Bint Aḥmad and the Politics of Religion", *Arabica*, 50 (2003), pp. 96–108.
- Triki, Ahmed. *Néoplatonisme et aspect mystique de la création de l'univers dans la philosophie des Iḫwān*. Lille and Algiers: al-Sharika al-Waṭaniyya li l-Nashr wa'l-Tawzī'/SNED, [1974]. pp. 104.
- Tritton, Arthur Stanley (1881–1973). "Notes on Some Ismaïli Manuscripts, from Information Supplied by Dr. Paul Kraus", *BSOS*, 7 (1933), pp. 33–39.
- Tritton, Arthur S. "Theology and Philosophy of the Isma'ilis", *JRAS* (1958), pp. 178–188.
- Troupeau, Gérard. "Un traité christologique attribué au calife Fatimide al-Mu'izz", *AI*, 15 (1979), pp. 11–24.
- Troussel, Marcel. "Notes sur quelques monnaies Fatimides, provenant des environs du Kouif (Région de Tébessa)", *Recueil des notices et mémoires de la Société Archéologique, Historique et Géographique de Constantine*, 70 (1957–59), pp. 67–71.
- Ṭu'ayma, Ṣābir. *al-'Aqā'id al-bāṭiniyya wa-ḥukm al-Islām fīhā*. Beirut: al-Maktaba al-Thaqāfiyya, 1406/1986. pp. 400.
- Ṭughiyānī, Isḥāq. "Janbahā-yi khiyālī-yi shi'r-i Ḥakīm Nāṣir-i Khusraw", *NP*, 8, no. 2 (1382 Sh./2003), pp. 175–189.
- Tutunji, Jenab. "Isma'ili Shi'ism", in *Encyclopedia of the Modern Middle East*, ed., Reeva S. Simon et al. New York: Macmillan Reference USA, 1996, vol. 2, p. 899.
- Tyabji, Faiz Badruddin (1877–1950). "Social Life in 1804 & 1929 amongst Muslims in Bombay", *JBBRAS*, NS, 6 (1930), pp. 286–300.

U

- Udovitch, Abraham L. "A Tale of Two Cities: Commercial Relations Between Cairo and Alexandria during the Second Half of the Eleventh Century", in Harry A. Miskimin, David Herlihy and A.L. Udovitch, ed., *The Medieval City*. New Haven: Yale University Press, 1977, pp. 143–162.
- Udovitch, Abraham L. "Merchants and *Amīrs*: Government and Trade in Eleventh-century Egypt", in *The Medieval Levant: Studies in Memory of Eliyahu Ashtor (1914–1984)* ; being, *Asian and African Studies*, 22 (1988), pp. 53–72.
- Udovitch, Abraham L. "Medieval Alexandria: Some Evidence from the Cairo Genizah Documents", in *Alexandria and Alexandrianism*. Malibu, CA: J. Paul Getty Museum, 1996, pp. 273–284.
- Udovitch, Abraham L. "Fatimid Cairo: Crossroads of World Trade – From Spain to India", in *EF*, pp. 681–691.
- al-ʿUshayrī, Muḥammad Riyāḍ. *al-Taṣawwur al-lughawī ʿinda al-Ismāʿīliyya: dirāsa fī Kitab al-zīna li-Abī Ḥātim al-Rāzī*. Alexandria: Mansha'at al-Maʿārif, 1985. pp. 342.
- ʿUthmān, Hāshim. *al-Ismāʿīliyya bayna al-ḥaqā'iq wa'l-abāṭīl*. Beirut: Mu'assasat al-Aʿlamī, 1419/1998. pp. 434.
- ʿUways, ʿAbd al-Ḥalīm. "Qaḍiyyat nasab al-Fāṭimiyyīn amām manhaj al-naqd al-ta'rīkhī", *Majallat Kulliyyat al-ʿUlūm al-Ijtimāʿiyya, Jāmiʿat al-Imām Muḥammad ibn Saʿūd al-Islāmiyya*, 6 (1982), pp. 137–89; 2nd ed., Cairo: Dār al-Ṣaḥwa, 1406/1985. pp. 56.
- Uysal, Enver. "Ihvân-i Safâ", in *IA*2, vol. 22, pp. 1–6.
- Üzün, Ilyas. "Hüccet", in *IA*2, vol. 18, pp. 451–452.
- Üzün, Mustafa. "Ezher", in *IA*2, vol. 12, pp. 53–58.

V

- Vāʿiẓ Zāda, Ḥusayn. "Muʿtaqidāt-i firqa-yi Ismāʿīliyya", *Mihr*, 8, no. 5 (1331 Sh./1952), pp. 295–298; no. 6 (1331 Sh./1952), pp. 363–366.
- Vāʿiẓ Zāda, Ḥusayn. "Munāẓara-yi Muḥammad b. Zakariyyā' Rāzī va Abū Ḥātim ʿAbd al-Raḥmān Rāzī", *Farhang-i Īrān Zamīn*, 2 (1333 Sh./1954), pp. 254–271.
- Vāʿiẓ Zāda, Ḥusayn Ḥakīm Ilāhī. "Hibat Allāh Shīrāzī", *Dānish*, 1 (1328

Sh./1949), pp. 501–508, 594–595, 635–641; 2 (1329 Sh./1950), pp. 22–23 (unfinished).

- Vajda, Georges (1908–1981). "Melchisédec dans la mythologie Ismaélienne", *JA*, 234 (1943–45), pp. 173–183; reprinted in G. Vajda, *Études de théologie et de philosophie Arabo-Islamiques à l'époque classique*, ed., Daniel Gimaret et al. Variorum Collected Studies Series, CS 228. London: Variorum, 1986, article I.
- Vajda, Georges. "Un opuscule Ismaélien en transmission Judéo-Arabe (*Risālat al-Jawharayn*)", *JA*, 246 (1958), pp. 459–466.
- Vajda, Georges. "Les lettres et les sons de la langue Arabe d'après Abû Ḥâtim al-Râzî", *Arabica*, 8 (1961), pp. 113–130; reprinted in G. Vajda, *Études de théologie et de philosophie Arabo-Islamiques à l'époque classique*, ed., Daniel Gimaret et al. Variorum Collected Studies Series, CS 228. London: Variorum, 1986, article IV.
- Vajda, Georges. "L'aventure tragique d'un cadi Maghrébin en Égypte Fāṭimide", *Arabica*, 15 (1968), pp. 1–5.
- Vajda, Georges. "La mašyaḫa d'Ibn al-Ḫaṭṭāb al-Rāzī: contribution à l'histoire du Sunnisme en Égypte Fāṭimide", *BEO*, 23 (1970), pp. 21–99.
- van Belle, Jan. "Travelogue of an Ethnomusicologist: Living Musical Traditions of the Ismailis in Afghan Badakhshan", International Institute for Asian Studies, *IIAS Newsletter*, 27 (March, 2002), pp. 9–10.

van Berchem, Max, *see* Berchem, Max van

- van den Berg, Gabrielle. "Poetry and Religion in Tajik Badakhshan", International Institute for the Study of Islam in the Modern World, *ISIM Newsletter*, 12 (1997), p. 10.
- van den Berg, Gabrielle. "Examples of Persian and Shughni Poetry from Tajik Badakhshan", in Charles Melville, ed., *Proceedings of the Third European Conference of Iranian Studies*, Part 2: *Mediaeval and Modern Persian Studies*. Beiträge zur Iranistik, 17. Wiesbaden: L. Reichert Verlag, 1999, pp. 135–144.
- van den Berg, Gabrielle. "Ismaili Poetry in Tajik Badakhshan: A Safavid Connection", *Persica*, 17 (2001), pp. 1–10.
- van den Berg, Gabrielle. "Shughni-Rushani", in *The Oxford Dictionary of Islam*, ed., John L. Esposito. Oxford: Oxford University Press, 2003, p. 293.

- van den Berg, Gabrielle, and Jan van Belle. "The Performance of Poetry and Music by the Ismāʿīlī People of Badakhshān: An Example of Madāh from the Shāhdara-Valley", *Persica*, 15 (1993–95), pp. 49–76.
- van Donzel, Emery. "Badr al-Jamālī, the Copts in Egypt and the Muslims in Ethiopia", in Ian R. Netton, ed., *Studies in Honour of Clifford Edmund Bosworth*, Volume I, *Hunter of the East: Arabic and Semitic Studies*. Leiden: E.J. Brill, 2000, pp. 297–309.

van Ess, Josef, *see* Ess, Josef van

- Van Nieuwenhuyse, Stijn. "The Uprising of Abū Rakwa and the Bedouins against the Fāṭimids", *Acta Orientalia Belgica*, 17 (2003), pp. 245–264.
- Van Reeth, J. "*Al-Qumāma* et le *Qā'im* de 400 H: le trucage de la lampe sur le tombeau du Christ", in *ESFAM2*, pp. 171–190.

See also under D. de Smet

- Vatikiotis, Panayiotis J. (1928–1997). "A Reconstruction of the Fatimid Theory of the State", *IC*, 28 (1954), pp. 399–409.
- Vatikiotis, Panayiotis J. "The Syncretic Origins of the Fatimid Daʿwa", *IC*, 28 (1954), pp. 475–491.
- Vatikiotis, Panayiotis J. "Al-Hakim bi-Amrillah: The God-King Idea Realised", *IC*, 29 (1955), pp. 1–8.
- Vatikiotis, Panayiotis J. *The Fatimid Theory of State*. Lahore: Orientalia Publishers, 1957. pp. viii + 222; reprinted, Lahore: Institute of Islamic Culture, 1981. pp. viii + 222.
- Vatikiotis, Panayiotis J. "The Rise of Extremist Sects and the Dissolution of the Fatimid Empire in Egypt", *IC*, 31 (1957), pp. 17–26.
- Vazīnpūr, Nādir. "Dalā'il manṭiqī-yi Nāṣir-i Khusraw barā-yi taghyyir-i madhhab-i khud chi būd?", *Majalla-yi Dānishkada-yi Adabiyyāt va ʿUlūm-i Insānī, Dānishgāh-i Tehran*, 24, nos. 3–4 (1358 Sh./1979), pp. 128–148.
- Venture, M. "Mémoire pour servir à l'histoire des Druses, peuple du Liban", *Annales des Voyages*, 4 (1808), pp. 325–372.
- Vercellin, Giorgio. "Ismāʿīliti", in *Grande Dizionario Enciclopedico*. Turin: Unione Tipografico-Editrice Torinese, 1988, vol. 11, p. 205.
- Verdia, H.S. "The Bohra Civil War", *New Quest*, 7 (1978), pp. 55–58.
- Verdia, H.S. "The Pains of Modernization: A Case Study of Bohras in Udaipur", *New Quest*, 7 (1978), pp. 51–54.

- Vermeulen, Urbain and Daniel de Smet (ed.), *Egypt and Syria in the Fatimid, Ayyubid and Mamluk Eras*. Orientalia Lovaniensia Analecta, 73. Louvain: Peeters, 1995. pp. 371.
- Vermeulen, Urbain and Daniel de Smet (ed.), *Egypt and Syria in the Fatimid, Ayyubid and Mamluk Eras II*. Orientalia Lovaniensia Analecta, 83. Louvain: Peeters, 1998. pp. 311.
- Vermeulen, Urbain and J. Van Steenbergen (ed.), *Egypt and Syria in the Fatimid, Ayyubid and Mamluk Eras III*. Orientalia Lovaniensia Analecta, 102. Louvain: Peeters, 2001. pp. xii + 471.
- Viguera, Maria J. "Los Fātimies de Ifrīqiya en el *Kitāb al-Ḥulla* de Ibn al-Abbār de Valencia", *Sharq al-Andalus*, 2 (1985), pp. 29–37.
- Villegas, Marcelino. "La narrativa Árabe contemporánea y sus fuentes: Mahdī ʿĪsà ṣ-Ṣaqr y los Ijwān aṣ-Ṣafāʾ", *Al-Qanṭara*, 7 (1986), pp. 287–299.
- Virani, Shafique Nizarali. "The Eagle Returns: Evidence of Continued Ismāʿīlī Activity at Alamūt and in the South Caspian Region Following the Mongol Conquests", *JAOS*, 123 (2003), pp. 351–370.
- Vire, François (d. 1999). "Le traité de l'art de volerie (*Kitāb al-bayzara*) rédigé vers 385/995 par le Grand-Fauconnier du calife Fāṭimide al-ʿAzīz bi-llāh", *Arabica*, 12 (1965), pp. 1–26, 113–139, 262–296; 13 (1966), pp. 39–76.
- Vives, Antonio Prieto. "Numismatica Qarmaṭa", *al-Andalus*, 1 (1933), pp. 301–305.

W

- al-Walī, Ṭāhā. *al-Qarāmiṭa: awwal ḥarakat ishtirākiyya fi'l-Islām*. Beirut: Dār al-ʿIlm li'l-Malāyīn, 1981. pp. 428.
- Walji, Shirin Remtulla. "Ismailis in Kenya: Some Perspectives on Continuity and Change", in Mohamed Bakari and Saad S. Yahya, ed., *Islam in Kenya: Proceedings of the National Seminar on Contemporary Islam in Kenya*. [Nairobi]: Mewa Publications, 1995, pp 1–18.
- Walker, John (1900–1964). "A Fatimid Kufic Tablet from Upper Egypt", *Le Muséon*, 51 (1938), pp. 335–340.
- Walker, John. "al-Mahdī ʿUbaid Allāh", "Sitt al-Mulk", "Ṭalāʾiʿ b. Ruzzīk", "Tamīm b. al-Muʿizz", in *EI*.

- Walker, Paul Ernest. "A Byzantine Victory over the Fatimids at Alexandretta (971)", *Byzantion*, 42 (1972), pp. 431–440.
- Walker, Paul E. "An Ismāʿīlī Answer to the Problem of Worshiping the Unknowable, Neoplatonic God", *American Journal of Arabic Studies*, 2 (1974), pp. 7–21; reprinted in *Ilm*, 2, no. 1 (1976), pp. 12–22.
- Walker, Paul E. "An Early Ismaili Interpretation of Man, History and Salvation", *Ohio Journal of Religious Studies*, 3, no. 2 (1975), pp. 29–35; reprinted in *Ilm*, 2, nos. 3–4 (1977), pp. 30–35.
- Walker, Paul E. "Cosmic Hierarchies in Early Ismāʿīlī Thought: The View of Abū Yaʿqūb al-Sijistānī", *MW*, 66 (1976), pp. 14–28.
- Walker, Paul E. "The Ismaili Vocabulary of Creation", *SI*, 40 (1974), pp. 75–85; reprinted in *Ilm*, 1, no. 4 (1976), pp. 24–30.
- Walker, Paul E. "The 'Crusade' of John Tzimisces in the Light of New Arabic Evidence", *Byzantion*, 47 (1977), pp. 301–327.
- Walker, Paul E. "Eternal Cosmos and the Womb of History: Time in Early Ismaili Thought", *IJMES*, 9 (1978), pp. 355–366.
- Walker, Paul E. "The Doctrine of Metempsychosis in Islam", in Wael B. Hallaq and Donald P. Little, ed., *Islamic Studies Presented to Charles J. Adams*. Leiden: E.J. Brill, 1991, pp. 219–238.
- Walker, Paul E. "The Universal Soul and the Particular Soul in Ismāʿīlī Neoplatonism", in Parviz Morewedge, ed., *Neoplatonism and Islamic Thought*. Studies in Neoplatonism: Ancient and Modern, 5. Albany, NY: State University of New York Press, 1992, pp. 149–166.
- Walker, Paul E. *Early Philosophical Shiism: The Ismaili Neoplatonism of Abū Yaʿqūb al-Sijistānī*. Cambridge Studies in Islamic Civilization. Cambridge: Cambridge University Press, 1993. pp. xvi + 203.
- Walker, Paul E. "The Ismaili Daʿwa in the Reign of the Fatimid Caliph al-Ḥākim", *Journal of the American Research Center in Egypt*, 30 (1993), pp. 161–182.
- Walker, Paul E. "Abū Tammām and his Kitāb al-Shajara: A New Ismaili Treatise from Tenth-century Khurasan", *JAOS*, 114 (1994), pp. 343–352.
- Walker, Paul E. "Succession to Rule in the Shiite Caliphate", *Journal of the American Research Center in Egypt*, 32 (1995), pp. 239–264.
- Walker, Paul E. *Abū Yaʿqūb al-Sijistānī: Intellectual Missionary*. Ismaili Heritage Series, 1. London: I.B. Tauris in association with The

Institute of Ismaili Studies, 1996, pp. xv + 132. Arabic trans., *Abū Yaʿqūb al-Sijistānī: al-mufakkir al-dāʿīya*, tr., M. ʿAyzūqī. Salamiyya: al-Ayādī, 1998. pp. 166. Persian trans., *Abū Yaʿqūb Sijistānī: mutifakkir va dāʿī-yi Ismāʿīlī*, tr., Farīdūn Badra'ī. Tehran: Farzān, 1377 Sh./1998. pp. 193.

- Walker, Paul E. "An Ismaʿili Version of the Heresiography of the Seventy-two Erring Sects", in *MIHT*, pp. 161–177. Arabic trans., "Riwāya Ismāʿīliyya min adab al-firaq al-ghāliya ḥawla al-firaq al-ithnatayn wa'l-sabʿīn al-khāṭi'a", in *IAW*, pp. 165–182. Persian trans., "Rivāyatī Ismāʿīlī az bidʿat-nigārī-yi haftād va du firqa-yi gumrāh", in *TAI*, pp. 202–221.
- Walker, Paul E. "Fatimid Institutions of Learning", *Journal of the American Research Center in Egypt*, 34 (1997), pp. 179–200.
- Walker, Paul E. "The Ismāʿīlī Daʿwa and the Fāṭimid Caliphate", in M.W. Daly, ed., *The Cambridge History of Egypt*: Volume 1, *Islamic Egypt, 640–1517*, ed., Carl F. Petry. Cambridge: Cambridge University Press, 1998, pp. 120–150, 557–560.
- Walker, Paul E. *Ḥamīd al-Dīn al-Kirmānī: Ismaili Thought in the Age of al-Ḥākim*. Ismaili Heritage Series, 3. London: I.B. Tauris in association with The Institute of Ismaili Studies, 1999. pp. xiv + 168. Arabic trans., *al-Fikr al-Ismāʿīlī fī ʿaṣr al-Ḥākim bi-Amr Allāh*, tr., Sayf al-Dīn al-Qaṣīr. Damascus: Dār al-Madā, 1980 [2000]. pp. 237. Persian trans., *Ḥamīd al-Dīn Kirmānī: tafakkur-i Ismāʿīlī dar dawra-yi al-Ḥākim bi-Amr Allāh*, tr., Farīdūn Badra'ī. Tehran: Farzān, 1379 Sh./2000. pp. 186.
- Walker, Paul E. "Another Family of Fatimid Chief Qadis: The al-Fāriqīs", *Journal of Druze Studies*, 1 (Fall, 2000), pp. 49–69.
- Walker, Paul E. "The Identity of one of the Ismaili *Dāʿīs* sent by the Fatimids to Ibn Ḥafṣūn", *Al-Qanṭara*, 21 (2000), pp. 387–388.
- Walker, Paul E. *Exploring an Islamic Empire: Fatimid History and its Sources*. Ismaili Heritage Series, 7. London: I.B. Tauris in association with The Institute of Ismaili Studies, 2002. pp. xv + 286.
- Walker, Paul E. "Al-Maqrīzī and the Fatimids", *Mamlūk Studies Review*, 7 (2003), pp. 83–97.
- Walker, Paul E. "Purloined Symbols of the Past: The Theft of Souvenirs and Sacred Relics in the Rivalry Between the Abbasids and Fatimids", in Farhad Daftary and Josef W. Meri, ed., *Culture and Memory in*

Medieval Islam: Essays in Honour of Wilferd Madelung. London: I.B. Tauris in association with The Institute of Ismaili Studies, 2003, pp. 364–387.

- Walker, Paul. E. "Aga Khan", "Alamut", "Bohras", "Isma'ili", in *Encyclopedia of Asian History*, ed., Ainslie T. Embree. New York: Charles Scribner's Sons, 1988.
- Walker, Paul E. "Abū Ya'qūb Sejestānī", "Ekwān al-Ṣafā'", "The Institute of Ismaili Studies", in *EIR*.
- Walpole, Frederick (1822–1876). *The Ansayrii (or Assassins), with Travels in the Further East, in 1850–51*. London: R. Bentley, 1851. 3 vols.
- Warner, Nicholas. "The Fatimid and Ayyubid Eastern Walls of Cairo: Missing Fragments", *AI*, 33 (1999), pp. 283–305.
- Wasserman, James. *The Templars and the Assassins: The Militia of Heaven*. Rochester, VT: Inner Traditions, 2001. pp. 318. Spanish trans., *Templarios y Asesinos*, tr., J.A. Bravo. Barcelona: Edicíones Martínez Roca, 2002. pp. 395.
- Wasserstein, David J. "An Unrecognized Hoard of Fāṭimid Silver from al-Andalus and a Phantom Caliph", *Al-Qanṭara*, 15 (1994), pp. 245–252.
- Wasserstein, David J. "The Coins in the Golden Hoard from Tiberias", *'Atiqot*, 36 (1998), pp. 10–14.
- Wasserstein, David J. "The Silver Coins in the Mixed Hoard from Tiberias", *'Atiqot*, 36 (1998), pp. 15–22.
- Wasserstein, David J. "Inventing Tradition and Constructing Identity: The Genealogy of 'Umar Ibn Hafsūn Between Christianity and Islam", *Al-Qanṭara*, 23 (2002), pp. 269–297.
- Watson, Oliver. "Fritware: Fatimid Egypt or Saljuq Iran?", in *EF*, pp. 299–307.
- Watt, William Montgomery. "Fatimids", in *Encyclopedia Americana*. New York: Americana Corporation, 1977, vol. 11, pp. 50–51.
- Wehr, Hans (1909–1981). "Zu den Schriften Ḥamza's im Drusenkanon", *ZDMG*, NS, 21 (1942), pp. 187–207.
- Weil, Gotthold. "Die Assassinen", *Historische Zeitschrift*, 9 (1863), pp. 418–434.
- Wickens, George Michael (b. 1918). "The Chronology of Nāṣir-i

Khusrau's *Safarnāma*", *Islamic Quarterly*, 4 (1957–58), pp. 66–77.

- Widengren, Geo. "The Gnostic Technical Language in the Rasā'il Iḫwān al-Ṣafā'", in *Actas IV Congresso de Estudos Árabes e Islâmicos, Coimbra-Lisboa 1 a 8 de setembro de 1968*. Leiden: E.J. Brill, 1971, pp. 181–203.
- Widengren, Geo. "La légende des Sept Dormants dans les écrits des Frères Purs", in Enrico Castelli, ed., *Démythisation et idéologie*. Actes du colloque organisé par le Centre International d'Études Humanistes et par l'Institut d'Études Philosophiques de Rome, Rome, 4–9 janvier 1973. Paris: Aubier-Montaigne, 1973, pp. 509–526.
- Widengren, Geo. "The Pure Brethren and the Philosophical Structure of their System", in Alford T. Welch and Pierre Cachia, ed., *Islam: Past Influence and Present Challenge*. Edinburgh: Edinburgh University Press, 1979, pp. 57–69.
- Widengren, Geo. "Macrocosmos – Microcosmos Speculation in the Rasa'il Ikhwan al-Safa and Some Hurufi Texts", *Esistenza mito ermeneutica: scritti per Enrico Castelli;* being, *Archivio di Filosofia*, 1 (1980), pp. 297–312.
- Widengren, Geo. "On Some Astrological Correspondences in the Writings of the Pure Brethren", in Gherardo Gnoli and Lionello Lanciotti, ed., *Orientalia Iosephi Tucci Memoriae Dicata*. Serie Orientale Roma, 56. Rome: Istituto Italiano per il Medio ed Estremo Oriente, 1988, vol. 3, pp. 1551–1557.
- Wiet, Gaston (1887–1971). "Deux pièces de céramique Égyptienne", *Ars Islamica*, 3 (1936), pp. 172–179.
- Wiet, Gaston. "Un nouveau tissu Fatimide", *Orientalia*, NS, 5 (1936), pp. 385–388.
- Wiet, Gaston. "Un dessin du XIe siècle", *BIE*, 19 (1936–37), pp. 223–227.
- Wiet, Gaston. *L'Égypte Arabe de la conquête Arabe à la conquête Ottomane 642–1517 de l'ère chrétienne*. Histoire de la nation Égyptienne, IV. Paris: Sociéte de l'Histoire Nationale; Librairie Plon, 1937, pp. 179–308.
- Wiet, Gaston. "Nouvelles inscriptions Fatimides", *BIE*, 24 (1941–42), pp. 145–158.
- Wiet, Gaston. "Un céramiste de l'époque Fatimide", *JA*, 241 (1953), pp. 249–253.

- Wiet, Gaston. "Une nouvelle inscription Fatimide au Caire", *JA*, 249 (1961), pp. 13–20.
- Wiet, Gaston. "Recherches sur les bibliothèques Égyptiennes aux Xe et XIe siècles", *Cahiers de Civilisation Médiéval*, 6 (1963), pp. 1–11.
- Wiet, Gaston. "Un proconsul Fatimide de Syrie: Anushtakin Dizbiri (m. en 433/1042)", *Mélanges de l'Université Saint-Joseph*, 46 (1970–71), pp. 385–407.
- Wiet, Gaston. "Shāwar", "Shīrkūh", "Yāzūrī" in *EI*.
- Wiet, Gaston. "al-ʿĀḍid li-Dīn Allāh", "al-ʿĀdil b. al-Salār", "al-Afḍal b. Badr al-Djamālī", in *EI2*.
- Wiet, Gaston. "Fāṭimides", in *Encyclopaedia Universalis*. Paris: Encyclopaedia Universalis, 1985, vol. 7, p. 796.
- Wiet, Gaston. "Fāṭimides", in *EUDI*, pp. 305–307.
- Wilckens, Leonie von. "Fatimidische Gewebe mit gewirktem Dekor im Vergleich mit spanischen und sizilischen", in *Islamische Textilkunst des Mittelalters: Aktuelle Probleme*. Riggisberger Berichte, 5. Riggisberg: Abegg-Stiftung, 1997, pp. 157–171.
- Willey, Peter R.E. "The Valley of the Assassins", *JRCA*, 48 (1961), pp. 147–151.
- Willey, Peter R.E. *The Castles of the Assassins*, with a Foreword by Sir Claude Auchinleck. London: George G. Harrap, 1963. pp. 328; reprinted, Fresno, CA: Linden Publishing Co., 2001. Persian trans., *Qilāʿ-i ḥashshāshīn*, tr., Muḥammad ʿAlī Sākī. Tehran: ʿIlmī, 1368 Sh./1989. pp. 422.
- Willey, Peter R.E. "Further Expeditions to the Valleys of the Assassins", *JRCA*, 54 (1967), pp. 156–162.
- Willey, Peter R.E. "The Assassins in Quhistan", *JRCA*, 55 (1968), pp. 180–183.
- Willey, Peter R.E. "Assassins of Qa'in", *Geographic Magazine*, 40 (1968), pp. 1294–1303.
- Willey, Peter R.E. "The Assassins, Brutal Myth or Living Sect?", *The Traveller*, 16, no. 3 (1986), pp. 42–46.
- Willey, Peter R.E. "The Ismaili Fortresses in Semnan and Khorasan", *University Lectures in Islamic Studies*, 2 (1998), pp. 167–181.
- Willey, Peter R.E., N.R. Jones and A.C. Garnett. "The 1972 Assassin Expedition", *Asian Affairs*, 61 (1974), pp. 60–70.

- Williams, Caroline. "The Cult of 'Alid Saints in the Fatimid Monuments of Cairo – Part I: The Mosque of al-Aqmar", *Muqarnas*, 1 (1983), pp. 37–52.
- Williams, Caroline. "The Cult of 'Alid Saints in the Fatimid Monuments of Cairo – Part II: The Mausolea", *Muqarnas*, 3 (1985), pp. 39–60.
- Williams, Patrick A. "The Assassination of Conrad of Montferrat: Another Suspect?", *Traditio*, 26 (1970), pp. 381–389.
- Wilson, Colin. *Order of Assassins: The Psychology of Murder*. London: R. Hart-Davis, 1972. pp. vii + 242.
- Worbs, Johann Gottlob. *Geschichte und Beschreibung des Landes der Drusen in Syrien*. Görlitz: C.G. Anton, 1799. pp. 262.
- Wright, Owen. "Music at the Fatimid Court: The Evidence of the Ibn al-Ṭaḥḥān Manuscript", in *EF*, pp. 537–545.
- Wright, Theodor P., Jr. "Competitive Modernization within the Daudi Bohra Sect of Muslims and its Significance for Indian Political Development", in Helen E. Ullrich, ed., *Competition and Modernization in South Asia*. New Delhi: Abhinav Publications, 1975, pp. 151–178.
- Wright, Theodor P., Jr. "Muslim Kinship and Modernization: The Tyabji Clan of Bombay", in Imtiaz Ahmad, ed., *Family, Kinship and Marriage among Muslims in India*. New Delhi: Manohar, 1976, pp. 217–238.
- Wüstenfeld, Ferdinand (1808–1899). *Geschichte der Faṭimiden Chalifen nach den Arabischen Quellen*, in *Abhandlungen der königlichen Gesellschaft der Wissenschaften zu Göttingen, Historisch-philologische Classe*, 26, Band 3 (1880), pp. 1–97; 27, Band 1 (1881), pp. 1–130; 27, Band 3 (1881), pp. 1–126. Published separately, Göttingen: Dieterich Verlag, 1881. pp. 352; reprinted, Hildesheim and New York: G. Olms, 1976. A history of the Fatimid caliphate drawing on numerous Arabic chronicles.
- Wüstenfeld, Ferdinand. "Fachr ed-dîn der Drusenfürst und seine Zeitgenossen" in *Abhandlungen der königlichen Gesellschaft der Wissenschaften zu Göttingen, Historisch-philologische Klasse*, 33, no. 2 (1886), pp. 1–178. Published separately, Göttingen: Dieterich Verlag, 1886. pp. 178. Arabic trans., *Fakhr al-Dīn amīr al-Durūz wa-muʿāṣirūhu*, tr., Buṭrus Shalfūn. Uṣūl wa-marājiʿ ta'rīkhiyya. Beirut: Dār Laḥd Khāṭir, 1981. pp. 235.

Y

- *Yādnāma-yi Nāṣir-i Khusraw*. Mashhad: Dānishkada-yi Adabiyyāt va ʿUlūm-i Insānī, Dānishgāh-i Firdawsī, 2535 [1355 Sh.]/1976. pp. 672.
- Yāḥaqqī, Muḥammad Jaʿfar. "Zamān, makān va māda dar Dīwān-i Nāṣir-i Khusraw", *Nashriyya-yi Dānishkada-yi Ilāhiyāt va Maʿārif-i Islāmī-yi Mashhad*, 26–27 (1357 Sh./1978), pp. 212–239.
- Yahia, Osman (1919–1997). "Ismaélisme", in *Encyclopaedia Universalis*. Paris: Encyclopaedia Universalis, 1985, vol. 10, pp. 277–279.
- Yahia, Osman. "Ismaélisme", in *EUDI*, pp. 439–445.

See also under Henry Corbin

- Yalaoui (al-Yaʿlāwī), Mohammed (Muḥammad). "Les relations entre Fāṭimides d'Ifriqiya et Omeyyades d'Espagne à travers le Dīwān d'Ibn Hānī", in *Actas del II Coloquio Hispano Tunccino dc Estudios Historicos. Madrid/Barcelona, mayo de 1972*. Madrid: Istituto Hispano-Arabe de Cultura, 1973, pp. 13–30.
- Yalaoui, Mohammed. "Sur une possible régence du prince Fatimide ʿAbdallah b. Muʿizz en Ifriqiya au IVᵉ/Xᵉ siècle", *CT*, 22, nos. 85–86 (1974), pp. 7–22.
- Yalaoui, Mohammed. *Un poète Chiite d'occident au IVème/Xème siècle: Ibn Hānī' al-Andalusī*. Université de Tunis, Faculté des Lettres et Sciences Humaines, 6e série, Philosophie-Litterature, IX. Tunis: Université de Tunis, 1976. pp. 474. Arabic trans., *Ibn Hānī' al-Maghribī al-Andalusī (973/362–931/320), shāʿir al-dawla al-Fāṭimiyya*, tr., Muḥammad al-Yaʿlāwī. Beirut: Dār al-Gharb al-Islāmī, 1405/1985. pp. 404.
- Yalaoui, Mohammed. "Ibn Hâni', poète Shîʿîte et chantre des Fât'imides au Maghreb", *Les Africains*, 6 (1977), pp. 101–125.
- Yalaoui, Mohammed. "Controverse entre le Fatimide al-Muʿizz et l'Omeyyade al-Nasir, d'après le 'Kitab al-Majalis w-al-Musayarat' du Cadi Nuʿman", *CT*, 26, nos. 103–104 (1978), pp. 7–33.
- Yalaoui, Mohammed. *al-Adab bi-Ifrīqiya fi'l-ʿahd al-Fāṭimī 296–365H*. Beirut: Dār al-Gharb al-Islāmī, 1986. pp. 396.
- Yalaoui, Mohammed. "Tarjamat al-Mahdī ʿUbayd Allāh min Kitāb al-Muqaffā li'l-Maqrīzī", *Ḥawliyyāt al-Jāmiʿa al-Tūnusiyya*, 25 (1986), pp. 37–92.
- Yalaoui, Mohammed. "al-Fazārī", in *EI2*, Supplement.

- Yāsīn, Anwar, Wā'il al-Sayyid and Bahā' al-Dīn Sayf Allāh. *Bayna al-ʿaql wa'l-nabī: baḥth fi'l-ʿaqīda al-Durziyya.* Paris: n.p., 1981. pp. 464. French trans., *Entre la raison et le prophète. Essai sur la religion des Druzes*, tr., Joseph Azzi. Questions d'Orient. Paris: J. Bertoin, 1992. pp. 320.
- Yazici, Tahsin. "Fidâî", in *IA*2, vol. 13, p. 53.
- Young, Gordon. *Golden Prince: The Remarkable Life of Prince Aly Khan.* London: R. Hale, 1955. pp. xii + 191.
- Youssef, Joseph N. "Dirāsa fī wathā'iq al-ʿaṣrayn al-Fāṭimī wa'l-Ayyūbī al-maḥfūẓa bi-maktabat dayr Sānt Kātrīn fī Sīnā", *Majallat Kulliyyat al-Ādāb, Jāmiʿat al-Iskandariyya/Bulletin of the Faculty of Arts, Alexandria University*, 18 (1964), pp. 179–203; English summary, "A Study of the Fāṭimid and Ayyūbid Documents in the Monastery of Mt. Sinai", pp. 204–208.
- Yūsuf (Yousef),ʿAbd al-Ra'ūf ʿAlī (Abd el-Ra'uf Ali). "Ṭabaq 'Ghabn' wa'l-khazaf al-Fāṭimī al-mubakkir", *Majallat Kulliyyat al-Ādāb, Jāmiʿat al-Qāhira/Bulletin of the Faculty of Arts, Cairo University*, 18, no. 1 (1956), pp. 87–106.
- Yūsuf, ʿAbd al-Ra'ūf ʿAlī. "Khazzāfūn min al-ʿaṣr al-Fāṭimī wa-asālībuhum al-fanniyya", *Majallat Kulliyyat al-Ādāb, Jāmiʿat al-Qāhira/Bulletin of the Faculty of Arts, Cairo University*, 20, no. 2 (1958), pp. 173–279.
- Yūsuf,ʿAbd al-Ra'ūf ʿAlī. "A Rock-crystal Specimen in the Museum of Islamic Art, Cairo, and the Seven Fatimid Domes in the Qarāfa al-Kubrā, Cairo", in *EF*, pp. 311–317.
- Yusuf Ali, A. "Khodja", in *EI*, vol. 2, pp. 960–962. Persian trans., "Firqa-yi Khuja", tr., Yaʿqūb Āzhand, in B. Lewis et al., *Ismāʿīliyān dar ta'rīkh*, pp. 397–401.
- Yūsufī, Ghulām Ḥusayn (1927–1990). "Nāṣir-i Khusraw, muntaqidī ijtimāʿī", in *YNK*, pp. 619–640.

Z

- Zabīs, Sulaymān Muṣṭafā. "Ilmāma ʿan aḥwāl al-Qāhira al-iqtiṣādiyya wa-ʿalāqatihā maʿā al-khārij fī ʿahd al-Fāṭimiyyīn", in *Abḥāth al-nadwa al-dawliyya li-ta'rīkh al-Qāhira.* Cairo: Wizārat al-Thaqāfa wa'l-Iʿlām, 1971, vol. 3, pp. 577–597.

- Zabīs (Zbiss), Sulaymān (Slimane) M. "Mahdia et Ṣabra-Manṣoûriya: nouveaux documents d'art Fatimite d'occident", *JA*, 244 (1956), p. 79–93.
- Zabīs, Sulaymān Muṣṭafā. "Ta'rīkh al-Qāhira al-iqtiṣādī", *Ta'rīkh al-'Arab wa'l-'Ālam*, 99–100 (1987), pp. 28–38.
- Zāhid 'Alī (1888–1958). *Ta'rīkh-i Fāṭimiyyīn-i Miṣr*. Hyderabad: Jāmi'at 'Uthmāniyya, 1367/1948. 2 vols; reprinted, Karachi: Nafīs Akīdīmī, 1963. 2 vols. (in Urdu).
- Zāhid 'Alī. *Hamāre Ismā'īlī madhhab kī ḥaqīqat awr uskā niẓām*. Academy of Islamic Studies, Publications, 1. Hyderabad: Nāmī Prīs, 1373/1954. pp. 664 (in Urdu).
- Ẓahīr, Iḥsān Ilāhī. *al-Ismā'īliyya, ta'rīkh wa-'aqā'id*. Lahore: Idārat Tarjamān al-Sunna, 1406/1986. pp. 757 (in Urdu).
- Ẓāhir, Sulaymān. *al-Shī'a wa'l-Ismā'īliyya*. Beirut: al-Dār al-Islāmiyya, 2002. pp. 163.
- al-Ẓāhirī, Fāliḥ. *Ḥusn al-wafā li-Ikhwān al-Ṣafā'*. Alexandria: Maṭba'at Sharikat al-Makārim, 1323/1906. pp. 69.
- Zakhoder, Boris Nikolaevich (1898–1960). "Muhammad Nakhshabi. K istorii karmatskogo dvizheniya v Sredney Azii v X veke" [Muḥammad Nakhshabī. Toward the History of the Qarmaṭī Movement in Central Asia in the 10th Century], *Uchyonïe zapiski Moskovskogo gosudarstvennogo universiteta* (Moscow), 1 (1940), pp. 96–112.
- Zakī, 'Abd al-Raḥmān. "Imtidād al-Qāhira min 'aṣr al-Fāṭimiyyīn ilā 'aṣr al-Mamālīk", in *Abḥāth al-nadwa al-dawliyya li-ta'rīkh al-Qāhira*. Cairo: Wizārat al-Thaqāfa wa'l-I'lām, 1971, vol. 3, pp. 617–643. French summary, "L'extension du Caire entre l'an 969 et 1517 (Résumé)", in *Colloque international sur l'histoire du Caire*, pp. 469–471.
- Zakī, Aḥmad. *Mawsū'āt al-'ulūm al-'Arabiyya wa-baḥth 'alā Rasā'il Ikhwān al-Ṣafā'*. Cairo: al-Markaz al-'Arabī li'l-Baḥth wa'l-Nashr, 1983. pp. 99.
- Zakuev, Akhmad Keredi. *Filosofiya "Brat'ev chistoti"* [Philosophy of the "Brethren of Purity"]. Baku: Izdatel'stvo Akademii Nauk Azerbaydzhanskoy SSSR, 1961. pp. 122.
- Zambaur, Eduard Karl Marx von (1866–1947). *Manuel de généalogie et de chronologie pour l'histoire de l'Islam*. Hannover: H. Lafaire, 1927, vol. 1, pp. 47 (Fatimids and Kalbids of Sicily), 94–96 (Fatimids), 103 (Bāṭinīs of Syria), 116 (Qarmaṭīs of Baḥrayn), 117 (Zuray'ids), 119

(Ṣulayḥids), 217–218 (Bāṭinīs of Persia); vol. 2, genealogical tables E (Ḥusaynid ʿAlids); reprinted, Bad Pyrmont: H. Lafaire/W. Behrens, 1955. 2 vols.; reprinted, Osnabrück: Biblio Verlag, 1976.

- Zanjānī, Barāt. "Tawḍīḥī dar bāra-yi mithālhā-yi riyaḍī ki Ḥakīm Nāṣir-i Khusraw barā-yi tafhīm-i maṭālib-i falsafī bikār burda ast", in *YNK*, pp. 246–252.
- al-Zarkilī, Khayr al-Dīn. "al-Ḥurra al-Ṣulayḥiyya", in his *al-Aʿlām*. Beirut: Khayr al-Dīn al-Zarkilī, 1969, vol. 1, pp. 279.
- Zarrīnkūb, ʿAbd al-Ḥusayn. "Shahrastānī va Majlis-i Farsī-yi ū", *Furūgh-i ʿIlm*, 1 (1329 Sh./1950), pp. 83–90.
- Zarrīnkūb, ʿAbd al-Ḥusayn. "Āvāra-yi Yumgān", *Sukhan*, 13, no. 1 (1341 Sh./1962), pp. 39–50.
- Zaryāb Khuʾī, ʿAbbās (1919–1995). "Baqaliyya", in *DDI*, vol. 3, pp. 637–638.
- Zaryāb Khuʾī, ʿAbbās. "Abū Yaʿqūb Sijzī (Sijistānī), Isḥāq b. Aḥmad", in *DMBI*, vol. 6, pp. 423–429.
- Zaryāb Khuʾī, ʿAbbās and Muḥammad Ḥusayn Mashāyikh Farīdanī. "Imām ʿAlī b. Abī Ṭālib", "Imām Ḥasan Mujtabā", "Imām Ḥusayn", "Imām Zayn al-ʿĀbidīn", "Imām Muḥammad Bāqir", "Imām Ṣādiq", in *DT*.
- Zayd, Usāma Zakī. *al-Ṣalībiyyūn wa-Ismāʿīliyyat al-Shām fī ʿaṣr al-ḥurūb al-Ṣalībiyya*. Alexandria: al-Hayʾa al-Miṣriyya al-ʿĀmma liʾl-Kitāb, 1980. pp. 351.
- Zaydān, Jurjī (1861–1914). *Ṣalāḥ al-Dīn wa-makāʾid al-ḥashshāshīn*. Cairo: Maṭbaʿat al-Hilāl, 1913, pp. 192. Persian trans., *Ṣalāḥ al-Dīn Ayyūbī va Ismāʿīliyān*, tr., Muḥammad ʿAlī Shīrāzī. Tehran: Gūtinbirg, 1339 Sh./1960. pp. 220. Ottoman Turkish trans., *Salaheddin Eyyubi we Ismaililer*, tr., Zeki Magamiz. Istanbul: Ikdam Matbasi, 1927. pp. 377.
- Zbiss, Slimane Mostfa. "La situation économique du Caire et ses relations exterieures au temps des Fāṭimides (Résumé)", in *Colloque international sur l'histoire du Caire*, pp. 473–474.
- Zéki Pacha, Ahmed., "Les nouveaux égouts du Caire et les passages souterrains des Khalifes Fatimites", *BIE*, 5 série, 6 (1912), pp. 1–10, 195–198.
- Zeller, J. "The Druses and their Religion", *Church Missionary Intelligencer*, NS, 12 (1887), pp. 536–549.

- Zetterstéen, Karl V. (b. 1866). "Zikrawaih b. Mihrawaih", in *EI*, vol. 4, pp. 1226–1227.
- Zghal, Hatem. "Substance et accident dans les *Rasā'il Iḫwān al-Ṣafā*", in Ahmad Hasnawi et al., ed., *Perspectives Arabes et médiévales sur le tradition scientifique et philosophique Grecque*. Orientalia Lovaniensia Analecta, 79. Louvain: Peeters; Paris: Institut du Monde Arabe, 1997, pp. 535–553.
- Zimpel, H. "Assassinen-Castel Kalaat el Alaid Sajuhm (Sahium) 8 Stunden Ritt östlich von Ladakia", *Das Ausland*, 23 (1850), pp. 129–130.
- Ziya, Yusuf. "Ihvân-ı Safâ", *DIFM*, 1, no. 1 (1925), pp. 183–192.
- al-Zuʿbī, Muḥammad ʿAlī. *al-Durūz: ẓāhiruhum wa-bāṭinuhum*. [Beirut]: Maktabat al-ʿIrfān, 1956. pp. 158; 2nd revised ed., n.p.: n.p., 1972. pp. 184.

5

Selected Theses

In this chapter are listed a selection of theses on Ismaili, or Ismaili-related, topics submitted in partial fulfillment of requirements for doctoral, masters' and other types of higher degrees, to American, Canadian, British, French and Italian universities, as well as higher institutions of learning in Iran and a few other countries. The theses published subsequently as books are indicated with PB.

- al-Abduljader (al-ʿAbd al-Jādir), Adel Salem (ʿĀdil Sālim). "Studies in the History and Thought of the Ismāʿīlī States in Mediaeval Yemen" (Ph.D. thesis, University of Edinburgh, 1997). pp. xi + 670. (PB)
- Abouzeid, Ola Abdelaziz. "A Comparative Study between the Political Theories of al-Farabi and the Brethren of Purity" (Ph.D. thesis, University of Toronto, 1988).
- Abu-Izzeddin, Nejla Mustafa. "The Racial Origins of the Druzes" (Ph.D. thesis, University of Chicago, 1934).
- Adrah, Hala. "Druze Identity in Perspective: A Case Study of Druze University Students" (M.A. thesis, University of London, School of Oriental and African Studies, 1991). pp. vii + 49.
- Aḥmadzāda, Fariyāl. "Falsafa-yi ijtimāʿī-yi Ḥasan-i Ṣabbāḥ" (M.A. thesis, Dānishkada-yi ʿUlūm-i Ijtimāʿī, Dānishgāh-i Tehran, 1363–64 Sh./1984–85). pp. 142.

- Ahmed, Shama S. "Religious Leadership and Social Change in the Ismaili Khoja Community" (M.Soc.Sc. thesis, University of Birmingham, 1975). pp. 83.
- Akbar Hussain, Faizah Ismail. "The Qarāmiṭa" (Ph.D. thesis, University of Exeter, 1984). pp. iv + 283.
- ʿAlībakhshī, Ruʾyā. "Barrasī-yi uḍāʿ-i siyāsī ijtimāʿī-yi junbish-i Nizāriyān-i Īrān" (M.A. thesis, Dānishkada-yi Adabiyyāt va ʿUlūm-i Insānī, Dānishgāh-i Shahīd Bihishtī, 1374–75 Sh./1995–96). pp. 212.
- Alibhai, Mohamed Abualy. "Abū Yaʿqūb al-Sijistānī and *Kitāb Sullam al-Najāt*: A Study in Islamic Neoplatonism" (Ph.D. thesis, Harvard University, 1983). pp. xiii + 172 (English) + 113 (Arabic).
- Amdouni, Hassan. "L'organisation sociale en Ifriqiya sous les Fatimides" (Thèse [de 3e cycle], Université de Paris-Sorbonne, Paris IV, 1986).
- Amīrismī, Kāmbīz. "Ismāʿīliyān-i Nizārī-yi Īrān az suqūṭ-i Alamūt tā āghāz-i imāmat-i Āqā Khān-i sivum" (M.A. thesis, Dānishkada-yi Adabiyyāt va ʿUlūm-i Insānī, Dānishgāh-i Shahīd Bihishtī, 1378 Sh./1999). pp. 219.
- Asani, Ali Sultaan Ali. "The Ismāʿīlī *ginān* Literature: Its Structure and Love Symbolism" (B.A. honors thesis, Harvard College, 1977). pp. i + 79.
- Asani, Ali Sultaan Ali. "*The Būjh Nirañjan*: A Critical Edition of a Mystical Poem in Medieval Hindustani with its Khojkī and Gujarati Recensions" (Ph.D. thesis, Harvard University, 1984). pp. xi + 500. (PB)
- Āshūrī, Muḥsin. "Buhra, firqaʾī az firaq-i Ismāʿīliyya" (M.A. thesis, Dānishkada-yi Tablīgh va Maʿārif-i Islāmī, Dānishgāh-i Imām Ṣādiq, 1370 Sh./1991). pp. 257.
- Assaad, Sadik Ismail. "The Reign of al-Ḥākim bi Amr Allāh, 386/996–411/1021: A Political Study" (Ph.D. thesis, University of London, School of Oriental and African Studies, 1971). pp. 329. (PB)
- Āzādī, Mīnā. "Ismāʿīliyya va taʾthīrāt-i ān dar ḥukūmathā-yi vaqt" (M.A. thesis, Dānishkada-yi ʿUlūm-i Iqtiṣādī va Siyāsī, Dānishgāh-i Shahīd Bihishtī, 1353 Sh./1974). pp. 181.
- Badakhchani, Jalal Hosseini. "The Paradise of Submission: A Critical Edition and Study of *Rawḍeh-i Taslīm* commonly known as *Taṣawwurāt* by Khwājeh Naṣīr al-Dīn-i Ṭūsī (1201–1275)" (Ph.D.

thesis, University of Oxford, 1989). pp. vi + 456 (English + Persian). (PB)

- Bāghistānī, Ismāʿīl. "Taʾrīkh-i tashkīlāt-i idārī va farhangī-yi dawlat-i Fāṭimiyān" (M.A. thesis, Dānishkada-yi Adabiyyāt va ʿUlūm-i Insānī, Dānishgāh-i Tehran, 1376 Sh./1997).
- Baiza, Yahia. "Issues and Challenges of Higher Education for Afghan Ismaili Refugees in Pakistan" (M.Sc. thesis, University of Oxford, 2002). pp. 105.
- Baṣīrī, Ḥusayn ʿAlī. "Dhikr-i taqrīr madhāhib-i Bāṭiniyān va Ismāʿīliyān va aḥvāl-i jamāʿat-i madhkūr" (M.A. thesis, Dānishkada-yi Adabiyyāt va ʿUlūm-i Insānī, Dānishgāh-i Tehran, 1344 Sh./1965). pp. 94.
- Ben Ammou, Samira. "Idéologie sous-jacente au terrorisme des Nizarites" (Thèse de 3e cycle, Université de la Sorbonne, Paris IV, 1978).
- Beshir, Beshir Ibrahim. "The Fatimid Caliphate, 386–487 A.H./996–1094 A.D." (Ph.D. thesis, University of London, School of Oriental and African Studies, 1970). pp. 266.
- Bhatia, Parviz. "The Early Nizari Ismaʿili Doctrine of *Taʿlim*: An Analytic Study of Hasan-i-Sabbah's Interpretation of the Ismaʿili Doctrine of Authoritative Teaching" (M.A. thesis, University of London, School of Oriental and African Studies, 1988). pp. iii + 70.
- Bhatia, Zarina G. "Social Changes in the Ismaili Society of East Africa, with Reference to the Imamat of Four Successive Aga Khans" (B. Litt. thesis, University of Oxford, 1974). pp. vii + 185.
- Bierman, Irene A. "Art and Politics: The Impact of Fatimid Uses of *Ṭirāz* Fabrics" (Ph.D. thesis, University of Chicago, 1980). pp. ix + 484.
- Blank, Jonah Bernard. "Mullahs on the Mainframe: Islamization and Modernity among the Daudi Bohras" (Ph.D. thesis, Harvard University, 1998). pp. xii + 636. (PB)
- Bloom, Jonathan Max. "Meaning in Early Fatimid Architecture: Islamic Art in North Africa and Egypt in the Fourth Century A.H. (Tenth Century A.D.)" (Ph.D. thesis, Harvard University, 1980). pp. xi + 359.
- Boivin, Michel. "Shiʿisme Ismaélien et modernité chez Sultan Muhammad Shah Aga Khan (1877–1957)" (Ph.D. thesis, Université de la Sorbonne Nouvelle Paris III, 1993). pp. iv + 960. (PB)

- Brett, Michael. "Fitnat'l-Qayrawān: A Study of Traditional Arabic Historiography" (Ph.D. thesis, University of London, School of Oriental and African Studies, 1970). pp. 547.
- Bryer, David R. W. "The Origins of the Druze Religion: An Edition of Ḥamza's Writings and an Analysis of his Doctrine" (D.Phil. thesis, University of Oxford, 1971). pp. 2 + xiii + 303 (English) + 318 (Arabic).
- Calderini, Simonetta. "La 'Risālat al-Mabda' wa al-Ma'ād' (Adamo ed il cosmo nell' Ismailismo)" (M.A. thesis, Istituto Universitario Orientale di Napoli, 1980–81). pp. xxvi + 168 (Italian) + 30 (Arabic).
- Calderini, Simonetta. "Studies in Ismaili Cosmology: The Role of Intermediary Worlds" (Ph.D. thesis, University of London, School of Oriental and African Studies, 1991). pp. vii + 247.
- Chiarelli, Leonard Charles. "Sicily during the Fatimid Age" (Ph.D. thesis, University of Utah, 1986). pp. ix + 266.
- Clarke, Peter B. "The Ismaili Khojas: A Sociological Study of an Islamic Sect in London" (M.Phil. thesis, King's College, London, 1974–75). pp. 208.
- Cortese, Delia. "I sette capitoli di Bābā Sayyid-nā (La figura di Melkisedeq nell'Ismailismo)" (M.A. thesis, Istituto Universitario Orientale di Napoli, 1980–81). pp. ix + 210 (Italian) + 42 (Persian).
- Cortese, Delia. "Eschatology and Power in Mediaeval Persian Ismailism" (Ph.D. thesis, University of London, School of Oriental and African Studies, 1993). pp. vii + 280.
- Desai, Madhavi. "The Traditional Houseform of Bohras in Gujarat: Architectural Response to Cultural Ethos" (M.A. thesis, Ahmedabad University, Department of Art and Architecture, 1992).
- Dossa, Parin Aziz. "Ritual and Daily Life: Transmission and Interpretation of the Ismaili Tradition in Vancouver" (Ph.D. thesis, University of British Columbia, 1985). pp. xi + 301.
- Douwes, Dick. "De Isma'ili's van Syrie, 1800–1920" (M.A. thesis, University of Nijmegen, 1984). pp. 65.
- Eboo, Nadia. "The Revolt of the Āghā Khān Maḥallātī and the Establishment of the Nizārī Imāmate in India" (B.A. thesis, Victoria University of Manchester, 1979). pp. 47.
- Eboo Jamal, Nadia. "The Continuity of the Nizari Ismaili *Da'wa* 1256–

1350" (Ph.D. thesis, New York University, 1996). pp. xiii + 317. (PB)

- Esmail, Aziz. "Satpanth Ismailism and Modern Changes within it, with Special Reference to East Africa" (Ph.D. thesis, University of Edinburgh, 1971). pp. vi + 560.
- Feki (al-Faqī), Habib (al-Ḥabīb). "Trois traités Ismaéliens Yéménites" (Thèse de doctorat de 3e cycle, Faculté des Lettres et Sciences Humaines de Paris, Sorbonne, 1970). pp. 330 (French) + 66 (Arabic). (PB)
- Gabrani, Majida. "The Multi-Media Approach to Religious Education in Ismaili Community" (M.A. thesis, University of London, Institute of Education, 1985). pp. i + 99.
- Gagnon, Jean François. "Gnose et philosophie: une étude du Ta'wil Ismaélien d'après le Livre des sources d'al-Sijistānī" (M.A. thesis, McGill University, Institute of Islamic Studies, 1995). pp. vii + 78.
- Ghadiali, Durriya Rozanna. "Forty Years of Female Rule in Medieval Yemen: Illuminating the Reign of al-Sayyida bint Ahmad al-Sulayhi (d. 532/1137)" (M.A. thesis, University of Texas at Austin, 1998). pp. vi + 94.
- Gharīb, Mīnā. "Firqa-yi Ismāʿīliyya va naqsh-i siyāsī-yi ān dar ḥukūmathā-yi Islāmī dar Īrān" (M.A. thesis, Dānishkada-yi ʿUlūm-i Siyāsī va Ijtimāʿī, [Dānishgāh-i Tehran], 1358 Sh./1979). pp. 152.
- Ḥā'irī, Muḥammad Ḥasan. "Ḥikmat-i naẓarī va ḥikmat-i ʿamalī dar āthār-i Nāṣir-i Khusraw" (Ph.D. thesis, University of Tehran, 1366 Sh./1987). pp. 361.
- Haji, Zebunisa A. "La doctrine Ismaélienne d'après l'oeuvre d'Abû Ishâq Qohestânî (fin du XVe siècle)" (Thèse de 3e cycle, Université de la Sorbonne, Paris IV, 1975). pp. 517.
- Hallam, Roger N.M. "The Shia Imami Ismaili Community in Britain" (M.Phil. thesis, University of London, School of Oriental and African Studies, 1971). pp. 189.
- Hamblin, William James. "The Fāṭimid Army during the Early Crusades" (Ph.D. thesis, University of Michigan, 1985). pp. iv + 323.
- al-Hamdani, Abbas H. "The Sīra of al-Mu'ayyad fi'd-Dīn ash-Shīrāzī" (Ph.D. thesis, University of London, School of Oriental and African Studies, 1950). pp. 198.
- al-Hamdānī, Ḥusain F. "The Doctrines and History of the Ismāʿīlī

Daʿwat in Yemen, as based on the Dāʿī Idrīs ʿImād u'd-Dīn's Kitāb Zahr u'l-Maʿānī and Other Works" (Ph.D. thesis, University of London, School of Oriental Studies, 1931). pp. xxii + 260.

- Hamdani, Sumaiya Abbas. "From *Daʿwa* to *Dawla*: Qadi al-Nuʿman's Ẓāhirī Construction of Fatimid Legitimacy" (Ph.D. thesis, Princeton University, 1995). pp. vi + 270.
- Hamiduddin, Rabab. "The Qaṣīdah of the Ṭayyibī Daʿwah and the Dīwān of Syedna ʿAlī b. Muḥammad al-Walīd (d. 612/1215)" (Ph.D. thesis, University of London, School of Oriental and African Studies, 2000). pp. 241.
- Hassan, Hassan Ibrahim. "Some Aspects of Shīʿīte Propaganda under the Fāṭimids in Egypt" (Ph.D. thesis, University of London, 1927). pp. 2 + xx + 180. (PB)
- Heck, Gene William. "Cairo or Baghdad? A Critical Re-examination of the Role of Egypt in the Fāṭimid Dynasty's Imperial Design" (Ph.D. thesis, University of Michigan, 1986). pp. viii + 337.
- Hickling, Carissa. "Disinheriting Daughters: Applying Hindu Laws of Inheritance to the Khoja Muslim Community in Western India, 1847–1937" (M.A. thesis, University of Manitoba, Winnipeg, 1998). pp. xii + 236.
- Hirji, Boustan. "A Study of *al-Risālah al-Bāhirah*" (Ph.D. thesis, McGill University, Institute of Islamic Studies, 1994). pp. ix + 248 (English) + 27 (Arabic).
- Huehns, Colin. "Music of Northern Pakistan" (D.Phil. thesis, University of Cambridge, 1991). pp. 651 + x + 448 (music notes) + 75.
- Hunsberger, Alice C. "Nāṣir-i Khusraw's Doctrine of the Soul: From the Universal Intellect to the Physical World in Ismāʿīlī Philosophy" (Ph.D. thesis, Columbia University, 1992). pp. vi + 235.
- Hunzai, Faquir Muhammad. "The Concept of Tawḥīd in the Thought of Ḥamīd al-Dīn al-Kirmānī (d. after 411/1021)" (Ph.D. thesis, McGill University, Institute of Islamic Studies, 1986). pp. x + 309.
- Hunzai, Ghulam Abbas. "The Concept of Pleasure Propounded by Nāṣir-i Khusraw" (M.A. thesis, McGill University, Institute of Islamic Studies, 1993). pp. 133.
- al-Imad, Leila Sami. "The Fatimid Vizierate, 969–1172" (Ph.D. thesis, New York University, 1985). pp. v + 177. (PB)

- Jamani, Hasina M. "Brahm Prakâsh: A Translation and Analysis" (M.A. thesis, McGill University, Institute of Islamic Studies, 1985). pp. vi + 111.
- Jiwa, Shainool. "The Initial Destination of the Fāṭimid Caliph ʿAbd Allāh al-Mahdī's *Dār al-Hijrah*: Yaman or Maghrib" (M.A. thesis, McGill University, Institute of Islamic Studies, 1984). pp. x + 197.
- Jiwa, Shainool. "A Study of the Reign of the Fifth Fāṭimid Imām/Caliph al-ʿAzīz Billāh" (Ph.D. thesis, University of Edinburgh, 1989). pp. xiv + 281.
- Jiwani, Karim. "The Challenge of Moral Education in a Secular Society: With Particular Reference to the Ismaili Community in Canada" (M.A. thesis, University of London, Institute of Education, 1986). pp. vi + 156.
- Kader, Themina. "Material Culture Studies and Art Education: Examining the Cultural Artifacts of the Bohra from Makaan to Masjid" (Ph.D. thesis, The Pennsylvania State University, 2000). pp. xi + 247.
- Kajani, Zaheed. "The Success of the Fatimid Daʿwah in Islam" (M.A. Thesis, University of California, Berkeley, 1993). pp. 106.
- al-Kange, Jaʿfar. "Ismâʿiliens, Nusayrites et Druzes en Syrie: Structure socio-religieuse et histoire de 1920 à nos jours" (Thèse de 3e cycle, Strasbourg 2, 1983).
- Karim, Alzim. "The Portrayal of Abū Yazīd in the *Iftitāḥ al-Daʿwa* of al-Qāḍī al-Nuʿmān" (M.A. thesis, University of London, School of Oriental and African Studies, 1987). pp. 66
- Karim, Alzim M.V. "Issues in Teacher Education in the Contemporary Ismaili Community" (M.A. thesis, University of London, Institute of Education, 1986). pp. 97.
- Kassam, Tazim Rahim. "Songs of Wisdom and Circles of Dance: An Anthology of Hymns by the Satpanth Ismāʿīlī Saint, Pīr Shams" (Ph.D. thesis, McGill University, Faculty of Religious Studies, 1992). pp. x + 402. (PB)
- Kassam, Zainool Rahim. "The Problem of Knowledge in Nāṣir-i Khusraw: An Ismāʿīlī Thinker of 4th/10th Century" (M.A. thesis, McGill University, Institute of Islamic Studies, 1985). pp. xii + 155.
- Kassam, Zainool Rahim. "Imam and Avatara: A Study of Divine-Human Configurations in Naṣīr al-Dīn Ṭūsī (d. 1274 CE) and Ramanuja (d. 1137 CE)" (Ph.D. thesis, McGill University, Faculty of Religious

Studies, 1995). pp. 500.

- Keshavjee, Rafique Habib. "The Quest for Gnosis and the Call of History: Modernization among the Ismailis of Iran" (Ph.D. thesis, Harvard University, 1981). pp. 23 + 51 + 45 + 75 + 42. (PB)
- Keshwani, Dilshad. "Curriculum Planning for Indian Ismāʿīlī Religions Schools, with Special Reference to the Islamic History Syllabus (Age Group 7–14)" (M.A. thesis, University of London, Institute of Education, 1982). pp. vi + 133 + 29.
- Kessler, Peter Edward. "The Reign of the Fatimid Caliph al-Mustansir Bi-llah 1027–1094 A.D.: A Discussion of Maqrizi's Portrayal in the *Ittiʿāẓ al-ḥunafā*" (B. Litt. thesis, University of Oxford, 1971). pp. 271.
- Khakee, Gulshan. "The Dasa Avatāra of the Satpanthi Ismailis and the Imam Shahis of Indo-Pakistan" (Ph.D. thesis, Harvard University, 1972). pp. v + 635.
- Khalatbari, Alahyar. "Recherche historique sur la secte religieuse Nizarite en Iran: Période d'Alamût" (Thèse de 3e cycle, Université de la Sorbonne, Paris IV, 1976).
- Khan, Dominique-Sila. "Bâbâ Râmdeo, dieu des Parias. Traditions religieuses et culturelles dans une communauté d'intouchables au Rajasthan" (Thèse de doctorat, Université de Paris VII-Jussieu, 1993). pp. 604 in 2 vols.
- Khanmohammad, Mumtaz. "The Fatimid Daʿwa in the Reign of al-Hakim Bi Amr Allah" (M.A. thesis, University of London, School of Oriental and African Studies, 1986). pp. 70.
- Khedoori, Elias. "Charters of Privileges Granted by the Fāṭimids and Mamlūks to St. Catherine's Monastery of Ṭūr Sinai (ca. 500 to 900 A.H.)" (M.A. thesis, University of Manchester, 1958). pp. iv + 245.
- Khemir, Sabiha. "The Palace of Sitt al-Mulk and Fāṭimid Imagery" (Ph.D. thesis, University of London, School of Oriental and African Studies, 1990). 2 vols.
- Kikuchi, Tatsuya. "Myth and Philosophy of Ismāʿīlīya" (Ph.D. thesis, Tokyo University, 1998).
- Kjellberg, Eva. "The Ismailis in Tanzania" (M.A. thesis, Institute of Public Administration, The University College, Dar es Salaam, 1967). pp. vii + 66.
- Kūpā, Fāṭima. "Barrasī-yi ʿaqāʾid-i kalāmī dar āthār-i Nāṣir-i Khusraw"

(M.A. thesis, Dānishkada-yi ʿUlūm-i Insānī, Dānishgāh-i Tarbiyat-i Mudarris, 1373 Sh./1994). pp. 463.

- Ladak, Hussain Akberali. "The Fāṭimid Caliphate and the Ismāʿīlī Daʿwa – From the Appointment of Mustaʿlī to the Suppression of the Dynasty" (Ph.D. thesis, University of London, School of Oriental and African Studies, 1971). pp. 279.
- Lev, Yaacov. "A Political Study of Egypt and Syria under the Early Fatimids 358/968–386/996. (Ph.D. thesis, University of Manchester, 1978). pp. 222.
- Lewis, Bernard. "Studies on the History of the Qarmaṭī and Ismāʿīlī Movements from the 8th till the 11th Century" (Ph.D. thesis, University of London, Faculty of Arts, 1939). (PB)
- Lokhandwalla, Shamoon T. "The Origins of Ismaili Law" (D.Phil. thesis, University of Oxford, 1950). pp. xii + 315.
- Lowe, John D. "Monetary Development in Fatimid Egypt and Syria (358–567/969–1171)" (M.A. thesis, University of Arizona, 1985). pp. viii + 114.
- Mahamid, H. "The Development of the Fatimid Administration" (M.A. thesis, University of Haifa, 1988).
- Marquet, Yves. "La philosophie des Iẖwân al-Ṣafâ'" (Thèse de Doctorat d'État, Université de Paris, IV-Sorbonne, 1971). pp. 680. (PB)
- Mascheroni, Grazia. "Magia e astrologia nella 52a Epistola deghli Iẖwān al-Ṣafā (B.A. thesis, Ca' Foscari Università, 1994–95).
- Mathssiges, Chantal. "A Comparative Study of the Evolution of Sufism and Ismailism in IX–XIIth c." (M.A. thesis, University of London, School of Oriental and African Studies, 1990). pp. 40.
- Mawani, Parin Ismail Velji. "The Jamat Khana as a Source of Cohesiveness in the Ismaili Community in Kenya" (M.A. thesis, University of Nairobi, 1975). pp. vi + 216.
- Mawji, Meera F.H. "An Open and Realistic Approach to Religious Education in the Ismaili Community" (M.A. thesis, University of London, Institute of Education, 1986). pp. iii + 97.
- Mawji, Meera F.H. "The Fāṭimids and the Ikhwān al-Ṣafā'" (M.A. thesis, University of London, School of Oriental and African Studies, 1987). pp. iii + 41.
- Mazagonwalla, Reshma. "An Ismaili Response to Innovation: The

Professional Development of Religious Teachers: A Reappraisal of Some Skills through Micro-Training" (M.A. thesis, University of London, Institute of Education, 1985). pp. 113.

- Merchant, Alnoor Jehangir. "Types and Uses of Argument in Anti-Ismāʿīlī Polemics" (M.A. thesis, McGill University, Institute of Islamic Studies, 1991). pp. viii + 218.
- Messier, Ronald Albert. "Muslim Exploitation of West African Gold during the Period of the Fāṭimid Caliphate" (Ph.D. thesis, University of Michigan, 1972). pp. xi + 215.
- Mirshahi, Gholam-Reza. "The 'Confessional Ode' of Nāṣir-i Khusrav and his Conversion to Ismāʿīlism" (M.A. thesis, University of London, School of Oriental and African Studies, 1989). pp. 141.
- Mirza, Nasseh Ahmad. "The Syrian Ismāʿīlīs at the Time of the Crusades" (Ph.D. thesis, University of Durham, 1963). pp. v + 201. (PB)
- Mitha, Farouk. "Re-reading al-Ghazālī: Orthodoxy, Reason and Authority in the *Kitāb al-Mustaẓhirī*" (M.A. thesis, McGill University, Institute of Islamic Studies, 1993), pp. 178. (PB)
- Morani, Hamida. "The Changing Role of the Ismaili Religion Teachers, with Special Reference to India" (M.A. thesis, University of London, Institute of Education, 1985). pp. 87.
- Morris, Harold Stephen. "Immigrant Indian Communities in Uganda" (Ph.D. thesis, University of London, 1963). pp. 639. (PB)
- Muḥaqqiq (Mohaghegh), Mahdī (Mehdi). "Taḥqīq dar Dīwān-i Nāṣir-i Khusraw va sabk va sharḥ va iṣṭilāḥāt-i ʿilmī va falsafī va abyāt-i mushkil-i ān" (Ph.D. thesis, University of Tehran, 1332 Sh./1953). pp. 338. (PB)
- Muʿizzī, Fāṭima. "Ismāʿīliyān-i Badakhshān" (Ph.D. thesis, Dānishkada-yi Adabiyyāt va ʿUlūm-i Insānī, Dānishgāh-i Tehran, 1381 Sh./2002).
- Muʿizzī, Maryam. "Ismāʿīliyān-i Īrān: az suqūṭ-i Alamūt tā imrūz bā takiyah bar dawrān-i muʿāṣir" (M.A. thesis, Dānishkada-yi Adabiyyāt, Firdawsī University, Mashhad, 1371–72 Sh./1992–93). pp. 446.
- Najib, Azizullah. "Kitāb Aʿlām al-Nubuwwa me Muḥammad ibn Zakariyā Rāzī aur Abū Ḥātim al-Rāzī ke afkār kā falsafayāna tajzaya" (M.Phil. thesis, Karachi University, 1991). pp. 389.
- Nakhai, Mandana. "The Safar Nāmih [Travel Journal] of the Persian

Nāṣir Khusrau (A.D. 1003–1072?). Translated into English with an Introduction and Notes" (Ph.D. thesis, University of Tennessee, 1979). pp. vi + 249.

- Nasser-Bush, Merun Hussein. "Differential Adjustment Between two Indian Immigrant Communities in Toronto: Sikhs and Ismailis" (Ph.D. thesis, University of Colorado, 1974). pp. xii + 197.
- Naẓīrī, ʿIshrat. "Sāzimān-i tarbiyatī-yi firqa-yi Ismāʿīliyya" (M.A. thesis, Dānishkada-yi Ravānshināsī va ʿUlūm-i Tarbiyatī, Dānishgāh-i Tehran, 1354 Sh./1975). pp. 132.
- Netton, Ian Richard. "The Syncretic Philosophy of the Rasāʾil of Ikhwān al-Ṣafāʾ" (Ph.D. thesis, University of Exeter, 1976). pp. 300. (PB)
- Nomoto, Shin. "Early Ismāʿīlī Thought on Prophecy According to the *Kitāb al-Iṣlāḥ* by Abū Ḥātim al-Rāzī (d. ca. 322/934–5)" (Ph.D. thesis, McGill University, Institute of Islamic Studies, 1999). pp. xvii + 364.
- Nooradin, Ubai. "The Concept of Language in the Tracts of the Brethren of Purity" (Ph.D. thesis, New York University, 1993).
- Noorally, Zawahir. "The First Agha Khan and the British, 1838–1868: A Study in British Indian Diplomacy and Legal History" (M.A. thesis, University of London, School of Oriental and African Studies, 1964). pp. 205.
- Nūḥ, ʿAlī. "Al-Khiṭāb al-Ismāʿīlī fīʾl-tajdīd al-fikr al-Islāmī al-muʿāṣir" (M.A. thesis, al-Jāmiʿa al-Lubnāniyya/University of Lebanon, 1993). pp. 202. (PB)
- Öz, Mustafa. "Nizârî Ismaili Mezhebinde Ağa Hanlar Dönemi" (Ph.D. thesis, Mü. Ilâhiyat Fakültesi, 1986).
- Papanek, Hanna. "Leadership and Social Change in the Khoja Ismaili Community" (Ph.D. thesis, Radcliffe College, 1962). pp. ix + 329 + 34.
- Peervani, Parveen. "Concept of Imamat with Special Reference to Nizari Ismailis" (M.A. thesis, American University of Beirut, 1967). pp. 80.
- Peerwani (Peervani), Parwin (Parveen). "Taṣḥīḥ-i intiqādī-yi Kitāb-i Khvān al-Ikhvān-i Nāṣir-i Khusraw Qubādiyānī (394 H. –482 H.), bā sharḥ-i ijmālī-yi aḥvāl va āthār-i Nāṣir-i Khusraw" (Ph.D. thesis, Dānishkada-yi Adabiyyāt va ʿUlūm-i Insānī, Dānishgāh-i Tehran, 1354 Sh./1975). pp. 346.

- Peterson, Daniel Carl. "Cosmogony and the Ten Separated Intellects in the 'Rāḥat al-'Aql' of Ḥamīd al-Dīn al-Kirmānī" (Ph.D. thesis, University of California, Los Angeles, 1990). pp. x + 598.
- Phillips, John G. "Qalʿat Maṣyāf: A Study in Islamic Military Architecture" (Ph.D. thesis, University of London, School of Oriental and African Studies, 1982). pp. 230 + 78 plates.
- Qutbuddin, Bazat Saifiyah. "A Section from the *ʿUyūn al-Akhbār wa Funūn al-Āthār* (Volume VII) of Dāʿī Idrīs ʿImād al-Dīn (d. 872/1468) and the Succession Controversy following the Death of the Fatimid Caliph al-Mustanṣir: The Claims of the Mustaʿliyya and the Nizāriyya" (M.A. thesis, American University in Cairo, 1993).
- Qutbuddin, Bazat Saifiyah. "The Political History of the Fāṭimid-Ṭayyibī Daʿwa in Yemen (ca. 524–832/1130–1429)" (D.Phil. thesis, University of Oxford, 1996). pp. ix + 256.
- Qutbuddin, Bazat Tahera. "Al-Muʾayyad fī al-Dīn al-Shīrāzī, Founder of a New Tradition of Fatimid *Daʿwa* Poetry" (Ph.D. thesis, Harvard University, 1999). pp. 388.
- Rahim, Hamshad. "The Aga Khan and the Khojas of India" (M.A. thesis, University of Chicago, 1958). pp. iii + 96.
- Rajput, Ali Mohammad. "Hassan-bin-Sabbah: His Life and Thought" (M.A. thesis, University of Birmingham, 1985). pp. vi + 204.
- Rajwani, Farida A. "The Development of Ismaʿili Religious Education in Canada" (M.A. thesis, McGill University, Department of Administration and Policy Studies in Education, 1983). pp. vi + 96.
- Rattansi, Diamond. "The Nizārī Ismāʿīlīs of Pakistan: Ismāʿīlism, Islam and Westernism Viewed through the Firmāns: 1936–1980" (M.A. thesis, McGill University, Institute of Islamic Studies, 1981). pp. 171.
- Rattansi, Diamond. "Islamization and the Khojah Ismāʿīlī Community in Pakistan" (Ph.D. thesis, McGill University, Institute of Islamic Studies, 1987). pp. ix + 245.
- Remtulla, Mehdi. "Educational and Social Adjustment of Francophone and Anglophone Khoja Ismailis in Montreal" (M.A. thesis, McGill University, 1979). pp. vi + 87.
- Richards, Edlyn Suzanne. "From the Shadows into the Light: The Disappearance of the Fāṭimid Caliph al-Ḥākim" (M.A. thesis, San Jose State University, 2002). pp. 123.

- Saleh, Marlis J. "Government Relations with the Coptic Community in Egypt During the Fāṭimid Period (358–567 A.H./969–1171 C.E.)" (Ph.D. thesis, University of Chicago, 1995). pp. vi + 337.
- Salinger, Gerard George. "The *Kitāb al-Jihād* from Qāḍī Nu'mān's *Da'ā'im al-Islām*, Translated with Introduction and Notes" (Ph.D. thesis, Columbia University, 1953). pp. 120.
- Sanders, Paula A. "The Court Ceremonial of the Fatimid Caliphate in Egypt" (Ph.D. thesis, Princeton University, 1984). pp. x + 260. (PB)
- Schaffner, David. "The Relations of the Order of the Assassins with the Crusaders during the Twelfth Century" (M.A. thesis, University of Chicago, 1939). pp. 71.
- Shah, Bulbul. "The Imām as Interpreter of the Qur'ān According to al-Qāḍī al-Nu'mān (d. 363/974)" (M.A. thesis, McGill University, Institute of Islamic Studies, 1984). pp. iii + 87.
- Shah, Parmesh. "Participatory Village Resource Management: Case Study of Aga Khan Rural Support Programme (AKRSP) India" (Ph.D. thesis, University of Sussex, 1997). pp. xv + 372.
- Shakir, Mohammed. "Sīrat al-Malik al-Mukarram: An Edition and Study" (Ph.D. thesis, University of London, School of Oriental and African Studies, n.d. [1990s]). 2 vols.
- Sheikh, Karim Sajjad. "Sir Aga Khan: A Political Biography" (M.Phil. thesis, Quaid-i-Azam University, Department of History, Islamabad, 2004). pp. 142.
- Shodan, Amrita "Legal Representations of Khojas and Pushtimārga Vaishnava Polities and Communities: The Aga Khan Case and the Maharaj Libel Case in Mid-Nineteenth Century Bombay" (Ph.D. thesis, University of Chicago, 1995). pp. 281. (PB)
- Steigerwald, Diane. "L'Imâmologie dans la doctrine Ismaélienne Nizârienne" (M.A. thesis, McGill University, Institute of Islamic Studies, 1987). pp. 185.
- Steigerwald, Diane. "Essai sur la pensée théologique et philosophique de Shahrastânî (m.548/1153)" (Ph.D. thesis, McGill University, Institute of Islamic Studies, 1994). pp. 343. (PB)
- Strick, Betsy Rebecca. "Ideology and Expressive Culture in the Druze Family" (Ph.D. thesis, University of California, San Diego, 1990). pp. 496.

- Sutūda, Manūchihr. "Ta'rīkh-i Ismā'īliyya dar rishta-yi Alburz" (Ph.D. thesis, Dānishkada-yi Adabiyyāt va 'Ulūm-i Insānī, Dānishgāh-i Tehran, 1338 Sh./1959). (PB)
- Swead [Swayd], Samy Shavit. "Lebanese Druze Identity: Change or Continuity? (1840s–1990s)" (Ph.D. thesis, University of California, Los Angeles, 1993). pp. 240.
- Tabarā, Ḥabīb. "Ta'thīr-i Ismā'īliyya dar adabiyyāt-i Fārsī" (Ph.D. thesis, Dānishkada-yi Adabiyyāt va 'Ulūm-i Insānī, Dānishgāh-i Tehran, 1344 Sh./1965). pp. 361.
- Talbani, Abdulaziz Shamsuddin. "The Debate about Prophecy in 'Kitāb A'lām al-Nubūwah': An Analytic Study" (M.A. thesis, McGill University, Institute of Islamic Studies, 1988). pp. xiii + 175.
- Tārum, Maytham. "Ta'rīkh va 'aqā'id-i Ismā'īliyya-yi Āqā Khāniyya" (M.A. thesis, Markaz-i Tarbiyat-i Mudarris, Ḥawza-yi 'Ilmiyya yi Qumm, 1372–73 Sh./1993–94). (PB)
- Tejani, Ashif. "The Devotional Literature of the Nizari Ismailis of the Indian Subcontinent and its Evolving Role within the Community" (M.A. thesis, University of London, School of Oriental and African Studies, 2000). pp. 34.
- Thobani, P.U. "Modernism in the Teachings of the Aga Khan and of Ameer Ali's 'The Spirit of Islam'" (M.A. thesis, University of Edinburgh, 1970).
- Traboulsi, Samer Farouk. "Gender, Authority and Legitimacy in Medieval Yemen: The Case of Arwā Bint Aḥmad" (M.A. thesis, American University of Beirut, 1998). pp. xii + 145.
- Valliani, Amin Muhammad. "Modernization and Social Change (A Study of the Ismaili Community of Pakistan)" (Ph.D. thesis, Hamdard University, Hamdard Institute of Education and Social Sciences, 2001). pp. iv + 175.
- van den Berg, Gabrielle. "Minstrel Poetry from the Pamir Mountains: A Study on the Songs and Poems of the Ismâ'îlîs of Tajik Badakhshan" (Ph.D. thesis, State University of Leiden, 1997). pp. 764.
- Vatikiotis, Panayiotis J. "The Fatimid Theory of State" (Ph.D. thesis, Johns Hopkins University, 1954). (PB)
- Virani, Hanif. "The Task of Curriculum Planning for a Modern Ismaili Religious Education Curriculum in the Canadian Context" (M.A. thesis, University of London, Institute of Education, 1982). pp. vii + 131.

- Virani, Shafiq Nizarali. "The Voice of Truth: Life and Works of Sayyid Nūr Muḥammad Shāh, a 15th/16th-century Ismāʿīlī Mystic" (M.A. thesis, McGill University, Institute of Ismaili Studies, 1995). pp. ix + 152.
- Virani, Shafiq Nizarali. "Seekers of Union: The Ismailis from the Mongol Debacle to the Eve of the Safavid Revolution" (Ph.D. thesis, Harvard University, 2001). pp. xii + 291.
- von Westphalen, Elisabeth Irene Graefin. "The Relationship of the Fatimids to Neoplatonism" (M.A. thesis, University of London, School of Oriental and African Studies, 1991). pp. 47.
- Walji, Shirin Remtulla. "A History of the Ismaili Community in Tanzania" (Ph.D. thesis, University of Wisconsin, Madison, 1974). pp. iv + 264.
- Walker, Paul Ernest. "Abū Yaʿqūb al-Sijistānī and the Development of Ismaili Neoplatonism" (Ph.D. thesis, University of Chicago, 1974). pp. viii + 226. (PB)
- al-Zāmil, Nāṣir b. Fūzān. "Qarāmiṭat al-Bahrain" (M.A. thesis, Imam Muḥammad b. Saʿūd University, 1982).

Appendix

Genealogical Tables and Lists

I
Early Imāmī and Ismaili Imams

1. ʿAlī b. Abī Ṭālib (d. 40/661)
Fāṭima (d. 11/632), daughter of the Prophet

1. al-Ḥasan (d. 49/669)

2. al-Ḥusayn (d. 61/680)

3. ʿAlī Zayn al-ʿĀbidīn (d. 95/714)

Zayd (d. 122/740)

4. Muḥammad al-Bāqir (d. ca. 114/732)

5. Jaʿfar al-Ṣādiq (d. 148/765)

Mūsā al-Kāẓim (d. 183/799)

Other Twelver Shiʿi imams

6. Ismāʿīl al-Mubārak (d. after 136/754)

ʿAbd Allāh al-Afṭaḥ (d. 149/766)

7. Muḥammad al-Maymūn (d. after 179/795)

8. ʿAbd Allāh (al-Akbar)

9. Aḥmad

10. al-Ḥusayn (d. ca. 268/881)

Abū ʿAlī Muḥammad Abu'l-Shalaghlagh (d. ca. 286/899)

11. ʿAlī b. (Saʿīd) ʿAbd Allāh al-Mahdī (d. 322/934) — daughter

12. Abu'l-Qāsim Muḥammad al-Qā'im (d. 334/946)

Other Fatimid caliph-imams

The list of imams for Nizārī Ismailis starts with ʿAlī and it excludes al-Ḥasan. For the Mustaʿlī Ismailis, ʿAlī has acquired the higher rank of *asās* and al-Ḥasan is counted as the first imam.

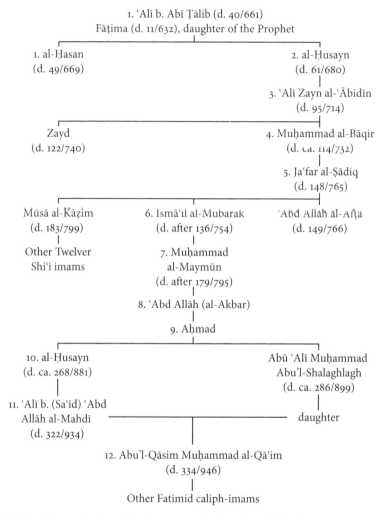

II
The Fatimid Ismaili Caliph-Imams

I-11. Abū Muḥammad ʿAbd Allāh al-Mahdī biʾllāh (d. 322/934)

II-12. Abuʾl-Qāsim Muḥammad al-Qāʾim bi-Amr Allāh (d. 334/946)

III-13. Abū Ṭāhir Ismāʿīl al-Manṣūr biʾllāh (d. 341/953)

IV-14. Abū Tamīm Maʿadd al-Muʿizz li-Dīn Allāh (d. 365/975)

V-15. Abū Manṣūr Nizār al-ʿAzīz biʾllāh (d. 386/996)

VI-16. Abū ʿAlī al-Manṣūr al-Ḥākim bi-Amr Allāh (d. 411/1021)

VII-17. Abuʾl-Ḥasan ʿAlī al-Ẓāhir li-Iʿzāz Dīn Allāh (d. 427/1036)

VIII-18. Abū Tamīm Maʿadd al-Mustanṣir biʾllāh (d. 487/1094)

Abuʾl-Qāsim Muḥammad

XI-21. ʿAbd al-Majīd al-Ḥāfiẓ (d. 544/1149)

XII-22. al-Ẓāfir (d. 549/1154)

XIII-23. al-Fāʾiz (d. 555/1160)

Yūsuf

XIV-24. al-ʿĀḍid (d. 567/1171)

25. Daʾūd (d. 604/1207-8)

Other Ḥāfiẓī imams

IX-19. al-Mustaʿlī biʾllāh (d. 495/1101)

X-20. al-Āmir bi-Aḥkām Allāh (d. 524/1130)

21. al-Ṭayyib

Hidden Ṭayyibī imams

19. Nizār (d. 488/1095)

Nizārī imams

Roman numbers designate the succession order of the Fatimid caliphs. Arabic numbers designate the order of the Ismaili imams. After al-Mustanṣir, the Nizārīs and Mustaʿlīs followed different lines of imams. After al-Āmir, the Mustaʿlīs themselves split into the Ṭayyibī and Ḥāfiẓī factions, recognizing different imams.

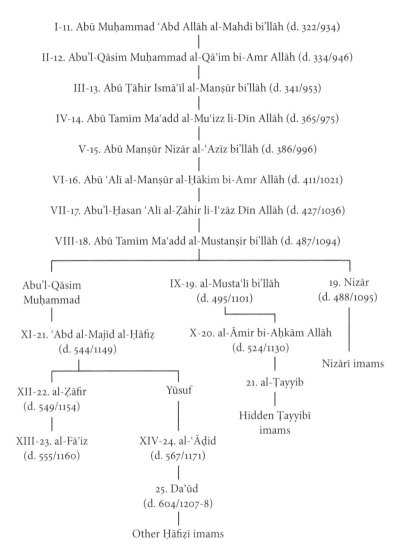

III
Nizārī Ismaili Imams
Qāsim-Shāhī Nizārī Imams

19. Nizār b. al-Mustanṣir bi'llāh (d. 488/1095)
20. al-Hādī
21. al-Muhtadī
22. al-Qāhir
23. Ḥasan II *'alā dhikrihi'l-salām* (d. 561/1166)
24. Nūr al-Dīn Muḥammad II (d. 607/1210)
25. Jalāl al-Dīn Ḥasan III (d. 618/1221)
26. 'Alā' al-Dīn Muḥammad III (d. 653/1255)
27. Rukn al-Dīn Khurshāh (d. 655/1257)
28. Shams al-Dīn Muḥammad (d. ca. 710/1310)
29. Qāsim Shāh
30. Islām Shāh
31. Muḥammad b. Islām Shāh
32. Mustanṣir bi'llāh II (d. 885/1480)
33. 'Abd al-Salām Shāh
34. Gharīb Mīrzā (Mustanṣir bi'llāh III) (d. 904/1498)
35. Abū Dharr 'Alī (Nūr al-Dīn)
36. Murād Mīrzā (d. 981/1574)
37. Dhu'l-Faqār 'Alī (Khalīl Allāh I) (d. 1043/1634)
38. Nūr al-Dahr (Nūr al-Dīn) 'Alī (d. 1082/1671)
39. Khalīl Allāh II 'Alī (d. 1090/1680)
40. Shāh Nizār II (d. 1134/1722)
41. Sayyid 'Alī (d. 1167/1754)
42. Ḥasan 'Alī
43. Qāsim 'Alī (Sayyid Ja'far)
44. Abu'l-Ḥasan 'Alī (Bāqir Shāh) (d. 1206/1792)
45. Shāh Khalīl Allāh III (d. 1232/1817)
46. Ḥasan 'Alī Shāh, Āghā Khān I (d. 1298/1881)
47. Āqā 'Alī Shāh, Āghā Khān II (d. 1302/1885)
48. Sulṭān Muḥammad Shāh, Aga Khan III (d. 1376/1957)
49. H.H. Shāh Karīm al-Ḥusaynī, Aga Khan IV, the present *ḥāḍir* imam

Muḥammad-Shāhī (Muʾminī) Nizārī Imams

19. Nizār b. al-Mustanṣir biʾllāh (d. 488/1095)
20. Ḥasan b. Nizār (d. 534/1139)
21. Muḥammad b. Ḥasan (d. 590/1194)
22. Jalāl al-Dīn Ḥasan b. Muḥammad (d. 618/1221)
23. ʿAlāʾ al-Dīn Muḥammad b. Ḥasan (d. 653/1255)
24. Rukn al-Dīn Maḥmūd b. Muḥammad (d. 655/1257)
25. Shams al-Dīn Muḥammad b. Maḥmūd (d. ca. 710/1310)*
26. ʿAlāʾ al-Dīn Muʾmin Shāh b. Muḥammad
27. Muḥammad Shāh b. Muʾmin Shāh
28. Raḍī al-Dīn b. Muḥammad Shāh
29. Ṭāhir b. Raḍī al-Dīn
30. Raḍī al-Dīn II b. Ṭāhir (d. 915/1509)
31. Shāh Ṭāhir b. Raḍī al Dīn II al-Ḥusaynī al-Dakkanī (d. ca. 956/1549)
32. Ḥaydar b. Shāh Ṭāhir (d. 994/1586)
33. Ṣadr al-Dīn Muḥammad b. Ḥaydar (d. 1032/1622)
34. Muʿīn al-Dīn b. Ṣadr al-Dīn (d. 1054/1644)
35. ʿAṭiyyat Allāh b. Muʿīn al-Dīn (Khudāybakhsh) (d. 1074/1663)
36. ʿAzīz Shāh b. ʿAṭiyyat Allāh (d. 1103/1691)
37. Muʿīn al-Dīn II b. ʿAzīz Shāh (d. 1127/1715)
38. Amīr Muḥammad b. Muʿīn al-Dīn II al-Musharraf (d. 1178/1764)
39. Ḥaydar b. Muḥammad al-Muṭahhar (d. 1201/1786)
40. Amīr Muḥammad b. Ḥaydar al-Bāqir, the final imam of this line

Some Muḥammad-Shāhī sources add the name of Aḥmad al-Qāʾim between the 24th and 25th imams.

IV
Ṭayyibī Mustaʿlī *Dāʿīs*

In Yaman

1. al-Dhu'ayb b. Mūsā al-Wādiʿī (d. 546/1151)
2. Ibrāhīm b. al-Ḥusayn al-Ḥāmidī (d. 557/1162)
3. Ḥātim b. Ibrāhīm al-Ḥāmidī (d. 596/1199)
4. ʿAlī b. Ḥātim al-Ḥāmidī (d. 605/1209)
5. ʿAlī b. Muḥammad b. al-Walīd (d. 612/1215)
6. ʿAlī b. Ḥanẓala al-Wādiʿī (d. 626/1229)
7. Aḥmad b. al-Mubārak b. Muḥammad b. al-Walīd (d. 627/1230)
8. al-Ḥusayn b. ʿAlī b. Muḥammad b. al-Walīd (d. 667/1268)
9. ʿAlī b. al-Ḥusayn b. ʿAlī b. al-Walīd (d. 682/1284)
10. ʿAlī b. al-Ḥusayn b. ʿAlī b. Ḥanẓala (d. 686/1287)
11. Ibrāhīm b. al-Ḥusayn b. ʿAlī b. al-Walīd (d. 728/1328)
12. Muḥammad b. Ḥātim b. al-Ḥusayn b. al-Walīd (d. 729/1329)
13. ʿAlī b. Ibrāhīm b. al-Ḥusayn b. al-Walīd (d. 746/1345)
14. ʿAbd al-Muṭṭalib b. Muḥammad b. Ḥātim b. al-Walīd (d. 755/1354)
15. ʿAbbās b. Muḥammad b. Ḥātim b. al-Walīd (d. 779/1378)
16. ʿAbd Allāh b. ʿAlī b. Muḥammad b. al-Walīd (d. 809/1407)
17. al-Ḥasan b. ʿAbd Allāh b. ʿAlī b. al-Walīd (d. 821/1418)
18. ʿAlī b. ʿAbd Allāh b. ʿAlī b. al-Walīd (d. 832/1428)
19. Idrīs b. al-Ḥasan b. ʿAbd Allāh b. al-Walīd (d. 872/1468)
20. al-Ḥasan b. Idrīs b. al-Ḥasan b. al-Walīd (d. 918/1512)
21. al-Ḥusayn b. Idrīs b. al-Ḥasan b. al-Walīd (d. 933/1527)
22. ʿAlī b. al-Ḥusayn b. Idrīs b. al-Walīd (d. 933/1527)
23. Muḥammad b. al-Ḥasan (al-Ḥusayn) b. Idrīs b. al-Walīd (d. 946/1539)

In India

24. Yūsuf b. Sulaymān (d. 974/1567)
25. Jalāl b. Ḥasan (d. 975/1567)
26. Dā'ūd b. ʿAjabshāh (d. 997/1589 or 999/1591)

After the Dāʾūdī-Sulaymānī Schism

Dāʾūdī *Dāʿīs*: In India

27. Dāʾūd Burhān al-Dīn b. Quṭbshāh (d. 1021/1612)
28. Shaykh Ādam Ṣafī al-Dīn b. Ṭayyibshāh (d. 1030/1621)
29. ʿAbd al-Ṭayyib Zakī al-Dīn b. Dāʾūd b. Quṭbshāh (d. 1041/1631)
30. ʿAlī Shams al-Dīn b. al-Ḥasan b. Idrīs b. al-Walīd (d. 1042/1632)
31. Qāsim Zayn al-Dīn b. Pīrkhān (d. 1054/1644)
32. Quṭbkhān Quṭb al-Dīn b. Dāʾūd (d. 1056/1646)
33. Pīrkhān Shujāʿ al-Dīn b. Aḥmadjī (d. 1065/1655)
34. Ismāʿīl Badr al-Dīn b. Mullā Rāj b. Ādam (d. 1085/1674)
35. ʿAbd al-Ṭayyib Zakī al-Dīn b. Ismāʿīl Badr al-Dīn (d. 1110/1699)
36. Mūsā Kalīm al-Dīn b. ʿAbd al-Ṭayyib Zakī al-Dīn(d. 1122/1710)
37. Nūr Muḥammad Nūr al-Dīn b. Mūsā Kalīm al-Dīn (d. 1130/1718)
38. Ismāʿīl Badr al-Dīn b. Shaykh Ādam Ṣafī al-Dīn (d. 1150/1737)
39. Ibrāhīm Wajīh al-Dīn b. ʿAbd al-Qādir Ḥakīm al-Dīn (d. 1168/1754)
40. Hibat Allāh al-Muʾayyad fi'l-Dīn b. Ibrāhīm Wajīh al-Dīn (d. 1193/1779)
41. ʿAbd al-Ṭayyib Zakī al-Dīn b. Ismāʿīl Badr al-Dīn (d. 1200/1785)
42. Yūsuf Najm al-Dīn b. ʿAbd al-Ṭayyib Zakī al-Dīn (d. 1213/1798)
43. ʿAbd ʿAlī Sayf al-Dīn b. ʿAbd al-Ṭayyib Zakī al-Dīn (d. 1232/1817)
44. Muḥammad ʿIzz al-Dīn b. Shaykh Jīwanjī Awrangābādī (d. 1236/1821)
45. Ṭayyib Zayn al-Dīn b. Shaykh Jīwanjī Awrangābādī (d. 1252/1837)
46. Muḥammad Badr al-Dīn b. ʿAbd ʿAlī Sayf al-Dīn (d. 1256/1840)
47. ʿAbd al-Qādir Najm al-Dīn b. Ṭayyib Zayn al-Dīn (d. 1302/1885)
48. ʿAbd al-Ḥusayn Ḥusam al-Dīn b. Ṭayyib Zayn al-Dīn (d. 1308/1891)
49. Muḥammad Burhān al-Dīn b. ʿAbd al-Qādir Najm al-Dīn (d. 1323/1906)
50. ʿAbd Allāh Badr al-Dīn b. ʿAbd al-Ḥusayn Ḥusam al-Dīn (d. 1333/1915)
51. Ṭāhir Sayf al-Dīn b. Muḥammad Burhān al-Dīn (d. 1385/1965)
52. Muḥammad Burhān al-Dīn b. Ṭāhir Sayf al-Dīn, the present *dāʿī*

Sulaymānī *Dāʿīs*: In India and Yaman

27. Sulaymān b. Ḥasan (d. 1005/1597)

28. Jaʿfar b. Sulaymān (d. 1050/1640)
29. ʿAlī b. Sulaymān (d. 1088/1677)
30. Ibrāhīm b. Muḥammad b. al-Fahd al-Makramī (d. 1094/1683)
31. Muḥammad b. Ismāʿīl (d. 1109/1697)
32. Hibat Allāh b. Ibrāhīm (d. 1160/1747)
33. Ismāʿīl b. Hibat Allāh (d. 1184/1770)
34. al-Ḥasan b. Hibat Allāh (d. 1189/1775)
35. ʿAbd al-ʿAlī b. al-Ḥasan (d. 1195/1781)
36. ʿAbd Allāh b. ʿAlī (d. 1225/1810)
37. Yūsuf b. ʿAlī (d. 1234/1819)
38. al-Ḥusayn b. al-Ḥusayn (d. 1241/1826)
39. Ismāʿīl b. Muḥammad (d. 1256/1840)
40. al-Ḥasan b. Muḥammad (d. 1262/1846)
41. al-Ḥasan b. Ismāʿīl (d. 1289/1872)
42. Aḥmad b. Ismāʿīl (d. 1306/1889)
43. ʿAbd Allāh b. ʿAlī (d. 1323/1905)
44. ʿAlī b. Hibat Allāh (d. 1331/1913)
45. ʿAlī b. Muḥsin (d. 1355/1936)
46. Ḥusām al-Dīn al-Ḥājj Ghulām Ḥusayn (d. 1357/1938)
47. Sharaf al-Dīn al-Ḥusayn b. Aḥmad al-Makramī (d. 1358/1939)
48. Jamāl al-Dīn ʿAlī b. Sharaf al-Dīn al-Ḥusayn al-Makramī (d. 1395/1975)
49. al-Sharafī al-Ḥasan b. al-Ḥusayn al-Makramī (d. 1413/1992)
50. al-Ḥusayn b. Ismāʿīl al-Makramī, the present *dāʿī*

ʿAlawī (ʿAlawiyya) *Dāʿīs*: In India

27. Dā'ūd Burhān al-Dīn b. Quṭbshāh (d. 1021/1612)
28. Shaykh Ādam Ṣafī al-Dīn b. Ṭayyibshāh (d. 1030/1621)
29. Shams al-Dīn ʿAlī b. Ibrāhīm (d. 1046/1637)
30. Zakī al-Dīn Ṭayyib b. Shaykh Ādam (d. 1047/1638)
31. Badr al-Dīn Ḥasan b. Walī (d. 1090/1679)
32. Ḍiyā' al-Dīn Jīwābhā'ī b. Nūḥ (d. 1130/1718)
33. Mu'ayyad al-Dīn Hibat Allāh b. Ḍiyā' al-Dīn (d. 1151/1738)
34. Shihāb al-Dīn Jalāl b. Nūḥ (d. 1158/1745)
35. Nūr al-Dīn Nūrbhā'ī b. Shaykh ʿAlī (d. 1178/1764)
36. Ḥamīd al-Dīn Shams al-Dīn b. Hibat Allāh (d. 1189/1775)
37. Shams al-Dīn Shaykh ʿAlī b. Shams al-Dīn (d. 1248/1832)
38. Ḥamīd al-Dīn Shams al-Dīn b. Shaykh ʿAlī (d. 1252/1836)

39. Mufīd al-Dīn Najm al-Dīn b. Shaykh ʿAlī (d. 1282/1865)
40. Amīn al-Dīn Amīr al-Dīn b. Najm al-Dīn (d. 1296/1879)
41. Fakhr al-Dīn Jīwābhāʾī b. Amīr al-Dīn (d. 1347/1929)
42. Badr al-Dīn Fidā ʿAlī b. Fakhr al-Dīn (d. 1377/1958)
43. Nūr al-Dīn Yūsuf b. Badr al-Dīn (d. 1394/1974)
44. Abū Ḥātim Ṭayyib Ḍiyāʾ al-Dīn b. Nūr al-Dīn Yūsuf, the present *dāʿī*

The list of the ʿAlawī *dāʿī*s was supplied to the author by their *daʿwa* headquarters in Vadodara, Gujarāt.

Index
(Chapters 1–2)

Index of Titles of Primary Sources